This reader is an education in itself. A student who reads this rich collection carefully will be able to think intelligently about the world in which we are living and where we are heading. Bravo.
Immanuel Wallerstein, Senior Research Scholar, Yale University, USA

Globalization achieves several important objectives: it destroys the naïve sociological belief that globalism is a recent development; it interweaves the historical rise and fall of empires with global processes; it gives due recognition to the interaction of culture, technology and war; and it puts pay to the notion that globalization is just westernization. With a feast of readings, it provides a comprehensive and interdisciplinary overview of the debates. Authoritative and judicious, *Globalization* is a significant achievement.
Bryan S. Turner, Presidential Professor of Sociology at the Graduate Center, the City University of New York, USA

A sparkling collection of gems from global history and from contemporary debates on globalization and society. The wide variety of original documents is admirable, and the careful annotation and commentary provide excellent guidance for students and teachers.
Raewyn Connell, Chair of Education, University of Sydney, Australia

This book provides a comprehensive coverage of globalization, both historically and geopolitically. Intriguingly, it also introduces a fascinating overview of the Japanese experience of globalism, and indeed of other Asiatic countries. The editors are combined exquisitely. I am sure that *Globalization* will become a classic work in the field.
Masataka Katagiri, Professor of Theoretical Sociology, Chiba University, Japan

Globalization: a reader is a significant and compelling new addition to the scholarly understanding of the processes and dynamics of globalization in the history of human social life. Its impressive collection of primary sources fills a number of important gaps in the study of globalization, highlighting otherwise neglected analytical perspectives and opening up new possibilities of interpretation for today's students and scholars. Its deep historical sense helps steer us away from superficial accounts of globalization as something completely new. Its sharp eye for both the relatively consistent aspects of globalization and the particular spin put on it in imperialism and colonialism gives us a stimulating appreciation of the full range of conceptual pathways that can be followed in the study of globalization. Above all, both the selection of sources and the accompanying commentary convey powerfully an especially profound and distinctive sociological sensibility that will enrich our conceptual appreciation of the place of globalization in the transformations of social life.
Robert van Krieken, Professor of Sociology, University College Dublin, Ireland

What a marvelous compendium! *Globalization: a reader* is a Wunderkammer, a social-critic's desk-book, a provocative yet elegantly expressed argument about history, especially as domination, and a serious effort to construct a canon useful across several academic disciplines. In short, for students in the broadest and best sense, there is a great deal of real education to be had here. But while *Globalization* surely has much to teach anyone, it is also a book to be savored. At least for an aging imperialist like me, the book's vaguely Edwardian stance, its insistence on decorum while discussing moral compromise, and worse, along with its dryly horrified tone and finely wrought diction, make *Globalization* an excellent choice for leafing through on a cold evening, in the library, preoccupied with sin and perhaps distracted by a good whisky. Well done indeed.

David Westbrook, Professor of Law, University of Buffalo, USA

This thoughtful and sophisticated reader offers students the opportunity to pass through all the vexing dichotomies in today's scholarly discourse: the universal and the particular, the historical and the contemporary, the classical and the postmodern views of globalization. Pedagogically sound. The right stuff for the wrong times.

Keith Doubt, Professor of Sociology, Wittenberg University, USA

This is the collection I have been waiting for. It puts globalization in its appropriate historical context: reaching from 5,000 years ago to the near future. It is only within this broad sweep of history that we can see what is truly new now in the twenty-first century. These readings and their careful introductions show that much of what passes for new in popular accounts, is not new at all, but has been going on for millennia. They illustrate that globalization or at least globalization-like processes have been occurring, with many variations for a long time. Furthermore, today is not the end of time as some have argued, only a prelude to what comes next. With this broad approach, we gain a better chance of figuring out what sorts of things might come next, and how to act in order to improve the chances of those changes we want, and prevent those we do not want.

Thomas Hall, Professor of Anthropology, Depauw University, USA

'Globalization' is now a mostly indispensable term to describe and discuss contemporary social and cultural issues which include not only world-wide public problems, but also touch on personal and private concerns in our everyday lives. This book will be a great guide, providing students with remarkably helpful and wide-ranging tools for creating their own understanding of the concept of globalization.

Atsushi Sawai, Professor of Sociology, Keio University, Japan

I have no doubts that *Globalization* will become the central text for the undergraduate and graduate studies in social sciences around the world, and that it will be of special value in post-Soviet Central Asia. It does a tremendous job of rethinking globalization and making sense of it in historical perspective. It is accessible to lay readers and informative for those who are not new to social sciences. The book's impressive scope has been masterly woven together into a structured study of the rapidly emerging phenomena that hitherto have been in danger of becoming 'everything for everybody, and nothing as a result'. This volume exposes the power of diverse voices that would have been unlikely to appear in one and the same place. They have magnified and brought to focus the debates and perspectives with unprecedented clarity.

Jamilya Jeenbaeva, Professor of Sociology, American University of Central Asia, Bishkek, Kyrgyzstan

GLOBALIZATION

This book is destined to become a classic in the field, and the classroom standard for teachers and their students. *Globalization* is the first all-inclusive reader that presents globalization as a contemporary, earth shaking force that has its foundations in ancient, classical, as well as modern civilizations.

Here, for the first time in print, is the full historical story of globalization – drawn from original sources, explained by accessible introductions and biographical commentaries, and clearly organized as a comprehensive textbook to guide students through the ins and outs of globalization.

With astonishing social, political and historical depth, the book ranges from the Babylonian and Persian empires in Mesopotamia to the global electronic economy of the twenty-first century, from ancient Greece and imperial Rome to transformations in contemporary state power and global inequalities. From Kenichi Ohmae to Al Gore, from Osama bin Laden to Timothy Garton Ash, from Amartya Sen to AbdouMaliq Simone: this is a dazzling collection of the most important academic and public statements on globalization.

Throughout, the editors expertly guide the reader through the complex terrain of globalization – its engaging histories, its transnational economies, its multiple cultures and cosmopolitan politics.

Charles Lemert, **Anthony Elliott**, **Daniel Chaffee**, and **Eric Hsu** are the founding associates of the International Research Consortium on Global Change (IRCGC) based at Flinders University, Australia, and Wesleyan University, USA.

GLOBALIZATION
A reader

Edited by

Charles Lemert,

Anthony Elliott,

Daniel Chaffee, and

Eric Hsu

 Routledge
Taylor & Francis Group

LONDON AND NEW YORK

First published 2010 by Routledge
2 Park Square, Milton Park, Abingdon, Oxon OX14 4RN

Simultaneously published in the USA and Canada
by Routledge
270 Madison Avenue, New York, NY 10016

Routledge is an imprint of the Taylor & Francis Group, an informa business

© 2010 Charles Lemert, Anthony Elliott, Daniel Chaffee and Eric Hsu for selection and editorial matter;
individual contributors their contribution

Typeset in Amasis and Akzidenz Grotesque by
RefineCatch Limited, Bungay, Suffolk
Printed and bound by
MPG Books Group in the UK

British Library Cataloguing in Publication Data
A catalogue record for this book is available from the British Library

Library of Congress Cataloging-in-Publication Data
Globalization : a reader / edited by Charles Lemert . . . [et al.].
        p. cm.
    Includes bibliographical references and index.
    1. Globalization.   I. Lemert, Charles C., 1937–
JZ1318.G5786229 2010
303.48′2—dc22   2009040070

ISBN13: 978-0-415-46477-2 (hbk)
ISBN13: 978-0-415-46478-9 (pbk)

ISBN10: 0-415-46477-3 (hbk)
ISBN10: 0-415-46478-1 (pbk)

Contents

Preface   xiii
Introduction: Globalization – Fluid Concept/Multiple Reality   xv
Acknowledgments   xxv
Notes on dates and selections   xxxv

PART ONE THE AGE OF EMPIRES   1

The Imperial Disposition and Civilizational Empires   10

Egypt: The Narmer Palette 10
Persia: Zarathustra, *Avesta* 11
India: Vedic Civilization, *Rig Veda* 12
Mesopotamia: *The Epic of Gilgamesh* 13
Ancient Israel: The Yahwist Myth of Creation and Fall 15
China: Zhou Dynasty, Mencius on the Mandate of Heaven 18
Arabia: Muhammad, *Qur'an* and the Treaty of Hudaybiyyah 19
The Americas: The Abenaki Creation Story 22
Greece: Homer, *Iliad* 23

Imperial Systems, Conflict, and Expansion   25

Egypt: Ramses II, The Battle of Kadesh 25
Babylonia: Cyrus the Great, the Achaemenid Empire 27
Greece and Persia: Thucydides, the Peloponnesian Wars 28
Macedonia: Plutarch, Alexander the Great 31
Post-Alexandrine Empires: Ptolemy I, the Rosetta Stone 33
India: the Mauryan Empire, the Edicts of Ashoka 36
Rome, the Republic: Cicero, *De re publica* 37
Rome, the Empire: Augustus, *Res gestae divi Augusti* 40
Korea: *Samguk Sagi,* Unified Silla and T'ang Dynasties 43
China: Fall of the Qin and the Rise of the Han Dynasties 45

Instability and Decline in Global Empires   47

The Americas: The Mayan Civilization, The Dresden Codex 47
Africa: Ibn Hawqal, the Empires of Ghana and Mali 48
Japan: The *Kojiki* to the Edo Period 50
The Americas: The Incan Empire, Pachacuti Inca Yupanqui 51
Rome, the Decline: Constantine and Augustine of Hippo 51
Mississippi Trading Zone: Cahokia Mounds 53

Eurasia: The Ottoman Empire's Breach to the West 54
Mesoamerica: Hernán Cortés, The Conquest of New Spain 56

PART TWO THE MODERN WORLD-SYSTEM AND INDUSTRIAL CAPITALISM   59

The European Voyages of Exploration and Discovery in the Sixteenth Century   76

Immanuel Wallerstein on the European World Economy 76
Scandinavian Probes to North America 79
Iberian Discoveries of the Americas 80
English Settlements in North America 82
Iberian Circumnavigation of the World: Ferdinand Magellan 85

The Interstate System and Colonization, after 1648   88

The Peace of Westphalia 88
America in the European Imagination: John Locke 90
Early Trade Routes to the East: Marco Polo 92
Colony as a Gulag of Undesirables: Australia 93
Colony as Wholly Owned Subsidiary: King Leopold and the Congo 95
Colonization of Civil Virtues: Pax Britannica 102

The New Sciences of Global Imagination, 1450–1884   104

Modern Psychology of the Migrating Self: René Descartes 104
Longitudinal Reckoning: The Greenwich Prime Meridian 106
Print and Literacy: Johannes Gutenberg and Martin Luther 110
Army as War Machine: Napoleon's Military Theory 111
Weights and Measures: The Scientific Forest 114
Thermodynamics and the Steam Engine: Robert Boyle and James Watt 119
Steel and Heavy Industry: Henry Bessemer 121
Evolutionary Sciences of Life: Charles Darwin 126

PART THREE THE SHORT TWENTIETH CENTURY: GLOBAL UNCERTAINTY AND RESTRUCTURING, AFTER 1914   129

Global Warfare and the New Imperia   142

Europe and the Balkans: The Assassination of Archduke Ferdinand 142
Europe's Lost Imperium: Paul Fussell on the Great War 143
China: End of Dynasty, Sun Yat-Sen and Nationalism 145
Germany: Thirty Years War in Europe, John Maynard Keynes on Versailles 149
Russia: Soviet Revolution, Vladimir Lenin 151
Japan: Hirohito and the Cult of the Emperor 153
Germany: Adolf Hitler and National Socialism 155
The American Century: Henry Luce 157

The Cold War as a Struggle for Global Control, 1946–1975   159

Cold War and the Iron Curtain: Winston Churchill 159

The American Threat and Stalinist Ideology: Joseph Stalin 160
The Soviet Threat and the Principle of Deterrence: George F. Kennan 164
Great Britain and Suez: The Protocol of Sèvres 166
Vietnam and Resistance to Hegemonic Intrusions: Hô Chí Minh 176

Decolonizing Movements Challenge the Euro-American World Order, 1947–1961   178

Africa, Negritude, and Violence: Frantz Fanon 178
India, Expulsion of the British, and Partition: Mohandas Gandhi 180
China, Leninism with Buddhist Pretensions: Mao Zedong 181
Congo, Independence from Belgium: Patrice Lumumba 183
Cuba, Thorn in the Flesh of American Hegemony: Fidel Castro 185

New Global Forces Erode the Modern, 1963–1991/2001   188

Asia and the American Civil Rights Movement: Martin Luther King and Malcolm X 188
Eastern Europe, the Velvet Revolution, and the End of the Modern: Václav Havel 190
Zaire, the Post-Colonial Nightmare in Africa: V.S. Naipaul 193
China, Revolt and Slaughter: Tiananmen's Beijing Spring 194
Russia, Perestroika and Glasnost: Mikhail Gorbachev 196
Brazil, Porto Alegre: The World Social Forum (WSF) 198

PART FOUR THE GREAT GLOBALIZATION DEBATE, 1989–2010   201

Globalists   209

The End of the Nation-State: Kenichi Ohmae 209
The Network Society: Manuel Castells 211
Global Shift: Peter Dicken 213
Cosmopolitans and World Culture: Ulf Hannerz 215
The Golden Straitjacket: Thomas Friedman 219

Anti-Globalists   221

Globalization in Question: Paul Hirst and Grahame Thompson 221
Reclaiming the Commons: Naomi Klein 225
The Challenge of Global Capitalism: Robert Gilpin 227
Globalization and International Interdependence: R.J. Barry Jones 230
The End of Global Strategy: Alan M. Rugman and Richard Hodgetts 232

Transformationalists   240

Runaway World: Anthony Giddens 240
Global Transformations: David Held and Anthony McGrew 243
Globalism as Americanization: Project for the New American Century 246
Neoliberalism as Exception: Aihwa Ong 247
States of Emergency: Al Gore 250
Globality and Globalization: Ulrich Beck 251

Post-Globalists   254

Human Consequences of Globalization: Zygmunt Bauman 254
The Global Cultural Economy: Arjun Appadurai 256
Globalization and Late Capitalism: Fredric Jameson 259
A Postmortem for Globalization: Justin Rosenberg 264

PART FIVE CONTEMPORARY GLOBALIZATION, 1996–2010   267

9/11 and its Aftermath   274

Global Jihad: Osama bin Laden 274
Traumas of the Global: Slavoj Žižek 276
Globalization's Democratic Deficit: Joseph S. Nye, Jr 279
Failed States: Noam Chomsky 281

Global Governance   284

Our Global Neighborhood: The Commission on Global Governance 284
Governance without Government: James N. Rosenau 287
Global Covenant: David Held 291
China and the Global Order: G. John Ikenberry 295
Realist Critique of Global Citizenship: Danilo Zolo 298

Cultural Globalization, Global Culture   302

Culture and Globalization: John Tomlinson 302
Creative Destruction: Tyler Cowen 304
The Local and the Global: Stuart Hall 306
Incorporating the Third World: Albert Paolini 310
Glocalization: Roland Robertson 314

Globalizing Regions   318

The End of History: Francis Fukuyama 318
Clash of Civilizations: Samuel Huntington 321
Clash of Globalizations: Stanley Hoffman 325
Globalizing Hong Kong: Peter Kwong and Dusanka Miscevic 328
Globalizing China: Doug Guthrie 331
Europe as Not-America: Timothy Garton Ash 333
The Future of Europe: Anthony Giddens and Ulrich Beck 336

PART SIX GLOBAL FUTURES: TIME AND TENSE, 1980–2010, AND BEYOND   339

Post-Contemporary Globalisms   356

Nomadology: Gilles Deleuze and Felix Guattari 356
Empire: Michael Hardt and Antonio Negri 358
Global Assemblages: Saskia Sassen 360
Global Complexity: John Urry 368

Global Civil Society in the Cosmopolitan Age   372

Global Civil Society: John Keane 372
Versions of Global Civil Society: Mary Kaldor 376
Cosmopolitan Patriots: Kwame Anthony Appiah 380
Violence, Identity, and Poverty: Amartya Sen 382
Spectral Nationality: Pheng Cheah 384

Globalization and Personal Life: Intimate Globalization   388

New Maladies of the Soul: Julia Kristeva 388
Global Sex: Dennis Altman 390
Turbulence of Migration: Nikos Papastergiadis 393
Everywhere and Anywhere: Jean-Luc Nancy 398
Precarious Life: Judith Butler 401

Information Technologies and Assemblages   404

The Integral Accident: Paul Virilio 404
Naked Life: Giorgio Agamben 406
Social Complexity and Assemblages: Manuel DeLanda 409
Necropolitics: Achille Mbembe 413
The Disappeared: AbdouMaliq Simone 417

An Inconclusive Word, After the Crash   422

Bibliography   425
Index   429

Preface

Globalization: A reader is not intended as yet another addition to the mounting pile of titles on globalism. Instead, it sets globalization – as both lived experience and arresting idea – in a rather more original *historical context*, one which allows the reader to inquire as to the myriad ways in which globalism runs from ancient Babylon to post-global Beijing. The version of globalization that we want to promote in this book – sociological, historical, political, cultural, philosophical – is one that challenges the very idea of versions. Historical social science may not be value neutral, but to the extent that the ideal still matters, it at least requires students of new and vast topics to set aside the temptations to work as if, in this case, globalization were somehow a recent occurrence or a self-evident phenomenon.

The book was conceived in 2005 in New Haven but the bulk of the research did not begin until 2007 after Daniel Chaffee and Eric Hsu joined Anthony Elliott and Charles Lemert. Anthony Elliott already had good reason to believe that Routledge would take on the project. After a few rounds of conversations, first locally, then in several combinations on several continents, we decided to do the work – a commitment that, at the time, was based more on our sense of the importance of the project than a precise idea of the turns and twists of research and thinking it would demand.

After a little time and more talk, an outline, then a formal proposal, came rather quickly together. We used as our model an anthology one of us had previously published on another subject in which agreed-upon classic texts were arrayed against ones not normally collected in anthologies in that field (social theory). The success of that book emboldened us to try a similar approach in editing and composing *Globalization*. There was, however, an exception to that general rule; namely, that the topic being different and newer, there was less consensus among experts as to which are the classics or, even, when exactly globalization began in the long history of regional trade routes and territorial aspirations of empires and thrones. This gave us our opening to include material on ancient empires, on the technologies of navigation and shipping, on the imperial disposition, and on other topics clearly evident now in the book itself as it has come to be.

The social aspects of our division of labor was carried forth in meetings of the editors at various times and places – sunny days at Glenelg, snowbound weeks in New Haven, a rainy weekend in McLaren Vale wine country (where, truth be told, we drank a life-changing Grenache that inspired more naps than work) – but mostly during many long hours indoors at Flinders and Wesleyan Universities.

We can honestly say that the work is truly collaborative. What divisions of labor there were broke out according to the strengths and abilities of various of us. Anthony Elliott, of course, wrote a good number of the commentaries on the selections and the entirety of two of the introductions. He also was the principal contact with Gerhard Boomgaarden, our Routledge publisher. Charles Lemert did his share of the composition, always with the sound advice of the others.

At the crucial final stages and at others along the way, Daniel Chaffee became the *de facto* managing editor of the Google.doc site to which we submitted work from wherever we were in the world at a given time, but even more he managed the final details with the Routledge production team and brought the whole thing into its final form. Though we could not get him to say it, it ought to be said that among us all none did more than Daniel Chaffee to discover and shape the intellectual and material labors of this project. Daniel also wrote the lion's share of the commentaries and, with Eric Hsu, did much of the hard research of determining the sources and contents of the selections. When it comes to attempting to represent, say, Ancient Chinese or Persian imperial philosophies, it is no mean trick to search all the options to find the one or few that seemed to us right for what we were attempting to do. Eric also wrote many of the commentaries that, it should be said, often took days of painstaking research.

The work consumed a good bit of our lives over some four years – during which time two babies were born, three others started to grow up, one marriage was consummated, and, though less momentous, bonds of scholarship and friendship among us were tied ever tighter. If someone wants to know if the order of the names on the cover page signifies something about who did what, the answer would be: not so much; or if it does none of us could possibly emerge from the web of work and companionship in which the book was made to say precisely what it might mean.

Institutionally, we thank the institutions that have supported this work, including, Wesleyan and Flinders universities, Academica Sinica, the Chinese Academy of Social Sciences, the State Council of the People's Republic of China, Seoul National University, the American University of Central Asia, the Open Society Institute, the Australian Research Council, as well as the British Academy, and the proprietors of a very special dance hall in Istanbul. We owe a special debt to everyone at Routledge, especially Gerhard Boomgaarden, Jennifer Dodd, and Sarah Enticknap. We should also like to thank Nicola Gerhaghty, Fiore Inglese, Condrad Meyer, Kriss McKie, Carmel Meiklejohn, Deborah Maxwell, John Urry, Nick Stevenson, Bryan Turner, Riaz Hassan, Robert Holton, Immanuel Wallerstein, Jamilya Jeenbaeva, David Levy, Joshua Scannell, Niki Atchitoff Gray, Will Runge, Sam Han, Sang-Jin Han, Patrick Lee, Anastasya Saepaeva, Huma Gohar Roti, the late Johanna Justin Jinich, Ming Yan, Geri Thoma, Tamara Warachinski, Tu Chi Nyugen, Ly Ngo, Pirya Gosh, Irene Bright-Dumm, Anthony Moran, Molly Birnbaum, Alan Chun, Kohei Saito, Makenna Goodman, Tim Schwartz, Galina Borborukova, Medina Aitieva, Gulnara Ibraeva, Mehrigiul Ablezova, José Corderu, Chuta Chuluunbat, Waverly Duck, Ming Jin and Lin Hsun Hsu, Peter Hsu, Jon Shestakofsky, Dan Mendelson, Christine Rabstenek, Lydia Bell, Ronald Lim, Sean Deel, Anna Duer, Ruth Chaffee, and Lauren Graber, among many others near and far who have touched this work intellectually and personally.

New Haven and Adelaide
November 8, 2009

Introduction: Globalization – Fluid Concept/Multiple Reality

There was a moment when a person living in Connecticut could Google the words "kingdom" and "empire," both in the same search, and come up with the address of a Chinese restaurant in Melbourne, Australia. There, at once, you have many of the basic problems associated with what has come to be called *globalization*. Search a concept, find food across the world. What in the world do these things have to do with each other? It is as if the order of things has collapsed and that everything is related in some odd fashion to everything else, with no discernible principle of organization.

Sometime just before or after the beginning of the current millennium, people in far corners of the globe began to realize that the worldly order they had grown accustomed to had changed in ways hard to define. A famous French historian famously quoted an even more famous Argentine poet on this problem of the order of things:

> A certain Chinese encyclopedia [states that] "animals" [are defined as a class] divided into (a) belonging to the Emperor, (b) embalmed, (c) tame, (d) sucking pigs, (d) sirens, (f) fabulous, (g) stray dogs, (h) included in the present classification, (i) frenzied, (j) innumerable, (k) drawn with a very fine camelhair brush, (l) *et cetera*.

If in such an ancient Chinese world stray dogs were related somehow to sucking pigs, then, in another, kingdoms can be far away places to eat. So imbued are we with the notion that the things of this world are orderly that we fail, more times that not, to consider the evidence right before us. Take, for example, the ease with which, in conversation, we direct the word "we" to those near about as if together we constituted a well-bonded group. More often than not those we address as a "we" are no such thing; sometimes there is no "we" even among those with whom we live. Familiarity with the ways and means of others is hard won and readily lost. We try to think ourselves as bound up with others because we desire a sense of coherence in life with others – a coherence that is hardly justified by the experience of the bumps and grinds, not to mention the misunderstandings, of daily life. When a search engine surprises us with a Chinese place in Melbourne, we take the mistake as a joke on us and suppose we were meant to get the point. The point to be taken is that global things are seldom as orderly as we wish they were.

For one thing, the surprise of globalization is not so much the technological wizardry so often put forth as capable of creating a global village. But to watch the world go by through any of the multiplying televisual tools at hand is not to put us in anything like a village. The figure of speech – *village* as the idealized intimate community – is a wish that not even the fastest, high definition media can make real. We do not minimize the miracle of globalizing technologies so much as emphasize the way results of this kind can put us somewhere we did not have in mind; put us there, that is, without really putting us anywhere necessarily out of the ordinary. Where we are put, when it comes to globalization, is not so much somewhere in particular but in states of human life we have seen before but never imagined to have been so raw in their familiarity.

In a quiet suburban park on the edge of New Haven, Connecticut, there is a remote corner where only the hardiest of day hikers might visit. For years, there was a simple tent in that corner, below a mound of earth hidden in the fair seasons with wild shrubs. The spot was always tidily arranged – a few cooking pots, spare clothes not entirely soiled, a sleeping bag. Those who knew of the place never reported seeing anyone inside. Yet, it was hard to escape the thought that the tent was, if not exactly a home, a shelter of sorts for the down-and-out, perhaps a rendezvous for lovers. Who knows? It was at least a domestic structure of a kind, set up on public land, used by someone or ones in their pursuit of the barest elements of human life.

Look more closely in almost any human settlement and you will find squatters – on river banks, under highway bridges, around grates and vents, along borders, on the outskirts of otherwise ultra-modern cities. From an apartment in Mumbai you can smell the rotting flesh of those who died in their tracks. On a rare clear day, from the sky-top suites of hotels in Hong Kong you can see the assemblage city, Shenzhen – a city of millions of mostly illegal immigrant workers scratching out a life, often living packed by the dozen in rooms meant for a few. Across the globe in Africa and Southeast Asia to the Americas and Central Asia, in Europe and North America there are, by one estimate, no fewer than a billion squatters – people living on the margins, building shanties on land they do not own, people at risk of being chased off to who knows where. Not all are desperately poor, but most are. They are, for the most part, people living without the rights of place or citizenship. They get by, when they do, by an astonishing ingenuity. According to Robert Neuwirth, every year some 70 million people leave rural villages for the uncertain life that has come to be called bare life – the expression inspired by Italian social theorist Giorgio Agamben.

To talk about globalization is to talk about trends that are fundamentally changing human life. It is very possible that the single most important trend today is not global information networks but human migrations from depleted countrysides to the new assemblage cities – to, that is, aggregations of people few of whom have a right to the places where they squat so long as they can, people who are live beings, however poor their circumstances; humans who are redefining the meaning of human being by surviving close to, but outside, the borders of privilege and inclusion.

No one can say exactly what this and other trends will tell the coming generations. Our children or grandchildren may or may not see the effects of globalizing forces as different in their natures as squatting and Googling. Thus, to present a book on globalization is to venture into new territory and to venture with ill-drawn maps. Much as the new-world explorers in the decades around 1500 navigated as best they could with oddly drawn charts and crude instruments of reckoning, so too must those who, early in the current millennium, seek to come to terms with globalization. We who are in that situation are, however, at a particular disadvantage. We think we know more than can be known about the new global realities. This may be a perverse consequence of technologies that allow us to key and click to find this or that map or fact. We who may have for the time being escaped the impoverished assemblages are ourselves caught in assemblages just as disorienting, if different in kind. In the flows of digitalized data, we spin (or are spun by) a web through which our keyed-in messages travel about, taking along some disconnected aspect of our being. We get angry in CAPS. We seduce in smiley faces. The information is thin as thin can be yet, like our children in their video-games, we enter assemblages of another nature – and there we think we know what to think and know about the world.

Globalization, whatever it turns out to be in the long run of human life, is here to stay. But where it stays (or where it puts us in the end) is hard to say. The conditions of bare life punch us in the gut. The poor have the advantage, if one can any longer speak of advantages, of knowing from their experiences and their migrations that they are among the living excluded. We others who are among the privileged who can read and use a keyboard are less likely to be clear about the conditions of our exclusions. In an almost philosophical sense, to be human is to be excluded – to be, that is, among the consciously living who will die on a date certain we cannot know in advance. To live is to live barely for the time we have. Our mortality is a bridge to nowhere we can imagine. Globalization is about the finely articulated deadliness of the human. What globalization seems to be doing is cutting away at the elaborate shelters people create – not just for warmth, but for protection against the winds of the final outcome of the time we cannot think even as it determines the course of our lives.

Another way to identify the effects of globalization is by reference to one of the most prominent of those structures that, it would seem, is beginning to fade fast. Globalization is about border crossings – whether on foot or by keyboard. Borders, in principle, are the territorial markers of the place where people of their own kind live out their days. In recent centuries the most important territorial borders in much of the world were the nations. Nation-states defined the more or less identifiable members of a culture associated with a set of governing institutions. States, in their glory days, were meant to settle disputes, assure that the cultural rules were well advertised, distribute (or allow to be distributed) the goods necessary for life, and police the borders within which these activities were meant to occur. States still operate in these ways but even the more powerful ones are clearly less able to settle, advertise, distribute, and police with any degree of efficiency. People without papers migrate across their borders looking for, and sometimes finding, work or income or at least shelter. Others migrate across the skies in technoships they do not quite comprehend to visit places they will never see where they will "talk" with others they will never meet. For the longest time, for a good many people, nations were the sheltering places that lent them a sense of who they were. To have a national identity is to have a passport to which is attached a home. Nations were the first address required before one buys a lot or squats in a corner in order to make a home. Even when tyrants take over the housing shelter or attack the national plot of the homeland, the home life of a people was assured by their rights of belonging – usually their citizenship, more recently a mere meager right to squat without too much trouble from local officials.

Globalization, it could be said, makes all of us homeless to some or another degree. It pulls or pushes us out of the well-trimmed national yards, forcing us to define ourselves by other means than once people did. Neither national nor ethnic claims assure the greater number of human beings any of the essentials of human survival. Some flee the fields and forests played out by poachers. Others search for a better life that recedes just behind the wake of corporate thirsts for cheaper labor.

It is far from clear that it is even possible to be a global citizen as it was to be a citizen of, say, the people's republics of one of the Koreas or of the Chinas or the Americas. In most places on the global citizenship, rights are as easily abraded as the local water supplies are fouled. Where they are not the once unquestioned vitality of a civil sphere into which individuals might enter to argue their causes is itself teased out by movements that thread their way from a locale to an abstract global. The very idea, appealing to some, of a global civil sphere would be a lovely thing to behold if only we could say where it might take place. If the model for a national civil society is the open forum or the fee marketplace, then where do we go precisely to change the debate or to sell our wares?

At the other extreme to those who are confident that the virtues of the national society can be made real amid a global society of sharp political and cultural changes are those who turn, at long last, away from the idealization of bourgeois society there to see the actual suffering of the excluded. On this end of the globalization debate are those who are exploring the conditions of bare life – of life in assemblages where no one has a legal right to belong; of lives that, remarkably, may be more vibrant than one supposes, but still they are lives lived amid global realties quite far beyond any world's ability to make them meaningful, beyond even the reach of the police, beyond any degree of wealth to buy off.

The extremes of global realities are many. Most of them unsettling the vocabularies of the social sciences to which we have grown accustomed. If we are to understand globalization in real, as distinct from familiar, terms, we must be willing to imagine worlds unable to provide homes as once they did, unable to assure inclusion in a stable civil sphere, unable even to point to a place to live that is not bare and barren.

To be willing to stretch in these ways is not to abandon all hope, nor to assume the thing itself cannot be known. It is only to admit that those who want to understand globalization want to understand global realities that may well have always been a central aspect of human society, yet, for whatever reason, are just now drawing fresh and vexed attentions. They must, thus, begin at the beginning.

WHAT IS GLOBALIZATION?

In the beginning was the globe. In time, there was a world. The distinction makes a difference.

A globe is a physical thing in space. The gases cooled and congealed into earth and waters. The lands moved as the waters rose and fell, froze and melted. The surface of this globe, like all other physical things, is extended in space, which means that anything that moved upon it took time to travel. Global things, being harshly material, create resistances to movement.

The world, by contrast, is an imaginary thing – an artifact of the human imagination. Worlds, thus, can be anywhere in an instant. Worlds resist not at all, except when living beings try to make them work. Then their imaginers must contend with globes that provide the friction that from time to time allows them to work more or less. Then as worlds spread upon the global surface, people meet up with differences of various kinds. Then and there, when imagined worlds encounter each other on physical globes, resistance grinds, making the work more difficult, sometimes impossible.

Globalization is a concept that can betray its strict meaning. Most, if not all, attempts to understand globalization are theories that are, in effect, attempts to imagine the movement of social worlds on the surface of the global whole. Theories are necessary and many of them are quite good. In this case, since they are made by people embedded in worlds, theories of globalization must work extra hard to overcome the globe's physical resistance to social movement.

Globes can endure without worlds. But *worlds*, being social things, cannot survive without globes. Globalization, therefore, is about the dependence of the one on the other. The relation stimulates the social imagination to rediscover the globe's worlds – its many and different worlds; to discover them, that is, as locales on a planet both small and large where people both similar and different must deal with each other, not always happily.

The physical distance that separates people populating different worlds can be, and usually is, a protective shield. Yet, when people dare to climb up and over the sacred mountain and there to find others who in the same instant find them, then the isolating shelter tatters. Why, one might ask, would people challenge their gods by climbing up and over a sacred mountain into a different world? The people were hungry and thirsty. They needed fresh food and water. The answer must be that their gods did not provide for them as they had been promised.

Insofar as globalization is a term arising from the information technologies that today allow people to climb the sacred mountains from an air-conditioned Starbucks, it is a term that means to account for the discovery of the global whole in all its sundry differences and tensions. But globalization cannot be narrowly conceived, as many have, as the magic of information technologies that make the global earth smaller. The ice caps are melting, the seas rising, the lands eroding. But the globe itself is much the same size and over-all shape as it always has been, give or take a few billion years here and there.

Globalization, thereby, is a theory that itself needs to be continuously reworked to account for a seeming endless supply of information about the global worlds. Chiefly this means thinking together, hard and long, about the realities of the humanized globe that are, as they always have been since humanoids first rose to walk on hind quarters. We live for a while in blissful isolation, then the scarcity of things force us to travel far and wide – for food, sex, shelter, air, water, more. There in time we are shocked to find that our world is other to others. Among social beings, there could hardly be a more upsetting realization.

Today, the important obstacle to thinking about global matters is not one of getting enough visual, verbal, and arithmetic information about them. Rather, it is that, still early in the 2000s, most people, even the young, grew up in worlds that have taught them that their world, whichever one it may be, is the best, even if it is not the only one. This occurs in all worlds of course. But one among these worlds has, over the last 500 years or so, become so capacious in its imagination and so powerful in its abilities to control or influence other worlds, that over time many quite different worlds have felt they must of necessity join forces with this one – or, at least, to pretend in its presence as if they were a strong ally. One powerful example of the extent to which this world has come to dominate the others is that others have all felt it in their interests to learn to speak its language.

As a result, *the* world is more or less accurately said to be centered in this one powerful instance of the worldly imagination. In and of itself, this is a common occurrence across the times and places of human history. Empires and civilizations are two instances of the extent to which worlds bend toward an imperial Center, there to find relief from what ails them.

Plus which, the transference of a local center to a global one is made easier by the happenstance that all, or nearly all, known worlds organize themselves locally around a center. The local centers may be as simple as a dominant totem, as fine as a sweat lodge where the elders prevail, or as mysterious as a sacred mountain whereupon their gods do whatever gods do when they are not promising and failing to deliver. In time, this habit of bowing to a sacred center took on more and more of the known and imaginable worlds of what in time came to be called a cosmology. A cosmology is a theory rich with symbolic and mythic contents of the organizing center of the cosmos. This sort of center is often symbolized by some recognizable sacred icon, building, object, or place; hence, nearly everywhere one goes, even today, you can see in the skyline or background of a settlement some such symbol of a people's sense of their Center – church steeples, minarets, a Mount of Olives, a Mecca, Mount Kailash, the Black Hills, World Trade Centers, ziggurats, football stadia, a Mount Olympus, and so on.

Generally speaking, these more ancient centers came to be called an *axis mundi* – a vector of the spiritual imagination whereby, as in ancient Mesopotamia, the surface of the earth was at the midpoint between the heavens above and a Sheol or Hades below.

As the more elemental versions of this kind of thinking began to fade early in modern times, the same cosmic logic arose in the form of expressions such as "*the* modern world." You can see right away, though many ignore it, that "*the* modern world" is itself a kind of half-baked cosmology – if only because it is more or less nonsense to the rational eye. Anyone with the least awareness of the other side of the mountain must realize that there can never be any one world – as in *the* world. Unless, of course, the expression is favored by people who believe they understand the other side of their sacred mountain, when in fact they have never gone there or heard anything but stories about these other places. Yet, stories always contain a kernel of truth amid the tares.

If there were a modern world, then how do we account for the wild, immutable social differences there to be seen? Plus which, how do we account for evidence that, whatever we might mean by "modern," there are worlds in various places on the globe that are so far from modern as to be unthinkable to moderns? In effect, there is no one world and it is not exhaustively modern; therefore we cannot accurately speak of "the" modern world. Yet, variations on the expression abound as though the modern world were a given.

Yet worlds, including the modern one, are not figments of the imagination. To say that a world is an imaginary is to do no more than describe the honest, even necessary, human need to think in an orderly way. We order our worlds according to a hierarchy of totems or hodge-podge of categories known only to the podges who belong to the hodge; or in modern times according to rules of scientific description – however we think of our worlds as ordered, we think according to some systematic method.

The method used by members of the modern world is one that assumes, but seldom admits, that an *axis mundi* is a line through imaginary time instead of cosmic space. The modern principle of the center has been, and may still be, that nearly everything that occurred before the present is inferior to everything that came after. As a result, moderns tend to think of their world as if it were *the* world. By their world they mean, but do not admit to, originally Western Europe and the United Kingdom (both, by the way, figures of speech taken to be literal places), then North America and other of Europe's colonies, then, in time, in urban centers over all the Americas, the Asias, the Middle East, and some, but not all, parts of the African continent.

Whatever might be concluded about the idea that there is a modern world, the indisputable fact is that it is reasonable to draw a sharp line in time dividing the modern era from all that came before – what some still call primitive and others call traditional societies. At the very least, this distinction confirms that there are times in human history where social forms are changed in ways that go far beyond a mere transformation. This is an important concession if only because it suggests that if global things changed once before then they could again as, indeed, they may have since 1991, as many say. This of course is one of the issues that must be addressed in any attempt to understand globalization. Is globalization a world- or globe-changing process or, less starkly, is it a readjustment within the terms and structures of the modern world? But, before addressing this question, another and similar one must be addressed – one that is in effect the bookend to the other.

If we were to agree with historians, prophets, and other sages that the modern world began as a deep global restructuring of the traditional, then how are we to measure the extent of the restructuring? Obviously, it goes almost without saying that *the* modern world, if we are to use the expression, is utterly and decisively different from the traditional one, but then we are at risk of making no sense whatsoever because it can hardly be denied that the modern remains deeply indebted to all that came before. In the modern West culture, law, and thought draw still on the Romans and the Greeks as, in China, the modernizing socialist program stands by as Confucian principles re-enter public life and private experience. No less, though it is seldom recognized, it would be foolish to suggest a comparison between say the totemic religions of elementary social groups and the proud religious steeples of moderns or the secular spires of their skyscrapers. Something comparable appears in the modern, even postmodern, worlds that can be confidently associated with the similar in long ago worlds. We may call it the universal appeal of religion or the social function of centering or the need of the human mind for order. Whatever we call it is what it is, and because it is, we must note that, however much worlds on globes change, they carry with them the recoverable past.

Turn this idea upside down and you have the second serious issue concerning globalization – one that, in this book, we address directly in the way the book is organized. In this respect, we are no doubt taking a controversial stand, but not one that cannot be explained and defended. That stand is that whatever else is common to modern and premodern social forms, globalization is, if not a fact in all cases, a discernible process. Thus we have organized the book to begin with a section of readings that represent the most ancient globalizing ideas of the classical and preclassical cultures around the globe. Compounding the controversy, though not as severely, we add another section of the decisively premodern, if not quite ancient, forms of globalization.

What then is the controversy? Let us state it with respect to one of today's first and most prolific students of globalization – one who does not need or seek to go about advertising himself as a globalist or the like. We refer to Immanuel Wallerstein, who articulates in the earliest volume of an already classic work what he calls the *modern world-system* (a locution that deploys the "the" but in excusable ways because he so thoroughly defends this system, as a system, with geographic and historical boundaries). The idea we have in mind is a linch pin of *The Modern World System, I*, where, in the concluding essay, Wallerstein distinguishes sharply between *world-empires* and *world-economies*.

The distinction carries with it the claim that, while both have occurred in premodern times (the Roman Empire in the one case, the Hanseatic League in the other), in the modern era the empire has all but disappeared before the emergence of the *modern* world-economy. This would be before the emergence of modern capitalism as a world-system – first, in the long sixteenth century, through subsequent stages, into the decisive moment in the nineteenth and twentieth centuries when industrial Britain then, after World War II, the United States became the dominant core powers in the world-system. Put all too simply, Wallerstein's idea is based on the widely agreed upon theory that capitalism is unlike all other economic systems in its skillful deployment of the appearance of calm, reason, and law behind which, as Marx put it, the capitalist, Mr Moneybags, exploits the worker and the resources of the globe to make his greedy profits.

Among other differences between a world-empire and a systemic world-economy is the suggestion that empires depend on force while modern economic systems use more covert forms of power. This is true of course; yet, we think, it may be too strong to say that there were not globalizing forces and effects at work in the long premodern periods where many more than a few local sacred mountains were traversed, then united under an imperial order, for economic as well as other social purposes.

MAPPING GLOBALIZATION

"Globalization" may be the defining buzzword of our era. In both the academy and public political life, it is difficult to think of a term that has gone global as quickly, and to such astonishing effect, as "globalization". From the staggering turnover of world foreign exchanges worth $1.4 trillion a day to the one billion international flights made each year, from the immense magnitude and geographical scale of trade, capital, and migrants to the incessant spread of new information technologies and digital media, from the growth of intricately layered transnational organizations – such as the International Red Cross, Amnesty International, Christian Aid, and Transparency International – that comprises the realm of global civil society to the emergence of new transnational terror networks such as Al-Qaeda, from the debates of comparative historians such as Jack Goldstone and John E. Willis II, as well as specialists on the Muslim world, concerning the multidimensional nature of global histories to the icons of transnational popular culture such as McDonalds, Coca-Cola, Starbucks, and Nokia: globalization is an idea whose time has come, shedding light as it does on the rapidly expanding scale, speed, magnitude and impact of transcontinental flows and inter-regional patterns of social interaction.

The term "globalization" is of relatively recent vintage, but the fact of it is as ancient as the earliest times – whenever settled peoples set out to colonize and incorporate economic, political, and cultural places foreign to their own. It is true of course that the globalization debate as we know it today – and as it is taught and written on – is distinctive to the present global situation. Yet, as Immanuel Wallerstein has repeatedly pointed out, globalization begins at least with the age of discovery and economic colonization in the long sixteenth century. We go somewhat further on his point (believing that he would not be in serious disagreement) by seeking to define the global ideal in its proper historical contexts. These would include, of course, the age of empires, a period of at least four millennia. But it would also include the core religious and cultural ideas, the traces of which are found through the many overlapping ideologies of modernity. What makes the modern period distinctive is that it is a radical hegemony of a series of Western world powers that had (and have) the effect of inventing the idea of one world or of global economies on the illusionary notion that the culture of the European Diaspora is the one and true culture of the human world. It is this illusion that has started to break down after the world revolutions of 1968 and that came to a head in the crucial period from the end of the Cold War in 1989–91 and 9/11. As a result, this book includes quite a few cultural and religious texts mixed with political ones on the conviction that, always, the idea to colonize distant territories is as much a religious or cultural ideal as it is a political and economic interest.

We have composed this book, collecting the various key statements from a variety of historical periods, political contexts, intellectual perspectives, and academic disciplines, in the belief that globalization has a central role to play in contemporary intellectual culture and a fundamental role within the social sciences. Our aim has been to offer a book that combines some originality by placing the debate over globalization in its wider historical context with a comprehensive treatment of both academic and popular accounts of the phenomenon. Throughout the book, we aim to cover the major theoretical perspectives in globalization studies and the major findings of contemporary research in a fair-minded, although not indiscriminate, fashion.

Whilst the debate over globalization has produced a voluminous literature, at once specialist and popular, this book advances a number of novel claims. Put simply, these are:

- Western exceptionalism is an illusion of the political mind.
- Globalization is not a uniform process. On the contrary, globalization is multidimensional – shaped by, and reshaping, complex forces of economic trade, state organization, and political ideologies.
- Globalization is intricately interwoven with the emergence of "multiple modernities." That is to say, Western globalization is in various respects quite different from, say, Islamic globalization or Chinese globalization.
- Globalization is not merely coterminous with the recent rise of new information technologies. On

the contrary, as sections examining the period of early modern globalization reveal, the world from the sixteenth through nineteenth centuries was more interconnected than many analysts have allowed.

EARLIER VERSIONS OF GLOBALIZATION

In its collection of diverse readings from various historical periods, political contexts, and economic transformations, this book seeks to stress the multicentered dimensions of intellectual and ideological production essential to processes of globalization. From the ancient worlds of civilizational empires through archaic or early modern globalization to more contemporary stages of global networks and complexity, the actors involved in the production and transformation of multiple globalizations have reflexively understood such processes in the context of diverse theoretical systems, doctrines, and traditions of thought – some overlapping, many remarkably different from each other. Ideological knowledge and techniques were equally central to Western radical secularism as to the religious beliefs and cyclical time of South and East Asia, and from which the social-historical and cultural-economic roots of global change could be considered anew. Clearly enough, this elementary sense of "globalization" referred to, among other things, an emerging *global history of ideas* – defined by a pioneer of globalization studies, Roland Robertson, as "the twofold process of the particularization of the universal and the universalization of the particular."

But what, exactly, was global about this twofold form of social transformation? As one example, the world takes a universalizing swerve – in which people began to share a single, common dream of how things should be. Thus, we might say that thinking about both the globe and the world in earlier historical circumstances always took place under social conditions in which individuals drew upon certain theoretical ideas about "globalization" (by which we mean, especially, the universalization of the particular) in order to think about the new society of which they were part. That is to say, consciousness of the Modern Age was one in which people could not help but think about the world in universal and multileveled ways with regard to politics and economics particularly, but just as immediately society and culture. And one key example of such global thinking would surely be the Eurocentric paradigm for understanding modernity itself. The story of what will happen to the globe under conditions of the Eurocentric horizon, as societies and cultures find themselves accorded either a central or peripheral role in a line of social development accorded universal significance, belongs to the narrative of Western civilization. In the Eurocentric paradigm, the globe becomes more or less synonymous with "civilization," in the sense of a universal process of material, cultural, and intellectual progress. Civilization, from this angle, appears largely as a European notion – in which, say, the Hegelian Spirit or Max Weber's "problem of universal history" is cast as the highroad to modernity.

GLOBALIZATION WARS: TODAY'S IDEA OF THE GLOBE

Today's intensively global conditions for living in, and thinking about, the globalized age have dramatically altered the hold on power of the Eurocentric horizon. That is to say, people are less in thrall to the normative force of European civilization as "the way of life" than once they were. The reasons for this are clear. Over recent years, dating from sometime around the world revolution of 1968 and certainly from the installation of satellites above the earth in 1973, there has been a dramatic enlargement of global communication, trade, and interaction – which in turn has led to major geopolitical changes in the relations between the local and the global, core states and periphery, and thus to novel conceptions of the shape of the world. Another way of putting this point is to say that the globalization of earlier periods, uncoupled from the force of the Eurocentric horizon, has modulated into "advanced" or "hyper" globalization. From this angle, communication linkages across the globe appear as both more dense and more extensive than in previous historical epochs – primarily as the result of remarkable innovations in new communication technologies and their applications to the new economy of global cities.

Whether celebrated or deplored, globalization as a concept becomes in our own time increasingly central to contemporary cultural outlooks – particularly as a means for explaining recent technological revolutions, but also for thinking about postmodern culture and the arts, the disappearance of History, the spread of terror networks and the war on terror, climate change, and such like. While there is no single adequate definition of globalization in the current age, consider the following list of random definitions currently in circulation:

- the Westernization, or Americanization, of the world;
- the rising interpenetration of economies that cross nation-state boundaries and which stretch social relations to bring people together and raise living standards;
- the highest stage of advanced, or multinational, capitalism;
- the stretching of social relations across space and time;
- the emergence of a "borderless world";
- the dominance of global communicational conglomerates promoting the "death of distance";
- the speeding-up of the world;
- the inevitable growing magnitude, and deepening impact, of transcontinental flows;
- a process transformational of the strict separation between domestic and international arenas, between internal and external affairs;
- that which leads to the creolization or hybridization of cultures;
- the production of empire and new mechanisms of multilateral control and surveillance;
- new structures inseparable from processes of complexity, fluidity, and liquidity possessing patterns and properties that are often far from equilibrium;
- the spread of networks and interrelated transnational technological, organizational, and cultural innovations.

There are a number of points that might be noted about this list of definitions. For example, some of these definitions rate globalization very positively, others negatively, and some are clearly ambiguous. The more positive of these definitions see globalization as an inevitable development in the geopolitics of social relations, emphasizing the benefits of an improved quality of life, raised living standards, and increased intercultural communication. In this sense, globalism is regarded as a social good – in much the same way as the coming of the telephone or motorcar might have been. Some of these definitions, however, view globalization pejoratively – as the ideology of multinational capitalism, for example – and thus emphasize the vested economic and political interests as well as uneven consequences of globalism. Anti-globalists, whether making the charge of Westernization or turbo-capitalist exploitation, view globalization as fundamentally responsible for the compounding of inequalities.

Another point is that this list of definitions carries a range of implications for understanding the world in which we live: not just in academic terms but also for everyday life. Some formulations identify profoundly transformative processes, such that the very existence of the "global" disrupts established paradigms, political orthodoxies, and traditional ways of understanding the character of social life. A number of conceptual approaches in this respect, from various positive globalists to postmodernists, suggest that the social sciences must radically rethink its subject-matter – as a world of "bounded" societies no longer exists, if indeed it ever once did. Other traditions of thought are much more cautious. Some argue that the significance of globalization has been exaggerated; others that the discourse of globalism is a myth.

Another interesting feature of this list is that the bulk of these definitions have been produced in only the last two decades or so. This is a reminder of the important point that the debate over globalization is still very much in its infancy. To date, globalization studies are only at a very early or elementary stage of mapping, classifying, and interrogating the multicentered forms of knowledge and ideological production essential to processes of globalism. Too often, local, national, and regional histories of globalism have been reductively conceptualized within the territorial boundaries of political states and ecological zones – rather than grasping the necessity of a global approach to all reorderings of society and historical change. One aim of this book is to clarify and to probe the possible connections between "societies" and the global – given that we argue globalization is less a singular causal force than a complex of interlocking connections, properties, and patterns.

This type of global approach to globalization studies is also a useful analytical tool for engaging with the major debates of our own time. In setting out and defending a multidimensional approach to globalization, we mean to underscore the following key points. First, that globalization can best be understood not as a static entity, but as comprising multidimensional social, cultural, economic, and political processes. Globalism does not reflect a top-heavy, one-way developmental logic, and nor does it prefigure a homogeneous world culture. Rather, it refers to the formation, reproduction, and transformation of interregional networks, as well as global systems of interaction and exchange. In this connection, the complex, contradictory interaction of national or societal systems and wider global processes can be analytically separated from any conception of global integration. Second, the temporal restructuring and spatial density wrought as a consequence of globalization spells multidimensional networks of relations between actors, communities, states, international institutions, non-governmental organizations, and multinational corporations which make up the global order. These new global networks define an evolving structure that at once empowers and constrains communities, states, and social forces.

Acknowledgments

The publishers would like to thank the following for permission to reprint their material:

Joseph H. Peterson for kind permission to reprint Zarathustra, *Avesta*, translation by Bartholomae, from I.J.S. Taraporewala, *The Divine Songs of Zarathustra*. Translation of excerpt from Zoroastrian text Yasna, by Joseph H. Peterson, copyright 1997. Used with permission. http://www.avesta.org/.

Chowkhamba Sanskrit Series Office, India for kind permission to reprint "Rig Veda 3.62 – Gayatri Mantra" in Ralph T.H. Griffith (1971) 'The Hymns of the Rig-Veda,' The *Chowkhamba Sanskrit Studies* vol. XXXV (Varanasi – 1 (India): The Chowkhamba Sanskrit Series Office, vol. 1, pp. 389–390).

Penguin Group for permission to reprint "The Epic of Gilgamesh: the Babylonian epic poem and other texts in Akkadian and Sumerian," translated with an introduction by Andrew George. Penguin Books, 1999; Penguin Classics 2000, Revised 2003. Copyright © Andrew George, 1999.

The University of Toronto Press for permission to reprint Dobson, W.A.C.H. (1963) *Mencius: a new translation arranged and annotated for the general reader*. University of Toronto Press. 'Reprinted with permission of the publisher.'

Bowman Books and Joseph Bruchac for permission to reprint "The Coming of Gluskabi" in *The Wind Eagle and Other Abenaki Stories*. Told by Joseph Bruchac. Greenfield Center, NY: Bowman Books, 1985.

University of Illinois Press for kind permission to reprint James Henry Breasted *Ancient Records of Egypt: VOL. 3: The Nineteenth Dynasty*, University of Illinois Press, 2001 [1906].

Princeton University Press for permission to reprint Pritchard, James B. (ed.) (1958) *Ancient Near East: An anthology of texts and pictures*. Princeton NJ: Princeton University Press. Pritchard, James; *The Ancient Near East*. © 1958 Princeton University Press, 1986 renewed PUP Reprinted by permission of Princeton University Press.

The Internet Classics Archive for kind permission to reprint Thucydides, "Funeral Oration of Pericles" in *History of the Peloponnesian War*, book 2. Translated by Richard Crawley in 1876. The Internet Classics Archive available online at http://classics.mit.edu.

Harvard University Press for kind permission to reprint Plutarch, Moralia. "On the Fortune or the Virtue of Alexander, bk. 1," *De Fortuna Alexandri by Plutarch* as published in Vol. IV of the Loeb Classical Library edition, 1936. Reprinted by permission of the publishers and the Trustees of the Loeb Classical Library from Velleius Paterculus, Loeb Classical Library Volume 152, translated by F. W. Shipley,

Cambridge, Mass.: Harvard University Press, Copyright © 1924 by the President and Fellows of Harvard College. The Loeb Classical Library® is a registered trademark of the President and Fellows of Harvard College.

The Trustees of the British Museum for kind permission to reprint the translation of the Greek section of the Rosetta Stone, which appears in the British Museum Press publication *The Rosetta Stone*, by Carol Andrews ISBN 0–7141–1931–2, pp. 25, 26, 27, 28. © 1981 The Trustees of the British Museum. http://pw1.netcom.com/~qkstart/rosetta.html.

The Buddhist Publication Society Inc. for permission to reprint Ven. Dhammika "Edicts of King Ashoka, Pillar 13."

Augustus, *Deeds of Augustus (Res Gestae Divi Augusti)*. Reprinted by permission of the publishers and the Trustees of the Loeb Classical Library from Velleius Paterculus, Loeb Classical Library Volume 152, translated by F.W. Shipley, Cambridge, Mass.: Harvard University Press, Copyright © 1924 by the President and Fellows of Harvard College. The Loeb Classical Library® is a registered trademark of the President and Fellows of Harvard College.

Columbia University Press for permission to reprint "Samguk Sagi: 41:394–43:406" from Peter Lee (ed). *Sourcebook of Korean Civilization*. From "Samguk Sagi: 41:394–43:406" in Peter Lee, Ed., *Sourcebook of Korean Civilization*, p. 111–112. Copyright © 1993 Columbia University Press. Reprinted with permission of the publisher.

The Australian National University, Faculty of Asian Studies and Mei-Kao Ku for kind permission to reprint Chinese Mirror for Magistrates: The Hsin-Yu of Lu Chia (Faculty of Asian Studies Monographs, 11) by Mei-Kao Ku July 1988, Australian National University, Faculty of Asian Studies.

Deutsche Fotothek / Staats- und Universitätsbibliothek Dresden (SLUB) for permission to reprint image of page 6 of the "Dresden Codex" reference SLUB Mscr.Dresd.R.310.

Cambridge University Press for permission to reprint "The Picture of the Earth," in *Corpus of Early Arabic Sources for West African History* translated by J.F.P. Hopkins, edited and annotated by N. Levtzion and J.F.P. Hopkins. Cambridge [Eng.] and New York: Cambridge University Press, 1981, pp. 44–46. Reproduced with permission.

Tuttle Publishing for kind permission to reprint Kojiki. Translation 1919 by Basil Hall Chamberlain. Vol. II. 1 (Sect. XLIV), p. 159–161. Reprinted with kind permission of Tuttle Publishing.

Bilingual Press/Editorial Bilingüe for permission to reprint "Hymn Seven, Prayer for the Inca" by John Curl (trans.), from *Ancient American Poets* by John Curl, translator, Bilingual Press/Editorial Bilingüe, 2005, Tempe, Arizona.

Christian Classics Ethereal Library for kind permission to reprint Augustine of Hippo, "The Folly of the Romans," City of God (I, 3) from Christian Classics Ethereal Library, www.ccel.org.

Cahokia Mounds State Historic Site, Illinois, for kind permission to reprint image of the Cahokia Mounds.

University of Utah Press for kind permission to reprint "Concerning other events that happened when the Mexicans, Tlatelolcans, and the lord of Mexico surrendered to the Spaniards," in *Conquest of New Spain: 1585 Revision* by Bernardino de Sahagún. *Reproductions of the Boston Public Library Manuscript and*

Carlos María de Bustamante 1840 Edition, translated by Howard F. Cline, edited with an introduction and notes by S.L. Cline. Salt Lake City: University of Utah Press, 1989, pp. 137–139.

Elsevier for permission to reprint Wallerstein, Immanuel (1974) *The Modern World System: Capitalist Agriculture and the Origins of the European World-Economy in the Sixteenth Century* (New York, San Francisco, London: Academic Press), pp. 15–17. Copyright © Elsevier 1974.

Random House, Inc. for permission to reprint Fernández-Armesto, Felipe (2003) *The Americas: A Hemispheric History* (New York: The Modern Library), pp. 90–95. From THE AMERICAS by Felipe Fernandez-Armesto, copyright © 2003 by Felipe Fernandez-Armesto. Used by permission of Modern Library, a division of Random House, Inc.

Massachusetts Historical Society's Collections for kind permission to reprint William Bradford, 'Of Plimouth Plantation' in *Collections of the Massachusetts Historical Society*, ser. 4, vol. 3, ed. Charles Deane (Boston: Little, Brown, and Company, 1856), 100–106, reprinted from the Massachusetts Historical Collections.

Avalon Project at the Yale Law Library for kind permission to reprint Treaty of Westphalia. http://avalon.law.yale.edu/17th_century/westphal.asp.

Random House, Inc. for permission to reprint Hughes, Robert (1966) *The Fatal Shore*. New York: Vintage Books, pp. 1–3. From *The Fatal Shore* by Robert Hughes, copyright © 1986 by Robert Hughes. Used by permission of Alfred A. Knopf, a division of Random House, Inc.

Houghton Mifflin Harcourt for permission to reprint Hochschild, Adam (1999) *King Leopold's Ghost*. Houghton Mifflin. pp. 6–18. Excerpt from KING LEOPOLD'S GHOST by Adam Hochschild. Copyright © 1998 by Adam Hochschild. Reprinted by permission of Houghton Mifflin Harcourt Publishing Company. All rights reserved.

Walker and Co. for permission to reprint Sobel, Dava (1995) *Longitude: The True Story of a Lone Genius Who Solved the Greatest Scientific Problem of His Times*. New York: Walker and Company, pp. 165–175.

Beinecke Rare Book and Manuscript Library, Yale University for kind permission to reprint image of the Gutenberg Bible (Biblia latina. Bible. Latin. Vulgate. 1454), pp. 146v–147r. Originally published Mainz: Johann Gutenberg, Call Number: ZZi 56, Bibliographic Record Number: 2020598.

University of California Press for permission to reprint "Napoleon, social and political thoughts," in Chaliand, Gérard (ed.) (1994) *The Art of War in World History from Antiquity to the Nuclear Age* (Berkeley: University of California Press), pp. 646–651.

Yale University Press for permission to reprint Scott, James C. (1998) *Seeing Like a State: How Certain Schemes to Improve the Human Condition Have Failed* (New Haven: Yale University Press), pp. 11–15, 25–29.

Houghton Mifflin Harcourt for permission to reprint Ruth Benedict (1946) *The Chrysanthemum and the Sword: Patterns of Japanese Culture*. Boston: Houghton Mifflin Company, pp. 29–33. Excerpt from THE CRYSANTHEMUM AND THE SWORD by Ruth Benedict. Copyright 1946 by Ruth Benedict;

Random House, Inc. for permission to reprint V.S. Naipaul "A New King for the Congo," *New York Review of Books*, Volume 22, Number 11 · June 26, 1975. From THE WRITER AND THE WORLD: ESSAYS by V. S. Naipaul, copyright © 2002 by V. S. Naipaul. Used by permission of Alfred A. Knopf, a division of Random House, Inc.

The World Social Forum for kind permission to reprint "Note from the Organizing Committee on the Principles that Guide the WSF." http://www.forumsocialmundial.org.br/main.php?id_menu=4_2&cd_language=2 (English text by volunteer translators Helena El Masri and Peter Lenny).

Simon and Schuster, Inc. and The Free Press for permission to reprint Ohmae, Kenichi (1995) *The End of the Nation State: The Rise of the Regional Economies*. New York: Free Press Paperbacks. pp. 7, 28–30, 141–2. Reprinted and edited with the permission of The Free Press, a Division of Simon and Schuster, Inc., from THE END OF THE NATION STATE: The Rise of the Regional Economies by Kenichi Ohmae. Copyright © 1995 by McKinsey and Company. All rights reserved.

The Johns Hopkins Center for Transatlantic Relations for kind permission to reprint Castells, Manuel (2006). "The Network Society: From Knowledge to Policy" in Castells, Manuel and Gustavo Cardoso (eds) *The Network Society: From Knowledge to Policy*. Washington DC: Johns Hopkins Center for Transatlantic Relations. pp. 3–5, 7, 15–16.

Sage Publications for permission to reprint Dicken, Peter (1992). *Global Shift: the internationalization of economic activity*. London: Paul Chapman, 1992. 2nd ed. pp. 5–6, 10–13. Reproduced by permission of SAGE Publications, London, Los Angeles, New Delhi and Singapore, from Peter Dicken, *Global Shift: the internationalization of economic activity*. © 1992 Peter Dicken.

Taylor & Francis Books UK for permission to reprint Hannerz, Ulf (1996). *Transnational Connections: Culture, People, Places*. London and New York: Routledge. pp. 102, 107–111. From *Transnational Connections: Culture, People, Places*, by Ulf Hannerz, Copyright © 1996, Routledge. Reproduced by permission of Taylor and Francis Books UK.

HarperCollins Publishers for permission to reprint Freidman, Thomas (2000) *The Lexus and the Olive Tree*. London: Harpers Collins Publishers, 2000, pp.104–6. Reprinted by permission of HarperCollins Publishers Ltd © Thomas Freidman 2000.

Polity Press for permission to reprint extracts from Hirst, Paul and Grahame Thompson (1990) *Globalization in Question*, Cambridge: Polity Press. pp. 1–7.

Klein Lewis Productions Ltd for permission to reprint Naomi Klein (2004) "Reclaiming the Commons" in ed. Tom Mertes, *A Movement of Movements*. London: Verso. pp. 219–229. This is a transcript of a talk given at the Center for Social Theory and Comparative History, UCLA, in April 2001, it has been abridged as marked by the editor. "Reclaiming the Commons" by Naomi Klein, copyright © 2001 by Naomi Klein.

Princeton University Press for permission to reprint Gilpin, Robert (2000) *The Challenge of Global Capitalism: The World Economy in the twenty-first Century*. Princeton NJ: Princeton University Press. pp. 3, 5–10. GILPIN, ROBERT G; *THE CHALLENGE OF GLOBAL CAPITALISM* © 2000 Princeton University Press. Reprinted by permission of Princeton University Press.

Continuum International Publishing Group for permission to reprint Jones, R.J. Barry (1995) *Globalization and Interdependence in the International Political Economy*. London: Pinter Publishers. pp. 219–221. By kind permission of Continuum International Publishing Group.

Reprinted from *European Management Journal*, Vol. 19, No. 4., Rugman, Alan and Richard Hodgetts, "The End of Global Strategy," pp. 333–343, Copyright 2001, with permission from Elsevier.

Profile Books for permission to reprint Giddens, Anthony (1999) *Runaway World*. Cambridge: Polity Press. pp. 6–10, 12–13, 15–19.

Routledge / Taylor & Francis Group LLC for permission to reprint Giddens, Anthony (1999) *Runaway World*. Cambridge: Polity Press. pp. 6–10,12–13, 15–19. RUNAWAY WORLD: HOW GLOBALIZATION IS RESHAPING OUR LIVES by Anthony Giddens. Copyright 1999 by Taylor & Francis Group LLC – Books. Reproduced with permission of Taylor and Francis Group LLC – Books in the format Other book via Copyright Clearance Center.

Polity Press for permission to reprint Held, David and Anthony McGrew (1999) *Global Transformations*. Cambridge: Polity Press. pp. 7–9.

New American Century for kind permission to reprint "Statement of Principles, June 3, 1997." From http://www.newamericancentury.org/statementofprinciples.htm.

Aihwa Ong, "Introduction (excerpts totaling 4 pages)", in *Neoliberalism as Exception: Mutations in Citizenship and Sovereignty*, pp. 1–27. Copyright, 2006, Duke University Press. All Rights Reserved. Used by permission of the publisher.

The Nobel Foundation for kind permission to reprint Gore, Al "The Nobel Peace Prize Lecture, 2007," Nobel Lecture, Oslo, 10 December 2007. © The Nobel Foundation 2007. http://nobelprize.org/nobel_prizes/peace/laureates/2007/gore-lecture_en.html.

Polity Press for permission to reprint Beck, Ulrich (1999) *What is Globalization*. Translated by Patrick Camiller, Cambridge: Polity Press. pp. 10–13.

Columbia University Press and Polity Press for permission to reprint Bauman, Zygmunt (1998) *Globalization: The Human Consequences*. New York: Columbia University Press. pp. 2–3, 9–10, 18–19.

Sage for permission to reprint Appadurai, Arjun, "Disjuncture and Difference in the Global Cultural Economy." *Theory, Culture and Society* Vol. 7. No. 2, pp. 296–300, 301–303, copyright © 1990 by Sage. Reprinted by Permission of SAGE.

Fredric Jameson, "Notes on Globalization as a Philosophical Issue (excerpts of 9 pages)" in *The Cultures of Globalization*, Fredric Jameson and Masao Miyoshi, Eds., pp 54–77. Copyright, 1998, Duke University Press. All rights reserved. Used by permission of the publisher.

Palgrave Macmillan for permission to reprint Rosenberg, Justin (2005) "Globalization Theory: A Postmortem," in *International Politics*, 42, pp. 11–15. Reprinted by permission from Macmillan Publishers Ltd: from *International Politics*, Justin Rosenberg, "Globalization Theory: A Postmortem," © 2005 Justin Rosenberg, published by Palgrave Macmillan.

Verso for permission to reprint Žižek, Slavoj (2001) "Welcome to the Desert of the Real."

Foreign Affairs for permission to reprint extracts from Nye, Joseph S. (2001) "Globalization's Democratic Deficit: How to Make International Institutions More Accountable." *Foreign Affairs* July/August, p. 2–6.

Allen & Unwin Book Publishers for permission to reprint Chomsky, Noam (2006) *Failed States: The Abuse of Power and the Assault on Democracy.* Allen & Unwin, 2006. pp. 1–2, 252, 263–4. www.allenandunwin.com.

Henry Holt & Co. LLC and the author for permission to reprint Chomsky, Noam (2006) *Failed States: The Abuse of Power and the Assault on Democracy.* Allen and Unwin, 2006. pp. 1–2, 252, 263–4. Text from FAILED STATES: The Abuse of Power and the Assault on Democracy by Noam Chomsky. Copyright © 2006 by Harry Chomsky as trustee of Chomsky Grandchildren Nominee Trust. Reprinted by arrangement with Henry Holt and Company, LLC.

Oxford University Press for permission to reprint The Commission on Global Governance (2002) *Our Global Neighborhood.* By permission of Oxford University Press.

Cambridge University Press and the author for permission to reprint Rosenau, James N. (1992) "Governance, Order and Change in World Politics," in J. Rosenau and E. Czempiel (eds) *Governance Without Government: Order and Change in World Politics.* Cambridge: Cambridge University Press. pp. 3–8. © Cambridge University Press 1992, reproduced with permission.

Polity Press for permission to reprint Held, David (2004) *Global Covenant: The Social Democratic Alternative to the Washington Consensus.* Cambridge: Polity Press. pp. 162–169.

Foreign Affairs for permission to reprint extracts from Ikenberry, G. John (2008) "The Rise of China and the Future of the West: Can the Liberal System Survive?" *Foreign Affairs* Jan/Feb 2008.

Polity Press for permission to reprint Tomlinson, John (1999) *Globalization and Culture.* Cambridge: Polity Press, pp. 27–31.

Cowen, Tyler (2002) *Creative Destruction: How Globalization is Changing the World Cultures.* Princeton, NJ: Princeton University Press. pp. 55–59. COWEN, TYLER; *CREATIVE DESTRUCTION.* Princeton University Press. Reprinted by permission of Princeton University Press.

Palgrave Macmillan for permission to reprint Hall, Stuart (1991) "The Local and the Global: Globalization and Ethnicity," in Anthony King (ed.) *Culture and Globalization and the World System: Contemporary Representation of Identity.* London: Macmillan, pp. 30–36.

Lynne Rienner for permission to reprint Paolini, Albert (1999) From *Navigating Modernity: Postcolonialism, Identity, and International Relations* by Albert J. Paolini, edited by Anthony Elliott and Anthony Moran. Copyright © 1999 by Lynne Rienner Publishers, Inc. Used with permission of the publisher.

Sage Publications Ltd for permission to reprint Robertson, Roland (1995) "Glocalization: Time-Space Homogeneity Heterogeneity," in Mike Featherstone *et al.* (eds) *Global Modernities.* London: Sage Publications. pp. 28–32. Reproduced by permission of SAGE Publications, London, Los Angeles, New Delhi and Singapore, from Roland Robertson, *Glocalization: Time-Space Homogeneity Heterogeneity* © 1995 Roland Robertson.

International Creative Management, Inc. for permission to reprint Fukuyama, Francis "The End of History?" in *The National Interest.* Summer 1989. Reprinted by permission of International Creative Mangement, Inc. Copyright © 1989 by Francis Fukuyama for The National Interest.

Foreign Affairs for permission to reprint extracts from Huntington, Samuel (1993). "The Clash of Civilizations?" *Foreign Affairs* 22, Summer, pp. 22–26, 39–41.

Foreign Affairs for permission to reprint extracts from Hoffman, Stanley (2002). "Clash of Globalizations," in *Foreign Affairs*, vol. 81, no. 4, July/August, pp. 110–115.

Taylor & Francis Ltd for kind permission to reprint Kwong, Peter and Duskana Miscevic (2002) "Globalization and Hong Kong's Future," *Journal of Contemporary Asia*, vol. 32, no. 3, pp. 323, 324, 325, 328, 335, 336. Reprinted by permission of the publisher (Taylor & Francis Ltd, http://www.tandf.co.uk/journals).

Taylor and Francis Books for permission to reprint Guthrie, Doug (2006) *China and Globalization: The Social, Economic and Political Transformation of Chinese Society*, New York; London: Routledge. pp. 3–4, 255, 329–331. Copyright © 2006 From *China and Globalization: The Social, Economic and Political Transformation of Chinese Society* by Doug Guthrie. Reproduced by permission of Taylor and Francis Group, LLC, a division of Informa plc. New York and London: Routledge. pp. 3–4, 255, 329–331.

Penguin Group (UK) for permission to reprint Garton Ash, Timothy (2004) *Free World: America, Europe, and the Surprising Future of the West*. New York: Random House. pp. 46–50, 80–82. From FREE WORLD by Timothy Garton Ash (Allen Lane 2004, Penguin Books 2005). Copyright © Timothy Garton Ash, 2004, 2005. Reproduced by permission of Penguin Books Ltd.

Random House, Inc for permission to reprint from FREE WORLD: AMERICA, EUROPE AND THE SURPRISING FUTURE OF THE WEST by Timothy Garton Ash, copyright © 2004 by Timothy Garton Ash. Used by permission of Random House, Inc.

Polity Press for permission to reprint Giddens, Anthony and Ulrich Beck (2007) "Open Letter on the Future of Europe," in Anthony Giddens *The Future of Europe*. Cambridge: Polity Press, pp. 231–234.

Semiotext(e) for permission to reprint Deleuze, Gilles, and Guattari, Felix (1986) *Nomadology: The War Machine*. New York: Semiotext(e). pp. 50–54. *Nomadology: the War Machine*. Copyright © 1986 by Semiotext(e). Used by permission of the publisher. http://www.semiotexte.com.

Harvard University Press for permission to reprint Hardt, Michael and Antonio Negri (2000) *Empire*. Reprinted by permission of the publisher from EMPIRE by Michael Hardt and Antonio Negri, pp. xi–xii, xv–xvi, 15, 392, Cambridge, Mass.: Harvard University Press, Copyright © 2000 by the President and Fellows of Harvard College.

Co-Action Publishing for permission to reprint Sassen, Saskia (2008) "Neither Global Nor National: Novel Assemblages of Territory, Authority and Rights," *Ethics and Global Politics*, Vol. 1, No. 2, pp. 61–71. http://journals.sfu.ca/coaction/index.php/egp/article/view/1814/1809.

Polity Press for permission to reprint Urry, John (2003) *Global Complexity*. Cambridge: Polity Press. pp. 93–101.

Verso for permission to reprint Davis, Mike (2007) *Planet of Slums*. London and New York: Verso. pp. 134–146.

Cambridge University Press and John Keane for permission to reprint Keane, John (2003) *Global Civil Society?* Cambridge: Cambridge University Press. pp. 8–12, 16–17. © John Keane 2003, published by Cambridge University Press, reproduced with permission.

Polity Press for permission to reprint Kaldor, Mary (2003) *Global Civil society: An Answer to War.* Cambridge: Polity Press. pp. 6–12.

The University of Chicago Press for permission to reprint Appiah, Kwame Anthony (1997) "Cosmopolitan Patriots," *Critical Inquiry* 23, spring, pp. 617–9, 633–4. Copyright © 1997, The University of Chicago Press.

Sage for permission to reprint Sen, Amartya "Violence, Identity and Poverty," *Journal of Peace Research* Vol. 45, No. 5, pp. 5–7, 13–15, copyright © 2008 by Sage. Reprinted by Permission of SAGE.

Pheng Cheah, "Spectral Nationality: The Living on [sur-vie] of the Postcolonial Nation in Neocolonial Globalization (excerpts of 4 pages)" in *Boundary 2*, volume 26, no. 3, pp. 225–252. Copyright, 1999, Duke University Press. All rights reserved. Used by permission of the publisher.

Columbia University Press for permission to reprint Kristeva, Julia (1995) *New Maladies of the Soul.* Translated by Ross Guberman. New York: Columbia University Press. pp. 6–10.

The University of Chicago Press and Dennis Altman for permission to reprint Altman, Dennis (2001) *Global Sex.* Chicago: University of Chicago Press. pp. 100–105, © 2001 The University of Chicago.

Polity Press for permission to reprint Papastergiadis, Nikos (2000) *Turbulence of Migration: Globalization, Deterritorialization and Hybridity.* Cambridge: Polity Press, pp. 40–41, 44, 46–50.

SUNY Press for permission to reprint Jean-Luc Nancy (2007) *The Creation of the World or Globalization.* Translated by Francois Raffoul and David Pettigrew. Albany, NY: State University of New York Press. pp. 33–37. Reprinted by permission from *The Creation of the World or Globalization* by Jean-Luc Nancy, translated by Francois Raffoul and David Pettigrew, the State University of New York Press © 2007, State University of New York. All rights reserved.

Verso for permission to reprint Butler, Judith (2004) *Precarious Life: The Powers of Mourning and Violence.* London and New York: Verso. pp. xi – xiii, xvii–xxi.

Verso for permission to reprint Virilio, Paul (2005) *The Information Bomb.* London: Verso, pp. 130–137, 139–140.

University of Minnesota Press for permission to reprint extracts from Giorgio Agamben (2000) *Means without End: Notes on Politics.* Translated by Vincenzo Binetti and Cesare Casarino. Minneapolis and London: University of Minnesota Press. pp. 3–12.

Continuum International Book Publishing for permission to reprint DeLanda, Manuel (2006) *A New Philosophy of Society: Assemblage Theory and Social Complexity.* London and New York: Continuum. pp. 95–6, 112–119. By kind permission of Continuum International Publishing Group.

Achille Mbembe, "Necropolitics (excerpts of 6 pages)" translated by Libby Meintjes, in *Public Culture*, Volume 15, No. 1, pp. 11–40. Copyright, 2003, Duke University Press. All rights reserved.

Simone, AbdouMaliq (2003) "The visible and the invisible: Remaking Cites in Africa," in *Under Siege: Four African Cities–Freetown, Johannesburg, Kinshasa, Lagos: Documenta11_Platform4.* Hatje Cantz Publishers. pp. 37–41.

Taylor & Francis Books (UK) for kind permission to reprint Zolo, Danilo (2007) "Global Citizenship: A Realist Critique" in Eds. Stephen Slaughter and Wayne Hudsons *Globalisation and Citizenship: The Transnational Challenge*. London and New York: Routledge, p. 80–3.

Disclaimer

Notes on Dates and Selections

Readers will find dates or date ranges for the selections in Parts One, Two, and Three, usually in the captions for each selection. These parts are historically sensitive, and dates are used here to guide the reader. In Parts Four, Five, and Six the selections are all relatively contemporary. In all cases where the date of a selected text or document is of particular importance it is mentioned in the commentary that introduces the selection.

Also, please note that these are literally selections, often with breaks in the text or document presented. These breaks are indicated by an ellipsis within square brackets, at the end of the material before the break. Where breaks are not indicated the material is continuous, though not the entirety of the text itself. See notes at the end of the selections for the source information.

PART ONE

The age of empires, 3000 BCE–1500 CE

INTRODUCTION TO PART ONE

To speak of an "Age of Empires" is to take the risks that must be taken if we are to understand the nature of globalization. The safer course would be to stipulate, as many do, that globalization is a historical process of relatively *recent times*. Yet, "recent times" is itself a troubling category. When "recent times" refers, let us say, to the last decade of the twentieth century and the first of the twenty-first, it is necessary to ask whether the times in question are *still-modern, late-modern*, or *post-modern*. Recent is as recent does! For those who believe the world as it is now is *still-modern*, "recent times" could stretch back through time to any of a number of truly modern events – 1914 (the Great War and the loss of innocence), or 1848 (Revolution and the emergence of liberal synthesis), or 1789 (Revolution and the end of the old political order), 1648 (the Peace of Westphalia, and the emergence of the nation-state), or, even, 1492 (the discovery of the Indies and beginning of a new world order). To think of this world now as modern is to conclude that one or another of the social structures that came into being after any of these turning-points is still viably salient. This is a hard line to hold in the face of changes abreast these days, but some give it their all.

Others, by contrast, tend to hedge their bets on the time of recent times by stipulating a *late-modern* which could be any time of another series of events after which some crucial aspect of the modern fell away to be replaced by something new and different, if not utterly beyond the modern. Thus, earlier to later: 1912 (Frederick Winslow Taylor's *Principles of Scientific Management*; hence Fordism), 1929 (Depression; hence the definitive collapse in the U.S. of naïve economic individualism), 1945 (Hiroshima; hence nuclear culture), 1947 (Gandhi and India; hence decolonization), 1968 (world revolution; hence, end of the liberal synthesis), 1989–1991 (end of the Cold War; hence globalism accelerated by the beginning of information age). The main point of *late-modern* ideas is to lay down a stake in the *still-modern* without denying that something important has turned against the drift of the modern. *Late-moderns* hate the locution *post-modern* even more than do *still-moderns*.

Then, too, there are some who continue to use *post-modern* even though it turns out to be an empirically empty category. To think of recent-times as *post-modern* is empty because, if one is to be historically serious, it is impossible to make strong claims about any recent from a point within that recent. As a result, the *post-modern* (as a historical term, as distinct from a theoretical movement) might just as well be late-modern; or, perhaps better, a way of marking an apparent but unverifiable claim that something big has changed in a major structural way. This is how many have come to use the term *globalization* – as code for *post-modern*, which in turn is a semantic marker for a conspicuous possibility that can be used in public without much risk of embarrassment over the facts that, by definition, cannot be hard enough to be had.

There are many word-games to be played in any attempt to describe recent times, ancient times, modern times, traditional times or, for that matter, any sort of time period whether nearby or remote. Word-games, however, are not idle play. They can be hard and serious work. To work a game is to engage a problem that may or may not have a solution and, in either case, whatever the outcome, the rules are not yours for the making any more than the result, if any, is for you alone to determine.

Word-games of the kind we have in mind are, thus, less like tennis than chess: prowess counts in the one, mental patience in the other. In tennis you are meant to put a ball in a box right before you; in chess you must put a piece in an indeterminate box not yet open. When it comes to modern-times, globalization is chess-like – a game ever more impossible to control or predict much less win. If globalization is as potent a force as most think it is, then players cannot be confident that the rules they have been taught still apply. At the extreme, to play with recent times is to game without knowing the rules; and globalization as a word-game aspect is a near-perfect instance of the troubles in store.

Thus it is that we dare to speak of empires as if they can be toyed with in relation to globalization. It is widely assumed, and for good reason, that while there are imperial features to global things, empires as such are features of the past. As in many matters, Immanuel Wallerstein has focused this distinction as well as anyone by defining the modern global economy as a world-system that was appreciably, hence definitively, more efficient in its methods than were world-empires. Certainly, empires are political, but they are also "primitive means of economic domination"; by contrast, modern world-economies, Wallerstein continues, "have invented the technology that makes it possible to increase the flow of the surplus ... by eliminating the 'waste' of too cumbersome a political superstructure."[1] Hence, the idea is that empires, because they dominate so clumsily, are confined to an impossibly primitive station on the curve of modern times. The systems of modern times have, in principle, become so technically competent as to do their evil with little waste and proportionately greater profit.

On the surface, the argument is persuasive – in large part because it is consistent with the social scientific dictum that modern times are different from any that may have come before them. What Wallerstein adds is that the difference is in the nature and scope of the economic element in modern times. Empires are predominantly political forms; and they are older than recent times by a good half-millennium. But it is the scope of the modern that accounts for the modern as at once old (or young) enough to date to the sixteenth century but also ambitious enough to have taken the world as it is for the taking (hence, the efficiency of surplus accumulation in the readiness to move relentlessly wherever labor and resource can be had on the cheap). The modern is by nature not just economic but economically driven to globalize in ways that render the political secondary if not irrelevant.

But here, in the wisdom of these ideas, is where the modern comes up against the empire – thus, to put considerations of recent times and globalization in a quandary. As regards their respective ambitions, empires and world-systems both were global in the sense of seeking out by any means necessary what territories they could gain and hold in order to exploit local human and natural resources. This is not global in the geographic sense, but it is global in what may be a more useful sense: the whole of available territories vulnerable to taking and exploitation.

Under the Han Dynasties (206 BCE–220 CE),[2] China controlled much of the territory of present-day China. In geographic size its reach was 6 million square kilometers, second only to the Persian Empire under Darius I. This was far less than later empires – the Mongols in the thirteenth century and the British in the nineteenth, for examples. Yet as a percentage of the world's population, Han China included a quarter of the world's population, about the same as the Mongols and more than the British.

Han China was in every sense of the word imperial. Its military strength and cultural confidence were great enough for the Hans to exercise diplomatic and virtual colonial control over Vietnam and Southeast Asia, part of Korea, north into Mongolia and the Gobi, west into Central Asia. Still today, the ethnic majority in China are the Han. This was the period that brought to an end the Warring States era and solidified ancient Chinese culture under the influence of Confucian and Taoist philosophies. In addition, the Hans developed an effective bureaucratic administrative system able to reach broadly across its territories and deep into local communities. In these respects, Han China was a classically traditional empire in that political authority and military force worked to consolidate large and diverse populations over a substantial territory and, in the process, to solidify important and continuing aspects of Chinese art, culture, and ethnic dominance.

In the Han period, the Silk Road became China's most important global link to the West. The Silk Road stretched from the northern urban centers in the East to Central Asia beyond the Tarim Basin and the Taklamakan Desert in far western China. It established military control that allowed the economic activity that eventually linked China to Africa, Rome, and Europe. More importantly, the Silk Road was the ancient template for the major trade networks of what Andre Gunder Frank argumentatively called the Asian world-system after 1400 CE.[3] Without judging the merits of Frank's claim that the only true original global economic system was Asian (as opposed to European, as Wallerstein argues), it is indisputable that, beginning with the Hans, China became the center of both an empire and an early version of a world-system. Today there is little reason to suspect that the Asian trade system was truly global and, if anything, vastly more efficient than Europe's modern world-system.

What came to pass is not, of course, the point at issue. It is fair enough to insist that Han China and certainly its major successor dynasties (notably, the Mongolian, the Ming, the Qing) were empires in a classic sense. But they were, as they came in time to be, important and enduring important economic trade systems. They were not global in the sense of spanning the geographic globe, but they were global in their economic ambition and reach.

Were the Hans economically less efficient than the Romans of the same period? Did they accumulate less capital? Can we speak of "capital" in reference to premodern economic systems? Did traditional empires plow back wealth gained from conquests and colonization into their core states? If they did, as surely they did, was their method rational? If their economic gains were secured with military support, are they any less properly called profits of a kind? These and others are open questions. But they are open enough to challenge the idea that globalization is entirely a modern or post-modern process marked by late-modern, if not post-modern, technologies that speed the flow of capital and goods.

Our purpose is not to settle these questions so much as to put the globalization question in broader historical terms. However seriously one games with words, in the end, if there is an end, when the outcomes are in question, we have only to apply the mental patience that allows us to study the board before us, there to imagine what is to be done in our next move that might – just might – open the ultimate box we might occupy, there to check the king.

If empires are to be considered early instances of globalization, then it is important to introduce the notion of an *imperial disposition*. A disposition is normally assumed to be a property of an individual's inclination to move in a certain direction or at least to feel in a certain way while moving about in their world. Individuals are, thus, disposed to hate those who hate them and to love those who love them – not necessarily with passions that match those of the others, and certainly not often with a particularly coherent sense of why these feelings are what they are. Dispositions are inclinations to feel, thence to act, in ways that may work well enough even when those disposed cannot say in so many words why they are so inclined.

Similarly, even large gatherings of individuals have surprisingly profound if often unruly dispositions. Ethnic strife, among other examples, is a deeply irrational disposition to hate a particular other. The Hutus and the Tutsis are disposed to mutual enmity to the point of engaging in mass killings. The example is of course a bit loaded in favor of our main idea. Still, it is sound enough to suggest that before there are empires there must be a disposition toward empire or an imperial impulse. While such a social disposition is not necessarily moved by hatred, it can be marked by passions widely shared. Peoples organized in great number are disposed to hold other peoples at a distance, to attack them if need be, thus to be ever at the ready to act against threats, real or perceived, that another people may pose.

Hence, another confusion: What might be the relation between an imperial disposition and actual empires? The question arises because you can find traces of the imperial disposition in ancient stories, sayings, legends, or texts that are frequently (perhaps even normally) handed down long before the cultures in which they originate become civilizations much less empires. In the West, for example, one of the prominent Judeo-Christian myths of origin was written into the form by which it is known today somewhat late in the settled history of the Jewish people – probably in the Davidic period in Israel early in the tenth century BCE. Yet, elements of the story are similar to themes present in earlier myths in ancient Mesopotamia. Most of the oldest biblical writings, including the stories of the earth's creation, of an original paradise, of humankind's moral failures, of cleansing floods were rooted in other cultures and carried forward by the early fathers of ancient Israel. Just the same, scribes in the Davidic era codified these stories at a time when David was king of Israel, then at the height of its civilizational maturity – but, if a kingdom, hardly a global empire. In a short time after the golden age of King David, Israel would split over tribal differences, which made Israel and Judah vulnerable to the greater empires of Mesopotamia – the Babylonians, the Syrians, and others to follow. A good deal of the ritual literature of Israel was actually written in a period of exile and captivity under the Babylonians. In their essential details they were redacted into the Torah, the Christian Old Testament, and the Qur'an, the sacred texts of the three great Abrahamic religions of the West – Judaism, Christianity, and Islam.

Over the centuries following the establishment of the early religions and the civilizations evolving thereupon, stories of an original paradise and fall came to be defining features of a general, eventually, secular myth of human history in the West. To be sure, the emphasis on aspects of the myths of the origin of human sin and trouble varied from faith to faith, but there was, and is, a remarkably common ground, which may explain the ease with which the religious myths slipped over into secular cultures. Even those without devotional ties to the traditional faiths of the West recognize the myth of a garden from which the first man and his woman were expelled for reason of their desire to be like their gods. Western thinking about history and the human race is deeply, if not universally, a story of paradise lost and the moral struggle to regain it. Whether in Marx's idea of paradise regained in the post-revolutionary classless society or in elements of secular Zionism or in any of the sects and ideologies that sprang up in opposition to the received faiths, even in neo-religions such as the American Church of the Latter Day Saints, among many others, the West thinks of historical time as if it were moving ever upward toward the good state lost.

Thus, it happened that, after many centuries, a good many modern civilizations appropriated their own versions of the Adamic myth as a metaphor for the original goodness of a certain people who had fallen from grace, thence condemned to a history of struggle to regain that grace. One consequence was the many subsequent ideologies of special peoples – of Israel as a light to the nations, of Rome as the seat of world Christianity, of Mecca as the center of global Islam, of America as a new world of chosen people; and, even, at the extreme of political evil, Hitler's National Socialism and Mao's cultural revolutions, not to mention Stalin's gulags. In some cases, such as late twentieth and early twenty-first-century American ideology of Christian duty to fight an ill-defined war in Iraq against poorly understood "terrorisms," are thinly veiled versions of the generic idea that some men are chosen to liberate others – chosen that is by a special providence that endows them with rights to invade sovereign states. These sorts of off-beat ideologies of righteousness are no less obnoxious in their consequences than those of Osama bin Laden's particular distortion of Sunni Islamic ideas. But, the point of the comparison is that in both instances imperializing actions taken in the period after 2001 drew upon an imperial disposition that can be traced back some four millennia to stories of a pre-Abrahamic yesteryear and legends of the fall of humankind.

The religious terms "sin" and "a fall" do not, by any means, appear in all the stories. But the key to those stories, as Nietzsche explained, is that good and evil are terms essential to the Western moral claim that, in human history, some thereby are chosen to defend the good from the insidious dangers of the evil ones. The good are those who endow themselves with the right perforce to use imperial measures to secure survival if not happiness. To be sure, the connection may seem remote at best but it is there to be seen in the stark differences between the religious ideas of the West and those of the ancient East. In the West, history is reasoned time moving forward; in the East, time is less the key to all things except as the history of the great civilizational centers, as in the case of the Han dynasty in China.

Thus, we propose a distinction between an imperial disposition and empire itself. In historical time, the two may be relatively close to each other or far removed. Either way, the one is a precondition of the other. This, in turn, raises an issue far beyond our purposes: Might it be that an imperial disposition is a universal, even structural, feature of human nature? The question, if starkly materialist, has several versions, each reasonable in its way. Is it that man, like the animal he is, is fundamentally aggressive? Or, perhaps that man, like the need-bound creature he is, must search without ceasing for food, water, and shelter, which requires a territorializing drive? Or that he is what he eats and, thus, will eat and kill what he can to be what he is? Each of these queries, and others of the type, are evidently based on recurring forms of human behavior – thus on an element of human nature hard to deny. When human beings came to organize their lives in groups which, in time, grew in size and range of inclusion, they faced the problem of collective survival.

Human groups have proven themselves highly adaptable. If they happen to live in a sufficiently fertile location, they may remain there for durations of time – in principle, for an *ever*. Yet, as things happen, should an unanticipated ecological imbalance such as sudden decline in water supply or a disturbance in the food chain, even a remote people is likely to be driven to range abroad perhaps into other territories to acquire the necessities of survival. This seems to be, shall we say, a reasonable aspect of group life. But it is also an aspect that can be volatile whenever the size of the group grows unexpectedly by sudden fluctuations in, say, the fertility health of its women or the lust of its men, and any number of similar circumstances. Events such as these occurring on the putative borders of the human and the natural surely stand behind something like the imperial disposition. But are they the sum and substance of the disposition? We think not.

A disposition whether private or collective is in fact enmeshed with factors that may include material necessity but are primarily immaterial – one might even say cultural were it not for the indefiniteness of what a culture is; still, let it be cultural for the time being. As high-minded as many cultures are, there are few that do not promote something like an imperial attitude. It is said – a point to which we shall return – that the high-minded cultures are exclusively modern. In fact, they are not. Ancient cultures or civilizations may attach their origins to the myths of origins that are not nearly so forgiving as the Judeo-Christian one of a mere expulsion from the perfect garden. The Sumerian legend of Gilgamesh, older by a good 1000 years than the Judeo-Christian one, is a story of oft-times vicious struggle consummating in a grotesque death that gives birth to the new order. Then, too, both involve ravenous floods that cleanse the earth. At the least, death is an aspect of many if not all myths of origin, which in turn are excellent sources of discerning cultural texts that exhibit the imperial disposition.

What might such an early trace of the imperial attitude look like? For one example, take a passage from the eleventh-century BCE *Avesta*, one of the sources for the story of Zarathustra that gave rise to Zoroastrianism, the oldest of the global religions:

> I want freedom of movement and freedom of dwelling for those with homesteads, to those who dwell evermore on the earth with their cattle. With reverence of Asha, and (offerings) offered up, I vow this: I shall nevermore damage or plunder the Mazdayasnian settlements, even if I have to risk life and limb.

The setting was the region that came to be known as Persia, later in our time as Iran. The passage itself is not unlike many of the ancient texts (and quite a few modern ones) in that it affirms the desire for peace at home while insisting on the freedom to risk life and limb to defend it, even to extend the lands for sake of homestead and livestock. Yet, the passage itself appears a good many centuries before Darius I (549–530 BCE) restored and solidified the Persian Empire of Cyrus the Great (*c.* 590–*c.* 530 BCE), which had itself overcome the Babylonians.

Deeper still, the inspiration of the *Avesta* for the Zarathustra legend may be two millennia before the largest empire in the ancient world. From the glimmer to the imperial reality there is no certain line of descent. The Zoroastrian creedal declaration of principles of freedom upon a right to defend homelands is, effectively, the glimmer of some primal element in the most primitive of human settlements. Yet, and the point is important, from the disposition to the reality there is a consistency of a striking sort. The many traditions that did and did not become empires may have relied on elements that recur not only in civilizations near in space if not time to each other. There are even claims to be made for universal symbols appearing at the foundations of civilizations remote in space and time from each other.[4] Still, traces of ancient dispositions are, if not perfectly so, consistent through time within more or less connected regional cultures. The Zoroastrian legends were radically Manichean in their belief that the universe is governed by two equal, opposing, and ultimate forces of good and evil. By the time of Cyrus the Great, the Manichean themes may have been more muted, but still they are found in the wording of Cyrus's justification for conquering the Babylonians (and, by the way, liberating the Hebrew captives):

> When I entered Babylon as a friend and [when] I established the seat of government in the palace of the ruler under jubilation and rejoicing, Marduk, the great lord [induced] the magnanimous inhabitants of Babylon [to love me], and I was daily endeavoring to worship him. My numerous troops walked around in Babylon in peace, I did not allow anybody to terrorize [any place] of the [country of Sumer] and Akkad. I strove for peace in Babylon and in all his [other] sacred cities. As to the inhabitants of Babylon, [who] against the will of the gods [had/were . . ., I abolished] the forced labor which was against their [social] standing. I brought relief to their dilapidated housing, putting [thus] an end to their [main] complaints. Marduk, the great lord, was well pleased with my deeds and sent friendly blessings to myself, Cyrus, the king who worships him.

Cyrus the Great, whose Babylonian empire was restored by the Persian Darius, who, like the Han Dynasties, established an enduring culture, political control over a vast region, and an empire that invaded Europe.

Does the Manichean element persist over so many centuries? Or is it that any given Imperium is as empires always are – extravagantly ambitious and ruthless in their territorial drive? Fortunately, for the present, this need not be decided. It is enough that the filaments of history and culture that link a primitive disposition to an ancient empire have a degree of coherence that remains in the full-blown empire. Present-day Iran, at best a regional threat, hardly a global empire, has been governed since the fall of the Pahlavi regime in 1979 as an Islamic republic. Yet, keeping in mind the extreme statements of one in particular of its recent presidents, Mahmoud Ahmadinejad, it is at least possible that the attributions of evil to Israel and the United States are to a degree also Manichean, hence ancient Persian. If the ancestors thought of good and evil as rival orders of power in the nature of being, why not their sons, however filtered their thinking may be by cultural transformations (from Babylonian to Persian to the quasi-secularized Pahlavi regimes to the Islamic republics) as they come down into the circumstances of their present times?

The texts that follow in the first part, "Imperial Disposition and Civilizational Empires," are meant to illustrate with a wide range of global historical examples that the Imperial Disposition was an evident feature found in many if not all of the earliest cultures in regions where great civilizational empires arose.

In the second part, "Imperial Systems, Conflict, and Expansion," it almost goes without saying that where there are empires there will be external conflict as powers compete for control of the regions nearby. But also, as can be seen in these texts, the Greek, Macedonian, Seleucid, Roman, Silla, and Gupta empires were, like the Chinese Han, also organized as economic systems with, perhaps of necessity, global aspirations. To control an empire is to supply one's troops, to pay the tax bills for maintenance of the Imperium itself, and to accumulate wealth. That the wealth may have been gained by corvée or slave labor pressed by ruthless means or by less-than-modern efficiency in the exploitation of naturally occurring resources does not mean that it was not accumulating wealth. Are not the remains of the Silk Road, the ports of the Mediterranean, or the aqueducts of the Romans among the constant capital bequeathed to time itself? That ancient wealth may have gone more to monuments than to reinvestment banks does not mean that the empires were not economic systems of a kind – however lesser their rational means for administration of the means and the modes of production of the surpluses.

In the third group of selections, "Instability and Decline in Global Empires," still another global aspect of ancient empires is suggested. Because empires, like world-systems, compete with each other as do rival elements interior to them, so thereby conflict, hence decline, is inevitable. If the Aztecs, Mayans, and Incans in the Americas were, in relative terms, more regional than global in the geographic sense and thus more vulnerable to external forces, it does not mean that there were no globalizing economic systems elsewhere – of which a prime example is the vast trading zone of the Mississippians, centered in Cahokia, that reached as far to the northeast into modern-day New York and Ontario as it did deep to the south and west on the Mississippi–Missouri river networks. Did Rome and the Ottomans – both mighty empires able to project cultural, political, and economic power – fall because of a fatal cyclical feature of all empires? If cyclical thinking can be made historical, then is not the decline of empires at least as much due to the same economic factors that ruined the Iberian, Dutch, French, and British systems? The modern core states, including, it now seems, the American one today, met their Waterloo. Whether military or economic, all global systems, however grand or regional, come to a point where they cannot supply their troops, provide safe passages for their booty, enforce the law of cheap labor, find new and renewable resources, keep the taxes within tolerable limits, and so on.

There is no dichotomy between geopolitics and economic systems. There may be differing balances between the two and these may indeed vary from the earlier and less efficient to the recent and more efficient. But efficiency can only produce greater and greater surpluses when there is no limit to growth. It is one thing to scold the ancients for their primitive economic methods in worlds where, from the perspective of later times, they had all the potential for growth that moderns in hindsight could imagine. It is quite another sort of foolishness for the moderns to have pretended for so long that their vaunted and proven technologies would somehow cause the world to stave off the natural limits that quell the vibrancy of states and empires, as they do the lives of ordinary creatures.

Notes

1 Immanuel Wallerstein (1974) *Modern World-System I: Capitalist Agriculture and the Origins of the European World-Economy in the Sixteenth Century*, New York, San Francisco, London: Academic Press, p. 15.
2 The Xin Dynasty (9–23 CE) was an interregnum after which Han domination passed from West to East.
3 Andre Gunder Frank, (1998) *ReOrient: Global Economy in the Asia Age*, University of California Press. In particular, Frank (pp. 94–95) charts the trade routes of the Asian system (1400–1800) for which the Silk Road is the major East–West axis.
4 Mircea Eliade (1971) *Myth of the Eternal Return: Cosmos and History*, Princeton University Press.

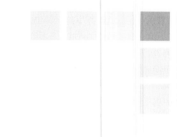

The Imperial Disposition and Civilizational Empires

EGYPT: THE NARMER PALETTE (c. 3100 BCE)

Discovered by British archaeologists in Hierakonpolis, at the site of the temple of Horus, the Narmer Palette, along with artifacts found close by, is considered important evidence of the beginning of statehood in Egypt. The two aspects of the palette depict Pharaoh Narmer wearing the crown of upper Egypt on the one and the crown of lower Egypt on the other. It is assumed that the palette was a donation to the temple to commemorate the unification of Egypt. It is not established that the palette depicts a real military event leading to the unification of Egypt. It may be purely ceremonial, marking the event. Some Egyptologists claim that the Pharaohs were actually from Mesopotamia. Whether the events commemorated were real or symbolic, the Narmer Palette is unquestionably one of the oldest and most important historical documents establishing the ancient origins of statehood and empire.

Narmer Palette, http://socrates.berkeley.edu/~mah/narmer_palette.htm.

PERSIA: ZARATHUSTRA, *AVESTA* (c. 1000–900 BCE)

The roots of Zoroastrian belief and practice can be traced to Indo-Iranian culture. Zoroastrianism is one of the world's oldest religions. It is based on the religious text, the *Avesta* (literally, "authoritative utterance") and takes its name from the prophet, Zarathustra, who lived sometime between 1700 BCE and 1500 BCE. While the original text of the *Avesta* is lost, much of it was reconstructed from surviving fragments, later transcriptions, oral histories, and commentaries. The 17 hymns attributed to Zarathustra are called *gathas*. They are written in Avestan, which is culturally and linguistically similar to the ancient Sanskrit of the Rig Veda. Zoroastrianism was first recognized by Herodotus in his written history of the Achaemenid Empire in 440 BCE.

The *Avesta* is divided into sections or hymns called *yasna* from the Indo-Iranian root *yaz* meaning "sacrifice, worship." Yasna 12, known as "The Zoroastrian Creed," was written after the murder of Zarathustra in the early years of the religion, and is an important prayer, said daily, and included in the marriage ceremony. Zoroastrians are followers of Ahura Mazda, the omniscient creator. Their religious philosophy is generally cited as the classic instance of Manichean dualism that holds the good and evil powers to be of distinct realms but of equivalent power. Zoroastrians thus reject evil powers (or *daevas*), while thinking of themselves as *spenta*, the ones possessing power and following love.

The following selection should be read as a ritual creed recited in worship by the faithful who declare their rejection of the evil powers and commitment to the good. The creed also exhibits traces of an imperial disposition aimed at protecting the faithful and their lands and elements of a creation myth. Also notice the parallels with Manichean aspects of later religions including Islam, Judaism, and Christianity as well as the significance of Zarathustra to philosophers, notably Nietzsche.

The Zoroastrian Creed, *Avesta*, Yasna 12

1. I curse the Daevas. I declare myself a Mazda-worshipper, a supporter of Zarathushtra, hostile to the Daevas, fond of Ahura's teaching, a praiser of the Amesha Spentas, a worshipper of the Amesha Spentas. I ascribe all good to Ahura Mazda, 'and all the best,' Asha-endowed, splendid, xwarena-endowed, whose is the cow, whose is Asha, whose is the light, 'may whose blissful areas be filled with light.'

2. I choose the good Spenta Armaiti for myself; let her be mine. I renounce the theft and robbery of the cow, and the damaging and plundering of the Mazdayasnian settlements.

3. I want freedom of movement and freedom of dwelling for those with homesteads, to those who dwell upon this earth with their cattle. With reverence for Asha, and (offerings) offered up, I vow this: I shall nevermore damage or plunder the Mazdayasnian settlements, even if I have to risk life and limb.

4. I reject the authority of the Crevasses, the wicked, no-good, lawless, evil-knowing, the most druj-like of beings, the foulest of beings, the most damaging of beings. I reject the Daevas and their comrades, I reject the demons (yatu) and their comrades; I reject any who harm beings. I reject them with my thoughts, words, and deeds. I reject them publicly. Even as I reject the head (authorities), so too do I reject the hostile followers of the druj.

5. As Ahura Mazda taught Zarathushtra at all discussions, at all meetings, at which Mazda and Zarathushtra conversed:

6. As Ahura Mazda taught Zarathushtra at all discussions, at all meetings, at which Mazda and Zarathushtra conversed – even as Zarathushtra rejected the authority of the Daevas, so I also reject, as Mazda-worshipper and supporter of Zarathushtra, the authority of the Daevas, even as he, the Asha-endowed Zarathushtra, has rejected them.

7. As the belief of the waters, the belief of the plants, the belief of the well-made (Original) Cow; as the belief of Ahura Mazda who created the cow and the Asha-endowed Man; as the belief of Zarathushtra, the

belief of Kavi Vishtaspa, the belief of both Frashaostra and Jamaspa; as the belief of each of the Saoshyants (saviors) – fulfilling destiny and Asha-endowed – so I am a Mazda-worshipper of this belief and teaching.

8. I profess myself a Mazda-worshipper, a Zoroastrian, having vowed it and professed it. I pledge myself to the well-thought thought, I pledge myself to the well-spoken word, I pledge myself to the well-done action.

9. I pledge myself to the Mazdayasnian religion, which causes the attack to be put off and weapons put down; [which upholds khvaetvadatha], Asha-endowed; which of all religions that exist or shall be, is the greatest, the best, and the most beautiful: Ahuric, Zoroastrian. I ascribe all good to Ahura Mazda. This is the creed of the Mazdayasnian religion.

Avesta, http://www.avesta.org/. This digital edition copyright © 1995 by Joseph H. Peterson. All rights reserved. Translation by Bartholomae, from I.J.S. Taraporewala, *The Divine Songs of Zarathushtra*. Notes in square brackets were added by JHP.

INDIA: VEDIC CIVILIZATION, *RIG VEDA* (1700–1000 BCE)

Civilization, as we understand it today, probably began in the Indus Valley around 5000 BCE. Archaeological excavations at present-day Harappa in Pakistan suggest there were cities in the region around 2500 BCE. Very little is known about them except that they traded with Mesopotamia. Vedic civilization probably began around 2000 BCE, apparently in the decline of Harappans. Most scholars place the Rig Vedic period from 1700 to 1000 BCE. Most notable during this period was the invasion of India and Iran by Aryan peoples. The name Aryan (from the Sanskrit *aryas*) comes from the Indo-European *ar* (roughly, "noble"). The Hindu caste system may have begun when Aryan invaders introduced a version of the class distinction between nobles and commoners – a social structure that was refined and fixed in the Later Vedic (or Brahman) period (1000–500 BCE). The surviving text of the *Rig Veda* (1000 BCE) dates from this transitional time and is the literary text from ancient India. The *Rig Veda* suggests a strong linguistic and cultural resemblance to the Iranian *Avesta*.

The selection is one of the most important Hindu passages in which the Gayatri Mantra praises the god Indra. The first English translator, Sir William James, paraphrased this verse as "Let us adore the supremacy of that divine sun, the god-head, who illuminates all from whom all proceed, to whom all must return, whom we invoke to direct our understandings aright in our progress towards this holy seat." Like the Iranian *Avesta*, the Mantra is a religious creed with evident elements of a territorial right derived from the origins of the earth itself.

Gayatri Mantra, *Rig Veda* 3.62

1 Your well-known prompt activities aforetime needed no impulse from your faithful servant.
Where, Indra-Varuna, is now that glory wherewith ye brought support to those who loved you?

2 This man [the worshipper], most diligent, seeking after riches, incessantly invokes you for your favour.
Accordant, Indra-Varuna, with Maruts, with Heaven and Earth, hear ye mine invocation.

3 O Indra-Varuna, ours be this treasure, ours be wealth, Maruts, with full store of heros.
May the Varûtrîs [guardian godess] with their shelter aid us, and Bhâratî and Hotrâ [goddesses presiding over worship] with the Mornings.

4 Be pleased with our oblations, though loved of all Gods, Brihaspati:
Give Wealth to him who brings thee gifts.

5 At sacrifices, with your hymns worship the pure Brihaspati – I pray for power which none may bend –

6 The Bull of men, whom none deceive, the wearer of each shape at will,
Brihaspati Most Excellent.

7 Divine, resplendent Pûshtan. this our newest hymn of eulogy
By us is chanted forth to thee.

8 Accept with favour this my song, be gracious to the earnest thought,
Even as a bridegroom to his bride.

9 May he who sees all, living things, sees them together at a glance,-
May he, may Pûshtan be our help.

10 May we attain that excellent glory of Savitar the God:
So may he stimulate our prayers.

11 With understanding, earnestly, of Savitar the God we crave
Our portion of prosperity.

12 Men, singers worship Savitar the God with hymn and holy rites,
Urged by the impulse of their thoughts.

13 Soma who gives success goes forth, goes to the gathering place of Gods [sacrifical chamber],
To seat him at the seat of Law [place where sacrific is performed].

14 To us and to our cattle may Soma give salutary food,
To biped some quadruped.

15 May Soma, strengthening our power of life, and conquering our foes,
In our assembly take his seat.

16 May Mitra-Varuna, sapient Pair, bedew our pasturage with oil [clarified butter, or fertilizing rain],
With meath [honey, or sweet dew] the regions of the air.

17 Far-ruling, joyful when adored, ye reign through majesty of might,
With pure laws everlastingly.

18 Lauded by Jamadagni's [may be the seer of the hymn] song, sit in the place of holy Law:
Drink Soma, ye who strengthen Law.

"Gayatri Mantra" in Ralph T. H. Griffith (1971) *The Hymns of the Rig-Veda*, The Chowkhamba Sanskrit Studies vol. XXXV (Varanasi – 1 (India): The Chowkhamba Sanskrit Series Office, vol. 1, pp. 389–390).

MESOPOTAMIA: *THE EPIC OF GILGAMESH* (c. 1300–1000 BCE)

Mesopotamia is often referred to as a "cradle of civilization." Its name derives from the Greek language and can be translated to "the land between the two rivers." As such, Mesopotamia is not a country or nation but a region located in between the Tigris and Euphrates rivers. As many scholars emphasize, Mesopotamia's history is varied and at times discontinuous. But even so, many still speak of a Mesopotamia as if it were a unified whole. In this regard, Mesopotamia is significant because it is said that many momentous events in world history took place in its lands. For instance, there is evidence to suggest that the turn to sedentary life first took place in Mesopotamia. Some surmise that this began sometime after the tenth millennium BCE alongside the concurrent rise of agriculture. Later on in the fifth millennium BCE during the Sumerian period, there is also evidence to suggest that some of the first urban centers of the world began to take form. This continued while new traditions such as the written word and mathematics, economic systems and new technologies started to develop.

One of the relics of this rich Mesopotamian history is *The Epic of Gilgamesh*, considered by many to be one of the oldest instances of fictional literature. It was written originally in Sumerian cuneiform, the earliest of all the Mesopotamian languages, which came about sometime around 3000 BCE. *The Epic of Gilgamesh* was later transcribed to other Mesopotamian languages such as Akkadian. This happened as the Sumerian

Era gradually gave way to other periods that would come after it. The selection and also the "standard version" of the Epic comes from these latter transcriptions.

Broadly speaking, what *The Epic of Gilgamesh* tells through a series of poems is the legend of Gilgamesh: a mythological hero-king who some scholars believe actually existed sometime during the Early Dynastic period (*c.* 2800 BCE). The story revolves around Gilgamesh and his half-beast companion, Enkidu. One particular notable section of the Epic recounts how they came to meet and exposes the traces of an imperial disposition. Enkidu, it is said, is created by the gods after complaints about King Gilgamesh are made by the people of Uruk. Initially, Enkidu is found wild, outside the walls of Uruk, and running with wild beasts and animals. However, after being seen by a hunter-trapper who sends a prostitute to direct Enkidu away from the city, Enkidu is seduced by the the harlot Shamhat and decides to leave behind his wild nature. In turn, Enkidu transforms himself from a being whom "knows not a people, nor even a country" to a person armed with reason and a desire to live with others. And because of this, he is welcomed into Uruk to live inside its imposing walls: a reminder that borders, even in most ancient of times, were things to be defended or enlarged.

Tablet 1. The Coming of Enkidu

Prologue and paean. King Gilgamesh tyrannizes the people of Uruk, who complain to the gods. To divert his superhuman energies the gods create his counterpart, the wild man Enkidu, who is brought up by the animals of the wild. Enkidu is spotted by a trapper, who lures him away from the herd with a prostitute. The prostitute shows him her arts and proposes to take him to Uruk, where Gilgamesh has been seeing him in dreams.

> He who saw the Deep, the country's foundation,
> [who] knew . . ., was wise in all matters!
> [Gilgamesh, who] saw the Deep, the country's foundation
> [who] knew . . ., was wise in all matters!
>
> [He] . . . Everywhere . . .
> and [learnt] of everything that sum of wisdom.
> He saw what was secret, discovered what was hidden,
> he brought back a tale of before the Deluge.
>
> He came a far road, was weary, found peace,
> and set all his labours on a tablet of stone.
> He built the rampart of Uruk-the-Sheepfold,
> of holy Eanna, the sacred storehouse.
>
> See its wall like a strand of wool,
> view its parapet that none could copy!
> Take the stairway of a bygone era,
> draw near to Eanna, seat of Ishtar the goddess,
> that no later king could ever copy!
>
> Climb Uruk's wall and walk back and forth!
> Survey its foundations, examine the brickwork!
> Were its bricks not fired in an oven?
> Did the Seven Sages not lay its foundations?

[A square mile is] city, [a square mile] date-grove, a square mile is
    clay-pit, half a square mile the temple of Ishtar:
[three square miles] and a half is Uruk's expanse.

[See] the tablet-box of cedar,
[release] its clasp of bronze!
[Lift] the lid of its secret,
    [pick] up the tablet of lapis lazuli and read out
the travails of Gilgamesh, all that he went through.

Surpassing all other kings, heroic in stature,
    brave scion of Uruk, wild bull on the rampage!
Going at the fore he was the vanguard,
    going at the rear, one his comrades could trust!

A mighty bank, protecting his warriors,
    a violent flood-wave, smashing a stone wall!
Wild bull of Lugalbanda, Gilgamesh, the perfect in strength,
    suckling of the august! Wild Cow, the goddess Ninsun!

Gilgamesh the tall, magnificent and terrible,
    who opened passes in the mountains,
who dug wells on the slopes of the uplands,
    and crossed the ocean, the wide sea to the sunrise;

who scoured the world ever searching for life,
    and reached through sheer force Uta-napishti the Distant;
who restored the cult-centres destroyed by the Deluge,
    and set in place for the people the rites of the cosmos.

The Epic of Gilgamesh: the Babylonian epic poem and other texts in Akkadian and Sumerian, translated with an introduction by Andrew George, Penguin Books, 1999.

ANCIENT ISRAEL: THE YAHWIST MYTH OF CREATION AND FALL (c. 1000 BCE)

The Jewish Torah comprises the first five books of the Christian Old Testament, of which Genesis is by far the most popular for the stories it offers of Adam and Eve, Abraham and Isaac, Sodom and Gomorrah, Noah and the Flood, Joseph and the Pharaohs of Egypt. Yet, like Homer's epic poems and most ancient texts, the Genesis narratives were edited out of many different sources. The story of the Garden of Eden and the ultimate expulsion of Adam and Eve for their sin of disobedience of their god, Yahweh, were part of the larger creation myth. Yet, this story (chapters 2 and 3) is different by a good measure from the account given of the creation of the earth and mankind in chapter 1, where the seven days of creation are each assigned a specific creative effort (light, land, seas, etc.), concluding with the seventh day of rest. This obviously is a more priestly account, written for ritual purposes. Chapters 2 and 3, by contrast, redact numerous local stories, many of which (such as Noah and the Flood) are borrowed from ancient Mesopotamian cultures. They were drawn together, probably in the Davidic period in the tenth century BCE, early in the settlement kingdom era of the Hebrew people. These stories are attributed to the Yahwist writers at a time of unity when Yahweh was the god of the predominant cult in Israel.

The first line of chapter 2 forms a seemingly smooth link to the chapter 1 account and may have been entered by a later editor since the priestly version was written some centuries after the Yahwist story. Still, as chapters 2 and 3 develop, they become a primordial theory of human history: mankind was cast in God's likeness and set in paradise; the primal figures, Adam and Eve, sinned by trying to possess the wisdom of their god, whereupon they were expelled into a world of evil, sin, struggle, and death. The actual history of ancient Israel of course reflects, first, the divisions of the kingdom, internal rivalries, and then wars with rival states, leading to the Babylonian captivity when the temple was demolished and the priestly leaders led into exile. The history of today's Palestine turns largely on a version of the story that God's people are by nature homeless and must therefore fight to protect their land.

Yahwist Creation Story, Genesis 2 and 3

1: Thus the heavens and the earth were finished, and all the host of them.

2: And on the seventh day God ended his work which he had made; and he rested on the seventh day from all his work which he had made.

3: And God blessed the seventh day, and sanctified it: because that in it he had rested from all his work which God created and made.

4: These are the generations of the heavens and of the earth when they were created, in the day that the LORD God made the earth and the heavens,

5: And every plant of the field before it was in the earth, and every herb of the field before it grew: for the LORD God had not caused it to rain upon the earth, and there was not a man to till the ground.

6: But there went up a mist from the earth, and watered the whole face of the ground.

7: And the LORD God formed man of the dust of the ground, and breathed into his nostrils the breath of life; and man became a living soul.

8: And the LORD God planted a garden eastward in Eden; and there he put the man whom he had formed.

9: And out of the ground made the LORD God to grow every tree that is pleasant to the sight, and good for food; the tree of life also in the midst of the garden, and the tree of knowledge of good and evil.

10: And a river went out of Eden to water the garden; and from thence it was parted, and became into four heads.

11: The name of the first is Pison: that is it which compasseth the whole land of Havilah, where there is gold;

12: And the gold of that land is good: there is bdellium and the onyx stone.

13: And the name of the second river is Gihon: the same is it that compasseth the whole land of Ethiopia.

14: And the name of the third river is Hiddekel: that is it which goeth toward the east of Assyria. And the fourth river is Euphrates.

15: And the LORD God took the man, and put him into the garden of Eden to dress it and to keep it.

16: And the LORD God commanded the man, saying, Of every tree of the garden thou mayest freely eat:

17: But of the tree of the knowledge of good and evil, thou shalt not eat of it: for in the day that thou eatest thereof thou shalt surely die.

18: And the LORD God said, It is not good that the man should be alone; I will make him an help meet for him.

19: And out of the ground the LORD God formed every beast of the field, and every fowl of the air; and brought them unto Adam to see what he would call them: and whatsoever Adam called every living creature, that was the name thereof.

20: And Adam gave names to all cattle, and to the fowl of the air, and to every beast of the field; but for Adam there was not found an help meet for him.

21: And the LORD God caused a deep sleep to fall upon Adam and he slept: and he took one of his ribs, and closed up the flesh instead thereof;

22: And the rib, which the LORD God had taken from man, made he a woman, and brought her unto the man.

23: And Adam said, This is now bone of my bones, and flesh of my flesh: she shall be called Woman, because she was taken out of Man.

24: Therefore shall a man leave his father and his mother, and shall cleave unto his wife: and they shall be one flesh.

25: And they were both naked, the man and his wife, and were not ashamed.

1: Now the serpent was more subtil than any beast of the field which the LORD God had made. And he said unto the woman, Yea, hath God said, Ye shall not eat of every tree of the garden?

2: And the woman said unto the serpent, We may eat of the fruit of the trees of the garden:

3: But of the fruit of the tree which is in the midst of the garden, God hath said, Ye shall not eat of it, neither shall ye touch it, lest ye die.

4: And the serpent said unto the woman, Ye shall not surely die:

5: For God doth know that in the day ye eat thereof, then your eyes shall be opened, and ye shall be as gods, knowing good and evil.

6: And when the woman saw that the tree was good for food, and that it was pleasant to the eyes, and a tree to be desired to make one wise, she took of the fruit thereof, and did eat, and gave also unto her husband with her; and he did eat.

7: And the eyes of them both were opened, and they knew that they were naked; and they sewed fig leaves together, and made themselves aprons.

8: And they heard the voice of the LORD God walking in the garden in the cool of the day: and Adam and his wife hid themselves from the presence of the LORD God amongst the trees of the garden.

9: And the LORD God called unto Adam, and said unto him, Where art thou?

10: And he said, I heard thy voice in the garden, and I was afraid, because I was naked; and I hid myself.

11: And he said, Who told thee that thou wast naked? Hast thou eaten of the tree, whereof I commanded thee that thou shouldest not eat?

12: And the man said, The woman whom thou gavest to be with me, she gave me of the tree, and I did eat.

13: And the LORD God said unto the woman, What is this that thou hast done? And the woman said, The serpent beguiled me, and I did eat.

14: And the LORD God said unto the serpent, Because thou hast done this, thou art cursed above all cattle, and above every beast of the field; upon thy belly shalt thou go, and dust shalt thou eat all the days of thy life:

15: And I will put enmity between thee and the woman, and between thy seed and her seed; it shall bruise thy head, and thou shalt bruise his heel.

16: Unto the woman he said, I will greatly multiply thy sorrow and thy conception; in sorrow thou shalt bring forth children; and thy desire shall be to thy husband, and he shall rule over thee.

17: And unto Adam he said, Because thou hast hearkened unto the voice of thy wife, and hast eaten of the tree, of which I commanded thee, saying, Thou shalt not eat of it: cursed is the ground for thy sake; in sorrow shalt thou eat of it all the days of thy life;

18: Thorns also and thistles shall it bring forth to thee; and thou shalt eat the herb of the field;

19: In the sweat of thy face shalt thou eat bread, till thou return unto the ground; for out of it wast thou taken: for dust thou art, and unto dust shalt thou return.

20: And Adam called his wife's name Eve; because she was the mother of all living.

21: Unto Adam also and to his wife did the LORD God make coats of skins, and clothed them.

22: And the LORD God said, Behold, the man is become as one of us, to know good and evil: and now, lest he put forth his hand, and take also of the tree of life, and eat, and live for ever:

23: Therefore the LORD God sent him forth from the garden of Eden, to till the ground from whence he was taken.

24: So he drove out the man; and he placed at the east of the garden of Eden Cherubims, and a flaming sword which turned every way, to keep the way of the tree of life.

"The Book of Genesis," *Holy Bible*, King James Version.

CHINA: ZHOU DYNASTY, MENCIUS ON THE MANDATE OF HEAVEN (c. 370–c. 290 BCE)

After Confucius, Mencius (*c.* 370–*c.* 290 BCE) is widely considered the most influential Chinese thinker in the Confucian tradition. Born a century after the death of Confucius (*c.* 479 BCE), Mencius lived during the Zhou Dynasty and the Warring States period. The Zhou Dynasty period was the longest in Chinese history (1122–256 BCE). Mencius taught near the end of the Zhous, in a period of disarray when China was a loose federation of rival territories, often at war over territorial claims and political power. After an interlude, the Han Dynasty (206 BCE–220 CE) asserted control over the vast expanse of once disorganized territories. It established the political and economic control that confirmed the Chinese ideal of itself as the Center of the Universe and also led to the Silk Road, a trade route that extended far to the West and permitted trade with Persia and, eventually, the West itself.

Confucius and Mencius were the philosophical masters of the latter Zhou period. Confucian influence continues today in China where it is enjoying a renaissance. As the selections reveal, they taught a philosophy of noble state craft founded on Tianmìng, the Mandate of Heaven, which is roughly equivalent to the European principle of the Divine Right of Kings. The Mandate of Heaven principle is the belief that rulers govern by divine right whereby their powers are based in personal virtue. Here the imperial impulse is directed toward the immortal aspects that permit an empire to endure. Hence, in the selections from the teachings of Mencius it is evident that the benevolence of the ruler is closely tied to his political and military rights. Still today in Beijing the restored Temple of Heaven is located on Tiananmen Square, the space of the Mandate of Heaven, on an axis leading to the Forbidden City, the palace of China's last dynasties before the nationalist rebellion in 1911.

One interesting side note is that the *lì* is a traditional unit of distance, roughly 500 meters, which would make a kingdom of 1000 *lì* about 500 kilometers across – not a very large kingdom, hence a rough, if poetic, hint at the number and size of the rival kingdoms in the latter Zhou period.

Book 1, Chapter 1

1. Mencius went to see king Hûi of Liang.
2. The king said, 'Venerable sir, since you have not counted it far to come here, a distance of a thousand lì, may I presume that you are provided with counsels to profit my kingdom?'
3. Mencius replied, 'Why must your Majesty use that word "profit?" What I am provided with, are counsels to benevolence and righteousness, and these are my only topics.
4. 'If your Majesty say, "What is to be done to profit my kingdom?" the great officers will say, "What is to be done to profit our families?" and the inferior officers and the common people will say, "What is to be done to profit our persons?" Superiors and inferiors will try to snatch this profit the one from the other, and the kingdom will be endangered. In the kingdom of ten thousand chariots, the murderer of his sovereign shall be the chief of a family of a thousand chariots. In the kingdom of a thousand chariots, the murderer of his prince shall be the chief of a family of a hundred chariots. To have a thousand in ten thousand, and a hundred in a thousand, cannot be said not to be a large allotment, but if righteousness be put last, and profit be put first, they will not be satisfied without snatching all.

5. 'There never has been a benevolent man who neglected his parents. There never has been a righteous man who made his sovereign an after consideration.

6. 'Let your Majesty also say, "Benevolence and righteousness, and let these be your only themes." Why must you use that word – "profit?".'

Book 1, Chapter 5

1. King Hûi of Liang said, 'There was not in the nation a stronger State than Tsin, as you, venerable Sir, know. But since it descended to me, on the east we have been defeated by Ch'i, and then my eldest son perished; on the west we have lost seven hundred lî of territory to Ch'in; and on the south we have sustained disgrace at the hands of Ch'û. I have brought shame on my departed predecessors, and wish on their account to wipe it away, once for all. What course is to be pursued to accomplish this?'

2. Mencius replied, 'With a territory which is only a hundred lî square, it is possible to attain to the royal dignity.

3. 'If Your Majesty will indeed dispense a benevolent government to the people, being sparing in the use of punishments and fines, and making the taxes and levies light, so causing that the fields shall be ploughed deep, and the weeding of them be carefully attended to, and that the strong-bodied, during their days of leisure, shall cultivate their filial piety, fraternal respectfulness, sincerity, and truthfulness, serving thereby, at home, their fathers and elder brothers, and, abroad, their elders and superiors, – you will then have a people who can be employed, with sticks which they have prepared, to oppose the strong mail and sharp weapons of the troops of Ch'in and Ch'û.

4. 'The rulers of those States rob their people of their time, so that they cannot plough and weed their fields, in order to support their parents. Their parents suffer from cold and hunger. Brothers, wives, and children are separated and scattered abroad.

5. 'Those rulers, as it were, drive their people into pit-falls, or drown them. Your Majesty will go to punish them. In such a case, who will oppose your Majesty?

6. 'In accordance with this is the saying, – "The benevolent has no enemy." I beg your Majesty not to doubt what I say.'

W.A.C.H. Dobson (1963) *Mencius: a new translation arranged and annotated for the general reader*, University of Toronto Press. Reprinted with permission of the publisher.

■ ■ ■ ■ ■ ■

ARABIA: MUHAMMAD, *QUR'AN* AND THE TREATY OF HUDAYBIYYAH (610–632 CE)

Muhammad (570–622 CE) is the founding and central figure of the religion of Islam. In the Muslim tradition, he is considered to be the last of the prophets and the messenger of Allah (God). Muhammad's teachings and interactions with Allah laid the foundations for the *Qur'an* (literally, the recitation), the central text of Islam. As such, Muhammad's life history has long been of great importance for the Muslim faith.

Muhammad was born sometime around 570 CE in the city of Mecca. Initially, his teachings did not take very well in his home town. This was especially true amongst the Quarysh, the ruling Meccans at the time. Because of this, Muhammad and his followers were forced to move elsewhere for refuge. Fearing for their safety, they left Mecca in 622 CE to settle down in the city of Yathrib, later renamed Medina. However, after several years and much conflict with the Quarysh, Muhammad did eventually return to Mecca. In 628 CE, Muhammad made an unarmed pilgrimage with some of his followers to the Holy City. This though proved to be an extremely risky maneuver, for at the same time the Quarysh had sent an armed group of soldiers to assassinate him. Hearing about this, Muhammad altered his plans and sought protection in the Hudaybiyyah, a nearby city. There, through peaceful means and popular Meccan support, he was able to negotiate a truce with the Quarysh. This came to be known as the Treaty of Hudaybiyyah and it allowed those of the Muslim faith to come and go to Mecca for their pilgrimage.

The following chapter (also known as a "Sura") from the *Qur'an* makes reference to and interprets these latter events. Here, the treaty is seen as a victory for and testament to the Muslim faith. Specifically, there is a distinction made between those who followed Muhammad on his unarmed pilgrimage and those who did not. For the former, the Sura celebrates their willingness to give their lives into the will of Allah; it suggests that their faith in Allah is what allowed them to go unharmed from the Quarysh. As for the latter, the Sura condemns these people to a life of conflict and punishment. This is because their selfishness amounts to a disbelief in Allah. One of the messages here is that peace follows those who are of true Muslim faith. Allah will always protect them from harm to the exclusion of unbelieving others in this and the next life.

Of course, it should be mentioned here that the Treaty of Hudaybiyyah perhaps involved more than divine intervention. Historians have noted that the Quarysh were under tremendous pressure from both their own populace and the threat of outside force to negotiate with Muhammad. This latter cause came to a head when, only two years after the Treaty of Hudaybiyyah was signed, forces allied with the Quarysh violated its terms and killed a Muslim caravan. In response, Muhammad led a Muslim army of over 10,000 soldiers to lay siege against the Quarysh. Confronted with such insurmountable odds, the Quarysh surrendered. Many of them converted to Islam, and Mecca, like many to come after, would become an Islamic city.

The Victory

In the name of Allah, the Beneficent, the Merciful.

48.1 Surely We have given to you a clear victory

48.2 That Allah may forgive your community their past faults and those to follow and complete His favor to you and keep you on a right way,

48.3 And that Allah might help you with a mighty help.

48.4 He it is Who sent down tranquillity into the hearts of the believers that they might have more of faith added to their faith – and Allah's are the hosts of the heavens and the earth, and Allah is Knowing, Wise

48.5 That He may cause the believing men and the believing women to enter gardens beneath which rivers flow to abide therein and remove from them their evil; and that is a grand achievement with Allah

48.6 And (that) He may punish the hypocritical men and the hypocritical women, and the polytheistic men and the polytheistic women, the entertainers of evil thoughts about Allah. On them is the evil turn, and Allah is wroth with them and has cursed them and prepared hell for them, and evil is the resort.

48.7 And Allah's are the hosts of the heavens and the earth; and Allah is Mighty, Wise.

48.8 Surely We have sent you as a witness and as a bearer of good news and as a warner,

48.9 That you may believe in Allah and His Apostle and may aid him and revere him; and (that) you may declare His glory, morning and evening.

48.10 Surely those who swear allegiance to you do but swear allegiance to Allah; the hand of Allah is above their hands. Therefore whoever breaks (his faith), he breaks it only to the injury of his own soul, and whoever fulfills what he has covenanted with Allah, He will grant him a mighty reward.

48.11 Those of the dwellers of the desert who were left behind will say to you: Our property and our families kept us busy, so ask forgiveness for us. They say with their tongues what is not in their hearts. Say: Then who can control anything for you from Allah if He intends to do you harm or if He intends to do you good; nay, Allah is Aware of what you do:

48.12 Nay! you rather thought that the Apostle and the believers would not return to their families ever, and that was made fairseeming to your hearts and you thought an evil thought and you were a people doomed to perish.

48.13 And whoever does not believe in Allah and His Apostle, then surely We have prepared burning fire for the unbelievers.

48.14 And Allah's is the kingdom. of the heavens and the earth; He forgives whom He pleases and punishes whom He pleases, and Allah is Forgiving, Merciful.

48.15 Those who are left behind will say when you set forth for the gaining of acquisitions: Allow us (that) we may follow you. They desire to change the world of Allah. Say: By no means shall you follow us; thus did Allah say before. But they will say: Nay! you are jealous of us. Nay! they do not understand but a little.

48.16 Say to those of the dwellers of the desert who were left behind: You shall soon be invited (to fight) against a people possessing mighty prowess; you will fight against them until they submit; then if you obey, Allah will grant you a good reward; and if you turn back as you turned back before, He will punish you with a painful punishment.

48.17 There is no harm in the blind, nor is there any harm in the lame, nor is there any harm in the sick (if they do not go forth); and whoever obeys Allah and His Apostle, He will cause him to enter gardens beneath which rivers flow, and whoever turns back, He will punish him with a painful punishment.

48.18 Certainly Allah was well pleased with the believers when they swore allegiance to you under the tree, and He knew what was in their hearts, so He sent down tranquillity on them and rewarded them with a near victory,

48.19 And many acquisitions which they will take; and Allah is Mighty, Wise.

48.20 Allah promised you many acquisitions which you will take, then He hastened on this one for you and held back the hands of men from you, and that it may be a sign for the believers and that He may guide you on a right path.

48.21 And others which you have not yet been able to achieve Allah has surely encompassed them, and Allah has power over all things.

48.22 And if those who disbelieve fight with you, they would certainly turn (their) backs, then they would not find any protector or a helper.

48.23 Such has been the course of Allah that has indeed run before, and you shall not find a change in Allah's course.

48.24 And He it is Who held back their hands from you and your hands from them in the valley of Mecca after He had given you victory over them; and Allah is Seeing what you do.

48.25 It is they who disbelieved and turned you away from the Sacred Mosque and (turned off) the offering withheld from arriving at its destined place; and were it not for the believing men and the believing women, whom, not having known, you might have trodden down, and thus something hateful might have afflicted you on their account without knowledge – so that Allah may cause to enter into His mercy whomsoever He pleases; had they been widely separated one from another, We would surely have punished those who disbelieved from among them with a painful punishment.

48.26 When those who disbelieved harbored in their hearts (feelings of) disdain, the disdain of (the days of) ignorance, but Allah sent down His tranquillity on His Apostle and on the believers, and made them keep the word of guarding (against evil), and they were entitled to it and worthy of it; and Allah is Cognizant of all things.

48.27 Certainly Allah had shown to His Apostle the vision with truth: you shall most certainly enter the Sacred Mosque, if Allah pleases, in security, (some) having their heads shaved and (others) having their hair cut, you shall not fear, but He knows what you do not know, so He brought about a near victory before that.

48.28 He it is Who sent His Apostle with the guidance and the true religion that He may make it prevail over all the religions; and Allah is enough for a witness.

48.29 Muhammad is the Apostle of Allah, and those with him are firm of heart against the unbelievers, compassionate among themselves; you will see them bowing down, prostrating themselves, seeking grace from Allah and pleasure; their marks are in their faces because of the effect of prostration; that is their description in the Taurat and their description in the Injeel; like as seed-produce that puts forth its sprout, then strengthens it, so it becomes stout and stands firmly on its stem, delighting the sowers that He may enrage the unbelievers on account of them; Allah has promised those among them who believe and do good, forgiveness and a great reward.

The Qur'an, http://quod.lib.umich.edu/cgi/k/koran/koran-idx?type=DIV0&byte=804189\.

THE AMERICAS: THE ABENAKI CREATION STORY (c. 100 CE ?)

The Abenaki Tribe is one of five tribes of the Wabanaki Confederacy that comprise the indigenous inhabitants of what is now the northeastern United States and southeastern Canada. While there are many individual Abenaki tribes, they not only are grouped geographically, but also speak a common language that is part of the Algonquin linguistic family. *Abenaki* is Algonquin for "people of the dawnland," a reference to the location at the eastern edge of the North American continent. Because of this positioning, they were the first indigenous Americans to come into contact with Europeans in the mid-1500s and suffered heavily from epidemics. The Abenaki tribes formed a political confederation in 1670, but by then it is estimated that at least 75 percent of the population had died from foreign diseases.

Stories are important for the Abenaki, not only for entertainment, but also for the transmission of cultural values. "The Coming of Gluskabi" is one of the Abenaki creation stories. *Tabaldak* is a word that is used interchangeably with Ktsi Nwaskw, the Abenaki name for "Great Mystery," the Creator. Some argue that the story of Tabaldak is relatively recent, and that it may be a mispronunciation of "Jesus Christ" and the story likewise. The name may also come from *Tolba* (turtle) and *Aki* (Earth), since some traditional stories say the American continent is balanced on the shell of a great turtle, and thus the name means "Earth Spirit."

Tabaldak created two men out of dust: Gluskonba (or Gluskabe) and Malsumis. They are the twin powers of good and evil: Gluskonba uses his power to protect man, and Malsumis to trick and do evil. Gluskonba vows to stop creating, and to become a transformer and protector of the earth. This story of the creation of earth is still being passed down today amongst the Abenaki.

The Coming of Gluskabi

Waudjoset ndatlokugan bizwakamigwi alnabe bimisigeniganiye agwedewabizun. Long ago my story was walking around, a forest lodge man with clothing made of sheets of moss and with strips of ashwood for his belt. And this is the place where my story decided to camp. And here this story of Gluskabi begins.

After Tabaldak had finished making human beings, he dusted his hands off and some of that dust sprinkled on the earth. From that dust Gluskabi formed himself. He sat up from the earth and said, 'Here I am.' So it is that some of the Abenaki people call Gluskabi by another name, 'Odzihozo,' which means 'The Man who made himself from something.' He was not as powerful as Tabaldak, but like his grandchildren, the human being, he had the power to change things, sometimes for the worst.

When Gluskabi sat up from the earth, The Owner was astonished. 'How did it happen now that you came to be?' he said.

Then Gluskabi said, 'Well, it is because I formed myself from this dust left over from the first humans that you made.'

'You are very wonderful,' The Owner told him.

'I am wonderful because you sprinkled me,' Gluskabi answered.

'Let us roam around now,' said The Owner. So they left that place and went uphill to the top of a mountain. There they gazed about, open-eyed, so far around they could see. They could see the lakes, the rivers, the tress, how all the land lay, the earth. Then The Owner said, 'Behold here how wonderful is my work. By the wish of my mind I created all this existing world, oceans, rivers, river lakes.' And he and Gluskabi gazed open-eyed.

Then Gluskabi said, 'Can not I also cause something to be created?'

And The Owner replied, 'Make whatever you can do according to your power.'

'Well,' Gluskabi said, 'Perhaps I can make the wind.' Then Gluskabi made the wind blow. It came up and blew so hard that the trees bent over and some were torn out by the roots. Gluskabi was very pleased.

'Enough,' said The Owner. 'I have seen how powerful you are and what you can do. Now, in return, I too will make the wind blow.' Then the wind rose. It blew so hard Gluskabi could not stand. It tangled up all the hair on Gluskabi's head and when he tried to smooth it down the wind blew the hair right off.

'Enough,' said Gluskabi. 'I have seen how powerful you are. No longer will I try to cause anything to be created.' So it was that Gluskabi had his first encounter with the wind and learned the limits of his own power.

But The Owner left Gluskabi the power to change things. 'Now you will be in charge of this earth,' The Owner said. 'You will work to make it a good place for your grandchildren, the human beings.'

And so Gluskabi began to do just that.

"The Coming of Gluskabi," *The Wind Eagle and Other Abenaki Stories*, retold by Joseph Bruchac, Greenfield Center, NY: Bowman Books, 1985.

GREECE: HOMER, *ILIAD* (c. 725–675 BCE)

The Trojan War is the foundational literary myth of Ancient Greece. It is unlikely that there was a historical event corresponding to the fall of Troy, but it is certain that the origins of Greek literature relied on myths handed down from the time of the alleged battle sometime in the thirteenth or twelfth centuries BCE. The undisputedly most important source of the story is Homer's *Iliad*, which was composed (probably in song) sometime late in the eighth or early in the seventh centuries BCE. On the other hand, there is an irresolvable dispute as to whether a single author, Homer, composed the epic poem some four centuries, at least, after the war was believed to have been waged.

These uncertainties serve to document the deep structural effects of an imperial disposition. For so great a poem as the *Iliad* (and its sequel, the *Odyssey*) to have taken on so vast a literary influence can only be because of a disposition for wonderment at the conflicting natures of society – the struggle for peace and worship against the necessity of war and conquest. Homer's *Iliad* may well be the single most quoted or copied story in all of Western literature. It is known to have influenced Sophocles and the other Greek dramatists, as well as Virgil – whose *Aeneid* is a remake of the Homeric epic.

The "Shield of Achilles" is the ornate description of the shield made by the god Hephaestus for Achilles before the battle with Hector outside the walls of Troy. Two great cities are pictured – one of peace and harmony, another of war and danger. While evidently a romantic description of the issues at stake in the Trojan War, if one takes the war itself as a myth depicting human nature, then the shield is a condensation of the Ancient Greece ideal in which conquest of rival kingdoms is a necessity to assure an idealized peace of human nature. Also, the elements of passion and revenge, typified in Achilles' killing of Hector, point to human nature's deepest inclination for conquest.

The Shield of Achilles, *Iliad*, Book 18

First he shaped the shield so great and strong, adorning it all over and binding it round with a gleaming circuit in three layers; and the baldric was made of silver. He made the shield in five thicknesses, and with many a wonder did his cunning hand enrich it. He wrought the earth, the heavens, and the sea; the moon also at her full and the untiring sun, with all the signs that glorify the face of heaven – the Pleiads, the Hyads, huge Orion, and the Bear, which men also call the Wain and which turns round ever in one place, facing Orion, and alone never dips into the stream of Oceanus.

He wrought also two cities, fair to see and busy with the hum of men. In the one were weddings and wedding-feasts, and they were going about the city with brides whom they were escorting by torchlight from their chambers. Loud rose the cry of Hymen, and the youths danced to the music of flute and lyre, while the women stood each at her house door to see them.

Meanwhile the people were gathered in assembly, for there was a quarrel, and two men were wrangling about the blood-money for a man who had been killed, the one saying before the people that he had paid damages in full, and the other that he had not been paid. Each was trying to make his own case good, and the people took sides, each man backing the side that he had taken; but the heralds kept them back, and the elders sate on their seats of stone in a solemn circle, holding the staves which the heralds had put into their hands. Then they rose and each in his turn gave judgement, and there were two talents laid down, to be given to him whose judgement should be deemed the fairest.

About the other city there lay encamped two hosts in gleaming armour, and they were divided whether to sack it, or to spare it and accept the half of what it contained. But the men of the city would not yet consent, and armed themselves for a surprise; their wives and little children kept guard upon the walls, and with them were the men who were past fighting through age; but the others sallied forth with Mars and Pallas Minerva at their head – both of them wrought in gold and clad in golden raiment, great and fair with their armour as befitting gods, while they that followed were smaller. . . . When they reached the place where they would lay their ambush, it was on a riverbed to which live stock of all kinds would come from far and near to water; here, then, they lay concealed, clad in full armour. Some way off them there were two scouts who were on the look-out for the coming of sheep or cattle, which presently came, followed by two shepherds who were playing on their pipes, and had not so much as a thought of danger. When those who were in ambush saw this, they cut off the flocks and herds and killed the shepherds. Meanwhile the besiegers, when they heard much noise among the cattle as they sat in council, sprang to their horses, and made with all speed towards them; when they reached them they set battle in array by the banks of the river, and the hosts aimed their bronze-shod spears at one another. With them were Strife and Riot, and fell Fate who was dragging three men after her, one with a fresh wound, and the other unwounded, while the third was dead, and she was dragging him along by his heel: and her robe was bedrabbled in men's blood. They went in and out with one another and fought as though they were living people haling away one another's dead.

He wrought also a fair fallow field, large and thrice ploughed already. Many men were working at the plough within it, turning their oxen to and fro, furrow after furrow. Each time that they turned on reaching the headland a man would come up to them and give them a cup of wine, and they would go back to their furrows looking forward to the time when they should again reach the headland. The part that they had ploughed was dark behind them, so that the field, though it was of gold, still looked as if it were being ploughed – very curious to behold.

"The Shield of Achilles," *The Iliad of Homer*, translated by Samuel Butler (1835–1902).

Imperial Systems, Conflict, and Expansion

■ ■ ■ ■ ■ ■ ■

EGYPT: RAMSES II, THE BATTLE OF KADESH (c. 1273 BCE)

The last Pharaoh of the eighteenth dynasty, Horemheb, began a new era of Egyptian imperial expansion through a revitalization of the military. The nineteenth dynasty, to which Ramses II belonged, was known for its expansion and the assertion of political dominance, running military campaigns against the Nubians in the south, the tribes of Libya in the west, and the Hebrews and the Hittites in the east. The Hittite Empire (c. 1750–1180 BCE) was an early Anatolian (Asia Minor) Empire that territorially encompassed much of what is modern-day Turkey. From 1400 to 1300 BCE, the Hittites were in a period of empire expanding, though they were known more for signing treaties and, according to some archaeologists, may have been the first constitutional democracy as they tended to annex territories and use treaties. Between 1180 and 1160 BCE the empire fell apart due to rival claims for the throne and the ensuing civil war. But in 1290 BCE, at the height of territorial expansion, the Hittite Empire encompassed lands in Assyria and Canaan, bordering on the Egyptian area of control.

Ramses II attacked the border town, Kadesh, which lies in modern-day Syria, in the fifth year of his reign. He was nearly captured and lost many men to Hittite forces. However, upon his return to Egypt he claimed a victory, but his army was nearly shattered and he had not claimed any new territory. Conflict between the Hittites and the Egyptians continued until both empires could not sustain the conflict due to other pressures.

In 1258 BCE, Hattusiliš III and Ramses II signed what is recognized as one of the earliest peace treaties. The treaty was written in both Egyptian hieroglyphs and Hittite governmental language, Akkadian cuneiform script, but the accounts are not identical. Each side claims that the other empire begged for peace. But it truly is an imperial document in that each side also claims that their gods demand peace. It also represents a resolution between two empires that were among the first to use statehood in their expansion, which is represented in their treaty which holds clauses for extradition, and mutual support and aid for internal conflicts. A mark of the importance this document holds for foreign affairs is that a copy of the treaty now resides in the United Nations building. Below is the Egyptian version that refers to Hattusiliš as Khetasar and to Hatti as "the kingdom of Kheta."

The Peace Treaty Between Ramses II and Hattusiliš III: The Egyptian Version

Year 21, first month of the second season, twenty-first day, under the majesty of the King of Upper and Lower Egypt: Usermare-Setepnere, Son of Re: Ramses-Meriamon, given life, forever and ever, beloved of

Amon-Re-Harakhte, Ptah-South-of-His-Wall, lord of 'Life-of-the-Two-Lands,' Mut, mistress of Ishru, and Khonsu-Neferhotep; shining upon the Horus-throne of the living, like his father, Harakhte, forever and ever.

On this day, lo, his majesty was at the city (called): 'House-of-Ramses-Meriamon,' performing the pleasing ceremonies of his father, Amon-Re-Harakhte-Atum, lord of the Two Lands of Heliopolis; Amon of Ramses-Meriamon, Ptah of Ramses-Meriamon, 'great in strength, son of Mut,' according as they gave to him eternity in jubilees, everlastingness in peaceful years, all lands, and all countries being prostrate beneath his sandals forever. There came the king's messenger, the deputy and butler, together with the king's messenger [bringing (?) to the king] Ramses II [the messenger (?)] of [Kheta, Ter]teseb and the [second messenger (?)] of Kheta [bearing (?) a silver tablet] which the great chief of the Kheta, Khetasar (xtAsrA) [caused] to be brought to Pharaoh, L. P. H., to crave peace [fro]m [the majesty] of the King of Upper and Lower Egypt, Ramses II, given life, forever and ever, like his father, Re, every day.

Copy of the silver tablet, which the great chief of Kheta, Khetasar (xtAsArA) caused to be brought to Pharaoh, L. P. H., by the hand of his messenger, Terteseb (tArAtysbw), and his messenger, Ramose, to crave peace from the majesty of Ramses II, the Bull of rulers, making his boundary as far as he desires in every land.

The treaty which the great chief of Kheta, Khetasar, the valiant, the son of Merasar (mrAsArA), the great chief of Kheta, the valiant, the grandson, of Seplel (sApA[rwrw]), [the great chief of Kheta, the val]iant, made, upon a silver tablet for Usermare-Setepnere (Ramses II), the great ruler of Egypt, the valiant, the son of Menmare (Seti II, the great ruler of Egypt, The valiant, the grandson of Menpehtire (Ramses I), the great ruler of Egypt, the valiant; the good treaty of peace and of brotherhood, setting peace [between them (?)], forever.

1. Now, at the beginning, since eternity, the relations of the great ruler of Egypt with the great chief of Kheta were (such) that the god prevented hostilities between them, by treaty. Whereas, in the time of Metella (mwTnrA), the great chief of Kheta, my brother, he fought w[ith Ramses II], the great ruler of Egypt, yet afterward, beginning with this day, behold, Khetasar, the great chief of Kheta, is [in] a treaty-relation for establishing the relations which the Re made, and which Sutekh made, for the land of Egypt, with the land of Kheta, in order not to permit hostilities to arise between them, forever.

2. Behold then, Khetasar, the great chief of Kheta, is in treaty relation with Usermare-Setepnere (Ramses II), the great ruler of Egypt, beginning with this day, in order to bring about good peace and good brotherhood between us forever, while he is in brotherhood with me, he is in peace with me; and I am in brotherhood with him, and I am in peace with him, forever. Since Metella (mwTnrA), the great chief of Kheta, my brother, succumbed to his fate, and Khetasar sat as great chief of Kheta upon the throne of his father, behold, I am together with Ramses-Meriamon, the great ruler of Egypt, and he is [with me in (?)] our peace and our brotherhood. It is better than the former peace and brotherhood which were in the land.

Behold, I, even the great chief of Kheta, am with [Ramses II], the great ruler of Egypt, in good peace and in good brotherhood.

The children of the children of the great chief of Kheta shall be in brotherhood and peace with the children of the children of Ramses-Meriamon, the great ruler of Egypt, being in our relations of brotherhood and our relations [of peace], that the [land of Egypt] may be with the land of Kheta in peace and brotherhood like ourselves, forever.

3. There shall be no hostilities between them, forever. The great chief of Kheta shall not pass over into the land of Egypt, forever, to take anything therefrom. Ramses-Meriamon, the great ruler of Egypt, shall not pass over into the land of Kheta, to take anything] therefrom, forever.

James Henry Breasted (2001/1906) *Ancient Records of Egypt, Vol. 3: The Nineteenth Dynasty*, University of Illinois Press.

BABYLONIA: CYRUS THE GREAT, THE ACHAEMENID EMPIRE (590–530 BCE)

Cyrus the Great (590–530 BCE) was the most active and successful military commander until Alexander the Great. After assuming the throne of Persia in 559 BCE, Cyrus brought political unification to the Iranian plateau by overthrowing the ruling Medians, and then proceeded to conquer the other empires in Asia Minor (Persian, Lydian, Neo-Babylonian, Neo-Assyrian, and Egyptian). Under the reign of Darius I, the Achaemenid Empire grew to be the second largest empire of classical antiquity, second to, and ending under, the invasion of Alexander the Great in 330 BCE.

Historians consider the Achaemenid Empire of Cyrus the Great to be a turning point in history between archaic and classical time periods. The previous rulers of Persia, the Medes, were semi-nomadic and tribal. Cyrus ushered in a new era of imperialism. While a highly successful general, he is not known for his military accomplishments, or imperial governance, so much as for his cultural policy of tolerance and respect. This is evidenced by his conquering of Babylon in 539/8 BCE that relied on propaganda as much as military planning. Upon conquering Babylon, in keeping with local customs, Cyrus had the inscriptions put on a cylinder and placed under the walls of Babylon. At the time he attacked, the reigning king, Nabonidus (from Chaldea in the south), did not allow the Babylonians to keep their festivals and traditions, and would not allow their deities to remain in temples. The text below outlines that he was not respectful of the local people nor as outlined in the book of Daniel in the bible, of the enslaved Jewish people. In the Cyrus Cylinder, Cyrus claims that the god of Babylon, Marduk, willed him to conquer the city, as he was the natural ruler. He returned the captured Babylonian deities to their cities and rebuilt the temples. He also freed the Hebrew peoples and allowed them to rebuild the temple in Jerusalem. Though calling himself "The Great King" and expression of divine right, he appeared to be more of a liberator than a conquerer, a trend that subsequent Persian rulers continued in their quest to expand into Asia.

Moderns claim that the Cyrus Cylinder is the first declaration of human rights (a copy resides at the UN headquarters). Whether it is indeed a call to "universal" rights, or a move that was necessitated out of a burgeoning empire, it is a mark of a new imperial system that relied on cultural trust and control rather than destruction and deportation.

Text of the Cyrus Cylinder

[one line destroyed] . . . [r]ims of the world . . . a weakling has been installed as the enu [Sumerian title for king] of his country; [the correct images of the gods he removed from their thrones, imi]tations he ordered to place upon them. A replica of the temple Esagila he has . . . for Ur and the other sacred cities inappropriate rituals . . . daily he did blabber [incorrect prayers]. He (furthermore) interrupted in a fiendish way the regular offerings, he did . . . he established within the sacred cities. The worship of Marduk, the king of the gods, he [chang]ed into abomination, daily he used to do evil against his (i.e. Marduk's) city . . . He [tormented] its [inhabitant]s with corvee-work (lit. a Yoke) without relief, he ruined them all.

Upon their complaints the lord of the gods became terribly angry and [he departed from] their region, (also) the (other) gods living among them left their mansions, wroth that he had brought (them) into Babylon. (but) Marduk [who does care for] . . . on account of (the fact that) the sanctuaries of all their settlements were in ruins and the inhabitants of Sumer and Akkad had become like (living) dead, turned back (his countenance) [his] an[ger] [abated] and he had mercy (upon them). He scanned and looked (through) all the countries, searching for a righteous ruler willing to lead him (i.e. Marduk) (in the annual procession). (Then) he pronounced the name of Cyrus, king of Anshan, declared him to be(come) the ruler of all the world. He made the Guti country and all the Manda-hordes bow in submission to his (i.e. Cyrus') feet. And he (Cyrus) did always endeavor to treat according the justice the black-headed whom he (Marduk) had made him conquer. Marduk, the great lord, a protector of his people/worshipers, beheld with pleasure his (i.e. Cyrus') good deeds and his upright mind (and therefore) ordered him to march against his city Babylon. He made him set out on the road to Babylon going at his side like a real friend. His widespread troops – their number, like that of the water of a river, could not be established – strolled along, their weapons packed away. Without any battle, he made him enter his town Babylon, sparing Babylon any calamity. He delivered into his (i.e. Cyrus') hands Nabonidus, the king who did not worship him (i.e. Marduk). All the inhabitants of Sumer and Akkad, princes and governors (included), bowed to him (Cyrus) and kissed his feet, jubilant that he (had received) the kingship, and with shining faces. Happily they greeted him as a master through whose help they had come (again) to life from death (and) had all been spared damage and disaster, and they worshiped his (very) name.

I am Cyrus, king of the world, great king, legitimate king, king of Babylon, king of Sumer and Akkad, king of the four riims (of the earth), son of Cambyses, great king, king of Anshan, grand-son of Cyrus, great king, king of Anshan, descendant of Teispes, great king, king of Anshan, of a family (which) always (exercised) kingship; whose rule Bel and Nebo love, whom they want as king to please their hearts.

When I entered Babylon as a friend and (when) I established the seat of government in the palace of the ruler under jubilation and rejoicing, Marduk, the great lord [induced] the magnanimous inhabitants of Babylon [to love me], and I was daily endeavoring to worship him. My numerous troops walked around in Babylon in peace, I did not allow anybody to terrorize (any place) of the [country of Sumer] and Akkad. I strove for peace in Babylon and in all his (other) sacred cities. As to the inhabitants of Babylon, [who] against the will of the gods [had/were . . ., I abolished] the corvee (lit.: yoke) which was against their (social) standing. I brought relief to their dilapidated housing, putting (thus) an end to their (main) complaints. Marduk, the great lord, was well pleased with my deeds and sent friendly blessings to myself, Cyrus, the king who worships him, to Cambyses, my son, the offspring of [my] loins, as well as to all my troops, and we all [praised] his great [godhead] joyously, standing before him in peace.

All the kings of the entire world from the Upper to the Lower Sea, those who are seated in throne rooms, (those who) live in other [types of buildings as well as] all the kings of the West land living in tents, brought their heavy tributes and kissed my feet in Babylon. (As to the region) from . . . as far as Ashur and Susa, Agade, Eshnunna, the towns of Zamban, Me-Turnu, Der as well as the region of the Gutians, I returned to (these) sacred cities on the other side of the Tigris, the sanctuaries of which have been ruins for a long time, the images which (used) to live therein and established for them permanent sanctuaries. I (also) gathered all their former inhabitants and returned (to them) their habitations. Furthermore, I resettled upon the command of Marduk, the great lord, all the gods of Sumer and Akkard whom Nabonidus has brought into Babylon to the anger of the lord of the gods, unharmed, in their (former) chapels, the places which made them happy.

May all the gods whom I have resettled in their sacred cities ask Bel and Nebo for a long life for me and may they recommend me (to him); to Marduk, my lord, they may say this: 'Cyrus, the king who worships you, and Cambyses, his son, . . .' . . . all of them I settled in a peaceful place . . . ducks and doves, . . . I endeavored to fortify/repair their dwelling places . . . [six lines destroyed]

James B. Pritchard (ed.) (1958) *Ancient Near East: An anthology of texts and pictures*, Princeton, NJ: Princeton University Press.

GREECE AND PERSIA: THUCYDIDES, THE PELOPONNESIAN WARS (c. 431–404 BCE)

The Greco-Persian wars of 490 BCE and 480–79 BCE brought into an alliance over 150 Greek states to form the Delian League. It acted to divide the spoils of war and to protect against further invasions. The Delian League was dominatd by Athenian control, and while it is unclear exactly when the league became the Athenian Empire, many place the date at 454 BCE when Athenian general, statesman, and politician Pericles moved the treasury to Athens. The time from the end of the Greco-Roman wars in 448 BCE until the start of the Peloponnesian War in 431 BCE is considered to be the Golden Age of Greek civilization, also known as "The Age of Pericles" for the aid that he gave in supporting the arts, literature, and a general cultural flourishing. The Peloponnesian War (431–404 BCE), actually a series of wars fought between rival Greek states vying for power, put an end to the cultural golden age. The war was instigated by the Peloponnesian League, a group of smaller states lead by Sparta, whom most believe began the war out of fear of Athenian imperialism and regional domination.

Thucydides (c. 460–401/395 BCE) is famous for writing a history of this terrible conflict. He was an Athenian naval commander who, fearing punishment for a lost battle with Sparta, went into exile in 423 BCE. His book, *History of the Peloponnesian War*, revered for its rigorous historical investigation and political realism, combines Thucydides' first-hand accounts, and research into the war until 411 BCE. This selection from the "Funeral Oration of Pericles," purportedly delivered at the end of the first year of the war in 431 BCE, was a eulogy for the war dead. Public mourning periods were an Athenian custom, but the speech of Pericles is anything but customary. Instead of speaking about military prowess of Athenian history, Pericles focuses on contemporary Athens and the democratic ideal of the system of Athenian imperialism. Praise for Athenian political innovation and the empire become intertwined with comfort for the bereaved. He admonishes those present to fight for the beliefs of Athens, and emulate the deeds of the dead. Some historians point out that Thucydides had a deep admiration for Pericles, so while the speech is not an exact recounting, and may not have happened in 431 BCE, it is probably correspondent to a real speech, and certainly representative of the key positions of Pericles' support of Athenian imperialism, as well as representing Greek political and public life.

Funeral Oration of Pericles

'Most of my predecessors in this place have commended him who made this speech part of the law, telling us that it is well that it should be delivered at the burial of those who fall in battle. For myself, I should have thought that the worth which had displayed itself in deeds would be sufficiently rewarded by honours also shown by deeds; such as you now see in this funeral prepared at the people's cost. And I could have wished that the reputations of many brave men were not to be imperilled in the mouth of a single individual, to stand or fall according as he spoke well or ill. For it is hard to speak properly upon a subject where it is even difficult to convince your hearers that you are speaking the truth. On the one hand, the friend who is familiar with every fact of the story may think that some point has not been set forth with that fullness which he wishes and knows it to deserve; on the other, he who is a stranger to the matter may be led by envy to suspect exaggeration if he hears anything above his own nature. For men can endure to hear others praised only so long as they can severally persuade themselves of their own ability to equal the actions recounted: when this point is passed, envy comes in and with it incredulity. However, since our ancestors have stamped this custom with their approval, it becomes my duty to obey the law and to try to satisfy your several wishes and opinions as best I may.

'I shall begin with our ancestors: it is both just and proper that they should have the honour of the first mention on an occasion like the present. They dwelt in the country without break in the succession from generation to generation, and handed it down free to the present time by their valour. And if our more remote ancestors deserve praise, much more do our own fathers, who added to their inheritance the empire which we now possess, and spared no pains to be able to leave their acquisitions to us of the present generation. Lastly, there are few parts of our dominions that have not been augmented by those of us here, who are still more or less in the vigour of life; while the mother country has been furnished by us with everything that can enable her to depend on her own resources whether for war or for peace. That part of our history which tells of the military achievements which gave us our several possessions, or of the ready valour with which either we or our fathers stemmed the tide of Hellenic or foreign aggression, is a theme too familiar to my hearers for me to dilate on, and I shall therefore pass it by. But what was the road by which we reached our position, what the form of government under which our greatness grew, what the national habits out of which it sprang; these are questions which I may try to solve before I proceed to my panegyric upon these men; since I think this to be a subject upon which on the present occasion a speaker may properly dwell, and to which the whole assemblage, whether citizens or foreigners, may listen with advantage.

'Our constitution does not copy the laws of neighbouring states; we are rather a pattern to others than imitators ourselves. Its administration favours the many instead of the few; this is why it is called a democracy. If we look to the laws, they afford equal justice to all in their private differences; if no social standing, advancement in public life falls to reputation for capacity, class considerations not being allowed to interfere with merit; nor again does poverty bar the way, if a man is able to serve the state, he is not hindered by the obscurity of his condition. The freedom which we enjoy in our government extends also to our ordinary life. There, far from exercising a jealous surveillance over each other, we do not feel called upon to be angry with our neighbour for doing what he likes, or even to indulge in those injurious looks which cannot fail to be offensive, although they inflict no positive penalty. But all this ease in our private relations does not make us lawless as citizens. Against this fear is our chief safeguard, teaching us to obey the magistrates and the laws, particularly such as regard the protection of the injured, whether they are actually on the statute book, or belong to that code which, although unwritten, yet cannot be broken without acknowledged disgrace. [. . .]

'Indeed if I have dwelt at some length upon the character of our country, it has been to show that our stake in the struggle is not the same as theirs who have no such blessings to lose, and also that the panegyric of the men over whom I am now speaking might be by definite proofs established. That panegyric is now in a great measure complete; for the Athens that I have celebrated is only what the heroism of these and their like have made her, men whose fame, unlike that of most Hellenes, will be found to be only commensurate with their deserts. And if a test of worth be wanted, it is to be found in their closing scene, and this not only in cases in which it set the final seal upon their merit, but also in those in which it gave the first intimation of their having any. For there is justice in the claim that steadfastness in his country's battles should be as a cloak to cover a man's other imperfections; since the good action has blotted out the bad, and his merit as a citizen more than outweighed his demerits as an individual. But none of these allowed either wealth with its prospect of future enjoyment to unnerve his spirit, or poverty with its hope of a day of freedom and riches to tempt him to shrink from danger. No, holding that vengeance upon their enemies was more to be desired than any personal blessings, and reckoning this to be the most glorious of hazards, they joyfully determined to accept the risk, to make sure of their vengeance, and to let their wishes wait; and while committing to hope the uncertainty of final success, in the business before them they thought fit to act boldly and trust in themselves. Thus choosing to die resisting, rather than to live submitting, they fled only from dishonour, but met danger face to face, and after one brief moment, while at the summit of their fortune, escaped, not from their fear, but from their glory.

'So died these men as became Athenians. You, their survivors, must determine to have as unfaltering a resolution in the field, though you may pray that it may have a happier issue. And not contented with ideas derived only from words of the advantages which are bound up with the defence of your country, though these would furnish a valuable text to a speaker even before an audience so alive to them as the present, you must yourselves realize the power of Athens, and feed your eyes upon her from day to day, till love of her fills your hearts; and then, when all her greatness shall break upon you, you must reflect that it was by courage, sense of duty, and a keen feeling of honour in action that men were enabled to win all this, and that no personal failure in an enterprise could make them consent to deprive their country of their valour, but they laid it at her feet as the most glorious contribution that they could offer. For this offering of their lives made in common by them all they each of them individually received that renown which never grows old, and for a sepulchre, not so much that in which their bones have been deposited, but that noblest of shrines wherein their glory is laid up to be eternally remembered upon every occasion on which deed or story shall call for its commemoration. For heroes have the whole earth for their tomb; and in lands far from their own, where the column with its epitaph declares it, there is enshrined in every breast a record unwritten with no tablet to preserve it, except that of the heart. These take as your model and, judging happiness to be the fruit of freedom and freedom of valour, never decline the dangers of war. For it is not the miserable that would most justly be unsparing of their lives; these have nothing to hope for: it is rather they to whom continued life may bring reverses as yet unknown, and to whom a fall, if it came, would be most tremendous in its consequences. And surely, to a man of spirit, the degradation of cowardice must be immeasurably more grievous than the unfelt death which strikes him in the midst of his strength and patriotism!

'Comfort, therefore, not condolence, is what I have to offer to the parents of the dead who may be here. Numberless are the chances to which, as they know, the life of man is subject; but fortunate indeed are they who draw for their lot a death so glorious as that which has caused your mourning, and to whom life has been so exactly measured as to terminate in the happiness in which it has been passed. Still I know that this is a hard saying, especially when those are in question of whom you will constantly be reminded by seeing in the homes of others blessings of which once you also boasted: for grief is felt not so much for the want of what we have never known, as for the loss of that to which we have been long accustomed. Yet you who are still of an age to beget children must bear up in the hope of having others in their stead; not only will they help you to forget those whom you have lost, but will be to the state at once a reinforcement and a security; for never can a fair or just policy be expected of the citizen who does not, like his fellows, bring to the decision the interests and apprehensions of a father. While those of you who have passed your prime must congratulate yourselves with the thought that the best part of your life was fortunate, and that the brief span that remains will be cheered by the fame of the departed. For it is only the love of honour that never grows old; and honour it is, not gain, as some would have it, that rejoices the heart of age and helplessness.

'Turning to the sons or brothers of the dead, I see an arduous struggle before you. When a man is gone, all are wont to praise him, and should your merit be ever so transcendent, you will still find it difficult not merely to overtake, but even to approach their renown. The living have envy to contend with, while those who are no longer in our path are honoured with a goodwill into which rivalry does not enter. On the other hand, if I must say anything on the subject of female excellence to those of you who will now be in widowhood, it will be all comprised in this brief exhortation. Great will be your glory in not falling short of your natural character; and greatest will be hers who is least talked of among the men, whether for good or for bad.

'My task is now finished. I have performed it to the best of my ability, and in word, at least, the requirements of the law are now satisfied. If deeds be in question, those who are here interred have received part of their honours already, and for the rest, their children will be brought up till manhood at the public expense: the state thus offers a valuable prize, as the garland of victory in this race of valour, for the reward both of those who have fallen and their survivors. And where the rewards for merit are greatest, there are found the best citizens.

'And now that you have brought to a close your lamentations for your relatives, you may depart.'

Thucydides, "Funeral Oration of Pericles," *History of the Peloponnesian War*, Book 21, translated by Richard Crawley in 1876. The Internet Classics Archive. Source: http://classics.mit.edu/Thucydides/pelopwar.2.second.html.

MACEDONIA: PLUTARCH, ALEXANDER THE GREAT (356–323 BCE)

Alexander the Great (356–323 BCE) is one of the best-known figures of history. Hated and revered, he created the largest empire of antiquity, conquering the Achemenid (Persian) Empire and extending his empire into India. Accounts of Alexander tend to vary between evil megalomaniac and beneficent liberator. Unsurprisingly, the Persians remember him as a destructive invader, and the Egyptians, whom he freed from the Persians (332–331 BCE), a liberator. Though speculative, it is worth suggesting that Alexander's actions and conquest were inspired by the cultural climate into which he was born. The city-states of Greece, following the Peloponnesian Wars, continued to vie for power, and form federal leagues to break apart attempts at imperialism. Aristotle asserted that if the Greeks could achieve unity, they could conquer the world.

Alexander's father, Philip II (382–336 BCE) became ruler of Macedon in 359 BCE at a time when Macedon had a struggling economy and was under constant threat from its neighbors with imperial aspirations. After consolidating power in Macedon, Philip II led an economic and social revolution, and was known for his policy of expansion and incorporation. In 346 BCE, with a powerful Macedon, instead of pursuing further fighting with Greek city-states, he promoted a general peace. He was elected general of the Grecian armies, and in 340 BCE he continued his expansionist policies by attacking Persia. He was assassinated – the circumstances were unclear – in 336 BCE. Alexander, though 20, had already shown himself to be a gifted general in his father's army, and he continued the invasion of Persia with similar expansionist and conciliatory politics as his father. He married Persians, and had his officers do the same. The retreating Persian army killed their king, Darius, and left his body to halt Alexander's advance. He is said to have paid the late king great respect by carrying the body with him to the Persian capital, Persepolis, and given him a state funeral following the local Zoroastrian customs.

In his teen years, Alexander was tutored by Aristotle, and may have taken on board his optimism about Greek unity and world domination. The Greek historian Plutarch (c. 46–120 CE) wrote a series of biographies of important Greek figures, exploring the influence of their character on history. This selection covers much of the biographical information in Plutarch's *Lives*, but explicitly links Alexander to a divine right to rule as a descendent of Zeus, and to the worldly philosophy of the Greeks. Alexander is often seen as a successor to Achilles and appears as a hero. He conquered the known civilized world, overtaking the Achaemenid Empire, beginning with Egypt and moving through Anatolia, Mesopotamia, and Bactria, and extended the empire beyond the former bounds of the Persian Achaemenid Empire into what is now India. He died of mysterious causes but probably from malaria, or another viral infection, alcoholism, or poisoning. His ability to conquer was in part due to the incorporation of foreigners into his armies. During the twelve years of campaigning, he would leave old soldiers to settle the new territories.

On the Fortune or the Virtue of Alexander

This is Fortune's discourse, who declares that Alexander is her own characteristic handiwork, and hers alone. But some rejoinder must be made on behalf of philosophy, or rather on Alexander's behalf, who would be vexed and indignant if he should be thought to have received as a pure gift, even at the hands of Fortune, the supremacy which he won at the price of much blood and of wounds that followed one after another; and

> *Many a night did he spend without sleeping,*
> *Many a blood-stained day did he pass amid combats unceasing*

against irresistible forces and innumerable tribes, against impassable rivers and mountain fastnesses whose summit no arrow could reach, furthered by wise counsels, steadfast purpose, manly courage, and a prudent heart.

I think that if Fortune should try to inscribe her name on his successes, he would say to her, 'Slander not my virtues, nor take away my fair name by detraction. Darius was your handiwork: he who was a slave and courier of the king, him did you make the mighty lord of Persia; and Sardanapalus, upon whose head you placed the royal diadem, though he spent his days in carding purple wool. But I, through my victory at Arbela, went up to Susa, and Cilicia opened the way for me into the broad land of Egypt; but to Cilicia I came by way of the Granicus which I crossed, using as a bridge the dead bodies of Mithridates and Spithridates. Adorn yourself, proud Fortune, and vaunt your dominion over kings that never felt a wound nor shed a drop of blood. For they have been Fortune's favourites, men such as Ochus was and Artaxerxes, whom at the very hour of their birth you placed upon the throne of Cyrus. But my body bears many a token of an opposing Fortune and no ally of mine. First, among the Illyrians, my head was wounded by a stone and my neck by a cudgel. Then at the Granicus my head was cut open by an enemy's dagger, at Issus my thigh was pierced by the sword. Next at Gaza my ankle was wounded by an arrow, my shoulder was dislocated, and I whirled heavily round and round. Then at Maracanda the bone of my leg was split open by an arrow. There awaited me towards the last also the buffetings I received among the Indians and the violence of famines. Among the Aspasians my shoulder was wounded by an arrow, and among the Gandridae my leg. Among the Mallians, the shaft of an arrow sank deep into my breast and buried its steel; and I was struck in the neck by a cudgel, when the scaling-ladders which we had moved up to the walls were battered down; and Fortune cooped me up alone, favouring ignoble barbarians and not illustrious adversaries with such an exploit. But if Ptolemy had not held his shield above me, and Limnaeus taking his stand before me had not fallen, a target for ten thousand shafts, and if my Macedonians had not overthrown the wall with spirit and main force, then that nameless village in a foreign land must needs have become the tomb of Alexander.'

Moralia Plutarch, "On the Fortune or the Virtue of Alexander, bk. 1," *De Fortuna Alexandri by Plutarch*, as published in vol. IV of the Loeb Classical Library edition, 1936.

POST-ALEXANDRINE EMPIRES: PTOLEMY I, THE ROSETTA STONE (196 BCE)

The Rosetta Stone has two imperial histories and has become an enduring icon of decryption and translation, from both its ancient and its modern histories. After Alexander the Great's death in 323 BCE, his generals fought for seven years over his empire. Eventually power was consolidated under three generals: Seleucid in 311/312 got much of the Achaemenian Empire, establishing the new capital at Babylon. During his reign, Ptolemy I (367–283 BCE) founded the library of Alexandria and sponsored Euclid. The Seleucids, Greeks, and the Ptolemaic Egyptians continued to struggle for power throughout the former empire of Alexander. The official language of the Ptolemaic Empire (305–30 BCE) was Demotic script. The text of the stone itself is a decree of Ptolemy V Epiphanes (204–181 BCE) that conveys thanks, by way of decreeing a tax amnesty, to the Egyptian priesthood for their aid in suppressing a native rebellion in 184/3 BCE. The text is carved in Demotic, Ancient Greek, and hieroglyphics, allowing for the modern translation of hieroglyphs. It was translated by Jean-François Champollion, a French Orientalist.

The stone was uncovered by French Forces in Egypt in 1799. It was taken from the French by British soldiers in 1801, and moved to the British Museum in London in 1802. The British added two sentences in white paint: "captured in Egypt by the British Army in 1801" and "Presented by King George III." Egypt asked for the return of the stone in 2003, and were given a replica by the British in 2005. As such, not only is it an enduring icon of translation, but of colonial domination from Ptolemaic, through French and British control.

Text of the Rosetta Stone

In the reign of the young one who has succeeded his father in the kingship, lord of diadems, most glorious, who has established Egypt and is pious towards the gods, triumphant over his enemies, who has restored the civilized life of men, lord of the Thirty Years Festivals, even as Ptah the Great, a king like Ra, great king of the Upper and Lower countries, offspring of the Gods Philopatores, one whom Ptah has approved, to whom Ra has given victory, the living image of Amun, son of Ra, Ptolemy, living for ever, beloved of Ptah, in the ninth year, when Aetos son of Aetos was priest of Alexander, and the Gods Soteres, and the Gods Adelphoi, and the Gods Euergetai, and the Gods Philopatores and the God Epiphanes Eucharistos; Pyrrha daughter of Philinos being Athlophoros of Berenike Euergetis, Areia daughter of Diogenes being Kanephoros of Arsinoe

Philadelphos; Irene daughter of Ptolemy being Priestess of Arsinoe Philopator; the fourth of the month of Xandikos, according to the Egyptians the 18th Mekhir.

Decree. There being assembled the Chief Priests and Prophets and those who enter the inner shrine for the robing of the gods, and the Fan-bearers and the Sacred Scribes and all the other priests from the temples throughout the land who have come to meet the king at Memphis, for the feast of the assumption by Ptolemy, the ever-living, the beloved of Ptah, the God Epiphanes Eucharistos, of the kingship in which he succeeded his father, they being assembled in the temple in Memphis on this day declared:

Whereas King Ptolemy, the ever-living, the beloved of Ptah, the God Epiphanes Eucharistos, the son of King Ptolemy and Queen Arsinoe, the Gods Philopatores, has been a benefactor both to the temple and to those who dwell in them, as well as all those who are his subjects, being a god sprung from a god and goddess like Horus the son of Isis and Osiris, who avenged his father Osiris, being benevolently disposed towards the gods, has dedicated to the temples revenues of money and corn and has undertaken much outlay to bring Egypt into prosperity, and to establish the temples, and has been generous with all his own means; and of the revenues and taxes levied in Egypt some he has wholly remitted and others has lightened, in order that the people and all the others might be in prosperity during his reign; and

whereas he has remitted the debts to the crown being many in number which they in Egypt and the rest of the kingdom owed; and

whereas those who were in prison and those who were under accusation for a long time, he has freed of the charges against them; and

whereas he has directed that the gods shall continue to enjoy the revenues of the temples and the yearly allowances given to them, both of corn and money, likewise also the revenue assigned to the gods from the vine land and from gardens and the other properties which belonged to the gods in his father's time; and

whereas he directed also, with regard to the priests, that they should pay no more as the tax for admission to the priesthood than what was appointed them throughout his father's reign and until the first year of his own reign; and has relieved the members of the priestly orders from the yearly journey to Alexandria; and

whereas he has directed that impressment for the navy shall no longer be employed; and of the tax on fine linen cloth paid by the temples to the crown he has remitted two-thirds; and whatever things were neglected in former times he has restored to their proper condition, having a care how the traditional duties shall be fittingly paid to the gods; and likewise has apportioned justice to all, like Thoth the great and great; and has ordained that those who return of the warrior class, and of others who were unfavourably disposed in the days of the disturbances, should, on their return be allowed to occupy their old possessions; and

whereas he provided that cavalry and infantry forces and ships should be sent out against those who invaded Egypt by sea and by land, laying out great sums in money and corn in order that the temples and all those who are in the land might be in safety; and having gone to Lycopolis in the Busirite nome, which had been occupied and fortified against a siege with an abundant store of weapons and all other supplies seeing that disaffection was now of long standing among the impious men gathered into it, who had perpetrated much damage to the temples and to all the inhabitants of Egypt, and having encamped against it, he surrounded it with mounds and trenches and elaborate fortifications; when the Nile made a great rise in the eighth year of his reign, which usually floods the plains, he prevented it, by damming at many points the outlets of the channels spending upon this no small amount of money, and setting cavalry and infantry to guard them, in a short time he took the town by storm and destroyed all the impious men in it, even as Thoth and Horus, the son of Isis and Osiris, formerly subdued the rebels in the same district; and as to those who had led the rebels in the time of his father and who had disturbed the land and done wrong to the temples, he came to Memphis to avenge his father and his own kingship, and punished them all as they deserved, at the time that he came there to perform the proper ceremonies for the assumption of the crown; and

whereas he remitted what was due to the crown in the temples up to his eighth year, being no small amount of corn and money; so also the fines for the fine linen cloth not delivered to the crown, and of those delivered, the several fees for their verification, for the same period; and he also freed the temples of the tax of the measure[1] of grain for every measure[2] of sacred land and likewise the jar of wine for each measure[2] of vine land; and

whereas he bestowed many gifts upon Apis and Mnevis and upon the other sacred animals in Egypt, because he was much more considerate than the kings before him of all that belonged to them; and for their burials he gave what was suitable lavishly and splendidly, and what was regularly paid to their special shrines, with sacrifices and festivals and other customary observances, and he maintained the honours of the temples and of Egypt according to the laws; and he adorned the temple of Apis with rich work, spending upon it gold and silver and precious stones, no small amount; and

whereas he has funded temples and shrines and altars, and has repaired those requiring it, having the spirit of a beneficent god in matters pertaining to religion; and

whereas after enquiry he has been renewing the most honourable of the temples during his reign, as is becoming; in requital of which things the gods have given him health, victory and power, and all other good things, and he and his children shall retain the kingship for all time.

With propitious fortune: It was resolved by the priests of all the temples in the land to increase greatly the existing honours of King Ptolemy, the ever-living, the beloved of Ptah, the God Epiphanes Eucharistos, likewise those of his parents the Gods Philopatores, and of his ancestors, the Great Euergatai and the Gods Adelphoi and the Gods Soteres and to set up in the most prominent place of every temple an image of the ever-living King Ptolemy, the beloved of Ptah, the God Epiphanes Eucharistos, which shall be called that of 'Ptolemy, the defender of Egypt,' beside which shall stand the principal god of the temple, handing him the scimitar of victory, all of which shall be manufactured in the Egyptian fashion; and that the priests shall pay homage to the images three times a day, and put upon them the sacred garments, and perform the other usual honours such as are given to the other gods in the Egyptian festivals; and to establish for King Ptolemy, the God Epiphanes Eucharistos, sprung of King Ptolemy and Queen Arsinoe, the Gods Philopatores, a statue and golden shrine in each of the temples, and to set it up in the inner chamber with the other shrines; and in the great festivals in which the shrines are carried in procession the shrine of the God Epiphanes Eucharistos shall be carried in procession with them. And in order that it may be easily distinguishable now and for all time, there shall be set upon the shrine ten gold crowns of the king, to which shall be added a cobra exactly as on all the crowns adorned with cobras which are upon the other shrines, in the centre of them shall be the double crown which he put on when he went into the temple at Memphis to perform therein the ceremonies for assuming the kingship; and there shall be placed on the square surface round about the crowns, beside the aforementioned crown, golden symbols eight in number signifying that it is the shrine of the king who makes manifest the Upper and the Lower countries. And since it is the 30th of Mesore on which the birthday of the king is celebrated, and likewise the 17th of Paophi on which he succeeded his father in the kingship, they have held these days in honour as name-days in the temples, since they are sources of great blessings for all; it was further decreed that a festival shall be kept in the temples throughout Egypt on these days in every month, on which there shall be sacrifices and libations and all the ceremonies customary at the other festivals and the offerings shall be given to the priests who serve in the temples. And a festival shall be kept for King Ptolemy, the ever-living, the beloved of Ptah, the God Epiphanes Eucharistos, yearly in the temples throughout the land from the 1st of Thoth for five days, in which they shall wear garlands and perform sacrifices and libations and the other usual honours, and the priests in each temple shall be called priests of the God Epiphanes Eucharistos in addition to the names of the other gods whom they serve; and his priesthood shall be entered upon all formal documents and engraved upon the rings which they wear; and private individuals shall also be allowed to keep the festival and set up the aforementioned shrine and have it in their homes; performing the aforementioned celebrations yearly, in order that it may be known to all that the men of Egypt magnify and honour the God Epiphanes Eucharistos the king, according to the law.

This decree shall be inscribed on a stela of hard stone in sacred and native and Greek characters and set up in each of the first, second and third rank temples beside the image of the ever-living king.

Notes

1 *artabe*, a Greek or Persian measure of 52 liters (1.48 bushel).
2 *aroura*, a Greek measure of 2,735 square meters (0.67 acre).

Text of the Rosetta Stone, http://pw1.netcom.com/~qkstart/rosetta.html, © 1981 The Trustees of the British Museum.

INDIA: THE MAURYAN EMPIRE, THE EDICTS OF ASHOKA (c. 262–232 BCE)

When Alexander the Great invaded India over the Ganges, a young Chandragupta Maurya (321–291 BCE) was watching. Chandragupta, following Alexander's style, raised an army and conquered the area around the Ganges basin. After Alexander withdrew from Gandhara, there was a power vacuum in India that Chandragupta took advantage of, spreading his empire into the Indus Valley, Gandhara, and Arachosia regions. He defeated Alexander's Persian successor's, the Seleucids, driving them out of India and forging the first unified Indian state. Mauryan law was harsh, and the penalty was death for a number of offenses. Chandragupta imposed tight economic control on his new territory.

King Ashoka (304–232 BCE) was the third and bloodiest of the Mauryan kings, ruling from 262 BCE until his death. After coming to power, he ruthlessly conquered the rest of the subcontinent and most of the territory that is now India during a war with the country of Kalinga. However, he was so troubled by the violence and bloodshed that his empire had imparted, that he underwent a religious conversion to Buddhism. His conversion from violent conquerer to peaceful and benevolent ruler prompted H.G. Wells to remark many years later "Amidst the tens of thousands of names of monarchs that crowd columns of history . . . the name of Ashoka shines, and shines almost alone, a star." Ashoka undertook a cultural conversion of India, eliminating the death penalty and undertaking to end violence by sending monks to all corners of the land. By the start of the following dynasty, the Gupta, most of India was vegetarian.

Little was known about Ashoka until the nineteenth century when stone carvings of his edicts − advice to followers − were found around the subcontinent. Before the discovery of the edicts, it was generally thought that Ashoka's transition from ruthless monarch to righteous Buddhist king was a myth that was too good to be true. However, with the discovery of the edicts, it is understood that these are evidence of Ashoka's attempt to run his empire based on the moral well-being of his subjects. The edicts, carved into rocks about 40–50 feet high are statements of the moral reforms that he outlined for the new empire. Additionally, he promises non-aggression to his neighbors and claims that he has no expansionist ideas. Although he was a Buddhist, and promoted Buddhism, he also showed a remarkable quality of religious tolerance. There were likely many stone carvings, but only ten survive, comprising some of the earliest written material of India.

Edicts of Ashoka, Pillar 13

Beloved-of-the-Gods, King Piyadasi, conquered the Kalingas eight years after his coronation.[1] One hundred and fifty thousand were deported, one hundred thousand were killed and many more died (from other causes). After the Kalingas had been conquered, Beloved-of-the-Gods came to feel a strong inclination towards the Dhamma, a love for the Dhamma and for instruction in Dhamma. Now Beloved-of-the-Gods feels deep remorse for having conquered the Kalingas.

Indeed, Beloved-of-the-Gods is deeply pained by the killing, dying and deportation that take place when an unconquered country is conquered. But Beloved-of-the-Gods is pained even more by this – that Brahmans, ascetics, and householders of different religions who live in those countries, and who are respectful to superiors, to mother and father, to elders, and who behave properly and have strong loyalty towards friends, acquaintances, companions, relatives, servants and employees – that they are injured, killed or separated from their loved ones. Even those who are not affected (by all this) suffer when they see friends, acquaintances, companions and relatives affected. These misfortunes befall all (as a result of war), and this pains Beloved-of-the-Gods.

There is no country, except among the Greeks, where these two groups, Brahmans and ascetics, are not found, and there is no country where people are not devoted to one or another religion.[2] Therefore the killing, death or deportation of a hundredth, or even a thousandth part of those who died during the conquest of Kalinga now pains Beloved-of-the-Gods. Now Beloved-of-the-Gods thinks that even those who do wrong should be forgiven where forgiveness is possible.

Even the forest people, who live in Beloved-of-the-Gods' domain, are entreated and reasoned with to act properly. They are told that despite his remorse Beloved-of-the-Gods has the power to punish them if necessary, so that they should be ashamed of their wrong and not be killed. Truly, Beloved-of-the-Gods desires non-injury, restraint and impartiality to all beings, even where wrong has been done.

Now it is conquest by Dhamma that Beloved-of-the-Gods considers to be the best conquest.[3] And it (conquest by Dhamma) has been won here, on the borders, even six hundred yojanas away, where the Greek king Antiochos rules, beyond there where the four kings named Ptolemy, Antigonos, Magas and Alexander rule, likewise in the south among the Cholas, the Pandyas, and as far as Tamraparni.[4] Here in the king's domain among the Greeks, the Kambojas, the Nabhakas, the Nabhapamkits, the Bhojas, the Pitinikas, the Andhras and the Palidas, everywhere people are following Beloved-of-the-Gods' instructions in Dhamma. Even where Beloved-of-the-Gods' envoys have not been, these people too, having heard of the practice of Dhamma and the ordinances and instructions in Dhamma given by Beloved-of-the-Gods, are following it and will continue to do so. This conquest has been won everywhere, and it gives great joy – the joy which only conquest by Dhamma can give. But even this joy is of little consequence. Beloved-of-the-Gods considers the great fruit to be experienced in the next world to be more important.

I have had this Dhamma edict written so that my sons and great-grandsons may not consider making new conquests, or that if military conquests are made, that they be done with forbearance and light punishment, or better still, that they consider making conquest by Dhamma only, for that bears fruit in this world and the next. May all their intense devotion be given to this which has a result in this world and the next.

Notes

1 Kalsi version, issued in 256 BCE. Kalinga corresponds roughly to the modern state of Orissa.
2 The Buddha pointed out that the four castes of Indian society likewise were not found among the Greeks; see Majjhima Nikaya, II:149.
3 Perhaps Ashoka had in mind Dhammapada 103–104.
4 Antiochos II Theos of Syria (261–246 BCE), Ptolemy II Philadelphos of Egypt (285–247 BCE), Antigonos Gonatos of Macedonia (278–239 BCE), Magas of Cyrene (300–258 BCE) and Alexander of Epirus (272–258 BCE).

Ashoka, 'Edicts of Ashoka, Pillar 13,' http://www.cs.colostate.edu/~malaiya/ashoka.html.

ROME, THE REPUBLIC: CICERO, *DE RE PUBLICA* (c. 54–51 BCE)

Marcus Tullius Cicero (106–43 BCE), born into the Equestrian class in the town of Arpinum outside Rome, was a famous orator, lawyer, political theorist, and senator who wrote many important works of moral and religious philosophy. He was consul of the Roman senate in 63 BCE. As a politician and political theorist, he was known for defending the Roman Republic against decay brought on by the increasing influence of the aristocracy. Roman senators were prohibited from engaging in trade, which meant that senators formed alliances with traders and other senators to solidify power into oligopolies. Cicero was invited to join the first triumverate, but declined, causing him to become an enemy of Julius Caesar. Cicero wrote *De re publica* as a defense of the republic he saw in decline due to the expansion of the Roman Republic and its transformation into an empire. First translated into English in 1842, it was translated as, "on the commonwealth." The title and style reflect its engagement with Plato's *Republic*, and it became an important basis for Augustine's *City of God*. While the first triumvirate had political power, they had operated outside the law. With the passage of *Lex Titia* in 43 BCE, triumvirates – essentially military dictatorships – were allowed to operate legally, and thus formally assumed most of the operating power of the senate. While the shift of power from the senate to ruling oligopolies had already taken place, the passage of this law formally ended the Roman Republic as such. Cicero was assassinated in 43 BCE by the second triumvirate, which included Gaius Julius Caesar Octavianus (later known as Augustus), Marcus Aemilius Lepidus, and Mark Antony.

The most famous passage, "The Dream of Scipio," is a fictional dream of Scipio Africanius in dialogue with his grandfather Scipio Africanus the elder in heaven. The choice of the Scipios is significant, as both were thought to possess second sight, and both Scipios were important generals in the Roman conquest of Carthage. Scipio, the elder, fought Hannibal and conquered Carthage, forcing them to pay heavy taxes to Rome. Upon his return from battle, he was offered the position of dictator of Rome, but declined. Scipio minor, acting on orders from the senate, burned Carthage to the ground in 146 BCE, ending the Punic Wars. Although receiving critical acclaim for his victory, he expressed horror for the destruction of humanity, and was criticized for returning art works recovered in Carthage to their original communities. In choosing the Scipios for his book, Cicero is invoking two figures of the republic who declined imperial aspirations and wealth. They were also central figures in the expansion of Roman territory and influence, which is the cause of the decline of the Republic. In including them in his dialogue on the Republic, Cicero was trying to buttress his notion of natural law.

De re publica, "The Dream of Scipio"

[The passage begins with Africanus appearing to Scipio, who finds himself taken to heaven and looking down on earth and the other spheres of the universe.]

'Do not fear, Scipio, but be calm. Note carefully all the things I will tell you. Do you see Carthage there? I was the one who made that city submit to Rome, though now they stir up all the ancient conflicts yet once more and refuse to live in peace with Rome.' From where he stood amid the brightness of the stars, Africanus pointed down at Carthage, and said, 'This is the city you have come to attack. At this moment, you are merely an ordinary soldier, but within two years you will be consul, and then you will utterly lay waste to this city. At that moment, your surname, which you've inherited from me, will belong to you by right. After you've destroyed Carthage, celebrated your triumph in Rome, held the office of censor, travelled to Egypt, Syria, Asia, Greece, you will become consul yet again, and you will win a great war and level Numantia. But when you are celebrating this triumph in Rome, you will find the government in a state of anarchy, the results of the plots of Tiberius Gracchus, my grandson.

'After that, it will be your duty to devote to your people the beneficence of your integrity, talent, and wisdom. At that juncture, I see two paths which destiny opens up for you. For when your life has completed seven times eight revolutions of the sun, and when these two numbers [seven and eight], each of which for different reasons possesses some quality of perfection, have in their natural course brought you to your highest destiny, that is the time when Rome will turn to you and everything you represent. At that time, the fate of the entire country will depend on you alone. It will be your duty to take on the burden of the dictatorship, and restore order to the fractured state; an event that will be prevented only if your own criminal kinsmen turn their murderous hands against you.'

He continued, 'Mark this, for this thought will steel your determination to rush to the defense of your homeland. Every man who has preserved or defended his country, or has made it greater, is reserved a special place in heaven, where he enjoys an eternal life of happiness. Of all those things one might do on earth, nothing is more pleasing to the Supreme God, ruler of the universe, than the gatherings of men who are bound together by law and custom in those communities we call states. In fact, it is from this place, here, in heaven, that the rulers and preservers of states come from, and to which they eventually return.'

I now saw my dead father, Paullus, approaching, and I burst into tears. My father put his arms around me and kissed me, telling me not to weep. When, with effort, I held back my tears, I managed to say, 'Since this, my dear father, is the true life, as Africanus declares, why must I remain on earth? Why can I not join you?'

'That cannot be,' my father replied, 'for unless God, who rules all you see around you here, frees you from your confinement in the body, you cannot gain entrance to this paradise. You see, humans are brought into existence in order to inhabit the earth, which is at the center of this holy place, this paradise. They have been given souls made out of the undying fire which make up stars and constellations, consisting of spherical bodies animated by the divine mind, each moving with marvelous speed, each in its own orbit and cycle. It is destined that you and other righteous men suffer your souls to be imprisoned with your bodies; you may not abandon life except when commanded by the Supreme God who bestowed it on you. Otherwise, you will have failed your duty, the duty which you, like every other human being, were meant to fulfill.

'Do upon earth as your grandfather did. Do as I have done, your father. Love justice and devotion. These are owed to both your parents and kinsmen; but more than anything else, they are owed to your country. Such is the life that leads to heaven, and to the company of those who, having finished their lives in the world, are now freed from their bodies and dwell in that region you gaze upon, the Milky Way.' As he said this, he pointed to a circle of light, flashing brilliantly among all the other fires of heaven. As I looked around from my vantage point in every direction, the whole view was complete and beautiful. I saw stars never seen from the earth, larger than anyone has ever imagined. The smallest of these stars was the one farthest from heaven and nearest to the earth, the moon, which shone only with a reflected light. The starry spheres were much larger than the earth. The earth, in fact, seemed so minute in relation to these spheres that I began to think less of this vast Roman Empire of ours which is only a pinpoint on the surface of this small earth. [. . .]

'So where do you get the idea that your fame, or anyone's fame, can ever be so great that it would extend beyond these inhabited lands? Your fame could never cross the Caucasus mountains you see there, nor could it ford the Ganges river. Not one person in these eastern regions, or the remote western regions, or the far north or south for that matter, will ever hear your name, let alone desire to remember it. Once you leave all these people out, you can see how small and trivial an area your glory will spread over. [. . .]

'Strive on,' he answered, 'secure in the knowledge that only your body is mortal and that your true self endures forever. The man you appear to be is not yourself at all, for your real self is not that corporeal, palpable, changing form you see, but the spirit inside. Remember that you are a god, you have a god's potential for life, sensation, memory, and foresight, a god's power to rule, to govern, and to direct the body which is given to you as a servant, in the same way God, who reigns over us, directs the entire universe. This sovereignty exercised by the eternal God over the universe is mirrored by the sovereignty your immortal soul exercises over your frail body. [. . .]

'Use this everlasting force, then, for the most resplendent deeds possible! And remember that the most splendid deeds you can do are those which serve your country. Those souls devoted to such deeds will find it easy to wing their way to this place, which is the true and genuine home for human souls. The soul's flight will be all the more quick if, during the period of confinement within the body, this soul has contemplatively roamed widely, thinking on what lies outside itself, and has contrived ways to detach itself from the body as much as possible. When one has failed to do this, and has abandoned the soul to bodily indulgence and enslaved it to the body, allowing those passions which are bonded to pleasure to persuade the soul to flout the laws of gods and men, this soul, after departing from the body, can only hover weakly above the earth. Nor does it return to its proper place in the heavens until it has suffered many ages of torment.'

At these words, Africanus vanished, and I awoke from my sleep.

http://www.wsu.edu/~dee/ROME/SCIPIO.HTM, translated from the Latin by Richard Hooker, © 1993, Richard Hooker.

■ ■ ■ ■ ■ ■

ROME, THE EMPIRE: AUGUSTUS, *RES GESTAE DIVI AUGUSTI* (c. 14 CE)

Augustus (63 BCE–14 CE), born Gaius Octavius Thurinus, and known as Octavian, was the first emperor of the Roman Empire (Augustine Empire). He was adopted by his great uncle Julius Caesar. After Caesar's assassination in 44 BCE, Augustus joined with Mark Antony and Marcus Aemilius Lepidus in the second triumvirate. With the passage of *Lex Titia* in 43 BCE, they ruled the Roman Empire. In a move called the "Roman revolution," the second triumvirate labeled over 300 senators and 2,000 equites "outlaws," confiscated their property, and replaced them with sympathetic supporters. In-fighting between Antony, Lepidus, and Augustus eventually ended with sole control of the empire passing to Augustus. In 31 BCE, after defeating Antony at the Battle of Actium, and Lepidus's suicide, Augustus became the de facto ruler of Rome. He refused to take on the role of dictator that was offered to him by the senate, and returned official control to the senate in 27 BCE. However, Augustus, through his control of the military, personal relationships, and vast personal wealth he accrued through political control of Rome, was the autocratic ruler of Rome. The system of imperial government that he developed is thought to have served as a model for all imperial governments, leaving a façade of democracy, and maintaining power through the accrual of wealth, military control, and bureaucracy handled through patronage. Also in 27 BCE, the senate gave him the name "Augustus," with religious connotations meaning "the illustrious one."

Augustus's rule ushered in an era of relative peace known as Pax Romana (also called Pax Augustus). The selection here, *Res Gestae Divi Augusti* (The Achievements of the Divine Augustus), is Augustus's account of his accomplishments. He wrote them in both Greek and Latin, and had the text carved into the walls of the temple in Rome. He details how he used his vast wealth to rebuild the city of Rome, raise a professional army and police force, build roads, and support the Roman treasury. Upon his death in 14 CE, he was voted a god by the senate and all subsequent emperors held the title Caesar Augustus.

Augustus – Monumentum Ancyranum (*Res Gestae Divi Augusti*)

1 At the age of nineteen,[1] on my own initiative and at my own expense, I raised an army[2] by means of which I restored liberty[3] to the republic, which had been oppressed by the tyranny of a faction.[4] For which service the senate, with complimentary resolutions, enrolled me in its order, in the consulship of Gaius Pansa and Aulus Hirtius, giving me at the same time consular precedence in voting; it also gave me the imperium.[5] As propraetor it ordered me, along with the consuls, 'to see that the republic suffered no harm.' In the same year, moreover, as both consuls had fallen in war,[6] the people elected me consul and a triumvir for settling the constitution.[7]

2 Those who slew my father[8] I drove into exile, punishing their deed by due process of law,[9] and afterwards when they waged war upon the republic I twice[10] defeated them in battle.

3 Wars, both civil and foreign, I undertook throughout the world, on sea and land, and when victorious I spared all citizens who sued for pardon.[11] The foreign nations which could with safety be pardoned I preferred to save rather than to destroy. The number of Roman citizens who bound themselves to me by military oath was about 500,000. Of these I settled in colonies or sent back into their own towns, after their term of service,

something more than 300,000, and to all I assigned lands, or gave money as a reward for military service.[12] I captured six hundred ships,[13] over and above those which were smaller than triremes.

4 Twice I triumphed with an ovation,[14] thrice I celebrated curule triumphs,[15] and was saluted as imperator twenty-one times.[16] Although the Senate decreed me additional triumphs I set them aside. When I had performed the vows which I had undertaken in each war I deposited upon the Capitol the laurels which adorned my fasces.[17] For successful operations on land and sea, conducted either by myself or by my lieutenants under my auspices, the senate on fifty-five occasions decreed that thanks should be rendered to the immortal gods. The days on which such thanks were rendered by decree of the senate numbered 890. In my triumphs there were led before my chariot nine kings or children of kings.[18] At the time of writing these words I had been thirteen times consul, and was in the thirty-seventh year of my tribunician power.[19]

5 The dictatorship[20] offered me by the people and the Roman Senate, in my absence and later when present, in the consulship of Marcus Marcellus and Lucius Arruntius[21] I did not accept. I did not decline at a time of the greatest scarcity of grain the charge of the grain-supply, which I so administered that, within a few days, I freed the entire people, at my own expense, from the fear and danger in which they were.[22] The consulship, either yearly or for life, then offered me I did not accept. [. . .]

25 I freed the sea from pirates. About thirty thousand slaves, captured in that war, who had run away from their masters and had taken up arms against the republic, I delivered to their masters for punishment.[23] The whole of Italy voluntarily took oath of allegiance to me and demanded me as its leader in the war in which I was victorious at Actium. The provinces of the Spains, the Gauls, Africa, Sicily, and Sardinia took the same oath of allegiance.[24] Those who served under my standards at that time included more than 700 senators,[25] and among them eighty-three who had previously or have since been consuls up to the day on which these words were written, and about 170 have been priests.

26 I extended the boundaries[26] of all the provinces which were bordered by races not yet subject to our empire. The provinces of the Gauls, the Spains, and Germany, bounded by the ocean from Gades to the mouth of the Elbe, I reduced to a state of peace.[27] The Alps, from the region which lies nearest to the Adriatic as far as the Tuscan Sea, I brought to a state of peace without waging on any tribe an unjust war.[28] My fleet sailed from the mouth of the Rhine eastward as far as the lands of the Cimbri to which, up to that time, no Roman had ever penetrated either by land or by sea, and the Cimbri and Charydes and Semnones and other peoples of the Germans of that same region through their envoys sought my friendship and that of the Roman people.[29] On my order and under my auspices two armies were led, at almost the same time, into Ethiopia and into Arabia which is called the 'Happy,' and very large forces of the enemy of both races were cut to pieces in battle and many towns were captured.[30] Ethiopia was penetrated as far as the town of Nabata,[31] which is next to Meroë. In Arabia the army advanced into the territories of the Sabaei[32] to the town of Mariba.

27 Egypt I added to the empire of the Roman people.[33] In the case of Greater Armenia, though I might have made it a province after the assassination of its King Artaxes, I preferred, following the precedent of our fathers, to hand that kingdom over to Tigranes, the son of King Artavasdes, and grandson of King Tigranes, through Tiberius Nero who was then my stepson.[34] And later, when the same people revolted and rebelled, and was subdued by my son Gaius,[35] I gave it over to King Ariobarzanes the son of Artabazus, King of the Medes, to rule, and after his death to his son Artavasdes. When he was murdered I sent into that kingdom Tigranes, who was sprung from the royal family of the Armenians.[36] I recovered all the provinces extending eastward beyond the Adriatic Sea, and Cyrenae, which were then for the most part in possession of kings,[37] and, at an earlier time,[38] Sicily and Sardinia, which had been seized in the servile war.

28 I settled colonies of soldiers in Africa, Sicily, Macedonia, both Spains, Achaea, Asia, Syria, Gallia Narbonensis, Pisidia. Moreover, Italy has twenty-eight colonies founded under my auspices which have grown to be famous and populous during my lifetime.[39]

Notes

1 Octavian was nineteen on September 23, 44 BCE.

2 During October, by offering a bounty of 500 denarii, he induced Caesar's veterans at Casilinum and Calatia to enlist, and in November the legions named Martia and Quarta repudiated Antony and went over to him. This activity of Octavian, on his own initiative, was ratified by the Senate on December 20, on the motion of Cicero.

3 In the battle of Mutina, April 43. Augustus may also have had Philippi in mind.

4 By 'faction' he means Antony, whom he never mentions by name.

5 On January 2, 43 BCE, the Senate decreed that Octavian should be classed as a quaestorius (Dio, XLVI.29, 41), should be a member of the Senate (Livy, Epit. cxviii), should have the consularia ornamenta, and for that reason should give his opinion along with the consuls (App. BCE iii.51); he was also given the rank of propraetor with imperium, i.e. the constitutional right to command soldiers.

6 Pansa died of his wounds, and Hirtius was killed in action in the operations about Mutina.

7 Octavian became consul August 19, 43 BCE, after marching his army from Cisalpine Gaul to intimidate the Senate. On November the appointment of Octavian, Antony, and Lepidus as triumvirs was brought about by their arrival in the city with armed forces.

8 Julius Caesar.

9 By the lex Pedia.

10 The two battles at Philippi.

11 He is referring in particular to the clemency which he showed after the battle of Actium, for which he received a crown of oak leaves in 27 BCE ob cives servatos.

12 Of the 300,000 soldiers who received honourable dismissal from the service, 120,000 had been settled in colonies by the year 29 BCE; the remaining 180,000 must consequently have been mustered out in the succeeding 42 years of his reign. They were in service at the death of Augustus 25 legions (Tac. Ann. IV.5), or about 150,000 men, exclusive of the praetorian and urban cohorts. Those who were killed in battle or died in service therefore numbered about 50,000.

13 From Sextus Pompeius at Mylae 30 ships (Appian v.108), and at Naulochus 283 (ib. 108); from Antony at Actium 300 (Plutarch, Ant. 68).

14 'Bis ovans ingressus est urbem, post Philippense (40 BCE) et rursus post Siculum bellum' (Nov. 13, 36 BCE), Suet. Aug. 22. An ovation was a minor triumph. In this the conqueror entered the city on foot or on horseback instead of in the four-horse chariot, as in the case of the curule triumph.

15 'Curulis triumphos tris egit Delmaticum, Actiacum, Alexandrinum continuo triduo omnes' (Aug. 13, 14, 15 of the year 29), Suet. Aug. 22. 'Tres triumphos egit, unum ex Illyrico, alterum ex Achaica victoria, tertium de Cleopatra' (Liv. Epit. 133).

16 These acclamations as imperator, for military successes, must not be confused with the title of imperator prefixed to the name of Augustus and succeeding emperors. Mommsen gives the list, Res gestae Divi Augusti, p.11.

17 Under the Republic the consul or praetor when starting on an expedition took his vows on the Capital; if acclaimed imperator by his troops he decked his fasces with laurel, and on his return deposited the wreath upon the Capitol.

18 In the three triumphs of the year 29 BCE the following names are known: Alexander of Emesa, Adiatorix the Galatian prince with his wife and sons, and Alexander and Cleopatra, children of Cleopatra, whose statue was borne in the procession of the Egyptian triumph (Gardthausen, Aug. i.473).

19 Augustus held his thirteenth consulship in 2 BCE. He held his thirty-seventh tribunicia potestas in AD 14.

20 Dio (LIV.1.4)° says in this connexion: 'As for the dictatorship, however, he did not accept the office, but went so far as to rend his garments when he found himself unable to restrain the people in any other way either by argument or enemy; for, since he was superior to dictators in the power and honours he already possessed, he properly guarded against the jealousy and hatred which the title would arouse' (Cary's trans.). See also Vell. II.89.5.

21 22 BCE

22 According to Dio (liv.1) the offer of the dictatorship and the request that Augustus become commissioner of the grain-supply were made at the same time. The crisis was caused by the conjunction of an overflow of the Tiber, a pestilence which interfered with agriculture in Italy, and consequent famine.

23 He is referring to the war with Sextus Pompey, terminated in 36 BCE Pompey's following was made up largely of runaway slaves, and his fleet, so manned, had cut off the grain fleets on their way to Rome. See Vell. II.73.

24 In other words, all the provinces in the half of the empire ruled by Octavianus.

25 The number of senators at that time was about 1000.

26 The extensions included: the temporary pushing forward of the German frontier from the Rhine to the Elbe; the creation of the new provinces of Pannonia and Moesia; the addition of the new provinces of Galatia and Paphlagonia in Asia Minor; the expedition of Aelius Gallus to Arabia Felix; and in Africa, in addition to the formal annexation of Egypt, some minor expeditions by the various pro-consuls.

27 In the Gallic and Cantabrian expeditions of Augustus himself, 27–25 BCE, in that of Carrinas against the Morini, of Messala against the Aquitani, 27 BCE, and the numerous campaigns in Germany, particularly of Drusus and Tiberius. Pacavi could apply to Germany for a very brief period only.

28 At Torbia (Tropaea Augusti), near Monaco, stood a monument, of which only fragments now exist, commemorating the subjugation of the Alpine peoples. Pliny, N. H. III.20.136, has preserved the inscription: 'The Senate and the Roman people to Caesar . . . Augustus . . . because under his leadership and auspices all the Alpine nations from the upper to the lower sea have been brought into subjection to the Roman people.' There follows a list of forty-six peoples.

29 For this naval expedition to the Elbe in AD 5 see Vell. II.106. The Cimbri inhabited the coast of Schleswig and Jutland, the Charudes (the Greek text gives 'Chalybes') were their close neighbours, and the Semnones were located between the Elbe and Weser.

30 The Arabian expedition of Aelius Gallus, 25–24 BCE. The two other portions were called Arabia petraea and Arabia deserta.

31 Queen Candace, taking advantage of the withdrawal of Egyptian garrisons for the Arabian expedition, captured some towns in upper Egypt. They were retaken by C. Petronius, 24–22 BCE His punitive expedition penetrated Aethiopia.

32 In southern Arabia.

33 In 30 BCE, after Actium. Before that time Egypt had been a nominally independent kingdom, though, in a sense, a Roman protectorate. Since 57 BCE, when Ptolemy Auletes was restored, a considerable Roman force had been maintained there. After Actium, Egypt, unlike other provinces, was treated as the personal domain of the emperor. For the peculiar status of Egypt as a part of the empire see Arnold, Roman Provincial Administration, p.113.

34 In 20 BCE See Vell. II.94.

35 It was in the factional struggle which followed the setting up of Artavasdes that Gaius received the wound from which he died in February, AD 4.

36 For the complicated question of the Armenian succession see Mommsen, Res Gestae, pp.109–117.

37 Antony had received by the treaty of Brundisium in 40 BCE Macedonia, Achaia, Asia, Pontus, Bithynia, Cilicia, Cyprus, Syria, Crete, the Cyrenaica. The last five he had given over to foreign kings. These alienations of foreign territory were the occasion of the civil war which ended at Actium.

38 By the defeat of Sextus Pompey in 36 BCE

39 For these colonies of Augustus see Mommsen, Res Gestae, pp.119–222; also Hermes, xviii.161 ff.

KOREA: *SAMGUK SAGI*, UNIFIED SILLA AND T'ANG DYNASTIES (c. 57 BCE–668 CE)

Said to be compiled sometime in the mid-twelfth century, the *Samguk Sagi* is considered to be the oldest collection of writings that concern the Korean Three Kingdoms period (c. 57 BCE–668 CE). Although the *Samguk Sagi* translates to "Chronicles of the Three Kingdoms," it primarily follows one particular point of view; much of the *Samguk Sagi* devotes itself to understanding how the Silla Kingdom came to assert itself as the primary authority in the Korean peninsula, to the exclusion of other kingdoms and tribes.

One of the histories that the *Samguk Sagi* recounts is how the Silla relied on military assistance from the then ascendant T'ang Dynasty of the Chinese Empire to defeat the Koguryo and Paekche Kingdoms. But as the following selection reveals, this "alliance" however, had some undesirable costs. After each defeat of the

Paekche in 660 CE and the Koguryo in 668 CE, the Silla soon found themselves in conflict with their once Chinese allies, who now desired to colonize the lands they helped to conquer. In part, this was driven by the Chinese belief that Imperial China was by its nature a more superior civilization.

In a move many historians call a turning point on Korea's path to independence, the Silla eventually drove the Chinese out of their lands after many years of sporadic fighting. Though the Silla would eventually fall a few centuries later to the Goryeo Dynasty (in 935 CE), the unification of Korea under the Silla set a precedent that the Korea peninsula could in principle fall under one authority. Of course, one interesting thing to note here is that the Chinese Empire retained influence long after they were forced away by the Silla. The *Samguk Sagi*, like other Korean literary texts of the times, was written in Classical Chinese. It was not until later, in the twelfth century CE, that the Korean language began to take form.

Samguk Sagi

During Great King T'aejong's seventh year, *kyongsin*, in summer, the sixth month, the Great King and the Crown Prince Pommin moved out with a huge army to attack Paekche, setting camp at Namch'on. At the same time, the P'ajinchin'an Kim Inmun, who had gone to T'ang requesting troop support, came along with the T'ang Great Generals Su Ting-fang and Liu Po-ying at the head of one hundred thirty thousand troops, crossing the sea and landing at Tongmul Island. They had first sent an attendant Munch'on on ahead to announce their arrival; and with receipt of this news, the king ordered the Crown Prince, Generals Yusin, Chinju, Ch'onjon, and others to take a hundred large vessels laden with troops to meet them. The Crown Prince met General Su Ting-fang, and Ting-fang said to him, 'I'll go by the sea route and you, Prince, go by land. We will meet at the walls of Sabi, Paekche's capital, on the tenth of the seventh month.' When the Crown Prince reported this, the Great King led his generals and warriors to an encampment at Sara. General Su Ting-fang and Kim Inmun came into Ibolp'o by sea but ran aground and were unable to proceed because of the thick coastal mud. Willow rush mats were spread permitting the armies to land, and T'ang and Silla joined in the attack on Paekche. They destroyed her.

Throughout that campaign, it was Yusin's merit that was greatest, and when the emperor of T'ang heard of it, he sent an emissary to praise and compliment him. General Su Ting-fang said to Yusin, Inmun, and Yangdo, 'My command allows me to exercise authority as conditions dictate, so I will now present to you as maintenance lands all of Paekche's territory that has been acquired, this as reward for your merit. How would that be?' Yusin answered, 'You came with Heavenly Troops, Great General, to help realize our unworthy prince's wish to avenge our small nation, and from our unworthy prince on down to all officials and people throughout the nation there is endless rejoicing. How could it be just for the three of us alone to enrich ourselves by accepting such a gift?' They did not accept it.

Once they defeated Paekche, the men of T'ang camped on the Sabi hills and secretly planned to invade Silla. When our king learned of it, he summoned all officials together to discuss a strategy. Lord Tami put forward his opinion, saying: 'Have our people disguise themselves as Paekche men – wear Paekche clothes and act as if they are going to rebel. The men of T'ang will surely strike at them, then we can use this as an excuse to fight and achieve our goal.' Yusin said, 'That idea is worth using. Let us follow that plan.' But the king said, 'The T'ang army has destroyed our enemy for us. If we turn about and fight them, would we have heaven's protection?' Yusin answered, 'A dog fears his master, but if the master steps on its paw, the dog bites him. Why shouldn't one save himself when endangered? I beg that the Great King grant permission.' But the men of T'ang, learning of our preparedness through spies, took the Paekche king, ninety-three officials, and twenty thousand soldiers as prisoners, and on the third day of the ninth month set sail from Sabi to return to T'ang. A group including Junior General Liu Jen-yüan was left behind to occupy the territory.

After Su Ting-fang had presented the prisoners, the Son of Heaven expressed words of commendation and indebtedness and then said, 'Why didn't you follow through with an attack on Silla?' Ting-fang said, 'The Silla sovereign is humane and loves his people, his officers serve their nation with loyalty, and those below serve those above as if they were their fathers or elder brothers. Even though it is a small country, one can't plot against them.'

Unknown (1993) "*Samguk Sagi*: 41:394–43:406," in Peter Lee (ed), *Sourcebook of Korean Civilization*, New York: Columbia University Press, pp. 111–112.

CHINA: FALL OF THE QIN AND THE RISE OF THE HAN DYNASTIES (221–206 BCE)

The start of the Han Dynasty (206 BCE–220 CE) in China began with the fall of the Qin Dynasty (221–206 BCE). The Qin were most notable for being the first to unify China. In part, they were able to do so because they were the first to institute a strict bureaucracy, one that made few exceptions and was rigorously applied to all. Through this strict legalistic approach, which created order among its own people, military, and government, the Qin were able to defeat the other warring states. Accordingly, this approach is how the First Emperor of China, also known as Shi Hwangdi, decided to rule his newly founded empire. Among other things, he standardized units of measurements and the Chinese writing system throughout the lands he now controlled. The downfall of the Qin Dynasty came when this mindset was pressed too far. The Qin Dynasty fell when they exhausted their resources and pushed for reform too quickly and forcefully. Peasants, soldiers, and intellectuals alike felt they were treated poorly and overworked. All of this came to a head when Shi Hwangdi died in 210 BCE and the Qin Dynasty was left without a clear successor. Within three years, there were armed uprisings and conflicts throughout China.

From this dire situation came the Han Dynasty. During this period of unrest, a peasant-born magistrate named Liu Bang from the Han province was able to rise to power. After the defeat of the Qin kingdom and other warring factions, Liu Bang assumed the position of emperor and also the new title of Han Gaozu. Whilst he retained much of the bureaucratic structure left by the Qin Dynasty, Gaozu took a different tact in how he ruled his empire. For instance, he listened to scholars who advocated a less rigid legalistic approach. This shift occurred along with, and in part also owing to the rise of Confucianism within the government. In essence, what this new line of thinking advocated was a more responsive state of affairs. Laws should be in the service of the people and not the other way around.

One of the more well-known advocates of this way of thinking during the Han Dynasty was Lu Jia, a Confucian scholar. In the selection below, which excerpts from his book Xinyu (literally "Speeches"), Lu Jia urges the newly founded Han Dynasty to learn from the mistakes of the Qin. Here, he explains that laws must not be too numerous or rigid. For him, they sometimes cause the conflicts which they were meant to set right. For empires to endure, Lu Jia advocates a more accessible form of governance. To avoid conflict, respect of the people must also be won.

Wu-Wei: on "Non-Action" . . .

Nothing in the teaching of the Way is greater than the principle of Non-Action, and nothing in the pattern of proper behaviour is greater than being cautious and careful. Why do we say so? In former times when Emperor Yü-shun 虞舜 governed the world, he did nothing but play the five stringed guitar and chant the poem of Nan-feng 南風. He was so still that it seems he had no intention of ruling the state, so free of care that it seemed he felt no concern in his heart for the empire, but yet the world was well governed. Again, the Duke of Chou 周公 instituted propriety and music, offered sacrifices to heaven and earth and to mountains and rivers. He did not maintain soldiers, the punishments were suspended and laws were not put into effect. Yet the states within the four seas came to pay homage with tribute, [and even] the ruler of Yüeh-shang 越裳 came to have an audience [with the king] through two lots of interpretation. So "Non-Action" is actually efficient action.

[On the other hand] Ch'in Shih-huang-ti established executions and put into practice the penalty of tearing culprits' bodies in pieces with chariots in order to control the wicked and the evil, and he also built the Great Wall along the frontier with the barbarians in order to make preparation against the *Hu* people. He sent punitive expeditions against the big states and he annexed the small states. His authority awed the people in the world, his generals despatched troops in all directions to bring the foreign states into submission. Meng T'ien 蒙恬 attacked the disorders without, Li Ssu 李斯 administered the laws within. And yet the more action they took in the empire, the more trouble developed, the more laws they legislated, the more evils were produced, with the result that the greater the army they established the more enemies they had. As to the Ch'in Dynasty, it was not that they did not want proper government, they failed because they set up too many laws and their punishments were too harsh.

Therefore the superior man will put emphasis on generosity for his own protection, and he will act in accordance with the middle way in order to gain control of the remote people. Then the people will respect his authority and will be influenced by his example. They will accept his virtue and flock to his territory, they will praise his administration and will never oppose his government. They will obey his command without fear of punishment and they will be happy to work without hope of reward. In this way they will be deeply influenced by his moral power and they will hold fast to the middle way.

Now laws and ordinances are set up to punish evildoers [but not to persuade people towards goodness]. Consider the filial piety of Tseng 曾 and Min 閔 the purity of I 貴 and Ch'i 齊. Did they act in this way because they were frightened? [Actually this was attained through the effects of education and influences.] In this way, as concerns the people of Emperors Yao 堯 and Shun 舜, every family of them was worthy of enfeoffment, while among the people of Emperor Chieh and Emperor Chou, every family of them deserved to be executed. Why should this be so? Because the influence [of the ruler] made it so. So the reason the place near a river is wet and the place near a hill is dry is that things of the same category influence one another. The reason that high mountains produce clouds and small hills produce mist, that the four (great) rivers flow east and not one of the hundred (small) rivers flow west, is because small things follow the great, the few follow numerous. Now in the capital of a king, the ruler faces south, and the people model themselves after him. So his actions and behaviour must conform to the laws and regulations. In former times King Hsiang of Chou 周象王 was unable to serve his stepmother, and when he fled to dwell in the state of Cheng there were many of his subordinates who abandoned their parents. Ch'in-shih-huang was arrogant and extravagant, he liked to build high terraces and spacious palaces and dwellings, so all the great and wealthy people in the empire built houses to imitate him. They built their gates as big as those of a palace and equipped their buildings with stables and arsenals. They delighted in items of carvings, applied bright and precious colours, and in this way they confused the proper gradation of high and low. Duke Huan of Ch'i 齊桓公 was fond of women, he took his aunts and sisters of the same kinship as his wives, and so in his state there were immoral relations between people of close kinship. Again, King P'ing of Ch'u 楚平王 was extravagant and arbitary and he could not control his subjects. He put levies upon his people to obtain wealth, he increased the number of his chariots by hundreds, and yet at the same time he wished to make the people in the world wealthy and prosperous. Obviously this was impossible. In this situation, the state of Ch'u became more extravagant and there was no distinction between the ruler and ministers.

So the ruler's influence on his people is just like that of the wind which sweeps over the grass. If the ruler worships warfare at his court, then the peasants will make armour and weapons in the fields. This is the way that the sovereign controls his subjects: if the people are extravagant, he responds with thrift, if the people are proud and licentious, he controls with his good conduct. In this way, it never happens that the sovereign is benevolent and his subjects are violent, and it never happens that when a ruler gives way to others on the road, his subjects will push themselves forward. . . .

Translated by Mei-kao Ku, "A Chinese mirror for magistrates."

THE AMERICAS: THE MAYAN CIVILIZATION, THE DRESDEN CODEX (c. 1100–1200 CE)

The Mayan civilization is the most significant Mesoamerican civilization, spanning *c.* 2000 BCE to 900 CE, lasting right up to the Spanish arrival in the 16th century. It continues to be a distinct cultural presence in Mexico today. At its peak (250–900) Mayan civilization developed a written language, calendar, mathematics, and astronomy, and many historians argue that it was one of the most densely populated civilizations in world history. Mayan civilization inhabited what is now southern Mexico, including the Yucatán Peninsula, Guatemala, Belize, El Salvador, and western Honduras. It reached its urban peak in the eigth and ninth centuries and then went into decline for unknown reasons. Some argue that it exceeded its agricultural capacity, and others suggest an extended drought, but the causes are unknown.

The Mayas developed paper at the same time as the Romans in the fifth century, but the huun paper of the Mayas made from tree bark was more durable than the Roman papyrus. This image is from the Dresden Codex, thought to be the most significant of Mayan codices, or painted folding books. Historians argue it was written just before the Spanish arrival, and is an important work of art, as well as containing ritual information.

Dresden Codex
Picture credit: SLUB Dresden/Deutsche Fotothek

AFRICA: IBN HAWQAL, THE EMPIRES OF GHANA AND MALI (c. 800–1240 CE)

Abu 'l-Qasim Muhammad al-Nusaybi, known commonly as Ibn Hawqal, was an Arabic geographer who traveled extensively in Asia, the Maghrib region of North Africa, and Spain. Not much is known of his life except what can be understood from his principal work, *Surat al-Ard* (*Picture of the Earth*). This book is an elaboration of al-Istakhri's Kitab al-masalik wa-'l-mamalik. Ibn Hawqal is thought to be the first Arabic geographer following al-Ya'qubi. One of Ibn Hawqal's most significant contributions to geography is his account and description of Sijilmasa, a central trading center of the Maghrib region. Sijilmasa was important in trans-Sahara trade, especially the trade of gold and salt between Egypt, Sudan, and the Ghana Empire (approximately 800–1240 CE).

The Ghana Empire gained wealth through the trade of gold, salt, and ivory to North Africa, the Middle East, and Europe. The camel made possible trans-Sahara trade, which brought wealth to Ghana but was ended by the Mali Empire in 1240 CE. The following passage from Ibn Hawqal describes the important trade route from Ghana through Sijilmasa to the salt hungry Sudan. The trade of salt was essential to the Ghana and Mali empires.

The Picture of the Earth

We have not mentioned the land of the Sūdān in the west, nor the Buja nor the Zanj, nor other peoples with the same characteristics, because the orderly government of kingdoms is based upon religious beliefs, good manners, law and order, and the organization of settled life directed by sound policy. These people lack all these qualities and have no share in them. Their kingdoms, therefore, do not deserve to be dealt with separately as we have dealt with other kingdoms. Some of the Sūdān, who live nearer to these well-known kingdoms, do resort to religious beliefs and practices and law, approaching in this respect the people of these kingdoms. Such is the case with the Nūba and the Ḥabasha, because they are Christians, following the religious tenets of the Rūm. Prior to the rise of Islam they were in neighbourly contact with the Byzantine Empire, because the land of Nūba borders on Egypt, and the Ḥabasha live on the Sea of al-Qulzum (the Red Sea). Between them [the Nūba and the Ḥabasha] and the land of Egypt is an inhabited [*sic*] desert in which there are gold mines. The Ḥabasha are linked to Egypt and Syria by way of the Red Sea.[1] [. . .]

The southern part of the earth includes the land of the Sūdān. Their land which is in the Furthest West on the Ocean is an encircled (*multaff*) land, which has no contact with other kingdoms. But one of its frontiers extends to the Ocean; another to the desert which separates it from the land of the Maghrib; another to the desert which extends over the Oases to the land of Egypt; and another frontier stretches to the desert which, as we have already said, puts forth no plants and has no population because of the extreme heat. The length of the land of the Sūdān is about 1,000 *farsakhs*, and its width about the same, except that [its length] to the sea, not to the back of the Oases (*ẓahr al-wāhāt*) is longer than its width [*sic*].[2] [. . .]

The southern ocean continues past Māssa, the western parts of Sijilmāsa, the confines of the Farthest Sūs (al-Sūs al-Aqṣā), and extends along the outer fringes of Awdaghust, Ghāna, Kūgha, and to the south-east of Sāma and Gharīwā,[3] in a country with innumerable inhabitants, until it reaches the desert which no one has yet crossed. Between its further part and the land of the Zanj are enormous deserts and sands which were crossed in olden times. The route from Egypt to Ghāna went over them but the winds blew continually upon the caravans, heavy and light, and more than one heavy caravan was annihilated and light one exterminated;[4] also the enemy attacked them and annihilated them on more than one occasion. So they abandoned this road and left it for [that of] Sijilmāsa. The caravans used to pass through the Maghrib to Sijilmāsa, which became inhabited by people from 'Irāq, and merchants from Baṣra and Kūfa, and the men from Baghdād, who used this road.[5] They, their children, and their trade flourish, their light caravans are constantly on the move and their heavy caravans are incessant to obtain enormous profits, fat gains, and abundant benefits. Merchants in the countries of Islam seldom approach them in affluence. I have seen a warrant written concerning a debt owed by Muḥammad b. Abī Sa'dūn in Awdaghust, and witnessed by assessors, for 42,000 dinars.[6] [. . .]

Besides what he exacts for the Sultan, the *amīr* of Ajdābiya levies tolls from the caravans going to and coming from the land of the Sūdān. [. . .]

In more than one place there [at Bāshū, between Tunis and Sousse] the water is obviously very unwholesome so that no stranger enters it without becoming ill; but if the Sūdān enter it it suits them. They are in good spirits and disposed to work.[7] [. . .]

That which is beyond him [the ruler of the Maghrib] and situated more deeply in the deserts of Sijilmāsa and Awdaghust and the territories of Lamṭa and Tādmakka towards the south and the territories of Fazzān contains water-points around which are tribes of unheeded[8] Berbers who are unacquainted with cereals (*ta'ām*) and have never seen wheat or barley or any other kind of grain. They are for the most part in a state of wretchedness and their dress is a piece of cloth worn sash-wise. Their staple diet is milk and flesh.[9] I shall mention this and describe it again after I have finished mentioning the distances exhaustively, if God wills.

Notes

1 This passage is borrowed, almost verbatim, from Al-Iṣṭakhrī (*Corpus of Early Arabic Sources of West African History*, pp. 40–1). But whereas Al-Iṣṭakhrī had almost nothing to say about the Sūdān, Ibn Hawqal certainly endeavoured to get information about them which he incorporated in his work. This passage therefore has little sense in the context of Ibn Hawqal's work. It demonstrates the consequences of wholesale borrowings from an earlier author.

2 Borrowed from Al-Iṣṭakhrī (*Corpus*, p. 41).

3 This passage, like the previous one, is a verbal description of the map. The terminology which Ibn Hawqal uses for that description is not always clear, e.g.: *ẓāhir al-Sūs al-aqṣā*, *'alā ẓawāhir Awdaghust, qabūl Sāma*.

4 *Mufrada* is another obscure term used by Ibn Hawqal. In the present translation *qāfila* and *mufrada* have already been rendered tentatively as 'heavy and light caravans'. In the translation of Kramers and Wiet (58) 'les caravans et les voyageurs sans bagages'. On the old route between Ghāna and Egypt see Ibn al-Faqīh (*Corpus*, p. 27).

5 See Al Ya'qūb (*Corpus*, p. 22) and Ibn al-Ṣaghīr (*Corpus*, p. 24) on traders from Kūfa and Baṣra, who were very likely Ibāḍīs, at Zawīla and Tāhart.

6 The story about the check from Awdaghust (repeated on p. 47) has led modern historials to assert that Ibn Hawqal visited Awdaghust himself. This assumption is now challenged by Levtzion (1968), who argues that Ibn Hawqal must have seen the check at Sijilmāsa and that he never crossed the Sahara.

7 Reference to expatriate Sūdān in various roles are fairly frequent, e.g. al-Nuwayrī in Ibn Khaldūn, *Berbères*, tr. De Slane I 400, 425 (under the Aghlabids); Ibn 'Idhārī, *Bayān*, Leiden 1948, I 244, 273, 274, 289, 291 (under the Zirids) Ikhall (pp. 164–5 at the battle of Zallāqa); IAZ 158.1 (not included in *Corpus*) etc. (at the battle of Las Navas). See also Ibn Hajar al-Asqalani, Sakh and Hopkins (1958), 72–3

8 The term *muhmal*, which we translate as 'unheeded', is later used also by Ibn Sa'īd (*Corpus*, 182, 185). The meaning seems to be that God has seen fit to leave these people without divine guidance.

9 This is a stereotyped description of the Saharan nomads, cf. Al-Ya'qūbī (*Corpus*, p. 22).

The Picture of the Earth, Corpus of Early Arabic Sources for West African History, translated by J.F.P. Hopkins; edited and annotated by N. Levtzion and J.F.P. Hopkins, Cambridge; New York: Cambridge University Press, 1981, pp. 44–46.

JAPAN: THE *KOJIKI* TO THE EDO PERIOD (c. 712 CE–1868 CE)

The *Kojiki* (*Record of Ancient Matters*), written in 712 CE, is the oldest surviving book in Japan. Along with *Nihon Shoki* (*Chronicles of Japan*), these books detail the beginning of the imperial line of emperors as beginning with the Sun Goddess. The legitimacy of the imperial throne is based on the myths in these texts. The second scroll of the *Kojiki*, called Nakatsumaki, is an account of the conquest and unification of Japan by a direct descendent of the Sun Goddess, Emperor Jimmu (whose name means "divine warrior"). From its presentation to the Emperor Temmu in 680, the *Kojiki* was bound with imperial aspirations, as it is thought to be part of the emperor's attempt to solidify his historical legitimacy and historically cleanse the Soga Clan and their attempted coup of any imperial rights.

The *Kojiki* re-emerged as an important text in Japanese culture during the Tokugawa, also known as the Edo period (1603–1868). The Battle of Sekigahara, won by Tokugawa Ieyasu, effectively ended the fighting of the Middle Ages and led to a long period of relative peace, albeit under a tyrannical government. During this time, culture flourished in Japan, and the mythical texts began to be questioned by scholars. The myths were reinforced by the ruling Tokugawa, who sought legitimacy for their position as shogun under the emperor, and they defended imperial right by rejecting trade outside China, consolidating power in Edo (now Tokyo), and suppressing Buddhism and Christianity. The *Kojiki*, *Nihon Shoki*, and their myths are not a complete explanation of Japanese imperialism and militarism, but are a major factor and the myths continued on until the end of World War II in 1945.

Reign of the Emperor Jim-Mu (Part I – His Progress Eastward, and Death of his Elder Brother)

The two Deities His Augustness Kamu-yamato-ihare-biko and his elder brother His Augustness Itsu-se, dwelling in the palace of Takachiho took counsel, saying: 'By dwelling in what place shall we quietly carry on the government of the Empire? It were probably best to go east.' Forthwith they left Himuka on their progress to Tsukushi. So when they arrived at Usa in the Land of Toyo, two of the natives, whose names were Usa-tsu-hiko and Usa-tsu-hime built a palace raised on one foot, and offered them a great august banquet. Removing thence, they dwelt for one year at the palace of Wokoda in Tsukushi. Again making a progress up from that land, they dwelt seven years at the palace of Takeri in the land of Agi. Again removing, and making a progress up from that land, they dwelt eight years at the palace of Takashima in Kibi. So when they made their progress up from that land, they met in the Hayasuhi Channel a person riding towards them on the carapace of a tortoise, and raising his wings as he angled. Then they called to him to approach, and asked him, saying: 'Who art thou?' He replied, saying: 'I am an Earthly Deity.' Again they asked him, saying: 'Knowest thou the sea-path?' He replied, saying: 'I know it well.' Again they asked him, saying: 'Wilt thou follow and respectfully serve us?' He replied, saying: 'I will respectfully serve you.' So they pushed a pole across to him, drew him into the august vessel, and forthwith conferred on him the designation of Sawa-ne-tsu-hiko. (This is the ancestor of the Rulers of the land of Yamato.) So when they went up from that land they passed the Namihaya Crossing, and brought up at the haven of Shirakata. At this time Nagasune-biko of Tomi raised an army, and waited to go out to fight [against them]. Then they took the shields that had been put in the august vessel, and disembarked. So they called that place by the name of Tate-dzu. It is what is now called the Tadetsu of Kusaka. Therefore when fighting with the Prince of Tomi, His Augustness Itsu-se was pierced in his august hand by the Prince of Tomi's hurtful arrow. So then he said: 'It is not right for me, an august child of the Sun-Deity, to fight facing the sun. It is for this reason that I am stricken by the wretched villain's hurtful hand. I will henceforward turn round, and smite him with my back to the sun.' Having [thus] decided, he, on making a progress round from the southern side, reached the sea of Chinu, and washed the blood on his august hand: so it is called the sea of Chinu. Making a progress round from thence, and arriving at the river-mouth of Wo in the land of Ki, he said: 'Ah! that

I should die stricken by the wretched villain's hand!' and expired as a valiant man. So that river-mouth was called the river mouth of Wo. The Mausoleum, too, is on Mount Kama in the land of Ki.

Kojiki, translation 1919 by Basil Hall Chamberlain, Vol. II. 1 (Sect. XLIV), pp. 159–161. Source: http://www.sacred-texts.com/shi/kj/index.htm.

THE AMERICAS: THE INCAN EMPIRE, PACHACUTI INCA YUPANQUI (1438–1471 CE)

Pachacuti Inca Yupanqui (1438–1471) was the establishing emperor of the Incan Empire, transforming a kingdom into an empire by extending Incan control over a region encompassing all of civilized South America (an area including the present-day countries of Peru, Ecuador, and Bolivia). Pachacuti (meaning literally "world transformer/turner") named his empire Tahuantinsuyu (meaning literally "The united four provences"), a name that reflects its political and military organization of four areas of control, each ruled by a governor. An astute military and political leader, Pachacuti ensured control over his empire by keeping the army and religious leaders separated. His rule was supported by divine blessings, a notion reinforced by his poetry, which are call *haillikuna*, or Sacred Hymns.

Hymn Seven: Prayer for the Inca

> O Lord Wiracocha,
> origin of all things,
> diligent Lord,
> Creator beyond measure,
> Fortunate Wiracocha
> Who says, "Let there be lords,
> let there be Incas:"
> Preserve the Lord you have raised,
> the Inca you have given life,
> preserve him blessed and safe.
> Let the people, his servants,
> live well.
> Bring victory over his enemies
> for ages without end.
> Do not shorten his days,
> or his children's or descendants',
> keep them fortunate, in peace,
> my Lord.

John Curl (2005) *Ancient American Poets*, Bilingual Press.

ROME, THE DECLINE: CONSTANTINE AND AUGUSTINE OF HIPPO (324–410 CE)

The question of the fall of the Roman Empire has intrigued Western historians. It is hard to identify a precise point at which the empire "fell" because the empire disintegrated for quite some time. The death of

Theodosius I in 395 was the last time the empire was unified, but the breaking apart of the empire began long before. The decline of Rome was bound up with the rise of Christianity. Emperor Dioclitian split the Roman Empire into four districts, each to be ruled by its own emperor. He is famous for his persecution of Christians (303–311), who he saw as a threat to unified power. Constantine I (272–337) emerged as the emperor, assuming sole power in 324 and is famous for making Christianity the preferred religion of the Roman Empire. After Rome was sacked by the Visigoths in 410, the first time in over 800 years, many offered the opinion that the reason was the abandonment of the Roman Gods by Constantine I.

In response to the moral turpitude of his fellow Romans, Augustine of Hippo (354–430) published *De Civitate Dei* (*The City of God*) shortly after the sacking of Rome to provide solace for his fellow Romans. The title makes reference to both Plato's *Republic*, and Cicero's *De re publica*, both concerned with government and natural law. Augustine is an important figure in the development of Western Christianity and philosophy. In particular, he is seen as a forefather of Reformation. He argues that there is a tension between the city of man, and the city of God (the church), but that divine justice is fixed, and history is the playing out of the preordained will of God. The city of man is tainted by original sin and there is no guarantee of salvation. Calvinists would later develop this point into the doctrine of predestination, and Max Weber links this to the rise of capitalism.

Augustine of Hippo, "The Folly of the Romans"

That the Romans Did Not Show Their Usual Sagacity When They Trusted that They Would Be Benefited by the Gods Who Had Been Unable to Defend Troy

And these be the gods to whose protecting care the Romans were delighted to entrust their city! O too, too piteous mistake! And they are enraged at us when we speak thus about their gods, though, so far from being enraged at their own writers, they part with money to learn what they say; and, indeed, the very teachers of these authors are reckoned worthy of a salary from the public purse, and of other honors. There is Virgil, who is read by boys, in order that this great poet, this most famous and approved of all poets, may impregnate their virgin minds, and may not readily be forgotten by them, according to that saying of Horace,

'The fresh cask long keeps its first tang.'[1]

Well, in this Virgil, I say, Juno is introduced as hostile to the Trojans, and stirring up Æolus, the king of the winds, against them in the words,

'A race I hate now ploughs the sea,
Transporting Troy to Italy,
And home-gods conquered'[2]

And ought prudent men to have entrusted the defence of Rome to these conquered gods? But it will be said, this was only the saying of Juno, who, like an angry woman, did not know what she was saying. What, then, says Æneas himself, – Æneas who is so often designated 'pious?' Does he not say,

'Lo! Panthus, 'scaped from death by flight,
Priest of Apollo on the height,
His conquered gods with trembling hands
He bears, and shelter swift demands?'[3]

ONE

Is it not clear that the gods (whom he does not scruple to call 'conquered') were rather entrusted to Æneas than he to them, when it is said to him,

'The gods of her domestic shrines
Your country to your care consigns?'[4]

If, then, Virgil says that the gods were such as these, and were conquered, and that when conquered they could not escape except under the protection of a man, what a madness is it to suppose that Rome had been wisely entrusted to these guardians, and could not have been taken unless it had lost them! Indeed, to worship conquered gods as protectors and champions, what is this but to worship, not good divinities, but evil omens?[5] Would it not be wiser to believe, not that Rome would never have fallen into so great a calamity had not they first perished, but rather that they would have perished long since had not Rome preserved them as long as she could? For who does not see, when he thinks of it, what a foolish assumption it is that they could not be vanquished under vanquished defenders, and that they only perished because they had lost their guardian gods, when, indeed, the only cause of their perishing was that they chose for their protectors gods condemned to perish? The poets, therefore, when they composed and sang these things about the conquered gods, had no intention to invent falsehoods, but uttered, as honest men, what the truth extorted from them. This, however, will be carefully and copiously discussed in another and more fitting place. Meanwhile I will briefly, and to the best of my ability, explain what I meant to say about these ungrateful men who blasphemously impute to Christ the calamities which they deservedly suffer in consequence of their own wicked ways, while that which is for Christ's sake spared them in spite of their wickedness they do not even take the trouble to notice; and in their mad and blasphemous insolence, they use against His name those very lips wherewith they falsely claimed that same name that their lives might be spared. In the places consecrated to Christ, where for His sake no enemy would injure them, they restrained their tongues that they might be safe and protected; but no sooner do they emerge from these sanctuaries, than they unbridle these tongues to hurl against Him curses full of hate.

Notes

1 Horace, *Ep.* I. ii. 69.
2 *Æneid*, i. 71.
3 *Ibid*, ii. 319.
4 *Ibid*. 293.
5 *Non numina bona, sed omina mala.*

Augustine of Hippo, "The Folly of the Romans," *City of God* (I, 3), Christian Classics Ethereal Library. Source: http://www.ccel.org/ccel/schaff/npnf102.iv.ii.iv.html.

MISSISSIPPI TRADING ZONE: CAHOKIA MOUNDS (c. 1000–1100 CE)

Cahokia Mounds is likely to have been the largest pre-Columbian settlement north of Mexico and part of the Mississippian culture. Little is known about the culture, except that they lived in the geographic area around the Mississippi River in what is now the United States, and they built mounds. Archeologists think that the culture developed and was able to expand via the cultivation of corn. The Mississippian Period reached its peak around 1000, and was abandoned around 1400. What is now the Cahokia Mounds is thought to have been a major regional city with a population of 10,000–20,000 people. It is unknown exactly why the civilization declined and disappeared, leaving only mounds and other archeological evidence. The largest mound, Monk's Mound (pictured below) is the largest prehistoric mound in the Western Hemisphere. Monk's, like the other mounds, are thought to have been temples and residences for the leaders, and a connection to the spirit world.

Monk's Mound
Photo: Cahokia Mounds State Historic Site, reprinted with permission.

EURASIA: THE OTTOMAN EMPIRE'S BREACH TO THE WEST (1683–1923 CE)

The Ottoman Empire (1299–1923) was best known for its position between the East and West. At its peak, it covered an area of what is now Turkey and the Middle East, North Africa, and Europe. The Ottoman Empire is most remembered by history for its stagnation and disintegration. Population pressures demanded more territory, but the empire fell behind Europe in the development of technology, particularly military technology. The Ottomans sought to control Vienna for its strategic position on the Danube, linking western Europe to the Black Sea. The first siege of Vienna was in 1529, and the second, more famous, in 1683. The period is often referred to as the "breach to the west." The second siege of Vienna, also called the "Battle of Vienna," was the decisive turn of power, with the Hapsburg and the Holy Alliance prevailing over the Ottomans in a 300-year struggle for control of central Europe. Defeat at Vienna began a period of stagnation and decline for the Ottoman Empire. The Treaty of Sèvres in 1920 at the end of World War I between the Allies and the Ottoman Empire stripped nearly all the territory from the Ottoman Empire except what is now Turkey, and excluded Turkey from Europe, fulfilling the dream of the Christian Holy League to finish the Ottoman Empire. The Turkish War of Independence (1919–1923) was waged by the Turkish National Movement, a revolutionary group fighting against the Allies, and eventually lead to the Treaty of Lausanne in July 1923. It is the final end of the Ottoman Empire, leading to the formation of the Republic of Turkey, a definition of the borders, and Turkey's renunciation of colonial claims in Libya.

Treaty of Peace with Turkey signed at Lausanne July 24, 1923: The Convention Respecting the Régime of the Straits and Other Instruments signed at Lausanne

The British Empire, France, Italy, Japan, Greece, Roumania and the Serb-Croat-Slovene State, of the one part, And Turkey, of the other part;

Being united in the desire to bring to a final close the state of war which has existed in the East since 1914,

Being anxious to re-establish the relations of friendship and commerce which are essential to the mutual well-being of their respective peoples,

And considering that these relations must be based on respect for the independence and sovereignty of States,

Have decided to conclude a Treaty for this purpose. [. . .]

Article I

From the coming into force of the present Treaty, the state of peace will be definitely re-established between the British Empire, France, Italy, Japan, Greece, Roumania and the Serb-Croat-Slovene State of the one part, and Turkey of the other part, as well as between their respective nationals. Official relations will be resumed on both sides and, in the respective territories, diplomatic and consular representatives will receive, without prejudice to such agreements as may be concluded in the future, treatment in accordance with the general principles of international law. [. . .]

Article 38

The Turkish Government undertakes to assure full and complete protection of life and liberty to all inhabitants of Turkey without distinction of birth, nationality, language, race or religion.

All inhabitants of Turkey shall be entitled to free exercise, whether in public or private, of any creed, religion or belief, the observance of which shall not be incompatible with public order and good morals.

Non-Moslem minorities will enjoy full freedom of movement and of emigration, subject to the measures applied, on the whole or on part of the territory, to all Turkish nationals, and which may be taken by the Turkish Government for national defence, or for the maintenance of public order. [. . .]

Article 44

Turkey agrees that, in so far as the preceding Articles of this Section affect non-Moslem nationals of Turkey, these provisions constitute obligations of international concern and shall be placed under the guarantee of the League of Nations. They shall not be modified without the assent of the majority of the Council of the League of Nations. The British Empire, France, Italy and Japan hereby agree not to withhold their assent to any modification in these Articles which is in due form assented to by a majority of the Council of the League of Nations.

Turkey agrees that any Member of the Council of the League of Nations shall have the right to bring to the attention of the Council any infraction or danger of infraction of any of these obligations, and that the Council may thereupon take such action and give such directions as it may deem proper and effective in the circumstances.

Turkey further agrees that any difference of opinion as to questions of law or of fact arising out of these Articles between the Turkish Government and any one of the other Signatory Powers or any other Power, a member of the Council of the League of Nations, shall be held to be a dispute of an international character under Article 14 of the Covenant of the League of Nations. The Turkish Government hereby consents that any such dispute shall, if the other party thereto demands, be referred to the Permanent Court of International Justice. The decision of the Permanent Court shall be final and shall have the same force and effect as an award under Article 13 of the Covenant.

Treaty of Peace with Turkey signed at Lausanne July 24, 1923.

MESOAMERICA: HERNÁN CORTÉS, THE CONQUEST OF NEW SPAIN (c. 1517 CE)

The Spanish colonization of New Spain was defended with the Spanish Requirement of 1513 – a declaration of the Spanish monarchy, endorsed by the Pope, that was read to Native Americans by the Conquistadors and pronounced the divine right to occupy territory, and to subjugate all who refused to convert to Christianity. Since the declaration was read in Spanish without translation, it was a thin moral and legal excuse for Spanish expansion. The conquest of New Spain is often associated with the conquering of the Aztec capital Tenochtitlan by Hernán Cortés (1485–1547). Cortés, a Spanish settler in Cuba led an expeditionary force to the mainland in 1519 and, defying the wishes of the colonial government, turned the expedition into a colonizing one. The Aztecs had only consolidated imperial power in 1428, and were in an ongoing war with the Tlaxcala called "The Flower War." The Aztecs believed it was their divine mission to fight wars and gain captives for sacrifice and death in battle, which was referred to as a "flowery death." Cortés found a good reception with the Mexican tribes chafing from Aztec rule and the "The Flower War."

Many historians argue that the Aztec Emperor Moctezuma II believed Cortés to be an incarnation of the war god Quetzalcóatl, and part of a series of signs indicating the end of the Aztec civilization. After forming an alliance with the Tlaxcala, Cortés marched to Tenochtitlan in November 1519, where Moctezuma welcomed him and his army. Relations swiftly deteriorated, in part from an Aztec dissatisfaction with the submission of Moctezuma. The Aztecs forced Cortés and his invading force to retreat and regroup in Tlaxcala. Under the leadership of Cuauhtémoc, the last Aztec emperor, the Aztecs continued to fight Spanish rule, but eventually fell, after waves of smallpox and an eight-month siege, leading to Spanish rule on August 13, 1521.

In 1585, Franciscan friar Bernadino de Sahagún published his collected accounts of the conquest of New Spain as related in the native language of Nahuatl by Aztec soldiers. The selection is from his collected accounts, and significantly mentions Cortés's translator, Marina, who provided Cortés with key knowledge and communication. She is known as Malinche, and her name is now synonymous with traitor in Mexico. The account relates that Spanish soldiers were killing fleeing Aztecs to get their gold.

Conquest of New Spain

*Concerning Other Events that Happened when the Mexicans, Tlatelolcans,
and the Lord of Mexico Surrendered to the Spaniards*

Other things, which are included here, also occurred when the Mexicans and their lord surrendered to Captain don Hernando Cortés. After the Mexicans, Tlatelolcans, and their ruler had arrived at the palace on whose rooftop Captain don Hernando Cortés was waiting, some of the Spaniards, whom the Captain commanded, went down and received [Cuauhtemoc], helping him out of the canoe and bringing him joyfully to the Captain's presence. They then fired the artillery, sounded the trumpets and drums, and raised the standard in token and celebration of victory.

All that day the Spaniards celebrated at seeing that war, which had been so prolonged and costly, come to an end. They embraced and comforted the lord of Mexico and the leaders of Mexico and Tlatelolco.

On the following morning, peace was publicly proclaimed. The [Spaniards] ordered that those who were penned up in the fort should come out safely and freely return to their homes to seek rest and solace.[1] Likewise, they proclaimed a decree to the Spaniards, Tlaxcalans, and all the other Indians, that they should not inflict any harm on them, or take any of their possessions, or enslave any men, women, boys, or girls. Having heard the proclamation that had been made, those within the fort emerged, and [when they were] arriving at the main road leading to the district called Coyonacazco, some Tlaxcalans attacked, and began to rob and kill some of those who were leaving. Seeing this, the Captain immediately sent Spaniards to protect the Mexicans, and to restrain and imprison those who were harming them.[2]

After this, those who were emerging began to go their separate ways, toward where they wanted to go,[3] whereas others left by water in canoes, and others waded through the water. As they came out on land, some soldiers[4] began to rob them and take them captive. They were looking only for the gold that they were carrying. They frisked the clothes of the men and women, and even made them open their mouths to see if they were carrying gold in them. They selected the best-looking young men and maidens and took them as slaves; some of them disguised themselves with torn cloaks to avoid being taken slaves. When this account reached the Captain, he immediately ordered that the offenders be stopped, arrested, and brought to him before they could do any further harm,[5] although already they had branded some good-looking young men and women on the face.

That evening,[6] [the Spaniards] placed the lord of Mexico and his Mexican and Tlatelolcan leaders aboard a brigantine and took them to the place called Acachinanco, where all the brigantines were assembled, which is on the edge of the Mexican lakeshore. The following day, the Spaniards returned to this district of Amaxac, fully armed but not geared for battle. When they arrived at this district of Amaxac and Coyonacazco, they all covered their noses with linen cloths brought for this purpose because of the great stench that there was in all these districts from the dead and rotting bodies that filled the whole place as well as the pestiferous canals. All came on foot and brought with them the Lord of Mexico, Cuauhtemoc, and the lord of Texcoco, called Coanacotzin, and the lord of the Tepanecans, called Tetlepanquetzatzin. All three came together, with Cuauhtemoc, lord of Mexico, in the middle. Behind them came the following leaders: Cihuacoatl,[7] Tlacotzin; Tlilancalqui[8] Petlauhtzin; Huitznahuatl,[9] Motelchiuhtzin; Mexicatl Achcauhtli,[10] Tecutlamacazqui, Coatzin; Tlatlatzin, Tlaçoliatitl. They had in their possession all the gold that had been assembled during the war.

Everybody went directly to the district of Atactzinco, here in Tlatelolco, where now stands the church of Santa Lucia. A host of Spaniards, arranged two by two, followed these leaders to guard them. Reaching the house of the leader called Coyohuehuetzin, they ascended to its rooftop garden, which was completely canopied with rich mantles to shade against the sun. There they had decked out the throne and canopy for Captain don Hernando Cortés, who brought his interpreter, Marina, with him. When the Captain was seated, the lord of Mexico, Cuauhtemoc, sat on his right hand,[11] and beside him sat the lord of Texcoco, Coanacotzin.[12]

Notes

Notes by S.L. Cline compare the 1585 revisions with the Spanish text of the *Florentine Codex* (FC) (Sahagún 1979).

1 FC reports this in its Chapter 40; see note 12 here in Chapter 40.
2 FC does not report this defense.
3 FC says they went "hazia Tlacuba y otros hazia sanct. Xpoual [Cristóbal]" (f. 81v).

4 FC indicates the soldiers were both Spaniards and their Indian allies: "Los españoles y sus amjgos pusieron se en todos los camjnos y robauan // a los que pasauan tomandolos el oro que lleuauan" (f.82r,v).

5 FC does not report Cortés intervening.

6 FC indicates the date by the Aztec calendar: "despartio se la guerra en la cuenta de los años, que se dize tres casas, y en la cuenta de los dias: en el signo que se llama Cecoatl" (f.83).

7 Cihuacoatl literally means "snake woman." The officeholder was the ruler's most important adviser. See Sahagún 1950–82; pt. 13. 2d ed.: 119 n.5.

8 Tlillancalqui seems to have been a religious specialist. See Sahagún 1950–82, pt. 13, 2d ed.: 119 n.6.

9 Huitznahuatl is the title of one of the major Mexica military commanders.

10 Achcauhtli literally means "elder brother." See also Sahagún 1950–82, pt. 4, 2d ed.:55. FC has Motelchiuhtzin as one person, the achcauhtli another, and mexicatl a third: "otro Motelchiuhtzin, otro Mexicatl, otro achcauhtli" (f.84).

11 FC indicates Cuauhtemoc's attire: "tenja cubierta vna manta que se llama Quetzalychpetzi" (f.84).

12 FC indicates Coanacotzin's attire: "tenja cubierta una manta de nequen que se llama Xoxochiteio" (f.84).

Bernardino de Sahagún "Concerning other events that happened when the Mexicans, Tlatelolcans, and the lord of Mexico surrendered to the Spaniards," *Conquest of New Spain: 1585 Revision*. Reproductions of the Boston Public Library Manuscript and Carlos María de Bustamante 1840 Edition. translated by Howard F. Cline, edited with an introduction and notes by S.L. Cline. Salt Lake City: University of Utah Press, 1989, pp. 137–139.

PART TWO

The modern world-system and industrial capitalism, 1500–1914 CE

INTRODUCTION TO
PART TWO

Every indication is that the English language word "modern" is one of those words that came into use in order to name something felt to be widely occurring, the meaning and nature of which was far from certain. In this respect, "modern" is a word of the same kind as "global" in "globalization" – also in our times a word for something everyone with an opinion on such things agrees is happening even when where it is leading would seem to be unclear. Thus as *the modern* commonly refers duplicitously to what is taken to be the new in the present, so *globalization*, when used colloquially (which is to say, without very much research), points to something new in a much later present – our own – which, being new, is, like the modern, different from its past.

Thus it is that modern things and global ones are, in some basic sense, things of the same kind. Their differences may turn out to be many but, at their most elemental, the modern and the global differ in respect to the pasts against which they are new. The English word "modern" came into use in the sixteenth century to distinguish what was then going on in the world from what had come before – the feudal, the traditional, the age of religion, the primitive, the backward, the despotic, and, of course, the dullest of all such names, the pre-modern. Ever since, it was thought that in all of the spheres of human endeavor modern things were somehow different from things that went before. Likewise, the global in globalization means to refer to new happenings said to be a fresh if not entirely happy departure from the modern which, in its first days, enjoyed its own relation to a past. Whether a global thing will retain features of its modern past is hard to say even if it is hard to imagine how any new thing could possibly be utterly and irrevocably different from its past. We know that very late in the long history of the modern there remained strong and vibrant forces of its past – feudal practices, village life, traditional holidays and cuisines, backward practices, despotic rulers, primitive worlds, and much more.

The foremost rule of historical change is that the new never springs all at once from a past. Indeed, new structural arrangements do not spring up so much as slither slowly out from under a long settled rock that itself remains fixed to the landscape as a kind of solid reminder of the pasts. As the global is today the snake that is coming out from the modern, so the modern, in its time, sneaked out from the feudal. The difference is that the global is the kind of time worm that has always been sneaking up on any number of pasts – the ancient and classical civilizations as well as the feudal. So too – and in much the same way – the modern came out of the dark as a strange combination of those classical qualities that had endured the darker ages that, somewhere late in the fifteenth and early in the sixteenth centuries, came to be seen as different in spirit, if not form, from what had gone before. It would take, thereafter, a good long while until well into the nineteenth century before industrial capitalism in its uncertain relation with the democratic state would seem to have melted down the classical and feudal social forms to such a degree that a modern spirit would become, as Max Weber put it, a "tremendous cosmos" – new, ubiquitous, overwhelming, and threatening to the spirit and values of the past.

The corollary to the first rule that historical changes are never a tsunami is that social changes, like glaciers, are slow moving structures carrying along the sediments of the past, grinding and shifting them into some new formation. Hence, the practice of identifying the first modern structures with certain already well-formed events (if event is the right word) that had poked their noses into the sixteenth and seventeenth centuries more or less.

Of these there were three structural developments that would mark the modern as a new kind of global order:

1 The ambitious *voyages of discovery* emanating from Iberia, then soon after from the rest of Europe that crossed the Atlantic, first, to the Americas, north and south, then unrelentingly across and beyond the Pacific to extend the European map of global things to cover the earth.
2 The *settlement and colonization* by rational, if cruel, methods of administration of the far-flung lands for the purposes of economic extraction and trade, organized eventually into a more or less rational system of accords resulting in a European division of colonizing labor.
3 The *new technologies* that lent moral force and productive efficiencies to navigation to and from the new worlds, and greased the subjugation of native lands and resources, in order to establish profitable trade routes along which speed and efficiencies of exchange were multiples greater than anything of the kind in their premodern past.

Ambitious voyages, rational colonial systems, and efficient technologies – these were the foundational structures of the modern. And, like all structures, none began pure and simple in the so-called modern era that began in the long sixteenth century, and all gathered force and form in the centuries after.

It is harder to say why it is that the Europeans who by hook or crook imposed themselves as the dominant core of a world economy are so readily considered the source of the modern. Even today, in spite of the terrible economic and social prospects of the capitalist system early in the twenty-first century, believers in the West as the universal system of the modern are not hard to find. Though shaken by the crash of 2009, world economic leaders forage in the East, North, and South while running (and exhausting) the global marketplaces according to principles of the modern West. Yet, at the same time, one need not revert to the instances of radical Islamic fundamentalists or Christian primitivist evangelicals to find skeptics as to the uniqueness of the European West.

Andre Gunder Frank is notable among economic and social historians who have argued that the European world-system was not only not the first but also not even a true world-system when compared to the trade routes and systems of Ancient China, Central Asia, and the Iberian Mediterranean. Frank puts it this way:

> Early modern Europe was neither more important in the world economy nor more advanced in any way than other regions of the world. This was not the case even counting all of its Atlantic outliers. Nor was Europe in any way "Central" to or a "core" of any world-embracing economy or system. ... If any economy had a "central" position and role in the world economy before 1800, they were in Asia. If any economy had a "central" position and role in the world economy and its possible hierarch of "centers," it was China.[1]

Frank took an aggressively contrarian position, most particularly against Immanuel Wallerstein. Still, quite apart from who, between them, may be correct (or, better, whether their differences can be reconciled), what remains on balance are two points: first, that the Asian or Afro-Asian world-system began to decline in favor of the European one after 1800; second, that whatever the differences between Ancient China as a core and the European cores, after 1800 there was a strong and undeniable movement toward industrial capitalism and that, in the long run, the European world-system – whatever its comparative limitations or advantages to an earlier Asian one – was (and remains) the indisputably *modern* system. These two differences (the second not directly addressed by Frank) do not wreck the world-system position associated with Wallerstein, nor do they alter in important ways the modifications we take from it and will soon explain. Asia: yes, undoubtedly globalization, including economic globalization, was rooted in Asia, broadly defined to include Central and Near Asia; but the modern as a new global form was something different altogether and that is the difference addressed here in Part Two.

A crucial (possibly *the* crucial) difference, theories aside, between the ancient, imperial global trade networks that were centered more in Asia and the modern world-system is that between globalizing programs based on land routes, such as the Silk Road, and sea routes, such as the Atlantic trade triangles. Though both systems overcame formidable unsettled and unsettleable spaces – the Talkla Makan Desert of Far and Central Asia and the North Atlantic seas – the European system was fundamentally a naval project requiring a navigational imagination, while the over-land system (fixed in time during the Han Dynasty) was, though risky and daunting to be sure, more down to earth. The one reckoned among the stars that could be hidden from view on open seas and storms that permitted no refuge; the other reckoned by the sun that, at the least set regularly, to provide relief from the open desert heat and rest from the travel. The northern and southern Silk Roads eventually expanded to include the shipping lanes close by the coastal markers on the Indian Ocean. This was the same navigational method that made the Mediterranean marine cultures, but coastal reckoning differs from open sea shipping for never venturing into open and uncharted seas.

The difference is not one of the dangers encountered, but of the extraordinary systematic imagination required, beginning with the hard-to-substantiate idea of the world as geographic space of extension. The Chinese and other classical civilizations were skillful mariners who developed early versions of the magnetic compass, but only the Europeans applied their ingenuity to seeking new worlds across indefinite global spaces, guided in large part by the idea that somewhere out there would be a new route to the East to be found by circumnavigation.

Immanuel Wallerstein's *Modern World System I* (1974) is fundamental to the position we take in this book in two ways – neither of which is exactly what Wallerstein himself meant to say when, in the 1970s, he established the concept of the modern world-system. First, by setting the European sixteenth century as the beginning of a global system of trade among unequal parts – the dominating core of capital accumulation and the dominated periphery from which labor and natural resource were ruthlessly extracted – Wallerstein was attacking the central principles of a theory of modern economic progress that was then, and today still is, the prominent theory of liberal markets and freedoms. This is the point that Andre Gunder Frank ignores – that the modern system that arose after 1800 arose under the mantle of a liberal geo-culture. In this aspect, we agree wholeheartedly with the general outlines of Wallerstein's analytic scheme, even while departing from his, we think, over strong principle of rational demarcation between world empires and the modern system. Here Frank may have a point. Just the same, Wallerstein's distinction allows for a general theory of globalization that reaches far beyond the vaguely post-modern theories that would locate the beginning of globalization sometime late in the twentieth century. But, on the other hand, as we have suggested in Part One, Wallerstein's idea of the modern as a systematic world-economy understates the accomplishments if not the method of world-empires such as those of China after the Han Dynasty and the classical Mediterranean. As Wallerstein puts it, the world-empire was limited as to duration by the attenuation of "effective control" by the dominant imperial order. The implication, as he works it out, is that the rational methods of the European world-economy provided a more efficient method for the virtual control of a global system based in a rationalized scheme for economic exchange as distinct from imperial or, in time, state control. Our difference on this point is slight but crucial (and only remotely one that buys into Frank's acerbic arguments). We, perhaps even more than Wallerstein (and certainly more than Frank), seek to reset the historical clock of globalization by, at one point, granting that the modern that begins to come out of its past in the sixteenth century, while it would not be fully systematic for a good two centuries (as, indeed, so many of the ancient and classical trade systems were not, ever), was already in early modern Europe inclined toward a principle of rational order. At the same time, this is a point of some value when it comes to assessing the current situation early in the twenty-first century when, to many if not all, the global is worming its way into the bowels of a system the modern invented. Wallerstein's strong theory of world-system, even with its many and subtle critical reservations, seems to us to place too much emphasis on, as he put it, the world system as the unit of analysis – an emphasis that for all intents and purposes leads to the conviction that in transformational times of uncertainty, such as the one we are evidently in, the failing system will in due if not near course reset itself into a new system of some or another kind. Hence, we think, two problems: first, that of overestimating the systemic qualities in the transition from the feudal to the modern over a span that could be as great as from the twelfth to the nineteenth centuries; second, that of being too optimistic as to the prospects that the global can or will lead to a new systemic arrangement. The second is important to Part Six of this book. The first is at issue in Part Two.

Thus, our second general point of appreciation and difference: as Wallerstein indeed came to do in the writings of the 1980s and later, we would identify as essential to the establishment of the modern world-economy distinctive European cultural sensibilities that, as he put it (following Weber in particular), arose in the rational aspects of the Renaissance and the Protestant Reformation. Our position is not any sort of the weary culturalist criticism of world-system analysis as somehow overly materialist. Wallerstein's method is, to be sure, materialist in the sense of being socio-economic history. But he certainly, even in the earliest statements of world-system analysis, from which the selection we include is taken, provides a robust consideration of the many elements necessary to the transition from loose federations of towns and regional markets characteristic of the feudal era in Europe to the modern capitalist world-system. The key figure in this transition, as many have said, was the merchant class; but Wallerstein is subtle on the point that the merchant class derived from a new class of agents both in and between domains and as representatives of more distant trading leagues:

> Agents of the landlords who sometimes became independent, as well as ... peasants who retained enough surplus after payment to the landlords to sell it on the market; ... and resident agents of long-distance merchants (based often in the Italian city-states and later in the Hanseatic cities) who capitalized on poor communications and hence high-disparities of prices.[2]

The structural roots of the trader agents were early in the feudal period, at least as early as the twelfth and thirteenth centuries. The key word, however, is "agents," suggesting thus aspects of a system that while avaricious, even ruthless, relied on a proto-entrepreneurial attitude that would, in the modern era, develop into the bourgeois class that formed the political pole in the economic clashes that would mark the capitalist period.

The very idea of an agent, and especially agents of distant regions, requires at the least a discernible quality of rational capacity for exchange and of reasonable representations of the qualities of goods and services offered and taken by the agents. If not trust, exactly, then the agents shared a certain will to generate agricultural surplus for exchange into capital surplus. The exchange, especially over distances, demanded agricultural efficiencies able to feed food-producing populations while also creating surpluses of potential wealth, including durable goods fungible in markets at some distance from domains on which they were produced. This much of Wallerstein's earliest statement of the origins of the modern system is both completely agreeable and utterly brilliant in the subtle anticipation of the role of the rational agent well before anything like rationalized market economics, whether local, regional, or global.

Certainly feudal Europe was not the first place to be acquainted with agents of various kinds. But, if one is to account for the fact that the modern system was inherently global from its inception the primitive agents of a merchant class had to have been imbued by a more general series of affects, if not subjective attitudes. We do not mean to exclude "culture" from the vocabulary of these affects, but we do mean to suggest that, well before the modern idea of culture came into its own in the nineteenth century, there were gross organizing structures neither simply political nor economic. Or to put it otherwise, well before liberal ideologies of the free individual there were powerful collective forces that were neither ancient fish nor modern fowl. Of these, the most prominent was a widely, if not universally, inviting commitment to the importance of the voyage or the journey that in turn required the supposition that, whatever the traditional goods of the region or village, they were lacking in some aspect that could only be found at a distance – at, that is, a distance that could only exist initially in the imagination. One might even say that before the modern came into its own as a global system, it was a theory of a world considered transcendent of the European here and now.

The modern world is, thus, a theory of extended space. Modern space was certainly politically organized, economically driven, and institutionally settled. But it was, and remains, a projected space – a dimension that seems to have outrun traditional ideas of cyclical time in order to inspire, among other aspects, the voyages of discovery that led to the projection of power into distant colonies that made efficiencies of travel of the essence of economic profit. As is well illustrated by the Norse adventures to Greenland and the Americas around 1000 CE and Marco Polo's to the East some two centuries later, the idea of distant place worthy of pursuit existed in some rudimentary form well before even the earliest of evidences of the actual places much less the assured means of finding them. The Norse settlements from the sea were gained by the then prevailing methods of coastal reckoning (as Marco Polo's were by land). Though primitive by modern standards, both entailed early ideas of the voyage or the journey as proper, even essential. Otherwise one would not find in the *Saga of Eirik the Red* the striking lines: "Leif set sail as soon as he was ready. He was tossed about a long time out at sea, and lightened upon lands of which before he had not expectation. There were fields of wild wheat, and the vine-tree full of growth." To be sure a key source of the idea of the necessary voyage was Christianity, as King Olaf Tryggvason stipulated in his orders to Leif: "Thou shalt go my errand, and preach Christianity in Greenland." The Norse errands to the wilderness were uncanny anticipations of the language attributed to the dissenting English Christians who, more than six centuries later, in a very different world, counted themselves as on God's errand into the wilderness of New England.

Though the distinctive features of Christianity as a religion of the earthly pilgrim toward a divine end is undoubtedly a prominent aspect of the European theory of the world, this doctrinal element is insufficient to account for the emergent theory of the westward voyages toward new and distant places. The Norse passage hints at the importance of sheer discovery: "After this there was much talk about making ready to go to land which Leif had discovered." Even more striking is another, more human, but still creative, aspect of the English colonies in Massachusetts. They were, in the words Perry Miller and other historians drew from the settlers along the New England coast, an errand into the wilderness that sought to extend God's promises of a new land flowing with milk and honey (or wild wheat and vine trees, in the *Saga of Eirik the Red*).

The New England colonies were thus a spiritual geography of this world – a world in which their God sought a new beginning for His people. Yet, Governor Bradford's *Of Plymouth Plantation* is filled with the most mundane particulars of the organization of life in the wilderness including the famous passage selected here on the encounters with the local peoples: "Having in some sorte ordered their bussines at home it was thought meete to send some abroad to see their new friend Massasoyet, . . . as also that hearby they might view ye countrie, and see in what manner he lived." Pious Christians they were, as they were colonizers whose new world would cruelly force their new "friends" into submission. Yet, from the earliest moment their voyage was, first of all, a flight from the sinful degradations of Europe and, second, as the passage suggests, a mission of encounter and discovery founded in the most basic of economic duties, survival, but also in sheer intrigue at the new people and their "countrie." In retrospect, the discoveries were pure and simple – the practice of a methodical subjugation of new and distant worlds to the rational will of the Europeans. This is fair enough, so long as it is kept well in mind that the motivation entailed an autonomous quality of curiosity, even courage. The courage required may have been necessary first in the crossings by sea but also, once settled, all the missions of discovery faced, most often overwhelming odds against the harsh natural conditions and hostile local people. The striking difference from Governor Bradford's more pacific encounters in Massachusetts is seen in the fact that the Spaniards a century earlier under Ferdinand Magellan encountered hostilities in the Philippines that led to their leader's death in 1521. The selection from *First Voyage around the World* describes the clever deceptions of the Mauthan natives who, after killing Magellan and turning back his attack, tricked the Spanish into believing they could negotiate a peace settlement. Aided by Magellan's interpreter and slave, who hated his Spanish captors, the Mauthan played the Spanish as fools, in the end causing them to abandon hope of recovering their captain's body and flee for home. Their ranks thinned by the defeat, Magellan's fleet were forced to ditch one of their ships to complete the homeward journey in two vessels.

A curiosity of the account is Magellan's appeal to his men as they faced daunting odds in the battle to "be of good cheer" by remembering the Spanish conquests in "Yucatan" (which is to say, Mexico) where, under Cortez, a small band of several hundred Spanish overwhelmed thousands of natives. Magellan's foolish confidence in the natural (that is, Christian) superiority of Iberian power reflects the naïvety that the terms of their defeat in the hands of natives could be renegotiated by reason of their belief in the justice of their ways.

Still, leaderless and defeated in the Philippines, Magellan's crew returned home to Spain laden with achievements – the first voyage around the world, the breaching of the Straits of Magellan at the cone of South America where Atlantic meets Pacific, and a considerable advance in understanding of the geography of global space (including, in time, the realization of the necessity of an adjustment in the calendar that become the International Date Line). The cultural logic of the Iberian voyage was flawed, as time would tell, but the scientific logic of their navigations would reset the calculus of global reckoning. Here, in point of practical accomplishment, lay the beginning of a true understanding of the nature and variety of global realities.

The Americas were, if not the sole preoccupation of the early European adventures, surely the most powerful example of their original intentions and long-term economic achievements. Felipe Fernández-Armesto, in his brilliantly succinct *The Americas* (2003), details how, in the two centuries after Magellan, the Europeans in the Americas reinvented the new worlds they discovered: "Long-range trade, on a scale unimaginable before the European conquests, expanded the area of cultural exchange to embrace the whole hemisphere." The Europeans, while ruthless in their way, did not obliterate indigenous economic zones. Rather, they used and expanded on them, as in the French appropriation of the fur trade in the North and, more generally, in the persistence that in time closed the space between the Atlantic and Pacific worlds by the breaching of the Isthmus of Panama (ultimately by the hard won digging of the canal).

The trajectory over time from the Norse probes to the North to the economic colonization of the entire hemisphere spanned a good millennium and continues into our day when European influences, cultural and economic, continue to define the Americas, if not unify them from Argentina and Chile in the south to the Arctic north where – as the Southern Cone was in Magellan's day – in the 2000s the most proximate and powerful of the northern tier of Euro-America competes in the search for oil resources and for a stake in opening of a Northwest passage by the melting Arctic ice.

Marco Polo is, surely, the icon of the prehistory of the modern, in respect to both his legendary journey to the East and his commentaries on the commercial wonders of the Far East. In the selection "Concerning the City of Cambaluc," the remarkable feature is his amazement before the real consequences of the Silk Road and the then (in the last quarter of the thirteenth century) robust international commercial activity. "To this city are brought articles of greater cost and rarity, and in greater abundance of all kinds, than to any other city in the world." A traveler from the Venetian Republic surely had to have been stunned by the economic bustle. Even if he could not possibly have possessed a serious measure of all the cities of the world, his astonishment is itself a good enough measure of the European economic imagination that would not rival the accomplishments of the East for centuries to come.

Against which, centuries later, when the modern was on the verge of discovering itself, one encounters John Locke's astonishing statement in 1690: "In the beginning all the world was America and more so than that is now; for no such thing as money was any where known." Locke's importance as author of a general philosophy of natural man, with all that the expression conveys, and of an (perhaps the most) influential liberal theory of the modern political order goes without saying. At a crucial juncture in his *Second Treatise of Government* (1690), written early in the colonizing period (and a near century before the American

Revolution), Locke identifies America with the primal state of nature, which catches one up short. Whether the line is to be taken as a metonym of his philosophical anthropology or as a historical recognition of the Americas in the coming global system is an open question. What is not is that the Americas were already, well before fully settled, the imaginative platform for the modern global scheme that would be essentially economic. Thus the riddle at the heart of the dream – that the Americas were somehow the pure form of the world precisely because they were dreamt before, as Marx would later say, the cash nexus came to organize the modern system. Here Locke was truly prophetic. What was coming already early in the colonizing period of European expansion had to do, for better or worse, with the economic measure of human value.

True measures of the world in a global sense became possible, in a scientific sense, after Magellan's circumnavigation. Still, the refinements of those measures would take centuries to mature. Yet, certainly by the seventeenth century it was evident that to speak of the new as the modern made it necessary to speak of a serious and potentially globally useful method for measuring the costs and values exchanged across distances in a global system. Measures, thus, are the essential practical applications of the modern as a global theory of systematic exchange, which among much else involved, as a political consideration, a measured sense of borders and limits.

The Peace of Westphalia in 1648 is commonly taken, against much historical dispute, as the symbolic beginning of such a system in Europe. Readers of the selection "The Treaty of Westphalia" would be right to laugh out loud at the long list of strange and irregular parties to the accord – from The Holy Roman Emperor and the King of France to a variety of "most illustrious and most excellent Lords" of various domains and principalities that in time would disappear into the nation-states of modern Europe. Yet behind the irregularities lay a principle of global importance – that the rights of authorities over their respective territories and the peoples therein must be measured by a calculus of the benefits of peace over the costs of war. Thus, at least symbolically, were established the accords from which would develop not just the modern nation-state but more importantly an international system of states defined by respect for the authorities of the several in their separate territories. It need not be said that, in the centuries to follow, the rule of peace was seldom kept for very long. Yet, the accords arising from a long history of land and sea war on and about the European continent that had exhausted rivals and sapped their competitive capital were the basis for a system of sorts that made all the difference in the world.

The wars meant to be ended by the Treaty were certainly not regionally confined to continental Europe. If there was a decisive event that prefigured the Treaty's necessity, that event occurred 60 years before in the defeat of the Spanish Armada by the English in 1588. The Anglo-Spanish war from 1585 to 1604, of which the defeat of the Spanish navy was the decisive turn, was in effect a war for dominance at sea and, thus, a war that would determine the terms of a global division of labor in the Americas and beyond. The apparent theme of the Treaty of 1648 was local but the effect was global. In the century between Magellan and the English colonies in Massachusetts (from the 1520s to the 1620s), the Spanish and the English as well as the French and the Dutch would compete unevenly for their stakes in the Americas – a competition that took the preliminary form of territorial acquisition but resulted ultimately in a hemispheric and global division of labor. The Treaty of 1648 was hardly an explicit mapping of global authorities, but its principled regard for territorial authority was obviously at least as much a condition for global rights of colonial authority as to proto-national ones on the continent. The Treaty may have led to the modern nation-state, but from there it led by way of the ground rules of an international system.

Just as the Peace in Europe was never stable, neither would be the global system already emerging in the sixteenth century. Yet in the two centuries after Westphalia, colonial wars and revolutions notwithstanding, the division of colonial administration would be well settled. The terms of those settlements were not, however, those of a rights of control over distinctive colonial settlements; more deeply, they were the considered calculation of the diminishing returns of aggression as a method for expanding territorial control in the wider world. It is not for nothing that, even now, so long after the colonial system of the Europeans came into its own, the geopolitical map of the world, drastically altered in many ways, bleeds with the traces of the European system of global control and its division of colonial labors that made it what the modern world was, and to a large extent still is: a system founded on the theoretical rule of a reasonable principle of true if unattainable regard for territorial rights and authorities.

All the more striking is that the global colonial system was a projection of the regional values behind the Peace of Westphalia which was, in further effect, an accord among national cultural differences that would manifest themselves in a weird but true respect for differences as to the ethics of the colonial administration. British Australia would serve as a penal colony that would purify the British Isles of uncivil aliens; hence Robert Hughes's riveting description in his *Fatal Shores* – "In Australia England drew the sketch of our own [20th] century's terrible fresco of repression, the Gulag." Then too, the general features of Pax Britannica would serve as a slogan since the colonial system would function as a crude attempt at what today is often called a global civil society. Thus, for one example, Britain's 1858 Treaty with China at Tientsin, so evidently skewed in its favor, was temperate at least in its confidence in its own regard for civility. If the English colonial system professed a virtue impossible to attain in any colonial system, then there was a wide variety of colonizing styles, of which King Leopold's may be the polar opposite in its overt ruthlessness. Adam Hochschild, in the selection from *King Leopold's Ghost* (1999), his chilling account of Belgian cruelty in Africa, characterizes the attitude that drove the European mind's idea of colonial spaces: "For Europeans, Africa remained the supplier of valuable raw materials – human bodies and elephant tusks." Otherwise, they saw it as they saw the far flung worlds of indigenous being – "faceless, bland, empty, a place on the map waiting to be explored."

Colonies were instruments of the European global imagination. They were various and evenly dispersed, whether falsely virtuous or excessively evil extensions of the rational will for ordering the world.

Strictly speaking, from the Oxford English Dictionary, one learns that a technology is a systematic study of an art or craft. Though this classical meaning has been eclipsed by the modern applied sciences of the arts of invention, it is worth noting that the term "technology" originally enjoyed a broad, one even might say, humanistic meaning.

It was Michel Foucault, in 1982, who coined the phrase "technologies of the self" which he introduced in a lecture at the University of Vermont with a conspicuous comment on the standard theory of the origins of the modern self and the one he came to sponsor:

> Max Weber posed the question: If one wants to behave rationally and regulate one's action according to true principles, what part of one's self should one renounce? What is the ascetic price of reason? ... I posed the opposite question: How have certain kinds of interdictions required the price of certain kinds of knowledge about oneself? What must one know about oneself in order to be willing to renounce anything?[3]

Either way, the art of self is itself a technology perfected in modern times as an ethic of renunciation. Whether this ethic, or self-knowledge, is understood as an ascetic discipline of the self or a reflexive knowledge of self there can be little doubt that the foundational technology of the modern world was and remains a technology of self – one that requires a reasoned and calculated renunciation of bodily and social temptations in order to form the general principle of a self, whether personal or general, able to move forward and ahead along the timeline of a linear history. Foucault's theory is that the art of self-knowledge arose early in the Christian era in the discipline of confession and repentance. Weber's is that it came to full bloom in the Calvinist ascetic of disciplined action in this world. Where the two not entirely opposite theories converge is on the historical fact that the self of the modern age is a self in motion in respect to which the moral individual understands life – hers and that of the collective – as on a journey.

School children are likely to have heard of René Descartes' "I think, therefore I am" even if their teachers find it hard to explain the point being made. What pupils are not often taught is that the famous line from his *A Discourse of Method* in 1637 was a key text of both the technique of modern scientific method and the technology of the self. *A Discourse on Method*, moreover, was framed in respect to Descartes' own personal journey to uncover the inner truth that could lead to systematic knowledge of the exterior worlds. In the selection, this is made plain in such lines as: "As soon as my age permitted me to pass from under the control of my instructors, I entirely abandoned the study of letters and resolved no longer to seek any other science than the knowledge of myself, or of the great book of the world." *Of myself . . . / . . . of the great book of the world!* Another striking juxtaposition formulated in 1637, well before Locke and well after the age of discovery had begun. To have settled on thinking itself as the first principle of thought – "I think, therefore I am" – was also to fold the classical philosophy of being into the consciousness of self as in modernizing effect of the ground of all being – again: the great book of the world. That this axiom of modern thinking would be derived from a journey, as Descartes says, is more than poetic license. As in respect to voyages of discovery, so too with respect to the technologies of the modern self, however they are understood. For a well-measured world colonized at great distance to be imagined, the modern required a theory of self as the agent of these migrations.

If Descartes' explicit formulation of the ideal of the migrating self was relatively late in the early history of the modern system, the kernel of the ideal was evident long before in the implicits of one of the modern age's most definitive historical convergences: the invention of the moveable type press (which made mass literacy possible) after 1440; and, after 1517, the Lutheran idea of the calling of all Christian believers to found their faith on their independent reading of Scripture. These two seemingly incongruous events on either side of the turn of the sixteenth century were together the technological and popular cultural precursors of the modern theory of the migrating self.

Gutenberg's press quickly led to the modern idea of publication and hence of writing and reading as arts meant for the masses. Though the moveable type method, such as today's keyboarding, is susceptible to errors, the printing press made the reproduction of written text fast, efficient, and above all available at once in quantities sufficient to mass distribution. In the fifteenth century, however, reading literacy was still a skill available only to the elite. It was not uncommon even for members of the priestly class to lack the essentials of literacy in the sense of writing and reading. Mass literacy, and the true economic and social value of Gutenberg's invention, required the revolution by which "the people" could come into being. Printing alone, as the lesson of the East where printing had long been in practice, was that necessary but insufficient technology unto the kind of changes that would mark the modern West. As Giorgio Agamben, among others, has recently pointed out, the popular idea of "the people" came into its own in the modern era in a duplicitous relation to "the People" – which is to say the projected ideal of the popular classes as the true source of authority. Of course, democracy in the sense of the rule of the people has always been, even in modern times, at best an approximation of the ideal. What came to be *the* People depended on the formation of *a* people able, in principle, to reason; hence, the importance of literacy as a sign and condition of modern political and economic order.

The revolution that lent possibility to the ideal of a rational people was Martin Luther's radical critique of scholastic Christianity. By challenging the exclusive right of the priestly class to control and interpret the terms of salvation, Luther argued the doctrine of the priesthood of all believers – an idea that would become central to all subsequent Protestant Christianity. What was meant by the priesthood of all believers varied wildly among sectarian groups that would form in the wake of Luther's revolution. The details of the theological argument are, like most theologies, complicated and, to the strictly rational mind, absurd. But the essentials are easily summarized: if the people were to be the authors of their own faith, then what is the decisive authority that, in Foucault's words, judges the knowledge by which a believing self might emerge? Luther's answer was, famously, the Bible. For Luther, faith's calling is to be founded in holy scripture to which the believer must turn for the wisdom of faith.

The practical problem was that, with rare exception, the people in this theory were unable to read. This was mainly the result of the Roman system keeping the scriptures and the ritual language in what to ordinary people was an esoteric language, Latin, which remained aloof from translation into the common languages. Hence, by contrast, the Protestant Reformation required a good degree of literacy among the faithful which is why, theories aside, one of the Luther's enduring accomplishments was the translation of the Bible into

German. Though it would be centuries before the actual level of literacy among the masses in the modern world would be passably beyond the minimum, the revolution in popular culture was the establishment of reading as necessary to faith, hence to salvation.

From Max Weber's famous argument in *Protestant Ethic and the Spirit of Capitalism* (1904–05) comes the notion that it was Calvin, not Luther, who was the true, if inadvertent, genius of the modern individual. It is true, of course, that Luther's religion, as a social philosophy, remained traditional. Still, without Luther, Calvin would hardly have mattered, and in the sphere of culture and its technologies of the self, Luther was far the more revolutionary. According to Luther's formula, the individual believer was, effectively, the first clear and distinct migrating self. More even than with Descartes, or anyone of the time, Luther's theories entailed, as a matter of public necessity, an individual self able to believe for himself if not exactly to think for himself. The indispensable entailment of the Protestant Reformation was the general idea of the religious authority of the individual.

The importance of Gutenberg's invention of a technology capable of creating a literate people lay in wait for the legitimate value of literacy itself. Though Descartes claims to have "abandoned the study of letters" to discover the thinking self, the very idea of the thinking and migrating self presupposed a kind of knowledge of self that, by 1637, was available normally and generally as a consequence of literacy. Not everywhere, to be sure, but widely enough across the sectors of Europe to set Descartes' more or less secular idea of the thinking self in its proper historical frame.

It is far too simple to conclude that the material technologies that would define the modern world-system as it would evolve depended in a straightforward causal line from the primitive early modern technologies of self. But it is not too simple to suppose that, without the distillation of Christian ideas of pilgrimage into secularizing ideas of the self always in motion, it would be hard to imagine the voyages of discovery and, ever after, the concatenation of new material technologies that would make the fully modern world-system possible.

The material technologies that fueled the motor of the modern system were not, by any means, sprung all at once in a miraculous age of the new. The mariner's astrolabe – a primitive computer for calculating distances, depths, and heights against the relations of sun, stars, and horizon – had been in common use well before the modern era and was still a standard navigating instrument into the seventeenth century, when more refined navigational measures replaced it. The astrolabe stands as a reminder that modern technologies evolved out of classical and medieval pasts, but also as instances of ingenuity that both served the earliest voyages to the far worlds and demonstrated their limitations.

If technology is, as the word originally meant, an art, it involves the art of imagination. Locke's imaginative figuring of America as there from the beginning of the world was an artist's probe beyond the already known facts that such a place existed. Though many of modernity's new material technologies appear to be nuts and bolts instruments of travel, communication, measurement, and production, none is ever applied to hard reality without a powerful imaginative leap.

John Harrison's marine chronometer may well have set the standard for technological imagination applied to hard material engineering. The problem he set out to solve was that the calculation of longitude required a reliable clock that could function accurately on rolling seas. Harrison, who died in 1776, was a self-taught inventor who devoted the bulk of his adult life to solving this problem. His chronometers were a succession of gradually more refined instruments of which the final wonder was in effect a pocket watch. His inventions changed navigation by allowing sea captains to calculate with reasonable accuracy the time of their positions at sea relative to a standard of universal time. They were, as the selection from Dava Sobel's *Longitude* (1995) explains, a bricolage of moving parts, many of which had no actual function. Still his clocks proved the workability of a counter-weight system for time machines in rough seas where pendulum clocks were useless. Harrison's marvelous time pieces were done the disservice of being stored away exposed to the elements until early in the twentieth century, when another English craftsman spent years of his life restoring them to working order for the world to see. By then, however, the chronometer was already superseded by modern radio technologies. Yet, Harrison's inventions run on today as a symbols of the ingenuity of their inventor.

Harrison's nuts and bolts chronometers were but the material devices that advanced pre-existing technologies. By making the estimate of longitude accurate at sea, he had grasped, as others had for years before him, the crucial difference between latitude and longitude and how the difference affected the reckoning of position at sea. Early in Dava Sobel's book she explains the issue in its starkest terms: "The zero-degree of latitude is fixed by the laws of nature, while the zero-degree of longitude shifts like the sands of time." The selection from Sobel's book is the telling conclusion of the story of the establishment of Greenwich Mean Time as the prime meridian of global time-space. Latitude is the measure of parallels encircling the global east and west. They are natural in that each parallel marks a series of degrees on a circumference that, at any given degree, is exactly the same at any point along the lateral measures of global space. The equator, thus, is the pure perfect maximum latitude measure against which all others, north and south, are reckoned. The mariner need only calculate the distance by observing his position, north or south, at high noon.

Yet, as Magellan's returning crew realized upon completing their circumnavigation, global time varies according to position. Their carefully kept logs recorded a one-day difference from the local date upon their return. This meant that, as anyone moves along the lateral space of the world, time must shift because, among other facts of the matter, the navigator's relation to the sun varies not just according to latitude but also according to a measure of global positioning that will be different in degrees of distance from the equator and also in respect to some fixed position that is more or less arbitrarily agreed upon by all mariners to be the zero-degree of global time. That measure from pole to pole in discrete degrees is longitude, which as Sobel puts it "shifts like the sands of time." Longitude, thus, was invented by a measuring intelligence that used time to calibrate location in relation to global space. Harrison, says Sobel, "wrested the world's whereabouts from the stars, and locked the secret in a pocket watch."

Even the primitive astrolabe could measure spatial distances; hence, latitude. But neither the starry skies above nor the intuitive moral compass of the mariner could measure global time. The answer was effectively simple – the agreement among voyagers whatever their region or nation of origin that Greenwich Mean Time would be the temporal standard from which all other time zones (that is, arbitrarily gathered degrees set against fixed temporal measures longitude) would vary. That agreement was formalized by the world's major maritime nation in 1884 and remains fixed in place today (in spite of some temporal rogue states such as China, which claims all of China to be of one time zone). Time shifts like sand because the globe rotates daily on its own axis while on its annual orbit of the sun – hence a day anywhere on earth is a day in earth's time.

Longitude thus set the global clock and completed the ordering of global measures. It is arbitrary as to its prime but, once it was fixed by accord in 1884, longitude, a temporal measure, organized global space such that navigators could locate their positions according to the exact degrees of latitude and longitude. Longitudinal reckoning had long been a crude estimate until Harrison perfected the apt technology in the eighteenth century. He died in 1776, the beginning of the age of modernizing revolutions. It would be a good many decades before either the American or the French Revolutions would settle into versions of their current democratic forms. Along the way, the global colonial system and the inter-state wars would continue to breach the Peace of Westphalia on land and also overseas, which is to say in the struggle for authority and power in the colonial worlds.

Napoleon was a flawed genius, brilliant at land war and its administration as in the imposition of modernizing reforms during the restoration of the Empire in France. No one better advanced the civil principles of the French Revolution and few did so much to settle the metric system as the language of measurement in the modern world. The selection from Napoleon's *Maxims* on warfare, "The War Machine: Land and Sea" (our title), captures his method of consolidating traditional military theory to organize his grand army into a technology for speed and efficiency able to strike fast and hard in land war. In respect to land, he could be said to have reinvented the army and its generals as a rationalized war machine. At the same time, Napoleon overestimated the genius of the general as opposed to the sea captain:

The art of war on land is an art of genius, of inspiration. On the sea everything is definite and a matter of experience. The admiral needs only one science, navigation. .... A general never knows anything with certainty, never sees his enemy clearly and never knows where he is.

What he meant, one supposes, is that on land, however brightly the battlefield is lit by the sun or moon, there is always a valley or prominence, even a distance, behind and beyond which the enemy can marshal an attack. Napoleon himself could not see across the distances of Russia in 1812, nor through the fog at Waterloo in 1815. What he failed to understand about navigation is that everything at sea must account for time, and time requires a science – but also a global imagination. The admiral sees the enemy fleet when he is put upon but first he must find or estimate its position which can only be efficiently plotted by creative use of longitudinal reckoning which, as mariners knew for centuries, is never, even after the mariner's chronometer, an exact science. Napoleon, in this respect, whatever his modern sensibilities, belonged to an older order of global understanding. He fashioned his armies as a mechanical technology for stolid defense and lightning-fast offense on land, where (he may have been right) there are always surprises, such as the rain that gave Wellington the advantage at Waterloo. The seas were the future – for naval power, to be sure, but also for global power. Napoleon was mistaken, at least about the sea. The admiral spends most of his time never seeing anything in particular except the sudden rise of land or of an enemy's sails on the horizon.

At sea everything is measurement. The technologies of positional reckoning changed as the modern age developed but there was never a time when the mariner was not required to measure his place at sea. Land can create the illusion of a vaster obscurity as it did for the great French general, but in modern times everything of value – commodities, resources, distances, speeds, shipping channels, and all the rest – requires their equivalent of the 1884 accords that Greenwich would be the prime meridian. The progress in over two centuries after 1648 was majestic. Westphalia set in place a principle of measured differences between and among territories, but it lacked a language. As Greenwich would be the zero-degree of global time-space after 1884, so too would everything of worth on God's earth seek its zero-degree value. The modern world was neither simply physical nor human but both at once and both were modern to the extent that they were eventually brought under the rule of measurement.

Karl Marx, more enduringly than any one, described the zero-degree value as the commodity – that queer thing abounding in metaphysical subtleties. He meant that any given commodity could express the whole world of fungible values exchangeable without limit on the condition that any and all commodities are traded according to quantitative equivalencies and qualitative differences – a quarter of wheat for a bale of cotton or 50 guilders. The equivalencies, including those arbitrarily assigned to any locally accepted currency, vary over time as do the qualities, but the working assumption is that somewhere behind the differences exchanged and their variations there is a more or less stable single commodity that serves as, in effect, the zero-degree – the Greenwich Mean Time of economic values – against which all others are clocked. For Marx that commodity was human labor power. His stipulation of the zero-degree of economic and social value has always been open to dispute, but even now, so long after, it is hard to imagine a way to define a general theory of human values. Value in the modern sense is measured value and measurement, as we have seen in other spheres, and is always ultimately global but global measures depend without exception on a zero-degree standard. The quibble with Marx is on the question of whether that standard is human labor power or some other such as the liberal ideal of a pure abstract, if invisible, market. Even a god will do as a zero-degree, as often one did. But that something must stand in as the unqualified measure is without question.

On this idea in *Capital I* (1867) Marx articulated the rhymes and reasons of the capitalist order. He could as well have been speaking, without the radical if optimistic edge he lent to the ultimate fatal consequences of that order, of the modern world as such. Indeed, that is exactly what he did with Engels, just less than 20 years before, in the *Manifesto of the Communist Party* (1848) in which the deep inner reasons of capitalism were identified as the endless revolutions in which all that is sold melts away. Divorced from the corruptions the years have imputed to him and his ideas, Marx's zero-degree entails a prospect that neither liberal theory nor Marx's own quite anticipate. If the zero-degree (money or market or a god) is the condition by which all given commodities, in their several quantities, can be traded in their equivalencies according to a calculus of exchanges, then ultimately there are no qualities. In this sense, Marx, not fully appreciating the implications of his theory, was the first mature theorist of measurement. The world that trades according to well-measured rules of similarities is the ultimate, this-worldly expression of the calculus of human worth. The zero-degree of value is, thus, inescapably a pure zero.

In *Seeing Like a State* (1998), James Scott used the German forest late in the eighteenth century as the prime (though not by any means exclusive) instance of the evidence that the emerging modern state, being able only to see what it could see when it came to extractable wealth, begged, like the business firm, for relief from an infinity of local measures.

> The achievement of German forestry science in standardizing techniques for calculating the sustainable yield of commercial timber hence revenue was impressive enough. What is decisive for our purposes, however, was the next logical step in forest management. That step was to create, through careful seeding, planting, and cutting a forest that was easier for state foresters to count, manipulate, measure, and assess.

Here, consistent with but beyond Marx's original theory, Marx's political-economy is forced into a relation with Westphalia's implicit theory of the rational border between nation-states. As Scott goes on to say, the achievement, not just of forest science but of the whole modern commodity trade, was to transcend local measures in favor of more general, ultimately universal ones. When the thing measured was a bushel of produce, a barrel of oil, or a plot of land, or almost anything else, the limits on the establishment of an international standard were, as always there are, the force of locals to play with the unit itself by adjusting the size of the bushel or barrel or claiming irregularities and exceptions to measures of land and its worth. There is little the modern system can do about the plasticity of the zero-measure except to do as would be done in the zero-degree of time: States must agree to a prime meridian of value. In respect to global time, Greenwich was relatively absolute; in respect to currencies and their worth, value is plastic but relatively stable. Gold or silver, USDs or Euros — whichever is not of the essence. The agreements today are so plastic that several currencies are good enough. But for there to be values there must be prime values.

Still for the modern world-system to work as it has, or claims to have, there must be passable inter-national measures for all things in the world — their weights, their volumes and mass, their sizes, their velocities, and all else that can figure in an exchange; otherwise: no commodities and no exchange, and hence no accumulated wealth. The unstable element of the equation is, of course, measures of quality for which a currency (or, universal value form) is itself, as Marx argued, a necessary but artificial commodity in the system of exchanges. Monies represent imputed values but, even when precious metal reserves stood behind a currency, the value imputed, at the point of exchange, was not liquid. As Zygmunt Bauman has said so well, the modern capitalist order is ultimately and decisively about liquidity. Unless everything solid can be melted down exchange will freeze, growth will stop, and the system will slow and finally expire for the lack of oxygen to fuel the system when the quota between intake and output is not efficient enough to feed the body. The health of the global economic body is measured ultimately by the waste it produces. The lungs and heart cannot survive without the bladder and bowels. The problem of course is that in naturally occurring plant and animal bodies waste replenishes life. Under capitalism, waste clogs the arteries and fouls the air and water.

Still efficiency is the final measure of capital accumulation. When the ration of rationally calculated inputs (normally, labors of various kinds and resources of all possible kinds), the product output cannot generate the excess of value added to value costs. The difference is, thus, profit, which is to say waste. The system requires for the sake of profit that the real wastes of its equation not add to the input costs. The principle of efficiency was well understood long before the industrial era of modern capitalism in the mid-nineteenth century. James Watt's eighteenth-century steam engine was the technology that drove the engine faster and faster — shipping and railroads, factory production and agricultural efficiencies were thus faster and less costly in the long run than, in particular, "mere" human and animal labor. But again the material technology of the steam engine relied heavily on the imagination, notably Watt's grasp of the already by-then vaguely realized laws of thermodynamics that derived from Robert Boyle's seventeenth century laws of pressure and heat in closed spaces. In respect to the engine, the lesson of the laws was: avoid heat-loss. Thus, in the selection from Watt's 1769 patent application for the steam engine, Watt's original description of his technology states: "Newly invented method of lessening the consumption of steam and fuel in fire engines." Steam was speed wrought in the efficiencies of burning fuel in a sealed space. The seal is never perfect, but perfect enough to reduce the fuel costs while augmenting the power, hence speed, of the engine.

As steam thus generated is a liquefying process, so too was the major advance at the mid-nineteenth century – the one that made heavy industry efficient, and hence possible. Henry Bessemer's 1856 paper reports the results of the applied and experimental work that led to efficiencies in steel production. Steel was an advance over iron because, impurities removed, it was stronger and more durable. It is not surprising, thus, that this efficiency, like Watt's, involved melting. Molten iron ore burns away the impurities, leaving steel. Bessemer's process (patented in 1855) was fast and efficient:

> Thus it will be seen that by a single process, requiring no manipulation or particular skill, and with only one workman, from three to five tons of crude passes into the condition of several piles of malleable iron in from 30 to 35 minutes, with the expenditure of about one-third part of the blast now used in a finery furnace and with the consumption of no other fuel than is contained in the crude iron.

Today, in the world's largest steel mills, one workman can run the mill entirely by monitoring computer-based technologies. Everything modern is in the efficiency – reducing labor and resource costs to expel waste, thus to produce the machinery that makes the product that, now more than ever, represents but does not embody actual human labor power, which is to say: value.

In 1859, just a few years after Bessemer's paper, Charles Darwin published what very probably was the greatest – certainly the most influential and controversial – scientific work of the nineteenth century. In one sense, *On the Origin of Species* was light years removed from the technologies of Watt and Bessemer, even from the modern theory of economic and social value. Yet, like every major advance that cumulatively drove the modern economic system unrelenting toward its global mission, Darwin's *On the Origin of Species* was precisely a theory of the origin of all life in "the mystery of all mysteries." Nor should it be a surprise that while the work was not formally numeric it was meant to consider "the distribution of organic beings over the face of the globe, the first great fact which strikes us is that neither the similarity nor dissimilarity of the inhabitants of the various regions can be accounted for by their climatic and other physical conditions." Measurement measures distributions according to agreed upon rules of similarities and differences. Darwin's *Origin* was the measure of life – its origins in a mystery, its migration across the surfaces of the globe, and the evolution of its differences that exceed the terms of sheer physical circumstances. On the one hand, Darwin was author of the nineteenth-century myth that the human is a discrete and supreme aspect of life itself. On the other, he set the terms of a standard that, only now early in the twenty-first century, is dawning on human consciousness – that man, whatever else he is, is inextricably alive to the extent that he sustains a vital relation to his animal nature. Man is, at least, animal, which, as we will discuss in Part Six, is not the same as lacking a soul.

From 1500 CE, plus or minus a century or two, the modern world discovered and asserted its newness. Half a millennium and more after, the world is a very different place than it was then. But all the discoveries and settlements, inventions and other technologies of progress led as surely to trouble as to good. None succeeded in proving that the human is life unto itself. None reined in the violence and death. None assured peace within the species or in its relations with other things and beings. The modern was, or is, not nothing. It is the reality in which we dwell. But whatever good it has done, it has failed its own measures of the sphere of human life. By cutting and calculating the parts of the world into distributed parts arraigned according to their values in respect to the measure of all things, the modern was new only in the sense that it refined the methods by which the waste of life and resources is displaced from workable consciousness. Eventually, when the human puts everything to the measure of its wealth, it cannot avoid the necessity of the destruction it requires in order to assure a progress that in the long run of things amounts only to what their zero-degree standards claim for them.

Notes

1   Andre Gunder Frank (1998) *ReOrient: Global Economy in the Asia Age*, University of California Press, p. 5.
2   Immanuel Wallerstein (1974) *The Modern World System: Capitalist Agriculture and the Origins of the European World-Economy in the Sixteenth Century*, New York, San Francisco, and London: Academic Press, p. 19.
3   Michel Foucault (1988) *Technologies of the Self: A Seminar With Michel Foucault*, Amherst, MA: University of Massachusetts Press, p. 17.

The European Voyages
of Exploration and
Discovery in the
Sixteenth Century

IMMANUEL WALLERSTEIN ON THE EUROPEAN WORLD ECONOMY (1500–1991)

Immanuel Wallerstein (1930–) is a Senior Research Scholar at Yale University. In the past he has been Distinguished Professor of Sociology at the State University of New York at Binghamton and Directeur d'etudes at the Ecole des Hautes en Sciences Sociales in Paris. He is most known for his work *The Modern World-System* (1974, 1980, 1989; 3 vols) which makes the argument that the modern world-system is distinct from empire, and linked to global capitalist enterprise. This selection from that work focuses on the European capitalist system of trade that emerged in the sixteenth century as a distinct change from the system of empire.

The Modern World-System (1974)

In the late fifteenth and early sixteenth century, there came into existence what we may call a European world-economy. It was not an empire yet it was as spacious as a grand empire and shared some features with it. But it was different, and new. It was a kind of social system the world has not really known before and which is the distinctive feature of the modern world-system. It is an economic but not a political entity, unlike empires, city-states and nation-states. In fact, it precisely encompasses within its bounds (it is hard to speak of boundaries) empires, city-states, and the emerging "nation-states." It is a "world" system, not because it encompasses the whole world, but because it is larger than any juridically-defined political unit. And it is a "world-*economy*" because the basic linkage between the parts of the system is economic, although this was reinforced to some extent by cultural links and eventually, as we shall see, by political arrangements and even confederal structures.

An empire, by contrast, is a political unit. For example, Shmuel Eisenstadt has defined it this way:

> The term "empire" has normally been used to designate a political system encompassing wide, relatively high centralized territories, in which the center, as embodied both in the person of the emperor and in the central political institutions, constituted an autonomous entity. Further, although empires have usually been based on traditional legitimation, they have often embraced some wider, potentially universal political and cultural orientation that went beyond that of any of their component parts.[1]

Empires in this sense were a constant feature of the world scene for 5,000 years. There were continuously several such empires in various parts of the world at any given point of time. The political centralization of an empire was at one and the same time its strength and its weakness. Its strength lay in the fact that it guaranteed economic flows from the periphery to the center by force (tribute and taxation) and by monopolistic advantages in trade. Its weakness lay in the fact that the bureaucracy made necessary by the political structure tended to absorb too much of the profit, especially as repression and exploitation bred revolt which increased military expenditures.[2] Political empires are a primitive means of economic domination. It is the social achievement of the modern world, if you will, to have invented the technology that makes it possible to increase the flow of the surplus from the lower strata to the upper strata, from the periphery to the center, from the majority to the minority, by eliminating the "waste" of too cumbersome a political superstructure.

I have said that a world-economy is an invention of the modern world. Not quite. There were world-economies before. But they were always transformed into empires: China, Persia, Rome. The modern world-economy might have gone in that same direction – indeed it has sporadically seemed as though it would – except that the techniques of modern capitalism and the technology of modern science, the two being somewhat linked as we know, enabled this world-economy to thrive, produce, and expand without the emergence of a unified political structure.[3]

What capitalism does is offer an alternative and more lucrative source of surplus appropriation (at least more lucrative over a long run). An empire is a mechanism for collecting tribute, which in Frederic Lane's pregnant image, "means payments received for protection, but payments in excess of the cost of producing the protection."[4] In a capitalist world-economy, political energy is used to secure monopoly rights (or as near to it as can be achieved). The state becomes less the central economic enterprise than the means of assuring certain terms of trade in other economic transactions. In this way, the operation of the market (not the *free* operation but nonetheless its operation) creates incentives to increased productivity and all the consequent accompaniment of modern economic development. The world-economy is the arena within which these processes occur.

A world-economy seems to be limited in size. Ferdinand Fried observed that:

> If one takes account of all the factors, one reaches the conclusion that the space of the 'world' economy in Roman antiquity could be covered in about 40 to 60 days, utilizing the best means of transport. . . . Now, in our times [1939], it also takes 40 to 60 days to cover the space of the modern world economy, if one uses the normal channels of transportation for merchandise.[5]

And Fernand Braudel adds that this could be said to be the time span of the Mediterranean world in the sixteenth century.[6]

The origins and the functioning of such a 60-day European world-economy[7] in the sixteenth century is our concern here. It is vital to remember, however, that Europe was not the only world-economy at the time. There were others.[8] But Europe alone embarked on the path of capitalist development which enabled it to outstrip these others. How and why did this come about? Let us start by seeing what happened in the world in the three centuries prior to 1450. In the twelfth century, the Eastern Hemisphere contained a series of empires and small worlds, many of which were interlinked at their edges with each other. At that time, the Mediterranean was one focus of trade where Byzantium, Italian city-states, and to some extent parts of northern Africa met. The Indian Ocean–Red Sea complex formed another such focus. The Chinese region was a third. The Central Asian land mass from Mongolia to Russia was a fourth. The Baltic area was on the verge of becoming a fifth. Northwest Europe was however a very marginal area in economic terms. The principal social mode or organization there was what has come to be called feudalism.

We must be very clear what feudalism was not. It was not a "natural economy," that is, an economy of self-subsistence. Western Europe feudalism grew out of the disintegration of an empire, a disintegration which was never total in reality or even *de jure*.[9] The myth of the Roman Empire still provided a certain cultural and even legal coherence to the area. Christianity served as a set of parameters within which social action took place. Feudal Europe was a "civilization," but not a world-system.

Notes

1   S.N. Eisenstadt, 'Empires,' International Encyclopedia of the Social Sciences (New York: Macmillan and Free Press, 1968), V, 41.

2   A discussion of the internal contradictions of empires which account for their decline is to be found in S.N. Eisenstadt, 'The Causes of Disintegration and Fall of Empires: Sociological and Historical Analyses,' Diogenes, No 34, Summer 1961, 82–107.

3   And it was a mark of political wisdom to realize this. The first such sign of wisdom was the refusal of Venice in the thirteenth century to take over the political burdens of the Byzantine Empire. Mario Abrate observes:

>   'The political organism which emerged from the Fourth Crusade, the Eastern Latin Empire, placed its entire hope of survival on the continuity of its links with the West.'
>   'Venice, the naval power which had supported the Crusade, and furnished the naval means to conduct it, did not wish to burden itself with the political governance of the Empire (Doge Enrico Dandolo refused in fact the throne that was offered to him) but assured itself, and that almost automatically, of the monopoly of naval communications and markets for all the territories controlled by the new Latin Dominion.' 'Creta, colonia veneziana nei secoli XIII–XV,' Economia e storia, IV, 3, lugl.sett. 1957, 251.

4   Frederic C. Lane, 'The Economic Meaning of War and Protection' in Venice and History (Baltimore: Johns Hopkins Press, 1966), 389.

5   Ferdinand Fried, Le tournant de l'économie mondiale (1942), cited in Fernand Braudel, La Méditerranée et le monde mediterranéen à l'époque de Philippe II, 2e édition revue et augmentée (Paris: Lib. Armand Colin, 1966), I, 339.

6   See Braudel, La Méditerranée, I, 339–340. As for Europe in the fifteenth century, Garrett Mattingly argues that it still required smaller-scale units: 'At the beginning of the fifteenth century Western society still lacked the resources to organize stable states on the national scale. On the scale of the Italian city state it could do so. Internally the smaller distances to be overcome brought the problems of transport and communication, and consequently the problems of collecting taxes and maintaining the central authority, within the range of practical solution.' Renaissance Diplomacy (London: Jonathan Cape, 1955), 59.

But, says Mattingly, this changes by the following century: '[I]n terms of commercial intercourse, or military logistics, or even of diplomatic communication, European distances were perceptibly greater in the fourteenth than in the sixteenth century.' [Ibid., p. 60].

7   'When one says "world", with reference to the sixteenth century . . . in fact, usually one means Europe by the world . . . On a world scale, geographically speaking, the Renaissance economy is a regional aspect, no doubt primordial, but nonetheless regional.' Michel Mollat, 'Y a-t-il une économie de la Renaissance?', in Actes du Colloque sur la Renaissance (Paris: Lib. Philosophique J. Vrin, 1958), 40.

8   Before the constitution of a truly world economy (still uncompleted in the twentieth century), each nucleus of population is found in the center of a communications network. . . . Each of these worlds corresponds . . . to a nucleus with a high population density. It is bounded by deserts, by seas, by virgin lands. The case of Europe and that of China are particularly clear.' Pierre Chaunu, L'expansion européenee du XIIIe au XVe siècle, Collection Nouvelle Clio, No. 26 (Paris: Presses Universitaires de France, 1969), 255.

9   Marc Bloch attacked the basic confusion head on: 'Clearly from the fact that a transaction stipulates a price in monetary equivalents or in kind, one cannot legitimately deduce, without more precise evidence, that the payment was really made or not in cash. . . .

Just as the political institutions of feudalism, characterized by a profound weakening of the State, presumed nonetheless the memory and bore the traces of a past when the State had been strong, so the economy, even when exchange had become minimal, never ended its attachment to a monetary schema, whose principles were inherited from preceding civilizations.' 'Economie-nature ou économie-argent: un pseudo-dilemme,' Annales d'histoire sociale, I, 1939, 13–14. Bloch further states:

>   'European feudalism should therefore be seen as the outcome of the violent dissolution of older societies It would in fact be unintelligible without the great upheaval of the Germanic invasions which, by forcibly uniting two societies originally at very different stages of development, disrupted both of them.' Feudal Society (Chicago, Illinois: Univ. of Chicago Press, 1961), 443.

On the issue of the 'money-economy,' see also M. M. Postan: 'Thus from the point of view of English history, and even from that of medieval and Anglo-Saxon history, the rise of the money economy in the sense of its first appearance has no historical meaning. Money was in use when documented history began, and its rise cannot be adduced as an explanation of any later phenomenon.' 'The Rise of a Money Economy.' *Economic History Review*, XIV, 2, 1944, 127.

Immanuel Wallerstein (1974) *The Modern World-System: Capitalist Agriculture and the Origins of the European World-Economy in the Sixteenth Century I*, New York, San Francisco, London: Academic Press, pp. 15–17.

SCANDINAVIAN PROBES TO NORTH AMERICA (c. 1000)

Vikings are often credited as being the first to discover pelagic navigation and to sail by astrological charts, as well as being famed ship builders. Their navigational skills and need for trade led to the discovery of Greenland in 876. In part, mass migrations from Norway began with the consolidation of power by King Harald in 872. These migrations led to the formation of a thriving culture in Iceland, including the establishment there of the first parliamentary system of government, the Althing. Eirik the Red was banned from Norway and Iceland and decided to move to Greenland, settling there in 982 and giving the appealing name to attract more settlers. Eirik's son Leif Ericson (*c.* 970–*c.* 1020) is thought to be the first European to visit North America in 1000. Much of what is known about these events is from two Norse sagas: The Graenlendinga Saga, and Eirik's Saga. Eirik's Saga was written much later around 1200–1300, probably from the point of view of the first settler, Leif's brother Thorfinn Karlsefni. While some historians still maintain Columbus to be the first European explorer, archeological evidence confirms the sagas about the establishment of a Norse colony at what is now L'Anse aux Meadows, Newfoundland, Canada. The sagas detail extensively the land, climate, and trade with the Native Americans. Norse men called the western land "Vinland" for the presence of grapes, but they detail other economic assets such as timber and skins. Historians surmise that a climatic event known as "The Little Ice Age" lasting from the twelfth to the fourteenth century may have made life in the northern climates too difficult to sustain a colony and trade with North America and the colony was abandoned.

The Saga of Eirik the Red

Eirik had a wife who was named Thjodhild, and two sons; the one was named Thorstein, and the other Leif. These sons of Eirik were both promising men. Thorstein was then at home with his father; and there was at that time no man in Greenland who was thought so highly of as he. Leif had sailed to Norway, and was there with King Olaf Tryggvason.

Now, when Leif sailed from Greenland during the summer, he and his men were driven out of their course to the Sudreyjar. They were slow in getting a favourable wind from this place, and they stayed there a long time during the summer . . . reaching Norway about harvest-tide.

He joined the body-guard of King Olaf Tryggvason, and the king formed an excellent opinion of him, and it appeared to him that Leif was a well-bred man. Once upon a time the king entered into conversation with Leif, and asked him, 'Dost thou purpose sailing to Greenland in summer?'

Leif answered, 'I should wish so to do, if it is your will.' The king replied, 'I think it may well be so; thou shalt go my errand, and preach Christianity in Greenland.'

Leif said that he was willing to undertake it, but that, for himself, he considered that message a difficult one to proclaim in Greenland. But the king said that he knew no man who was better fitted for the work than he. 'And thou shalt carry,' said he, 'good luck with thee in it.' 'That can only be,' said Leif, 'if I carry yours with me.'

Leif set sail as soon as he was ready. He was tossed about a long time out at sea, and lighted upon lands of which before he had no expectation. There were fields of wild wheat, and the vine-tree in full growth. There were also the trees which were called maples; and they gathered of all this certain tokens; some trunks so large that they were used in house-building. Leif came upon men who had been shipwrecked, and took them home with him, and gave them sustenance during the winter. Thus did he show his great munificence and his graciousness when he brought Christianity to the land, and saved the shipwrecked crew. He was called Leif the Lucky. [. . .]

After this there was much talk about making ready to go to the land which Leif had discovered.

The Saga of Eirik the Red (1880) English, trans. J. Sephton, from the original '*Eiríks saga rauða*' Source: Icelandic Saga Database, http://www.sagadb.org/eiriks_saga_rauda.en

IBERIAN DISCOVERIES OF THE AMERICAS (THE LONG SIXTEENTH CENTURY)

Felipe Fernández-Armesto (1950–) is a British historian who currently holds the Prince of Asturias Chair in Spanish Culture and Civilization at Tufts University and is a member of the Faculty of Modern History at Oxford University. He was formerly the Professor of Global Environmental History, Queen Mary, University of London and Director of the Programme in Global History, Institute of Historical Research, University of London. In *The Americas: A Hemispheric History*, Armesto argues that the Americas cannot be understood in isolation, but must be taken as a cultural whole. In this selection, he looks at the Iberian influence in colonizing South America, and the effect of trade not only on new agriculture and economic goods back to Europe, but also around the Americas as a whole.

The Americas: A Hemispheric History (2003)

Long-range trade, on a scale unimaginable before the European conquests, expanded the area of cultural exchange to embrace the whole hemisphere. It is not generally realized that in the colonial New World precolonial patterns of exchange often remained intact; European merchants joined existing trading communities, extending the reach or increasing the volume of traffic, enhancing what Indian Ocean venturers called "country trades," which involved local or regional exchanges that never touched Europe. In colonial North America, trade in deerskins and beaver pelts extended precolonial practice. The *coureurs des bois* and buckskin-clad frontiersmen slotted into an existing framework, which linked hunting grounds and routes of trade and tribute. The Huron, farmers and traders who did not need to hunt except as means of traditional exercise and dietary supplement, were the middlemen of the early-seventeenth-century fur trade, supplying French buyers in Québec. During the 1620s they supplied ten to twelve thousand pelts a year. A few years ago I stumbled across a fascinating document, now over four hundred years old, from colonial Venezuela. It had ended up in – of all places – the Public Record Office in London, where, presumably, it had arrived via an English pirate ship, which must have captured the mail vessel in which, in about 1594, the document was bound for Spain. It explains how Spanish entrepreneurs took part in a profitable canoe-borne trade in local textiles, natural pharmaceuticals, and dyestuffs along the coast of Venezuela in the 1590s. Similarly, the economy that sustained the conquerors of Yucatán was no trans-oceanic affair of precious goods but an extension of the age-old trade with central Mexico, based largely on cacao for consumption in Mexico City.

Of course, Spanish activity was not confined to modest ventures of these kinds, along traditional grooves. The Spanish monarchy was a great inaugurator of new intra-American trade routes. New cities, founded in places never settled on a large scale before, especially on the Pacific and Atlantic coasts, became magnets for the supply of foodstuffs, cotton textiles, and building materials. The conquest of Peru from 1527 to 1533 demanded a new transcontinental route across the Isthmus of Panama, which became, like the alternative later opened from Bolivia to the Atlantic via the River Plate, a major silver-bearing artery of the Spanish Empire. The new mining ventures in remote hinterlands were served by mule-train routes, which the indigenous civilizations had never required. The conquest of much of Chile in the mid-sixteenth century stimulated the creation of a heroic new seaborne route, far into the Pacific, to overcome the Humboldt Current; it took longer for sailing ships to get from Lima to Concepción than from Seville to Santo Domingo.

The slow but inexorable spread of Spanish frontiers brought regions formerly unknown to one another into touch; the link between Mexico and Peru is the most startling case, since it seems incredible – yet true – that the civilizations of those areas never had any significant mutual contact until the Spaniards arrived. Although the places Spaniards occupied in New Mexico, Arizona, and Texas had shown some signs of Mexican cultural influences in the past, California was a genuinely new discovery, where Spanish missions in the eighteenth century created for the first time ventures in settlement and agriculture that made the region a potential trading partner for other parts of the monarchy. It would have been possible for indigenous merchants to navigate the Amazon and the Orinoco before the coming of the Spaniards, but as far as we know, they never did so. Those mighty and mysterious waterways were not fully exploited as arteries of commerce until well into the seventeenth century, after the efforts of such heroic explorers as Pedro Teixeira, who in 1639 demonstrated that the Amazon could be navigated upriver from the Atlantic to the vicinity of Quito, or Miguel de Ochogavia, "the Columbus of the Apure," who in 1647 celebrated his own achievement in doggerel:

> I came, I saw, I conquered, and returned in glory
> From Orinoco – crystals cleft and fears allayed.
>
> To God I dedicate, in thanks, my wondrous story,
>   To you, my readers, all the benefits to trade.

Historians of the new commerce opened up by the Spanish Empire have traditionally concentrated on the world-changing transoceanic trades: the *carrera de Indias*, which linked Spain to America and injected Europe's specie-starved economies with veins of bullion; the slave suppliers' *asientos*, which let other European merchants into the Spanish Main and linked the Americas to Africa; and the route of the Manila galleon, which made an annual crossing of the Pacific to Acapulco, facilitating the direct exchange of Mexican silver for Chinese manufactures. But from the point of view of American history, the new *intra*-American ventures were more important; the routes laced together formerly sundered parts of the hemisphere, making it possible to think of an ever-bigger area as a whole. In North America the fur traders – though Eurasian markets were overwhelmingly the ultimate destination of their wares – were also developers of "country trades," gradually pushing their supply routes further into the interior. Toward the end of the colonial period it was the development of the Mississippi–Missouri river system as a new highway of trade that made the Louisiana question so vital and led to the bewildering turnover in sovereignty claims, until they were resolved in favor of the United States in 1803.

Trade's tendency to mesh ever-growing parts of the Americas together accelerated in the postcolonial period. Richard Henry Dana's famous experience of his *Two Years Before the Mast* (1840) illustrates the remarkable initiative that linked California and New England by sea. After a voyage around the continent via Cape Horn – a notoriously backbreaking route that compelled sailors to strain at the yards, hauling to beat the wind – they stretched hides on the beach near Los Angeles and attended the wedding of a Yankee businessman, tight-lipped and stovepipe-hatted, to a beguiling señorita; this was how California began to be linked, culturally and commercially, into the life of the United States before the continent could be safely or reliably crossed by land. The meshing and melding of the Americas continued with the pioneers – explorers, scientists, trappers, Jesuits, Mormons, and miners – who painfully picked out transcontinental and interriver routes in the early nineteenth century. The wagon trains and railway surveyors followed.

Where trade routes grow, transfers of biota follow. The ecological exchanges that accompanied and followed colonialism happened across the Americas as well as across the oceans. Today the same varieties of maize are grown in North Dakota as in Mexico and Argentina. Turkeys, unknown outside Mesoamerica at the time of the conquest, have become the Thanksgiving Day dish of the United States. Chiles have conquered northern palates. The defining ingredients of Mexican cuisine stake out ever more of the culinary territory. Chili is the hot brand of this cuisine, corn and black beans its solid symbols; limes provide its lashings; filmy expanses of cheese form its flag. Chili con carne is its signature dish. Chili is part of the story of the Americanization of America, made from the repertoire of ingredients that predated the American annexation of the Southwest and that, since then, have gradually conquered the conquerors.

Felipe Fernández-Armesto (2003) *The Americas: A Hemispheric History*, New York: The Modern Library, pp. 90–95.

ENGLISH SETTLEMENTS IN NORTH AMERICA (1620–1691)

The English colonial settlement at Plymouth (1620–1691) is one of the first permanent English settlements in North America. The land was surveyed by Captain John Smith and settled by a group of English religious dissidents known colloquially as the Pilgrims. Unlike much of the scattered settlements along the northeastern coast, which were primarily fishing, logging, and hunting/trapping camps, and the major settlement at Jamestown, which was primarily entrepreneurial in nature, the Plymouth Colony was established as a religious haven for a separatist group from the English Anglican Church. William Bradford (1590–1657) was one of the community leaders, and eventually elected governor of the colony. His diaries from 1620 to 1647 were published under the title *History of Plymouth Plantation*, and give an account of the mundane reality of life in the colony, including assistance provided by a Native American, Squanto, and an allusion to the celebration now known as Thanksgiving – an emblem of what is now considered to be typically "American."

History of Plymouth Plantation

In this month of *April* whilst they were bussie about their seed, their Gov[r] (M[r]. John Carver[1]) came out of y[e] feild very sick, it being a hott day; he complained greatly of his head, and lay downe, and within a few howers his sences failed, so as he never spake more till he dyed, which was within a few days after. Whoss death was much lamented, and caused great heavines amongst them, as ther was cause. He was buried in y[e] best maner they could, with some vollies of shott by all that bore armes; and his wife, being a weak woman, dyed within 5. or 6. weeks after him.

Shortly after William Bradford was chosen Gove[r] in his stead, and being not yet recovered of his ilnes, in which he had been near y[e] point of death, Isaak Allerton was chosen to be an Asistante unto him, who, by renewed election every year, continued sundry years togeather,[2] which I hear note once for all.

May 12. was y[e] first mariage in this place,[3] which, according to y[e] laudable custome of y[e] Low-Cuntries, in which they had lived, was thought most requisite to be performed by the magistrate, as being a civill thing, upon which many questions aboute inheritances doe depende, with other things most proper to their cognizans, and most consonante to y[e] scripturs, Ruth 4. and no wher found in y[e] gospell to be layed on y[e] ministers as a part of their office. "This decree or law about mariage was published by y[e] Stats of y[e] Low-Cuntries An[o]: 1590. That those of any religion, after lawfull and open publication, coming before y[e] magistrats, in y[e] Town or Stat-house, were to be orderly (by them) maried one to another." Petets Hist.[4] fol: 1029. And this practiss hath continued amongst, not only them, but hath been followed by all y[e] famous churches of Christ in these parts to this time, – An[o]: 1646.

Haveing in some sorte ordered their bussines at home, it was thought meete to send some abroad to see their new freind Massasoyet, and to bestow upon him some gratuitie to bind him y[e] faster unto them; as also that hearby they might veiw y[e] countrie, and see in what maner he lived, what strength he had aboute him, and how ye ways were to his place, if at any time they should have occasion. So ye 2. *of July*[5] they sente M^r. Edward Winslow & M^r. Hopkins, with ye foresaid Squanto for ther guid, who gave him a suite of cloaths, and a horsemans coate, with some other small things, which were kindly accepted; but they found but short comõns, and came both weary and hungrie home. For ye Indeans used then to have nothing so much corne as they have since ye English have stored them with their hows, and seene their industrie in breaking up new grounds therwith. *They found his place to be* 40. *myles from hence*, ye soyle good, & ye people not many, being dead and abundantly wasted in ye late great mortalitie which fell in all these parts aboute *three years* before ye coming of ye English, wherin thousands of them dyed, they not being able to burie one another; ther sculs and bones were found in many places lying still above ground, where their houses & dwellings had been; a very sad spectackle to behould. But they brought word that ye Narighansets lived but on ye other side of that great bay, & were a strong people, and many in number, living compacte togeather, and had not been at all touched with this wasting plague.

Aboute y^e *later end of this month*, one John Billington[6] lost him selfe in ye woods, & wandered up and downe some 5. days, living on beries and what he could find. At length he light on an Indean plantation, 20. mils south of this place, called *Manamet*, they conveid him furder of, to *Nawsett*, among those peopl that had before set upon ye English when they were costing, whilest ye ship lay at ye Cape, as is before noted. But ye Gove^r caused him to be enquired for among ye Indeans, and at length Massassoyt sent word wher he was, and ye Gove^r sent a shalop for him, & had him delivered. Those people also came and made their peace; and they gave full satisfaction to those whose corne they had found & taken when they were at Cap-Codd.[7]

Thus ther peace and aquaintance was pretty well establisht wth the natives aboute them; and ther was an other Indean called *Hobamack* come to live amongst them, a proper lustie man, and a man of accounte for his vallour & parts amongst ye Indeans, and continued very faithfull and constant to ye English till he dyed. He & Squanto being gone upon bussines amonge ye Indeans, at their returne (whether it was out of envie to them or malice to the English) ther was a Sachem called Corbitant, alyed to Massassoyte, but never any good freind to ye English to this day, mett with them at an Indean towne caled Namassakett 14 miles to ye west of this place, and begane to quarell wth them, and offered to stabe Hobamack; but being a lusty man, he cleared him selfe of him, and came runing away all sweating and tould ye Govr what had befalne him, and he feared they had killed Squanto, for they threatened them both, and for no other cause but because they were friends to ye English, and servisable unto them. Upon this ye Gove^r taking counsell, it was conceivd not fitt to be borne; for if they should suffer their friends & messengers thus to be wronged, they should have none would cleave unto them, or give them any inteligence, or doe them serviss afterwards; but nexte they would fall upon them selves. Whereupon it was resolved to send ye Captaine and 14. men well armed, and to goe and fall upon them in ye night; and if they found that Squanto was kild, to cut of Corbitants head, but not to hurt any but those that had a hand in it. Hobamack was asked if he would goe & be their guid, and bring them ther before day. He said he would, and bring them to ye house wher the man lay, and show them which was he. So they set forth ye 14. *of August*, and beset ye house round; the Captin giving charg to let none pass out, entred ye house to search for him. But he was goone away that day, so they mist him; but understood ye Squanto was alive, & that he had only threatened to kill him, and made an offer to stabe him but did not. So they withheld and did no more hurte, & ye people came trembling, and brought them the best provissions they had, after they were aquainted by Hobamack what was only intended. Ther was 3.[8] sore wounded which broak out of ye house, and asaid to pass through ye garde. These they brought home with them, & they had their wounds drest and cured, and sente home. After this they had many gratulations from diverce sachims, and much firmer peace; yea, those of ye Iles of Capawack sent to make frendship; and this Corbitant him selfe used ye mediation of Massassoyte to make his peace, but was shie to come neare them a longe while after.

After this, ye 18. of Sepemb^r: they sente out ther shalop to the Massachusets, with 10. men, and Squanto for their guid and interpreter, to discover and veiw that bay, and trade with ye natives; the which they performed, and found kind entertainement. The people were much affraid of ye Tarentins, a people to ye eastward which used to come in harvest time and take away their corne, & many times kill their persons. They returned in saftie, and brought home a good quanty of beaver, and made reporte of ye place, wishing they had been ther seated; (but it seems ye Lord, who assignes to all men ye bounds of their habitations, had apoynted it for an other use.) And thus they found y[e] Lord to be with them in all their ways, and to blesse their outgoings and incomings, for which let his holy name have y[e] praise for ever, to all posteritie.[9]

They begane now to gather in y[e] small harvest they had, and to fitte up their houses and dwellings against winter, being all well recovered in health and strength, and had all things in good plenty; for as some were thus imployed in affaires abroad, others were exersised in fishing, aboute codd, & bass, & other fish, of which y[e] tooke good store, of which every family had their portion. All y[e] somer ther was no wante. And now begane to come in store of foule, as winter aproached, of which this place did abound when they came first (but afterward decreased by degrees). And besids water foule, ther was great store of wild Turkies, of which they tooke many, besids venison, &c. Besids they had aboute a peck a meale a weeke to a person, or now since harvest, Indean corne to y[t] proportion. Which made many afterwards write so largly of their plenty hear to their friends in England, which were not fained, but true reports.[10]

In Novemb[r], about y[t] time twelfe month that them selves came, ther came in a small ship[11] to them unexpected or loked for,[12] in which came M[r]. Cushman (so much spoken of before) and with him 35. persons[13] to remaine & live in y[e] plantation; which did not a litle rejoyce them. And they when they came a shore and found all well, and saw plenty of vitails in every house, were no less glade. For most of them were lusty yonge men, and many of them wild enough, who litle considered whither or aboute what they wente, till they came into y[e] harbore at Cap-Codd, and ther saw nothing but a naked and barren place. They then begane to thinke what should become of them, if the people here were dead or cut of by y[e] Indeans. They begane to consulte (upon some speeches that some of y[e] sea-men had cast out) to take y[e] sayls from y[e] yeard least y[e] ship should gett away and leave them ther. But y[e] m[r]. hereing of it, gave them good words, and tould them if any thing but well should have befallne y[e] people hear, he hoped he had vitails enough to cary them to Virginia, and whilst he had a bitt they should have their parte; which gave them good satisfaction. So they were all landed; but ther was not so much as bisketcake or any other victialls[14] for them, neither had they any beding, but some sory things they had in their cabins, nor pot, nor pan, to drese any meate in; nor overmany cloaths, for many of them had brusht away their coats & cloaks at Plimoth as they came. But ther was sent over some burching-lane[15] suits in y[e] ship, out of which they were supplied. The plantation was glad of this addition of strength, but could have wished that many of them had been of beter condition, and all of them beter furnished with provissions; but y[t] could not be helpte.

Notes

1 What is known concerning Carver is derived from this History, Mourt's Relation, and Morton's Memorial. Contrary to the general impression, he left no descendants. See list of passengers in the Mayflower, in the Appendix, No. I. – ED.

2 In 1624, it will be seen, the Assistants were increased to five, giving the Governor a double voice. – ED.

3 This was the marriage of Edward Winslow, – whose former wife, Elizabeth, died on the 24th of March preceding, – to Mrs. Susannah White, the mother of Peregrine and the widow of William White, who died on the twenty-first of February. See Prince, 1. 76, 98, 103, 105. – ED.

4 The work here cited is probably "La grande Chronique ancienne et moderne de Holland, Zelande, Westfrise, Utrecht," &c., by Jean-François le Petit, 1601 and 1611. No copy of this work exists in any of the public libraries in this neighborhood. – ED.

5 For a full account of this visit to Massasoit, written probably by Winslow, see Mourt, in Young, pp. 202–213. It is there stated that the party set forward on their journey the 10th of June, which Prince thinks an error, and follows Bradford. – ED.

6 He was the brother of Francis, who discovered Billington Sea, and a son of the notorious John. – ED.

7 For the narrative of the expedition in search of the boy Billington, see Mourt, in Young, pp. 214–218. There is a discrepancy in the dates, but Prince follows this History. – ED.

8 "One man and a woman that were wounded went home with us." Mourt, in Young, where is a more full narrative of this visit to Namasket. – ED.

9 For a more full "relation of our voyage to the Massachusetts, and what happened there," see Mourt, in Young, pp. 224–229. – ED.

10 Reference is here made, doubtless, to letters of Winslow and Hilton, sent to England by the Fortune, in which they give a flattering description of the country, and speak of the colony as in a prosperous condition. "We are so far free from

want," writes the former, "that we often wish you partakers of our plenty." Winslow's letter was printed in Mourt's Relation, which was probably sent over at the same time. Hilton's letter first appeared in New England's Trials. – ED.

11 The Fortune, of fifty-five tons. She sailed from London "in the beginning of July, but it was the end of August ere they could pass Plymouth, and arrived at New Plymouth in New England the eleventh of November." Smith's New England's Trials, p. 16. – ED.

12 She came yᵉ 9. to yᵉ Cap.

13 For a list of the passengers who came in the Fortune, see Young, p. 235; Russell's Pilgrim Memorials, pp. 151, 153. – ED.

14 Nay, they were faine to spare yᵉ shipe some to carry her home.

15 "*Birchover lane*, so called of *Birchover*, the first builder and owner thereof, now corruptly called *Birchin* lane.
"This lane and the high street near adjoining, hath been inhabited (for the most part) with wealthy Drapers, from Birchover's lane on that side the street, down to the *stockes*. In the reign of Henry the sixth, had ye (for the most part) dwelling there, Frippers or Upholders, that sold apparel and old household stuff." Stow's Survey of London, ed. 1633, p. 215. – ED.

William Bradford *History of Plymouth Plantation*, edited by Charles Deane, reprinted from the Massachusetts Historical Collections. Google Books, pp. 100–106.

IBERIAN CIRCUMNAVIGATION OF THE WORLD: FERDINAND MAGELLAN (1519–1521)

Ferdinand Magellan (1480–1521) was born Portuguese, but after disgrace in the court became a subject of the Spanish to lead an expedition to the Spice Islands. The 1494 Treaty of Tordesillas divided the non-Christian world, most of it unseen by European eyes, between Portugal and Spain, forcing the Spanish to discover a western trade route to Asia. Magellan set out with five ships and 237 men in 1519, eventually reaching the Philippines in 1521. They established a camp on Homonhon Island, and the local chief converted to Christianity. Magellan had a plan to use this as a base, and to subvert other local leaders to Christian rule, beginning with the neighboring island (known as Mactan). Some 1,500 Mactans led by Datu Lapu-lapu easily repelled Magellan and his total force of 49 men, and Magellan was killed in the battle. Juan Sebastián Elcano took over as commander of the expedition, eventually returning to Spain with one ship, and 18 of the original 237 men, completing the first circumnavigation of the world. Magellan, because of a previous expedition to the east, became the first man to cross all the meridians of the world. The log book from Magellan's voyage survives, and was important as a contribution to understanding global time as critical to longitude, as well as a testament of the cultural imperialism and the implicit dogmatic domination of the age of exploration.

First Voyage Around the World

The King of Mauthan, seeing our men coming, draws up about three thousand of his subjects in the field, and Magellan draws up his on the shore, with their guns and warlike engines, though only a few; and though he saw that he was far inferior to the enemy in number, yet he thought it better to fight this warlike race, which made use of lances and other long weapons, than either to return or to use the soldiers from Subuth. So he orders his men to be of good cheer and brave hearts, and not to be alarmed at the number of the enemy, for they had often seen, as formerly, so in quite recent times, two hundred Spaniards in the island of Yucatan put sometimes two or three hundred thousand men to flight. But he pointed out to the Subuth islanders that he had brought them, not to fight, but to watch their bravery and fighting power (robur in acie). So, having charged the enemy, both sides fought valiantly: but, as the enemy were more numerous, and used longer weapons, with which they did our men much damage, Magellan himself was at last thrust through and slain. But the rest of our men, though they did not seem quite conquered, yet retreated, having lost their leader. And the enemy dared not follow them, as they were retreating in good order.

So the Spaniards, having lost their admiral, Magellan, and seven of their comrades, returned to Subuth, where they chose another commander, John Serrano, a man not to be despised. He immediately renewed with fresh gifts the alliance that had been made with the King of Subuth, and promised to subdue the King of Mauthan.

Magellan had a slave, born in the Moluccas, whom he had bought in Malacca some time back; this man was a perfect master of the Spanish language, and, with the assistance of one of the islanders of Subuth as interpreter, who knew the language of the Moluccas, our men managed all their communications. This slave had been present at the battle of Mauthan, and had received some slight wounds in it. For which reason he lay all day long nursing himself. Serrano, who could manage nothing without him, spoke to him very harshly, and told him that he had not ceased to be a slave and bondsman because Magellan was dead, but that the yoke of slavery would be heavier, and that he would be severely flogged unless he did the services required of him more zealously.

This slave conceived an intense hatred of us from these words; but, concealing his anger, he went a few days after to the Chief of Subuth, and told him that the greed of the Spaniards was insatiable, that they had resolved and determined, after they had conquered the King of Mauthan, to make a quarrel with him and take him away prisoner, and there was no other remedy possible than to anticipate their treachery by treachery. The savage believed it all. He made peace secretly with the King of Mauthan and the others, and they plotted our destruction. Serrano, the commander, with all the rest of his officers, who were about twenty-seven in number, were invited to a solemn banquet. They, suspecting no evil – for the savages had cunningly dissimulated in everything – land, careless and unsuspecting, as men who were going to dine with the chief would do. Whilst they were feasting they were set upon by those who had been placed in ambush. Shouts were raised on all sides, and news flew to the ships that our men were murdered, and that everything on the island was hostile to us. Our men see from the ships that the beautiful cross which they had hoisted on a tree was hurled to the ground, and kicked to pieces by the savages with great fury. But the remaining Spaniards, who had stopped on board, when they knew of their comrades' murder, feared some still greater treachery. Wherefore, when they had weighed anchor, they begin to set sail quickly. Shortly after, Serrano was brought down to the shore bound most cruelly, and he begged them to redeem him from so harsh a captivity. He said he had prevailed upon them to permit his being ransomed, if our men would only do it.

Though our men thought it shameful to leave their commander in this way, yet, fearing fraud and treachery, they put out to sea, leaving Serrano on the shore, weeping bitterly, and imploring the help and assistance of his fellow-countrymen with great and grievous lamentation. The Spaniards sailed along, sad and anxious, having lost their commander and their shipmates, not only alarmed by their loss and by the slaughter of their mates, but because their number was reduced so low that it was quite insufficient for the management of three ships. Wherefore they hold a council, and, having taken the votes, they agree that there was nothing better to do than to burn some one of the three ships, and keep only two.

CHRONOLOGY
OF THE
FIRST VOYAGE ROUND THE WORLD

Magellan arrives at Seville	–	–	–	–	–	October 20,	1518
Magellan's fleet sails from Seville	–	–	–	Monday,[1]	August 10,		1519
Magellan sails from San Lucar de Barrameda,		–	–	Tuesday,	September 20,		,,
„ arrives at Tenerife	–	–	–	–	–	September 26,	,,
„ sails from Teuerife	–	–	–	–	Monday,	October 3,	,,
„ arrives at Rio de Janeiro	–	–	–	–	–	December 13,	,,
„ sails from Rio	–	–	–	–	–	December 26,	,,
„ sails from Rio de la Plata	–	–	–	–	–	February 2,	1520
„ arrives at Port St. Julian	–	–	–	–	–	March 31,	,,
Eclipse of Sun	–	–	–	–	–	April 17,	,,
Loss of *Santiago*							
Magellan sails from Port St. Julian	–	–	–	–	August 24,		,,
„ sails from river of Sauta Cruz	–	–	–	–	October 18,		,,
„ makes Cape of the Virgins, entrance of Straits	–			–	October 21,		,,
Desertion of *San Antonio*	–	–	–	–	November		,,
Magellan issues from Straits into the Pacific,	–		–	Wednesday,	November 28,		,,
Magellan fetches San Pablo Island	–	–	–	–	January 24,		1521
„ fetches Tiburones Island	–	–	–	–	February 4,		,,
„ reaches the Ladrone Islands,	–		–	Wednesday,	March 6,		,,
„ reaches Samar Island of the Philippines	–		–	Saturday,	March 16,		,,
„ reaches Mazzava Island,	–	–	–	–	Thursday,	March 28,	,,
„ arrives at Sebu Island	–	–	–	–	–	April 7,	,,
Death of Magellan at Matan	–	–	–	–	Saturday,	April 27,	,,
Burning of *Conception*	–	–	–	–	–	May,	,,
Arrival of *San Antonio* at Seville	–	–	–	–	–	May 6,	,,
Arrival of *Victoria* and *Trinity* at Tidore,	–	–	–	Friday,	November 8,		,,
Victoria sails from Tidore	–	–	–	–	–	December 21,	,,
„ discovers Amsterdam Island,	–	–	–	Tuesday,	March 18,		1522
„ doubles the Cape of Good Hope	–	–	–	–	May 18,[1]		,,
„ arrives at Cape Verde Islands,[2]	–	–	–	Wednesday,	July 9,		,,
„ arrives at Sau Lucar	–	–	–	–	Saturday,[2]	September 6,	,,
„ casts anchor at Seville	–	–	–	–	Monday,[2]	September 8,	,,
Thanksgiving at Church of Our Lady of Victory	–		–	Tuesday,[2]	September 9,		,,

1 The 10th of August was a Wednesday, and Monday was the 8th of August: all the other dates of the week and month agree and are consistent with each other.

2 According to Albo's Log-Book; according to Pigafetta, May 6.

3 These dates are according to the ship's time, which differed by a day from the time at the Cape Verde Islands and Seville.

Ferdinand Magellan *First Voyage Around the World*, pp. Chronology and 200–202.

THE PEACE OF WESTPHALIA (1648)

The Peace of Westphalia is a term given to the collective treaties of Osnabrück (15 May 1648) and Münster (24 October 1648) that had lasting political and economic ramifications for Europe and its colonial aspirations. The signing of these treaties ended the Thirty Years War (1618–1648) in the Holy Roman Empire and the Eighty Years' War between Spain and the Republic of the Seven United Netherlands (1568–1648). The Thirty Years War involved most of Europe and was destructive both of the populations involved and to economic and political aspirations. Primarily the Peace of Westphalia is seen as key to establishing the modern concept of the sovereign nation-state, both through fixing many of the present national borders in Europe and, more importantly, by clarifying the concept of the relationship of citizens to their rulers. The sovereigns who signed the Treaty (the first diplomatic conference of its kind) agreed among themselves that citizens were expected to be loyal to their states and not to overlap political or religious interests. Globally speaking, Spanish world influence declined along with the Habsburg Empire, as the French, British and Dutch all began to rise. The Dutch separated from the Holy Roman Empire, and with Spanish embargoes on Dutch commerce lifted, they emerged as a major colonial power involved in trade, shipping, and the spread of global capitalism (a point noted by Wallerstein).

Treaty of Westphalia: Peace Treaty between the Holy Roman Emperor and the King of France and their Respective Allies

In the name of the most holy and individual Trinity: Be it known to all, and every one whom it may concern, or to whom in any manner it may belong, That for many Years past, Discords and Civil Divisions being stir'd up in the Roman Empire, which increas'd to such a degree, that not only all Germany, but also the neighbouring Kingdoms, and France particularly, have been involv'd in the Disorders of a long and cruel War: And in the first place, between the most Serene and most Puissant Prince and Lord, Ferdinand the Second, of famous Memory, elected Roman Emperor, always August, King of Germany, Hungary, Bohemia, Dalmatia, Croatia, Slavonia, Arch-Duke of Austria, Duke of Burgundy, Brabant, Styria, Carinthia, Carniola, Marquiss of Moravia, Duke of Luxemburgh, the Higher and Lower Silesia, of Wirtemburg and Teck, Prince of Suabia, Count of Hapsburg, Tirol, Kyburg and Goritia, Marquiss of the Sacred Roman Empire, Lord of Burgovia, of the Higher and Lower Lusace, of the Marquisate of Slavonia, of Port Naon and Salines, with his Allies and Adherents on one side; and the most Serene, and the most Puissant Prince, Lewis the Thirteenth, most Christian King of France and Navarre, with his Allies and Adherents on the other side. And after their Decease, between the most Serene and Puissant Prince and Lord, Ferdinand the Third, elected Roman Emperor, always August, King of Germany, Hungary, Bohemia, Dalmatia, Croatia, Slavonia, Arch-Duke of Austria, Duke of Burgundy, Brabant, Styria, Carinthia, Carniola, Marquiss of Moravia, Duke of Luxemburg, of the Higher and Lower Silesia, of Wirtemburg and Teck, Prince of Suabia, Count of Hapsburg, Tirol, Kyburg and Goritia, Marquiss of the Sacred Roman Empire, Burgovia, the Higher and Lower Lusace, Lord of the Marquisate of Slavonia, of Port Naon and Salines, with his Allies and Adherents on the one side; and the most Serene and most Puissant Prince and Lord, Lewis the Fourteenth, most Christian King of France and Navarre, with his Allies and Adherents on the other side: from whence ensu'd great Effusion of Christian Blood, and the Desolation of several Provinces. It has at last happen'd, by the effect of Divine Goodness, seconded by the Endeavours of the most Serene Republick of Venice, who in this sad time, when all Christendom is imbroil'd, has not ceas'd to contribute its Counsels for the publick Welfare and Tranquillity; so that on the side, and the other, they have form'd Thoughts of an universal Peace. And for this purpose, by a mutual Agreement and Covenant of both Partys, in the year of our Lord 1641. the 25th of December, N.S. or the 15th O.S. it was resolv'd at Hamburgh, to hold an Assembly of Plenipotentiary Ambassadors, who should render themselves at Munster and Osnabrug in Westphalia the 11th of July, N.S. or the 1st of the said month O.S. in the year 1643. The Plenipotentiary Ambassadors on the one side, and the other, duly establish'd, appearing at the prefixt time, and on the behalf of his Imperial Majesty, the most illustrious and most excellent Lord, Maximilian Count of Trautmansdorf and Weinsberg, Baron of Gleichenberg, Neustadt, Negan, Burgau, and Torzenbach, Lord of Teinitz, Knight of the Golden Fleece, Privy Counsellor and Chamberlain to his Imperial Sacred Majesty, and Steward of his Houshold; the Lord John Lewis, Count of Nassau, Catzenellebogen, Vianden, and Dietz, Lord of Bilstein, Privy Counsellor to the Emperor, and Knight of the Golden Fleece; Monsieur Isaac Volmamarus, Doctor of Law, Counsellor, and President in the Chamber of the most Serene Lord Arch-Duke Ferdinand Charles. And on the behalf of the most Christian King, the most eminent Prince and Lord, Henry of Orleans, Duke of Longueville, and Estouteville, Prince and Sovereign Count of Neuschaftel, Count of Dunois and Tancerville, Hereditary Constable of Normandy, Governor and Lieutenant-General of the same Province, Captain of the Cent Hommes d'Arms, and Knight of the King's Orders, &c. as also the most illustrious and most excellent Lords, Claude de Mesmes, Count d'Avaux, Commander of the said King's Orders, one of the Superintendents of the Finances, and Minister of the Kingdom of France &c. and Abel Servien, Count la Roche of Aubiers, also one of the Ministers of the Kingdom of France. And by the Mediation and Interposition of the most illustrious and most excellent Ambassador and Senator of Venice, Aloysius Contarini Knight, who for the space of five Years, or thereabouts, with great Diligence, and a Spirit intirely impartial, has been inclin'd to be a Mediator in these Affairs. After having implor'd the Divine Assistance, and receiv'd a reciprocal Communication of Letters, Commissions, and full Powers, the Copys of which are inserted at the end of this Treaty, in the presence and with the consent of the Electors of the Sacred Roman Empire, the other Princes and States, to the Glory of God, and the Benefit of the Christian World, the following Articles have been agreed on and consented to, and the same run thus.

That there shall be a Christian and Universal Peace, and a perpetual, true, and sincere Amity, between his Sacred Imperial Majesty, and his most Christian Majesty; as also, between all and each of the Allies, and Adherents of his said Imperial Majesty, the House of Austria, and its Heirs, and Successors; but chiefly between the Electors, Princes, and States of the Empire on the one side; and all and each of the Allies of his said Christian Majesty, and all their Heirs and Successors, chiefly between the most Serene Queen and Kingdom of Swedeland, the Electors respectively, the Princes and States of the Empire, on the other part. That this Peace and Amity be observ'd and cultivated with such a Sincerity and Zeal, that each Party shall endeavour to procure the Benefit, Honour and Advantage of the other; that thus on all sides they may see this Peace and Friendship in the Roman Empire, and the Kingdom of France flourish, by entertaining a good and faithful Neighbourhood.

That there shall be on the one side and the other a perpetual Oblivion, Amnesty, or Pardon of all that has been committed since the beginning of these Troubles, in what place, or what manner soever the Hostilitys have been practis'd, in such a manner, that no body, under any pretext whatsoever, shall practice any Acts of Hostility, entertain any Enmity, or cause any Trouble to each other; neither as to Persons, Effects and Securitys, neither of themselves or by others, neither privately nor openly, neither directly nor indirectly, neither under the colour of Right, nor by the way of Deed, either within or without the extent of the Empire, notwithstanding all Covenants made before to the contrary: That they shall not act, or permit to be acted, any wrong or injury to any whatsoever; but that all that has pass'd on the one side, and the other, as well before as during the War, in Words, Writings, and Outrageous Actions, in Violences, Hostilitys, Damages and Expences, without any respect to Persons or Things, shall be entirely abolish'd in such a manner that all that might be demanded of, or pretended to, by each other on that behalf, shall be bury'd in eternal Oblivion.

Treaty of Westphalia, Avalon Project, Yale University. Source: http://avalon.law.yale.edu/17th_century/westphal.asp.

AMERICA IN THE EUROPEAN IMAGINATION: JOHN LOCKE (1690)

John Locke (1632–1704) was a British philosopher and political theorist associated with a range of theories and standpoints. In philosophy he is the founder of British empiricism, and in political theory he is best known for liberalism and the social contract. His theory of mind as a *tabula rasa*, "blank slate," argues that people are born without innate ideas, and knowledge is formed by experience. Politically his writings became important to American revolutionaries. In particular, his assertion that government should be "with the consent of the governed." The concept of consent is part of his theory of the state of nature, which is modified through reason and the Christian belief in not harming others. Those familiar with the American Declaration of Independence will recognize Locke in the assertion that individuals should not be constrained in their pursuit of life, liberty, and the owning of property.

Second Treatise of Government

41. There cannot be a clearer demonstration of any thing, than several nations of the Americans are of this, who are rich in land, and poor in all the comforts of life; whom nature having furnished as liberally as any other people, with the materials of plenty, i.e. a fruitful soil, apt to produce in abundance, what might serve for food, raiment, and delight; yet for want of improving it by labour, have not one hundredth part of the conveniencies we enjoy: and a king of a large and fruitful territory there, feeds, lodges, and is clad worse than a day-labourer in England.

42. To make this a little clearer, let us but trace some of the ordinary provisions of life, through their several progresses, before they come to our use, and see how much they receive of their value from human industry. Bread, wine and cloth, are things of daily use, and great plenty; yet notwithstanding, acorns, water and leaves, or skins, must be our bread, drink and cloathing, did not labour furnish us with these more useful commodities: for whatever bread is more worth than acorns, wine than water, and cloth or silk, than leaves, skins or moss, that is wholly owing to labour and industry; the one of these being the food and raiment which unassisted nature furnishes us with; the other, provisions which our industry and pains prepare for us, which how much they exceed the other in value, when any one hath computed, he will then see how much labour makes the far greatest part of the value of things we enjoy in this world: and the ground which produces the materials, is scarce to be reckoned in, as any, or at most, but a very small part of it; so little, that even amongst us, land that is left wholly to nature, that hath no improvement of pasturage, tillage, or planting, is called, as indeed it is, waste; and we shall find the benefit of it amount to little more than nothing. This shews how much numbers of

men are to be preferred to largeness of dominions; and that the increase of lands, and the right employing of them, is the great art of government: and that prince, who shall be so wise and godlike, as by established laws of liberty to secure protection and encouragement to the honest industry of mankind, against the oppression of power and narrowness of party, will quickly be too hard for his neighbours: but this by the by. To return to the argument in hand,

43. An acre of land, that bears here twenty bushels of wheat, and another in America, which, with the same husbandry, would do the like, are, without doubt, of the same natural intrinsic value: but yet the benefit mankind receives from the one in a year, is worth 5l. and from the other possibly not worth a penny, if all the profit an Indian received from it were to be valued, and sold here; at least, I may truly say, not one thousandth. It is labour then which puts the greatest part of value upon land, without which it would scarcely be worth any thing: it is to that we owe the greatest part of all its useful products; for all that the straw, bran, bread, of that acre of wheat, is more worth than the product of an acre of as good land, which lies waste, is all the effect of labour: for it is not barely the plough-man's pains, the reaper's and thresher's toil, and the baker's sweat, is to be counted into the bread we eat; the labour of those who broke the oxen, who digged and wrought the iron and stones, who felled and framed the timber employed about the plough, mill, oven, or any other utensils, which are a vast number, requisite to this corn, from its being feed to be sown to its being made bread, must all be charged on the account of labour, and received as an effect of that: nature and the earth furnished only the almost worthless materials, as in themselves. It would be a strange catalogue of things, that industry provided and made use of, about every loaf of bread, before it came to our use, if we could trace them; iron, wood, leather, bark, timber, stone, bricks, coals, lime, cloth, dying drugs, pitch, tar, masts, ropes, and all the materials made use of in the ship, that brought any of the commodities made use of by any of the workmen, to any part of the work; all which it would be almost impossible, at least too long, to reckon up.

44. From all which it is evident, that though the things of nature are given in common, yet man, by being master of himself, and proprietor of his own person, and the actions or labour of it, had still in himself the great foundation of property; and that, which made up the great part of what he applied to the support or comfort of his being, when invention and arts had improved the conveniencies of life, was perfectly his own, and did not belong in common to others.

45. Thus labour, in the beginning, gave a right of property, wherever any one was pleased to employ it upon what was common, which remained a long while the far greater part, and is yet more than mankind makes use of. Men, at first, for the most part, contented themselves with what unassisted nature offered to their necessities: and though afterwards, in some parts of the world (where the increase of people and stock, with the use of money, had made land scarce, and so of some value) the several communities settled the bounds of their distinct territories, and by laws within themselves regulated the properties of the private men of their society, and so, by compact and agreement, settled the property which labour and industry began; and the leagues that have been made between several states and kingdoms, either expresly or tacitly disowning all claim and right to the land in the others possession, have, by common consent, given up their pretences to their natural common right, which originally they had to those countries, and so have, by positive agreement, settled a property amongst themselves, in distinct parts and parcels of the earth; yet there are still great tracts of ground to be found, which (the inhabitants thereof not having joined with the rest of mankind, in the consent of the use of their common money) lie waste, and are more than the people who dwell on it do, or can make use of, and so still lie in common; tho' this can scarce happen amongst that part of mankind that have consented to the use of money.

46. The greatest part of things really useful to the life of man, and such as the necessity of subsisting made the first commoners of the world look after, as it cloth the Americans now, are generally things of short duration; such as, if they are not consumed by use, will decay and perish of themselves: gold, silver and diamonds, are things that fancy or agreement hath put the value on, more than real use, and the necessary support of life. Now of those good things which nature hath provided in common, every one had a right (as hath been said) to as much as he could use, and property in all that he could effect with his labour; all that his industry could extend to, to alter from the state nature had put it in, was his. He that gathered a hundred

bushels of acorns or apples, had thereby a property in them, they were his goods as soon as gathered. He was only to look, that he used them before they spoiled, else he took more than his share, and robbed others. And indeed it was a foolish thing, as well as dishonest, to hoard up more than he could make use of. If he gave away a part to any body else, so that it perished not uselesly in his possession, these he also made use of. And if he also bartered away plums, that would have rotted in a week, for nuts that would last good for his eating a whole year, he did no injury; he wasted not the common stock; destroyed no part of the portion of goods that belonged to others, so long as nothing perished uselesly in his hands. Again, if he would give his nuts for a piece of metal, pleased with its colour; or exchange his sheep for shells, or wool for a sparkling pebble or a diamond, and keep those by him all his life he invaded not the right of others, he might heap up as much of these durable things as he pleased; the exceeding of the bounds of his just property not lying in the largeness of his possession, but the perishing of any thing uselesly in it.

47. And thus came in the use of money, some lasting thing that men might keep without spoiling, and that by mutual consent men would take in exchange for the truly useful, but perishable supports of life.

48. And as different degrees of industry were apt to give men possessions in different proportions, so this invention of money gave them the opportunity to continue and enlarge them: for supposing an island, separate from all possible commerce with the rest of the world, wherein there were but an hundred families, but there were sheep, horses and cows, with other useful animals, wholsome fruits, and land enough for corn for a hundred thousand times as many, but nothing in the island, either because of its commonness, or perishableness, fit to supply the place of money; what reason could any one have there to enlarge his possessions beyond the use of his family, and a plentiful supply to its consumption, either in what their own industry produced, or they could barter for like perishable, useful commodities, with others? Where there is not some thing, both lasting and scarce, and so valuable to be hoarded up, there men will not be apt to enlarge their possessions of land, were it never so rich, never so free for them to take: for I ask, what would a man value ten thousand, or an hundred thousand acres of excellent land, ready cultivated, and well stocked too with cattle, in the middle of the inland parts of America, where he had no hopes of commerce with other parts of the world, to draw money to him by the sale of the product? It would not be worth the enclosing, and we should see him give up again to the wild common of nature, whatever was more than would supply the conveniencies of life to be had there for him and his family.

49. Thus in the beginning all the world was America, and more so than that is now; for no such thing as money was any where known. Find out something that hath the use and value of money amongst his neighbours, you shall see the same man will begin presently to enlarge his possessions.

John Locke (1690) "Second Treatise of Government" in *Two Treatises of Government*, Project Gutenberg.

EARLY TRADE ROUTES TO THE EAST: MARCO POLO (1271–1293)

Marco Polo (*c.* 1254–*c.* 1324), an Italian explorer and trader, was one of the first Westerners to travel to China. His travels were documented in the work *The Travels of Marco Polo* by the poet Rustichello da Pisa. Soon after the book was published, Polo became a rather (in)famous figure. Readers were fascinated by the things that Polo said that he saw in China. So much so that to most of Medieval Europe, what Polo described was considered unbelievable. This is what led *The Travels of Marco Polo* to gain the nickname, *Il Millione* (literally, The Million), which was meant to suggest that the work was filled with a million lies or exaggerations. Nevertheless, Polo's work was still immensely influential. At the time, it was still the only account of China that many Westerners had access to.

One of the consequences of Polo's writings was to make known to the West just how much trading took place in China, which Polo called "Cathay." In the selection, Polo makes the bold claim that more precious articles of all sorts are brought to Cambaluc (now known as Beijing) than to any other city in the world, a claim he buttresses by pointing to the large quantity of goods that flow in and out of the city gates daily.

Another consequence of Polo's writings was to increase European interest in trade and travel to China and the Far East in general. This led to a slightly unforeseen outcome as some historians believe that it also inadvertently inspired Europeans to come across the New World. In the pursuit for new routes to the Far East, European explorers would later come upon the Americas. One of those was Christopher Columbus, who had a copy of *The Travels of Marco Polo* with him on his many voyages.

Concerning the City of Cambaluc, and its Great Traffic and Population

You must know that the city of Cambaluc hath such a multitude of houses, and such a vast population inside the walls and outside, that it seems quite past all possibility. There is a suburb outside each of the gates, which are twelve in number; and these suburbs are so great that they contain more people than the city itself [for the suburb of one gate spreads in width till it meets the suburb of the next, whilst they extend in length some three or four miles]. In those suburbs lodge the foreign merchants and travellers, of whom there are always great numbers who have come to bring presents to the Emperor, or to sell articles at Court, or because the city affords so good a mart to attract traders. [There are in each of the suburbs, to a distance of a mile from the city, numerous fine hostelries for the lodgment of merchants from different parts of the world, and a special hostelry is assigned to each description of people, as if we should say there is one for the Lombards, another for the Germans, and a third for the Frenchmen.] And thus there are as many good houses outside of the city as inside, without counting those that belong to the great lords and barons, which are very numerous. . . .

To this city also are brought articles of greater cost and rarity, and in greater abundance of all kinds, than to any other city in the world. For people of every description, and from every region, bring things (including all the costly wares of India, as well as the fine and precious goods of Cathay itself with its provinces), some for the sovereign, some for the court, some for the city which is so great, some for the crowds of Barons and Knights, some for the great hosts of the Emperor which are quartered round about; and thus between court and city the quantity brought in is endless.

As a sample, I tell you, no day in the year passes that there do not enter the city 1000 cart-loads of silk alone, from which are made quantities of cloth of silk and gold, and of other goods. And this is not to be wondered at; for in all the countries round about there is no flax, so that everything has to be made of silk. It is true, indeed, that in some parts of the country there is cotton and hemp, but not sufficient for their wants. This, however, is not of much consequence, because silk is so abundant and cheap, and is a more valuable substance than either flax or cotton.

Round about this great city of Cambaluc there are some 200 other cities at various distances, from which traders come to sell their goods and buy others for their lords; and all find means to make their sales and purchases, so that the traffic of the city is passing great.

Marco Polo, "Concerning the City of Cambaluc, and its great traffic and population," *The Travels of Marco Polo – Volume 2*, Project Gutenberg. Source: http://www.gutenberg.org/files/10636/10636-8.txt.

COLONY AS A GULAG OF UNDESIRABLES: AUSTRALIA (1788–1850)

Robert Hughes (1938–) was born and educated in Sydney where, at university, his interest in art flourished. Since then Hughes has lived in Europe and the United States. His books, essays, and media presentations have made him known the world over for his art criticism and for his non-fiction history. *Fatal Shore* (1986), his history of the founding of Australia as a penal colony, is widely considered the foremost account of early Australia's history as well as a brilliant literary achievement in its own right.

The Fatal Shore: "The Harbor and the Exiles"

In 1787, the twenty-eighth year of the reign of King George III, the British Government sent a fleet to colonize Australia.

Never had a colony been founded so far from its parent state, or in such ignorance of the land it occupied. There had been no reconnaissance. In 1770 Captain James Cook had made landfall on the unexplored east coast of this utterly enigmatic continent, stopped for a short while at a place named Botany Bay and gone north again. Since then, no ship had called: not a word, not an observation, for seventeen years, each one of which was exactly like the thousands that had preceded it, locked in its historical immensity of blue heat, bush, sandstone and the measured booming of glassy Pacific rollers.

Now this coast was to witness a new colonial experiment, never tried before, not repeated since. An unexplored continent would become a jail. The space around it, the very air and sea, the whole transparent labyrinth of the South Pacific, would become a wall 14,000 miles thick.

The late eighteenth century abounded in schemes of social goodness thrown off by its burgeoning sense of revolution. But here, the process was to be reversed: not Utopia, but Dystopia; not Rousseau's natural man moving in moral grace amid free social contracts, but man coerced, exiled, deracinated, in chains. Other parts of the Pacific, especially Tahiti, might seem to confirm Rousseau. But the intellectual patrons of Australia, in its first colonial years, were Hobbes and Sade.

In their most sanguine moments, the authorities hoped that it would eventually swallow a whole class – the "criminal class," whose existence was one of the prime sociological beliefs of late Georgian and early Victorian England. Australia was settled to defend English property not from the frog-eating invader across the Channel but from the marauder within. English lawmakers wished not only to get rid of the "criminal class" but if possible to forget about it. Australia was a cloaca, invisible, its contents filthy and unnameable. Jeremy Bentham, inveighing against the "thief-colony" in 1812, argued that transportation

> was indeed a measure of *experiment* ... but the subject-matter of experiment was, in this case, a peculiarly commodious one; a set of *animae viles*, a sort of excrementitious mass, that could be projected, and accordingly was projected – projected, and as it should seem purposely – as far out of sight as possible.

To most Englishmen this place seemed not just a mutant society but another planet – an exiled world, summed up in its popular name, "Botany Bay." It was remote and anomalous to its white creators. It was strange but close, as the unconscious to the conscious mind. There was as yet no such thing as "Australian" history or culture. For its first forty years, everything that happened in the thief-colony was English. In the whole period of convict transportation, the Crown shipped more than 160,000 men, women and children (due to defects in the records, the true number will never be precisely known) in bondage to Australia. This was the largest forced exile of citizens at the behest of a European government in pre-modern history. Nothing in earlier penology compares with it. In Australia, England drew the sketch for our own century's vaster and more terrible fresco of repression, the Gulag. No other country had such a birth, and its pangs may be said to have begun on the afternoon of January 26, 1788, when a fleet of eleven vessels carrying 1,030 people, including 548 male and 188 female convicts, under the command of Captain Arthur Phillip in his flagship *Sirius*, entered Port Jackson or, as it would presently be called, Sydney Harbor.

One may liken this moment to the breaking open of a capsule. Upon the harbor the ships were now entering, European history had left no mark at all. Until the swollen sails and curveting bows of the British fleet came round South Head, there were no dates. The Aborigines and the fauna around them had possessed the landscape since time immemorial, and no other human eye had seen them. Now the protective glass of distance broke, in an instant, never to be restored.

To imagine the place, one should begin at North Head, the upper mandible of the harbor. Here, Australia stops, its plates of sandstone break off like a biscuit whose crumbs, the size of cottages, lie jumbled 250 feet below, at the surging ultramarine rim of the Pacific. A ragged wall of creamy-brown sandstone, fretted by the incessant wind, runs north to a glazed horizon. To the east, the Pacific begins its 7,000-mile arc toward South America. Long swells grind into the cliff in a boiling white lather, flinging veils of water a hundred feet into the air. At the meetings of its ancient planes of rock, sea and sky – mass, energy and light – one can grasp why the Aborigines called North Head *Boree*, "the enduring one."

The sandstone is the bone and root of the coast. On top of the cliff, the soil is thin and the scrub sparse. There are banksia bushes, with their sawtooth-edge leaves and dried seed-cones like multiple, jabbering mouths. Against this austere gray-green, the occasional red or blue scribble of a flower looks startling. But further back to the west, the sandstone ledges dip down into the harbor, separating it into scores of inlets. In 1788 these sheltered coves were densely wooded. The largest trees were eucalypts: red gums, angophoras, scribbly gums and a dozen others. Until the late eighteenth century no European had ever seen a eucalypt, and very strange they must have looked, with their strings of hanging, halfshed bark, their smooth wrinkling joints (like armpits, elbows or crotches), their fluent gesticulations and haze of perennial foliage. Not evergreens, but evergrays: the soft, spatially deceitful background color of the Australian bush, monotonous-looking at first sight but rippling with nuance to the acclimatized eye.

In the gullies, where streams of water slid from pool to pool leaving beards of rusty algae on their sandstone lips, giant cabbage-tree palms grew, their damp shade supporting a host of ferns and mosses. Yellow sprays of mimosa flashed in the sun along the ridges, and there were stands of blackboy trees, their dry spear of a stalk shooting up from a drooping hackle of fronds.

Robert Hughes (1986) *The Fatal Shore*, New York: Vintage Books, pp. 1–3.

COLONY AS WHOLLY OWNED SUBSIDIARY: KING LEOPOLD AND THE CONGO (1888–1903)

Adam Hochschild (1942–) is a writer and journalist whose work has appeared in leading magazines and other media. He lives in San Francisco and teaches writing at the Graduate School of Journalism at Berkeley. *King Leopold's Ghost* (1999) is a much-admired and thoroughly reliable account of the cruelty with which King Leopold of Belgium ruled Congo as its sole "owner."

King Leopold's Ghost: Prologue – The Traders are Kidnapping our People

When Europeans began imagining Africa beyond the Sahara, the continent they pictured was a dreamscape, a site for fantasies of the fearsome and the supernatural. Ranulf Higden, a Benedictine monk who mapped the world about 1350, claimed that Africa contained one-eyed people who used their feet to cover their heads. A geographer in the next century announced that the continent held people with one leg, three faces, and the heads of lions. In 1459, an Italian monk, Fra Mauro, declared Africa the home of the roc, a bird so large that it could carry an elephant through the air.

In the Middle Ages, almost no one in Europe was in a position to know whether Africa contained giant birds, one-eyed people, or anything else. Hostile Moors lived on Africa's Mediterranean coast, and few Europeans dared set foot there, much less head south across the Sahara. And as for trying to sail down the west

African coast, everyone knew that as soon as you passed the Canary Islands you would be in the Mare Tenebroso, the Sea of Darkness.

> In the medieval imagination [writes Peter Forbath], this was a region of uttermost dread . . . where the heavens fling down liquid sheets of flame and the waters boil . . . where serpent rocks and ogre islands lie in wait for the mariner, where the giant hand of Satan reaches up from the fathomless depths to seize him, where he will turn black in face and body as a mark of God's vengeance for the insolence of his prying into this forbidden mystery. And even if he should be able to survive all these ghastly perils and sail on through, he would then arrive in the Sea of Obscurity and be lost forever in the vapors and slime at the edge of the world.

It was not until the fifteenth century, the dawn of the age of ocean navigation, that Europeans systematically began to venture south, the Portuguese in the lead. In the 1440s, Lisbon's shipbuilders developed the caravel, a compact vessel particularly good at sailing into the wind. Although rarely more than a hundred feet long, this sturdy ship carried explorers far down the west coast of Africa, where no one knew what gold, spices, and precious stones might lie. But it was not only lust for riches that drove the explorers. Somewhere in Africa, they knew, was the source of the Nile, a mystery that had fascinated Europeans since antiquity. They were also driven by one of the most enduring of medieval myths, the legend of Prester John, a Christian king who was said to rule a vast empire in the interior of Africa, where, from a palace of translucent crystal and precious stones, he reigned over forty-two lesser kings, in addition to assorted centaurs and giants. No traveler was ever turned away from his dinner table of solid emerald, which seated thousands. Surely Prester John would be eager to share his riches with his fellow Christians and to help them find their way onward, to the fabled wealth of India.

Successive Portuguese expeditions probed ever farther southward. In 1482, an experienced naval captain named Diogo Cão set off on the most ambitious voyage yet. As he sailed close to the west African coast, he saw the North Star disappear from the sky once his caravel crossed the equator, and he found himself much farther south than anyone from Europe had ever been.

One day Cão came upon something that astounded him. Around his ship, the sea turned a dark, slate-tinged yellow, and brownish-yellow waves were breaking on the nearby beaches. Sailing toward the mouth of an inlet many miles wide, his caravel had to fight a current of eight to nine knots. Furthermore, a taste of the water surrounding the ship revealed that it was fresh, not salt. Cão had stumbled on the mouth of an enormous silt-filled river, larger than any a European had ever seen. The impression its vastness made on him and his men is reflected in a contemporary account:

> For the space of 20 leagues [the river] preserves its fresh water unbroken by the briny billows which encompass it on every side; as if this noble river had determined to try its strength in pitched battle with the ocean itself, and alone deny it the tribute which all other rivers in the world pay without resistance.

Modern oceanographers have discovered more evidence of the great river's strength in its "pitched battle with the ocean": a hundred-mile-long canyon, in places four thousand feet deep, that the river has carved out of the sea floor.

Cão went ashore at the river's mouth and erected a limestone pillar topped with an iron cross and inscribed with the royal coat of arms and the words: "In the year 6681 of the World and in that of 1482 since the birth of our Lord Jesus Christ, the most serene, the most excellent and potent prince, King João II of Portugal did order this land to be discovered and this pillar of stone to be erected by Diogo Cão, an esquire in his household."

The river where he had landed would be known by Europeans for most of the next five hundred years as the Congo. It flowed into the sea at the northern end of a thriving African kingdom, an imperial federation of two to three million people. Ever since then, geographers have usually spelled the name of the river and the eventual European colony on its banks one way, and that of the people living around its mouth and their indigenous kingdom another.

The Kingdom of the Kongo was roughly three hundred miles square, comprising territory that today lies in several countries. Its capital was the town of Mbanza Kongo – *mbanza* means "court" – on a commanding hilltop some ten days' walk inland from the coast and today just on the Angolan side of the Angola–Congo border. In 1491, nine years and several voyages after Diogo Cão's landfall, an expedition of awed Portuguese priests and emissaries made this ten-day trek and set up housekeeping as permanent representatives of their country in the court of the Kongo king. Their arrival marked the beginning of the first sustained encounter between Europeans and a black African nation.

The Kingdom of the Kongo had been in place for at least a hundred years before the Portuguese arrived. Its monarch, the ManiKongo, was chosen by an assembly of clan leaders. Like his European counterparts, he sat on a throne, in his case made of wood inlaid with ivory. As symbols of royal authority, the ManiKongo carried a zebra-tail whip, had the skins and heads of baby animals suspended from his belt, and wore a small cap.

In the capital, the king dispensed justice, received homage, and reviewed his troops under a fig tree in a large public square. Whoever approached him had to do so on all fours. On pain of death, no one was allowed to watch him eat or drink. Before he did either, an attendant struck two iron poles together, and anyone in sight had to lie face down on the ground.

The ManiKongo who was then on the throne greeted the Portuguese warmly. His enthusiasm was probably due less to the Savior his unexpected guests told him about than to the help their magical fire-spouting weapons promised in suppressing a troublesome provincial rebellion. The Portuguese were glad to oblige.

The newcomers built churches and mission schools. Like many white evangelists who followed them, they were horrified by polygamy; they thought it was the spices in the African food that provoked the dreadful practice. But despite their contempt for Kongo culture, the Portuguese grudgingly recognized in the kingdom a sophisticated and well-developed state – the leading one on the west coast of central Africa. The ManiKongo appointed governors for each of some half-dozen provinces, and his rule was carried out by an elaborate civil service that included such specialized positions as *mani vangu vangu*, or first judge in cases of adultery. Although they were without writing or the wheel, the inhabitants forged copper into jewelry and iron into weapons, and wove clothing out of fibers stripped from the leaves of the raffia palm tree. According to myth, the founder of the Kongo state was a blacksmith king, so ironwork was an occupation of the nobility. People cultivated yams, bananas, and other fruits and vegetables, and raised pigs, cattle, and goats. They measured distance by marching days, and marked time by the lunar month and by a four-day week, the first day of which was a holiday. The king collected taxes from his subjects and, like many a ruler, controlled the currency supply: cowrie shells found on a coastal island under royal authority.

As in much of Africa, the kingdom had slavery. The nature of African slavery varied from one area to another and changed over time, but most slaves were people captured in warfare. Others had been criminals or debtors, or were given away by their families as part of a dowry settlement. Like any system that gives some human beings total power over others, slavery in Africa could be vicious. Some Congo basin peoples sacrificed slaves on special occasions, such as the ratification of a treaty between chiefdoms; the slow death of an abandoned slave, his bones broken, symbolized the fate of anyone who violated the treaty. Some slaves might also be sacrificed to give a dead chief's soul some company on its journey into the next world.

In other ways, African slavery was more flexible and benign than the system Europeans would soon establish in the New World. Over a generation or two, slaves could often earn or be granted their freedom, and free people and slaves sometimes intermarried. Nonetheless, the fact that trading in human beings existed in any form turned out to be catastrophic for Africa, for when Europeans showed up, ready to buy endless shiploads of slaves, they found African chiefs willing to sell.

Soon enough, the slave-buyers came. They arrived in small numbers at first, but then in a flood unleashed by events across the Atlantic. In 1500, only nine years after the first Europeans arrived at Mbanza Kongo, a Portuguese expedition was blown off course and came upon Brazil. Within a few decades, the Western Hemisphere became a huge, lucrative, nearly insatiable market for African slaves. They were put to work by the millions in Brazil's mines and on its coffee plantations, as well as on the Caribbean islands where other European powers quickly began using the lush, fertile land to grow sugar.

In the Kingdom of the Kongo, the Portuguese forgot the search for Prester John. Slaving fever seized them.

Men sent out from Lisbon to be masons or teachers at Mbanza Kongo soon made far more money by herding convoys of chained Africans to the coast and selling them to the captains of slave-carrying caravels.

The lust for slave profits engulfed even some of the priests, who abandoned their preaching, took black women as concubines, kept slaves themselves, and sold their students and converts into slavery. The priests who strayed from the fold stuck to their faith in one way, however; after the Reformation they tried to ensure that none of their human goods ended up in Protestant hands. It was surely not right, said one, "for persons baptized in the Catholic church to be sold to peoples who are enemies of their faith."

A village near Diogo Cão's stone pillar on the south shore of the Congo River estuary became a slave port, from which more than five thousand slaves a year were being shipped across the Atlantic by the 1530s. By the next century, fifteen thousand slaves a year were exported from the Kingdom of the Kongo as a whole. Traders kept careful records of their booty. One surviving inventory from this region lists "68 head" of slaves by name, physical defects, and cash value, starting with the men, who were worth the most money, and ending with: "Child, name unknown as she is dying and cannot speak, male without value, and a small girl Callenbo, no value because she is dying; one small girl Cantunbe, no value because she is dying."

Many of the slaves shipped to the Americas from the great river's mouth came from the Kingdom of the Kongo itself; many others were captured by African slave-dealers who ranged more than seven hundred miles into the interior, buying slaves from local chiefs and headmen. Forced-marched to the coast, their necks locked into wooden yokes, the slaves were rarely given enough food, and because caravans usually traveled in the dry season, they often drank stagnant water. The trails to the slave ports were soon strewn with bleaching bones.

Once they were properly baptized, clothed in leftover burlap cargo wrappings, and chained together in ships' holds, most slaves from this region were sent to Brazil, the nearest part of the New World. Starting in the 1600s, however, a growing demand tempted many ship captains to make the longer voyage to the British colonies in North America. Roughly one of every four slaves imported to work the cotton and tobacco plantations of the American South began his or her journey across the Atlantic from equatorial Africa, including the Kongo kingdom. The KiKongo language, spoken around the Congo River's mouth, is one of the African tongues whose traces linguists have found in the Gullah dialect spoken by black Americans today on the coastal islands of South Carolina and Georgia.

*   *   *

When the Atlantic slave trade began decimating the Kongo, that nation was under the reign of a ManiKongo named Nzinga Mbemba Affonso, who had gained the throne in 1506 and ruled as Affonso I for nearly forty years. Affonso's life spanned a crucial period. When he was born, no one in the kingdom knew that Europeans existed. When he died, his entire realm was threatened by the slave-selling fever they had caused. He was a man of tragic self-awareness, and he left his mark. Some three hundred years later, a missionary said, "A native of the Kongo knows the name of three kings: that of the present one, that of his predecessor, and that of Affonso."

He was a provincial chief in his early thirties when the Portuguese first arrived at Mbanza Kongo, in 1491. A convert to Christianity, he took on the name Affonso and some Portuguese advisers, and studied for ten years with the priests at Mbanza Kongo. One wrote to the king of Portugal that Affonso "knows better than us the prophets, the Gospel of our Savior Jesus Christ, all the lives of the saints and all that has to do with our holy mother Church. If Your Highness saw him, You would be astonished. He speaks so well and with such assurance that it always seems to me that the Holy Spirit speaks through his mouth. My Lord, he does nothing but study; many times he falls asleep over his books and many times he forgets to eat or drink because he is speaking of our Savior." It is hard to tell how much of this glowing portrait was inspired by the priest's attempt to impress the Portuguese king and how much by Affonso's attempt to impress the priest.

In the language of a later age, King Affonso I was a modernizer. He urgently tried to acquire European learning, weapons, and goods in order to strengthen his rule and fortify it against the destabilizing force of the white arrival. Having noticed the Portuguese appetite for copper, for example, he traded it for European products that would help him buy the submission of outlying provinces. Clearly a man of unusual intelligence, Affonso tried to do something as difficult in his time as in ours: to be a *selective* modernizer. He was an enthusiast for the church, for the written word, for European medicine, and for woodworking, masonry, and other skills to be learned from Portuguese craftsmen. But when his fellow king in Lisbon sent an envoy to urge the adoption of Portugal's legal code and court protocol, Affonso wasn't interested. And he tried hard to keep out prospectors, fearing total takeover of his land if Europeans found the gold and silver they coveted.

Because virtually everything we know about this part of Africa for the next several hundred years comes to us from its white conquerors, King Affonso I provides something rare and valuable: an African voice. Indeed, his is one of the very few central African voices that we can hear at all before the twentieth century. He used his fluency in Portuguese to dictate a remarkable series of letters to two successive Portuguese kings, the first known documents composed by a black African in any European language. Several dozen of the letters survive, above his signature, with its regal flourish of double underlinings. Their tone is the formal one of monarch to monarch, usually beginning "Most high and powerful prince and king my brother . . ." But we can hear not just a king speaking; we hear a human being, one who is aghast to see his people taken away in ever greater numbers on slave ships.

Affonso was no abolitionist. Like most African rulers of his time and later, he owned slaves, and at least once he sent some as a present to his "brother" king in Lisbon, along with leopard skins, parrots, and copper anklets. But this traditional exchange of gifts among kings seemed greatly different to Affonso from having tens of thousands of his previously free subjects taken across the sea in chains. Listen to him as he writes King João III of Portugal in 1526:

> Each day the traders are kidnapping our people – children of this country, sons of our nobles and vassals, even people of our own family. . . . This corruption and depravity are so widespread that our land is entirely depopulated. . . . We need in this kingdom only priests and schoolteachers, and no merchandise, unless it is wine and flour for Mass. . . . It is our wish that this kingdom not be a place for the trade or transport of slaves.

Later the same year:

> Many of our subjects eagerly lust after Portuguese merchandise that your subjects have brought into our domains. To satisfy this inordinate appetite, they seize many of our black free subjects. . . . They sell them . . . after having taken these prisoners [to the coast] secretly or at night. . . . As soon as the captives are in the hands of white men they are branded with a red-hot iron.

Again and again Affonso speaks about the twin themes of the slave trade and the alluring array of cloth, tools, jewelry, and other knickknacks that the Portuguese traders used to buy their human cargoes:

> These goods exert such a great attraction over simple and ignorant people that they believe in them and forget their belief in God. . . . My Lord, a monstrous greed pushes our subjects, even Christians, to seize members of their own families, and of ours, to do business by selling them as captives.

While begging the Portuguese king to send him teachers, pharmacists, and doctors instead of traders, Affonso admits that the flood of material goods threatened his authority. His people "can now procure, in much greater quantity than we can, the things we formerly used to keep them obedient to us and content." Affonso's lament was prescient; this was not the last time that lust for Europe's great cornucopia of goods undermined traditional ways of life elsewhere.

The Portuguese kings showed no sympathy. King João III replied: "You . . . tell me that you want no slave-trading in your domains, because this trade is depopulating your country. . . . The Portuguese there, on the contrary, tell me how vast the Congo is, and how it is so thickly populated that it seems as if no slave has ever left."

Affonso pleaded with his fellow sovereigns as one Christian with another, complete with the prejudices of the day. Of the priests turned slave-traders, he wrote:

In this kingdom, faith is as fragile as glass because of the bad examples of the men who come to teach here, because the lusts of the world and lure of wealth have turned them away from the truth. Just as the Jews crucified the Son of God because of covetousness, my brother, so today He is again crucified.

Several times Affonso sent his appeals for an end to the slave trade directly to the Pope in Rome, but the Portuguese detained his emissaries to the Vatican as they stepped off the boat in Lisbon.

Affonso's despair reached its depth in 1539, near the end of his life, when he heard that ten of his young nephews, grandsons, and other relatives who had been sent to Portugal for a religious education had disappeared en route. "We don't know whether they are dead or alive," he wrote in desperation, "nor how they might have died, nor what news we can give of them to their fathers and mothers." We can imagine the king's horror at being unable to guarantee the safety even of his own family. Portuguese traders and sea captains along the long route back to Europe sidetracked many a cargo between the Kongo kingdom and Lisbon; these youngsters, it turned out, ended up in Brazil as slaves.

His hatred for the overseas slave trade and his vigilance against its erosion of his authority won Affonso the enmity of some of the Portuguese merchants living in his capital. A group of eight made an attempt on his life as he was attending Mass on Easter Sunday in 1540. He escaped with only a bullet hole in the fringe of his royal robe, but one of his nobles was killed and two others wounded.

After Affonso's death, the power of the Kongo state gradually diminished as provincial and village chiefs, themselves growing rich on slave sales, no longer gave much allegiance to the court at Mbanza Kongo. By the end of the 1500s, other European countries had joined in the slave trade; British, French, and Dutch vessels roamed the African coast, looking for human cargo. In 1665, the army of the weakened Kingdom of the Kongo fought a battle with the Portuguese. It was defeated, and the ManiKongo was beheaded. Internal strife further depleted the kingdom, whose territory was all taken over by European colonies by the late 1800s.

*   *   *

Except for Affonso's letters, the written record of these times still shows them entirely through white men's eyes. How did the Europeans, beginning with Diogo Cão and his three ships with faded red crosses on their sails, appear to the people living at the great river's mouth? To see with their eyes, we must turn to the myths and legends that have filtered down over the centuries. At first, Africans apparently saw the white sailors not as men but as *vumbi* – ancestral ghosts – since the Kongo people believed that a person's skin changed to the color of chalk when he passed into the land of the dead. And it was obvious that this was where these menacing white *vumbi* had come from, for people on the shore saw first the tips of an approaching ship's masts, then its superstructure, then its hull. Clearly the ship had carried its passengers up from their homes beneath the surface of the earth. Here is how the Portuguese arrival was recounted by Mukunzo Kioko, a twentieth-century oral historian of the Pende people:

> Our fathers were living comfortably. . . . They had cattle and crops; they had salt marshes and banana trees.
>
> Suddenly they saw a big boat rising out of the great ocean. This boat had wings all of white, sparkling like knives.
>
> White men came out of the water and spoke words which no one understood.
>
> Our ancestors took fright; they said that these were *vumbi*, spirits returned from the dead.
>
> They pushed them back into the ocean with volleys of arrows. But the *vumbi* spat fire with a noise of thunder. Many men were killed. Our ancestors fled.
>
> The chiefs and wise men said that these *vumbi* were the former possessors of the land. . . .
>
> From that time to our days now, the whites have brought us nothing but wars and miseries.

The trans-Atlantic slave trade seemed further confirmation that Europeans had come from the land of the dead, for after they took their shiploads of slaves out to sea, the captives never returned. Just as Europeans would be long obsessed with African cannibalism, so Africans imagined Europeans practicing the same thing.

The whites were thought to turn their captives' flesh into salt meat, their brains into cheese, and their blood into the red wine Europeans drank. African bones were burned, and the gray ash became gunpowder. The huge, smoking copper cooking kettles that could be seen on sailing vessels were, it was believed, where all these deadly transformations began. The death tolls on the packed slave ships that sailed west from the Congo coast rose higher still when some slaves refused to eat the food they were given, believing that they would be eating those who had sailed before them.

As the years passed, new myths arose to explain the mysterious objects the strangers brought from the land of the dead. A nineteenth-century missionary recorded, for example, an African explanation of what happened when captains descended into the holds of their ships to fetch trading goods like cloth. The Africans believed that these goods came not from the ship itself but from a hole that led into the ocean. Sea sprites weave this cloth in an "oceanic factory, and, whenever we need cloth, the captain . . . goes to this hole and rings a bell." The sea sprites hand him up their cloth, and the captain "then throws in, as payment, a few dead bodies of black people he has bought from those bad native traders who have bewitched their people and sold them to the white men." The myth was not so far from reality. For what was slavery in the American South, after all, but a system for transforming the labor of black bodies, via cotton plantations, into cloth?

*   *   *

Because African middlemen brought captives directly to their ships, Portuguese traders seldom ventured far from the coast. For nearly four centuries, in fact, after Diogo Cão came upon the Congo River, Europeans did not know where the river came from. It pours some 1.4 million cubic feet of water per second into the ocean; only the Amazon carries more water. Besides its enormous size and unknown course, the Congo posed another puzzle. Seamen noticed that its flow, compared with that of other tropical rivers, fluctuated relatively little during the year. Rivers such as the Amazon and the Ganges had phases of extremely high water and low water, depending on whether the land they drained was experiencing the rainy or the dry season. What made the Congo different?

The reason several centuries' worth of visitors failed to explore the Congo's source was that they couldn't sail upstream. Anyone who tried found that the river turned into a gorge, at the head of which were impassable rapids.

Much of the Congo River basin, we now know, lies on a plateau in the African interior. From the western rim of this plateau, nearly a thousand feet high, the river descends to sea level in a mere 220 miles. During this tumultuous descent, the river squeezes through narrow canyons, boils up in waves 40 feet high, and tumbles over 32 separate cataracts. So great is the drop and the volume of water that these 220 miles have as much hydroelectric potential as all the lakes and rivers of the United States combined.

For any sailor bold enough to get out of his ship and walk, the land route around the rapids wound uphill through rough, rocky country feared for its treacherous cliffs and ravines and for malaria and the other diseases to which Europeans had no immunity. Only with enormous difficulty did some Capuchin missionaries twice manage to get briefly inland as far as the top of the great rapids. A Portuguese expedition that tried to repeat this trek never returned. By the beginning of the nineteenth century, Europeans still knew nothing about the interior of central Africa or about where the river began.

In 1816, a British expedition, led by Captain James K. Tuckey of the Royal Navy, set off to find the Congo's origins. His two ships carried a wonderfully odd assortment of people: Royal Marines, carpenters, blacksmiths, a surgeon, a gardener from the royal gardens at Kew, a botanist, and an anatomist. The anatomist was directed, among other things, to make a careful study of the hippopotamus and to "preserve in spirits and if possible in triplicate, the organ of hearing of this animal." A Mr. Cranch was entered on the ship's log as Collector of Objects of Natural History; another expedition member was simply listed as Volunteer and Observant Gentleman.

When he arrived at the Congo's mouth, Tuckey counted eight slave ships from various nations at anchor, awaiting their cargoes. He sailed his own ships as far up the river as he could and then set off to skirt the thunderous rapids overland. But he and his exhausted men grew discouraged by endless "scrambling up the sides of almost perpendicular hills, and over great masses of quartz." These came to be called the Crystal

Mountains. The river was a mass of foaming rapids and enormous whirlpools. At a rare calm stretch Tuckey observed, rather provincially, that "the scenery was beautiful and not inferior to any on the banks of the Thames." One by one, the Englishmen began to suffer from an unknown illness, most likely yellow fever, and after about 150 miles, Tuckey lost heart. His party turned around, and he died shortly after getting back to his ship. By the time the shaken survivors of the expedition made their way back to England, twenty-one of the fifty-four men who had set out were dead. The source of the Congo River and the secret of its steady flow was still a mystery. For Europeans, Africa remained the supplier of valuable raw materials – human bodies and elephant tusks. But otherwise they saw the continent as faceless, blank, empty, a place on the map waiting to be explored, one ever more frequently described by the phrase that says more about the seer than the seen: the Dark Continent.

Adam Hochschild (1999) *King Leopold's Ghost*, Houghton Mifflin, pp. 6–18.

COLONIZATION OF CIVIL VIRTUES: PAX BRITANNICA (1815–1914)

For the UK and China, the signing of the Treaty of Tien Tsin marked a significant end to the Second Opium War (which lasted from 1856 to 1860). Having been defeated, China was forced to agree that it would open its ports and lands, almost unconditionally, to the merchants of the victors. This, as the selection below illustrates, occurred without a reciprocal offer. By and large, the British Empire was able to capture control of such resources because of its superior maritime forces, which for a century (from 1815 to 1914) went unrivaled. This era of British maritime dominance became known as Pax Britannica, which in Latin means the "British peace." However, as some have pointed out, this term is something of a misnomer, for whatever "peace" the British brought about came at the cost of continual bloodshed and warfare. Throughout the period of Pax Britannica, only a handful of those years can actually be considered peaceful for the British Empire. The rest were occupied with conflicts ranging from the Second Boer War in South Africa to the Crimean War, which was fought on and around the Crimean peninsula.

Treaty Between Her Majesty and the Emperor of China – signed, in the English and Chinese Languages, at Tien-tsin, June 26, 1858

Her Majesty the Queen of the United Kingdom of Great Britain and Ireland, and His Majesty the Emperor of China, being desirous to put an end to the existing misunderstanding between the two countries, and to place their relations on a more satisfactory footing in future, have resolved to proceed to a revision and improvement of the Treaties existing between them. . . .

X. British merchant ships shall have authority to trade upon the Great River (Yang-tse). The Upper and Lower Valley of the river being, however, disturbed by outlaws, no port shall be for the present opened to trade, with the exception of Chin-kiano, which shall be opened in a year from the date of the signing of this Treaty. . . .

XI. In addition to the cities and towns of Canton, Amoy, Fochow, Ningpo, and Shanghai, opened by the Treaty of Nanking, it is agreed that British subjects may frequent the cities and ports of New-Chwang, Tang-Chow, Tai-Wau (Formosa), Chau-Chow (Swatow) and Kiung-Chow (Hainan).

They are permitted to carry on trade with whomsoever they please, and to proceed to and fro at pleasure with their vessels and merchandise.

They shall enjoy the same privileges, advantages, and immunities, at the said towns and ports, as they enjoy at the ports already opened to trade, including the right of residence, of buying or renting houses, of leasing land therein, and of building churches, hospitals, and cemeteries.

XII. British subjects, whether at the ports or at other places, desiring to build or open houses, warehouses, churches, hospitals, or burial-grounds, shall make their agreement for the land or buildings they require, at the rates prevailing among the people, equitably, and without exaction on either side.

XIII. The Chinese Government will place no restrictions whatever upon the employment, by British subjects, of Chinese subjects in any lawful capacity. . . .

XV. All questions in regard to rights, whether of property or person, arising between British subjects, shall be subject to the jurisdiction of the British authorities. . . .

XXV. Import duties shall be considered payable on the landing of the goods, and duties of export on the shipment of the same. . . .

L. All official communications addressed by the Diplomatic and Consular Agents of Her Majesty the Queen to the Chinese authorities shall, henceforth, be written in English. They will for the present be accompanied by a Chinese version, but it is understood that, in the event of there being any difference of meaning between the English and Chinese text, the English Government will hold the sense as expressed in the English text to be the correct sense. This provision is to apply to the Treaty now negotiated, the Chinese text of which has been carefully corrected by the English original.

LI. It is agreed, that henceforward the character 'I' [a Chinese character signifying 'barbarian'] shall not be applied to the Government or subjects of Her Britannic Majesty, in any Chinese official document issued by the Chinese authorities, either in the capital or in the provinces.

LII. British ships of war coming for no hostile purpose, or being engaged in the pursuit of pirates, shall be at liberty to visit all ports within the dominions of the Emperor of China, and shall receive every facility for the purchase of provisions, procuring water, and, if occasion require, for the making of repairs. The commanders of such ship shall hold intercourse with the Chinese authorities on terms of equality and courtesy. . . .

LVI. The ratifications of this Treaty, under the hand of Her Majesty the Queen of Great Britain and Ireland, and His Majesty the Emperor of China, respectively, shall be exchanged at Pekin, within a year from this day of signature. . . .

In token whereof, the respective Plenipotentiaries have signed and sealed this Treaty.

Done at Tien-tsin, this twenty-sixth day of June, in the year of our Lord one thousand eight hundred and fifty-eight: corresponding with the Chinese date, the sixteenth day, fifth moon, of the eighth year of Hien Fung.

"Treaty of Tien-Tsin," http://web.jjay.cuny.edu/~jobrien/reference/ob28.html.

The New Sciences of Global Imagination, 1450–1884

■

MODERN PSYCHOLOGY OF THE MIGRATING SELF: RENÉ DESCARTES (1637)

René Descartes (1596–1650) was born in provincial France where he spent his early years before moving to the Netherlands. A mathematician and philosopher, Descartes is often said to be the founder of modern philosophy. In 1637, after years of personal and intellectual pilgrimage, he published *A Discourse on Method*, which contains the famous line *Cogito ergo sum* (I think therefore I am) – which so obviously challenges traditional thought by rejecting scholastic metaphysics. Thereafter, modern philosophy was forced to deal with the consciousness of the thinking individual as source of knowledge.

Discourse on the Method of Rightly Conducting the Reason, and Seeking Truth in the Sciences

Part I

Good sense is, of all things among men, the most equally distributed; for every one thinks himself so abundantly provided with it, that those even who are the most difficult to satisfy in everything else, do not usually desire a larger measure of this quality than they already possess. And in this it is not likely that all are mistaken the conviction is rather to be held as testifying that the power of judging aright and of distinguishing truth from error, which is properly what is called good sense or reason, is by nature equal in all men; and that the diversity of our opinions, consequently, does not arise from some being endowed with a larger share of reason than others, but solely from this, that we conduct our thoughts along different ways, and do not fix our attention on the same objects. For to be possessed of a vigorous mind is not enough; the prime requisite is rightly to apply it. The greatest minds, as they are capable of the highest excellences, are open likewise to the greatest aberrations; and those who travel very slowly may yet make far greater progress, provided they keep always to the straight road, than those who, while they run, forsake it.

For myself, I have never fancied my mind to be in any respect more perfect than those of the generality; on the contrary, I have often wished that I were equal to some others in promptitude of thought, or in clearness and distinctness of imagination, or in fullness and readiness of memory. And besides these, I know of no other qualities that contribute to the perfection of the mind; for as to the reason or sense, inasmuch as it is that alone which constitutes us men, and distinguishes us from the brutes, I am disposed to believe that it is to be found complete in each individual; and on this point to adopt the common opinion of philosophers, who say that the difference of greater and less holds only among the accidents, and not among the forms or natures of individuals of the same species.

I will not hesitate, however, to avow my belief that it has been my singular good fortune to have very early in life fallen in with certain tracks which have conducted me to considerations and maxims, of which I have formed a method that gives me the means, as I think, of gradually augmenting my knowledge, and of raising it by little and little to the highest point which the mediocrity of my talents and the brief duration of my life will permit me to reach. For I have already reaped from it such fruits that, although I have been accustomed to think lowly enough of myself, and although when I look with the eye of a philosopher at the varied courses and pursuits of mankind at large, I find scarcely one which does not appear in vain and useless, I nevertheless derive the highest satisfaction from the progress I conceive myself to have already made in the search after truth, and cannot help entertaining such expectations of the future as to believe that if, among the occupations of men as men, there is any one really excellent and important, it is that which I have chosen.

After all, it is possible I may be mistaken; and it is but a little copper and glass, perhaps, that I take for gold and diamonds. I know how very liable we are to delusion in what relates to ourselves, and also how much the judgments of our friends are to be suspected when given in our favor. But I shall endeavor in this discourse to describe the paths I have followed, and to delineate my life as in a picture, in order that each one may also be able to judge of them for himself, and that in the general opinion entertained of them, as gathered from current report, I myself may have a new help towards instruction to be added to those I have been in the habit of employing.

My present design, then, is not to teach the method which each ought to follow for the right conduct of his reason, but solely to describe the way in which I have endeavored to conduct my own. They who set themselves to give precepts must of course regard themselves as possessed of greater skill than those to whom they prescribe; and if they err in the slightest particular, they subject themselves to censure. But as this tract is put forth merely as a history, or, if you will, as a tale, in which, amid some examples worthy of imitation, there will be found, perhaps, as many more which it were advisable not to follow, I hope it will prove useful to some without being hurtful to any, and that my openness will find some favor with all.

From my childhood, I have been familiar with letters; and as I was given to believe that by their help a clear and certain knowledge of all that is useful in life might be acquired, I was ardently desirous of instruction. But as soon as I had finished the entire course of study, at the close of which it is customary to be admitted into the order of the learned, I completely changed my opinion. For I found myself involved in so many doubts and errors, that I was convinced I had advanced no farther in all my attempts at learning, than the discovery at every turn of my own ignorance. And yet I was studying in one of the most celebrated schools in Europe, in which I thought there must be learned men, if such were anywhere to be found. I had been taught all that others learned there; and not contented with the sciences actually taught us, I had, in addition, read all the books that had fallen into my hands, treating of such branches as are esteemed the most curious and rare. I knew the judgment which others had formed of me; and I did not find that I was considered inferior to my fellows, although there were among them some who were already marked out to fill the places of our instructors. And, in fine, our age appeared to me as flourishing, and as fertile in powerful minds as any preceding one. I was thus led to take the liberty of judging of all other men by myself, and of concluding that there was no science in existence that was of such a nature as I had previously been given to believe. [. . .]

For these reasons, as soon as my age permitted me to pass from under the control of my instructors, I entirely abandoned the study of letters, and resolved no longer to seek any other science than the knowledge of myself, or of the great book of the world. I spent the remainder of my youth in traveling, in visiting courts and armies, in holding intercourse with men of different dispositions and ranks, in collecting varied experience, in proving myself in the different situations into which fortune threw me, and, above all, in making such reflection on the matter of my experience as to secure my improvement. For it occurred to me that I should find much more truth in the reasonings of each individual with reference to the affairs in which he is personally interested, and the issue of which must presently punish him if he has judged amiss, than in those conducted by a man of letters in his study, regarding speculative matters that are of no practical moment, and followed by no consequences to himself, farther, perhaps, than that they foster his vanity the better the more remote they are from common sense; requiring, as they must in this case, the exercise of greater ingenuity and art to render them probable. In addition, I had always a most earnest desire to know how to distinguish the true from the false, in order that I might be able clearly to discriminate the right path in life, and proceed in it with confidence.

It is true that, while busied only in considering the manners of other men, I found here, too, scarce any ground for settled conviction, and remarked hardly less contradiction among them than in the opinions of the philosophers. So that the greatest advantage I derived from the study consisted in this, that, observing many things which, however extravagant and ridiculous to our apprehension, are yet by common consent received and approved by other great nations, I learned to entertain too decided a belief in regard to nothing of the truth of which I had been persuaded merely by example and custom; and thus I gradually extricated myself from many errors powerful enough to darken our natural intelligence, and incapacitate us in great measure from listening to reason. But after I had been occupied several years in thus studying the book of the world, and in essaying to gather some experience, I at length resolved to make myself an object of study, and to employ all the powers of my mind in choosing the paths I ought to follow, an undertaking which was accompanied with greater success than it would have been had I never quitted my country or my books. [. . .]

Part IV

I am in doubt as to the propriety of making my first meditations in the place above mentioned matter of discourse; for these are so metaphysical, and so uncommon, as not, perhaps, to be acceptable to every one. And yet, that it may be determined whether the foundations that I have laid are sufficiently secure, I find myself in a measure constrained to advert to them. I had long before remarked that, in relation to practice, it is sometimes necessary to adopt, as if above doubt, opinions which we discern to be highly uncertain, as has been already said; but as I then desired to give my attention solely to the search after truth, I thought that a procedure exactly the opposite was called for, and that I ought to reject as absolutely false all opinions in regard to which I could suppose the least ground for doubt, in order to ascertain whether after that there remained aught in my belief that was wholly indubitable. Accordingly, seeing that our senses sometimes deceive us, I was willing to suppose that there existed nothing really such as they presented to us; and because some men err in reasoning, and fall into paralogisms, even on the simplest matters of geometry, I, convinced that I was as open to error as any other, rejected as false all the reasonings I had hitherto taken for demonstrations; and finally, when I considered that the very same thoughts (presentations) which we experience when awake may also be experienced when we are asleep, while there is at that time not one of them true, I supposed that all the objects (presentations) that had ever entered into my mind when awake, had in them no more truth than the illusions of my dreams. But immediately upon this I observed that, whilst I thus wished to think that all was false, it was absolutely necessary that I, who thus thought, should be somewhat; and as I observed that this truth, I think, therefore I am (COGITO ERGO SUM), was so certain and of such evidence that no ground of doubt, however extravagant, could be alleged by the sceptics capable of shaking it, I concluded that I might, without scruple, accept it as the first principle of the philosophy of which I was in search.

René Descartes, 'Discourse on the Method of Rightly Conducting the Reason, and Seeking Truth in the Sciences,' in *A Discourse on Method*. Project Gutenberg.

■ ■ ■ ■ ■ ■

LONGITUDINAL RECKONING: THE GREENWICH PRIME MERIDIAN (1884)

Dava Sobel (1947–) is a science writer of much acclaim. *Longitude* (1995) is a best-selling, prize-winning book that tells the story of the painstaking work that led to the establishment of the prime meridian at

Greenwich, England. Though Greenwich Mean Time (GMT) is an arbitrary prime, its international acceptance, which continues today, made longitudinal reckoning accurate and oceanic navigation efficient.

Longitude: In the Meridian Courtyard

I am standing on the prime meridian of the world, zero degrees longitude, the center of time and space, literally the place where East meets West. It's paved right into the courtyard of the Old Royal Observatory at Greenwich. At night, buried lights shine through the glass-covered meridian line, so it glows like a man-made midocean rift, splitting the globe in two equal halves with all the authority of the Equator. For a little added fanfare after dark, a green laser projects the meridian's visibility ten miles across the valley to Essex.

Unstoppable as a comic book superhero, the line cuts through the nearby structures. It appears as a brass strip on the wooden floors of the Meridian House, then transforms into a single row of red blips that recall an airplane's emergency exit lighting system. Outside, where the prime meridian threads its way among the cobblestones, concrete slab stripes run alongside it, with brass letters and tick marks announcing the names and latitudes of the world's great cities.

A strategically placed machine offers to issue me a souvenir ticket stamped with the precise moment – to one-hundredth of a second – when I straddled the prime meridian. But this is just a sideshow attraction, with a price of £1 per ticket. Actual Greenwich Mean Time, by which the world sets its watch, is indicated far more precisely, to within millionths of seconds, inside the Meridian House on an atomic clock whose digital display changes too fast for the eye to follow.

Nevil Maskelyne, fifth astronomer royal, brought the prime meridian to this location, seven miles from the heart of London. During the years he lived on the Observatory site, from 1765 to his death in 1811, Maskelyne published forty-nine issues of the comprehensive *Nautical Almanac*. He figured all of the lunar-solar and lunar-stellar distances listed in the *Almanac* from the Greenwich meridian. And so, starting with the very first volume in 1767, sailors all over the world who relied on Maskelyne's tables began to calculate their longitude from Greenwich. Previously, they had been content to express their position as degrees east or west of any convenient meridian. Most often they used their point of departure – "three degrees twenty-seven minutes west of the Lizard," for example – or their destination. But Maskelyne's tables not only made the lunar distance method practicable, they also made the Greenwich meridian the universal reference point. Even the French translations of the *Nautical Almanac* retained Maskelyne's calculations from Greenwich – in spite of the fact that every other table in the *Connaissance des Temps* considered the Paris meridian as the prime.

This homage to Greenwich might have been expected to diminish after chronometers triumphed over lunars as the method of choice for finding longitude. But in fact the opposite occurred. Navigators still needed to make lunar distance observations from time to time, in order to verify their chronometers. Opening to the appropriate pages in the *Nautical Almanac*, they naturally computed their longitude east or west of Greenwich, no matter where they had come from or where they were going. Cartographers who sailed on mapping voyages to uncharted lands likewise recorded the longitudes of those places with respect to the Greenwich meridian.

In 1884, at the International Meridian Conference held in Washington, D.C., representatives from twenty-six countries voted to make the common practice official. They declared the Greenwich meridian the prime meridian of the world. This decision did not sit well with the French, however, who continued to recognize their own Paris Observatory meridian, a little more than two degrees east of Greenwich, as the starting line for another twenty-seven years, until 1911. (Even then, they hesitated to refer directly to Greenwich Mean Time, preferring the locution "Paris Mean Time, retarded by nine minutes twenty-one seconds.")

Since time is longitude and longitude time, the Old Royal Observatory is also the keeper of the stroke of midnight. Day begins at Greenwich. Time zones the world over run a legislated number of hours ahead of or behind Greenwich Mean Time (GMT). Greenwich time even extends into outer space: Astronomers use GMT to time predictions and observations, except that they call it Universal Time, or UT, in their celestial calendars.

Half a century before the entire world population began taking its time cues from Greenwich, the observatory officials provided a visual signal from the top of Flamsteed House to ships in the Thames. When naval captains were anchored on the river, they could set their chronometers by the dropping of a ball every day at thirteen hundred hours – 1 P.M.

Though modern ships rely on radio and satellite signals, the ceremony of the ball continues on a daily basis in the Meridian Courtyard, as it has done every day since 1833. People expect it, like teatime. Accordingly, at 12:55 P.M., a slightly battered red ball climbs halfway up the mast to the weather vane. It hovers there for three minutes, by way of warning. Then it ascends to its summit and waits another two minutes. Mobs of school groups and self-conscious adults find themselves craning their necks, staring at this target, which resembles nothing so much as an antiquated diving bell. It's a far cry, indeed, from the glitz of Times Square on New Year's Eve.

This more frequent, oddly anachronistic event has a genteel feel. How lovely the red metal looks against the blue October sky, where a stout west wind drives puffs of clouds over the twin observatory towers. Even the youngest children are quiet, expectant.

At one o'clock, the ball drops, like a fireman descending a very short pole. Nothing about the motion even suggests high technology or precision timekeeping. Yet it was this ball and other time balls and time guns at ports around the world that finally gave mariners a way to reckon their chronometers – without resorting to lunars more than once every few weeks at sea.

Inside Flamsteed House, where Harrison first sought the advice and counsel of Edmond Halley in 1730, the Harrison timekeepers hold court in their present places of honor. The big sea clocks, H-1, H-2, and H-3, were brought here to Greenwich in a rather dishonorable fashion, after being rudely removed from Harrison's house on May 23, 1766. Maskelyne never wound them, nor tended to them after testing them, but simply consigned them to a damp storage area where they were forgotten for the rest of his lifetime – and where they remained for another twenty-five years following his death. By the time one of John Roger Arnold's associates, E. J. Dent, offered to clean the big clocks for free in 1836, the necessary refurbishing required a four-year effort on Dent's part. Some of the blame for the sea clocks' deterioration lay with their original cases, which were not airtight. However, Dent put the cleaned timekeepers back in their cases just as he'd found them, inviting a new round of decay to commence immediately.

When Lieutenant Commander Rupert T. Gould of the Royal Navy took an interest in the timekeepers in 1920, he later recalled, "All were dirty, defective and corroded – while No. 1, in particular, looked as though it had gone down with the *Royal George* and had been on the bottom ever since. It was completely covered – even the wooden portions – with a bluish-green patina."

Gould, a man of great sensitivity, was so appalled by this pitiful neglect that he sought permission to restore all four (the three clocks and the Watch) to working order. He offered to do the work, which took him twelve years, without pay, and despite the fact that he had no horological training.

"I reflected that, so far as that was concerned, Harrison and I were in the same boat," Gould remarked with typical good humor, "and that if I started with No. 1 I could scarcely do that machine any further harm." So he set to right away with an ordinary hat brush, removing two full ounces of dirt and verdigris from H-1.

Tragic events in Gould's own life inured him to the difficulty of the job he had volunteered for. Compared to the mental breakdown he suffered at the outset of World War I, which barred him from active duty, and his unhappy marriage and separation, described in the *Daily Mail* in such lurid detail that he lost his naval commission, the years of attic seclusion with the strange, obsolete timepieces were positively therapeutic for Gould. By putting them to rights, he nursed himself back to health and peace of mind.

It seems only proper that more than half of Gould's repair work – seven years by his count – fell to H-3, which had taken Harrison the longest time to build. Indeed, Harrison's problems begat Gould's:

"No. 3 is not merely complicated, like No. 2," Gould told a gathering of the Society for Nautical Research in 1935, "it is abstruse. It embodies several devices which are entirely unique – devices which no clockmaker has ever thought of using, and which Harrison invented as the result of tackling his mechanical problems as an engineer might, and not as a clock-maker would." In more than one instance, Gould found to his chagrin that "remains of some device which Harrison had tried and subsequently discarded had been left *in situ*." He had to pick through these red herrings to find the devices truly deserving of salvage.

Unlike Dent before him, who had merely cleaned the machines and sawed off the rough edges of broken pieces to make them look neat, Gould wanted to make everything whir and tick and keep perfect time again.

While he worked, Gould filled eighteen notebooks with meticulous colored-ink drawings and elaborate verbal descriptions far clearer than any Harrison ever wrote. These he intended for his own use, to guide him through repetitions of difficult procedures, and to save himself the needless repetition of costly mistakes. The removal or replacement of the escapements in H-3, for example, routinely took eight hours, and Gould was forced to go through the routine at least forty times.

As for H-4, the Watch, "It took me three days to learn the trick of getting the hands off," Gould reported. "I more than once believed that they were welded on."

Although he cleaned H-1 first, he restored it last. This turned out to be a good thing, since H-1 was missing so many pieces that Gould needed the experience of exploring the others before he could handle H-1 with confidence: "There were no mainsprings, no mainspring-barrels, no chains, no escapements, no balance-springs, no banking-springs, and no winding gear. ... Five out of the twenty-four anti-friction wheels had vanished. Many parts of the complicated gridiron compensation were missing, and most of the others defective. The seconds-hand was gone and the hour-hand cracked. As for the small parts – pins, screws, etc. – scarcely one in ten remained."

The symmetry of H-1, however, and Gould's own determination, allowed him to duplicate many absent parts from their surviving counterparts.

"The worst job was the last," he confessed, "adjusting the little steel check-pieces on the balance-springs; a process which I can only describe as like trying to thread a needle stuck into the tailboard of a motor-lorry which you are chasing on a bicycle. I finished this, with a gale lashing the rain on to the windows of my garret, about 4 P.M. on February 1st, 1933 – and five minutes later No. 1 had begun to go again for the first time since June seventeenth, 1767: an interval of 165 years."

Thanks to Gould's efforts, the clock is still going now, in the observatory gallery. The restored time-pieces constitute John Harrison's enduring memorial, just as St. Paul's Cathedral serves as monument to Christopher Wren. Although Harrison's actual remains are entombed some miles northwest of Greenwich, in the cemetery of St. John's Church, Hampstead, where his wife, the second Elizabeth, and his son, William, lie buried with him, his mind and heart are here.

The Maritime Museum curator who now cares for the sea clocks refers to them reverently as "the Harrisons," as though they were a family of people instead of things. He dons white gloves to unlock their exhibit boxes and wind them, early every morning, before the visitors arrive. Each lock admits two different keys that work in concert, as on a modern safe deposit box – and reminiscent of the shared-key safeguards that prevailed in the clock trials of the eighteenth century.

H-1 requires one deft, downward pull on its brasslink chain. H-2 and H-3 take a turn with a winding key. That keeps them going. H-4 hibernates, unmoving and untouchable, mated for life with K-1 in the see-through cave they share.

Coming face-to-face with these machines at last – after having read countless accounts of their construction and trial, after having seen every detail of their insides and outsides in still and moving pictures – reduced me to tears. I wandered among them for hours, until I became distracted by a little girl about six years old, with a tussle of blond curls and a big Band-Aid angled above her left eye. She was viewing an automatically repeating color animation of the H-1 mechanism, over and over, sometimes staring intently at it, sometimes laughing out loud. In her excitement, she could hardly keep her hands off the small television screen, although her father, when he caught her at this, pulled them away. With his permission, I asked her what it was she liked so much about the film.

"I don't know," she answered. "I just like it."

I liked it, too.

I liked the way the rocking, interconnected components kept their steady beat, even as the cartoon clock tilted to climb up and then slide down the shaded waves. A visual synecdoche, this clock came to life not only as the true time but also as a ship at sea, sailing mile after nautical mile over the bounding time zones.

With his marine clocks, John Harrison tested the waters of space-time. He succeeded, against all odds, in using the fourth – temporal – dimension to link points on the three-dimensional globe. He wrested the world's whereabouts from the stars, and locked the secret in a pocket watch.

Dava Sobel (1995) *Longitude: The True Story of a Lone Genius Who Solved the Greatest Scientific Problem of His Times*, New York: Walker and Company, pp. 165–175.

PRINT AND LITERACY: JOHANNES GUTENBERG AND MARTIN LUTHER (1450–1517)

Johannes Gutenberg (1398–1468) was born in Mainz, Germany. He is known for having invented the first moveable type press in the West. The most important issue of his printing device was the Gutenberg Bible. A print run of but 180 copies were so magnificently reproduced that the surviving exemplars are today treasured museum pieces. As Gutenberg's printing machine made mass production of books and other printed matter possible, it remained for a cultural movement to encourage literacy. That movement was the Protestant Reformation that took root, also in Germany, after 1517. Martin Luther (1583–1646), a priest and scholar, broke with Pope Leo in the famous 95 Theses of 1517, which led to the Protestant movement – a central principle of which was that the Christian individual is the sole source of religious faith, the authority for which was not the Church but the Bible. Protestantism as it developed thus implied mass literacy. Luther himself translated the Bible into German, thereby by-passing Latin, the official language of the Church, and inspiring other translations into common language such as the King James version in English; hence, the impetus to literacy as a normal expectation of common people.

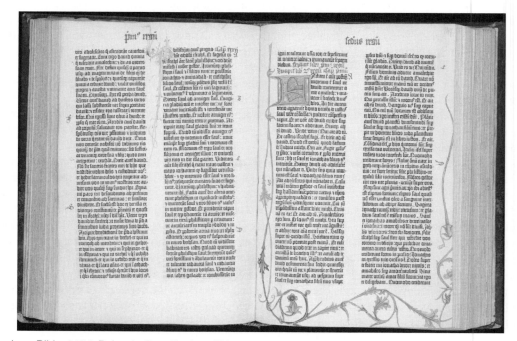

Gutenberg Bible, 1454. Beinecke Rare Book and Manuscript Library, Yale University.

ARMY AS WAR MACHINE: NAPOLEON'S MILITARY THEORY (1796–1815)

Napoleon Bonaparte (1769–1821) was born in Corsica. Bonaparte's military career progressed through the ranks such that, after successful campaigns in the 1790s, he staged the *coup d'état* in 1799 that led, five years later, to his assumption of the title of Emperor. Though his was a restoration government, Napoleon is credited with many political and legal reforms that, after the chaos in post-revolutionary France, solidified the foundations of the modern French state. His greatest fame, of course, was as the Commander of the Grand Army of France that was justifiably feared by France's enemies until, that is, he overextended his reach in the War of 1812 with Russia. Still, after defeat and exile, Napoleon returned to power. His defeat in 1815 at Waterloo by the English spelt the end of his career. In addition to the Napoleonic Code, Bonaparte's theory of total land war became a model for modern warfare. By contrast, his appreciation of naval warfare was less acute.

Napoleon, Social and Political Thoughts

In war, the commander alone understands the importance of certain things and can alone, through his will and greater insight, conquer and overcome all difficulties.

A collective government has less simple ideas and takes longer to make up its mind.

Do not hold a council of war, but take the advice of each one individually.

A man of war must have as much character as spirit; men who have much spirit and little character are the least suited [to war; such a man resembles] a ship whose masting is disproportionate to its ballast; it is better to have much character and little spirit. Men who have only an average amount of spirit and a proportionate character often succeed in this profession; one needs as much base as height. Caesar, Hannibal, Prince Eugene, and Frederick [the Great] were generals who had a lot of spirit and character in proportion.

The art of war consists, with an inferior army, in always having more forces than one's enemy at the point where one is attacking or the point where one is being attacked; but this art is to be learned neither from books nor from habit; it is delicacy of touch that strictly speaking constitutes the genius of war.

The art of war lies in positioning one's troops so that they are everywhere at once. The art of positioning troops is the great art of war. Distribute your troops in such a way that, whatever the enemy does, you can reassemble them within a few days.

Do not frontally attack positions that you can secure by flanking them.

Do not do what the enemy wishes simply because he wishes it; avoid the field of battle that he has reconnoitred and studied. Be even more careful to avoid one that he has fortified and where he has entrenched himself.

What are the conditions that make an army superior? First, its organization; second, how much experience of war the officers and men have; third, how much self-confidence they all have – that is, how much boldness, patience, and all the moral resources supplied by the idea of self.

The passage from defense to offense is one of the most delicate operations of war.

You should never leave the defensive line where the troops reform and rest without having a definite plan that leaves no uncertainty about the operations to follow. It would be a great misfortune to leave this line only to be obliged later to resume it. Three-quarters of war is a matter of morale; the balance of forces counts as only one-quarter.

In mountain war, he who attacks is at a disadvantage; even in offensive war, the art consists in only fighting on the defensive and forcing the enemy to attack.

As for moral courage, it is very rare, the courage of two o'clock in the morning – the courage of the unexpected, which, even when something happens totally out of the blue, nevertheless retains freedom of spirit, judgment, and decision making.

Loss of time is irreparable in war; the reasons alleged are always bad, since operations only fail through delays.

In the occupation of a country, the principal points should be occupied, and from them mobile columns should set out to pursue brigands. The experience of the Vendée [uprisings against the French revolutionary regime] proved that it was best to have large numbers of mobile columns scattered everywhere, and not stationary units.

The falling out of a battle is the result of an instant, a thought; the two sides come closer in various combinations, they clash, they fight for a while, the decisive moment occurs, a spark of morale declares itself, and the smallest reserve finishes it.

Caesar's principles were the same as Hannibal's; keep your forces united; do not be vulnerable at any point; move speedily to the important points; rely on morale, the reputation of your arms, the fear you inspire, and also on political means to keep your allies faithful and conquered peoples submissive.

Military genius is a gift from heaven, but the essential quality of a commander is firmness of character and the resolve to conquer at any cost.

Commanders are guided by their own experience or by genius. Tactics, movements, the science of the engineer and the artilleryman can be learned from treatises, rather like geometry; but knowledge of the higher realms of war is only acquired by experience and by study of the wars and battles of the great generals. Does one learn in grammar to compose a book of the *Iliad* or a tragedy by Corneille?

Military science consists first in accurately calculating the odds and then weighing up exactly, almost mathematically, the contribution of chance. On this point there must be no mistake; a decimal point more or less can change everything. But this distinction between science and work can only be found in the head of a genius, for it is needed wherever there is creation, and, of course, the greatest improvisation of the human spirit is that which gives existence to what has none. Chance thus always remains a mystery for mediocre spirits and becomes a reality for superior men. [. . .]

The art of war does not require complicated maneuvers; the simpler ones are to be preferred. Above all, what is needed is common sense. In those terms, it is hard to see how generals make mistakes; it is because they want to be clever. The most difficult thing is to divine the enemy's plans, to see what is true in all the reports one receives. The rest only requires common sense, it is like a bout of fisticuffs: the more blows you give, the better it will be. [. . .]

Remember these three things: union of forces, activity, and firm resolution to perish with glory. These are the three great principles of the art of war that have always given me favorable fortune in all my undertakings. Death is nothing; but to live defeated and without glory is to die every day.

The whole art of war consists in a defense that is well thought out and extremely circumspect and an offense that is bold and rapid.

You must be slow in deliberation and swift in execution.

The art of war is a simple art and everything lies in the execution; there is nothing vague about it; everything in it is common sense, nothing is ideology.

Winning is nothing, you must know how to profit from your success.

At the beginning of a campaign, you must consider carefully whether to advance or not; but once you have taken the offensive, you must maintain it to the last extremity; for apart from the honor of arms and the morale of the army, which are lost in a retreat, and the courage it gives the enemy, retreats are more disastrous and cost more in men and equipment than the most bloody engagements, with this difference, that in a battle the enemy loses almost as much as you, while in a retreat you lose without him losing anything.

With a few exceptions, victory goes to the largest force. The art of war thus consists in being superior in numbers at the point where you want to fight. If your army is smaller than the enemy's, do not give him time to unite his forces; surprise him in his movements; fall rapidly on the various regiments you have taken care to isolate, and combine your maneuvers so as to be able in all encounters to have your whole army face divisions of the [enemy's] army. In that way, with an army half the size of the enemy's, you will always be stronger than him on the field of battle.

It is exceptional and difficult to find all the qualities of a great general combined in one man. What is most desirable and distinguishes the exceptional man, is the balance of intelligence and ability with character or courage. If courage is predominant, the general will hazard far beyond his conceptions; and on the contrary, he will not dare to accomplish his conceptions if his character or his courage are below his intelligence. [. . .]

In a battle like in a siege, skill consists in converging a mass of fire on a single point: once the combat is opened, the commander who is adroit will suddenly and unexpectedly open fire with a surprising mass of artillery on one of these points, and is sure to seize it. [. . .]

War is composed of nothing but accidents, and, although holding to general principles, a general should never lose sight of everything to enable him to profit from these accidents; that is the mark of genius.

In war there is but one favorable moment; the great art is to seize it [. . .]

War on land, in general, consumes more men than naval warfare; it is more dangerous. The sailor in a fleet fights but once during a campaign; the ground soldier fights every day. The sailor, whatever may be the fatigues and dangers of the sea, suffers much less than the soldier: his is never hungry nor thirsty; he always has a place to sleep, his kitchen, his hospital and his pharmacy. There are fewer sick in the English and French fleets, where discipline maintains cleanliness and experience has discovered all the means of preserving health, than in armies. Besides the perils of battle, the sailor risks those of tempests; but seamanship has so much diminished the latter that it cannot be compared with those on land, such as popular uprisings, partial assassinations and surprises by hostile light troops.

An admiral commanding a fleet and a general commanding an army are men who need different qualities. One is born with the qualities proper to command an army, while the necessary qualities to command a fleet are acquired only by experience.

The art of war on land is an art of genius, of inspiration. On the sea everything is definite and a matter of experience. The admiral needs only one science, navigation. The general needs all or a talent equal to all, that of profiting by all experience and all knowledge. An admiral needs to divine nothing; he knows where his enemy is and he knows his strength. A general never knows anything with certainty, never sees his enemy clearly and never knows positively where he is. When armies meet, the least accident of the terrain, the smallest wood, hides a portion of the army. The most experienced eye cannot state whether he sees the entire enemy army or only three quarters of it. It is by the eyes of the mind, by reasoning over the whole, by a species of inspiration that the general sees, knows and judges. The admiral needs only an experienced glance; nothing of the enemy force is hidden from him. What makes the general's function difficult is the necessity of nourishing so many men and animals; if he permits himself to be guided by administrators, he will never budge and his expeditions will fail. The admiral is never bothered since he carries everything with him. An admiral has neither reconnaissances to make, terrain to examine nor fields of battle to study. Indian Ocean, American Ocean or North Sea – it is always a liquid plain. The most skillful will have no advantage over the least, except for his knowledge of prevailing winds in such and such coastal waters, by foresight of those which should prevail or by atmospheric signs: qualities which are acquired by experience and by experience only.

The general never knows the field of battle on which he may operate. His understanding is that of inspiration; he has no positive information; data to reach a knowledge of localities are so contingent on events that almost nothing is learned by experience. It is a faculty to understand immediately the relations of the terrain according to the nature of different countries; it is, finally, a gift, called a *coup d'oeil militaire* [the ability to take in the military situation at a glance] which great generals have received from nature. However the observations that can be made from topographic maps and the facility which education and habit give in reading maps, can be of some assistance.

An admiral depends more on the captains of his ships than a general on his generals. The latter has the opportunity to take direct command of the troops himself, to move to any point and to repair false movements. An admiral can influence personally only the men on the vessel on which he finds himself; smoke prevents signals from being seen and winds change or vary over the space occupied by his line. It is thus of all professions that in which subalterns should use the largest initiative.

"Napoleon," in Gérard Chaliand (ed.) (1994) *The Art of War in World History: From Antiquity to the Nuclear Age*, Berkeley: University of California Press, pp. 646–651.

■ ■ ■ ■ ■ ■

WEIGHTS AND MEASURES: THE SCIENTIFIC FOREST (1765–1800)

James C. Scott (1936–) teaches political science at Yale. He lives on a farm in Durham, Connecticut. He is noted for his research and writings on many subjects in and around political theory and history including *Weapons of the Weak* (1985) and *Domination and the Arts of Resistance* (1990), as well as *Seeing Like a State* (1998) which, among other contributions, is an important scholarly study of the centrality of measures and measurement to modern political and economic institutions.

Seeing Like a State: Nature and Space

Certain forms of knowledge and control require a narrowing of vision. The great advantage of such tunnel vision is that it brings into sharp focus certain limited aspects of an otherwise far more complex and unwieldy reality. This very simplification, in turn, makes the phenomenon at the center of the field of vision more legible and hence more susceptible to careful measurement and calculation. Combined with similar observations, an overall, aggregate, synoptic view of a selective reality is achieved, making possible a high degree of schematic knowledge, control, and manipulation.

The invention of scientific forestry in late eighteenth-century Prussia and Saxony serves as something of a model of this process.[1] Although the history of scientific forestry is important in its own right, it is used here as a metaphor for the forms of knowledge and manipulation characteristic of powerful institutions with sharply defined interests, of which state bureaucracies and large commercial firms are perhaps the outstanding examples. Once we have seen how simplification, legibility, and manipulation operate in forest management, we can then explore how the modern state applies a similar lens to urban planning, rural settlement, land administration, and agriculture.

The State and Scientific Forestry: A Parable

> I [Gilgamesh] would conquer in the Cedar Forest. . . . I will set my hand to it and will chop down the Cedar.
> – *Epic of Gilgamesh*

The early modern European state, even before the development of scientific forestry, viewed its forests primarily through the fiscal lens of revenue needs. To be sure, other concerns – such as timber for ship-building, state construction, and fuel for the economic security of its subjects – were not entirely absent from official management. These concerns also had heavy implications for state revenue and security.[2] Exaggerating only slightly, one might say that the crown's interest in forests was resolved through its fiscal lens into a single number: the revenue yield of the timber that might be extracted annually.

The best way to appreciate how heroic was this constriction of vision is to notice what fell outside its field of vision. Lurking behind the number indicating revenue yield were not so much forests as commercial wood, representing so many thousands of board feet of saleable timber and so many cords of firewood fetching a certain price. Missing, of course, were all those trees, bushes, and plants holding little or no potential for state revenue. Missing as well were all those parts of trees, even revenue-bearing trees, which might have been useful to the population but whose value could not be converted into fiscal receipts. Here I have in mind foliage and its uses as fodder and thatch; fruits, as food for people and domestic animals; twigs and branches, as bedding, fencing, hop poles, and kindling; bark and roots, for making medicines and for tanning; sap, for making resins; and so forth. Each species of tree – indeed, each part or growth stage of each species – had its unique properties and uses. A fragment of the entry under "elm" in a popular seventeenth-century encyclopedia on aboriculture conveys something of the vast range of practical uses to which the tree could be put.

> Elm is a timber of most singular use, especially whereby it may be continually dry, or wet, in extremes; therefore proper for water works, mills, the ladles and soles of the wheel, pumps, aqueducts, ship planks below the water line, . . . also for wheelwrights, handles for the single handsaw, rails and gates. Elm is not so apt to rive [split] . . . and is used for chopping blocks, blocks for the hat maker, trunks and boxes to be covered with leather, coffins and dressers and shovelboard tables of great length; also for the carver and those curious workers of fruitage, foliage, shields, statues and most of the ornaments appertaining to the orders of architecture. . . . And finally . . . the use of the very leaves of this tree, especially the female, is not to be despised, . . . for they will prove of great relief to cattle in the winter and scorching summers when hay and fodder is dear. . . . The green leaf of the elms contused heals a green wound or cut, and boiled with the bark, consolidates bone fractures.[3]

In state "fiscal forestry," however, the actual tree with its vast number of possible uses was replaced by an abstract tree representing a volume of lumber or firewood. If the princely conception of the forest was still utilitarian, it was surely a utilitarianism confined to the direct needs of the state.

From a naturalist's perspective, nearly everything was missing from the state's narrow frame of reference. Gone was the vast majority of flora: grasses, flowers, lichens, ferns, mosses, shrubs, and vines. Gone, too, were reptiles, birds, amphibians, and innumerable species of insects. Gone were most species of fauna, except those that interested the crown's gamekeepers.

From an anthropologist's perspective, nearly everything touching on human interaction with the forest was also missing from the state's tunnel vision. The state did pay attention to poaching, which impinged on its claim to revenue in wood or its claim to royal game, but otherwise it typically ignored the vast, complex, and negotiated social uses of the forest for hunting and gathering, pasturage, fishing, charcoal making, trapping, and collecting food and valuable minerals as well as the forest's significance for magic, worship, refuge, and so on.[4]

If the utilitarian state could not see the real, existing forest for the (commercial) trees, if its view of its forests was abstract and partial, it was hardly unique in this respect. Some level of abstraction is necessary for virtually all forms of analysis, and it is not at all surprising that the abstractions of state officials should have reflected the paramount fiscal interests of their employer. The entry under "forest" in Diderot's *Encyclopédie* is almost exclusively concerned with the *utilité publique* of forest products and the taxes, revenues, and profits that they can be made to yield. The forest as a habitat disappears and is replaced by the forest as an economic resource to be managed efficiently and profitably.[5] Here, fiscal and commercial logics coincide; they are both resolutely fixed on the bottom line.

The vocabulary used to organize nature typically betrays the overriding interests of its human users. In fact, utilitarian discourse replaces the term "nature" with the term "natural resources," focusing on those aspects of nature that can be appropriated for human use. A comparable logic extracts from a more generalized natural world those flora or fauna that are of utilitarian value (usually marketable commodities) and, in turn, reclassifies those species that compete with, prey on, or otherwise diminish the yields of the valued species. Thus, plants that are valued become "crops," the species that compete with them are stigmatized as "weeds," and the insects that ingest them are stigmatized as "pests." Thus, trees that are valued become "timber," while species that compete with them become "trash" trees or "underbrush." The same logic applies to fauna. Highly valued animals become "game" or "livestock," while those animals that compete with or prey upon them become "predators" or "varmints."

The kind of abstracting, utilitarian logic that the state, through its officials, applied to the forest is thus not entirely distinctive. What is distinctive about this logic, however, is the narrowness of its field of vision, the degree of elaboration to which it can be subjected, and above all, as we shall see, the degree to which it allowed the state to impose that logic on the very reality that was observed.[6]

Scientific forestry was originally developed from about 1765 to 1800, largely in Prussia and Saxony. Eventually, it would become the basis of forest management techniques in France, England, and the United States and throughout the Third World. Its emergence cannot be understood outside the larger context of the centralized state-making initiatives of the period. In fact, the new forestry science was a subdiscipline of what was called cameral science, an effort to reduce the fiscal management of a kingdom to scientific principles that would allow systematic planning.[7] Traditional domainal forestry had hitherto simply divided the forest into roughly equal plots, with the number of plots co-inciding with the number of years in the assumed growth cycle.[8] One plot was cut each year on the assumption of equal yields (and value) from plots of equal size. Because of poor maps, the uneven distribution of the most valuable large trees (*Hochwald*), and very approximate cordwood (*Bruststaerke*) measures, the results were unsatisfactory for fiscal planning.

The achievement of German forestry science in standardizing techniques for calculating the sustainable yield of commercial timber and hence revenue was impressive enough. What is decisive for our purposes, however, was the next logical step in forest management. That step was to attempt to create, through careful seeding, planting, and cutting, a forest that was easier for state foresters to count, manipulate, measure, and assess. The fact is that forest science and geometry, backed by state power, had the capacity to transform the real, diverse, and chaotic old-growth forest into a new, more uniform forest that closely resembled the administrative grid of its techniques. To this end, the underbrush was cleared, the number of species was reduced (often to monoculture), and plantings were done simultaneously and in straight rows on large tracts. These management practices, as Henry Lowood observes, "produced the monocultural, even-age forests that eventually transformed the Normalbaum from abstraction to reality. The German forest became the archetype for imposing on disorderly nature the neatly arranged constructs of science. Practical goals had encouraged mathematical utilitarianism, which seemed, in turn, to promote geometric perfection as the outward sign of the well-managed forest; in turn the rationally ordered arrangements of trees offered new possibilities for controlling nature."[9]

The tendency was toward regimentation, in the strict sense of the word. The forest trees were drawn up into serried, uniform ranks, as it were, to be measured, counted off, felled, and replaced by a new rank and file of lookalike conscripts. As an army, it was also designed hierarchically from above to fulfill a unique purpose and to be at the disposition of a single commander. At the limit, the forest itself would not even have to be seen; it could be "read" accurately from the tables and maps in the forester's office.

Forging the tools of legibility: Popular measures, state measures

Nonstate forms of measurement grew from the logic of local practice. As such, they shared some generic features despite their bewildering variety – features that made them an impediment to administrative uniformity. Thanks to the synthesis of the medievalist Witold Kula, the reasoning that animated local practices of measurement may be set out fairly succinctly.[10]

Most early measures were human in scale. One sees this logic at work in such surviving expressions as a "stone's throw" or "within earshot" for distances and a "cartload," a "basketful," or a "handful" for volume. Given that the size of a cart or basket might vary from place to place and that a stone's throw might not be precisely uniform from person to person, these units of measurement varied geographically and temporally. Even measures that were apparently fixed might be deceptive. The *pinte* in eighteenth-century Paris, for example, was equivalent to .93 liters, whereas in Seine-en-Montagne it was 1.99 liters and in Precy-sous-Thil, an astounding 3.33 liters. The *aune*, a measure of length used for cloth, varied depending on the material (the unit for silk, for instance, was smaller than that for linen), and across France there were at least seventeen different aunes.[11]

Local measures were also relational or "commensurable."[12] Virtually any request for a judgment of measure allows a range of responses depending on the context of the request. In the part of Malaysia with which I am most familiar, if one were to ask "How far is it to the next village?" a likely response would be "Three rice-cookings." The answer assumes that the questioner is interested in how much time it will take to get there, not how many miles away it is. In varied terrain, of course, distance in miles is an utterly unreliable guide to travel time, especially when the traveler is on foot or riding a bicycle. The answer also expresses time not in minutes – until recently, wristwatches were rare – but in units that are locally meaningful. Everyone knows how long it takes to cook the local rice. Thus an Ethiopian response to a query about how much salt is required for a dish might be "Half as much as to cook a chicken." The reply refers back to a standard that everyone is expected to know. Such measurement practices are irreducibly local, inasmuch as regional differences in, say, the type of rice eaten or the preferred way of cooking chicken will give different results.

Many local units of measurement are tied practically to particular activities. Marathi peasants, as Arjun Appadurai notes, express the desired distance between the onion sets they plant in terms of hand-breadths. When one is moving along a field row, the hand is, well, the most handy gauge. In similar fashion, a common measure for twine or rope is the distance between the thumb and elbow because this corresponds with how it is wrapped and stored. As with setting onions, the process of measuring is embedded in the activity itself and requires no separate operation. Such measurements, moreover, are often approximate; they are only as exact as the task at hand requires.[13] Rainfall may be said to be abundant or inadequate if the context of the query implies an interest in a particular crop. And a reply in terms of inches of rainfall, however accurate, would also fail to convey the desired information; it ignores such vital matters as the timing of the rain. For many purposes, an apparently vague measurement may communicate more valuable information than a statistically exact figure. The cultivator who reports that his rice yield from a plot is anywhere between four and seven baskets is conveying more accurate information, when the focus of attention is on the variability of the yield, than if he reported a ten-year statistical average of 5.6 baskets.

There is, then, no single, all-purpose, correct answer to a question implying measurement unless we specify the relevant local concerns that give rise to the question. Particular customs of measurement are thus situationally, temporally, and geographically bound.

The politics of measurement

Thus far, this account of local measurement practices risks giving the impression that, although local conceptions of distance, area, volume, and so on were different from and more varied than the unitary abstract standards a state might favor, they were nevertheless aiming at objective accuracy. That impression would be false. Every act of measurement was an act marked by the play of power relations. To understand measurement practices in early modern Europe, as Kula demonstrates, one must relate them to the contending interests of the major estates: aristocrats, clergy, merchants, artisans, and serfs.

A good part of the politics of measurement sprang from what a contemporary economist might call the "stickiness" of feudal rents. Noble and clerical claimants often found it difficult to increase feudal dues directly; the levels set for various charges were the result of long struggle, and even a small increase above the customary level was viewed as a threatening breach of tradition.[14] Adjusting the measure, however, represented a roundabout way of achieving the same end. The local lord might, for example, lend grain to peasants in smaller baskets and insist on repayment in larger baskets. He might surreptitiously or even boldly enlarge the size of the grain sacks accepted for milling (a monopoly of the domain lord) and reduce the size of the sacks used for measuring out flour; he might also collect feudal dues in larger baskets and pay wages in kind in smaller baskets. While the formal custom governing feudal dues and wages would thus remain intact (requiring, for example, the same number of sacks of wheat from the harvest of a given holding), the actual transaction might increasingly favor the lord.[15] The results of such fiddling were far from trivial. Kula estimates that the size of the bushel (boisseau) used to collect the main feudal rent (taille) increased by one-third between 1674 and 1716 as part of what was called the réaction féodale.[16]

Even when the unit of measurement – say, the bushel – was apparently agreed upon by all, the fun had just begun. Virtually everywhere in early modern Europe were endless micropolitics about how baskets might be adjusted through wear, bulging, tricks of weaving, moisture, the thickness of the rim, and so on. In some areas the local standards for the bushel and other units of measurement were kept in metallic form and placed in the care of a trusted official or else literally carved into the stone of a church or the town hall.[17] Nor did it end there. How the grain was to be poured (from shoulder height, which packed it somewhat, or from waist height?), how damp it could be, whether the container could be shaken down, and, finally, if and how it was to be leveled off when full were subjects of long and bitter controversy. Some arrangements called for the grain to be heaped, some for a "half-heap," and still others for it to be leveled or "striked" (*ras*). These were not trivial matters. A feudal lord could increase his rents by 25 percent by insisting on receiving wheat and rye in heaped bushels.[18] If, by custom, the bushel of grain was to be striked, then a further micropolitics erupted over the strickle. Was it to be round, thereby packing in grain as it was rolled across the rim, or was it to be sharp-edged? Who would apply the strickle? Who could be trusted to keep it?

A comparable micropolitics, as one might expect, swirled around the unit of land measurement. A common measure of length, the ell, was used to mark off the area to be plowed or weeded as a part of feudal labor dues. Once again, the lengths and widths in ells were "sticky," having been established through long struggle. It was tempting for a lord or overseer to try raising labor dues indirectly by increasing the length of the ell. If the attempt were successful, the formal rules of corvée labor would not be violated, but the amount of work extracted would increase. Perhaps the stickiest of all measures before the nineteenth century was the price of bread. As the most vital subsistence good of premodern times, it served as a kind of cost-of-living index, and its cost was the subject of deeply held popular customs about its relationship to the typical urban wage. Kula shows in remarkable detail how bakers, afraid to provoke a riot by directly violating the "just price," managed nevertheless to manipulate the size and weight of the loaf to compensate to some degree for changes in the price of wheat and rye flour.[19]

Notes

1 Henry E. Lowood, 'The Calculating Forester: Quantification, Cameral Science, and the Emergence of Scientific Forestry Management in Germany,' in Tore Frangsmyr, J. L. Heilbron, and Robin E. Rider, eds, *The Quantifying Spirit in the Eighteenth Century* (Berkeley: University of California Press, 1991), pp. 315–42. The following account is largely drawn from Lowood's fine analysis.

2 The most striking exception was the royal attention to the supply of 'noble game' (e.g., deer, boars, foxes) for the hunt and hence to the protection of its habitat. Lest one imagine this to be a quaint premodern affectation, it is worth recalling the enormous social importance of the hunt to such recent 'monarchs' as Erich Honeker, Nicolae Ceauşescu, Georgy Zhuvkov, Władysław Gomułka, and Marshal Tito.

3 John Evelyn, *Sylva, or A Discourse of Forest Trees* (London, 1664, 1679), p. 118, cited in John Brinckerhoff Jackson, *A Sense of Place, a Sense of Time* (New Haven: Yale University Press, 1994), pp. 97–98.

4 Ramachandra Guha reminds me that the verb 'ignore' is inadequate here, for the state typically sought to control, regulate, and extinguish those practices that interfered with its own management policies. For much of my (admittedly limited) early education in the history of forestry, I am grateful to Ramachandra Guha and his two books, *The Unquiet Woods: Ecological Change and Peasant Resistance in the Himalaya* (Berkeley: University of California Press, 1989), and, with Madhav Gadgil, *This Fissured Land: An Ecological History of India* (Delhi: Oxford University Press, 1992). For an evocative and wide ranging exploration of the changing cultural meaning of the forest in the West, see Robert Pogue Harrison, *Forests: The Shadow of Civilization* (Chicago: University of Chicago Press, 1992).

5 Harrison, *Forests*, p. 121.

6 This last is a kind of twist on the Heisenberg principle. Instead of altering the phenomenon observed through the act of observation, so that the pre-observation state of the phenomenon is unknowable in principle, the effect of (interested) observation in this case is to alter the phenomenon in question over time so that it, in fact, more closely resembles the stripped down, abstract image the lens had revealed.

7 See Keith Tribe, *Governing Economy: The Reformation of German Economic Discourse, 1750–1840* (Cambridge: Cambridge University Press, 1988). The more general process of codifying the principles of state administration in seventeenth- and eighteenth-century Europe is examined by Michel Foucault under the (misleading) heading of 'police state'

(from *Polizeiwissenschaft*) in this lectures on 'governmentality,' delivered at the Collège de France. See Graham Burchell, Colin Gordon, and Peter Miller, eds. *The Foucault Effect: Studies in Governmentality* (London: Harvester Wheatsheaf, 1991), especially chap. 4.

8   In the late seventeenth century, Jean-Baptiste Colbert had extensive plans to 'rationalize' forest administration in order both to prevent poaching and to generate a more reliable revenue yield. To this end, Etienne Dralet's *Traité du regime forestier* proposed regulated plots (*tire-aire*) 'so that the growth is regular and easy to guard.' Despite these initiatives, nothing much came of it in France until 1820, when the new German techniques were imported. See Peter Sahlins, *Forest Rites: The War of the Demoiselles in Nineteenth-Century France*, Harvard Historical Studies no. 115 (Cambridge: Harvard University Press, 1994).

9   Lowood, 'The Calculating Forester,' p. 341. See also Harrison, *Forests*, pp. 122–3.

10   Witold Kula, *Measures and Men*, trans. R. Szreter (Princeton: Princeton University Press, 1986).

11   J. L. Heilbron, 'The Measure of Enlightenment,' in Tore Frangsmyr, J. L. Heilbron, and Robin E. Rider, eds., *The Quantifying Spirit in the Eighteenth Century* (Berkeley: University of California Press, 1991), pp. 207–8.

12   For an illuminating discussion along these lines, see Arjun Appadurai, 'Measurement Discourse in Rural Maharastra,' in Appadurai et al., *Agriculture, Language, and Knowledge in South Asia: Perspectives from History and Anthropology* (forthcoming).

13   Ibid., p. 14.

14   What was seen as customary might not have had a very long pedigree. It was always in the interests of at least one party, who feared a disadvantageous renegotiation, to treat the existing arrangement as fixed and sacrosanct.

15   Occasionally, the balance of power might swing in the other direction. See, in this connection, the evidence for a long decline in tithe payments in France: Emanuel LeRoi Ladurie and Joseph Gay, *Tithe and Agrarian History from the Fourteenth Century to the Nineteenth Century: An Essay in Comparative History,* trans. Susan Burke (Cambridge: Cambridge University Press, 1982), p. 27.

16   Kula, *Measures and Men*, p. 150. In Lower Bruma in the 1920s and '30s, the landlord's paddy basket for receiving tenants' rent in kind was nicknamed 'the cartbreaker' (James C. Scott, *The Moral Economy of the Peasant: Rebellion and Subsistence in Southeast Asia* [New Haven: Yale University press, 1976], p. 71).

17   The famous iron *toise* of Paris, for example, was set in one of the walls of the Grand Chatelet; see Ken Alder, 'A Revolution Made to Measure: The Political Economy of the Metric System in France,' in Norton W. Wise, ed., *Values of Precision* (Princeton: Princeton University Press, 1995), p. 44.

18   Marsenne, in the seventeenth-century spirit of exactitude, calculated that a striked boisseau held 172,000 grains of wheat, whereas a heaped measure held 220,160 (Kula, *Measures and Men*, p. 172). The advantage with oats, a larger grain is less.

19   Ibid., pp. 73–4. As with other challenges to customary measures, this one provoked municipal authorities and the populace to insist on weighing and measuring, in this case bakers' loaves, to prevent such practices.

James C. Scott (1998) *Seeing Like a State: How Certain Schemes to Improve the Human Condition Have Failed*, New Haven: Yale University Press, pp. 11–15, 25–29.

THERMODYNAMICS AND THE STEAM ENGINE: ROBERT BOYLE AND JAMES WATT (1662–1769)

Robert Boyle (1627–1691) published his law of thermodynamics in 1662, stating that for a gas at a constant temperature, there is an inverse relationship between pressure and volume ($k = PV$). While Boyle's law is for a constant, this principle is behind the development of steam power and the more recent internal combustion engines where a rising temperature increases pressure. James Watt (1736–1819), a Scottish engineer, is famous for refining the Newcomen steam engine by adding a separate steam condenser. This refinement, combined with more precise tooling of engine parts, made a more efficient and powerful engine that could be used for mining, industrial power, and locomotion. The steam engine, developed with Boyle's constant, was a driver of the industrial revolution and mechanized transportation.

Watt's Steam Engine Patent (1769)

TO ALL TO WHOM THESE PRESENTS SHALL COME, I, JAMES WATT, of Glasgow, in Scotland, Merchant, send greeting.

WHEREAS His most Excellent Majesty King George the Third, by His Letters Patent under the Great Seal of Great Britain, bearing date the Fifth day of January, in the ninth year of His said Majesty's reign, did give and grant unto me, the said James Watt, His special licence, full power, sole priviledge and authority, that I, the said James Watt, my exõrs, admõrs, and assigns, should and lawfully might, during the term of years therein expressed, use, exercise, and vend, throughout that part of His Majesty's Kingdom of Great Britain called England, the Dominion of Wales, and Town of Berwick upon Tweed, and also in His Majesty's Colonies and Plantations abroad, my "NEW INVENTED METHOD OF LESSENING THE CONSUMPTION OF STEAM AND FUEL IN FIRE ENGINES;" in which said recited Letters Patent is contained a proviso obliging me, the said James Watt, by writing under my hand and seal, to cause a particular description of the nature of the said Invention to be inrolled in His Majesties High Court of Chancery within four calendar months after the date of the said recited Letters Patent, as in and by the said Letters Patent, and the Statute in that behalf made, relation being thereunto respectively had, may more at large appear.

NOW KNOW YE, that in compliance with the said provisoe, and in pursuance of the said Statute, I, the said James Watt, do hereby declare that the following is a particular description of the nature of my said Invention, and of the manner in which the same is to be performed (that is to say): –

My method of lessening the consumption of steam, and consequently fuel, in fire engines consists of the following principles: –

First, that vessell in which the powers of steam are to be employed to work the engine, which is called the cylinder in common fire engines, and which I call the steam vessell, must during the whole time the engine is at work be kept as hot as the steam that enters it, first, by enclosing it in a case of wood or any other materials that transmit heat slowly; secondly, by surrounding it with steam or other heated bodies; and, thirdly, by suffering neither water or any other substance colder than the steam to enter or touch it during that time.

Secondly, in engines that are to be worked wholly or partially by condensation of steam, the steam is to be condensed in vessells distinct from the steam vessells or cylinders, although occasionally communicating with them. These vessells I call condensers, and whilst the engines are working, these condensers ought at least to be kept as cold as the air in the neighbourhood of the engines by application of water or other cold bodies.

Thirdly, whatever air or other elastic vapour is not condensed by the cold of the condenser, and may impede the working of the engine; is to be drawn out of the steam vessells or condensers, by means of pumps wrought by the engines themselves, or otherwise.

Fourthly, I intend in many cases to employ the expansive force of steam to press on the pistons, or whatever may be used instead of them, in the same manner as the pressure of the atmosphere is now employed in common fire engines. In cases where cold water cannot be had in plenty, the engines may be wrought by this force of steam only, by discharging the steam into the open air after it has done its office.

Fifthly, where motions round an axis are required, I make the steam vessells in form of hollow rings or circular channels, with proper inletts and outletts for the steam, mounted on horizontal axles like the wheels of a water mill; within them are placed a number of valves that suffer any body to go round the channell in one direction only. In these steam vessells are placed weights, so fitted to them as intirely to fill up a part or portion of their channels, yet rendered capable of moving freely in them by the means herein-after mentioned or specified. When the steam is admitted in these engines between these weights and the valves, it acts equally on both, so as to raise the weight to one side of the wheel, and by the reaction on the valves successively to give a circular motion to the wheel, the valves opening in the direction in which the weights are pressed, but not in the contrary. As the steam vessel moves round it is supplied with steam from the boiler, and that which has performed its office may either be discharged by means of condensers, or into the open air.

Sixthly, I intend in some cases to apply a degree of cold not capable of reducing the steam to water, but of contracting it considerably, so that the engines shall be worked by the alternate expansion and constraction of the steam.

Lastly, instead of using water to render the piston or other parts of the engines air and steam tight, I employ oils, wax, rosinous bodies, fat of animals, quicksilver and other metalls, in their fluid state.

In witness whereof, I have hereunto set my hand and seal, this Twenty-fifth day of April, in the year of our Lord One thousand seven hundred and sixty-nine.

JAMES WATT. (L.S.)

Sealed and delivered in the presence of
COLL. WILKIE.
GEO. JARDINE.
JOHN ROEBUCK.

Be it remembered, that the said James Watt doth not intend that any thing in the fourth article shall be understood to extend to any engine where the water to be raised enters the steam vessell itself, or any vessell having an open communication with it.

JAMES WATT.

Witnesses,
COLL. WILKIE.
GEO. JARDINE.

AND BE IT REMEMBERED, that on the Twenty-fifth day of April, in the year of our Lord 1769, the aforesaid James Watt came before our said Lord the King in His Chancery, and acknowledged the Specification aforesaid, and all and every thing therein contained and specified, in form above written. And also the Specification aforesaid was stampt according to the tenor of the Statute made in the sixth year of the reign of the late King and Queen William and Mary of England, and so forth.

Inrolled the Twenty-ninth day of April, in the year of our Lord One thousand seven hundred and sixty-nine.

James Watt, Patent, 1855. Printed by George Edward Eyre and William Spottiswoode.

STEEL AND HEAVY INDUSTRY: HENRY BESSEMER (1856)

Sir Henry Bessemer (1813–1898) was an English engineer and inventor with over 129 patents. Most significantly, he is known for the Bessemer Process of making steel. He presented his process to the British Association on August 24, 1856, in a talk entitled "The Manufacture of Iron without Fuel." This process revolutionized the making of steel, utilizing a "Bessemer Converter" and involves bubbling air through pig iron to expunge impurities. The Bessemer Process made the production of steel both easier and cost effective, allowing steel to replace cast iron as a building material. While the process has been abandoned today, the Bessemer Process was an important and critical contribution to the industrial world, in particular the development of heavy industry, as steel is more resilient than iron. Quality steel is necessary for guns, railroads, bridges, and other industrial applications.

On the Manufacture of Malleable Iron and Steel without Fuel

MR. H. BESSEMER read the following paper at the British Association on Monday last: –

The manufacture of iron in this country has attained such an important position, that any improvement in this branch of our national industry cannot fail to be a source of general interest, and will, I trust, be a sufficient excuse for the present brief, and I fear, imperfect paper. I may mention, that for the last two years my attention has been almost exclusively directed to the manufacture of malleable iron and steel, in which, however, I had made but little progress, until within the last eight or nine months. The constant pulling down and rebuilding of furnaces, and the toil of daily experiments with large charges of iron, had already begun to exhaust my stock of patience; but the numerous observations I had made during this very unpromising period, all tended to confirm an entirely new view of the subject, which at that time forced itself upon my attention, viz – that I could produce a much more intense heat without any furnace or fuel, than could be obtained by either of the modifications I had used, and consequently that I should not only avoid the injurious action of mineral fuel on the iron under operation, but that I should at the same time avoid also the expense of the fuel. Some preliminary trials were made on from 101b. to 201b. of iron, and although the process was fraught with considerable difficulty, it exhibited such unmistakeable signs of success, as to induce me at once to put up an apparatus capable of converting about 7 cwt. of crude pig iron into malleable iron in 30 minutes. With such masses of metal to operate on, the difficulties which beset the small laboratory experiments of 101b. entirely disappeared. On this new field of inquiry, I set out with the assumption, that crude iron contains about 5 per cent. of carbon; that carbon cannot exist at a white heat in the presence of oxygen, without uniting therewith, and producing combustion; that such combustion would proceed with a rapidity dependent on the amount of surface of carbon exposed; and, lastly, that the temperature which the metal would acquire would be also dependent on the rapidity with which the oxygen and carbon were made to combine, and consequently that it was only necessary to bring the oxygen and carbon together in such a manner, that a vast surface should be exposed to their mutual action, in order to produce a temperature hitherto unattainable in our largest furnaces. With a view of testing practically this theory, I constructed a cylindrical vessel of three feet in diameter, and five feet in height, somewhat like an ordinary cupola furnace, the interior of which is lined with fire bricks, and at about two inches from the bottom of it, I insert five tuyère pipes, the nozzles of which are formed of well-burnt fire clay, the orifice of each tuyère being about three-eighths of an inch in diameter; they are so put into the brick lining (from the outer side) as to admit of their removal and renewal in a few minutes when they are worn out. At one side of the vessel, about half way up from the bottom, there is a hole made for running in the crude metal, and in the opposite side there is a tap-hole stopped with loam, by means of which the iron is run out at the end of the process. In practice this converting vessel may be made of any convenient size, but I prefer that it should not hold less than one, or more than five tons of fluid iron at each charge. The vessel should be placed so near to the discharge hole of the blast furnace as to allow the iron to flow along a gutter into it; a small blast cylinder will be required capable of compressing air to about 81b. or 101b. to the square inch. A communication having been made between it and the tuyères before named, the converting vessel will be in a condition to commence work; it will, however, on the occasion of its first being used after relining with firebricks be necessary to make a fire in the interior with a few baskets of coke, so as to dry the brickwork and heat up the vessel for the first operation, after which the fire is to be all carefully raked out at the tapping hole, which is again to be made good with loam. The vessel will then be in readiness to commence work, and may be so continued without any use of fuel until the brick lining in the course of time becomes worn away and a new lining is required. I have before mentioned that the tuyères are situated nearly close to the bottom of the vessel; the fluid metal will therefore rise some 18 inches or 2 feet above them. It is therefore necessary, in order to prevent the metal from entering the tuyère holes, to turn on the blast before allowing the fluid crude iron to run into the vessel from the blast furnace. This having been done, and the fluid iron run in, a rapid boiling up of the metal will be heard going on within the vessel, the metal being tossed violently about and dashed from side to side, shaking the vessel by the force with which it moves, from the throat of the converting vessel. Flame will then immediately issue, accompanied by a few bright sparks. This state of things will continue for about 15 or 20 minutes, during which time the oxygen in the atmospheric air combines with the carbon contained in the iron, producing carbonic acid gas, and at the same time evolving a powerful heat. Now, as this heat is generated in the interior of, and is diffusive in innumerable fiery bubbles through, the whole fluid mass, the vessel absorbs the greater part of it, and its temperature becomes immensely increased, and by the expiration of the 15 or 20 minutes before named that part of the carbon which appears mechanically mixed and diffused through the crude iron has been entirely consumed. The temperature, however, is so high that the chymically combined carbon now begins to separate from the metal, as is at once indicated by an immense increase in the volume of flame rushing out of the throat of the vessel. The metal in the vessel now rises several inches above its natural level, and a light frothy slag makes its appearance, and is thrown out in large foam-like masses. This violent eruption of cinder generally lasts about five or six minutes, when all further appearance of it ceases, a steady and powerful flame replacing the shower of sparks and cinders which always accompanies the boil. The rapid union of carbon and oxygen which thus takes place adds still further to the temperature of the metal, while the diminished quantity of carbon present allows a part of the oxygen to combine with the iron, which undergoes a combustion and is converted into an oxide. At the excessive temperature that the metal has now acquired the oxide as soon as formed undergoes fusion, and forms a powerful solvent of those earthy bases that are associated with the iron. The violent ebullition which is going on mixes most intimately the scoria and metal, every part of which is thus brought in contact with the fluid oxide, which will thus wash and cleanse the metal most thoroughly from the silica and other earthy bases which are combined with the crude iron, while the sulphur and other volatile matters which cling so tenaciously to iron at ordinary temperatures are driven off, the sulphur combining with the oxygen and forming sulphurous acid gas. The loss in weight of crude iron during its conversion into an ingot of malleable iron was found on a mean of four experiments to be 12½ per cent, to which will have to be added the loss of metal in the finishing rolls. This will make the entire loss probably not less than 18 per cent., instead of about 28 per cent, which is the loss on the present system. A large portion of this metal is, however, recoverable by treating with carbonaceous gases the rich oxides thrown out of the furnace during the boil. These slags are found to contain innumerable small grains of metallic iron, which are mechanically held in suspension in the slags, and may be easily recovered. I have before mentioned that after the boil has taken place a steady and powerful flame succeeds, which continues without any change for about 10 minutes, when it rapidly falls off. As soon as this diminution of flame is apparent the workman will know that the process is completed, and that the crude iron has been converted into pure malleable iron, which he will form into ingots of any suitable size and shape by simply opening the tap hole of the converting vessel and allowing the fluid malleable iron to flow into the iron ingot moulds placed there to receive it. The masses of iron thus formed will be perfectly free from any admixture of cinder, oxide, or other extraneous matters, and will be far more pure and in a forwarder state of manufacture than a pile formed of ordinary puddle bars. And thus it will be seen that by a single process, requiring no manipulation or particular skill, and with only one workman, from three to five tons of crude iron passes into the condition of several piles of malleable iron in from 30 to 35 minutes, with the expenditure of about one-third part the blast now used in a finery furnace with an equal charge of iron, and with the consumption of no other fuel than is contained in the crude iron. To those who are best acquainted with the nature of fluid iron, it may be a matter of surprise that a blast of cold air forced into melted crude iron is capable of raising its temperature to such a degree as to retain it in a perfect state of fluidity after it has lost all its carbon, and is in the condition of malleable iron, which in the highest heat of our forges only becomes a pasty mass. But such is the excessive temperature that I am enabled to arrive at with a properly shaped converting vessel and a judicious distribution of the blast, that I am enabled not only to retain the fluidity of the metal, but to create so much surplus heat as to re-melt the crop ends, ingot runners, and other scrap that is made throughout the process, and thus bring them without labour or fuel into ingots of a quality equal to the rest of the charge of new metal. For this purpose a small arched chamber is formed immediately over the throat of the converting vessel, somewhat like the tunnel head of the blast furnace. This chamber has two or more openings on the sides of it, and its floor is made to slope down words to the throat. As soon as a charge of fluid malleable iron has been drawn off from the connecting vessel, the workman will take the scrap intended to be worked into the next charge and proceed to introduce the several pieces into the small chamber, piling thom up around the opening of the throat. When this is done, he will run in his charge of crude metal, and again commence the process. By the time the boil commences the bar ends or other scrap will have acquired a white heat, and by the time it is over most of them will have been melted and run down into the charge. Any pieces, however, that remain, may then be pushed in by the workmen, and by the time the process is completed they will will all be melted, and ultimately combined with the rest of the charge, so that all scrap iron, whether cast or malleable, may thus be used up without any loss or expense. As an example of the power that iron has of generating heat in this process, I may mention a circumstance that occurred to me during my experiments. I was trying how small a set of tuyères could be used; but the size chosen proved to be too small, and after blowing into the metal for one hour and three-quarters I could not get up heat enough with them to bring on the boil. The experiment was therefore discontinued, during which time two-thirds of the metal solidified, and the rest was run off. A larger set of tuyère pipes were then put in, and a fresh charge of fluid iron run into the vessel, which had the effect of entirely remelting the former charge; and when the whole was tapped out it exhibited, as usual, that intense and dazzling brightness peculiar to the electric light.

To persons conversant with the manufacture of iron, it will be at once apparent that the ingots of malleable metal which I have described will have no hard or steely parts, such as is found in puddling iron, requiring a great amount of rolling to blend them with the general mass, nor will such ingots require an excess of rolling to expel cinder from the interior of the mass, since none can exist in the ingot, which is pure and perfectly homogeneous throughout, and hence requires only as much rolling as is necessary for the development of fibre; it therefore follows that, instead of forming a merchant bar or rail by the union of a number of separate pieces welded together, it will be far more simple and less expensive to make several bars or rails from a single ingot; doubtless, this would have been done long ago had not the whole process been limited by the size of the ball which the puddler could make.

The facility which the new process affords of making large masses will enable the manufacturer to produce bars that on the old mode of working it was impossible to obtain; while, at the same time, it admits of the use of some powerful machinery whereby a great deal of labour will be saved, and the process be greatly expedited. I merely mention this fact in passing, as it is not my intention at the present moment to enter upon any details of the improvements I have made in this department of the manufacture, because the patents which I have obtained for them are not yet specified. Before, however, dismissing this branch of the subject, I wish to call the attention of the meeting to some of the peculiarities which distinguish cast-steel from all other forms of iron, namely, the perfect homogeneous character of the metal, the entire absence of sand-cracks or flaws, and its greater cohesive force and elasticity as compared with the blister steel from which it is made, qualities which it derives solely from its fusion and formation into ingots, all of which properties malleable iron acquires in like manner by its fusion and formation into ingots in the new process. Nor must it be forgotten that no amount of rolling will give to blistered steel (although formed of rolled bars) the same homogeneous character that cast-steel acquires by a mere extension of the ingot to some 10 or 12 times its original length.

One of the most important facts connected with the new system of manufacturing malleable iron is that all the iron so produced will be of that quality known as charcoal iron, not that any charcoal is used in its manufacture, but because the whole of the processes following the smelting of it are conducted entirely without contact with or the use of any mineral fuel; the iron resulting therefrom will, in consequence, be perfectly free from those injurious properties which that description of fuel never fails to impart to iron that is brought under its influence. At the same time, this system of manufacturing malleable iron offers extraordinary facility for making large shafts, cranks, and other heavy masses; it will be obvious that any weight of metal that can be founded in ordinary cast-iron by the means at present at our disposal may also be founded in molten malleable iron, and be wrought into the forms and shapes required, provided that we increase the size and power of our machinery to the extent necessary to deal with such large masses of metal. A few minutes' reflection will show the great anomaly presented by the scale on which the consecutive processes of iron-making are at present carried on. The little furnaces originally used for smelting ore have from time to time increased in size, until they have assumed colossal proportions, and are made to operate on 200 or 300 tons of materials at a time, giving out 10 tons of fluid metal at a single run. The manufacturer has thus gone on increasing the size of his smelting furnaces, and adapting to their use the blast apparatus of the recquisite proportions, and has, by this means, lessened the cost of production in every way; his large furnaces require a great deal less labour to produce a given weight of iron than would have been required to produce it with a dozen furnaces, and in like manner he diminishes his cost of fueel blast and repairs, while he insures a uniformity in the ressult that never could have been arrived at by the use of a multiplicity of small furnaces. While the manufacturer has shown himself fully alive to these advantages, he has still been under the necessity of leaving the succeeding operations to be carried out on a scale wholly at variance with the principles he has found so advantageous in the smelting department. It is true that hitherto no better method was known than the puddling process, in which from 400 to 500 weight of iron is all that can be operated upon at a time, and even this small quantity is divided into homœpathic doses of some 70lb. or 80lb., each of which is moulded and fashioned by human labour, carefully watched and tended in the furnace, and removed therefrom one at a time, to be carefully manipulated and squeezed into form. When we consider the vast extent of the manufacture, and the gigantic scale on which the early stages of the progress is conducted, it is astonishing that no effort should have been made to raise the after processes somewhat nearer to a level commensurate with the preceding ones, and thus rescue the trade from the trammels which have so long surrounded it.

Before concluding these remarks I beg to call your attention to an important fact connected with the new process, which affords peculiar facilities for the manufacture of cast-steel.

At that stage of the process immediately following the boil, the whole of the crude iron has passed into the condition of cast-steel of ordinary quality; by the continuation of the process the steel so produced gradually loses its small remaining portion of carbon, and passes successively from hard to soft steel, and from soft steel to steely iron, and eventually to very soft iron; hence at a certain period of the process any quality of metal may be obtained; there is one in particular, which by way of distinction I call semi-steel, being in hardness about mid-way between ordinary cast-steel and soft malleable iron. This metal possesses the advantage of much greater tonsile strength than soft iron; it is also more elastic, and does not readily take a permanent set, while it is much harder, and is not worn or indented so easily as soft iron; at the same time it is not so brittle or hard to work as ordinary cast-steel. These qualities render it eminently well adapted to purposes where lightness and strength are specially required, or where there is much wear, as in the case of railway bars, which from their softness and lamellar texture soon become destroyed. The cost of semi-steel will be a fraction less than iron, because the loss of metal that takes place by oxidation in the converting vessel is about 2½ per cent. less than it is with iron; but, as it is a little more difficult to roll, its cost per ton may fairly be considered to be the same as iron; but, as its tensile strength is some 30 or 40 per cent. greater than bar iron, it follows that for most purposes a much less weight of metal may be used, so that taken in that way the semi-steel will form a much cheaper metal than any that we are at present acquainted with.

In conclusion, allow me to observe that the facts which I have had the honour of bringing before the meeting have not been elicited from mere laboratory experiments, but have been the result of working on a scale nearly twice as great as is pursued in our largest iron works, the experimental apparatus doing 7 cwt. in 30 minutes, while the ordinary puddling furnace makes only 4½ cwt. in two hours, which is made into six separate balls, while the ingots or blooms are smooth even prisms, 10 inches square by 30 inches in length, weighing about equal to 10 ordinary puddle balls.

THE Central Italian Railway Company have just deposited five millions of francs at Modena as a guarantee for the execution of the line in accordance with the contract signed at Vienna on the seventeenth March last.

ASSISTANT OBSERVER AT THE KEW OBSERVATORY. – The managers of the Kew Observatory having applied to the Council of the Society of Arts to recommend to them one of their candidates at the late examinations qualitied to undertake the duties of assistant observer, the Council have nominated Mr. Charles Chambers, of Leeds, who has accordingly been appointed to the office. Mr. Chambers obtained a certificate of the first grade in mathematics at the examinations held in June last at the Society's house in the Adelphi.

THE GREAT BELL FOR THE NEW PALACE AT WESTMINSTER. – The vicinity of the picturesque village of Norton, near Stockton-on-Tees, on the morning of the 6th instant, was the scene of an event of considerable national interest, – the casting of the great bell for the clock tower of the new palace at Westminster, which was accomplished at Messrs. Warner, Lucas, and Barrett's furnaces, by Messrs. Warner and Sons, of the Crescent Foundry, Jewin-street, London, well-known as the patentees of an improved method of casting church and turret bells. The mould has been in course of preparation for the last six weeks, and two reverberatory furnaces, capable of melting ten tons of metal each, have been built expressly for the purpose of casting this monster bell. The whole of the night previous was a scene of busy industry, and early in the morning the furnaces having attained the requisite heat, their doors were opened, and the operation of charging, or putting in the metal commenced, occupying about an hour, and in less than two and a half hours the whole of the metal required – 18 tons – was in a state of perfect fusion. At the signal being given, the furnaces were tapped, and the metal flowed from them into a pool prepared to hold it, before being admitted into the bell mould. The shutter or gate was then lifted, and the metal allowed to flow, which in five minutes completed the casting of (he bell, the successful termination of which delighted all present, who cordially joined the workpeople in three hearty cheers.

THE SUEZ CANAL – M. Ferdinand de Lesseps has been at Turin, and also at Genoa, on his way to Alexandria. His object has been to visit M. Paleocapa, the minister of public works, an engineer who gained great reputation by carrying out successfully the pier at Malamoco. The motive of this visit has not been to consult M. Paleocapa on the construction of the works of the Suez canal, but in order to overcome a greater difficulty – the opposition, namely, of the Sultan to the project; an opposition encouraged, it is said, by Lord Stratford de Radcliffe; and grounded on the fear that the transit of the East Indian, and Chinese commerce, by way of the Isthmus, will so greatly increase the wealth of the Viceroy, as to make him practically independent. The Sultan had put his veto on the convention concluded between the Canal Company and the Viceroy; this veto M. Ferdinand Lesseps wants to remove, and he resorts to M. Paleocapa, because he is aware that that gentleman stands very well with his Majesty Napoleon III, in consequence of a recent visit which he paid to Paris, on the subject of embanking the Rhone and the Loire. It is in order to induce M. Paleocapa to employ his influence with Louis Napoleon, in opposition to the Sultan's veto on the canal project, that M. Lesseps has paid his recent visit.

Henry Bessemer. "On the Manufacture of Malleable Iron and Steel without Fuel," in *The Engineer*. August 15, 1856.

EVOLUTIONARY SCIENCES OF LIFE: CHARLES DARWIN (1859)

Charles Darwin (1809–1882) was born in Shropshire, England. His father, Robert Darwin, was a wealthy doctor. At the age of 16, he went to the University of Edinburgh to pursue a career in medicine. However, he soon lost interest in his medical studies and instead developed a passion for the natural sciences. This interest continued when he transferred to the University of Cambridge three years later. There, he was taken under the wing of John Stevens Henslow, a young botany professor who made it possible for Darwin to go on a five-year surveying journey aboard the HMS *Beagle*, under the command of Captain Robert Fitzroy. During this voyage, which took him around the world to Northern Africa, South America, Australia, and back, Darwin collected and analyzed many different natural history specimens. He also provided counsel to Captain Fitzroy as an expert in geology. From this trip came many of the ideas for which Darwin is now known: specifically, his theory of biological evolution. This theory contends that populations evolve over generations through the process of natural selection, so that whichever species possess heritable traits that are best adapted to their environment are those that are "selected" by nature to continue their existence.

Although he had written about it previously in a shorter form, Darwin's clearest and most sustained articulation of this theory of evolution is found in his seminal 1859 work, *On the Origin of Species*, from which the selection is drawn. Here, it is interesting to note that Darwin is interested in many of the same questions that seem to plague many social thinkers today in the twenty-first century. Specifically, he asks what provokes natural life to constantly renew itself? The solution he offers is a sentiment that many of us are now familiar with: because of the inevitable interchange that occurs between different environments, species must adapt to new surroundings, thus producing moments of discord, destruction, creativity, and equilibrium.

On the Origin of Species by Means of Natural Selection

When on board H.M.S. 'Beagle,' as naturalist, I was much struck with certain facts in the distribution of the inhabitants of South America, and in the geological relations of the present to the past inhabitants of that continent. These facts seemed to me to throw some light on the origin of species – that mystery of mysteries, as it has been called by one of our greatest philosophers. [. . .]

In considering the distribution of organic beings over the face of the globe, the first great fact which strikes us is, that neither the similarity nor the dissimilarity of the inhabitants of various regions can be accounted for by their climatal and other physical conditions. Of late, almost every author who has studied the subject has come to this conclusion. The case of America alone would almost suffice to prove its truth: for if we exclude the northern parts where the circumpolar land is almost continuous, all authors agree that one of the most fundamental divisions in geographical distribution is that between the New and Old Worlds; yet if we travel over the vast American continent, from the central parts of the United States to its extreme southern point, we meet with the most diversified conditions; the most humid districts, arid deserts, lofty mountains, grassy plains, forests, marshes, lakes, and great rivers, under almost every temperature. There is hardly a climate or condition in the Old World which cannot be paralleled in the New – at least as closely as the same species generally require; for it is a most rare case to find a group of organisms confined to any small spot, having conditions peculiar in only a slight degree; for instance, small areas in the Old World could be pointed out hotter than any in the New World, yet these are not inhabited by a peculiar fauna or flora. Notwithstanding this parallelism in the conditions of the Old and New Worlds, how widely different are their living productions! [. . .]

A second great fact which strikes us in our general review is, that barriers of any kind, or obstacles to free migration, are related in a close and important manner to the differences between the productions of various regions. We see this in the great difference of nearly all the terrestrial productions of the New and Old Worlds, excepting in the northern parts, where the land almost joins, and where, under a slightly different climate, there might have been free migration for the northern temperate forms, as there now is for the strictly arctic productions. We see the same fact in the great difference between the inhabitants of Australia, Africa, and South America under the same latitude: for these countries are almost as much isolated from each other as is possible. On each continent, also, we see the same fact; for on the opposite sides of lofty and continuous mountain-ranges, and of great deserts, and sometimes even of large rivers, we find different productions; though as mountain-chains, deserts, &c., are not as impassable, or likely to have endured so long as the oceans separating continents, the differences are very inferior in degree to those characteristic of distinct continents.

Turning to the sea, we find the same law. No two marine faunas are more distinct, with hardly a fish, shell, or crab in common, than those of the eastern and western shores of South and Central America. [. . .]

This bond, on my theory, is simply inheritance, that cause which alone, as far as we positively know, produces organisms quite like, or, as we see in the case of varieties, nearly like each other. The dissimilarity of the inhabitants of different regions may be attributed to modification through natural selection, and in a quite subordinate degree to the direct influence of different physical conditions. The degree of dissimilarity will depend on the migration of the more dominant forms of life from one region into another having been effected with more or less ease, at periods more or less remote; – on the nature and number of the former immigrants; – and on their action and reaction, in their mutual struggles for life; – the relation of organism to organism being, as I have already often remarked, the most important of all relations. Thus the high importance of barriers comes into play by checking migration; as does time for the slow process of modification through natural selection. Widely-ranging species, abounding in individuals, which have already triumphed over many competitors in their own widely-extended homes will have the best chance of seizing on new places, when they spread into new countries. In their new homes they will be exposed to new conditions, and will frequently undergo further modification and improvement; and thus they will become still further victorious, and will produce groups of modified descendants. [. . .]

Authors of the highest eminence seem to be fully satisfied with the view that each species has been independently created. To my mind it accords better with what we know of the laws impressed on matter by the Creator, that the production and extinction of the past and present inhabitants of the world should have been due to secondary causes, like those determining the birth and death of the individual. When I view all beings not as special creations, but as the lineal descendants of some few beings which lived long before the first bed of the Silurian system was deposited, they seem to me to become ennobled. Judging from the past, we may safely infer that not one living species will transmit its unaltered likeness to a distant futurity. And of the species now living very few will transmit progeny of any kind to a far distant futurity; for the manner in which all organic beings are grouped, shows that the greater number of species of each genus, and all the species of many genera, have left no descendants, but have become utterly extinct. We can so far take a prophetic glance into futurity as to foretel that it will be the common and widely-spread species, belonging to the larger and dominant groups, which will ultimately prevail and procreate new and dominant species. As all the living forms of life are the lineal descendants of those which lived long before the Silurian epoch, we may feel certain that the ordinary succession by generation has never once been broken, and that no cataclysm has desolated the whole world. Hence we may look with some confidence to a secure future of equally inappreciable length. And as natural selection works solely by and for the good of each being, all corporeal and mental endowments will tend to progress towards perfection.

It is interesting to contemplate an entangled bank, clothed with many plants of many kinds, with birds singing on the bushes, with various insects flitting about, and with worms crawling through the damp earth, and to reflect that these elaborately constructed forms, so different from each other, and dependent on each other in so complex a manner, have all been produced by laws acting around us. . . . There is grandeur in this view of life, with its several powers, having been originally breathed by the Creator into a few forms or into one; and that, whilst this planet has gone cycling on according to the fixed law of gravity, from so simple a beginning endless forms most beautiful and most wonderful have been, and are being, evolved.

Charles Darwin, *On the Origin of Species by Means of Natural Selection* (2nd edition). Source: http://www.gutenberg.org/files/22764/22764-h/22764-h.htm.

PART THREE

The short twentieth century: global uncertainty and restructuring, after 1914

INTRODUCTION TO
PART THREE

Between empire and modern world-system there is a difference, but a difference that allows for globalization as, at least, a consequence of an imperial disposition and, at most, a formal, more-or-less rational, structure in the case of a world-system. The allowance, as we have argued, gives wide berth to the idea of globalization as it is currently used.

That the global, as distinct from the modern, can sneak up on any particular system of geopolitical order would seem to confound current theories of globalization. Yet, we propose, the distinction between the global and the modern clarifies the current state of globalization. It is not a contradiction to suggest that the modern European system after, say, 1800 is a scrupulous discrimination – both conceptually and historically – in the long enduring history of global processes. What the modern global added to prior global systems, including both economic systems (in Andre Gunder Frank's sense) and empires, was (or is), as we have said, a definite species of rationalizing logic – one that led to a variety of technologies including the technologies of self that were either prerequisites for or entailments of a global culture of modern systems.

Globalization, as we speak of it today early in the 2010s, has come out from under the modern but its manner of sneaking up on the world has been different from the modern's departure from its past. The modern, if one were to suppose it knew what it was doing, intended to build itself out of the premodern past – its religions, its agents, its astrolabes, its navigational skills, its imperial dispositions, its ready-made trade routes along the Silk Road and in the New Worlds, and much else.

Globalization, as it is discussed in our time, has a much less definite relation to *its* past, the modern. If it turns out to be something utterly different, it is far too soon to tell. This will be the theme of Part Four where the many and various positions in the Great Globalization Debate are presented. For the present, in Part Three, we join issues that are betwixt and between the rise of the modern as a unique form of globalization and a period of modern history that was meant to have been the grand fulfillment of the modern when, as things turned out, it was not.

Having quit the twentieth century for the twenty-first, we who have lived in both are sometimes tempted to say goodbye to all that and good riddance. The twentieth century, in retrospect, was at least disappointing and at worse a disaster. Though the twentieth was a century of astonishing advancements in learning, culture, science, and technology, it was also, and at the same time, a period in which whatever good was done all too often turned to evil. From an earlier vantage point located somewhere in the secure bourgeois classes of the nineteenth century it would have been logical to look to the future of a twentieth century as a time of unbridled progress, a perfection of what had begun for the better-off or otherwise rising classes in Europe and North America. In fact, against expectations, the twentieth century was one of the more disappointing centuries of the modern era.

Anyone who seeks in modern times a brighter century than the twentieth would do better choosing almost any of the others from among the sixteenth through to the nineteenth centuries. As the sixteenth century in the West was one of astounding adventures and the nineteenth one of no less remarkable technological and economic advances relative to what had come before them, the twentieth was a rather sordid affair in the bed of progress. Some might suppose, alternatively, that the seventeenth and eighteenth centuries were, on balance, more enlightened. This would be true, and to a degree is, except for the wars and revolutions that were good in respect to new, more civil, state and interstate systems but appallingly bad for the violence and other forms of suffering they failed to relieve; then too one might find these two middle centuries of the modern era impressive for the settlement of far reaches of the world in ways that led to a vast expansion of global wealth but the impression dims against the reality that the modern global economy was purchased on the backs of slaves and the colonized. Still, as mixed as the prior record of the Euro-American modern age was, the twentieth is the best example of the triumph of evil over good – or, better put, for the improbable odds against which the marvels of science, technology, and culture were trumped by stupidity, violence, and just plain human evil.

To say such a thing of any one epoch in human history demands a greater measure of precision than can usually be afforded the assessment of chunks of time as big as centuries. Centuries never quite fit the measures assigned them. Many of them begin before the turn of the centennial calendar, some exceed this normal allotment of time, and a few begin and end well within their calendrical century. Of all the many and necessary metrics of measurement that were important to the modern era, the one most regularly violated was the idea that 100 years was the metric for organizing nature's 365+ daily rotations. Curiously the Gregorian calendar, decreed in 1582, was meant to correct for the confusions in the prior Julian calendar with respect to the days in a year. Nice idea for calendars; not so much for actual social histories.

Thus, it happens that social historians tend to assess various centuries according to the unity of their gross historical structures and achievements. The sixteenth century, for example, is considered long. Immanuel Wallerstein, following Fernand Braudel, is among those who argue that the sixteenth is the foundational century of the modern capitalist system, thus longishly from 1450 to 1648. In terms less economic than general, one might mark the sixteenth century as from Gutenberg and the first overseas adventures to the English Civil War or to the Treaty of Westphalia in the 1640s. Likewise, Eric Hobsbawm considers the nineteenth century from 1789 to 1917 – roughly from the French Revolution to the Great War in Europe – to be longish. Any who would accept these reasonable parsings of modern historical time would thereby be required either to think of the seventeenth and eighteenth as short centuries or, were it not for the authority of the Gregorian calendar, simply to eliminate one of them (probably the seventeenth) to establish a long eighteenth century from roughly the Dutch Revolt to the French Revolution which could reasonably be considered a long century of Enlightenment applied to the emergence of the bourgeois state.

Whichever way one cuts the centuries, the twentieth is a short one. Wallerstein and Hobsbawm agree for similar if not identical reasons that 1914 to 1989/91 are the outer limits of this century of about 75 years. They, and others (ourselves included), agree, but still the question would be why? In the *Age of Extremes, 1914–1991*,[1] Hobsbawm describes the short twentieth century as an age of catastrophe that began with the Great War in Europe and stumbled along through the Second World War and its aftermath until the collapse of the Cold War in 1991. At the least, this twentieth century was a period of wars unceasing, whether hot or cold. Then too it was a century of violence of other and extreme kinds – decolonizing struggles, civil strife, ethnic genocides, urban violence, holocausts and gulags, political assassinations and worse. It is not that atrocities like these were unique to the twentieth century. What was, however, were the atrocities that occurred with such intensity in so painfully short a time. A century that was supposed to be the capstone of social progress was anything but.

Before and beneath the catastrophic inhumanities of the twentieth century stood the enduring fact that, whatever good or evil was done, what drove much of the period's events was a shift in global structures, in at least four important aspects: 1) the rise of global warfare and the restructuring of empires; 2) a protracted cold war and struggles for global control; 3) decolonizing movements and structural challenges to the Euro-American world order; 4) new global forces and the deterioration of the modern nation-state.

From one point of view the major structural event of the twentieth century was the emergence, in the words of Henry Luce, of the American Century. The famous expression appeared in *Time* magazine early in the 1940s, which was near the beginning of the American involvement in World War II in Europe – an involvement required, in part, by the evidence that Britain, the dominant world power until then, could not defeat the Nazi threat on its own nor even afford the cost of what by 1941 was already the second of the century's global wars. Luce's "century" was thereby very late to begin and, when he coined the phrase, it was far from clear that, even with the Americans, the Allies could defeat Hitler. Still, the idea was planted, and stuck, and turned out to be true in a sense not quite the same as Luce's. The idea of an American century was built on an exceptional American confidence in its moral superiority. But, as the war moved on to its conclusion, American power would not be like the powers of old. Global realities were changing all that.

By the 1940s, when the full-throated wrath of a new kind of warfare had enveloped the world, it was already evident that, American Century or not, the ancient norms of imperial aggression were radically changed in several ways. One of the changes was, of course, the global nature of warfare – global, that is, in both senses of the word: engulfing the world as a whole; total in the sense of involving entire populations including innocents who were not even remotely enemy combatants. The former might seem to be a merely technical discrimination in that world wars may be said to have been in evidence whenever great powers of any historic period confront each other on several fronts (for example, the Macedonians under Alexander and the Persian Empire; the Romans and the Goths). On the other hand, it is possible to say that World War I was a world war only insofar as its reach beyond Europe was mostly a defense of the colonial interests of the several European powers on both sides of the conflict.

Still, as Paul Fussell remarks in "The Trenches – What They Were Really Like," the dramatic Christmas truce of 1914, when German and British troops stepped out of their trenches to share Christmas greetings, was the "last gesture" of the nineteenth century. He meant that the few hours of truce were nothing more than a moment in a war so cruel that, Fussell adds, "the nineteenth century idea that human beings are getting better the longer the race goes on" was forever demolished.

Americans, especially, would find the failure of nineteenth century values a hard pill to swallow and some have argued that the nineteenth century would endure much longer in the United States – until, as Reinhold Niebuhr once said, the Depression of 1929; or, even 1941, as Luce might have better meant to say; or, at the extreme, in the aftermath of 2001 (which of course would have meant that, in America, the twentieth century in moral terms was a negative number.

Whichever, what remained on balance was that the Great War, or World War I, by whatever name, was warfare as never before. Long gone was Napoleon's theory of the field army as a military machine of overwhelming force. By mid-nineteenth century, notably in the American Civil War, the classical practice of armies aligned on strategic fronts was already broken if not eliminated by crucial technological advances. The railroad, for one, made the movement of troops and supplies more mobile (and, given the North's industrial advantage, this was one reason the Union was able to put down the rebellion). Another was the significant improvement in the power and range of canon and side arms. Thus, while the armies of the Confederacy and the Union faced each other on battlefields such as Gettysburg, snipers and trenches were increasingly the norm. As to military theory, Clausewitz's idea (apparently based in part on Napoleon's successes) that war was an extension of politics was eclipsed. The trenches of the Great War "smelled bad" as Fussell remarked. But as terrible as it was for young men to be confined to rat-infested, water-logged trenches within shouting distance of the enemy, the lesson of the Great War was one implied by the Civil War in America. Still today, the Americans, no strangers to war, have yet to give up so many lives to death and casualty. The carnage consumed the Republic that would be reunited in 1865. What would not be re-knit was Napoleon's ideal of the army as a machine.

By the time of the Great War of 1914, warfare had turned evil in ways hitherto neither technically possible nor ethically thinkable. The submarine, chemical warfare, saturation bombing, and air combat were methods of warfare that introduced the practise of killing at a distance, a practise that all subsequent wars, whether declared or insurgent, whether along mappable fronts or by guerilla sneak attacks from the bushes or tunnels, would become common if not commonly acceptable; hence the necessity of continual refinement in the Geneva Conventions. International accords that began in 1864 as general principles of "respect" for combatants were regularly revised in the twentieth century to cover the treatment of the wounded in battle and of prisoners, as well as prohibitions against chemical warfare, terrorism, crimes against humanity, and genocide. Needless to say, none was ever perfectly obeyed.

Much as the Treaty of Westphalia in 1648 was an accord vulnerable to state and military interests, so too were the international conventions meant to govern extremes of evil in armed conflict. States breached the peace Westphalia meant to establish; militants and militaries used what methods there were. Dunkirk implied Dresden thus also Hiroshima. The erosion of early modern ideals of civility and reason even in conflict was, of course, a consequence of the technologies that made impersonal long-distance warfare possible. After the appalling futilities of the trenches in the Great War, armed warfare would be increasingly and literally inhuman. "Don't shoot till you see the whites of their eyes" then became a slogan of old. Personal courage began to disappear as a warrior virtue, then, when the enemy was ever more an indiscriminate mass of abstract human and material targets. Even the ancient siege gradually took on a different military meaning. Unlike Troy of old, or even the Alamo, Marne in World War I and Leningrad in World War II were three-year sieges that ended in frustration and devastation on both sides. The futility only encouraged unproven and ultimately more violent methods. There is, for remarkable example, no evidence that the saturation bombings of Dresden in February 1945, nor of Hanoi after February 1965, nor of the more surgical Shock and Awe attacks on Baghdad in January 2003 had any discernible long-range effects on the wars that were already established as trench to trench, jungle to jungle, alley to alley. Hiroshima and Nagasaki did but only because the Japanese were already defeated in the Pacific after the fall of Okinawa early the summer of 1945.

Still, the global nature of warfare in the twentieth century retained an important cultural disposition typical of the ancient empires. One remote, if surprising, piece of evidence of this fact of late modern life was the recurrence of the idea of empire in both metaphoric and more or less literal senses. One thinks of the political slogan, "evil empire," invoked by Ronald Reagan against the last vestiges of the Soviet Imperium. Right-wing rhetoric would not matter all that much were it not that, upon the decline of the Soviet Union in 1991, there would arise a considerable number of arguments on both sides for and against the theme already implicit to the American Century ideology that the United States was that last true world-power. This was true, however, mostly in the sense that the American military was the largest by far in the world and one eager to reassert itself after failure in Vietnam. This it tried to do early in 1991 in the first Persian Gulf War — a stunning display of military technology that achieved very little more than did, subsequently, America's entanglements in Iraq and Afghanistan. In a somewhat more serious sense, the ideology and theory of post-modern empires is reflected in inexplicably well-regarded theoretical sketches of the new form of empire based on an alleged informational mode of production suggested, most famously, in Michael Hardt's and Antonio Negri's *Empire* (2000) which is selected in Part Six.

Yet, well before these rhetorical and theoretical adventures, the fact of empire remained a significant force at the beginning of the short twentieth century in 1914. There is some debate as to the real, as opposed to figurative, cause of World War I. Still, if a figurative event is needed, the assassination in Sarajevo of Archduke Ferdinand of the Austro-Hungarian Empire on June 28, 1914 is as good as any. One need only read, in the selection, the demands of the "Imperial and Royal Government" in Vienna to the Serbian Government. The Austro-Hungarians had not the least qualm about laying down demands upon the Serbs as if a decree by the then second-largest European Empire would be threat enough to move their unsettled Balkan territories. War ensued, after which the Hapsburgs lost their empire. Not only that but so too did the Ottomans and the Russian Czars, as also Germany would lose the last remnants of Bismarck's unified German Empire; as also the sun would set on the British Empire. The short twentieth century spelled the definitive end of the last vestiges of regional and global empires. The Great War was a world war because the European conflict necessarily extended to attack on and defense of the global interests of the several empires in colonies in Africa, Asia, and the Pacific.

Yet, the collapse of formal empires as a result of World War I did not mean the end of the imperial disposition that, as in ancient and classical geo-politics, would assume the force of empire, in effect if not name. Why Woodrow Wilson's war to end all wars would fail to settle the peace is a question of many answers. One surely is that the imperial disposition is ubiquitous, if not exactly universal. But still another is that, from the start (setting aside questions of the nature of state power), the twentieth century defied the idealism of earlier moments in the modern age.

If there is a single series of events that would typify the degradations into which the modern fell in the twentieth century, it would be the series that led, as if inevitably, from World War I to World War II. The misery and disgust of the first was, it could be said, more moral and psychological than pure practical evil. The second, by contrast, was the outbreak of wickedness. The deeper dispositions of the modern to ruthless cruelty inflicted against fellows of the species was, to be sure, aggravated by the new methods of long-distance warfare but, just as much, they were, as theologians often say, form-destroying irruptions of the good. From *Kristallnacht* in 1938 to Pearl Harbor in 1941 to Hiroshima in 1945, World War II, as it came to be, was malevolence turned loose on the world at large. Whatever heroism and tragedy there was, and whatever was great about the generations of men and women who fought the evil forces, the concluding reality is that from among holocausts, sneak attacks, and nuclear devastations it would be hard to choose one less brutal than the others. Even the Nazis would argue for a nationalist necessity behind the crematoria, as the Americans claimed a military necessity to their nuclear crematorium, so also the Japanese would claim the necessity of opportunity at Pearl Harbor. In the end, whatever the moral justifications, these were the signposts along the way toward the revelation that the modern age, with all its genteel sensibilities, was at the last no different from any other and may have been very much worse by being so very global in its effects.

The Japanese cult of the Emperor and Hitler's fanatic idea of the German state as the state of the pure Aryan *volk* were reversions to a grossly exaggerated imperial disposition, if not empires in the classic sense. Certainly they aimed to establish imperial orders through military and police violence. Yet, as Ruth Benedict, in the selection in this section shows, the grip of the Japanese Empire over the people was, if not the primary force in Japanese aggression in World War II, at least a factor. And, in this respect, a crucial aspect of both Imperial Japan and the Fascist Axis in Europe was a regression to the mythologies of original and superior folk – that is: of *the people* in a premodern, emotional, and romantic sense as the source of State power. This is strikingly evident already in 1924 in the selection from Hitler's speech before the Munich Court. "The State, however, is not an economic organization, it is a 'volkic' organism" – hence, the extreme of nationalist ideology. But also, added Hitler, the State "can maintain itself only when it places a power-policy (*machtpolitik*) ruthlessly in the foreground" – hence, the reality of a nationalist imperial disposition.

As the century would turn from war to war, two things became clear, if not clear enough to dispel the magical thinking of nineteenth century liberal culture. One was that the modern ideals of individual freedoms were insufficient to the good society; the other was that the State, hitherto an auxiliary of the market and an invention of the myth of the people, would step to the center of the global stage, for better or worse. What began in the Great War was to be the awkward truth of global things by the end of World War II.

No one would give better account of the failure of the Great War in Europe than John Maynard Keynes, who quit the British delegation to the Versailles Peace Treaty in 1919. Keynes's "Economic Consequences of the Peace" is one of the more astute early documents predicting what came to pass – that World War I would lead to World War II; that the severe punishments inflicted by the Allies on Germany would provoke them to further aggressions; that Europe herself, having suffered so in the Great War, would not soon regain its economic equilibrium; and (most striking of all for a liberal economist) that capitalism would be sorely threatened. "Perhaps it is historically true," said Keynes, "that no order of society ever perishes save by its own hand." In this, Keynes went far beyond the end of empire rhetoric. It was the economic and social system of modern Europe he had in mind. At the very least, he insisted that the days of uncomplicated *laissez-faire* market freedoms in the nineteenth century sense were at an end. By consequence, the modern state would of necessity take an active role in the management of fiscal and monetary markets – a reality that, after the Crash of 1929, would intrude on the exceptionalist perfection-ism of the United States.

After 1917, to take the striking example of the Soviet Union, the State would have to be very much more than one among other lesser actors. Dramatically in the USSR but clearly also in the West, the State became a central force in the global political economy. In the West, and especially in the United States, this develop-ment would, in time, be taken as proof positive of the virtue of the older nineteenth-century free-market values. Just the same, the continuous experiences of economic depression and world war required that even the United States, with its long traditions of hostility toward the federal State, would be forced, under Franklin Delano Roosevelt, to accept the activist State. Even though Roosevelt died just before the end of World War II, thus just before the beginning of the Cold War, he, though ill, saw at Yalta what was to become of a global conflict of rival state powers.

The October Revolution of 1917 planted the seeds for the Cold War that would follow hard on the heels of World War II. Yet, already in the early years of the twentieth century it was evident to those who were perceptive that before and eventually quite outside of the Cold War rivals came into conflict, there were other movements beholden, on the one hand, to the liberal ideologies that prevailed in the United States and, on the other hand, those that would prevail in the USSR.

These earlier movements were nationalism and socialism, both of which had deep roots in the nineteenth century prior to 1848. Nationalisms and socialism, in their ways, were both liberation movements, formed against the lingering aspects of premodern ideologies and practices – notably the Qing Dynasty in China and the Czarist regime in Russia. Both would, as the twentieth century unraveled, spread unevenly across the world into Africa, the Latin Americas and the Caribbean, and much of Asia. Yet, the two focal states of these movements remained Russia and China. Later, during the Cold War, in the West (and more acutely in the United States), the Union of Soviet Socialist Republics and the People's Republic of China were naïvely considered part and parcel of the same international communist movement. In point of fact, the histories of the two movements began differently and followed distinctive, if not exactly divergent, histories. Of the two revolutionary lines, the one in China was the more complicated and thus interesting in respect to developments beyond the Euro-American sphere of influence.

Modern China was established in a revolutionary overthrow of the last of the old-regime dynasties in China, the Qing. It began thus as a vibrant modernizing movement, based to a good degree on Western Enlightenment values. Its political form was republican, but its political destiny was nationalism. The selection here from the philosophical teachings of Sun Yat-Sen, the political leader of nationalism in China, illustrates just how complicated the origins of revolutionary China were.

Sun Yat-Sen's three principles were nationalism, democracy, and socialism. If democracy reflected his education in the United States, thus his exposure to liberal democratic values, then nationalism reflected Sun's not entirely unreasonable view of the practical necessities of a modern China. In 1911, as before during the long Qing rule, China was a federation of regions and ethnicities – Manchu, Mongol, Tartar, Tibetan, and Han Chinese. The Qing Dynasty, established in 1644, was in fact Manchu-Mongolian by ethnicity. The Manchu invaders of Beijing simply declared themselves the official Chinese, thus displacing by edict the at-the-time more ancient and traditional Han people's idea of republican democracy which was, as the text makes clear, based on direct electoral rights. In Sun's view, electoral rights were impossible given the relative weakness of the smaller groups that were true demographic minorities relative to the (then) 400 million Chinese people. This may well have been right, if not inherently true. The effect was a reassertion of Han dominance after the Qing period. The Han are the largest single ethnic group in China; still today, however, Han majority dominance contends with the long unsettled tensions between Beijing and the Uyghur and Tibetan minorities. Both minority groups claim political and cultural independence and both are well justified in these claims. The Uyghurs, in particular, are descendents of the Tartars, who are decidedly more Turkic than Han – a difference now made all the more acute by the prominent role of Sunni Islam in Uyghur religious culture. Hence, in the early decades of the Republic of China, Sun Yat-Sen claimed, more or less prudently, that democracy required national unity. "We must raise the prestige of the Chinese people, and unite all the races inhabiting China to form one Chinese people in Eastern Asia, a

Chinese National state." If the logic does not follow as day from night, it does represent the real politics of many modernizing liberation movements. To overthrow a traditional regime or dynasty is to require principles of national identity and political organization. This was as true in early republican China as it was in the formative decades of the United States. National liberation movements promote nationalism, and nationalism can, and often does, promote the worst sort of extremes as, say, in Mobutu Sese Seko's role in the 1961 overthrow of Patrice Lumumba's overthrow of the Belgians to reinvent the Belgian Congo as Zaire, a deeply pathological national entity; not to mention, of course, the twentieth century's definitively ugly nationalism, Nazi Germany.

Sun Yat-Sen's third principle, socialism, was honest, in its way, but also a practical attitude required in the 1920s by the emerging challenge of the communist movement. Mao Zedong himself is known to have been inspired by the republican overthrow of the Qing before he set his own political course that would lead to civil war with the nationalists. Sun's nationalist party, the Kuomintang, backed by the United States, would rule China under Chiang Kai-Shek after Sun's death. Then in 1949, the nationalists were defeated by the communists. They retreated to Taiwan when Mao established the People's Republic of China.

The deep structural conflict in China after 1911 until 1949 between nationalist and socialist liberation movements is in many ways the near perfect historical example of the global tensions that long prevailed in the world outside of the stable, capitalist states in the West. If, as we suggest, China from Sun until at least the death of Mao in 1976, represented the embodiment of the inherent tensions in the so-called developing and underdeveloped worlds, the Soviet Union from 1917 to 1991 embodied the tensions *within* the socialist ideal of communist society.

Vladimir Lenin was, needless to say, the leader and theoretician of a state governed by "the people" – by, that is, the common people of the working classes. The dilemma of a socialist revolution is how to maintain the purity of revolutionary ideals or, better put, how to organize a state on the basis of a permanent revolution. How can a modern industrial state truly bring about the passage of state power to "the proletariat and the poorest sections of the peasants aligned with the proletariat"? The challenge, as things turned out, would be in the defining goal of Lenin's theory in his "April Theses" – "that a complete break be effected in actual fact with all capitalist interests." In 1991, these capitalist interests were quick to say that the collapse of the Soviet Union was evidence of the effect of capitalism's inherent superiority. But this was a hasty conclusion that ignored the deeper structural fact that, whatever the merits of the liberal ideology of free markets, the global order had for long been directed by capitalist interests which, since the long sixteenth century, were global in reach.

"From Stettin in the Baltic to Trieste in the Adriatic an iron curtain has descended across the Continent." Of all the eloquent lines inspired by World War II, these on March 5, 1946, by Winston Churchill, were certainly among the most important even for one of the century's most eloquent leaders. Churchill thereby publically announced the beginning of the Cold War. Stalin did not miss the opportunity to accuse Churchill and his "friends" in the United States of war-mongering by likening his English-speaking former allies to Hitler's Germanic nationalism.

Just days before Churchill's speech, in a secret US State Department, a then relatively young and junior attaché to the American Embassy in Moscow transmitted his now famous Long Telegram outlining what was to become his nation's Cold War policy of containment of the Soviet Union. Seldom does one come across a document like this one in which the deeper interior thoughts of one side of a diplomatic divide are so starkly revealed. Kennan was a Princeton-educated gentleman – an intellectual and a diplomat. Yet, just one year after the Big Three meeting at Yalta settled the terms of the war in Europe, Kennan's telegram exposed the dark, half-baked prejudices Americans held against the Soviets. True, Stalin had shown himself to have been brutal in the treatment of his own people and, even, a bully of sorts with the Allied leaders at Yalta. Granting this, there remains room to marvel at the aggressively negative attitude Kennan and the US diplomatic corps had of the Soviets: "At bottom of Kremlin's neurotic view of world affairs is traditional and instinctive Russian sense of insecurity." Kennan possessed the best available knowledge of Stalin's ambitions and ideology, based (as the telegram puts it) on anything but an "objective picture of outside world." Ignorant or not of Anglo-American cultures, Stalin's interview with *Pravda*, republished in the *New York Times* days after Churchill spoke in Missouri, shows him to have been a shrewd politician, perfectly aware of how to strike to the moral heart of the Americans and the British, who but months before had been allies in victory if not in political culture.

These opening salvos of the Cold War indicate well enough the extent of the misperceptions and deceptions that motivated the cold threats that clouded the world over for much of the half-century after 1946. Global things are inherently structural, which is to say that to speak of a global war, whether hot or cold, is to speak in terms that demand a theory of world order itself. It is not surprising that the Americans and the Soviets took hard and extreme lines toward each other – lines that achieved the high point of danger in the Cuban Missile Crisis in October, 1962. Opponents in this kind of world war, even if cold, are forced to attribute global aspirations and motivations to their rivals for world dominance. In retrospect, what shocks is how little the ideologies were true to the respective liberal and socialist values that were the sources of Anglo-American and Soviet achievements, as different in kind and degree as they were. More remarkable still is the extent to which wild global thinking divorced from historical evidence can drive powerful and otherwise sensible nations to engage in stupid enterprises – of which, the American war in Vietnam after 1965 and the Soviet invasion of Afghanistan in 1979 were the supreme examples. As Vietnam broke the back of America's claims to moral superiority, so Afghanistan uncovered the inherent limits of the Soviet system to pursue its international goals at the expense of domestic prosperity.

The external skin of Cold War tension was, to be sure, the competition between, in particular, the Americans and the Soviets supported variously by lesser powers from within their respective spheres of influence – Western Europe in the American case, and Eastern Europe in the Soviet case, with China as a bit of a loose canon on the Soviet side. The People's Republic of China advanced the communist cause, initially, in its role in the Korean War after October, 1950; then later as a proxy in support of the North in Vietnam's civil war. As early as 1946, Ho Chi Minh warned the French, and through them the West, that its "war of resistance will be a long and hard one." When, late in the 1950s, the French had been defeated by Ho's forces and the Americans slowly moved to take up their war in Indochina, the US was still preoccupied with global communism – on the Korean peninsula (still divided today; still without a declaration of peace) and around the world.

Once more, the Cold War inspired an abstract global logic: the communists are aggressive; they do not understand "our" ways; they must be contained. The Chinese incursion in Korea seemed to support this logic. Yet, in Korea, China had, and has, a strategic interest. As close as Pyongyang is to Seoul, it is even closer (fewer than 200 miles) to China's border. This is not to say that the People's Republic was not motivated by its own brand of the communist theory of world order; it does point to the geopolitical reality that early in the 2000s China's interests in North Korea are less in its role as a strategic buffer and more as a nuclear and economic threat to East Asia. But, even more, today one looks back on the US military engagement in South Vietnam after 1965 and wonders just what were the direct ideological grounds for the American involvement. The French had already proven Ho Chi-Minh's determination to fight all foreigners who refused to see the struggle in Vietnam as a civil war more than it was part of a global struggle between two rival political systems.

The lessons not very well learned, even today, from the American failure in Vietnam were lessons of the degree to which the Cold War led to global competition for control and influence around the world. But, also, the competition, in turn, so deeply distracted the great power rivals as to cause them to ignore another underlying lesson of Vietnam, if not Korea. For the less well developed and poorer nations of the world, the foremost consideration is not ideological purity so much as economic benefits. There could be no better example – an example even better than Vietnam in the 1960s – than Cuba in 1959. Fidel Castro's revolution was nothing more than a liberation movement and, initially, not at all directed by socialist values. His turn to the Soviets for economic and military support was taken only after the Americans refused their support and, worse yet, attempted to destroy the revolution in the foolish and futile invasion at the Bay of Pigs in April 1961. Socialism was the ideological equipment used to sustain the revolution which, as things turned out, remained officially socialist but was more profoundly a nationalism of the *Cubanidad*, a restoration of José Martí's vision of Cuban national identity.

The Cold War, thus, as a conflict between variant theories of global history was a double-edged sword. It led the principals into direct action (as in Vietnam) which, in addition, caused them to misperceive the true interests of the nations and regions they sought to pull into their spheres of influence. The Soviets held their own in the Eastern Bloc and a good bit of Central Asia, as the Americans held theirs in the Caribbean and the Americas. Neither, however, won definitively in Africa or the Middle East. Where strategic military or economic interests were at issue, both sides engaged in all too crafty undercover tactics to protect their interests. The selection, here, from a top secret British Foreign Office memorandum on the intrigues surrounding European and Western interests in Egypt and the Suez Canal very well illustrates, as does Kennan's containment telegram, the extent to which conspiracy theories infected the ideological theories of global structures, including the suspicions that arose between and among those on the same side.

Beyond the conspiracies that both caused and doomed the Cold War, it was evident that in the cracks and crevices between the distracted global powers other movements were tearing at the foundations of their all too tidy theories of each other. After Vietnam, the Americans were bewildered by their global failure, as after their Afghanistan the Soviets would have given it all up, and after the terrors of the Cultural Revolution China under Deng Xiaoping would be transformed into a weirdly successful mixed economic system under formal socialist rule. Dislocations such as these opened the way for new and, in the long run, ever more potent global movements. The decolonizing movements that began in earnest more or less at the moment the Cold War broke the back of the modern world-system would prove more of a threat to the post-war programs for world order than would either the liberal capitalist or socialist state programs.

White folk who consider themselves wise to Black ways can often be heard using the expression "Don't you Mau Mau me" – this is usual when a Black person calls them out for some or another racially insensitive remark. The retort is thought to be way cool, even when used by whites who have no idea where it came from. In 1952, the Mau Mau were a political movement that led peasant-based attacks on the British colonizers in the central highlands of Kenya. Among their first victims was a family of British whites who were known to have been "generous" toward their native Kenyan workers. The Mau Mau method of attack was to slaughter by hacking with machetes, a weapon subsequently used with regularity against ethnic as well as white enemies.

Mau Mau violence in Kenya struck terror in the hearts of colonizers. But, as terrible as the slaughter was in 1952 in Kenya, the Mau Mau uprising was in fact late in the global decolonizing movements. In 1945–1946, just as the Cold War began, Vietnam declared independence from the French as did the Philippines from the United States – both more technical than factual events. The true and effective beginning of the rejection of Euro-American colonial rule was the year following, 1947, when Gandhi led the successful struggle against British rule in India. The Kenyan uprising was, therefore, notorious for native violence; hence, for representing the worst possible nightmare of the colonizers – that the people they have colonized, far from being grateful for their colonizing benevolence, were capable of violent means to overthrow their white oppressors. Ho Chi Minh's declamation that same year that the war of resistance would be "long and hard" was directed at the French who refused to accept Vietnam's independence – and through them to all the colonizing powers. As things would turn out, Ho's resistance movement, not to mention Gandhi's, would be the least of the colonizing world's worries.

In 1952, the year of the Mau Mau uprising, Frantz Fanon would publish *Black Skin, White Masks* the first of two great books of his short life. In this, the first, and relatively more philosophical of them, Fanon would put the lie to the colonizers' innocence that the colonized were, if not exactly lesser men, of a different order from the allegedly munificent white civilization. Fanon's point was that white colonial culture aimed to turn people of Black skin into dark reflections of their whiteness. In 1961, the year of his death, Fanon upped the ante with respect to violence. *The Wretched of the Earth* would become one of the handbooks of the revolutionary 1960s. In it Fanon would state in no uncertain terms that "the colonial world is a world cut in two"; that the colonial world is itself a world of violence; that behind the claims of civilized "peace" the white colonizers are "the bringer of violence into the home and into the mind of the native." In a time of rebellion, the colonized thus uses the very tool the colonizer used on them. Colonizing by its very nature, not to mention its means, is violent. Fanon, in the selection from *Wretched of the Earth*, was but one, though a notable one, of the decolonizing intellectuals and leaders who would reject the modern world order as it came to be in Africa and around the colonial world.

Patrice Lumumba was foremost among the pure political leaders of decolonization in Africa. In June 1960, he had led the successful overthrow of Belgian rule in Congo in the name of "the 'lost greatness' for the Congolese." Lumumba's words, reported in the selection here from an American newspaper, is one reason that, a year later (1961, the year of Fanon's *Wretched of the Earth*), Lumumba was assassinated, probably with the participation of the American CIA. Mobutu Sese Seko, an evidently insane oppressor, was installed in his place. Violence begat by the colonial powers was turned back on them, who then reverted to the violent nature of their controlling interests.

In 1960, the year following his overthrow of Fulgencio Batista, the American corporate puppet in Havana, Fidel Castro, speaking to the United Nations in New York City, uttered the words that could have been Fanon's, words that would anticipate by almost 30 years Gayatri Chakrovorty Spivak's famous question of the post-colonial world: "Can the subaltern speak?" "Colonies do not speak," said Castro in 1960. "Colonies are not known until they have the opportunity to express themselves." Decolonization was, and remains, violence, bred by violence, but it began in the colonizeds' bold declaration of the right to speak outside of the dominant languages of the colonizers and to speak to them in terms they could not understand.

But the colonizers would not have all the time in the world to figure out what was being said. Within a few years, still early in the 1960s, the words of the colonial world would break the mold of modern language and culture. In the United States, Martin Luther King Jr's Civil Rights Movement was, as he says in the selection here, influenced by Gandhi's anti-colonizing movement, fortified by the hard-edged political ideas of Reinhold Niebuhr. Comparably, Malcolm X, until 1964 a minister in the Nation of Islam, drew upon Islam and Asia in parting ways with Martin Luther King's more integrationist movement. Malcolm was murdered on February 21, 1965, within days of the start of America's expansion of the war in Vietnam. King was assassinated in 1968, shortly after that war was known to have been futile. If neither was killed because of that war against the decolonizing struggle in Southeast Asia, it is certain that, had they survived, both would have moved closer to each other's attitude toward racial violence. King already had, and this may be why he was killed by forces still not known.

One of the surprising sources of opposition to the white world's resistances to decolonization was the twentieth century's most famous, and arguably most talented, athletes, Muhammad Ali. On February 25, 1964 (just a year before Malcolm X's murder), as Cassius Clay, he defeated Sonny Liston to become heavyweight champion of the world. A few days later Clay announced that he was a follower of the Nation of Islam and that henceforth he was to be known as Muhammad Ali. Clay, now Ali, had been tutored in the Nation's Islamic principles by Malcolm X. The furor across the United States was insane – no doubt a resonant effect of the fear of confusion at the decolonizing movement. The United States government sought to punish Ali by drafting him into military duty in Vietnam, even though he had twice failed the intelligence test for induction. In 1967, Ali, having refused to accept the draft, was banished from boxing until 1971 when the Supreme Court overturned the judgments against him. Outside the ring, Ali's most famous contribution to decolonizing politics were words put into his mouth to the effect that he would not fight in Vietnam because "no Viet Cong ever called me nigger." The words were actually proven to have been words broadcast to American troops in Vietnam by Ho Chi Minh's forces. Ali had said something similar but not those words. The impression was that he could have. He regained his world championship in 1964 by defeating George Foreman in Zaire, Mobutu Sese Seko's Congo.

One of the reasons the Congo appears several times in this book is that, in many ways, it is the near perfect case study of the inherent violence of the colonial system, of the trials of resistance by the colonized, and of the aftermath of the white world's attempts to turn back the decolonizing movements. Mobutu Sese Seko was a farcical figure or, better put, he would have been were it not for the extent to which the Zaire period of his vicious rule in the Congo prolonged the agony of the long suffering of the Congolese people. It is all too easy to see the misery today in Congo as a regional "problem" of the long-troubled Sub-Saharan Africa. Yet, it would be a mistake to assume that the troubled parts of the African continent are somehow exceptions to the dreadful ruin the globalization of colonizing greed visited upon the world as a whole.

What began nearly at the same moment as the Cold War endured until its end in 1991 with the collapse in the Soviet Union. Is it a mere coincidence that the early 1990s were the high-water mark of talk of a post-modern world order? Vaclav Havel's words in "The End of the Modern Era" reflect a wider global movement to "seek new and better ways of managing society, the economy, and the world"? And why not, given the nightmarish twentieth century? At the same time, the early 1990s, if not post-modern, were at least when globalization entered public discussion. And, again, why not when the shifting and shaking of the modern system was subjected to challenges that were, indeed, local but also global in their inspiration? Was not the Tiananmen rebellion in China in 1989 a failure but, 20 years after, an inspiring coming to terms with the remnants of the old two-world order that pre-occupied the twentieth century? Was not Mikhail Gorbachev's Glasnost speech to the United Nations in 1988 more than a promise of the end of the Cold War − closer, that is, to a different sort of reckoning with the failures of the modern era?

Read the foundational declaration of principles of the World Social Forum in 2001 Porto Alegre: "The WSF [is an] opening meeting place [that is] plural, diversified, non-confessional, non-governmental and non-party." From Gandhi in 1947 in India through Fanon in 1962 in Algeria to the students in Tiananmen in 1989 could there be a better summary of the ideal, if not actual, results of the decolonizing of the modern world and, by contrast, could there be a better way of illuminating the high hopes of the modern age that began in the long sixteenth century in global voyages of discovery and may have ended, or at least become something different, in the globalizing forces of the short twentieth century?

Note

1 E.J. Hobsbawn (2001) *The Age of Extremes: A History of the World, 1914–1991*, Gloucester, MA: Peter Smith Pub Inc.

Global Warfare and the New Imperia

EUROPE AND THE BALKANS: THE ASSASSINATION OF ARCHDUKE FERDINAND (JUNE 28, 1914)

While there are many possible causes of World War I, most of these are linked to rising nationalism in Europe, a declining system of empire, and a series of international treaties. The 1878 Treaty of Berlin created the Kingdom of Serbia as an independent country and gave control of Bosnia and Herzegovina to the Austro-Hungarian Empire. Rising nationalism in Serbia and a desire to rebuild Serbian control led to a series of conflicts with the Austro-Hungarian Empire, including several wars and Serbia's annexation of Macedonia (from the Ottoman Empire) and Kosovo (from Bulgaria). A group of assassins, backed by members of the Serbian military, desired restoration of Serbian control of Balkan provinces and assassinated Archduke Ferdinand, heir to the Austro-Hungarian throne, and his wife Sophie, Duchess of Hohenberg, while they were inspecting troops in Sarajevo on June 28, 1914. The Austro-Hungarian Empire sent a letter, partially reproduced below, known as "The July Ultimatum" that demanded Serbia respect its commitments to Austria-Hungary. When it did not, Austria-Hungary cut off diplomatic relations, mobilized and declared war on July 28, 1914. Russia and France had a secret treaty with Serbia (signed in 1892), and all other powers went to war within a month, except Italy. The specific assassination of Ferdinand is less important than the complex web of international treaties, and the competition for imperial control in a globalizing Europe.

The Austro-Hungarian Minister for Foreign Affairs, Berchtold, to the Minister at Belgrade, von Giesl: Vienna, July 22, 1914

Your Excellency will present the following note to the Royal Government on the afternoon of Thursday, July 23: On the 31st of March, 1909, the Royal Serbian Minister at the Court of Vienna made, in the name of his Government, the following declaration to the Imperial and Royal Government:

Serbia recognizes that her rights were not affected by the state of affairs created in Bosnia, and states that she will accordingly accommodate herself to the decisions to be reached by the Powers in connection with Article 25 of the Treaty of Berlin. Serbia, in accepting the advice of the Great Powers, binds herself to desist from the attitude of protest and opposition which she has assumed with regard to the annexation since October last, and she furthermore binds herself to alter the tendency of her present policy toward Austria-Hungary, and to live on the footing of friendly and neighborly relations with the latter in the future.

Now the history of the past few years, and particularly the painful events of the 28th of June, have proved the existence of a subversive movement in Serbia, whose object it is to separate certain portions of its territory from the Austro-Hungarian Monarchy. This movement, which came into being under the very eyes of the

Serbian Government, subsequently found expression outside of the territory of the Kingdom in acts of terrorism, in a number of attempts at assassination, and in murders.

Far from fulfilling the formal obligations contained in its declaration of the 31st of March, 1909, the Royal Serbian Government has done nothing to suppress this movement. It has tolerated the criminal activities of the various unions and associations directed against the Monarchy, the unchecked utterances of the press, the glorification of the authors of assassinations, the participation of officers and officials in subversive intrigues; it has tolerated an unhealthy propaganda in its public instruction; and it has tolerated, finally, every manifestation which could betray the people of Serbia into hatred of the Monarchy and contempt for its institutions.

This toleration of which the Royal Serbian Government was guilty, was still in evidence at that moment when the events of the twenty-eighth of June exhibited to the whole world the dreadful consequences of such tolerance.

It is clear from the statements and confessions of the criminal authors of the assassination of the twenty-eighth of June, that the murder at Sarajevo was conceived at Belgrade, that the murderers received the weapons and the bombs with which they were equipped from Serbian officers and officials who belonged to the Narodna Odbrana, and, finally, that the dispatch of the criminals and of their weapons to Bosnia was arranged and effected under the conduct of Serbian frontier authorities.

The results brought out by the inquiry no longer permit the Imperial and Royal Government to maintain the attitude of patient tolerance which it has observed for years toward those agitations which center at Belgrade and are spread thence into the territories of the Monarchy. Instead, these results impose upon the Imperial and Royal Government the obligation to put an end to those intrigues, which constitute a standing menace to the peace of the Monarchy.

In order to attain this end, the Imperial and Royal Government finds itself compelled to demand that the Serbian Government give official assurance that it will condemn the propaganda directed against Austria-Hungary, that is to say, the whole body of the efforts whose ultimate object it is to separate from the Monarchy territories that belong to it; and that it will obligate itself to suppress with all the means at its command this criminal and terroristic propaganda.

The Austro-Hungarian Ultimatum to Serbia (English translation), World War I Document Archive. Source: http://wwi.lib.byu.edu/index.php/The_Austro-Hungarian_Ultimatum_to_Serbia_(English_translation).

EUROPE'S LOST IMPERIUM: PAUL FUSSELL ON THE GREAT WAR (CHRISTMAS 1914)

Imperium is a Roman militaristic conception of power, and the root of the English word "emperor" from the Latin *imperator*, or commander of the armed forces. There is a connection to the divine, and when rulers have both early political control and divine covenant, their ruling position is theocratic. It is a concept inherited by early modern Europe from the Holy Roman and Byzantine Empires, where the Roman emperor was the ruler of all persons, their souls, and the world. The Great War spelled the end for imperial empires, already declining in the face of rising nationalist sentiments. The Austrian, Russian, and Ottoman Empires were broken after the war, leaving a number of new and unstable states: the abdication of Kaiser Wilhelm II, and the declaration of the Republic of Germany on November 9, 1919; the Bolshevik revolution in Russia; and the continued allied war on the Ottoman Empire, ending with the establishment of Turkey. Imperial power succumbed to mechanized warfare; power as divine and holy right ceased, and with it the last flickers of the imperium. Historians remark on the horrors of the warfare and the high number of soldier deaths for the small amount of territory gained or lost. Paul Fussell (1924–) is an American historian, social critic, and Professor Emeritus at the University of Pennsylvania. He relays the situation of the men fighting in the trenches and indicates the last moment of the nineteenth century and imperial assumptions of life and warfare as Christmas 1914 when British and German troops met in no-man's land to celebrate on Christmas day, the last day when imperial expectations were realized and respected. The Germans and British met in the middle to play a football match, and interacted as friendly and civilized comrades before returning to the trenches to fight for another four years.

The Trenches – What They Were Really Like

The first thing was it smelled bad.

It smelled bad because there were open latrines everywhere. There were bodies rotting everywhere. Nothing could be done about them. You could throw a shovel full of quick lime on them to take some of the smell away, but the odor of the trenches was appalling.

It's hard to imagine people living for years in the middle of that smell. That's what they had to endure. For the most part there were no bunks, no places to lie down when you weren't on duty; so you lay in the mud, in a hole cut in the side of the trench, or in a dugout if you were an officer or an NCO.

The best time for attacking is in the early morning; partly because you have the advantage of darkness in forming the troops up.

You also have the advantage of a full day in which you can prosecute the development of the attack before it gets dark again. Both the Germans and the British had morning stand-to, which is short for stand-to-arms.

In the darkness as dawn was just about to open up, they would each stand on their firing steps in the trenches, which puts you about this high above the trench. You stood there with your loaded rifle waiting for an attack from the Germans. The Germans did the same thing.

When it was fully light, and it was clear that no attack was going to happen that morning, you stood down and had breakfast. Eating it on the firing trench, which was like a building bench in the trench you were occupying.

Then there's nothing to do all day, except listen to the bangs as the shells went off everywhere.

The object of each side was to try to put mortar shells into the enemy trench and blow it up, or kill the people in it. So there's constant noise and bombardment all day long. Now one couldn't stay forever in the trenches. You stayed usually about a week. Then you were rotated back with another unit, and a fresh unit came up for its week of trench duty.

There were rats the size of cats.

Both the Germans and the British were troubled with rats. The rats ate corpses, then they came in and snuggled next to you while you were sleeping. And they ate your own food, and they were filthy creatures. They also carried disease – bubonic plague primarily.

Many people think that the great flu epidemic of 1919, which affected the United States, had something to do with bubonic plague, which was being carried by these trench rats. Actually, more American troops died of flu than of bullets and shell fragments in the war.

Sky study becomes one of your few amusements.

You never see your enemy and the only thing you can see is the sky up above. You look at the sky constantly from the opening of the trench, because you can't look out to the side. All of your view is vertical. You consequently get very interested in birds for the first time, because those are the only animated things you can see, except for rats and lice, or other human beings.

You never see the enemy except when he's attacking, or you're attacking and you get close to him. So it's a curious, almost studious isolation that the troops are in. They're isolated from the setting and they're isolated, of course, from home, from normal pursuits, and so on. You could read in the trenches sometimes, but it was pretty hard to do with all the explosions going off all the time.

The Christmas Truce – The Last Twitch

The Christmas truce was the last twitch of the nineteenth Century.

By that I mean it was the last public moment in which it was assumed that people were nice, and that the Dickens view of the world was a credible view.

What happened was this: on Christmas morning, 1914, the German troops were dug in over there, and the British troops were dug in here. Somebody, some bright boy, sent a message over. (Probably threw it wrapped around a grenade without the pin pulled.) And it said something like: "Let's have a party. Let's meet in the middle. We won't shoot. And don't shoot us if we come between the lines."

The British soldiers thought this was a good idea.

A few people got up tentatively, left their rifles behind, and found they were not shot at. The Germans came out too. Probably only a dozen at first, but gradually it spread all the way up and down the line. Gradually, battalions and regiments were fraternizing between the lines.

A wonderful ironic moment.

They were exchanging cigarettes and addresses, exchanging insignias – treating each other like friends. It was a high emotional moment. It's the last gesture of the nineteenth Century idea that human beings are getting better the longer the human race goes on. Nobody could believe that after the First World War, and certainly not after the Second.

Paul Fussell, interview on PBS, http://www.pbs.org/greatwar/historian/hist_fussell_03_trenches.html and http://www.pbs.org/greatwar/historian/hist_fussell_04_xmas.html.

CHINA: END OF DYNASTY, SUN YAT-SEN AND NATIONALISM (1911)

Sun Yat-Sen (c. 1866/1870–1925) is commonly known as the person who modernized China. He did so by organizing the overthrow of China's imperial order in favor of a republican system. After which, Sun became China's on-and-off ideological and political leader (from 1911 until his death in 1926). Though his time as China's leader was almost never without controversy or conflict, Sun's ideas have been and still are of great importance. This is especially true of his doctrine known as the "Three Principles of the People," which exalts the ideals of nationalism, democracy, and socialism in the hopes of China becoming a powerful and wealthy nation.

However, as the selection demonstrates, these beliefs were informed by Western influences. In espousing the three principles, Sun had partly in mind Western thinkers such as Abraham Lincoln and Woodrow Wilson. This perhaps is due to the fact that Sun's own life was spent among American and European peoples since as some historians have noted, a good part of his early formative years were spent in places such as Hawaii and boarding schools run by the Church of England.

Interestingly, it is Sun's articulation of nationalism that has arguably received the most attention from his most notable followers. This is true of both those who went to Taiwan under Chiang Kai-Shek and those who stayed in mainland China under Mao Zedong that count Sun as one their ideological mentors. Yet, it is said by some that both parties have not stayed truly faithful to Sun's message. They have only taken parts of it to promote feelings of ultra-nationalism for their own ends and not the sort of "civic-nationalism" that was more inclusive and free from imperial aspirations that Sun also spoke of.

The Teachings of Sun Yat-Sen: The Three Principles of the People (San Min Chu I)

Our Republic is already ten years old, but we still cannot consider that our aim has been achieved. Our work is not yet completed: we must continue the struggle.

Our Party is radically different from all the other parties of China. Thus, there was a party which strove for the overthrow of the Tsing dynasty and the establishment of another dynasty, Ming. Of course, the principles of this party were opposed to ours. When in the last years of the Tsing dynasty, we were forced to establish ourselves in Tokyo, we determined the following as the fundamental principles of our Party: Nationalism, Democracy and Socialism. At that time, power in China was still in the hands of the Manchus and the Revolution had only arrived at this first stage, nationalism, passing over the other two principles.

The principles of President Lincoln completely coincide with mine. He said: "A government of the people, elected by the people and for the people." These principles have served as the maximum of achievement for the Europeans as well as Americans. Words which have the same sense can be found in China: I have translated them: "Nationalism, Democracy and Socialism." Of course, there can be no other interpretations.

I now wish to speak of *Nationalism*.

What meaning do we impart to the word "nationalism"? With the establishment of the Manchu dynasty in China, the people remained under an incredible yoke for over two hundred years. Now that dynasty has been overthrown, and the people, it would seem, ought to enjoy complete freedom. But does the Chinese people enjoy all the blessings of liberty? No. Then what is the reason? Why, that our Party has as yet far from fulfilled its appointed tasks, and has carried out only the negative part of its work, without doing anything of its positive work.

After the overthrow of the monarchy and the establishment of the republican system in the territory populated by the five nationalities (Chinese, Manchus, Mongols, Tartars and Tibetans), a vast number of reactionary and religious elements appeared. And here lies the root of the evil. Numerically, these nationalities stand as follows: there are several million Tibetans, less than a million Mongols, about ten million Tartars, and the most insignificant number of Manchus. Politically their distribution is as follows: Manchuria is in the sphere of Japanese influence, Mongolia, according to recent reports, is under the influence of Russia, and Tibet is the booty of Great Britain. These races have not sufficient strength for self-defence, but they might unite with the Chinese to form a single State.

There are four hundred million Chinese: if they cannot organise a single nation, a united State, this is their disgrace, and moreover a proof that we have not given complete effect even to the first principle, and that we must fight for a long while yet to carry out our tasks to the full. We shall establish a united Chinese Republic in order that all the peoples – Manchus, Mongols, Tibetans, Tartars and Chinese – should constitute a single powerful nation. As an example of what I have described, I can refer to the people of the United States of America, constituting one great whole, but in reality consisting of many separate nationalities: Germans, Dutch, English, French, etc. The United States are an example of a united nation. Such a nationalism is possible, and we must pursue it.

Or take another case of a nation of mingled races – Switzerland. It is situated in the heart of Europe: on one side it borders on France, on another on Germany, on a third, Italy. Not all the parts of this State have a common tongue, yet they constitute one nation. And only the wise cultural and political life of Switzerland makes its people of many races united and strong. All this is the consequence of the citizens of this Republic enjoying equal and direct electoral rights. Regarding this country from the aspect of international policy, we see that it was the first to establish equal and direct electoral rights for all the population. This is an example of nationalism.

But let us imagine that the work of uniting all the tribes who inhabit China has been completed, and one nation, "Chunhua" has been formed. Still the object has not been achieved. There are still many peoples suffering from unjust treatment: the Chinese people must assume the mission of setting free these people from their yoke, in the sense of direct aid for them or uniting them under the banner of a single Chinese nation. This would give them the opportunity to enjoy the feeling of equality between man and man, and of a just international attitude, that is, that which was expressed in the declaration of the American President Wilson by the words "self-determination of nations." Up to the moment of reaching this political stage, our work cannot be considered as finished. Everyone who wishes to join China must be considered Chinese. This is the meaning of nationalism – but "positive" nationalism, and to this we must give special attention.

As regards *democracy* I have already said that in Switzerland democracy has reached its highest point of development; but at the same time the system of representation prevailing there does not constitute real democracy, and only the direct right of the citizen fully answers to the requirements of democracy. Although revolutions took place at various times in France, America and England, and resulted in the establishment of the existing representative system, nevertheless that system does not mean direct and equal rights for all citizens, such as we are fighting for to-day. The most essential of such rights are: the franchise for all citizens: the right of recall (the officials elected by the people can be dismissed by them at will): the right of referendum (if the legislative body passes a law contrary to the wishes of the citizens, the latter may reject the law): the right of initiative (the citizens may propose draft laws, to be carried and adopted by the legislative body).

These four fundamental clauses constitute the basis of what I call "direct electoral right."

Lastly about *Socialism*. The theory of Socialism has become known in China comparatively recently. Its chief advocates usually limit their knowledge of this tendency to a few empty words, without having any definite programme. By long study I have formed a concrete view of this question. The essence of Socialism amounts to solving the problem of land and capital.

Summing up the above, I want also to make a few observations.

1. *Nationalism.* – Since the overthrow of the Tsing dynasty, we have carried out only one part of our obligations: we have fulfilled only our passive duty, but have done nothing in the realm of positive work. We must raise the prestige of the Chinese people, and unite all the races inhabiting China to form one Chinese people in Eastern Asia, a Chinese National State.

2. *Democracy.* – To bring about this ideal we must first of all adopt all the four points of direct electoral rights: universal suffrage, the referendum, the initiative and the rights of recall.

3. *Socialism.* – Here I have my plan.

The first task of my plan is to bring about the proportional distribution of the land. During my stay at Nanking (as Provisional President), I tried to carry out this proposal, but my desire was not fulfilled, as I was not understood. Social questions arise from the inequality between rich and poor. What do we understand by inequality? In ancient times, although there was a distinction between rich and poor, it was not so sharp as to-day. To-day the rich own all the land, while the poor have not even a little plot. The reason for this inequality is the difference in productive power. For example, in ancient times timber-cutters used axes, knives, etc. for their work, whereas to-day industry is greatly developed, machines have replaced human labour, and the result is that a much greater quantity of products is secured at the expense of much less human energy.

Take another example, from the sphere of agriculture. In ancient times only human labour was employed in this industry; but with the introduction of ploughing with horses and oxen, the process of tilling became more speedy and greatly reduced human effort. In Europe and America mechanised energy is now used to till the soil, which affords the opportunity of ploughing in the best possible way more than a thousand acres a day, thus eliminating the use of horses and oxen. This has created a truly amazing difference expressed by the ratio of a thousand to one. If we take the means of communication, however, we see that the introduction of steamships and railways has made communications more than a thousand times more rapid in comparison with human energy.

First we shall speak of the socialisation of land. The land systems of Europe and America are very different. In England up to this day the feudal system of land-holding has survived, whereas in the United States all the land is private property. But my social theory advocates the proportionalisation of the land, as a means of providing against future evils. We can see the latter beginning even at the present day. Take what is going on under our very eyes since the reorganisation of the Canton municipality: communications have improved, and in consequence the price of land along the embankment and in other most thickly populated districts has begun to increase daily, some estates selling for tens of thousands of dollars per *mu*. And all this belongs to private persons, living by the labour of others.

The old Chinese land system partially conforms to the principle of proportionalisation of land. In the event of this principle being applied, the two following conditions must be observed: taxation according to the value of the land, and compensation according to declared value. In China up to this day the so-called three-grade system of collection of land taxes has been preserved; but, owing to the inadequate development of transport and industry, land values were not so high in the past as they are to-day. Well-developed means of communication and developing industry have led, owing to the maintenance of the old system, to an extremely unequal rise in the value of the land. There are, for example, lands worth 2,000 dollars per *mu*, while there are also lands worth 20,000 dollars per *mu*, while between these two extremes of values there are a large number of the most varying values. But if taxes continue to be collected on the old system, both the tax collectors and the taxpayers will be put in such a position that dishonest collectors and landowners can make easy profits thereby.

Therefore if we want to abolish this evil and introduce the graduation of taxes, we must adopt the following method: to collect one per cent of the value of the land. For example, if a given piece of land is worth 2,000 dollars, its owner pays 20 dollars. The collection of further taxes will depend on an increase in the value of the land. The process of State purchase of the land must begin with the establishment of its definite value.

So much about the land question. There remains the issue of how to settle the problem of capital.

Recently I published a book entitled: *The International Development of China*. In this book I discussed the question of utilising foreign capital for the purpose of developing Chinese industry and commerce. Look at the Pekin-Hankow and Pekin-Mukden railways, and also at the Tientsin-Pukow line, built by foreign capital and yielding enormous profits. At the present time the total length of the Chinese railways is 5,000–6,000 miles, and their profits amount to 70–80 millions – more even than the land tax. But if the total length is increased to 50 or 60 thousand miles, the profits will also increase considerably. My opinion about the application of foreign capital to our industry is the following: all branches of our industry, for example mining, which represent, with any management worth its salt, profitable undertakings, are awaiting foreign capital.

When I speak of a loan in this connection, I mean the procuring of various machines and other necessary appliances for our industry. For example, after the construction of the Pekin-Hankow railway, the profits of which were enormous, the foreigners would have given us the chance to acquire it, with its future profit-making possibilities. These were so great that we could have completed the Pekin-Kalgan line, which now reaches Sunyang. In brief, we can easily incur debt to foreign capital, but the question is – how shall we utilise it, productively or otherwise?

We must admit that the degrees of sacrifice required for the social revolution will be higher than for the political. The Revolution of 1911 and the overthrow of the Manchus only partially realised the principle of Nationalism, while neither the theory of Democracy nor the theory of Socialism left any impression. But we must strive our utmost not only to secure the triumph of our first Party principle, but, in accordance with modern world ideas, to develop if possible the principles of democracy, which are also principles of our Party. Although both England and America are politically developed, political authority there still remains in the hands, not of the people as a whole, but of a political party.

During the great European War, President Wilson put forward the watchword: "self-determination of peoples." This corresponds to our Party principle of nationalism. After the Peace Conference at Versailles, a number of small but independent republics were formed, living without any common tie. This must clearly show you the principal tendency in the modern life of nations. Now the time is approaching to carry into effect our great principles of Nationalism, Democracy and Socialism. Only by the transformation of all three principles into reality can our people live and develop freely. But the explanation and application of these principles depend very largely on the display of your forces and the degree of energy shown in your propaganda. *Speech, March 6th, 1921, at a meeting of the Executive Committee of the Kuomintang in Canton.*

Sun Yat-Sen (1945) *The Teachings of Sun Yat-Sen: Selections From his Writings*, compiled and introduced by Professor N. Gangulee, London: The Sylvan Press, pp. 57–63.

GERMANY: THIRTY YEARS WAR IN EUROPE, JOHN MAYNARD KEYNES ON VERSAILLES (1919)

John Maynard Keynes (1883–1946) was born in Cambridge, England, where he grew up and studied at the university from which he earned a degree in mathematics in 1904. In early adult life, he worked as a civil servant intermittently. When not doing so, he was in Cambridge working on the general subject of probability theory that led to his eminence as an economist. During World War I he returned to the civil service in the war effort and at its conclusion was appointed to the British delegation to Versailles where the terms of the peace agreement with Germany were drawn up and handed down. As the selection from *The Economic Consequences of the Peace* shows, he was appalled by the economic disaster he foretold if, as happened, the Peace was to exact the severe penalties in the form of impossibly large reparation payments on Germany that it did. He resigned the delegation in disgust. Keynes could not have been more prophetic. Crippled by war and the demands imposed at Versailles, Germany fell into economic ruin that notoriously opened the door for Hitler and World War II; hence, 1914–1945 is often referred to as a Thirty Years War with Germany. The selection also displays Keynes's conclusion that the free market ideologies of the nineteenth century had to be qualified and supplemented by State activism in financial and monetary markets. To non-specialists this was the source of his fame as an economist.

The Economic Consequences of the Peace: Europe after the Treaty

The treaty includes no provisions for the economic rehabilitation of Europe – nothing to make the defeated Central empires into good neighbours, nothing to stabilise the new states of Europe, nothing to reclaim Russia; nor does it promote in any way a compact of economic solidarity amongst the Allies themselves; no arrangement was reached at Paris for restoring the disordered finances of France and Italy, or to adjust the systems of the Old World and the New.

The Council of Four paid no attention to these issues, being preoccupied with others – Clemenceau to crush the economic life of his enemy, Lloyd George to do a deal and bring home something which would pass muster for a week, the President to do nothing that was not just and right. It is an extraordinary fact that the fundamental economic problem of a Europe starving and disintegrating before their eyes, was the one question in which it was impossible to arouse the interest of the Four. Reparation was their main excursion into the economic field, and they settled it as a problem of theology, of politics, of electoral chicane, from every point of view except that of the economic future of the states whose destiny they were handling.

I leave, from this point onwards, Paris, the conference, and the treaty, briefly to consider the present situation of Europe, as the war and the peace have made it; and it will no longer be part of my purpose to distinguish between the inevitable fruits of the war and the avoidable misfortunes of the peace.

The essential facts of the situation, as I see them, are expressed simply. Europe consists of the densest aggregation of population in the history of the world. This population is accustomed to a relatively high standard of life, in which, even now, some sections of it anticipate improvement rather than deterioration. In relation to other continents Europe is not self-sufficient; in particular it cannot feed itself. Internally the population is not evenly distributed, but much of it is crowded into a relatively small number of dense industrial centres. This population secured for itself a livelihood before the war, without much margin of surplus, by means of a delicate and immensely complicated organisation, of which the foundations were supported by coal, iron, transport, and an unbroken supply of imported food and raw materials from other continents. By the destruction of this organisation and the interruption of the stream of supplies, a part of this population is deprived of its means of livelihood. Emigration is not open to the redundant surplus. For it would take years to transport them overseas, even, which is not the case, if countries could be found which were ready to receive them. The danger confronting us, therefore, is the rapid depression of the standard of life of the European populations to a point which will mean actual starvation for some (a point already reached in Russia and approximately reached in Austria). Men will not always die quietly. For starvation, which brings to some lethargy and a helpless despair, drives other temperaments to the nervous instability of hysteria and to a mad despair. And these in their distress may overturn the remnants of organisation, and submerge civilisation itself in their attempts to satisfy desperately the overwhelming needs of the individual. This is the danger against which all our resources and courage and idealism must now co-operate.

On 13 May 1919 Count Brockdorff-Rantzau addressed to the peace conference of the Allied and Associated Powers the Report of the German economic commission charged with the study of the effect of the conditions of peace on the situation of the German population. 'In the course of the last two generations,' they reported, 'Germany has become transformed from an agricultural state to an industrial state. So long as she was an agricultural state, Germany could feed 40 million inhabitants. As an industrial state she could ensure the means of subsistence for a population of 67 millions; and in 1913 the import-ation of foodstuffs amounted, in round figures, to 12 million tons. Before the war a total of 15 million persons in Germany provided for their existence by foreign trade, navigation, and the use, directly or indirectly, of foreign raw material.' After rehearsing the main relevant provisions of the peace treaty the report continues: 'After this diminution of her products, after the economic depression resulting from the loss of her colonies, her merchant fleet and her foreign investments, Germany will not be in a position to import from abroad an adequate quantity of raw material. An enormous part of German industry will, therefore, be condemned inevitably to destruction. The need of importing foodstuffs will increase consider-ably at the same time that the possibility of satisfying this demand is as greatly diminished. In a very short time, therefore, Germany will not be in a position to give bread and work to her numerous millions of inhabitants, who are prevented from earning their livelihood by navigation and trade. These persons should emigrate, but this is a material impossibility, all the more because many countries and the most important ones will oppose any German immigration. To put the peace conditions into execution would logically involve, therefore, the loss of several millions of persons in Germany. This catastrophe would not be long in coming about, seeing that the health of the population has been broken down during the war by the blockade, and during the armistice by the aggravation of the blockade of famine. No help, however great, or over however long a period it were continued, could prevent these deaths en masse.' 'We do not know, and indeed we doubt,' the Report concludes, 'whether the delegates of the Allied and Associated Powers realise the inevitable consequences which will take place if Germany, an industrial state, very thickly populated, closely bound up with the economic system of the world, and under the necessity of importing enormous quantities of raw material and foodstuffs, suddenly finds herself pushed back to the phase of her development which corresponds to her economic condition and the numbers of her population as they were half a century ago. Those who sign this treaty will sign the death sentence of many millions of German men, women and children.' [. . .]

The significant features of the immediate situation can be grouped under three heads: first, the absolute falling off, for the time being, in Europe's internal productivity; second, the breakdown of transport and exchange by means of which its products could be conveyed where they were most wanted; and third, the inability of Europe to purchase its usual supplies from overseas. [. . .]

The problem of the re-inauguration of the perpetual circle of production and exchange in foreign trade leads me to a necessary digression on the currency situation of Europe.

Lenin is said to have declared that the best way to destroy the capitalist system was to debauch the currency. By a continuing process of inflation, governments can confiscate, secretly and unobserved, an important part of the wealth of their citizens. By this method they not only confiscate, but they confiscate arbitrarily; and, while the process impoverishes many, it actually enriches some. The sight of this arbitrary rearrangement of riches strikes not only at security, but at confidence in the equity of the existing distribution of wealth. Those to whom the system brings windfalls, beyond their deserts and even beyond their expect-ations or desires, become 'profiteers,' who are the object of the hatred of the bourgeoisie, whom the inflation-ism has impoverished, not less than of the proletariat. As the inflation proceeds and the real value of the currency fluctuates wildly from month to month, all permanent relations between debtors and creditors, which form the ultimate foundation of capitalism, become so utterly disordered as to be almost meaningless; and the process of wealth-getting degenerates into a gamble and a lottery.

Lenin was certainly right. There is no subtler, no surer means of overturning the existing basis of society than to debauch the currency. The process engages all the hidden forces of economic law on the side of destruction, and does it in a manner which not one man in a million is able to diagnose.

In the latter stages of the war all the belligerent governments practised, from necessity or incompetence, what a Bolshevist might have done from design. Even now, when the war is over, most of them continue out of weakness the same malpractices. But further, the governments of Europe, being many of them at this moment reckless in their methods as well as weak, seek to direct on to a class known as 'profiteers' the popular indignation against the more obvious consequences of their vicious methods. These 'profiteers' are, broadly speaking, the entrepreneur class of capitalists, that is to say, the active and constructive element in the whole capitalist society, who in a period of rapidly rising prices cannot but get rich quick whether they wish it or desire it or not. If prices are continually rising, every trader who has purchased for stock or owns property and plant inevitably makes profits. By directing hatred against this class, therefore, the European governments are carrying a step further the fatal process which the subtle mind of Lenin had consciously conceived. The profiteers are a consequence and not a cause of rising prices. By combining a popular hatred of the class of entrepreneurs with the blow already given to social security by the violent and arbitrary disturbance of contract and of the established equilibrium of wealth which is the inevitable result of inflation, these govern-ments are fast rendering impossible a continuance of the social and economic order of the nineteenth century. But they have no plan for replacing it.

We are thus faced in Europe with the spectacle of an extra-ordinary weakness on the part of the great capitalist class, which has emerged from the industrial triumphs of the nineteenth century, and seemed a very few years ago our all-powerful master. The terror and personal timidity of the individuals of this class is now so great, their confidence in their place in society and in their necessity to the social organism so diminished, that they are the easy victims of intimidation. This was not so in England twenty-five years ago, any more than it is now in the United States. Then the capitalists believed in themselves, in their value to society, in the propriety of their continued existence in the full enjoyment of their riches and the unlimited exercise of their power. Now they tremble before every insult – call them pro-Germans, international financiers, or profiteers, and they will give you any ransom you choose to ask not to speak of them so harshly. They allow themselves to be ruined and altogether undone by their own instruments, governments of their own making, and a Press of which they are the proprietors. Perhaps it is historically true that no order of society ever perishes save by its own hand.

John Maynard Keynes (1919) *The Economic Consequences of the Peace.* Source: http://socserv2. socsci. mcmaster.ca~econ/ugcm/3ll3/keynes/peace.

RUSSIA: SOVIET REVOLUTION, VLADIMIR LENIN (1917)

Vladimir Lenin (1870–1924), the Soviet revolutionary leader, discovered Marxism in his youth. He studied law at the University of Saint Petersburg, but never practiced as a lawyer. Instead, he devoted himself to political and theoretical work. Among Lenin's important contributions to the theory of the revolutionary state was the *April Theses* (1917) that inspired the October 1917 revolution which the Bolsheviks won, leading to the founding of the Soviet Union of which Lenin became the first head of state. Lenin's earlier tract, *What Is to Be Done?* (1903) is famous for his ideas on the vanguard party and his later *Imperialism, the Highest Stage of Capitalism* (1916) is noteworthy for its analysis of World War I as struggle among capitalist interests. John Maynard Keynes, among others, who were not, like Lenin, revolutionaries, appreciated many of his points on the economic crisis of the world war.

April Theses

1) In our attitude towards the war, which under the new [provisional] government of Lvov and Co. unquestionably remains on Russia's part a predatory imperialist war owing to the capitalist nature of that government, not the slightest concession to 'revolutionary defencism' is permissible.

The class-conscious proletariat can give its consent to a revolutionary war, which would really justify revolutionary defencism, only on condition: (a) that the power pass to the proletariat and the poorest sections of the peasants aligned with the proletariat; (b) that all annexations be renounced in deed and not in word; (c) that a complete break be effected in actual fact with all capitalist interests.

In view of the undoubted honesty of those broad sections of the mass believers in revolutionary defencism who accept the war only as a necessity, and not as a means of conquest, in view of the fact that they are being deceived by the bourgeoisie, it is necessary with particular thoroughness, persistence and patience to explain their error to them, to explain the inseparable connection existing between capital and the imperialist war, and to prove that without overthrowing capital it is impossible to end the war by a truly democratic peace, a peace not imposed by violence.

The most widespread campaign for this view must be organised in the army at the front.

Fraternisation

2) The specific feature of the present situation in Russia is that the country is passing from the first stage of the revolution – which, owing to the insufficient class-consciousness and organisation of the proletariat, placed power in the hands of the bourgeoisie – to its second stage, which must place power in the hands of the proletariat and the poorest sections of the peasants.

This transition is characterised, on the one hand, by a maximum of legally recognised rights (Russia is now the freest of all the belligerent countries in the world); on the other, by the absence of violence towards the masses, and, finally, by their unreasoning trust in the government of capitalists, those worst enemies of peace and socialism.

This peculiar situation demands of us an ability to adapt ourselves to the special conditions of Party work among unprecedentedly large masses of proletarians who have just awakened to political life.

3) No support for the Provisional Government; the utter falsity of all its promises should be made clear, particularly of those relating to the renunciation of annexations. Exposure in place of the impermissible, illusion-breeding 'demand' that this government, a government of capitalists, should cease to be an imperialist government.

4) Recognition of the fact that in most of the Soviets of Workers' Deputies our Party is in a minority, so far a small minority, as against a bloc of all the petty-bourgeois opportunist elements, from the Popular Socialists and the Socialist-Revolutionaries down to the Organising Committee (Chkheidze, Tsereteli, etc.), Steklov, etc., etc., who have yielded to the influence of the bourgeoisie and spread that influence among the proletariat.

The masses must be made to see that the Soviets of Workers' Deputies are the only possible form of revolutionary government, and that therefore our task is, as long as this government yields to the influence of the bourgeoisie, to present a patient, systematic, and persistent explanation of the errors of their tactics, an explanation especially adapted to the practical needs of the masses.

As long as we are in the minority we carry on the work of criticising and exposing errors and at the same time we preach the necessity of transferring the entire state power to the Soviets of Workers' Deputies, so that the people may overcome their mistakes by experience.

5) Not a parliamentary republic – to return to a parliamentary republic from the Soviets of Workers' Deputies would be a retrograde step – but a republic of Soviets of Workers', Agricultural Labourers' and Peasants' Deputies throughout the country, from top to bottom.

Abolition of the police, the army and the bureaucracy

The salaries of all officials, all of whom are elective and displaceable at any time, not to exceed the average wage of a competent worker.

6) The weight of emphasis in the agrarian programme to be shifted to the Soviets of Agricultural Labourers' Deputies.

Confiscation of all landed estates

Nationalisation of all lands in the country, the land to be disposed of by the local Soviets of Agricultural Labourers' and Peasants' Deputies. The organisation of separate Soviets of Deputies of Poor Peasants. The setting up of a model farm on each of the large estates (ranging in size from 100 to 300 dessiatines, according to local and other conditions, and to the decisions of the local bodies) under the control of the Soviets of Agricultural Labourers' Deputies and for the public account.

7) The immediate union of all banks in the country into a single national bank, and the institution of control over it by the Soviet of Workers' Deputies.

8) It is not our immediate task to 'introduce' socialism, but only to bring social production and the distribution of products at once under the control of the Soviets of Workers' Deputies.

9) Party tasks:

(a) Immediate convocation of a Party congress;
(b) Alteration of the Party Programme, mainly:
   1. On the question of imperialism and the imperialist war;
   2. On our attitude towards the state and our demand for a 'commune state';
   3. Amendment of our out-of-date minimum programme;
(c) Change of the Party's name.

"The Tasks of the Proletariat in the Present Revolution [a.k.a. The April Theses.]" First published: April 7, 1917 in *Pravda* no. 26. Signed: N. Lenin. Published according to the newspaper text. *Lenin's Collected Works*, vol. 24, Moscow: Progress Publishers, 1964, pp. 19–26. Translated by Isaacs Bernard. Retrieved from Marxists Internet Archive.

JAPAN: HIROHITO AND THE CULT OF THE EMPEROR (1926–1945)

In the wake of Emperor Yoshisoto's death in 1926 came the ascension of Prince Hirohoto (1901–1989) to the throne of Emperor of Japan. At which point, Hirohoto was renamed Showa (translated, Enlightened Peace) to mark the passing of a new era. However, instead of ushering in the era of his newly given name, Emperor Showa presided over one of the bloodiest periods in Japanese history. From 1931 to 1945, Japan fought a war of imperial conquest against China and other neighboring lands. This resulted in the involvement of Japan in World War II and its eventual defeat at the hands of the allied forces.

While some recent historical accounts hold Emperor Showa at least slightly personally responsible for the decision to commit these acts of aggression, the cultural significance of the imperial throne was also a considerable factor. In *The Chrysanthemum and the Sword*, from which the selection is taken, Ruth Benedict (1887–1948) touches upon this very subject. Here, she makes the observation that Western allied forces during World War II did not properly understand how the Emperor was viewed in the eyes of his subjects. It was mistakenly believed that the Japanese people could renounce the imperial throne without also renouncing the idea of Japan as a nation, when in fact for many the two entities were coterminous. Indeed, as Benedict notes, many Japanese people held the view that "a Japan without the Emperor is not Japan." Such a sentiment had been in place since the Meiji Restoration of 1868, when imperial rule was re-established. Benedict, an anthropologist, wrote *The Chrysanthemum and the Sword* at the conclusion of war with Japan as a contribution to understanding the causes of the war and of Japan's part in it.

The Chrysanthemum and the Sword: 'The Japanese in the War' (1946)

The most famous question about Japanese attitudes concerned His Imperial Majesty, the Emperor. What was the hold of the Emperor on his subjects? Some American authorities pointed out that through all Japan's seven feudal centuries the Emperor was a shadowy figurehead. Every man's immediate loyalty was due to his lord, the *daimyo*, and, beyond that, to the military Generalissimo, the Shogun. Fealty to the Emperor was hardly an issue. He was kept accluded in an isolated court whose ceremonies and activities were rigorously circumscribed by the Shogun's regulations. It was treason even for a great feudal lord to pay his respects to the Emperor, and for the people of Japan he hardly existed. Japan could only be understood by its history, these American analysts insisted; how could an Emperor who had been brought out from obscurity within the memory of still living people be the real rallying point of a conservative nation like Japan? The Japanese publicists who again and again reiterated the undying hold of the Emperor upon his subjects were over-protesting, they said, and their insistence only proved the weakness of their case. There was no reason, therefore, that American policy during the war should draw on kid gloves in dealing with the Emperor. There was every reason rather why we should direct our strongest attacks against this evil Fuehrer concept that Japan had recently concocted. It was the very heart of its modern nationalistic Shinto religion and if we undermined and challenged the sanctity of the Emperor, the whole structure of enemy Japan would fall in ruins.

Many capable Americans who knew Japan and who saw the reports from the front lines and from Japanese sources were of the opposite persuasion. Those who had lived in Japan well knew that nothing stung the Japanese people to bitterness and whipped up their morale like any depreciatory word against the Emperor or any outright attack on him. They did not believe that in attacking the Emperor we would in the eyes of the Japanese be attacking militarism. They had seen that reverence for the Emperor had been equally strong in those years after the First World War when 'de-mok-ra-sie' was the great watchword and militarism was so discredited that army men prudently changed to mufti before they went out on the streets of Tokyo. The reverence of the Japanese for their Imperial chief could not be compared, these old Japanese residents insisted, with Heil-Hitler veneration which was a barometer of the fortunes of the Nazi party and bound up with all the evils of a fascist program.

Certainly the testimony of Japanese prisoners of war bore them out. Unlike Western soldiers, these prisoners had not been instructed about what to say and what to keep silent about when captured and their responses on all subjects were strikingly unregimented. This failure to indoctrinate was of course due to Japan's no-surrender policy. It was not remedied until the last months of the war, and even then only in certain armies or local units. The prisoners' testimony was worth paying attention to for they represented a cross-section of opinion in the Japanese Army. They were not troops whose low morale had caused them to surrender – and who might therefore be atypical. All but a few were wounded and unconscious soldiers unable to resist when captured.

Japanese prisoners of war who were out-and-out bitter-enders imputed their extreme militarism to the Emperor and were 'carrying out his will,' 'setting his mind at rest,' 'dying at the Emperor's command.' 'The Emperor led the people into war and it was my duty to obey.' But those who rejected this present war and future Japanese plans of conquest just as regularly ascribed their peaceful persuasions to the Emperor. He was all things to all men. The war-weary spoke of him as 'his peace-loving Majesty'; they insisted that he 'had always been liberal and against the war.' 'He had been deceived by Tojo.' 'During the Manchurian incident he showed that he was against the military.' 'The war was started without the Emperor's knowledge or permission.

The Emperor does not like war and would not have permitted his people to be dragged into it. The Emperor does not know how badly treated his soldiers are.' These were not statements like those of German prisoners of war who, however much they complained that Hitler had been betrayed by his generals or his high command, nevertheless ascribed war and the preparations for war to Hitler as supreme inciter. The Japanese prisoner of war was quite explicit that the reverence given the Imperial Household was separable from militarism and aggressive war policies.

The Emperor was to them, however, inseparable from Japan. 'A Japan without the Emperor is not Japan.' 'Japan without the Emperor cannot be imagined.' 'The Japanese Emperor is the symbol of the Japanese people, the center of their religious lives. He is a super-religious object.' Nor would he be blamed for the defeat if Japan lost the war. 'The people did not consider the Emperor responsible for the war.' 'In the event of defeat the Cabinet and the military leaders would take the blame, not the Emperor.' 'Even if Japan lost the war ten out of ten Japanese would still revere the Emperor.'

All this unanimity in reckoning the Emperor above criticism appeared phoney to Americans who are accustomed to exempt no human man from skeptical scrutiny and criticism. But there was no question that it was the voice of Japan even in defeat. Those most experienced in interrogating the prisoners gave it as their verdict that it was unnecessary to enter on each interview sheet: 'Refuses to speak against the Emperor'; all prisoners refused, even those who co-operated with the Allies and broadcast for us to the Japanese troops. Out of all the collected interviews of prisoners of war, only three were even mildly anti-Emperor and only one went so far as to say: 'It would be a mistake to leave the Emperor on the throne.' A second said the Emperor was 'a feeble-minded person, nothing more than a puppet.' And the third got no farther than supposing that the Emperor might abdicate in favor of his son and that if the monarchy were abolished young Japanese women would hope to get a freedom they envied in the women of America.

Japanese commanders, therefore, were playing on an all but unanimous Japanese veneration when they distributed cigarettes to the troops 'from the Emperor,' or led them on his birthday in bowing three times to the east and shouting 'Banzai'; when they chanted with all their troops morning and evening, 'even though the unit was subjected to day and night bombardment,' the 'sacred words' the Emperor himself had given to the armed forces in the Rescript for Soldiers and Sailors while 'the sound of chanting echoed through the forest.' The militarists used the appeal of loyalty to the Emperor in every possible way. They called on their men to 'fulfill the wishes of His Imperial Majesty,' to 'dispel all the anxieties of your Emperor,' to 'demonstrate your respect for His Imperial benevolence,' to 'die for the Emperor.' But this obedience to his will could cut both ways. As many prisoners said, the Japanese 'will fight unhesitatingly, even with nothing more than bamboo poles, if the Emperor so decrees. They would stop just as quickly if he so decreed'; 'Japan would throw down arms tomorrow if the Emperor should issue such an order'; 'Even the Kwantung Army in Manchuria' – most militant and jingoistic – 'would lay down their arms'; 'only his words can make the Japanese people accept a defeat and be reconciled to live for reconstruction.'

Ruth Benedict (1946) *The Chrysanthemum and the Sword: Patterns of Japanese Culture*, Boston: Houghton Mifflin Company, pp. 29–33.

GERMANY: ADOLF HITLER AND NATIONAL SOCIALISM (1924–1945)

Adolf Hitler (1889–1945) rose to political power from humble beginnings in post-World War I Germany. After the war, like many from the military, Hitler settled in Munich, a hotbed of conservative and right-wing politics. Germany was suffering economically from the Treaty of Versailles, and suffering ideologically by the displacement of the army and the famed officer corps. One of the popular sentiments of the time, often cited as a cause of Hitler's rise to power, was *Der Dolchstoß*, that the German Army had been stabbed in the back. This, of course, overlooks that it was the German Army that called for the armistice and for Wilhelm to step down. Despite the Weimar constitution (established August 31, 1919) being the most democratic ever, the army wanted to maintain the power and prestige that it had under the former empire and the Hohenzollen militarist autocracy. There was a resurfacing of Pan-German nationalistic sentiment that had begun in the multinational Austro-Hungarian Empire. Adolf Hitler became leader of the newly formed NSDAP, Nazi Party on April 1, 1920. In its formation, the party called for a strong central German state for all Germans, and the abrogation of the Treaty of Versailles and the Treaty of Saint-Germain-en-Laye, Austria's treaty that prevented Austria from forming any alliances.

The Nazi Party came to national attention with its attempted *coup d'état* in Munich of the Bavarian State, "The Beer Hall Putsch" (November 8–9, 1924). The Nazis were inspired by Mussolini's fascist control of Rome, and though they failed to seize power and Nazi leaders were either exiled or imprisoned, the ensuing trial catapulted the Nazi Party into the national spotlight. Hitler used the trial (February 26, 1924) as a platform to promote his political agenda and to distribute propaganda.

Hitler's Speech Before the Munich Court: Speech of March 27, 1924

When did the ruin of Germany begin? You know the watchword of the old German system in its foreign policy: it ran – maintenance of world peace, economic conquest of the world. With both these principles one cannot govern a people. The maintenance of world peace cannot be the purpose and aim of the policy of a State. The increase and maintenance of a people – that alone can be the aim. If you are going to conquer the world by an economic policy, other peoples will not fail to see their danger.

What is the State? Today the State is an economic organization, an association of persons, formed, it would seem, for the sole purpose that all should co-operate in securing each other's daily bread. The State, however, is not an economic organization, it is a 'volkic' organism. The purpose, the aim of the State is to provide the people with its food-supply and with the position of power in the world which is its due. Germany occupies in Europe perhaps the most bitter situation of any people. Militarily, politically, and geographically it is surrounded by none but rivals: it can maintain itself only when it places a power-policy (machtpolitik) ruthlessly in the foreground.

Two Powers are in a position to determine the future development of Europe: England and France. England's aim remains eternally the same: to balkanize Europe and to establish a balance of power in Europe so that her position in the world will not be threatened. England is not on principle an enemy of Germany, it is the power which seeks to gain the first place in Europe. The declared enemy of Germany is France. Just as England needs the balkanization of Europe, so France needs the balkanization of Germany in order to gain hegemony in Europe. After four and a half years of bitter struggle at last through the Revolution the scale of victory turned in favor of the coalition of these two Powers, with the following result: France was faced with the question: Was she to realize her eternal war-aim or not? That means: Could France destroy Germany and deprive it of all the sources whereby its people was fed? Today France watches the ripening to fulfillment of her age-old plan: it matters not what Government will be at the helm in France: the supreme aim will remain – the annihilation of Germany, the extermination of twenty million Germans, and the dissolution of Germany into separate States. . . .

The army which we have formed grows from day to day; from hour to hour it grows more rapidly. Even now I have the proud hope that one day the hour is coming when these untrained bands will become battalions, when the battalions will become regiments and the regiments divisions, when the old cockade will be raised from the mire, when the old banners will once again wave before us: and then reconciliation will come in that eternal last Court of Judgment – the Court of God – before which we are ready to take our stand. Then from our bones, from our graves will sound the voice of that tribunal which alone has the right to sit in judgment upon us. For, gentlemen, it is not you who pronounce judgment upon us, it is the eternal Court of History which will make its pronouncement upon the charge which is brought against us. The judgment that you will pass, that I know. But that Court will not ask of us: 'Have you committed high treason or not?' That Court will judge us . . . . who as Germans have wished the best for their people and their Fatherland, who wished to fight and to die. You may declare us guilty a thousand times, but the Goddess who presides over the Eternal Court of History will with a smile tear in pieces the charge of the Public Prosecutor and the judgment of the Court: for she declares us guiltless.

Hitler's Speech Before the Munich Court, Speech of March 27, 1924. Source: http://www.humanitas-international.org/showcase/chronography/speeches/1924–03–27.html.

THE AMERICAN CENTURY: HENRY LUCE (1941)

Henry Luce (1898–1967) was born to American missionaries in China. After studying at Yale, Luce eventually entered publishing as a founder of a series of important American magazines, including *Fortune*, *Life*, *Time*, and *Sports Illustrated*. His American Century idea appeared in *Time* in 1941.

The Ambiguous Legacy: "The American Century"

The 20th Century is the American Century

[. . .] *Some facts about our time*

Consider the 20th Century. It is ours not only in the sense that we happen to live in it but ours also because it is America's first century as a dominant power in the world. So far, this century of ours has been a profound and tragic disappointment. No other century has been so big with promise for human progress and happiness. And in no one century have so many men and women and children suffered such pain and anguish and bitter death.

It is a baffling and difficult and paradoxical century. No doubt all centuries were paradoxical to those who had to cope with them. But, like everything else, our paradoxes today are bigger and better than ever. Yes, better as well as bigger – inherently better. We have poverty and starvation – but only in the midst of plenty. We have the biggest wars in the midst of the most widespread, the deepest and the most articulate hatred of war in all history. We have tyrannies and dictatorships – but only when democratic idealism, once regarded as the dubious eccentricity of a colonial nation, is the faith of a huge majority of the people of the world.

And ours is also a revolutionary century. The paradoxes make it inevitably revolutionary. Revolutionary, of course, in science and in industry. And also revolutionary, as a corollary in politics and the structure of society. But to say that a revolution is in progress is not to say that the men with either the craziest ideas or the angriest ideas or the most plausible ideas are going to come out on top. The Revolution of 1776 was won and established by men most of whom appear to have been both gentlemen and men of common sense.

Clearly a revolutionary epoch signifies great changes, great adjustments. And this is only one reason why it is really so foolish for people to worry about our "constitutional democracy" without worrying or, better, thinking hard about the world revolution. For only as we go out to meet and solve for our time the problems of the world revolution, can we know how to re-establish our constitutional democracy for another 50 or 100 years.

This 20th Century is baffling, difficult, paradoxical, revolutionary. But by now, at the cost of much pain and many hopes deferred, we know a good deal about it. And we ought to accommodate our outlook to this knowledge so dearly bought. For example, any true conception of our world of the Twentieth Century must surely include a vivid awareness of at least these four propositions.

First: our world of 2,000,000,000 human beings is for the first time in history one world, fundamentally indivisible. Second: modern man hates war and feels intuitively that, in its present scale and frequency, it may even be fatal to his species. Third: our world, again for the first time in human history, is capable of producing all the material needs of the entire human family. Fourth: the world of the 20th Century, if it is to come to life in any nobility of health and vigor, must be to a significant degree an American Century.

Henry Luce (1999) "The American Century," in Michael J. Hogan (ed.) *The Ambiguous Legacy: U.S. Foreign Relations in the American Century*, New York: Cambridge University Press, pp. 11–30. © Henry Luce/Life Magazine, Time Inc. pp. 22–24.

The Cold War as a Struggle for Global Control, 1946–1975

COLD WAR AND THE IRON CURTAIN: WINSTON CHURCHILL (1946)

Winston Churchill (1874–1965) was a public servant, a military man and politician, a leader of his country, a Nobel Prize-winning author, and, very possibly, one of two men (Franklin Delano Roosevelt being the other) who held the world together in the worst days of World War II. His wit and ironic habits were an offspring of qualities of character and intelligence that are nowhere better exemplified than in his famous Iron Curtain Speech of 1946: "From Stettin in the Baltic to Trieste in the Adriatic an iron curtain has descended across the Continent." These are plain but chilling words, pronounced in Fulton, Missouri, just months after the conclusion of the long world war. With George Kennan's philosophical containment theory and Joseph Stalin's defiant retort to Churchill, the Iron Curtain Speech defined the terms and conditions of a global struggle that would endure until late 1991.

Iron Curtain Speech – 1946

A shadow has fallen upon the scenes so lately light by the Allied victory. Nobody knows what Soviet Russia and its Communist international organization intends to do in the immediate future, or what are the limits, if any, to their expansive and proselytizing tendencies. I have a strong admiration and regard for the valiant Russian people and for my wartime comrade, Marshall Stalin. There is deep sympathy and goodwill in Britain – and I doubt not here also – towards the peoples of all the Russias and a resolve to persevere through many differences and rebuffs in establishing lasting friendships. We understand the Russian need to be secure on her western frontiers by the removal of all possibility of German aggression. We welcome Russia to her rightful place among the leading nations of the world. We welcome her flag upon the seas. Above all, we welcome, or should welcome, constant, frequent and growing contacts between the Russian people and our own people on both sides of the Atlantic. It is my duty however, for I am sure you would wish me to state the facts as I see them to you. It is my duty to place before you certain facts about the present position in Europe.

From Stettin in the Baltic to Trieste in the Adriatic an iron curtain has descended across the Continent. Behind that line lie all the capitals of the ancient states of Central and Eastern Europe. Warsaw, Berlin, Prague, Vienna, Budapest, Belgrade, Bucharest and Sofia, all these famous cities and the populations around them lie in what I must call the Soviet sphere, and all are subject in one form or another, not only to Soviet influence but to a very high and, in some cases, increasing measure of control from Moscow. Athens alone – Greece with its immortal glories – is free to decide its future at an election under British, American and French observation. The Russian-dominated Polish Government has been encouraged to make enormous and wrongful inroads upon Germany, and mass expulsions of millions of Germans on a scale grievous and undreamed-of are now taking place. The Communist parties, which were very small in all these Eastern States of Europe, have been raised to pre-eminence and power far beyond their numbers and are seeking everywhere to obtain totalitarian control. Police governments are prevailing in nearly every case, and so far, except in Czechoslovakia, there is no true democracy.

Turkey and Persia are both profoundly alarmed and disturbed at the claims which are being made upon them and at the pressure being exerted by the Moscow Government. An attempt is being made by the Russians in Berlin to build up a quasi-Communist party in their zone of occupied Germany by showing special favors to groups of left-wing German leaders. At the end of the fighting last June, the American and British Armies withdrew westward, in accordance with an earlier agreement, to a depth at some points of 150 miles upon a front of nearly four hundred miles, in order to allow our Russian allies to occupy this vast expanse of territory which the Western Democracies had conquered.

If now the Soviet Government tries, by separate action, to build up a pro-Communist Germany in their areas, this will cause new serious difficulties in the American and British zones, and will give the defeated Germans the power of putting themselves up to auction between the Soviets and the Western Democracies. Whatever conclusions may be drawn from these facts – and facts they are – this is certainly not the Liberated Europe we fought to build up. Nor is it one which contains the essentials of permanent peace.

The safety of the world, ladies and gentlemen, requires a new unity in Europe, from which no nation should be permanently outcast. It is from the quarrels of the strong parent races in Europe that the world wars we have witnessed, or which occurred in former times, have sprung. Twice in our own lifetime we have seen the United States, against their wishes and their traditions, against arguments, the force of which it is impossible not to comprehend, twice we have seen them drawn by irresistible forces, into these wars in time to secure the victory of the good cause, but only after frightful slaughter and devastation have occurred. Twice the United State has had to send several millions of its young men across the Atlantic to find the war; but now war can find any nation, wherever it may dwell between dusk and dawn. Surely we should work with conscious purpose for a grand pacification of Europe, within the structure of the United Nations and in accordance with our Charter. That I feel opens a course of policy of very great importance.

Winston Churchill, "Iron Curtain Speech – 1946." Source: http://www.nationalcenter.org/ChurchillIronCurtain.html.

THE AMERICAN THREAT AND STALINIST IDEOLOGY: JOSEPH STALIN (1946)

Joseph Stalin (1878–1953) was the leader of the Soviet Communist Party, and thus of the Soviet Union, from 1922 until his death. His reign was marked by totalitarian brutality toward dissenters, real and imagined. Millions were lost or died in the Gulags. But there were also moments of triumph – from the initial hope that the Soviet Union seemed to offer those drawn to socialist ideals to the decisiveness of the Soviet army in the defeat of Germany and the Nazis on the Eastern Front. No Soviet leader was more the symbol of the evils attributed to global communism during the Cold War. The selection was Stalin's rapid-fire opening salvo in that ideological struggle, coming just days after Winston Churchill's famous "Iron Curtain" speech in Missouri.

Stalin Interview with *Pravda* on Churchill

LONDON, March 13 (U.P.) – The text of a Moscow broadcast on Generalissimo Stalin's statement follows:

A few days ago a Pravda correspondent approached Stalin with a request to clarify a series of questions connected with the speech of Mr. Churchill. Comrade Stalin gave clarifications, which are set out below in the form of answers to the correspondent's questions.

Q. How do you assess the last speech of Mr. Churchill which was made in the United States?

A. I assess it as a dangerous act calculated to sow the seed of discord among the Allied governments and hamper their cooperation.

Q. Can one consider that the speech of Mr. Churchill is damaging to the cause of peace and security?

A. Undoubtedly, yes. In substance, Mr. Churchill now stands in the position of a fire-brand of war. And Mr. Churchill is not alone here. He has friends not only in England but also in the United States of America.

Reminds Stalin of Hitler

In this respect, one is reminded remarkably of Hitler and his friends. Hitler began to set war loose by announcing his racial theory, declaring that only people speaking the German language represent a fully valuable nation. Mr. Churchill begins to set war loose also by a racial theory, maintaining that only nations speaking the English language are fully valuable nations, called upon to decide the destinies of the entire world.

The German racial theory brought Hitler and his friends to the conclusion that the Germans, as the only fully valuable nation, must rule over other nations. The English racial theory brings Mr. Churchill and his friends to the conclusion that nations speaking the English language, being the only fully valuable nations, should rule over the remaining nations of the world.

In substance, Mr. Churchill and his friends in England and the United States present nations not speaking the English language with something like an ultimatum: "Recognize our lordship voluntarily and then all will be well. In the contrary case, war is inevitable."

But the nations have shed their blood during five years of cruel war for the sake of liberty and the independence of their countries, and not for the sake of exchanging the lordship of Hitler for the lordship of Churchill.

It is, therefore, highly probable that the nations not speaking English and which, however, make up an enormous majority of the world's population, will not consent to go into a new slavery. The tragedy of Mr. Churchill lies in the fact that he, as a deep-rooted Tory, cannot understand this simple and obvious truth.

Sees a call to war

There is no doubt that the setup of Mr. Churchill is a set-up for war, a call to war with the Soviet Union. It is also clear that such a set-up as that of Mr. Churchill is incompatible with the existing treaty of alliance between England and the U.S.S.R. It is true that Mr. Churchill, in order to confuse his readers, declares in passing that the length of the Anglo-Soviet treaty for mutual aid and cooperation could easily be extended to fifty years.

But how can one reconcile such a statement by Mr. Churchill with his set-up for war against the Soviet Union, his preaching of war against the Soviet Union? It is clear that these things can in no way be compatible.

If Mr. Churchill, calling for war against the Soviet Union, still considers it possible to extend the duration of the Anglo-Soviet treaty to fifty years, then it means that he considers this treaty as an empty piece of paper, to be used in order to conceal and disguise his anti-Soviet set-up.

On this account, one cannot consider seriously the declaration of Mr. Churchill's friends in England about the extension of the Soviet-English treaty to fifty years or more. Problems of the duration of a treaty have no sense if one of the parties violates the treaty and turns it into an empty scrap of paper.

Q. How do you assess that part of Mr. Churchill's speech in which he attacks the democratic regime of the European countries which are our neighbors and in which he criticizes the good neighborly relations established between these countries and the Soviet Union?

Churchill "rude," lacks "tact"

A. This part of Mr. Churchill's speech is a mixture of the elements of the libel with the elements of rudeness and lack of tact. Mr. Churchill maintains that Warsaw, Berlin, Prague, Vienna, Budapest, Belgrade, Bucharest and Sofia, all these famous cities and the populations of those areas, are within the Soviet sphere and are all subjected to Soviet influence and to the increasing control of Moscow.

Mr. Churchill qualifies this as the "boundless expansionist tendencies of the Soviet Union." It requires no special effort to show that Mr. Churchill rudely and shamelessly libels not only Moscow but also the above-mentioned States neighborly to the U.S.S.R.

To begin with, it is quite absurd to speak of the exclusive control of the U.S.S.R. in Vienna and Berlin, where there are Allied control councils with representatives of four States, where the U.S.S.R. has only one-fourth of the voices.

It happens sometimes that some people are unable to refrain from libel, but still they should know a limit.

Secondly, one cannot forget the following fact: the Germans carried out an invasion of the U.S.S.R. through Finland, Poland, Rumania, Bulgaria and Hungary. The Germans were able to carry out the invasion through these countries by reason of the fact that these countries had governments inimical to the Soviet Union.

As a result of the German invasion, the Soviet Union has irrevocably lost in battles with the Germans, and also during the German occupation and through the expulsion of Soviet citizens to German slave labor camps, about 7,000,000 people. In other words, the Soviet Union has lost in men several times more than Britain and the United States together.

It may be that some quarters are trying to push into oblivion these sacrifices of the Soviet people which insured the liberation of Europe from the Hitlerite yoke.

But the Soviet Union cannot forget them. One can ask, therefore, what can be surprising in the fact that the Soviet Union, in a desire to ensure its security for the future, tries to achieve that these countries should have governments whose relations to the Soviet Union are loyal? How can one, without having lost one's reason, qualify these peaceful aspirations of the Soviet Union as "expansionist tendencies" of our Government?

"Rude, offensive libel"

Mr. Churchill further maintains that the Polish Government under Russian lordship has been spurred to an unjust and criminal spoliation against Germany. Here, every word is a rude and offensive libel. Contemporary, democratic Poland is led by outstanding men. They have shown in deeds that they know how to defend the interests and worth of their homeland, as their predecessors failed to do.

What reason has Mr. Churchill to maintain that the leaders of contemporary Poland can submit their country to a lordship by representatives of any country whatever? Does Mr. Churchill here libel the Russians because he has intentions of sowing the seeds of discord between Poland and the Soviet Union?

Mr. Churchill is not pleased that Poland should have turned her policy toward friendship and alliance with the U.S.S.R. There was a time when in the mutual relations between Poland and the U.S.S.R. there prevailed an element of conflict and contradiction. This gave a possibility to statesmen, of the kind of Mr. Churchill, to play on these contradictions, to take Poland in hand under the guise of protection from the Russians, to frighten Russia by specters of a war between Poland and herself, and to take for themselves the role of arbiters.

But this time is past. For enmity between Poland and Russia has given place to friendship between them, and Poland, present democratic Poland, does not wish any longer to be a playing-ball in the hands of foreigners. It seems to be that this is just what annoys Mr. Churchill and urges him to rude, tactless outbursts against Poland. After all, it is no laughing matter for him. He is not allowed to play for other people's stakes.

As for Mr. Churchill's attack on the Soviet Union in connection with the extending of the western boundaries of Poland, as compensation for the territories seized by the Germans in the past, there it seems to me that he quite blatantly distorts the facts.

As is known, the western frontiers of Poland were decided upon at the Berlin conference of the three powers, on the basis of Poland's demands.

The Soviet Union repeatedly declared that it considered Poland's demands just and correct. It may well be that Mr. Churchill is not pleased with this decision. But why does Mr. Churchill, not sparing his darts against the Russians in the matter, conceal from his readers the fact that the decision was taken at the Berlin conference unanimously, that not only the Russians voted for this decision but also the English and Americans?

On growth of Communists

Why did Mr. Churchill have to delude people? Mr. Churchill further maintains that the Communist parties were very insignificant in all these Eastern European countries but reached exceptional strength, exceeding their numbers by far, and are attempting to establish totalitarian control everywhere; that police-government prevailed in almost all these countries, even up to now, with the exception of Czechoslovakia, and that there exists in them no real democracy.

As is known in Britain at present there is one party which rules the country – the Labor party. The rest of the parties are barred from the Government of the country. This is called by Churchill a true democracy, meanwhile Poland, Rumania, Yugoslavia, Bulgaria and Hungary are governed by several parties – from four to six parties. And besides, the opposition, if it is loyal, is guaranteed the right to participate in the Government. This, Churchill calls totalitarian and the Government of police.

On what grounds? Do you expect an answer from Churchill? Does he not understand the ridiculous situation he is putting himself in by such speeches on the basis of totalitarianism and police rule. Churchill would have liked Poland to be ruled by Sosnkowski and Anders, Yugoslavia by Mikhailovitch, Rumania by Prince Stirbey and Radescu, Hungary and Austria by some king from the House of Habsburg, and so on.

Mr. Churchill wants to assure us that these gentlemen from the Fascist servants' hall can ensure true democracy. Such is the Democracy of Mr. Churchill. Mr. Churchill wanders around the truth when he speaks of the growth of the influence of the Communist parties in eastern Europe. It should, however, be noted that he is not quite accurate. The influence of Communist parties grew not only in Eastern Europe but in almost every country of Europe where fascism has ruled before: Italy, Germany, Hungary, Bulgaria, Rumania, Finland, and in countries which have suffered German, Italian or Hungarian occupation. France, Belgium, Holland, Norway, Denmark, Poland, Czechoslovakia, Yugoslavia, Greece, the Soviet Union and so on.

The growth of the influence of communism cannot be considered accidental. It is a normal function. The influence of the Communists grew because during the hard years of the mastery of fascism in Europe, Communists showed themselves to be reliable, daring and self-sacrificing fighters against fascist regimes for the liberty of peoples.

Mr. Churchill sometimes recalls in his speeches the common people from small houses, patting them on the shoulder in a lordly manner and pretending to be their friend. But these people are not so simple-minded as it might appear at first sight. Common people, too, have their opinions and their own politics. And they know how to stand up for themselves.

It is they, millions of these common people, who voted Mr. Churchill and his party out in England, giving their votes to the Labor party. It is they, millions of these common people, who isolated reactionaries in Europe, collaborators with fascism, and gave preference to Left democratic parties.

Says people fully back Reds

It is they, millions of these common people, having tried the Communists in the fire of struggle and resistance to fascism, who decided that the Communists deserve completely the confidence of the people. Thus grew the Communists' influence in Europe. Such is the law of historical development.

Of course, Mr. Churchill does not like such a development of events. And he raised the alarm, appealing to force. But he also did not like the appearance of the Soviet regime in Russia after the First World War. Then, too, he raised the alarm and organized an armed expedition of fourteen states against Russia with the aim of turning back the wheel of history.

But history turned out to be stronger than Churchill's intervention and the quixotic antics of Churchill resulted in his complete defeat. I do not know whether Mr. Churchill and his friends will succeed in organizing after the Second World War a new military expedition against eastern Europe. But if they succeed in this, which is not very probable, since millions of common people stand on guard over the peace, then one man confidently says that they will be beaten, just as they were beaten twenty-six years ago.

Joseph Stalin, "Stalin Interview with *Pravda* on Churchill," *New York Times*, March 14, 1946, p. 4.

THE SOVIET THREAT AND THE PRINCIPLE OF DETERRENCE: GEORGE F. KENNAN (1946)

George F. Kennan (1904–2005) was one of America's most distinguished and notable diplomats and public intellectuals. A Princeton man from Wisconsin, Kennan began his career in the US Foreign Service in 1926 and was eventually posted to the Soviet Union. The selection is from his justly famous "Long Telegram" (decoded from secret Foreign Service lines but transcribed in telegraph style). Thus, it was that in February 1946 (two weeks before Churchill's Iron Curtain speech in the US) that a junior American diplomat in Moscow laid down the intellectual underpinnings of the American policy of containment in the Cold War against the USSR. Kennan later expanded his influential theories, again under the veil of the pseudonym "X" as "Sources of Soviet Conduct," published in *Foreign Affairs* in 1947.

The Long Telegram

861.00/2–2246: Telegram
The Charge in the Soviet Union (Kennan) to the Secretary of State
SECRET
Moscow, February 22, 1946–9 p.m. [Received February 22–3: 52 p.m.] . . .
I apologize in advance for this burdening of telegraphic channel; but questions involved are of such urgent importance, particularly in view of recent events, that our answers to them, if they deserve attention at all, seem to me to deserve it at once. There follows:
Part 1: Basic Features of Post War Soviet Outlook, as Put Forward by Official Propaganda Machine
Are as Follows:

(a) USSR still lives in antagonistic 'capitalist encirclement' with which in the long run there can be no permanent peaceful coexistence. As stated by Stalin in 1927 to a delegation of American workers:

'In course of further development of international revolution there will emerge two centers of world significance: a socialist center, drawing to itself the countries which tend toward socialism, and a capitalist center, drawing to itself the countries that incline toward capitalism. Battle between these two centers for command of world economy will decide fate of capitalism and of communism in entire world.'

(b) Capitalist world is beset with internal conflicts, inherent in nature of capitalist society. These conflicts are insoluble by means of peaceful compromise. Greatest of them is that between England and US.

(c) Internal conflicts of capitalism inevitably generate wars. Wars thus generated may be of two kinds: intra-capitalist wars between two capitalist states, and wars of intervention against socialist world. Smart capitalists, vainly seeking escape from inner conflicts of capitalism, incline toward latter.

(d) Intervention against USSR, while it would be disastrous to those who undertook it, would cause renewed delay in progress of Soviet socialism and must therefore be forestalled at all costs.

(e) Conflicts between capitalist states, though likewise fraught with danger for USSR, nevertheless hold out great possibilities for advancement of socialist cause, particularly if USSR remains militarily powerful, ideologically monolithic and faithful to its present brilliant leadership.

(f) It must be borne in mind that capitalist world is not all bad. In addition to hopelessly reactionary and bourgeois elements, it includes (1) certain wholly enlightened and positive elements united in acceptable communistic parties and (2) certain other elements (now described for tactical reasons as progressive or democratic) whose reactions, aspirations and activities happen to be 'objectively' favorable to interests of USSR. These last must be encouraged and utilized for Soviet purposes.

(g) Among negative elements of bourgeois-capitalist society, most dangerous of all are those whom Lenin called false friends of the people, namely moderate-socialist or social-democratic leaders (in other words, non-Communist left-wing). These are more dangerous than out-and-out reactionaries, for latter at least march under their true colors, whereas moderate left-wing leaders confuse people by employing devices of socialism to serve interests of reactionary capital.

[. . .] At bottom of Kremlin's neurotic view of world affairs is traditional and instinctive Russian sense of insecurity. Originally, this was insecurity of a peaceful agricultural people trying to live on vast exposed plain in neighborhood of fierce nomadic peoples. To this was added, as Russia came into contact with economically advanced West, fear of more competent, more powerful, more highly organized societies in that area. But this latter type of insecurity was one which afflicted rather Russian rulers than Russian people; for Russian rulers have invariably sensed that their rule was relatively archaic in form fragile and artificial in its psychological foundation, unable to stand comparison or contact with political systems of Western countries. For this reason they have always feared foreign penetration, feared direct contact between Western world and their own, feared what would happen if Russians learned truth about world without or if foreigners learned truth about world within. And they have learned to seek security only in patient but deadly struggle for total destruction of rival power, never in compacts and compromises with it.

It was no coincidence that Marxism, which had smoldered ineffectively for half a century in Western Europe, caught hold and blazed for first time in Russia. Only in this land which had never known a friendly neighbor or indeed any tolerant equilibrium of separate powers, either internal or international, could a doctrine thrive which viewed economic conflicts of society as insoluble by peaceful means. After establishment of Bolshevist regime, Marxist dogma, rendered even more truculent and intolerant by Lenin's interpretation, became a perfect vehicle for sense of insecurity with which Bolsheviks, even more than previous Russian rulers, were afflicted. In this dogma, with its basic altruism of purpose, they found justification for their instinctive fear of outside world, for the dictatorship without which they did not know how to rule, for cruelties they did not dare not to inflict, for sacrifice they felt bound to demand. In the name of Marxism they sacrificed every single ethical value in their methods and tactics. Today they cannot dispense with it. It is fig leaf of their moral and intellectual respectability. Without it they would stand before history, at best, as only the last of that long succession of cruel and wasteful Russian rulers who have relentlessly forced country on to ever new heights of military power in order to guarantee external security of their internally weak regimes. This is why Soviet purposes must always be solemnly clothed in trappings of Marxism, and why no one should underrate importance of dogma in Soviet affairs. Thus Soviet leaders are driven [by?] necessities of their own past and present position to put forward which [apparent omission] outside world as evil, hostile and menacing, but as bearing within itself germs of creeping disease and destined to be wracked with growing internal convulsions until it is given final coup de grace by rising power of socialism and yields to new and better world. This thesis provides justification for that increase of military and police power of Russian state, for that isolation of

Russian population from outside world, and for that fluid and constant pressure to extend limits of Russian police power which are together the natural and instinctive urges of Russian rulers. Basically this is only the steady advance of uneasy Russian nationalism, a centuries old movement in which conceptions of offense and defense are inextricably confused. But in new guise of international Marxism, with its honeyed promises to a desperate and war torn outside world, it is more dangerous and insidious than ever before.

It should not be thought from above that Soviet party line is necessarily disingenuous and insincere on part of all those who put it forward. Many of them are too ignorant of outside world and mentally too dependent to question [apparent omission] self-hypnotism, and who have no difficulty making themselves believe what they find it comforting and convenient to believe. Finally we have the unsolved mystery as to who, if anyone, in this great land actually receives accurate and unbiased information about outside world. In atmosphere of oriental secretiveness and conspiracy which pervades this Government, possibilities for distorting or poisoning sources and currents of information are infinite. The very disrespect of Russians for objective truth – indeed, their disbelief in its existence – leads them to view all stated facts as instruments for furtherance of one ulterior purpose or another. There is good reason to suspect that this Government is actually a conspiracy within a conspiracy; and I for one am reluctant to believe that Stalin himself receives anything like an objective picture of outside world. Here there is ample scope for the type of subtle intrigue at which Russians are past masters. Inability of foreign governments to place their case squarely before Russian policy makers – extent to which they are delivered up in their relations with Russia to good graces of obscure and unknown advisors whom they never see and cannot influence – this to my mind is most disquieting feature of diplomacy in Moscow, and one which Western statesmen would do well to keep in mind if they would understand nature of difficulties encountered here.

George F. Kennan, "The Long Telegram," 1946. Source: http://en.wikisource.org/wiki/The_Long_Telegram.

■ ■ ■ ■ ■ ■

GREAT BRITAIN AND SUEZ: THE PROTOCOL OF SÈVRES (1956)

Sir Patrick Dean (1909–1994), an Assistant Under-Secretary at the Foreign Office for Britain, recounted in 1978 his role in the signing of the Protocol of Sèvres (October 22–24, 1956). Dean was sent by British Prime Minister Sir Anthony Eden to get a signed copy of the secret agreement, which stipulated military invasion of parts of Egypt in reaction to the Egyptian nationalization of the Suez Canal. The conflict is known as the Suez Crisis (also Tripartite Aggression, *Crise du canal de Suez*, The Sinai War). Control of the canal was important to the British because of the link to the empire and for its geopolitical importance, especially for the flow of oil. The invasion (beginning October 29, 1956) was brought to a rapid end by international political pressure from the UN and NATO who blocked the sale of oil to the UK and France. The US put financial pressure on the UK when President Eisenhower threatened to sell the US sterling bond holdings, an action that would have devalued the UK currency. The Chancellor of the Exchequer, Harold Macmillan, is remembered for his role in realizing that such a move by the US would prevent Britain from importing sufficient food. Thus the Suez Crisis was a crisis of a crumbling empire, the rise of the geopolitical importance of the Middle East and its oil reserves, and the role of international governmental organizations.

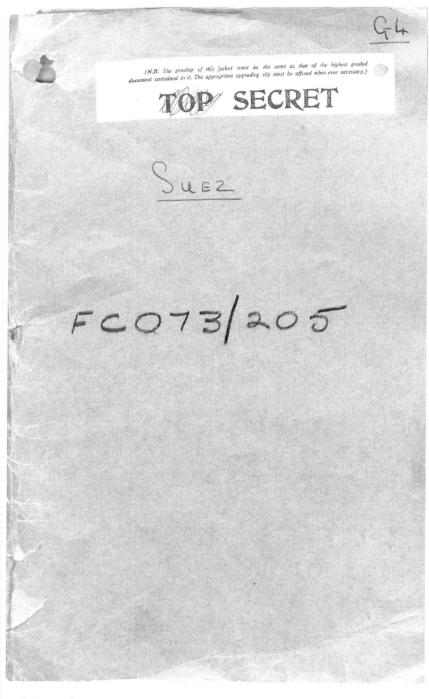

1) Get RA's informal steer [Float
idea of Bushell giving an
opinion subject to Dean's agreement]

2) Ask Dean if Logan knows &
if not if I can tell him.

3) Consult Logan. He may have a
view on sensitivity. ? Mention
asking Bushell if Dean agrees

4) If thought good idea – get Dean's
agreement to seeking Bushell's
views

5) Make recommendations on whether
to release Dean's record at
same time as other pp.

Catalogue Reference:FCO/73/205

ec

In the months preceding the Suez crisis in 1956 I was serving as Assistant Under Secretary in the Foreign Office in charge of the Permanent Under Secretary's Department.   In that capacity I was responsible inter alia for liaison with the Chiefs of Staff for Defence Planning and for Intelligence, being also Chairman of the Joint Intelligence Committee (JIC).   In practice most of my time was taken up with intelligence matters and the planning functions were carried out by the Head of the P.U.S. Department, at that time Geoffrey McDermott who regularly attended meetings of the Military Planners or their deputies.   The system in the Foreign Office was that when planning involved any particular country in detail the geographical department concerned was closely involved and also attended meetings of the Planners. I only came into the planning mechanism when either the Chiefs of Staff or the Planners themselves were discussing major questions of politico/strategic policy.   On the other hand I was closely in touch through the JIC machinery with the American Intelligence Representatives both civilian and military and in London and Washington.   This exchange was well-established and covered all parts of the world.

In the months following the seizure of the Suez Canal by Nasser I was generally aware that a great deal of detailed planning of various sorts for the recovery of the Suez Canal was going forward within the Ministry of Defence and that the Eastern Department and the P.U.S. Department were concerned.   I cannot now remember very much about the details, with which I was never closely concerned, although I do remember hearing about possible plans for the use of Cyprus as a staging point.   This was quite normal procedure.   In particular I never heard of any plans which involved joint plans or discussions with either the French or the Israelis and I have no reason to believe that there were any.

On the morning of 24th October I was woken in the small hours (I can't be more precise) by Sir Norman Brook whom I knew very well and was told that I was required to proceed to Paris later in the morning and that I was to be very careful not to let anyone else know and keep very quiet about it. I was also told to report to No. 10 Downing Street at, I think, about 8.30 a.m. as the Prime Minister, Sir Anthony Eden wished to see me.   I accordingly did so having first booked an air passage to Paris directly and not through the Foreign Office.

-1-

At No. 10 I was taken upstairs and saw the Prime Minister who was in bed for about 15-20 minutes, as far as I can remember. I cannot now remember all that he said but he impressed upon me his great anxiety about Nasser's policy and aims and his fear that he intended and was able to inflict great damage on British interests in the Middle East. It was already widely known how strongly he felt on this subject. He told me, without going into any details, that the French and the Israelis shared his opinion and that it might be necessary for the three countries to take action if at any time Nasser became a threat to the Canal or if, as a result of hostilities between Israel and Egypt, the Canal itself was threatened. He said that in that event British Forces might have to intervene but that it was most important that they should not do so or become involved in military operations unless a threat to the Canal had already clearly developed and Israeli forces had already advanced outside their frontier towards the Canal. At that point it would probably be necessary for the British and the French to issue a public warning that, unless hostilities ceased and the threat to the Canal was immediately removed, British and French forces would actively intervene between the Israelis and the Egyptians to ensure the safety of the Canal.

Sir Anthony Eden then said that although this plan had been generally discussed between the British, French and the Israelis (he made no mention of any specific meetings) it was essential to make absolutely sure before final decisions were taken that the Israelis and French had no doubt whatever in their minds that British Forces would not move unless the Israelis had advanced beyond their frontiers against Egypt and a threat to the Canal had clearly emerged. He then said that a meeting was due to take place that afternoon in Paris between the French and the Israelis which he wanted me to attend and make it absolutely clear to both of them what the British attitude and intentions were and to obtain their acceptance of them. If they did not accept them I should make it plain that there would be no acceptance on our side of any contingency military plan. He said that it was very important to keep the visit secret because it involved possible military operations and he told me that a private military aeroplane would be ready later in the morning to fly me to Paris and bring me back to report the same evening.

-2-

I went across to the Foreign Office and managed to cancel the flight that I had booked to Paris and then went to see Sir Ivone Kirkpatrick, the Permanent Under Secretary. I found him very depressed and in a bad temper, but I knew him well and was quite used to that as he often felt ill and in pain. I told him briefly what had happened but he displayed very little interest and it became clear to me that he was not enthusiastic about Sir A. Eden's ideas. Again I was not surprised as this was often the case. He told me however that as the Prime Minister had charged me with undertaking this mission I must carry it out and that I should report to the Secretary of State before leaving. This I did at 10 a.m. and Mr. Selwyn Lloyd told me that I would be accompanied by Mr. Donald Logan who was his Assistant Private Secretary. I was pleased about this particularly because it was clearly going to be difficult to make sure that I on my own properly conveyed Sir A. Eden's instructions and also accurately remembered all that might happen and be said at the meeting; and also because I knew Logan well and his French was particularly good.

At this point I should make it clear that:

(a) although the Prime Minister had told me that he agreed with the French and the Israelis about the possibility of military action being required if a threat to the security of the Canal developed as a result of hostilities between Egypt and Israel, I was told and knew nothing about any previous personal contacts or meetings at any level between the British, French and Israelis beyond the fact (which was common knowledge) that he and the Secretary of State had had a meeting with the French, M. Mollet and M. Pineau, in Paris on October 16th. I now believe that it was not until very shortly before October 16th that Sir A. Eden learned that joint military planning between the French and the Israelis had been going on for some time and had reached an advanced stage by October 16th when they went to Paris.

(b) I had no written instructions whatever and only knew what the Prime Minister had told me. My knowledge that some plans had been for some time under consideration within the Ministry of Defence was, as I have said, only general. So at this stage was my knowledge (? lack of knowledge) of political contacts with France and Israel. I was in no position to relate the one to the other.

-3-

(c)   I regarded my mission - and regarded it throughout - purely as a part of a military contingency plan upon which the Prime Minister wished to make sure that the other parties fully understood and accepted the two essential points upon the basis of which any plans for possible British military intervention would have to be drawn up.

(d)   I never at any time regarded what the Prime Minister asked me to do as authorising me to conclude in any sense a formal inter-Government agreement constituting a Treaty or anything like it between Governments, but merely as an occasion to make sure that British intentions were properly understood and embodied in any military contingency plan which might be drawn up.

(e)   I also regarded the Prime Minister's insistence on secrecy as being the normal adjunct of all forms of military planning.

The above was my understanding at the beginning and throughout.

After I had told Geoffrey McDermott that I should be out of my office all day, without stating the reason, Donald Logan and I left London about 10 a.m. in his car and drove to (I think) Hendon aerodrome whence we took off in a light military aircraft with a crew of two R.A.F. members and arrived at Villacoublay Airport as far as I remember soon after 1 p.m.   On the journey we discussed our mission and I learned from Donald for the first time that there had been a previous meeting in Paris between the French (I think M. Mollet, M. Bourges-Manourey and M. Pineau), the Israelis (Mr. Ben Gurion, Mr. Dayan and Mr. Peres) and Sir A. Eden and Mr. Selwyn Lloyd which had taken place two days earlier on 22nd October.   I found this interesting as I had tried to see Mr. Lloyd myself on that day but had been told that he was not available.

We were met at Villacoublay by General Challe, who was at that time unknown to me, but who I gathered was a Senior Staff Officer, and who explained that as we had some time to spare we would have lunch on the way to our destination. This we did at a roadside restaurant and eventually arrived at a villa in Sèvres (I learned this from the signposts) at as far as I remember soon after 4 p.m.

-4-

After a short wait we were ushered into a fairly large room, furnished like
a salon, where there were already gathered about ten other people, including
Mollet, Pineau and Bourges-Manoury, Minister of Defence for the French
and for the Israelis Ben Gurion, Dayan and Peres. The atmosphere was
correct but not very friendly and it was obvious to us that the French and the
Israelis had been talking together for a considerable time before we arrived.

I cannot remember much about the conversation which did not cover any major
points of policy but concentrated on the details of the military plan if a decision
were ever taken to put it into operation in certain eventualities. I confined
myself to emphasising more than once the two main points which the Prime
Minister had instructed me to make very clear to the others and Donald Logan
supported me sometimes speaking in French.

During the discussions we sought information about Israeli intentions as
regards a strike against Egypt, but were told nothing except that they
contemplated an act of war. It became clear to both of us that the French,
and even more the Israelis, were deeply suspicious of British intentions and
asked a number of questions which we answered in accordance with our
instructions. After a brief suspension a paper was suddenly produced from
the next room where it had apparently been very recently typed. It was about
4 small pages long. I cannot remember its contents but it took the form of an
outline plan of action and certainly neither in form or content purporting or appearing to be other than that.

Logan and I had not expected this as we had been proceeding on the basis that
the discussions were to be oral and that I should be reporting orally on them
to the Prime Minister on my return to London. We discussed whether we ought
to sign the paper as I was asked to do. We considered consulting London by
telephone but recognised that apart from the security risk involved to do so
would certainly increase the suspicion of British intentions. Logan was
satisfied that the paper accurately represented the course of the previous
discussions. I judged that the plan of action contemplated fell within the Prime
Minister's instructions to me and covered the two points which particularly

-5-

concerned the Prime Minister, namely that British Forces would not move until after a threat to the Canal had clearly emerged as the result of the Israelis crossing their frontier and a public warning calling on both the Israelis and the Egyptians to withdraw had been given. The paper was in fact a record of the action which the three Governments had said they were willing to take in the Middle East situation then current and as it would in certain eventualities evolve. As such it enabled me to make an accurate report to the Prime Minister on the precise intentions of the other two Governments (and the Prime Minister clearly wanted as much precision as possible about Israeli intentions). I accordingly initialled each page of the document and signed at the end and the French and the Israelis did the same by the hand of I think, but am not sure Mr. Ben Gurion and M. Mollet. I made it clear that I was signing ad referendum.

We then left leaving the others in the room and flew back to London arriving at Downing Street at I think about 10.30 pm. Several Ministers including the Prime Minister were already there or came in shortly after and I remember seeing among others Mr. Butler, Mr. Macmillan, Sir A. Douglas-Home, Sir A. Head (I think) and Lord Mountbatten. When I handed the document to Sir A. Eden and explained what had happened he clearly was surprised because he had not expected any written document, but he was satisfied with the contents which covered the points which he regarded as essential and he thanked me for that. Ministers then went in to a meeting and after a while I was allowed to go home.

I have been told since then that Sir A. Eden was at times critical of my action in signing the document, but though he was clearly surprised and not very pleased when I gave it to him and told him what had happened, he did not criticise me at the time (which, as I know well, he was very well capable of doing if somebody had displeased him) and he never said anything critical to me thereafter. On the contrary he once apologised to me for having put me into such an embarrassing situation and therefore subjected me to criticism in subsequent years.

-6-

On 25th October, the day after Donald Logan and I had visited Sèvres on the Prime Minister's instructions to impress upon the French and the Israelis certain points in connection with the plan for action in the event of a threat developing to the security of the Suez Canal, we were instructed again orally by (I believe) the Prime Minister to return to Paris to ask M. Pineau (or M. Mollet) to destroy the document which I had signed the day before at the meeting at Sèvres. We accordingly flew back by the same route to France and were driven to the Quai D'Orsay to whom a request had already been sent from London for an interview to be arranged.

At the Quai we explained the Prime Minister's request to M. Pineau who received it rather coldly and questioned the need or advisability of any such action, pointing out that the Israelis had a third copy and that they had already returned to Israel on the preceding evening very soon after Logan and I had left the villa at Sèvres. M. Pineau said however that he would give us a full answer later and we were then taken to a furnished apartment or suite on the upper floors and the key was turned in the door. We were left in the suite with a little mineral water and as far as I remember practically nothing to eat. We stayed there for at least four hours without anyone coming near us and then were taken down again to see Pineau who told us that the French Government would not accept Sir A. Eden's proposal partly because as already stated the Israelis already had a third copy of the document in Israel and partly because the French saw no reason to destroy the document. From the way they spoke both Logan and I got the clear impression that they distrusted the motives behind the Prime Minister's request and suspected that the real reason for it was that the Prime Minister might find it easier and more convenient to deny that there had been any previous planning or to refuse to act in accordance with the contingency plan, if it suited him, if no written documents existed in Paris or London.

Logan and I then returned to London and reported the outcome of our visit to the Secretary of State downstairs at No. 10 Downing Street.

-7-

Catalogue Reference:FCO/73/205   Image Reference:2

Patrick Dean, an Assistant Under-Secretary at the Foreign Office for Britain, "The Protocol of Sèvres, 1956" relayed to government in 1978. National Archive, Crown Copyright. Catalogue Reference: FCO/73/205.

VIETNAM AND RESISTANCE TO HEGEMONIC INTRUSIONS: HÔ CHÍ MINH (1946)

Hô Chí Minh [Nguyễn Sinh Cung] (1890–1969) was modern Vietnam's most important revolutionary leader and head of state. He was the architect of Hanoi's defeat of the French colonizers in 1954 and of the American colonial pretenders who, at the time of Hô's death in 1969, were all but defeated save for the terms of what the Americans called an honorable peace. In his youth, Hô traveled and lived in France, the United States, England, and the Soviet Union. He founded the Việt Minh national liberation movement from South China in 1941. The selection illustrates Hô's revolutionary fervor and the principles that moved his liberation movement against long odds to defeat the Western powers. Decades after his death, Vietnam is still officially ruled by the Communist Party even as it has entered the global economy as one of Asia's most recent developing economies.

To the Vietnamese People, the French People and the Peoples of the Allied Nations (December 21, 1946)

We, the Vietnamese Government and people, are determined to struggle for our country's independence and reunification, but we are also ready for friendly co-operation with the French people. That is why we signed the Preliminary Agreement of March 6, 1940, and the Modus Vivendi of September 14, 1946.

But the French reactionary colonialists lacked sincerity and regarded those agreements as scraps of paper.

In Nam Bo they continued to arrest and massacre Vietnamese patriots and to engage in provocations. They bullied honest Frenchmen who advocated sincerity, and set up a puppet government in order to divide our people.

In southern Trung Bo they continued to terrorize our compatriots, attack the Vietnamese army, and invade our territory.

In Bac Bo, they provoked clashes to occupy Bac Ninh, Bac Giang, Lang Son and many other localities. They blockaded the port of Haiphong, thus making it impossible for Vietnamese, Chinese, other foreigners and also French residents to carry out their businesses. They tried to strangle the Vietnamese people and wreck our national sovereignty. They used tanks, aircraft, heavy artillery and warships to massacre our compatriots, and occupied the port of Haiphong and other towns along the rivers.

That was not all. They put their naval, land and air forces on the alert and sent us ultimatum upon ultimatum. They massacred old people, women and children in the capital city of Hanoi itself.

On December 19, 1946, at 8 p.m. they attacked Hanoi, the capital of Viet Nam.

The French colonialists' aim to reconquer our country is obvious and undeniable.

The Vietnamese people are now facing these alternatives: either to fold their arms and bow their heads and fall hack into slavery, or to struggle to the end for freedom and independence.

No! The Vietnamese people will never again tolerate foreign domination.

No! The Vietnamese people will never again be enslaved. They would rather die than lose their independence and freedom.

French people!

We are your friends and want sincere co-operation with you within the French Union because we share a common ideal: freedom, equality and independence.

It is the reactionary French colonialists who have sullied France's honour and sought to divide us by provoking a war. As soon as France clearly understands our aspirations to independence and reunification and calls back the bellicose French colonialists, friendly relations and co-operation between the peoples of Viet Nam and France will be restored immediately.

French soldiers!

We have no grudge against each other. Only selfish interests have driven the reactionary colonialists to provoke clashes. Profits are for them, death for you, and decorations for the militarists. For you and your families, only suffering and destitution. Think the matter over. Are you going to shed your blood and lay down your lives for the reactionaries? Join us, you will be treated as friends.

Peoples of the Allied nations!

At a time when the democratic countries are striving to organize peace following the end of the World War the French reactionaries are trampling underfoot the Atlantic and San Francisco Charters. They are waging an aggressive war in Viet Nam for which they must bear full responsibility. The Vietnamese people ask you to intervene.

Fellow-countrymen!

The war of resistance will be a long and hard one. What ever sacrifices we must endure and however long the war of resistance will last, we are determined to fight to the end, until Viet Nam is completely independent and reunified. We are 20 million against 100,000 colonialists. We are bound to win.

On behalf of the Government of the Democratic Republic of Viet Nam, I give the following orders to the Army, self defence corps, militia and to the people of all three parts of Viet Nam:

1. If the French troops attack us, we must fight back hard with all available weapons. Let our entire people stand up to defend their Fatherland!

2. We must protect the lives and property of foreign residents and give the prisoners of war good treatment.

3. Those who collaborate with the enemy will be punished. Those who help the resistance and participate in the defence of their country will be rewarded.

Fellow-countrymen!

The Fatherland is in danger, let all of us stand up!

Long live independent and reunified Viet Nam!

Long live the victorious war of resistance!

Hô Chí Minh, Part Two (1945–1954): To the Vietnamese People, the French People and the Peoples of the Allied Nations (December 21, 1946), The Gioi Publishers. Source: http://www.cpv.org.vn/cpv/index_E.html.

Decolonizing Movements Challenge the Euro-American World Order, 1947–1961

AFRICA, NEGRITUDE, AND VIOLENCE: FRANTZ FANON (1961)

Frantz Fanon (1925–1961) was born in Martinique. He studied medicine in France and became a practicing psychiatrist at the notorious Blida hospital in Algiers where he treated the French white colonizers during the day and the Algerian colonized at night. He was certainly the most radical and probably the most important theorist of decolonization. His ideas were particularly powerful because they were, in addition to being philosophically subtle and historically serious, grounded in first-hand clinical knowledge of the subject position of the colonized. The selection is from the second of his two greatest books, published in French the year after his death from cancer. The first was *Black Skin, White Masks* (1952). Among the many of his supporters and, one might say, admirers were Jean Paul Sartre, who introduced Fanon to a French reader-ship, and Immanuel Wallerstein, who claims him as a major early influence on his world-systems analytic method.

Wretched of the Earth: Concerning Violence

NATIONAL liberation, national renaissance, the restoration of nationhood to the people, commonwealth: what-ever may be the headings used or the new formulas introduced, decolonization is always a violent phenom-enon. At whatever level we study it – relationships between individuals, new names for sports clubs, the human admixture at cocktail parties, in the police, on the directing boards of national or private banks – decoloniza-tion is quite simply the replacing of a certain 'species' of men by another 'species' of men. Without any period of transition, there is a total, complete and absolute substitution. It is true that we could equally well stress the rise of a new nation, the setting up of a new state, its diplomatic relations, and its economic and political trends. But we have precisely chosen to speak of that kind of *tabula rasa* which characterizes at the outset all decolonization. Its unusual importance is that it constitutes, from the very first day, the minimum demands of the colonized. To tell the truth, the proof of success lies in a whole social structure being changed from the bottom up. The extraordinary importance of this change is that it is willed, called for, demanded. The need for this change exists in its crude state, impetuous and compelling, in the consciousness and in the lives of the men and women who are colonized. But the possibility of this change is equally experienced in the form of a terrifying future in the consciousness of another 'species' of men and women: the colonizers.

Decolonization, which sets out to change the order of the world, is, obviously, a programme of complete disorder. But it cannot come as a result of magical practices, nor of a natural shock, nor of a friendly understanding. Decolonization, as we know, is a historical process: that is to say that it cannot be understood, it cannot become intelligible nor clear to itself except in the exact measure that we can discern the movements which give it historical form and content. Decolonization is the meeting of two forces, opposed to each other by their very nature, which in fact owe their originality to that sort of substantification which results from and is nourished by the situation in the colonies. Their first encounter was marked by violence and their existence together – that is to say the exploitation of the native by the settler – was carried on by dint of a great array of bayonets and cannon. The settler and the native are old acquaintances. In fact, the settler is right when he speaks of knowing 'them' well. For it is the settler who has brought the native into existence and who perpetuates his existence. The settler owes the fact of his very existence, that is to say his property, to the colonial system.

Decolonization never takes place unnoticed, for it influences individuals and modifies them fundamentally. It transforms spectators crushed with their inessentiality into privileged actors, with the grandiose glare of history's floodlights upon them. It brings a natural rhythm into existence, introduced by new men, and with it a new language and a new humanity. Decolonization is the veritable creation of new men. But this creation owes nothing of its legitimacy to any supernatural power; the 'thing' which has been colonized becomes man during the same process by which it frees itself.

In decolonization, there is therefore the need of a complete calling in question of the colonial situation. If we wish to describe it precisely, we might find it in the well-known words: 'The last shall be first and the first last.' Decolonization is the putting into practice of this sentence. That is why, if we try to describe it, all decolonization is successful.

The naked truth of decolonization evokes for us the searing bullets and bloodstained knives which emanate from it. For if the last shall be first, this will only come to pass after a murderous and decisive struggle between the two protagonists. That affirmed intention to place the last at the head of things, and to make them climb at a pace (too quickly, some say) the well-known steps which characterize an organized society, can only triumph if we use all means to turn the scale, including, of course, that of violence.

You do not turn any society, however primitive it may be, upside-down with such a programme if you are not decided from the very beginning, that is to say from the actual formulation of that programme, to overcome all the obstacles that you will come across in so doing. The native who decides to put the pro-gramme into practice, and to become its moving force, is ready for violence at all times. From birth it is clear to him that this narrow world, strewn with prohibitions, can only be called in question by absolute violence.

The colonial world is a world divided into compartments. It is probably unnecessary to recall the existence of native quarters and European quarters, of schools for natives and schools for Europeans; in the same way we need not recall Apartheid in South Africa. Yet, if we examine closely this system of compartments, we will at least be able to reveal the lines of force it implies. This approach to the colonial world, its ordering and its geographical lay-out will allow us to mark out the lines on which a decolonized society will be reorganized.

The colonial world is a world cut in two. The dividing line, the frontiers are shown by barracks and police stations. In the colonies it is the policeman and the soldier who are the official, instituted go-betweens, the spokesmen of the settler and his rule of oppression. In capitalist societies the educational system, whether lay or clerical, the structure of moral reflexes handed down from father to son, the exemplary honesty of workers who are given a medal after fifty years of good and loyal service, and the affection which springs from harmonious relations and good behaviour – all these aesthetic expressions of respect for the established order serve to create around the exploited person an atmosphere of submission and of inhibition which lightens the task of policing considerably. In the capitalist countries a multitude of moral teachers, counsellors and 'bewil-derers' separate the exploited from those in power. In the colonial countries, on the contrary, the policeman and the soldier, by their immediate presence and their frequent and direct action maintain contact with the native and advise him by means of rifle-butts and napalm not to budge. It is obvious here that the agents of government speak the language of pure force. The intermediary does not lighten the oppression, nor seek to hide the domination; he shows them up and puts them into practice with the clear conscience of an upholder of the peace; yet he is the bringer of violence into the home and into the mind of the native.

Frantz Fanon (1968) *Wretched of the Earth*, translated by Constance Farrington, New York: Grove Press, pp. 35–39.

INDIA, EXPULSION OF THE BRITISH, AND PARTITION: MOHANDAS GANDHI (1942–1948)

Mohandas K. Gandhi (1869–1948) was born in India, studied law in England, and then moved to South Africa to practice law. There he first developed his philosophy of *ahimsa* (non-violence) as an instrument of political resistance to colonial rule. When ultimately he returned to India, Gandhi applied this spiritual principle against British rule that, largely due to his leadership, ended in 1947. He was assassinated in 1948 but his political ideals lived on to influence, among countless others, Martin Luther King, Jr and the American Civil Rights Movement. "Quit India" conveys the rigor of his spiritually based political philosophy. Importantly, his success in liberating India from British rule may be said to be the first major step toward decolonization. It is not incidental that the British quit India just when the Cold War took shape.

The "Quit India" speeches by Mohandas K. Gandhi (1942)

[The following is the concluding portion of Gandhiji's speech before the A.I.C.C. at Bombay on 8 August 1942 which was delivered in English.]

[. . .] I want to declare to the world, although I may have forfeited the regard of many friends in the West and I must bow my head low; but even for their friendship or love I must not suppress the voice of conscience – promoting of my inner basic nature today. There is something within me impelling me to cry out my agony. I have known humanity. I have studied something of psychology. Such a man knows exactly what it is. I do not mind how you describe it. That voice within tells me, 'You have to stand against the whole world although you may have to stand alone. You have to stare in the face the whole world although the world may look at you with bloodshot eyes. Do not fear. Trust the little voice residing within your heart.' It says : 'Forsake friends, wife and all; but testify to that for which you have lived and for which you have to die. I want to live my full span of life. And for me I put my span of life at 120 years. By that time India will be free, the world will be free.

Let me tell you that I do not regard England or for that matter America as free countries. They are free after their own fashion, free to hold in bondage coloured races of the earth. Are England and America fighting for the liberty of these races today? If not, do not ask me to wait until after the war. You shall not limit my concept of freedom. The English and American teachers, their history, their magnificent poetry have not said that you shall not broaden the interpretation of freedom. And according to my interpretation of that freedom I am constrained to say they are strangers to that freedom which their teachers and poets have described. If they will know the real freedom they should come to India. They have to come not with pride or arrogances but in the spite of real earnest seekers of truth. It is a fundamental truth which India has been experimenting with for 22 years.

Unconsciously from its very foundations long ago the Congress has been building on non-violence known as constitutional methods. Dadabhai and Pherozeshah who had held the Congress India in the palm of their hands became rebels. They were lovers of the Congress. They were its masters. But above all they were real servants. They never countenanced murder, secrecy and the like. I confess there are many black sheep amongst us Congressmen. But I trust the whole of India today to launch upon a non-violent struggle. I trust because of my nature to rely upon the innate goodness of human nature which perceives the truth and prevails during the crisis as if by instinct. But even if I am deceived in this I shall not swerve. I shall not flinch. From its very inception the Congress based its policy on peaceful methods, included Swaraj and the subsequent generations added non-violence. When Dadabhai entered the British Parliament, Salisbury dubbed him as a black man; but the English people defeated Salisbury and Dadabhai went to the Parliament by their vote. India was delirious with joy. These things however India has outgrown.

It is, however, with all these things as the background that I want Englishmen, Europeans and all the United Nations to examine in their hearts what crime had India committed in demanding Independence. I ask, is it right for you to distrust such an organization with all its background, tradition and record of over half a century and misrepresent its endeavours before all the world by every means at your command? Is it right that by hook or by crook, aided by the foreign press, aided by the President of the U.S.A., or even by the Generalissimo of China who has yet to win his laurels, you should present India's struggle in shocking caricature? I have met the Generalissimo. I have known him through Madame Shek who was my interpreter; and though he seemed inscrutable to me, not so Madame Shek; and he allowed me to read his mind through her. There is a chorus of disapproval and righteous protest all over the world against us. They say we are erring, the move is inopportune. I had great regard for British diplomacy which has enabled them to hold the Empire so long. Now it stinks in my nostrils, and others have studied that diplomacy and are putting it into practice. They may succeed in getting, through these methods, world opinion on their side for a time; but India will speak against that world opinion. She will raise her voice against all the organized propaganda. I will speak against it. Even if all the United Nations opposed me, even if the whole of India forsakes me, I will say, 'You are wrong. India will wrench with non-violence her liberty from unwilling hands.' I will go ahead not for India's sake alone, but for the sake of the world. Even if my eyes close before there is freedom, non-violence will not end. They will be dealing a mortal blow to China and to Russia if they oppose the freedom of non-violent India which is pleading with bended knees for the fulfillment of debt along overdue. Does a creditor ever go to debtor like that? And even when, India is met with such angry opposition, she says, 'We won't hit below the belt, we have learnt sufficient gentlemanliness. We are pledged to non-violence.' I have been the author of non-embarrassment policy of the Congress and yet today you find me talking this strong language. I say it is consistent with our honour. If a man holds me by the neck and wants to drawn me, may I not struggle to free myself directly? There is no inconsistency in our position today.

There are representatives of the foreign press assembled here today. Through them I wish to say to the world that the United Powers who somehow or other say that they have need for India, have the opportunity now to declare India free and prove their bona fides. If they miss it, they will be missing the opportunity of their lifetime, and history will record that they did not discharge their obligations to India in time, and lost the battle. I want the blessings of the whole world so that I may succeed with them. I do not want the United Powers to go beyond their obvious limitations. I do not want them to accept non-violence and disarm today. There is a fundamental difference between fascism and this imperialism which I am fighting. Do the British get from India which they hold in bondage. Think what difference it would make if India was to participate as a free ally. That freedom, if it is to come, must come today. It will have no taste left in it today you who have the power to help cannot exercise it. If you can exercise it, under the glow of freedom what seems impossible, today, will become possible tomorrow. If India feels that freedom, she will command that freedom for China. The road for running to Russia's help will be open. The Englishmen did not die in Malaya or on Burma soil. What shall enable us to retrieve the situation? Where shall I go, and where shall I take the forty crores of India? How is this vast mass of humanity to be aglow in the cause of world deliverance, unless and until it has touched and felt freedom. Today they have no touch of life left. It has been crushed out of them. Its lustre is to be put into their eyes, freedom has to come not tomorrow, but today.

I have pledged the Congress and the Congress will do or die.

Mohandas K. Gandhi, "Quit India," August 8, 1942, Bombay. Source: http://en.wikisource.org/wiki/The_%22Quit_India%22_Speeches.

CHINA, LENINISM WITH BUDDHIST PRETENSIONS: MAO ZEDONG (1949)

Mao Zedong (1893–1976), the son of a peasant farmer in the Chinese province of Hunan, was a seminal figure in the Chinese communist movement and in the founding of the People's Republic of China. In his eventful life, Mao occupied many roles: writer, teacher, librarian, journalist, community organizer, politician and, finally, national leader. One of the more notable events in Mao's life was when he attended the First Congress of the Chinese Communist Party in 1921 at the urging of his mentor, Yang Changji. Initially, Mao's view of China was not entirely in line with those of his communist contemporaries. Instead of focusing on industrial workers, Mao put particular emphasis on the revolutionary potential of the peasantry class. This move would have been quite controversial within the Chinese Communist Party if not for the fact that communism itself was under attack when Mao made such remarks. In 1927, the Chinese Nationalist Party (Kuomintang) waged a violent campaign to drive communism away from China. This operation, however, was not entirely successful as the Communists were eventually able to claim a foothold in the countryside despite being ushered out from the urban areas. Accordingly, this is what enabled Maoism to become the dominant ideology within the Chinese Communist Party. When Mao came to assume the position of party leader, he was initially challenged by "orthodox" and Soviet-trained Marxists. But soon this power struggle subsided as the base for communist support came overwhelmingly from the northern Chinese peasantry.

In 1949, Mao's belief in a revolutionary peasantry class was fully realized when his Red Army, along with peasant soldiers, defeated the bulk of Generalissimo Chiang Kai-Shek's nationalist forces, thus 'liberating' the whole of China to a communist existence. The selection is excerpted from one of Mao's speeches during this period. Here, we find Mao celebrating the fact that the Chinese people are no longer under the yoke of old imperial system – a fact he attributes to the ability of the Community Party to fend off "foreign imperialists" and "domestic reactionaries." But at the same time, Mao is also extremely cautious. For in the same breath, he warns that the Communist revolution can be undone by those who wish to "re-oppress" the Chinese people. Thus, Mao proposes that the Communist Party must remain vigilant. One way to do so would be to turn to various foreign allies, who "marvel" at the things that the Chinese people have been able to accomplish.

The Chinese People have Stood Up! September 21, 1949

[Opening address at the First Plenary Session of the Chinese People's Political Consultative Conference.]
Fellow Delegates,
The Political Consultative Conference so eagerly awaited by the whole nation is herewith inaugurated. . . .
It is because we have defeated the reactionary Kuomintang government backed by U.S. imperialism that this great unity of the whole people has been achieved. In a little more than three years the heroic Chinese People's Liberation Army, an army such as the world has seldom seen, crushed all the offensives launched by the several million troops of the U.S.-supported reactionary Kuomintang government and turned to the counter-offensive and the offensive. At present the field armies of the People's Liberation Army, several million strong, have pushed the war to areas near Taiwan, Kwangtung, Kwangsi, Kweichow, Szechuan and Sinkiang, and the great majority of the Chinese people have won liberation. In a little more than three years the people of the whole country have closed their ranks, rallied to support the People's Liberation Army, fought the enemy and won basic victory. And it is on this foundation that the present People's Political Consultative Conference is convened.

Our conference is called the Political Consultative Conference because some three years ago we held a Political Consultative Conference with Chiang Kai-shek's Kuomintang. The results of that conference were sabotaged by Chiang Kai-shek's Kuomintang and its accomplices; nevertheless the conference left an indelible impression on the people. It showed that nothing in the interest of the people could be accomplished together with Chiang Kai-shek's Kuomintang, the running dog of imperialism, and its accomplices. . . . The only gain from that conference was the profound lesson it taught the people that there is absolutely no room for compromise with Chiang Kai-shek's Kuomintang, the running dog of imperialism, and its accomplices – overthrow these enemies or be oppressed and slaughtered by them, either one or the other, there is no other choice. In a little more than three years the Chinese people, led by the Chinese Communist Party, have quickly awakened and organized themselves into a nation-wide united front against imperialism, feudalism, bureaucrat-capitalism and their general representative, the reactionary Kuomintang government, supported the People's War of Liberation, basically defeated the reactionary Kuomintang government, overthrown the rule of imperialism in China and restored the Political Consultative Conference.

The present Chinese People's Political Consultative Conference is convened on an entirely new foundation; it is representative of the people of the whole country and enjoys their trust and support. Therefore, the conference proclaims that it will exercise the functions and powers of a National People's Congress. . . .

Fellow Delegates, we are all convinced that our work will go down in the history of mankind, demonstrating that the Chinese people, comprising one quarter of humanity, have now stood up. The Chinese have always been a great, courageous and industrious nation; it is only in modern times that they have fallen behind. And that was due entirely to oppression and exploitation by foreign imperialism and domestic reactionary governments. For over a century our forefathers never stopped waging unyielding struggles against domestic and foreign oppressors, including the Revolution of 1911 led by Dr. Sun Yat-sen, our great forerunner in the Chinese revolution. Our forefathers enjoined us to carry out their unfulfilled will. And we have acted accordingly. We have closed our ranks and defeated both domestic and foreign oppressors through the People's War of Liberation and the great people's revolution, and now we are proclaiming the founding of the People's Republic of China. From now on our nation will belong to the community of the peace-loving and freedom-loving nations of the world and work courageously and industriously to foster its own civilization and well-being and at the same time to promote world peace and freedom. Ours will no longer be a nation subject to insult and humiliation. We have stood up. Our revolution has won the sympathy and acclaim of the people of all countries. We have friends all over the world.

Our revolutionary work is not completed, the People's War of Liberation and the people's revolutionary movement are still forging ahead and we must keep up our efforts. The imperialists and the domestic reactionaries will certainly not take their defeat lying down; they will fight to the last ditch. After there is peace and order throughout the country, they are sure to engage in sabotage and create disturbances by one means or another and every day and every minute they will try to stage a come-back. This is inevitable and beyond all doubt. . . .

Our state system, the people's democratic dictatorship, is a powerful weapon for safeguarding the fruits of victory of the people's revolution and for thwarting the plots of domestic and foreign enemies for restoration, and this weapon we must firmly grasp. Internationally, we must unite with all peace-loving and freedom-loving countries and peoples, and first of all with the Soviet Union and the New Democracies, so that we shall not stand alone in our struggle to safeguard these fruits of victory and to thwart the plots of domestic and foreign enemies for restoration. As long as we persist in the people's democratic dictatorship and unite with our foreign friends, we shall always be victorious. . . .

Hail the victory of the People's War of Liberation and the people's revolution!

Hail the founding of the People's Republic of China!

Mao Tse-tung, The Chinese People have Stood Up!, September 21, 1949. Source: http://www.marxists.org/reference/archive/mao/selected-works/volume–5/mswv5_01.htm.

CONGO, INDEPENDENCE FROM BELGIUM: PATRICE LUMUMBA (1960)

Patrice Lumumba (1925–1961) was born in the Belgian Congo, easily the most brutal of European colonies. He led the resistance movement to Belgian rule culminating in the Congo's independence in 1960. The following year he was assassinated – no doubt with the collusion of American as well as Belgian authorities, who installed Mobuto Sese Seko as the dictator of the Congo which he, quite insanely, renamed Zaire. After Mobuto was forced to flee Zaire dying of cancer, there followed a series of barely less brutal governments that have made the Congo the ideal type of failed post-colonial nation "underdeveloped" by the core and semi-peripheral states of the capitalist world-system.

Lumumba assails colonialism as Congo is freed

Leopoldville, Republic of Congo, June 30 – An attack on colonialism by the Premier of the new Republic of Congo marred the ceremonies today in which King Baudouin of the Belgians proclaimed the territory's independence. [Early Friday the republic of Somalia was proclaimed.] The Congo independence ceremony before the two chambers of Parliament was attended by leading Belgian officials and diplomats from all over the world. It began in an atmosphere of friendship but was abruptly transformed by the militant speech of Premier Patrice Lumumba, who cited the sufferings of the African people at the hands of the whites.

Two hours later at a state dinner however, Mr. Lumumba toasted King Baudouin and praised Belgium for the magnificent work she had done in building the Congo. He said the Congolese people were grateful that Belgium had given them freedom without delay and then he said the two countries would remain friendly.

The ceremonies were held in the beautifully draped circular hall of the National Palace that was to have been the residence of the Belgian Governor General.

Kasavubu expresses goodwill

Joseph Kasavubu, the new nation's Chief of State, expressed goodwill toward Belgium and won hearty applause from the members of Parliament. Apparently as a result of behind-the-scenes discussion. Mr. Kasavubu dropped the last section of his prepared address, which was to have ended with the declaration: 'I proclaim in the name of the nation the birth of the Republic of the Congo!'

Instead, Mr. Lumumba moved from his place alongside Premier Gaston Eyskens of Belgium and went to the lectern to speak. He wore the maroon sash of the Order of the Crown, Belgium's highest decoration, which he received last night.

He said that June 30, 1960 would be known for the 'glorious history of our struggle for liberty.' He asserted that no Congolese would ever forget the struggle in which 'we have not spared our strength, our privations, our sufferings or our blood.'

Cites 'wounds' of colonialism

It was a struggle that was indispensable, he said, for putting an end to the 'humiliating slavery which had been imposed on us by force.' He commented that colonialism had left wounds too keen and too painful to be wiped from memory.

Premier Lumumba reminded the members of the new Parliament of 'the ironies, the insults, the blows that we had to submit to morning, noon and night because we were Negroes.'

He declared Congo must be made the 'rallying point of all Africa' and that the nation must put an end to the oppression of free thought and give to all citizens the fundamental liberties guaranteed in the United Nations Declaration of the Rights of Man.

He said Belgium had finally understood the meaning of history and had not tried to oppose Congo's independence. He noted that Belgium was ready to provide help and friendship and that a treaty had been signed that would be profitable to both countries. [. . .]

Premier Lumumba's speech produced comments of surprise and disappointment among Belgian and other Western representatives. The Soviet diplomats present seemed to be enjoying the occasion. [. . .]

Congo rises from stone age to statehood in few decades

Fifty-five years ago, in the heartland of darkest Africa, which formally became the independent Republic of Congo today, the wheel was not used, language was not written, cannibalism and witchcraft were common, and the site of the capital, Leopoldville, was still a dense jungle.

That area became known to the outside world only eighty-five years ago. At that time the British-born American newspaper man Sir Henry Morton Stanley, who had earlier tracked down the missing Dr. David Livingstone, undertook a long exploration of the Congo River.

Sir Henry later tried to interest the British in the new land but failed. However, he succeeded with King Leopold II of Belgium, who decided to use his own great wealth to develop the Congo as a kind of personal estate after the Belgian Government had refused to show interest. King Leopold set up the Independent State of the Congo, which lasted until 1908, when the Belgian Parliament took it over as a colony.

The Belgian Government set out to substitute the carpenter's hammer for the tribal drum, introducing the twentieth century overnight to a primitive people divided into many warring tribes.

The 13,600,000 Congolese, scattered over an immense area of equatorial forest and savanna about a third as large as the United States, are still divided into about 200 tribes, some of them still warring.

More than 400 dialects are still spoken in the Republic of Congo. The range of social evolution almost covers the range of human growth, starting with the Stone Age aborigines in the Pygmy tribes, who use arrows and spears dipped in poison. The new state is home not only to the world's smallest human beings – the four-foot Pygmies – but also to some of the world's tallest – the seven-foot-tall Watusis.

There is also a 'lost greatness' for the Congolese to remember in their new struggles. The Kingdom of the Congo flourished from the fourteenth century and even exchanged envoys with Portugal, the Vatican, Brazil and the Netherlands. But the kingdom fell victim to the slave traffic and began a rapid decline in the eighteenth century.

Today barely half of the Congolese can read and write, and only sixteen Congolese are university or college graduates. There are no Congolese doctors, lawyers or engineers, and no African officers in the 25,000-man Congolese Army.

The independence movement began among Congolese working for the colonial administration or for commercial companies in a land that is rich in copper and cobalt and industrial diamonds. At first, after World War II, the Congolese talked only of 'equal pay for equal work,' but following quickly upon this came talk of political rights.

In December, 1957, the Belgian colonial administration gave the Congolese their first measure of self-rule by holding elections in Leopoldville, Elisabethville and Jadotville. A year later the cry for 'immediate independence and departure of all the Belgians' had become common.

The Belgian Government tried to carry out a plan for independence by stages, but rioting in Leopoldville in January, 1959, aroused pressure for early independence. That independence was agreed upon at a roundtable conference in Brussels earlier this year.

Harry Gilroy (1960) "Lumumba Assails Colonialism as Congo is Freed," *New York Times*, July 1. Source: http://partners. nytimes.com/library/world/africa/600701lumumba.html.

CUBA, THORN IN THE FLESH OF THE AMERICAN HEGEMONY: FIDEL CASTRO (1960)

Fidel Castro (1926–), a lawyer, became the true inspiration and leader of the revolt of the Cuban people against a government corrupted by the influence of American wealth and corporate greed. The first signs of rebellion occurred in 1953, but the legends associated with Castro's movement are attached to the descent of rebel groups from the Sierra Maestra Mountains in 1956. Three years later, in 1959, the revolutionaries entered Havana as Fulgencio Batista fled the country. Though Castro's government soon became a client state of the Soviet Union, thus officially communist, Castro himself at the moment of the movement's triumph was not ideologically committed either way and, some say, would have preferred an American sponsorship. As things played out, Cuba was a major factor in global cold war politics as the Soviets made important military and financial investments in Cuba as a stake in the new world meant to counter America's sphere of hegemonic influence. Even today, well after the Cold War, Cuba remains a lesser but real thorn in the flesh of conservative American interests.

Fidel Castro, "To the U.N. General Assembly, The Problem of Cuba and its Revolutionary Policy," September 26, 1960

How did our country become a colony of the United States? It was not because of its origins; the same men did not colonize the United States and Cuba. Cuba has a very different ethnical and cultural origin, and the difference was widened over the centuries. Cuba was the last country in America to free itself from Spanish colonial rule, to cast off, with due respect to the representative of Spain, the Spanish colonial yoke; and because it was the last, it also had to fight more fiercely.

Spain had only one small possession left in America and it defended it with tooth and nail. Our people, small in numbers, scarcely a million inhabitants at that time, had to face alone, for almost thirty years, an army considered one of the strongest in Europe. Against our small national population the Spanish Government mobilized an army as big as the total forces that had fought against South American independence. Half a million Spanish soldiers fought against the historic and unbreakable will of our people to be free.

For thirty years the Cubans fought alone for their independence; thirty years of struggle that strengthened our love for freedom and independence. But Cuba was a fruit – according to the opinion of a President of the United States at the beginning of the past century, John Adams – it was an apple hanging from the Spanish tree, destined to fall, as soon as it was ripe enough, into the hands of the United States. Spanish power had worn itself out in our country. Spain had neither the men nor the economic resources to continue the war in Cuba; Spain had been defeated. Apparently the apple was ripe, and the United States Government held out its open hands.

Not one but several apples fell in to the hands of the United States. Puerto Rico fell – heroic Puerto Rico, which had begun its struggle for independence at the same time as Cuba. The Philippine Islands fell, and several other possessions. However, the method of dominating our country could not be the same. Our country had struggled fiercely, and thus had gained the favor of world public opinion. Therefore the method of taking our country had to be different.

The Cubans who fought for our independence and at that very moment were giving their blood and their lives believed in good faith in the joint resolution of the Congress of the United States of April 20, 1898, which declared that 'Cuba is, and by right ought to be, free and independent.'

The people of the United States were sympathetic to the Cuban struggle for liberty. That joint declaration was a law adopted by the Congress of the United States through which war was declared on Spain. But that illusion was followed by a rude awakening. After two years of military occupation of our country, the unexpected happened: at the very moment that the people of Cuba, through their Constituent Assembly, were drafting the Constitution of the Republic, a new law was passed by the United States Congress, a law proposed by Senator Platt, bearing such unhappy memories for the Cubans. That law stated that the constitution of Cuba must have an appendix under which the United States would be granted the right to intervent in Cuba's political affairs and, furthermore, to lease certain parts of Cuba for naval bases or coal supply station.

In other words, under a law passed by the legislative body of a foreign country, Cuban's Constitution had to contain an appendix with those provisions. Our legislators were clearly told that if they did not accept the amendment, the occupation forces would not be withdrawn. In other words, an agreement to grant another country the right to intervene and to lease naval bases was imposed by force upon my country by the legislative body of a foreign country.

It is well, I think, for countries just entering this Organization, countries just beginning their independent life, to bear in mind our history and to note any similar conditions which they may find waiting for them along their own road. And if it is not they, then those who came after them, or their children, or grandchildren, although it seems to us that we will not have to wait that long.

Then began the new colonization of our country, the acquisition of the best agricultural lands by United States firms, concessions of Cuban natural resources and mines, concessions of public utilities for exploitation purposes, commercial concessions of all types. These concessions, when linked with the constitutional right – constitutional by force – of intervention in our country, turned it from a Spanish colony into an American colony.

Colonies do not speak. Colonies are not known until they have the opportunity to express themselves. That is why our colony and its problems were unknown to the rest of the world. In geography books reference was made to a flag and a coat of arms. There was an island with another color on the maps, but it was not an independent republic. Let us not deceive ourselves, since by doing so we only make ourselves ridiculous. Let no one be mistaken. There was no independent republic; there was only a colony where orders were given by the Ambassador of the United States.

We are not ashamed to have to declare this. On the contrary: we are proud to say that today no embassy rules our country; our country is ruled by its people!

Once against the Cuban people had to resort to fighting in order to achieve independence, and that independence was finally attained after seven bloody years of tyranny, who forced this tyranny upon us? Those who in our country were nothing more than tools of the interests which dominated our country economically.

How can an unpopular regime, inimical to the interests of the people, stay in power unless it is by force? Will we have to explain to the representatives of our sister republics of Latin America what military tyrannies are? Will we have to outline to them how these tyrannies have kept themselves in power? Will we have to explain the history of several of those tyrannies which are already classical? Will we have to say what forces, what national and international interests support them?

The military group which tyrannized our country was supported by the most reactionary elements of the nation, and, above all, by the foreign interests that dominated the economy of our country. Everybody knows, and we understand that even the Government of the United States admits it, that that was the type of government favored by the monopolies. Why? Because by the use of force it was possible to check the demands of the people; by the use of force it was possible to suppress strikes for improvement of living standards; by the use of force it was possible to crush all movements on the part of the peasants to own the land they worked; by the use of force it was possible to curb the greatest and most deeply felt aspirations of the nation.

That is why governments of force were favored by the ruling circles of the United States. That is why governments of force stayed in power for so long, and why there are governments of force still in power in America. Naturally, it all depends on whether it is possible to secure the support of the United States.

Fidel Castro, "To the U.N. General Assembly, The Problem of Cuba and its Revolutionary Policy," September 26, 1960. Castro Speech Database [Embassy of Cuba]. Castro Internet Archive (Marxists.org) 2000. Source: http:/www.marxists.org/history/cuba/archive/castro/1960/09/26.htm.

New Global Forces
Erode the Modern,
1963–1991/2001

ASIA AND THE AMERICAN CIVIL RIGHTS MOVEMENT:
MARTIN LUTHER KING AND MALCOLM X (1959–1965)

Martin Luther King, Jr (1929–1968) was born of bourgeois Black parentage in Atlanta, Georgia. The relative affluence of his family allowed him to pursue higher education at the best schools then open to Black people. Soon after finishing his doctoral studies at Boston University, King was called to be pastor of the Dexter Avenue Baptist Church in Montgomery, Alabama. At the age of 27, he was thus thrown into the thick of the 1955 bus boycott, the first movement in the American Civil Rights Movement. There he applied the spiritual and political philosophies of Gandhi and of the American theological Reinhold Niebuhr. As the Civil Rights Movement began to fade after 1965, King turned more and more to anti-war and poverty issues, which many think led to his assassination in Memphis, Tennessee in 1968.

Malcolm X (1925–1965) was born of poor circumstances in Omaha, Nebraska. At an early age he turned to a life of crime then, as now, one the few economic "opportunities" for young Black men. In prison, he is said to have read the dictionary late at night, which in turn is thought to be the education that made him one of America's most eloquent Black revolutionary leaders. He became a leading minister in the Nation of Islam and a disciple of its leader, Elijah Muhammad. In this role, Malcolm was considered a leader of the Islamic wing of the Black Power movement and thus, in principle, an opponent of Martin Luther King. Yet, a trip to Mecca in 1964 caused him to reconsider his more primitive racial views, which led to his expulsion from the Nation of Islam and his détente with King. Malcolm X was assassinated on February 21, 1965, apparently by individuals associated with Elijah Muhammad. As King was influenced, in part, by the ideas of South Asia, Malcolm was in effect influenced by decolonizing ideas and non-Western theories of the modern world.

A Testament of Hope: "My Trip to the Land of Gandhi" – Martin Luther King, Jr. (1959)

The trip had a great impact upon me personally. It was wonderful to be in Gandhi's land, to talk with his son, his grandsons, his cousins and other relatives; to share the reminiscences of his close comrades, to visit his ashrama, to see the countless memorials for him and finally to lay a wreath on his entombed ashes at Rajghat. I left India more convinced than ever before that nonviolent resistance is the most potent weapon available to oppressed people in their struggle for freedom. It was a marvelous thing to see the amazing results of a nonviolent campaign. The aftermath of hatred and bitterness that usually follows a violent campaign was found nowhere in India. Today a mutual friendship based on complete equality exists between the Indian and British people within the commonwealth. The way of acquiescence leads to moral and spiritual suicide. The way of violence leads to bitterness in the survivors and brutality in the destroyers. But, the way of nonviolence leads to redemption and the creation of the beloved community.

The spirit of Gandhi is very much alive in India today. Some of his disciples have misgivings about this when they remember the drama of the fight, for national independence and when they look around and find nobody today who comes near the stature of the Mahatma. But any objective observer must report that Gandhi is not only the greatest figure in India's history but that his influence is felt in almost every aspect of life and public policy today.

India can never forget Gandhi. For example, the Gandhi Memorial Trust (also known as the Gandhi Smarak Nidhi) collected some $130 million soon after the death of "*the father of the nation.*" This was perhaps the largest, spontaneous, mass monetary contribution to the memory of a single individual in the history of the world. This fund, along with support from the Government and other institutions, is resulting in the spread and development of Gandhian philosophy, the implementing of his constructive program, the erection of libraries and the publication of works by and about the life and times of Gandhi. Posterity could not escape him even if it tried. By all standards of measurement, he is one of the half-dozen greatest men in world history.

I was delighted that the Gandhians accepted us with open arms. They praised our experiment with the nonviolent resistance technique at Montgomery. They seem to look upon it as an outstanding example of the possibilities of its use in Western civilization. To them as to me it also suggests that nonviolent resistance *when planned and positive in action* can work effectively even under totalitarian regimes.

We argued this point at some length with the groups of African students who are today studying in India. They felt that nonviolent resistance could only work in a situation where the resisters had a potential ally in the conscience of the opponent. We soon discovered that they, like many others, tended to confuse passive resistance with nonresistance. This is completely wrong. True nonviolent resistance is not unrealistic submission to evil power. It is rather a courageous confrontation of evil by the power of love, in the faith that it is better to be the recipient of violence than the inflictor of it, since the latter only multiplies the existence of violence and bitterness in the universe, while the former may develop a sense of shame in the opponent, and thereby bring about a transformation and change of heart.

Nonviolent resistance does call for love, but it is not a sentimental love. It is a very stern love that would organize itself into collective action to right a wrong by taking on itself suffering. While I understand the reasons why oppressed people often turn to violence in their struggle for freedom, it is my firm belief that the crusade for independence and human dignity that is now reaching a climax in Africa will have a more positive effect on the world, if it is waged along the lines that were first demonstrated in that continent by Gandhi himself.

February 1965: The Final Speeches: "The Black Muslim Movement" – Malcolm X

STAN BERNARD: And what is the [Black Muslim] movement? Is it a bona fide religion or just a terror organization? Tonight on Stan Bernard "Contact" we're going to have a look at the Muslims and the Black nationalists in general. And my guests tonight: Malcolm X, once the number-two man in the Black Muslims, now broken with Elijah Muhammad; he says he's a marked man and that a number of attempts have been made on his life. And also in the studio, or we hope very shortly, Aubrey Barnette. There's been some difficulty tonight, just before air time, and Aubrey may join us and he may not. He's also split from the organization, and he's written an article in this week's *Saturday Evening Post* labeled simply "The Black Muslims a Fraud." And here is Aubrey Barnette now. And my third guest tonight, Gordon Hall, an expert on extremist organizations.

Aubrey Barnette, in your article you call the Black Muslims a fraud. Now does this just apply to the mosque's methods of raising money or what? Do you think it's a religious fraud as well?

AUBREY BARNETTE: I think the entire Black Muslim movement is a fraud. And Webster's Dictionary defines a fraud as deceit trickery, or a trick. The Black Muslims have deceived the public. They've used trickery on trying to attract the Negroes and they have outright tricked the poor Black Muslim members. That's why I say they are a fraud.

BERNARD: Now, okay, they've tricked them. Now this is in terms of the religion itself as well as the money raising?

BARNETTE: Well, as far as the religion of Islam is concerned, I might say right here that any similarity between the Black Muslim and the true religion of Islam is purely coincidental.

BERNARD: Malcolm X, I said at the outset that you were once the number-two man. I think I can rightfully say that, easily you were certainly as well known as, almost as well known, or as well known as Elijah Muhammad.

MALCOLM X: But I never was the number-two man.

BERNARD: You never were the number-two man?

MALCOLM X: The press said I was the number-two man, but there were others ahead of me.

BERNARD: How do you feel about this comment from Aubrey Barnette?

MALCOLM X: What he's saying is true, especially about the first, especially about the religion. The religion of Islam itself is a religion that is based upon brotherhood and a religion in which the persons who believe in it in no way judge a man by the color of his skin. The yardstick of measurement in Islam is one's deeds, one's conscious behavior. And the yardstick of measurement that was used by Elijah Muhammad was based upon the color of the skin.

BERNARD: Malcolm, it wasn't too long ago that you were preaching separation, Black supremacy, you were – or separation at any rate; if not Black supremacy, it sounded like Black supremacy to a lot of people. How do you equate that now with what you're saying today?

MALCOLM X: There's not one person who is a Muslim who believes in Elijah Muhammad today who believes in him more strongly than I did. When I was with him I believed in him 100 percent. And it was my strong belief in him that made me go along with everything he taught. And I think if you check back on my representation of him while I was with him, I represented him 100 percent.

BERNARD: What is your status now, Malcolm?

MALCOLM X: How do you mean?

BERNARD: Right now. Have you broken –

MALCOLM X: I'm a Muslim. When I – You must understand that the Black Muslim movement, although it claimed to be a religious movement, based upon Islam, it was never acceptable to the orthodox Muslim world. Although at the same time it attracted the most militant, the most dissatisfied of the Black community into it. And by them getting into it and the movement itself not having a real action program, it comprised a number of persons who were extremely young and militant but who could not – and who were activists by nature but who couldn't participate in things. So the inactivity of the movement caused a great deal of dissatisfaction until finally dissension broke in and division, and those of us who left regrouped into a Muslim movement based upon orthodox Islam.

Malcolm X (1992) "The Black Muslim Movement," *February 1965: The Final Speeches*, New York: Pathfinder, pp. 16–19.

■ ■ ■ ■ ■ ■

EASTERN EUROPE, THE VELVET REVOLUTION, AND THE END OF THE MODERN: VÁCLAV HAVEL (1989)

Václav Havel (1936–) was a leading force in Czechoslovakia's resistance to Soviet-installed rule in Prague, for which he suffered imprisonment. Yet, Havel's gifts as a poet, philosopher, and playwright were instrumental to his leadership of what in 1989 surfaced as the Velvet Revolution in Czechoslovakia and Eastern

Europe. He was elected president of independent Czechoslovakia, then of the Czech Republic in 1993 after the reversion of Czechs and Slovakians to separate nations. The selection exemplifies one of the post-Cold War world's most subtle analysts of what some call postmodernism which, in fact, turned out to be a challenging historical departure from naïve modern liberalism with its cagey hegemonic principles of world-order.

The End of the Modern Era

The end of Communism is, first and foremost, a message to the human race. It is a message we have not yet fully deciphered and comprehended. In its deepest sense, the end of Communism has brought a major era in human history to an end. It has brought an end not just to the nineteenth and twentieth centuries, but to the modern age as a whole.

The modern era has been dominated by the culminating belief, expressed in different forms, that the world – and Being as such – is a wholly knowable system governed by a finite number of universal laws that man can grasp and rationally direct for his own benefit. This era, beginning in the Renaissance and developing from the Enlightenment to socialism, from positivism to scientism, from the Industrial Revolution to the information revolution, was characterized by rapid advances in rational, cognitive thinking.

This, in turn, gave rise to the proud belief that man, as the pinnacle of everything that exists, was capable of objectively describing, explaining and controlling everything that exists, and of possessing the one and only truth about the world. It was an era in which there was a cult of depersonalized objectivity, an era in which objective knowledge was amassed and technologically exploited, an era of belief in automatic progress brokered by the scientific method. It was an era of systems, institutions, mechanisms and statistical averages. It was an era of ideologies, doctrines, interpretations of reality, an era in which the goal was to find a universal theory of the world, and thus a universal key to unlock its prosperity.

Communism was the perverse extreme of this trend. It was an attempt, on the basis of a few propositions masquerading as the only scientific truth, to organize all of life according to a single model, and to subject it to central planning and control regardless of whether or not that was what life wanted.

The fall of Communism can be regarded as a sign that modern thought – based on the premise that the world is objectively knowable, and that the knowledge so obtained can be absolutely generalized – has come to a final crisis. This era has created the first global, or planetary, technical civilization, but it has reached the limit of its potential, the point beyond which the abyss begins. The end of Communism is a serious warning to all mankind. It is a signal that the era of arrogant, absolutist reason is drawing to a close and that it is high time to draw conclusions from that fact.

Communism was not defeated by military force, but by life, by the human spirit, by conscience, by the resistance of Being and man to manipulation. It was defeated by a revolt of color, authenticity, history in all its variety and human individuality against imprisonment within a uniform ideology.

This powerful signal is coming at the 11th hour. We all know civilization is in danger. The population explosion and the greenhouse effect, holes in the ozone and AIDS, the threat of nuclear terrorism and the dramatically widening gap between the rich north and the poor south, the danger of famine, the depletion of the biosphere and the mineral resources of the planet, the expansion of commercial television culture and the growing threat of regional wars – all these, combined with thousands of other factors, represent a general threat to mankind.

The large paradox at the moment is that man – a great collector of information – is well aware of all this, yet is absolutely incapable of dealing with the danger. Traditional science, with its usual coolness, can describe the different ways we might destroy ourselves, but it cannot offer us truly effective and practicable instructions on how to avert them. There is too much to know; the information is muddled or poorly organized; these processes can no longer be fully grasped and understood, let alone contained or halted.

We are looking for new scientific recipes, new ideologies, new control systems, new institutions, new instruments to eliminate the dreadful consequences of our previous recipes, ideologies, control systems, institutions and instruments. We treat the fatal consequences of technology as though they were a technical defect that could be remedied by technology alone. We are looking for an objective way out of the crisis of objectivism.

Everything would seem to suggest that this is not the way to go. We cannot devise, within the traditional modern attitude to reality, a system that will eliminate all the disastrous consequences of previous systems. We cannot discover a law or theory whose technical application will eliminate all the disastrous consequences of the technical application of earlier laws and technologies.

What is needed is something different, something larger. Man's attitude to the world must be radically changed. We have to abandon the arrogant belief that the world is merely a puzzle to be solved, a machine with instructions for use waiting to be discovered, a body of information to be fed into a computer in the hope that, sooner or later, it will spit out a universal solution.

It is my profound conviction that we have to release from the sphere of private whim such forces as a natural, unique and unrepeatable experience of the world, an elementary sense of justice, the ability to see things as others do, a sense of transcendental responsibility, archetypal wisdom, good taste, courage, compassion and faith in the importance of particular measures that do not aspire to be a universal key to salvation. Such forces must be rehabilitated.

Things must once more be given a chance to present themselves as they are, to be perceived in their individuality. We must see the pluralism of the world, and not bind it by seeking common denominators or reducing everything to a single common equation.

We must try harder to understand than to explain. The way forward is not in the mere construction of universal systemic solutions, to be applied to reality from the outside; it is also in seeking to get to the heart of reality through personal experience. Such an approach promotes an atmosphere of tolerant solidarity and unity in diversity based on mutual respect, genuine pluralism and parallelism. In a word, human uniqueness, human action and the human spirit must be rehabilitated.

The world today is a world in which generality, objectivity and universality are in crisis. This world presents a great challenge to the practice of politics, which, it seems to me, still has a technocratic, utilitarian approach to Being, and therefore to political power as well. Many of the traditional mechanisms of democracy created and developed and conserved in the modern era are so linked to the cult of objectivity and statistical average that they can annul human individuality. We can see this in political language, where cliché often squeezes out a personal tone. And when a personal tone does crop up, it is usually calculated, not an outburst of personal authenticity.

Sooner or later politics will be faced with the task of finding a new, postmodern face. A politician must become a person again, someone who trusts not only a scientific representation and analysis of the world, but also the world itself. He must believe not only in sociological statistics, but also in real people. He must trust not only an objective interpretation of reality, but also his own soul; not only an adopted ideology, but also his own thoughts; not only the summary reports he receives each morning, but also his own feeling.

Soul, individual spirituality, first-hand personal insight into things; the courage to be himself and go the way his conscience points, humility in the face of the mysterious order of Being, confidence in its natural direction and, above all, trust in his own subjectivity as his principal link with the subjectivity of the world – these are the qualities that politicians of the future should cultivate.

Looking at politics 'from the inside,' as it were, has if anything confirmed my belief that the world of today – with the dramatic changes it is going through and in its determination not to destroy itself – presents a great challenge to politicians.

It is not that we should simply seek new and better ways of managing society, the economy and the world. The point is that we should fundamentally change how we behave. And who but politicians should lead the way? Their changed attitude toward the world, themselves and their responsibility can give rise to truly effective systemic and institutional changes.

Václav Havel (1992) "The End of the Modern Era," *The New York Times*, March 1.

ZAIRE, THE POST-COLONIAL NIGHTMARE IN AFRICA: V.S. NAIPAUL (1975)

V.S. Naipaul (1932–) was born in Trinidad of an East Asian family. He grew to become one of the most distinguished literary figures of the late twentieth and early twenty-first centuries. Naipaul won the Nobel Prize for Literature in 2001. The selection is, in his case, an instance of a seriously engaged man of letters, but also of a telling narrative on the enduring saga of the Congo as the epitome of European colonization's evil.

A New King for the Congo

The Congo, which used to be a Belgian colony, is now an African kingdom and is called Zaire. It appears to be a nonsense name, a sixteenth-century Portuguese corruption, some Zairois will tell you, of a local word for 'river.' So it is as if Taiwan, reasserting its Chinese identity, were again to give itself the Portuguese name of Formosa. The Congo River is now called the Zaire, as is the local currency, which is almost worthless.

The man who has made himself king of this land of the three Zs – pays, fleuve, monnaie – used to be called Joseph Mobutu. His father was a cook. But Joseph Mobutu was educated; he was at some time, in the Belgian days, a journalist. In 1960, when the country became independent, Mobutu was thirty, a sergeant in the local Force Publique. The Force Publique became the Congolese National Army. Mobutu became the colonel and commander, and through the mutinies, rebellions, and secessions of the years after independence he retained the loyalty of one paratroop brigade. In 1965, as General Mobutu, he seized power; and as he has imposed order on the army and the country so his style has changed, and become more African. He has abandoned the name of Joseph and is now known as Mobutu Sese Seko Kuku Ngbendu Wa Za Banga.

As General Mobutu he used to be photographed in army uniform. Now, as Mobutu Sese Seko, he wears what he has made, by his example, the Zairois court costume. It is a stylish version of the standard two-piece suit. The jacket has high, wide lapels and is buttoned all the way down; the sleeves can be long or short. A boldly patterned cravat replaces the tie, which has more or less been outlawed; and a breast-pocket handkerchief matches the cravat. On less formal occasions – when he goes among the people – Mobutu wears flowered shirts. Always, in public, he wears a leopard-skin cap and carries an elaborately carved stick.

These – the cap and the stick – are the emblems of his African chieftaincy. Only the chief can kill the leopard. The stick is carved with symbolic figures: two birds, what looks like a snake, a human figure with a distended belly. No Zairois I met could explain the symbolism. One teacher pretended not to know what was carved, and said, 'We would all like to have sticks like that.' In some local carving, though, the belly of the human figure is distended because it contains the fetish. The stick is accepted by Zairois as the stick of the chief. While the chief holds the stick off the ground the people around him can speak; when the chief sets his stick on the ground the people fall silent and the chief gives his decision. [. . .]

It is said that the last five words of Mobutu's African name are a reference to the sexual virility which the African chief must possess: he is the cock that leaves no hen alone. But the words may only be symbolic. Because, as chief, Mobutu is 'married' to his people – 'The Marriage of Sese [Mobutu]' is a 'revolutionary' song – and, as in the good old days of the ancestors, comme au bon vieux temps de nos ancêtres, the chief always holds fast to his people. This marriage of the chief can be explained in another, more legalistic way: the chief has a 'contract' with his people. He fulfills his contract through the apparatus of a modern state, but the ministers and commissioners are only the chief's 'collaborators,' 'the umbilical cord between the power and the people.' [. . .]

But it is in the nature of a powerful chief that he should be unpredictable. The chief threatens; the people are cowed; the chief relents; the people praise his magnanimity. The days passed; daytime and even morning drinking didn't stop; many Africans continued to spend their days in that red-eyed vacancy that at first so mystifies the visitor. The nightclubs and movie houses didn't close; the prostitutes continued to be busy around the Memling Hotel. So that it seemed that in this matter of public morals, at least, the chief had relented. The ordinary people had been spared.

But the nervousness higher up was justified. Within days the axe fell on many of the chief's 'collaborators.' There was a shake-up; the circle of power around the chief was made smaller; and Zairois who had ruled in Kinshasa were abruptly dismissed, packed off to unfamiliar parts of the bush to spread the word of the revolution. Elima sped them on their way. 'The political commissioner will no longer be what he was before the system was modified. That is to say, a citizen floating above the day-to-day realities of the people, driving about the streets and avenues of Kinshasa in a Mercedes and knowing nothing of the life of the peasant of Dumi. The political commissioners will live with the people. They will be in the fields, not as masters but as peasants. They will work with the workers, they will share their joys and sorrows. They will in this way better understand the aspirations of the people and will truly become again children of the people.'

Words of terror. Because this was the great fear of so many of the men who had come by riches so easily, by simple official plunder, the new men of the new state who, in the name of Africanization and the dignity of Africa, were so often doing jobs for which they were not qualified and often were drawing salaries for jobs they were not doing at all; this, for all their talk of authenticity and the ways of the ancestors, was their fear: to be returned from the sweet corruptions of Kinshasa to the older corruption of the bush, to be returned to Africa.

And the bush is close. It begins just outside the city and goes on forever. The airplane that goes from Kinshasa to Kisangani flies over 800 miles of what still looks like virgin forest.

V.S. Naipaul (1975) "A New King for the Congo," *New York Review of Books*, vol. 22, no. 11, June 26.

CHINA, REVOLT AND SLAUGHTER: TIANANMEN'S BEIJING SPRING (1989)

The protests at Tiananmen Square in 1989 marked a major turning point in Chinese history. During April of that year, protestors, mainly students, came to Tiananmen Square to mourn the death of a pro-democracy advocate Hu Yaobang. They did so by demanding reforms that would further democratize the central government. However, they were met by strict opposition from the ruling Communist Party of China. Protests which once began peacefully soon turned violent, with some estimates putting the number of student fatalities from 200 to 3,000.

Caught in the midst of this conflict was the prominent role of the global news media. For perhaps one of the first times ever, images of the non-Western world were being fed "live" to audiences all over the world to witness what was happening. This led to an immediate response of condemnation from almost all Western nations. Besides the picture of the "Unknown Rebel" which shows an unidentified man standing in front of a column of tanks, the other most enduring image of the Tiananmen Square incident was the sympathetic speech given by then Communist Party General Secretary Zhao Ziyang to protesting students. As the selection reveals, this is when he asked the students to remain patient with the Communist Party, since they, the youth of China, would eventually take power. However, this subsequently led to Zhao's dismissal as General Secretary, since the party elites thought this act overly exposed their potential weaknesses. However, nearly 20 years later, Zhao's words have become somewhat prophetic. China is now arguably more democratic than it ever was, and this is in part because the old guard of the Communist Party has given some way to a new era of party leaders, some of whom were even partly involved in the 1989 protests.

Beijing Spring, 1989

[Video report, captioned "Important News: Zhao Ziyang and Li Peng Visit Fasting Students at Tiananmen Square"]

[Announcer] Zhao Ziyang, general secretary of the CPC Central Committee, and Li Peng, premier of the State Council, at 4:45 this morning [19:45 GMT, May 18] went to Tiananmen Square to see students who are on a hunger strike and to sincerely urge them to end their fast in order to protect their health.

[Begin recording] [Video report begins by showing Zhao Ziyang and Li Peng shaking hands with fasting students seated on a bus. Zhao and Li extend regards to the students.]

[Li Peng] Where do you go to school?

[Unidentified student] I am from Teachers' University.

[Li Peng] And you?

[Second unidentified student] Teachers' University.

[Li Peng] You are all students at Teachers' University.

[Third unidentified student] [Video shows one of the students maintaining order asking fellow students to make way for Zhao Ziyang and Li Peng to step off the bus.] Back up, please.

[Zhao Ziyang] [Video shows a very tired Zhao Ziyang, speaking through a small megaphone handed to him by a student.] I want to say a few words to the students. We have come too late.

[Fourth unidentified student] You have finally come.

[Zhao Ziyang] I am sorry, fellow students. No matter how you have criticized us, I think you have the right to do so. We do not come here to ask you to excuse us. All I want to say is that the fasting students are physically very weak now. Your fasting has entered its seventh day. This simply cannot go on. If the fasting lasts longer, the damage to the students' health will be irremediable, and their lives will be in danger. This is understood by everyone. The only thing – the most important thing – to do now is to immediately terminate the fasting.

I know your fasting is aimed at obtaining a very satisfactory answer to the issues you put forward to the government and the party. I think that a satisfactory answer is obtainable because the channel for our dialogue is still open. Some issues can be solved only through a process. Some issues – for example, the nature of your action – I feel can be eventually solved. We can reach a consensus. As you all know, many things involve complicated situations. It takes a process to solve them. You just cannot fast for six or seven days and adhere to the idea that your fast will not be terminated unless you receive a satisfactory answer, because if you end your fast only when you receive a satisfactory answer, it will be too late.

Your health will be irreparable. You are still young, fellow students. You still have ample time. You should live healthily and live to see the day when China completes the four modernizations. You are not like us, who are old. It is not easy for the state and your parents to nurture you and send you to college. How can you, at the age of only eighteen or nineteen, or in your twenties, sacrifice your lives like this? Just use your head and think. I am not here today to hold a dialogue with you. Today I just want you fellow students to use reason and try to understand what a serious situation is now facing us.

You all know the party and the state are now very worried. The entire society is [words indistinct]. All of Beijing is talking about your action. Moreover, as you all know, this situation in Beijing simply cannot go on anymore. This city of ours, the capital of China, is facing more and more grave situations every day. You comrades all have good intentions to do something good for the country, but this strike which has happened and is out of control, has affected everything – communications, transport, work, and the regular patients who want to see doctors.

In short, when you end your fast, the government will never close the door to dialogues, never. If you have questions, we will solve them. Despite what you say and the fact that we are a 'little late, we are getting closer to solving the problems. We are getting there step-by-step. That is all for now. My main purpose is to see the comrades here and express my feelings. I hope you comrades soberly think about this question. Those comrades who have organized the fast should also think soberly. Fasting is not something that can go on without reason.

We were once young, and we all had such a burst of energy. We also staged demonstrations, and I know the situation at that time. We did not think of the consequences. You should soberly think of things in the future. The sixth day is gone and the seventh day is here. Will the fasting really go on for the eighth, ninth, and tenth days? I say many things can eventually be solved. If you want to wait for that day, the day you receive a satisfactory answer, then you should end the fast early. Thank you, comrades. I just wanted to see you all. [Video shows students surrounding Zhao Ziyang and asking for his autograph; Zhao is shown signing his name on a handkerchief, a notebook, and a piece of cloth handed to him by students.] [End recording]

Michel Oksenberg, Lawrence R. Sullivan, and Marc Lambert (eds) *Beijing Spring, 1989: Confrontation and Conflict: The Basic Documents*, London: East Gate Book, M.E. Sharpe Inc, pp. 288–290. 'Beijing Television Service, 22:30 GMT, May 18, 1989.'

RUSSIA, PERESTROIKA AND GLASNOST: MIKHAIL GORBACHEV (1988)

Mikhail Gorbachev (1931–) was the last head of state, the General Secretary of the Communist Party of the Soviet Union (CPSU). He was elected to the post in March 1985, and was elected the first executive president in March 1990, from which he resigned declaring the position to be extinct on December 25, 1991. He has a reputation for being a reformer of communism and is well known for introducing major reforms during his leadership of the Soviet Union. Glasnost ("openness") was a freedom of information act and Perestroika ("restructuring") was an economic restructuring that allowed private ownership and foreign trade. Glasnost began as a governmental willingness to inform the people of economic troubles, but with the explosion of Chernobyl quickly changed into a "powerful modernizing force." Taken together, Glasnost and Perestroika are thought to be drivers of political change that led to the collapse of the Soviet Union. While it is clear that they played a role, it is important to note that the Soviet Union's economy was on the brink of collapse in the late 1980s, at least in part due to falling behind in the development of information technology and in the arms race with the U.S. Gorbachev's address to the United Nations in 1988 points to the world economy, and in particular scientific and informational technologies, and global communication as the most important drivers of world order.

Mikhail Gorbachev Addresses the United Nations

The role played by the Soviet Union in world affairs is well known and, in view of the revolutionary *perestroika* under way in our country, which has a tremendous potential for peace and international cooperation, we are now particularly interested in being properly understood.

That is why we have come here to address this most authoritative world body and to share our thoughts with its members. We want it to be the first to learn of our important new decisions.

What will humankind be like as it enters the twenty-first century? People are already fascinated by this not too distant future. We are looking forward to it with hopes for the best and yet with feelings of concern.

The world in which we live today is radically different from what it was at the beginning or even in the middle of this century. And it continues to change, as do all its components.

The advent of nuclear weapons was a tragic reminder of the fundamental nature of all these changes. A material symbol and expression of absolute military power, nuclear weapons at the same time revealed the absolute limits of that power. The problem of humankind's survival and self-preservation has come to the fore.

Profound social changes are taking place.

Whether in the East or the South, the West or the North, hundreds of millions of people, new nations and states, new public movements and ideologies have moved to the forefront of history.

Broad-based and frequently turbulent popular movements have given expression, in a multidimensional and contradictory way, to a longing for independence, democracy and social justice. The idea of democratizing the entire world order has become a powerful sociopolitical force.

At the same time, the scientific and technological revolution has turned many economic, food, energy, environmental, information and demographic problems, which only recently we treated as national or regional problems, into global concerns.

Thanks to the advances in mass media and means of transportation, the world seems to have become more visible and tangible. International communication has become easier than ever before. Today it is virtually impossible for any society to remain "closed." We need a radical review of approaches to the totality of the problems of international cooperation, which is a major element of universal security.

The world economy is becoming a single organism, and no state, whatever its social system or economic status, can normally develop outside it.

This places on the agenda the need to devise a fundamentally new machinery for the functioning of the world economy, a new structure of the international division of labor.

At the same time, the growth of the world economy reveals the contradictions and limits inherent in the traditional type of industrialization. Its further extension and intensification spell environmental catastrophe.

But there are still many countries without sufficiently developed industries, and some have not yet industrialized. One of the major problems is whether the process of their economic growth will follow the old technological patterns or whether they can join in the search for environmentally clean production.

Another problem is the widening gap between the developed and most of the developing countries, which is increasingly becoming a serious global threat.

Hence the need to begin a search for a fundamentally new type of industrial progress that would meet the interests of all peoples and states.

In a word, the new realities are changing the entire international situation. The differences and contradictions inherited from the past are diminishing or being displaced. But new ones are emerging.

Some former differences and disputes are losing their importance. But conflicts of a different kind are taking their place.

Life is making us abandon traditional stereotypes and outdated views; it is making us discard illusions.

The very concepts of the nature of and criteria for progress are changing.

It would be naive to think that the problems plaguing humankind today can be solved with the means and methods that were applied or seemed to work in the past.

This is one of the signs of the crucial nature of the current phase in history.

The greatest philosophers sought to grasp the laws of social development and to find an answer to the main question: how to make human life happier, fairer and more secure. Two great revolutions, the French Revolution of 1789 and the Russian Revolution of 1917, had a powerful impact on the very nature of history and radically changed the course of world developments.

These two revolutions, each in its own way, gave a tremendous impetus to humankind's progress. To a large extent, the two revolutions shaped the way of thinking that is still prevalent in social consciousness. It is a precious intellectual heritage.

But today we face a different world, and we must seek a different road to the future. In seeking it, we must, of course, draw on the accumulated experience and yet be aware of the fundamental differences between the situation yesterday and what we are facing today.

But the novelty of the tasks before us, as well as their difficulty, goes beyond that. Today we have entered an era when progress will be shaped by universal human interests.

The awareness of this dictates that world politics, too, should be guided by the primacy of universal human values.

The history of past centuries and millennia was a history of wars that raged almost everywhere, or of frequent desperate battles to the point of mutual annihilation. They grew out of clashes of social and political interests, national enmity, and ideological or religious incompatibility. All this did happen.

And even today many people would like these vestiges of the past to be accepted as inexorable law.

But concurrently with wars, animosities and divisions among peoples and countries, another objective trend has been gaining momentum – the emergence of a mutually interdependent and integral world.

Today, further world progress is only possible through a search for universal human consensus as we move forward to a new world order.

Isaac J. Tarasulo (ed. and trans.) (1989) "Mikhail Gorbachev Addresses the United Nations," *Gorbachev and Glasnost: Viewpoints from the Soviet Press*, Wilmington, DE: Scholarly Resources, pp. 330–333. Speech delivered December 7, 1988. First appeared in *Soviet Life*, special supplement no. 2, February 1989.

BRAZIL, PORTO ALEGRE: THE WORLD SOCIAL FORUM [WSF] (2001)

Originally founded in 2001 at Port Alegre, Brazil, the World Social Forum was organized by a variety of groups around the world – most notably, the Association for the Taxation of Financial Transactions for the Aid of Citizens (ATTAC), a coalition of mainly European unions, thinkers, and farmers who came to be known for their opposition to neo-liberalism and corporate globalization. The Forum's first inaugural conference was chosen to be held in Port Alegre partly because it was sponsored by the left-leaning Brazilian Workers' Party (PT). The event attracted more than 10,000 people from around the world and it was largely driven by the goal of offering alternatives to neo-liberal ideals and policies. The World Social Forum is also seen as a counterpoint to international financial and political meetings which typically do not allow widespread partici-pation and open discussion, most notably the World Economic Forum. Since the inaugural meeting which set the tone for future conferences, the World Social Forum has grown considerably in size and has also been held in other cities besides Port Alegre such as Mumbai and Nairobi. It has also been at the heart of much debate concerning the future direction of those social movements which oppose corporate and neo-liberal driven globalization.

Note from the Organizing Committee on the principles that guide the WSF

The World Social Forum (WSF) 2002 achieved major political impact, sparking wide-ranging debate to assess the event, which can be followed at our website. Nonetheless, we feel we should reiterate that the WSF is organized on the basis of the Charter of Principles approved by the International Council on 10th July, 2001.

Amongst the points of the Charter of Principles, we would like to recall the following:

a) The WSF defines itself as an 'open meeting place' (point 1), one which is 'plural, diversified, non-confessional, non-governmental and non-party' (point 8).

b) The WSF delimits itself politically as a space 'of groups and movements of civil society opposed to neoliberalism and to domination of the world by capital and any form of imperialism' (point 1). Its proposals 'stand in opposition to a process of globalization commanded by the large multinational corpor-ations and by the governments and international institutions at the service of those corporations interests, with the complicity of national governments' (point 4).

c) WSF events are non-deliberative for the WSF as a body. This point of method is frequently misunderstood, and requires special note: the WSF 'does not constitute a locus of power to be disputed by the participants in its meetings' and no one will be 'authorized, on behalf of (. . .) the Forum, to express positions claiming to be those of all its participants. The participants (. . .) shall not be called on to take decisions as a body, whether by vote or acclamation' (point 6). Nonetheless, 'organizations or groups of organizations that participate in the Forums meetings are assured the right (. . .) to deliberate on declarations or actions they may decide on', which the Forum will disseminate widely (point 7).

d) 'The WSF will always be a forum open to pluralism and to diversity of activities and ways of engaging' (point 9), which is a source of wealth and strength in the movement for another world. The Forum will coexist with contradictions and will always be marked by conflicting opinions among the organizations and movements whose positions lie within the bounds of its Charter of Principles.

e) The WSF is open to all and does not operate on the basis of invitations. It arranges the conditions necessary for all those interested in promoting their activities to be able to do so, under whatever name (workshops, seminars, meetings, forums, etc). The only activities organized at WSF 2002, on the collective responsibility of the Organizing Committee and the International Council, were 27 conferences (whose participants were chosen jointly with the facilitators) and testimonies from 15 personalities. No group or organization whose profile conforms to WSF principles has been or will be denied the right to participate in WSF events.

f) The World Parliamentary Forum and the Forum of Local Authorities dialogue with the WSF and its participants, but were organized as autonomous events with the same status as the other seminars, the first by a Parliamentary Commission and the second by the Porto Alegre City Government, not by the Organizing Committee and by the International Council. The WSF 'brings together and interlinks only organizations and movements of civil society from all the countries in the world' (point 5) and 'party representations or military organizations shall not participate in the Forum' (point 9). This does not mean, 'that government leaders and parliamentarians who abide by this Charter cannot be invited to participate, in a personal capacity' (point 9). This year, however, the Organizing Committee did not invite any heads of leaders or parliamentarians to the World Social Forum.

São Paulo, March 7th, 2002
Brazilian Organizing Committee

"Note from the Organizing Committee on the principles that guide the WSF," English text by volunteer translators Helena El Masri and Peter Lenny. http://www.forumsocialmundial.org.br/main.php?id_menu=4_2&cd_language=2.

PART FOUR

The great globalization debate, 1989–2010

INTRODUCTION TO
PART FOUR

Debate, if passionate, is rarely cosy or relaxed. Genuine debate begins in passionate awakenings – from the dawning realization that a given set of social arrangements are unfair and exploitative, or from first-hand experience of cultural encounters that teaches the world is not what one believed it to be. It would not be too far wrong to say that the debate over globalization in our own time has arisen from the soils of passionate awakenings – some radical, others profoundly skeptical, still others ambivalent – while managing along the way to raise the anxiety-provoking and tension-filled nature of dialogue to the second degree. What kind of cultural tension, though? Some of the most apprehensive persons-in-the-street worrying over the state and direction of globalization are known as sociologists, many of whom have been all too keenly aware of the economic and cultural unevenness of globalism as it unfolds across the planet. The belief that globalization is deeply corrosive of culture and character, as well as diminutive of national identities and the political sovereignty of states, forms part of a more popular wisdom which has in recent times been elaborated into a comprehensive social theory. Others, seeking to widen the scope of globalism to encompass images, ideology, and information culture, have sought to concentrate on the stretching of social relations which some regard as significant and even beneficial. Even so, such viewpoints are only the tip of the iceberg as regards the globalization debate. Indeed, it is fair to say that there has been a virtual explosion of competing approaches, theories, doctrines, and ideologies pertaining to the concept of globalization – ranging from economics and culture to governance and information technologies.

But not everything to do with the globalization debate of recent years might be said to be only discursive. Equally, the debate over globalization – anchored as it is within academic settings and the public political sphere – has become a source of great controversy in everyday life. Beyond the academy, the globalization debate has been carried out in the streets – through social protest, civil unrest, cultural uprisings, and various social movements such as the anti-globalization protestors. On the streets in Seattle, Rio, Geneva, and Cancun, the anti-globalization movement – from anti-capitalists and anarchists to environmentalists and people just generally worried about the plight of the planet – staged mass protests at the summits of the major transnational political and economic forums, such as the World Bank, the G8, and the International Monetary Fund. Tina Rosenberg, writing in *The New York Times*, summarizes well this political contest over globalization:

> Globalization is meant to signify integration and unity – yet it has proved, in its way, to be no less polarizing than the cold-war divisions it has supplanted. The lines between globalization's supporters and its critics run not only between countries but also through them, as people struggle to come to terms with the defining economic force shaping the planet today. The two sides in the discussion – a shouting match, really – describe what seem to be two completely different forces. Is the globe being knit together by the Nikes and Microsofts and Citigroups in a dynamic new system that will eventually lift the have-nots of the world up from medieval misery? Or are ordinary people now victims of ruthless corporate

domination, as the Nikes and Microsofts and Citigroups roll over the poor in nation after nation in search of new profits?[1]

Rosenberg rightly draws our attention to the line – certainly not always easy to spot, and no doubt a good deal harder to keep in mind – that runs from Nike to the small neglected child whose mother labors throughout a fifty-hour week for a pittance. How globalization, in its remaking of the economies of every nation, touches on the lives of the billions that now comprise our planet is what lies at the core of the major globalization debate that unfolded toward the end of the twentieth century. A debate that involved much more than simply supporters and critics, Part Four of this reader now turns to consider the intricacies of the theoretical and political architecture of what political theorist David Held has called "the great globalization debate."

THE GREAT GLOBALIZATION DEBATE

In seeking to capture the essentials of "the great globalization debate," it is useful to discriminate between two broad "levels" of general orientation – positive and negative versions of globalism. Beyond these broad dividing lines, it can further be said that the key points of argument cluster around the following groupings or theoretical positions:

- the globalists (pro-globalists, or hyperglobalizers)
- the anti-globalists
- the transformationalists
- post-globalists (including radical globalists).

In what follows, we look at and consider these very different ways of thinking about the forces of globalization. Our review of these theoretical doctrines and political positions is not intended as comprehensive, and nor do we consider some of the more subtle variations between social theorists of globalization. Rather, we wish to underscore the key trends in recent debates on globalization.

As early as the 1990s, it was becoming clear to public intellectuals (and most academics in their number) that the structure of advanced capitalism was changing. For a group of thinkers who have been variously dubbed "pro-globalists" or "hyperglobalizers," the arrival of truly global capital, finance, and trade with planetary reach was the inevitable concomitant of profit-maximizing transnational corporations exporting production to low-wage labor spots around the world. The pro-globalists argued that the global spread of globalization processes was increasingly impacting everywhere. Moreover the global marketplace, they argued, was not only transformed through a new openness, flexibility, and outsourcing in conventional industrial manufactures; rather, the biggest economic transformation heralded by globalization concerned the rise of finance, capital, and information flows. Service industries such as finance and telecommunications began to equal, and sometimes outstrip, conventional manufactures in terms of the volume of world trade. Against the backdrop of the information technology revolution and the know-how bound up with new communicational networks, finance became increasingly geared toward electronic money floating in extra-territorial cyberspace. At the click of a mouse, and in virtual real-time, corporations, banks, and fund managers could now transfer vast amounts of capital from one side of the world to the other. Notwithstanding the new social insecurities and short-termist world-view promoted by such global finance, the emergence of the information economy and opening up of the service sectors – notably telecommunications and finance – was celebrated by pro-globalists, for the most part, as marking the dawn of a new era for human progress.

Indeed, globalization was for the pro-globalists irreversible and inescapable. For writers as diverse in political orientation and theoretical temperament as Manuel Castells, Peter Dicken, and Ulf Hannerz, globalization not only reshaped industry and transformed every national economy, but it also touched upon the very fabric of daily life – often in surprising and complex ways. The arrival of a single global market was with us, and for many pro-globalists this was clearly a preferred form of life to anything that had existed previously. To pro-globalists (especially the hyperglobalists among them), the world had simply reinvented itself – consigning previous models of social coordination and the "good society" to the dustbin. Keniche Ohmae, the celebrated Japanese management guru, pronounced the arrival of a "borderless world." The pursuit of profitability by transnational corporations able to outsource production and to reshape trade and finance flows through the deployment of new communications technologies accompanied the "death" of distance and, effectively, the modern era. For pro-globalists, the process of globalization slices through the political authority of nation-states. Indifferent to national borders, globalization transforms not only economic mechanisms but also political power and cultural patterns. The result has been a "denationalization" of state economies – as politicians and policy-makers nowadays have less and less power to influence, let alone shape, transnational networks of production, trade, and finance.

There was, however, another side to the debate – one much more critical. These thinkers were labeled *skeptics*. The skeptics argued that globalization promised a great deal, but merely remained at the level of promise. The skeptics tended to doubt not only the liberationist, transformative zeal of the pro-globalists, but also questioned whether the so-called "new times" of advanced globalization are all that different from previous historical eras. The skeptics big question then was this: what evidence is there to indicate that the world is actually becoming more integrated? Is there evidence to show that the world is more globalized?

If there was a general theoretical pessimism informing the skeptics' response to the idea that we now live in "new times," then such doubt was raised to the second power after reviewing available evidence for the claim that we now all live in one single world. Indeed, if anything, global markets are intensifying North–South inequalities – marginalizing or excluding many "Third World" states from the economic benefits of trade deregulation and liberalization. An especially interesting version of the argument put by global skeptics is that of Paul Hirst and Graeme Thompson, reproduced here in the reading "Globalization in Question." Hirst and Thompson see little that's actually "new" in globalization – at least as described in various sectors of the media, as well as some of the arguments advanced by radical globalists. Against this backdrop, Hirst and Thompson reject nearly every claim associated with the globalization thesis. While acknowledging that there is today more cultural and communicational contact between nations than in previous periods, Hirst and Thompson contend that such contact does not amount to a truly globalized economy. Studying the period from 1890 to 1914, for example, they note that trade and investment flows were higher for that period than for today, that national borders were not as restricted and that, consequently, there were higher levels of transnational immigration. In a related fashion, Hirst and his colleagues questioned the scope of one of the key institutional emblems of globalization: the multinational corporation. So-called global transnational corporations (TNCs) were not really "global" at all, they said; they were instead nationally based companies at the center of international networks of subsidiaries. In contrast to the notion of "footloose capital" in flight around the globe seeking out ever greater profits, the majority of economic activity across the international economy occur primarily in the Organization for Economic Co-operational and Development (OECD) countries.

Other critics of the "myth of globalization" have pointed out that, in contrast to the colonizing spirit of the age of world empires, the majority of economic activity across the international economy has been occurring primarily in the OECD countries. Here the contributions of Robert Gilpin, R.J.B. Jones, and Alan Rugman are key. For in different ways, each of these writers has questioned whether globalization is a universal process experienced uniformly across all countries. Regionalization rather than globalization, it was argued from this standpoint, defined the shape of the worldwide economy. Some went so far as to claim that, because of the heavy regionalization of such trading blocs as the European Union and North America, the world economy was becoming less, not more, global. Most agreed, at any rate, that nation-states were not becoming progressively less sovereign – on the contrary, internationalization was regarded as fundamentally dependent on the regulatory control of national governments.

Alongside the skeptics of globalization were to be found the anti-globalizers. The anti-globalization brigade have been notoriously diverse, stretching from anti-capitalist protestors and anarchists to unionists and the traditional political Left to those campaigning for fair development in the "Third" world. This remarkably broad coalition of forces, dubbed largely by the media as the anti-globalization movement, developed over time a list of powerful charges cataloguing the sins of globalization. From low-paid sweat-shop workers in cheap wage countries such as China, India, Vietnam, and the like to the corporate domination of planet-wide commercial forces such as Microsoft, Nike, and Citigroup, and from the privatiza-tion of state industry to qualify for World Bank and IMF loans to the imposition of GM seeds on farmers in the developing world, the economic pressures of globalization were presented as menacing, corrosive, and soul-destroying. Globalism, according to certain versions of the anti-globalization case, has empowered multinational corporations and speculative finance, compounded inequalities, and eroded democracy, pro-moted Western imperialism and the Americanization of the world, destroyed environmental standards, as well as brutalized the public political sphere. The emergence of a planetary-scale global market with ever-decreasing tariffs, ever greater international production, as well as more integrated financial markets with higher trade flows, has unleashed a turbo-charged capitalism of unprecedented forms of economic exploitation and political oppression. Or, at least, this is globalization's reality according to the anti-globalizers.

The link between global Westernization or Americanization on the one hand and turbo-capitalist exploit-ation on the other in the anti-globalization discourse is sometimes explicit, sometimes implicit. A neo-Marxist conviction that capitalism exhibits a pathological expansionist logic, one which now expands the geographical reach of Western corporations and markets to the nth degree, informs this argument. The imperial West, it is suggested, has carved up and redivided the world into exclusive trade, investment, and financial sectors and flows, with new institutions – such as the G8 and World Bank – exercising global surveillance and domination. As a result, globalization is seen as a top-down process, its effects uniform. The weakness of this case, however, it that it cannot adequately justify the grounds of its own social critique: if globalization were really so omnipotent, all-powerful and manipulating, how would the social theorist ever find a position from which to launch an objective critique? In any event, the assumption that the globe is always geared to perfectly integrated markets is certainly deficient. That is to say, such critics have reduc-tively equated globalization with an economistic version of world markets. Yet, as we will see, concentrating solely on processes of economic integration, and thus neglecting current social, cultural, and political transformations, leads to an impoverished understanding of how globalization is constituted, contested, and shaped.

Yet there is another way of thinking about globalization that does not reduce to the zeal of the globalists, nor the pessimism of the anti-globalists. This is the theoretical position of *transformationalists*. The transfor-mationalist position is essentially a "Third"-way in political orientation, seeking to avoid the pitfalls of charac-terizing globalism as wholly positive or negative, and also avoiding the trap of conceiving of globalism in terms of the economy alone (as with the skeptics). For transformationalists, globalization inaugurates a "shake-out" within the realms of economics, politics, culture, and personal life. This is less the heralding of a completely new age (as argued by radical globalists), and rather an adjustment to a world that transforms previous structures, a world that shakes up distinctions between domestic and international, internal and external affairs.

The theory of transformational globalization has been developed and extended by a number of leading social theorists, including Lord Anthony Giddens (formerly director of the London School of Economics), German sociologist Ulrich Beck, and the political theorist David Held. This general standpoint – that globalization transforms, but does not necessarily overturn, modern structures – has also been given powerful political capital through its embracement by various public policy forums as well as the political administrations of the Blair Government in the UK and former President Bill Clinton in the USA during the 1990s.

In their pathbreaking work *Global Transformations* (1999), Held and his associates delineate, with con-siderable precision, what is truly "global" about globalization. In order to say anything meaningful about patterns of contemporary globalization, and particularly of how today's world order differs from previous historical forms of globalization, Held sets out four analytical dimensions of analysis:

- the extensity of global networks
- the intensity of global interconnectedness
- the velocity of global flows
- the impact propensity of global interconnectedness.

For Held, globalization certainly involves a *stretching* of social relations. What he means to underscore with this notion of stretching or extensity is that decisions or events occurring in one part of the world come to have ramifications for people living elsewhere. From global labor markets to global warming, it is nearly impossible today not to live with the consequences of the widening reach of networks of social activity and political power. But still there is more. For globalization implies not only a stretching of activities across frontiers, but also a rapid *intensification of interconnectedness* between peoples, institutions, and states. Here the networked world of high-speed telecommunications is the most obvious example. Stretching and intensity of social relations are thus key for Held; but there are also two other forces at work in the play of global things. One is velocity, by which Held seeks to underscore the *speeding up of social life*. This refers to the emergence of a 24/7 media culture, in which breaking news – from terrorist attacks to the fighting of wars – is relayed virtually instantly around the globe. But it also refers to the speeding up of transport, travel, and the global communication of information. The other concerns impact, in particular the magnification of local events or decisions into issues of global import.

Such global transformations spell, in turn, major changes for the nation-state. And Held and his associates provide some dramatic statistics to prove that the growth of transnational organizations alters the dynamics of both state and civil society. At the beginning of the twentieth century there were only 37 intergovernmental organizations (IGOs) and 176 international non-government organizations (INGOs) in force. Today, in addition to the many millions of private firms doing business across state borders, there are an estimated 7000 IGOs and some 50,000 non-governmental, not-for-profit organizations operating around the globe. These bodies – from Amnesty International and Christian Aid to the International Red Cross and Transparency International – make up a vast, multi-layered structure of global civil society. To this pattern of extensive non-governmental interconnectedness can also be added a thick web of key global policy-making bodies, including the United Nations, IMF, G8, World Trade Organization, European Union, and Asia Pacific Economic Cooperation.

Whither the nation-state? Not necessarily according to Held, and in this connection he outlines a highly nuanced theoretical position – one which puts him at some distance from those radical globalists for whom the state is, more or less, finished. Held certainly recognizes that many traditional domains of state activity have been eroded. As he develops this point: "individual states on their own can no longer be conceived of as the appropriate political units for either resolving key policy problems or managing effectively a broad range of public functions." But he thinks it a mistake to deny the ongoing relevance of the state to world affairs – witness, for example, the ongoing power of states such as the United States and China in global politics. Globalization in this sense is less about an erosion than a reshaping of the nation-state. "The modern state," suggest Held and McGrew, "is increasingly embedded in webs of regional and global interconnectedness permeated by supranational, intergovernmental and transnational forces, and unable to determine its own fate."

There are still many other social theorists who find themselves in yet another position (at once theoretical and political) on the globalization debate. These theorists are neither hyperglobalists nor skeptics; and certainly not transformationalists for that matter either. These are public intellectuals and writers who are willing to acknowledge the essential importance of globalization to the current age, while nonetheless retaining a critical perspective toward globalism. In the broader framework of the globalization debate, these writers can be dubbed "radical globalists."

Why radical? Because, according to this critical attitude, the world's rich network of global interdependence both nourishes and destroys. Globalization puts itself forth as transformative – space and time no longer limit the consequences of human action; our interconnections are always global, with the results of decisions and actions in one place influencing the lives and life-chances of people in other places throughout the world. The global electronic economy, however, appears to make all the more difficult – if not unthinkable – the sharing of collective responsibility for the living conditions and consequences of various forms of life across the planet. Our mutual dependency may be planetwide; and yet the growing, seemingly unstoppable forces of privatization, deregulation, consumerism, and new individualism appear to eat away at the very social co-ordinates of "togetherness" that globalism elsewhere promotes.

But still, readers may ask, what is radical in this political position of radical globalists? First, radical globalists take globalization with full seriousness. Yes, the world has entered a new social encounter – one for which existing maps and social memories are of no useful guide – and there is no turning back from globalism. Globalization, or so say radical globalists, functions on a planetary, global scale. Second, and without proclaiming that the new global realities are either good or bad, radical globalists argue that the coordinates of globalization processes are post-societal – cutting across established political positions and cultural patterns. The global reach of capital, culture, and communications now seems to operate in the planetary "space of flows" (to invoke Castells). Flows, informationalism, disjunction, difference: new terms of analysis are required, argue radical globalists, for the critique of globalization.

But, still, why radical? Because while the globalization process has bitten deeply into the culture and communications of finance and trade – thus resulting in the emergence of a new global electronic economy – there has been no parallel transformation of the philosophical, moral, or ethical forms of contemporary living. As Zygmunt Bauman, one of the most prolific and profound of the radical globalists, says in the reading in this section ("Globalization: The Human Consequences"), globalism as condition and consequence in lopsided. Globalism may have expanded the planetary reach of our geopolitical "sight" – thanks to 24/7 media culture we witness the misery, pain, and indignity of people suffering in faraway lands – but it has not produced a global extension of our "hands" in order to do something together for the moral good of humanity. As Bauman elsewhere sums up this global lopsidedness: "The planetary reach of capital, finances and trade – the forces that decide the range of choices and the effectiveness of human action, the way humans live and the limits of their dreams and hopes – has not been matched on a similar scale by the resources that humanity developed to control those forces that control human lives."[2] Bauman's idea of the unevenness of the globalization process is at the center of the social analysis of radical globalists – even if the focus of critique varies widely, from a fascination with cultural disjunction to the cultural studies of informationalism. Still, what *is* radical here remains the underscoring of the *human* in the conditions and consequences of globalization. As Bauman captures this: "Our mutual dependency is planetwide and so we are already, and will remain indefinitely, objectively responsible for one another. There are, however, few if any signs that we who share the planet are willing to take up in earnest the subjective responsibility for that objective responsibility of ours." The contest over globalization, after the case put by radical globalists, could not be more profound.

Notes

1   Tina Rosenberg (2002) "Globalization," *The New York Times*, August 18.
2   Zygmunt Bauman (2008) *Does Ethics Have a Chance in a World of Consumers*, Harvard University Press, p. 73.

Globalists

THE END OF THE NATION-STATE: KENICHI OHMAE (1995)

Kenichi Ohmae (1943–), founder of Ohmae and Associates, is a world-renowned Japanese management consultant who has advised corporations and governments about how to persevere in the current age of globalization. Ohmae has also written a number of influential books on this topic, including *The End of the Nation State*, *Borderless World*, and *The Mind of the Strategist*. He is commonly considered to be a one of the leading voices of the "hyperglobalist" position. Within social thought and in the broader public, his account of globalization is typically employed to argue how national borders no longer predominate as they once did.

The Old World has Fallen Apart

A funny – and, to many observers, a very troubling – thing has happened on the way to former U.S. President Bush's so-called "new world order": the old world has fallen apart. Most visibly, with the ending of the Cold War, the long-familiar pattern of alliances and oppositions among industrialized nations has fractured beyond repair. Less visibly, but arguably far more important, the modern nation state itself – that artifact of the eighteenth and nineteenth centuries – has begun to crumble.

For many observers, this erosion of the long-familiar building blocks of the political world has been a source of discomfort at least and, far more likely, of genuine distress. They used to be confident that they could tell with certainty where the boundary lines ran. These are our people; those are not. These are our interests; those are not. These are our industries; those are not. It did not matter that little economic activity remained truly domestic in any sense that an Adam Smith or a David Ricardo would understand. Nor did it matter that the people served or the interests protected represented a small and diminishing fraction of the complex social universe within each set of established political borders. [. . .]

On old economic maps, the most important cartographic facts had to do with things like the location of raw material deposits, energy sources, navigable rivers, deep-water ports, railroad lines, paved roads – and national borders. On today's maps, by contrast, the most salient facts are the footprints cast by TV satellites, the areas covered by radio signals, and the geographic reach of newspapers and magazines. Information has replaced both propinquity and politics as the factor most likely to shape the flows of economic activity. Physical terrain and political boundaries still matter, of course, but neither – and especially not political boundaries – matters as much as what people know or want or value.

In a sense, the intangibles of local knowledge, taste, and preference have always played a critical shape-giving role. Long before nation states existed, long before the cities, towns, and villages out of which they grew took recognizable form, groups of people linked by social and cultural ties regularly exchanged what they could hunt, fish, grow, gather, extract, or make. The meaningful horizons of their lives were circumscribed not by the artifice of formal political institutions, but by the land on which they lived and the social webs that enclosed them. Even in the modern world, with its crazy quilt of political borders, hundreds of millions of people – rural peasants, for example, in remote areas of China – exist in much the same fashion. Political dividing lines got added late, indeed, to these venerable maps of local experience. The ink is barely dry.

Even so, it is fading. And it is fading ever more quickly. Better information, made possible by better technology, is the reason. As the quality, range, and availability of information improve, growing numbers of people – no matter what their geographical location – come to know in ever finer detail how other people in other places live. At the same time, they come to know what kinds of economic choices can be made and what levels of value attach to those choices. Such knowledge and awareness, in turn, inevitably work to undermine the tyranny of both physical distance and government edict. The larger the field of known possibilities, the harder it is for a central authority to limit that field arbitrarily – or to make those limitations stick.

Centuries ago, the first Western travelers to reach Asia returned with goods and spices and artworks that forever changed the universe of possibilities out of which tastes and preferences at home would later crystallize. On this road of discovery, there is no going back. Or going more slowly. Indeed, in recent years, when the Silk Road is no longer a dangerous route through uncharted terrain but merely a degree of access to global media, like Fox TV, the time required for exposure to new dimensions of choice has shrunk to virtually nothing. And the barriers to such exposure have either disappeared or proven endlessly porous.

Even given the irreducibly local portion in any mix of customs and preferences, a newly shared knowledge of what is possible cannot help but lead across geographies to at least a partial convergence of tastes and preferences. Global brands of blue jeans, colas, and stylish athletic shoes are as much on the mind of the taxi driver in Shanghai as they are in the kitchen or the closet of the schoolteacher in Stockholm or São Paulo.

For several decades now, this process of California-ization has provided much of the market-driven support for the development of a genuinely borderless global economy. But this kind of convergence, important as it is, goes only so far. It overlays new tastes on an established, but largely unaffected, base of social norms and values. It adds new elements to the local mix of goods and services, but leaves the worldview of the people who purchase them unchanged. It expands the universe of what is desirable, but does nothing to shift the fundamental mind-set of those who experience those pangs of desire. The contents of kitchens and closets may change, but the core mechanisms by which cultures maintain their identity and socialize their young remain untouched. Political borders may offer little meaningful resistance to invasion by new constellations of consumer taste, but social borders limit their scope and effectively quarantine them within the superficial layers of culture. [. . .]

In the broad sweep of history, nation states have been a transitional form of organization for managing economic affairs. Their right – their prerogative – to manage them grew, in part, out of the control of military strength, but such strength is now an uncomfortably great burden to maintain. (It has also largely been exposed as a means to preserve the positions of those in power, not to advance the quality-of-life interests of their people.) Their right grew out of the control of natural resources and colonies, but the first is relatively unimportant as a source of value in a knowledge-intensive economy, and the second is less a source of low-cost resources than a bottomless drain on the home government's treasury. It grew out of the control of land, but prosperous economies can spread their influence through neighboring territories without any need for adjustment in formal divisions of sovereignty. And it grew out of the control of political independence, but such independence is of diminishing importance in a global economy that has less and less respect for national borders.

Moreover, as it grew, the nation state's organizational right to manage economic affairs fell victim to an inescapable cycle of decay. This should occasion no surprise. It comes as close to being a natural law as the messy universe of political economy allows. Whatever the form of government in power and whatever the political ideology that shapes it, demands for the civil minimum, for the support of special interests, and for the subsidization and protection of those left behind inexorably rise. In different circumstances, under different regimes, and during different eras, the speed of escalation varies. Good policy can slow the pace, bad policy can accelerate it. But no policy can stop it altogether. Nation states are political organisms, and in their economic bloodstreams cholesterol steadily builds up. Over time, arteries harden and the organism's vitality decays.

History, of course, also records the kinds of catastrophic, equilibrium-busting events that can stop or even reverse this aging process. Wars can do it, as can natural disasters like plagues, earthquakes, and volcanic eruptions. They have certainly done so in the past. But even for the most cold-blooded practitioners of *realpolitik*, these are hardly credible as purposeful instruments of economic policy.

Thus, in today's borderless economy, with its rapid cross-border migration of the four I's, there is really only one strategic degree of freedom that central governments have to counteract this remorseless buildup of economic cholesterol, only one legitimate instrument of policy to restore sustainable and self-reinforcing vitality, only one practical as well as morally acceptable way to meet their people's near-term needs without mortgaging the long-term prospects of their children and grandchildren. And that is to cede meaningful operational autonomy to the wealth-generating region states that lie within or across their borders, to catalyze the efforts of those region states to seek out global solutions, and to harness their distinctive ability to put global logic first and to function as ports of entry to the global economy. The only hope is to reverse the postfeudal, centralizing tendencies of the modern era and allow – or better, encourage – the economic pendulum to swing away from nations and back toward regions.

Ohmae, Kenichi (1995) *The End of the Nation State: The Rise of the Regional Economies*, New York: Free Press Paperbacks, pp. 7, 28–30, 141–2.

THE NETWORK SOCIETY: MANUEL CASTELLS (2006)

Manuel Castells (1942–) was born in Spain, active in the anti-Franco movement, and educated in France. He has worked all over the world and currently holds the Wallis Annenberg Chair in Communication Technology and Society at the University of Southern California, is Research Professor at the Open University of Catalonia in Barcelona, and Professor Emeritus, University of California, Berkeley. He is widely known for his groundbreaking research on networks and information technology, presented in three volumes, *The Information Age*. More recently he has worked in the area of communications and culture. This selection outlines his arguments about the structure of global networks.

Informationalism and Networks

I have conceptualized as the network society the social structure resulting from the interaction between the new technological paradigm and social organization at large.

Often, the emerging society has been characterized as information society or knowledge society. I take exception with this terminology – not because knowledge and information are not central in our society, but because they have always been so, in all historically known societies. What is new is the microelectronics-based, networking technologies that provide new capabilities to an old form of social organization: networks. Networks throughout history had a major advantage and a major problem vis-a-vis other forms of social organization. On the one hand, they are the most adaptable and flexible organizational forms, so following very efficienctly the evolutionary path of human social arrangements. On the other hand, in the past they could not master and coordinate the resources needed to accomplish a given task or fulfill a project beyond a certain size and complexity of the organization required to perform the task. Thus, in the historical record, networks were the domain of the private life, while the world of production, power, and war was occupied by large, vertical organizations, such as states, churches, armies, and corporations that could marshall vast pools of resources around the purpose defined by a central authority. Digital networking technologies enable networks to overcome their historical limits. They can, at the same time, be flexible and adaptive thanks to their capacity to decentralize performance along a network of autonomous components, while still being able to coordinate all this decentralized activity on a shared purpose of decision making. Digital communication networks are the backbone of the network society, as power networks (meaning energy networks) were the infrastructure on which the industrial society was built, as it was demonstrated by historian Thomas Hughes. To be sure, the network society manifests itself in many different forms, according to the culture, institutions, and historical trajectory of each society, as the industrial society encompassed realities as different as the United States, and the Soviet Union, England or Japan, while still sharing some fundamental features that were recognized as defining industrialism as a distinct form of human organization – not determined by the industrial technologies, but unthinkable without these technologies.

Furthermore, because the network society is based on networks, and communication networks transcend boundaries, the network society is global, it is based on global networks. So, it is pervasive throughout the planet, its logic transforms extends to every country in the planet, as it is diffused by the power embedded in global networks of capital, goods, services, labor, communication, information, science, and technology. So, what we call globalization is another way to refer to the network society, although more descriptive and less analytical than what the concept of network society implies. Yet, because networks are selective according to their specific programs, because they can simultaneously communicate and incommunicate, the network society diffuses in the entire world, but does not include all people. In fact, in this early twenty-first century, it excludes most of humankind, although all of humankind is affected by its logic, and by the power relationships that interact in the global networks of social organization. [. . .]

The network society, in the simplest terms, is a social structure based on networks operated by information and communication technologies based in microelectronics and digital computer networks that generate, process, and distribute information on the basis of the knowledge accumulated in the nodes of the networks. A network is a formal structure (see Monge and Contractor, 2004). It is a system of interconnected nodes. Nodes are, formally speaking, the points where the curve intersects itself. Networks are open structures that evolve by adding or removing nodes according to the changing requirements of the programs that assign performance goals to the networks. Naturally, these programs are decided socially from outside the network. But once they are inscripted in the logic of the network, the network will follow efficiently these instructions, adding, deleting, and reconfigurating, until a new program replaces or modifies the codes that command its operational system. [. . .]

There is an even deeper transformation of political institutions in the network society: **the rise of a new form of state** that gradually replaces the nation-states of the industrial era. This is related to globalization, that is the formation of a network of global networks than link selectively across the planet all functional dimensions of societies. Because the network society is global, the state of the network society cannot operate only or primarily in the national context. It has to engage in a process of global governance but without a global government. The reasons why there is not a global government, and it is unlikely it will be one in the foreseeable future, are rooted in the historical inertia of institutions, and of the social interests and values embedded in these institutions. Simply put, neither current political actors nor people at large want a world government, so it will not happen. But since global governance of some sort is a functional need, nation-states are finding ways to co-manage the global processes that affect most of the issues related to their governing practice. To do so, they increasingly share sovereignty while still proudly branding their flags. They form networks of nation-states, the most integrated and significant of which is the European Union. But they are around the world a number of state associations more or less integrated in their institutions and their practice that structure specific processed of transnational governance. In addition, nation-states have spurred a number of formal and informal international and supranational institutions that actually govern the world. Not only the United Nations, and verious military alliances, but also the International Monetary Fund and its ancillary agency, the World Bank, the G-8 club of leading countries in the world (with the permission of China), and a number of ad hoc groupings.

Furthermore, to connect the global and the local, nation-states have asserted or fostered a process of decentralization that reaches out to regional and local governments, and even to NGOs, often associated to political management. Thus, the actual system of governance in our world is not centered around the nation-state, although nation-states are not disappearing by any means. Governance is operated in a network of political institutions that shares sovereignty in various degrees an reconfigurates itself in a variable geopolitical geometry. This is what I have conceptualized as **the network state**. It is not the result of technological change, but the response to the structural contradiction between a global system and a national state. However, globalization is the form that takes the diffusion of the network society in its planetary reach, and new communication and transportation technologies provide the necessary infrastructure for the process of globalization. New communication technologies also help the actual operation of a complex network state, but this is a tool of performance rather than a determining factor. The transition from the nation-state to the network state is an organizational and political process prompted by the transformation of political management, representation and domination in the conditions of the network society.

Castells, Manuel (2006) "The Network Society: From Knowledge to Policy" in Manuel Castells and Gustavo Cardoso (eds) *The Network Society: From Knowledge to Policy*, Washington DC: Johns Hopkins Center for Transatlantic Relations, pp. 3–5, 7, 15–16.

GLOBAL SHIFT: PETER DICKEN (1992)

The British geographer Peter Dicken (1938–) is Emeritus Professor of Geography at University of Manchester. First published in 1986, his work *Global Shift*, from which the selection is taken, has been influential within social thought for its distinctly globalist perspective. Dicken here is interested in how certain conceptualizations of the world no longer predominate in the current globalized landscape. To this end, he investigates the emergence of transnational corporations and other globalizing trends beginning in the twentieth century.

A New Geo-economy

It is important to distinguish between processes of *internationalization* and processes of *globalization:*

- *Internationalization processes* involve the simple extension of economic activities across national boundaries. It is, essentially, a *quantitative* process which leads to a more extensive geographical pattern of economic activity.
- *Globalization processes* are *qualitatively* different from internationalization processes. They involve not merely the geographical extension of economic activity across national boundaries but also – and more importantly – the *functional integration* of such internationally dispersed activities.

Both processes – internationalization and globalization – coexist. In some cases, what we are seeing is no more than the continuation of long-established international dispersion of activities. In others, however, we are undoubtedly seeing an increasing dispersion and integration of activities across national boundaries. The pervasive internationalization, and growing globalization, of economic life ensure that changes originating in one part of the world are rapidly diffused to others. We live in a world of increasing complexity, inter-connectedness and volatility; a world in which the lives and livelihoods of every one of us are bound up with processes operating at a global scale.

However, although we are often led to believe that the world is becoming increasingly homogenized economically (and perhaps even culturally) with the use of such labels as 'global village', 'global market-place' or 'global factory', we need to treat such all-embracing claims with some caution. The 'globalization' tag is too often applied very loosely and indiscriminately to imply a totally pervasive set of forces and changes with uniform effects on countries, regions and localities. There are, indeed, powerful forces of global-ization at work . . . – but we need to adopt a sensitive and discriminating approach to get beneath the hype and to lay bare the reality. Change does not occur everywhere in the same way and at the same rate; the processes of globalization are not geographically uniform. The particular character of individual countries, of regions and of localities interacts with the larger-scale general processes of change to produce quite specific out-comes. Reality is far more complex and messy than many of the grander themes and explanations tend to suggest. [. . .]

'The end of geography'; 'the death of distance'. These two phrases resonate, either explicitly or implicitly, throughout much of the globalization literature. According to this view, dramatic developments in the tech-nologies of transport and communication have made capital – and the firms controlling it – 'hyper-mobile', freed from the 'tyranny of distance' and no longer tied to 'place'. In other words, it implies that economic activity is becoming 'deterritorialized'. The sociologist Manuel Castells argues that the forces of globalization, especially those driven by the new information technologies, are replacing this 'space of places' with a 'space of flows'.[1] Anything can be located anywhere and, if that does not work out, can be moved somewhere else with ease. Seductive as such ideas might be, a moment's thought will show just how misleading they are. Although transport and communications technologies have indeed been revolutionized both geographical distance and, especially, *place* remain fundamental. Every component in the production chain, every firm, every economic activity is, quite literally, 'grounded' in specific locations. Such grounding is both physical, in the form of sunk costs,[2] and less tangible in the form of localized social relationships.

The geo-economy, therefore, can be pictured as a geographically uneven, highly complex and dynamic web of production chains, economic spaces and places connected together through threads of flows. But the spatial *scale* at which these processes operate is, itself, variable. So, too, is the meaning which different scales have for different actors within the global economic system. The tendency is to collapse the scale dimension to just two: the global and the local and much has been written about the *global – local tension* at the interface between the two. Firms, states, local communities, it is argued, are each faced with the problem of resolving that tension.

There is no doubt that this is a real problem. However, it is not always the case that the terms 'global' and, especially, 'local', mean the same thing in different contexts. In the international business literature, for example, the term 'local' generally refers to the national, or even the larger regional, scale (i.e. at the level of Europe, Asia, North America). But for most people, 'local' refers to a very much smaller spatial scale: that of the local community in which they live. However, it is a mistake to focus only on the two extremes of the scale – the global and the local – at which economic activities occur. It is more realistic to think in terms of inter-related scales of activity and of analysis: for example, the local, the national, the regional (i.e. supranational) and the global. These have meaning both as activity spaces in which economic and political actors operate and also as analytical categories which more accurately capture some of the complexity of the real world.

However, we need to bear in mind that the scales are not independent entities. Figure 4.1 captures the major dimensions of these relationships. Individual industries (production/commodity chains) can be regarded as vertically organized structures which operate across increasingly extensive geographical scales. Cutting across these vertical structures are the territorially defined political-economic systems which, again, are manifested at different geographical scales. It is at the points of intersection of these dimensions in 'real' geographical space where specific outcomes occur, where the problems of existing within a globalizing economy – whether as a business firm, a government, a local community or as an individual – have to be resolved.

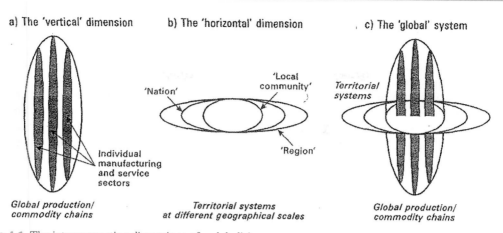

a) The 'vertical' dimension   b) The 'horizontal' dimension   c) The 'global' system

Individual manufacturing and service sectors

'Nation'   'Local community'   'Region'

Territorial systems

Global production/ commodity chains

Territorial systems at different geographical scales

Global production/ commodity chains

Figure 4.1 The interconnecting dimensions of a globalizing economy.
Source: Based, in part, on Humbert (1994, Figure 1)

Notes

1 Castells's arguments were developed initially in his book *The Informational City* (1989) and have been elaborated more recently in *The Rise of the Network Society. Volume 1* (1996).
2 Clark (1994), Clark and Wrigley (1995), Schoenberger (1997) explore the nature and significance of sunk costs in corporate decision-making and corporate restructuring in specifically spatial contexts.

Peter Dicken (1992) *Global Shift: the Internationalization of Economic Activity*, 2nd edn, London: Paul Chapman, pp. 5–6, 10–13.

COSMOPOLITANS AND WORLD CULTURE: ULF HANNERZ (1996)

Ulf Hannerz (1942–) is Professor of Anthropology at Stockholm University. He is best known for his multidisciplinary research on cultural circulation and globalization that brings together anthropological, socio-logical, and historical perspectives. Hannerz is credited with pioneering study on a number of new terms within social debates surrounding globalization – most notably "creolization." He is also known for his work on cosmopolitans, which the selection reveals. This is where Hannerz defines the qualities of a global cosmopolitan ethos.

Transnational Connections between Cosmopolitans and Locals

There is now a world culture, but we had better make sure we understand what this means: not a replication of uniformity but an organization of diversity, an increasing interconnectedness of varied local cultures, as well as a development of cultures without a clear anchorage in any one territory. And to this inter-connected diversity people can relate in different ways. For one thing, there are cosmopolitans, and there are locals.[1] [. . .]

The transnational and the territorial cultures of the world are entangled with one another in manifold ways. Some transnational cultures are more insulated from local practices than others; that of diplomacy as compared with that of commerce, for example. The transnational cultures are also as wholes usually more marked by some territorial culture than by others. Most of them are in different ways extensions or transform-ations of the cultures of western Europe and North America. If even the transnational cultures have to have physical centers somewhere, places in which, or from where, their particular meanings are produced and disseminated with particular intensity, or places to which people travel in order to interact in their terms, this is where such centers tend to be located. But even away from these centers, the institutions of the transnational cultures tend to be organized so as to make people from western Europe and North America feel as much at home as possible (by using their languages, for one thing). In both ways, the organization of world culture through center-periphery relationships is made evident. [. . .]

The real significance of the growth of transnational cultures, however, is often not the new cultural experi-ence that they themselves can offer people – for it is frequently rather restricted in scope – but their mediating possibilities. The transnational cultures are bridgeheads for entry into other territorial cultures. Instead of remaining within them, one can use the mobility connected with them to make contact with the meanings of other rounds of life, and gradually incorporate this experience into one's personal perspective.

Cosmopolitanism and cultures of critical discourse

The readiness to seize such opportunities and cosmopolitanize is no doubt often a very personal character trait. On the other hand, different transnational cultures may also relate in different ways to these opportunities. Here and there, and probably especially where the occupational practices themselves are not well insulated from the cultures of varied local settings, the development of competences in alien cultures has appeared too important to be left to chance and to personal whim; in the last few decades, we have seen the rapid growth of a culture shock prevention industry. Cross-cultural training programs have been developed to inculcate sensitiv-ity, basic *savoir-faire*, and perhaps an appreciation of those other cultures which are of special strategic importance to one's goals (from the occidental point of view, particularly those of Japan and the oil-rich Arab world). There is also a burgeoning do-it-yourself literature in this field.[2] Skeptics, of course, may dismiss these programs and this literature as a "quick cosmopolitan fix." They would be inclined to doubt that course-work for a couple of days or weeks, or a characteristically unsubtle handbook genre, can substitute for the personal journey of discovery. And they may be committed to the notion that cosmopolitans, as such, should be self-made.

Some transnational cultures, on the other hand, may have a kind of built-in relationship to that type of openness and striving toward mastery that I have referred to above. George Konrad, in the statement which I have already quoted, proposes that intellectuals have a particular predilection toward making themselves at home in other cultures. This is evidently more true in some instances than others; the French academia in its New York exile, we have seen, tended to keep to itself. Nonetheless, it may be worth considering the possibility that there is some kind of affinity between cosmopolitanism and the culture of intellectuals.

When locals were influential, Robert Merton (1957: 400) found in his classic study, their influence rested not so much on what they knew as on whom they knew. Cosmopolitans, in contrast, based whatever influence they had on a knowledge less tied to particular others, or to the unique community setting. They came equipped with special knowledge, and they could leave and take it with them without devaluing it.

Not surprisingly, there has been more attention given to such people recently.[3] They are "the new class," people with credentials, decontextualized cultural capital. Within this broad social category some would distinguish, as Alvin Gouldner (1979) has done, between intelligentsia and intellectuals. This is hardly necessary for my purposes here; in any case, according to Gouldner, they share a "culture of critical discourse."

Certainly these are a type of people who now stand a particularly good chance of becoming involved with the transnational cultures. Their decontextualized knowledge can be quickly and shiftingly recontextualized in a series of different settings. (Which is not to say that the transnational cultures consist of nothing but such knowledge – they may well evolve their own particularisms as well, of the kind which are elsewhere the special resource of locals: biographical knowledge of individuals, anecdotal knowledge of events and even of the constellations of locales which form the settings of these cultures.) What they carry, however, is not just special knowledge, but also that overall orientation toward structures of meaning to which the notion of the "culture of critical discourse" refers. This orientation, according to Gouldner's (1979: 28 ff.) description, is reflexive, problematizing, concerned with metacommunication; I would also describe it as generally expansionist in its management of meaning. It pushes on and on in its analysis of the order of ideas, striving toward explicitness where common sense, as a contrasting mode of meaning management, might come to rest comfortably with the tacit, the ambiguous, and the contradictory.[4] In the end, it strives toward mastery.

Obviously it cannot be argued that such an orientation to structures of meaning is in any way likely to show a particularly close fit with those alien cultures in themselves which the cosmopolitan desires to explore. These are probably as full of contradictions, ambiguities, and tendencies toward inertia as any other local culture, including that in which the cosmopolitan himself originates. Yet as a mode of approach, it seems to include much of that openness and drive toward greater competence which I have suggested are also characteristic of cosmopolitanism. It is not a way of becoming a local, but rather of simulating local knowledge.

The special relationship between intellectuals and cosmopolitanism, if there is one, could also be described in another way, hardly unrelated to what I have just said. Intellectuals in the narrower sense are involved in a particular way with what we might see as the center-periphery relationships of culture itself. Kadushin (1974: 6), in his study of American intellectuals, has suggested that each culture has certain central "value concepts" which give meaning to experience and action, and that most members of society manipulate these concepts easily enough because they tend to be defined mostly in their concrete applications rather than through abstract formulations. Intellectuals, however, have the special task of finding the relationship between value concepts, and tracing the application of these concepts over time. Such concepts, Kadushin notes, are for example "rights of man," "justice," or freedom of speech."

In their inquiries, the intellectuals traffic between the core of culture and the peripheral, ephemeral facts of everyday life. If they are vocationally in the habit of doing so, they would appear to have an advantageous point of departure for explorations of other cultures as well, when the opportunity of cosmopolitanism presents itself. And this advantage is surely not lost when different cultures in fact turn out to have central value concepts in common; George Konrad's transnational intellectuals, forming alliances across frontiers, tend to get together precisely over such shared concerns.

This has mostly been a sketch of the cosmopolitan abroad. Much of the time, even cosmopolitans are actually at home. Yet what does that mean in their case?

Perhaps real cosmopolitans, after they have taken out membership in that category, are never quite at home again, in the way real locals can be. Home is taken-for-grantedness, but after their perspectives have been irreversibly affected by the experience of the alien and the distant, cosmopolitans may not view either the seasons of the year or the minor rituals of everyday life as absolutely natural, obvious, and necessary. There may be a feeling of detachment, perhaps irritation with those committed to the local common sense and unaware of its arbitrariness. Or perhaps the cosmopolitan makes "home" as well one of his several sources of personal meaning, not so different from the others which are further away; or he is pleased with his ability to both surrender to and master this one as well.

Or home is really home, but in a special way; a constant reminder of a precosmopolitan past, a privileged site of nostalgia. This is where once things seemed fairly simple and straightforward. Or it is again really home, a comfortable place of familiar faces, where one's competence is undisputed and where one does not have to prove it to either oneself or others, but where for much the same reasons there is some risk of boredom.

At home, for most cosmopolitans, most others are locals. This is true in the great majority of territorially based cultures. Conversely, for most of these locals, the cosmopolitan is someone a little unusual, one of us and yet not quite one of us. Someone to be respected for his experiences, possibly, but equally possibly not somebody to be trusted as a matter of course. Trust tends to be a matter of shared perspectives, of "I know, and I know that you know, and I know that you know that I know." And this formula for the social organization of meaning does not necessarily apply to the relationship between local and cosmopolitan.

Some cosmopolitans are more adept at making it apply again. "*Wenn jemand eine Reise tut, dann kann er 'was erzählen*," the saying goes, and there are those who make a specialty out of letting others know what they have come across in distant places. So the cosmopolitan can to some extent be channeled into the local; and precisely because these are on the whole separate spheres the cosmopolitan can become a broker, an entrepreneur who makes a profit. Yet there is a danger that such attempts to make the alien easily accessible only succeeds in trivializing it, and thereby betraying its nature and the character of the real first-hand encounter. So in a way the more purely cosmopolitan attitude may be to let separate things be separate.[5]

Despite all this, home is not necessarily a place where cosmopolitanism is in exile. It is natural that in the contemporary world many local settings are increasingly characterized by cultural diversity. Those of cosmopolitan inclinations may make selective use of their habitats to maintain their expansive orientation toward the wider world. Other cosmoplitans may be there, whether they in their turn are at home or abroad, and strangers of other than cosmopolitan orientations. Apart from the face-to-face encounters, there are the media – both those intended for local consumption, although they speak of what is distant, and those which are really part of other cultures, like foreign books and films. What McLuhan once described as the implosive power of the media may now make just about everybody a little more cosmopolitan. And one may in the end ask whether it is now even possible to become a cosmopolitan without going away at all.

Conclusion: the dependence of cosmopolitans on locals, and their shared interests

To repeat, there is now one world culture; all the variously distributed structures of meaning and expression are becoming interrelated, somehow, somewhere. And people like the cosmopolitans have a special part in bringing about a degree of coherence; if there were only locals, world culture would be no more than the sum of its separate parts.

As things are now, on the other hand, it is no longer so easy to conform to the ideal type of a local. Some people, like exiles or migrant workers, are indeed taken away from the territorial bases of their local culture, but may try to encapsulate themselves within some approximation of it. Yet it is a greater number who, even staying home, find their local cultures less pervasive, less to be taken for granted, less clearly bounded toward the outside. If, through a terminal process of global homogenization, that other kind of world culture were ever to come about, locals would become extinct; or, seen differently, through the involvement with the one existing culture, everyone would be the same kind of local, at the global level.

Here, however, today's cosmopolitans and locals have common interests in the survival of cultural diversity. For the latter, diversity itself, as a matter of personal access to varied cultures, may be of little intrinsic interest. It just so happens that it is the survival of diversity that allows all locals to stick to their respective cultures. For the cosmopolitans, in contrast, there is value in diversity as such, but they are not likely to get it, in anything like the present form, unless other people are allowed to carve out special niches for their cultures, and keep them. Which is to say that there can be no cosmopolitans without locals.

Notes

1   This chapter was first published in a volume (Featherstone 1990) which has been more widely available than most of the publications where some of the other chapters first appeared, and therefore I had at first planned not to include it here. It seems, however, that some readers who may have come across this article in isolation have somehow assumed that it stands for a comprehensive view toward globalization, which it certainly does not (or at least not the view which they may think they see in it); and for that reason it may be useful to place it in the context of the other chapters.

To take one example, Buell (1994: 291 ff.) uses it to contrast generalized theories which depict "the global" as a separate layer on top of prior local formations with another, "more sophisticated line of inquiry," where globalization is seen as at work within older social and cultural formations. In Buell's view, I, together with Anthony D. Smith, represent the former type. I would hope that the difference between my view and Smith's is made sufficiently clear in Chapter 7 of this book, also published in its first version well before Buell's book. I might note that Buell refers elsewhere to another book (King 1991), in which I have a contribution discussing creolization and related matters in terms similar to those in Chapter 6 (Hannerz 1991). This would suggest that he should be aware of at least one of my publications where I formulate quite a different view than that which he is so quick to ascribe to me. But I recognize that the literature is large, and that it may be difficult to keep track of everything. (Elsewhere in his book, Buell refers repeatedly to one Anthony Tambiah, which may suggest that he has some difficulty keeping his Appiahs and Tambiahs apart.)

2   See for example the volume *Do's and Taboos Around the World*, issued by the Parker Pen Company (Axtell 1985), which describes its goals in the foreword: "Ideally, this book will help each world traveler grow little invisible antennae that will sense incoming messages about cultural differences and nuances. An appreciation and understanding of these differences will prevent embarrassment, unhappiness, and failure. In fact, learning through travel about these cultural differences can be both challenging and fun."

3   Randall Collins' (1979: 60 ff.) contrast between "indigenous" and "formal" production of culture is a related conception.

4   On common sense, see for example Geertz (1975), and Bourdieu's (1977: 164 ff.) discussion of the "doxic mode."

5   The cosmopolitan, that is to say, would tend not to be an active agent of creolization (cf. Chapter 6).

Ulf Hannerz (1996) *Transnational Connections: Culture, People, Places*, London and New York: Routledge, pp. 102, 107–111.

THE GOLDEN STRAITJACKET: THOMAS FRIEDMAN (2000)

Thomas Friedman (1953–) is an acclaimed, Pulitzer Prize-winning American journalist and author. He is an op-ed contributor for *The New York Times* and is well known for his writings on foreign affairs. Since 1999, he has written three books that explicitly deal with globalization: *The Lexus and the Olive Tree*, *The World is Flat*, and *Hot, Flat and Crowded*. Because of Friedman's penchant for coining neologisms, his oeuvre has played an influential role in shaping popular globalization discourse. This is true of the selection below which is taken from *The Lexus and the Olive Tree*. Here, through his term "the golden straitjacket," he contends that even though globalization forces every country to cede some of their political sovereignty to the new global economy, it is nevertheless still advantageous to do so. This is because buying into the new global order makes countries more financially prosperous. All gain when all participate in the system. In turn, this also means that countries have less incentive to go to war because their own wealth is dependent on one another.

Globalization and the Golden Straitjacket

The Golden Straitjacket is the defining political-economic garment of this globalization era. The Cold War had the Mao suit, the Nehru jacket, the Russian fur. Globalization has only the Golden Straitjacket. If your country has not been fitted for one, it will be soon. [. . .]

To fit into the Golden Straitjacket a country must either adopt, or be seen as moving toward, the following golden rules: making the private sector the primary engine of its economic growth, maintaining a low rate of inflation and price stability, shrinking the size of its state bureaucracy, maintaining as close to a balanced budget as possible, if not a surplus, eliminating and lowering tariffs on imported goods, removing restrictions on foreign investment, getting rid of quotas and domestic monopolies, increasing exports, privatizing state-owned industries and utilities, deregulating capital markets, making its currency convertible, opening its industries, stock and bond markets to direct foreign ownership and investment, deregulating its economy to promote as much domestic competition as possible, eliminating government corruption, subsidies and kickbacks as much as possible, opening its banking and telecommunications systems to private ownership and competition and allowing its citizens to choose from an array of competing pension options and foreign-run pension and mutual funds. When you stitch all of these pieces together you have the Golden Straitjacket.

Unfortunately, this Golden Straitjacket is pretty much "one size fits all." So it pinches certain groups, squeezes others and keeps a society under pressure to constantly streamline its economic institutions and upgrade its performance. It leaves people behind quicker than ever if they shuck it off, and it helps them catch up quicker than ever if they wear it right. It is not always pretty or gentle or comfortable. But it's here and it's the only model on the rack this historical season.

As your country puts on the Golden Straitjacket, two things tend to happen: your economy grows and your politics shrinks. That is, on the economic front the Golden Straitjacket usually fosters more growth and higher average incomes – through more trade, foreign investment, privatization and more efficient use of resources under the pressure of global competition. But on the political front, the Golden Straitjacket narrows the political and economic policy choices of those in power to relatively tight parameters. That is why it is increasingly difficult these days to find any real differences between ruling and opposition parties in those countries that have put on the Golden Straitjacket. Once your country puts it on, its political choices get reduced to Pepsi or Coke – to slight nuances of taste, slight nuances of policy, slight alterations in design to account for local traditions, some loosening here or there, but never any major deviation from the core golden rules. Governments – be they led by Democrats or Republicans, Conservatives or Labourites, Gaullists or Socialists, Christian Democrats or Social Democrats – that deviate too far from the core rules will see their investors stampede away, interest rates rise and stock market valuations fall. The only way to get more room to maneuver in the Golden Straitjacket is by enlarging it, and the only way to enlarge it is by keeping it on tight. That's its one virtue: the tighter you wear it, the more gold it produces and the more padding you can then put into it for your society.

Thomas Friedman (2000) *The Lexus and the Olive Tree*, London: HarperCollins Publishers, pp. 104–6.

Anti-Globalists

GLOBALIZATION IN QUESTION: PAUL HIRST AND GRAHAME THOMPSON (1990)

Paul Hirst (1943–2003) was Professor of Social Theory at Birkbeck University. He is well known for his brand of Athusserian Marxism and his contributions to the field of critical legal theory. Later in his academic career, Hirst would shift his attention to the topic of globalization. Grahame Thompson is Professor of Political Economy at the Open University. His research is mainly focused on economic networks and international governance systems. Collectively, Hirst and Thompson are most well known for their seminal book, *Globalization in Question*, which is their skeptical critique of the globalized economy thesis. The selection, which is taken from this work, sets out some of their reasons for disbelieving that globalization is inevitably upon us. These reasons address and overturn the supposed historical novelty and empirical basis of the hyperglobalist theory.

Globalization a Necessary Myth?

Globalization has become a fashionable concept in the social sciences, a core dictum in the prescriptions of management gurus, and a catch-phrase for journalists and politicians of every stripe. It is widely asserted that we live in an era in which the greater part of social life is determined by global processes, in which national cultures, national economies and national borders are dissolving. Central to this perception is the notion of a rapid and recent process of economic globalization. A truly global economy is claimed to have emerged or to be in the process of emerging, in which distinct national economies and, therefore, domestic strategies of national economic management are increasingly irrelevant. The world economy has internationalized in its basic dynamics, it is dominated by uncontrollable market forces, and it has as its principal economic actors and major agents of change truly transnational corporations that owe allegiance to no nation-state and locate wherever on the globe market advantage dictates.

This image is so powerful that it has mesmerized analysts and captured political imaginations. But is it the case? This book is written with a mixture of scepticism about global economic processes and optimism about the possibilities of control of the international economy and about the viability of national political strategies. One key effect of the concept of globalization has been to paralyse radical reforming national strategies, to see them as unfeasible in the face of the judgement and sanction of international markets. If, however, we face economic changes that are more complex and more equivocal than the extreme globalists argue, then the possibility remains of political strategy and action for national and international control of market economies in order to promote social goals.

We began this investigation with an attitude of moderate scepticism. It was clear that much had changed since the 1960s, but we were cautious about the more extreme claims of the most enthusiastic globalization theorists. In particular it was obvious that radical expansionary and redistributive strategies of national economic management were no longer possible in the face of a variety of domestic and international constraints. However, the closer we looked the shallower and more unfounded became the claims of the more radical advocates of economic globalization. In particular we began to be disturbed by three facts. First, the absence of a commonly accepted model of the new global economy and how it differs from previous states of the international economy Second, in the absence of a clear model against which to measure trends, the tendency to casually cite examples of the internationalization of sectors and processes as if they were evidence of the growth of an economy dominated by autonomous global market forces. Third, the lack of historical depth, the tendency to portray current changes as unique and without precedent and firmly set to persist long into the future.

To anticipate, as we proceeded our scepticism deepened until we became convinced that globalization, as conceived by the more extreme globalizers, is largely a myth. Thus we argue that:

1 The present highly internationalized economy is not unprecedented: it is one of a number of distinct conjunctures or states of the international economy that have existed since an economy based on modern industrial technology began to be generalized from the 1860s. In some respects, the current international economy is *less* open and integrated than the regime that prevailed from 1870 to 1914.
2 Genuinely transnational companies appear to be relatively rare. Most companies are based nationally and trade multinationally on the strength of a major national location of assets, production and sales, and there seems to be no major tendency towards the growth of truly international companies.
3 Capital mobility is not producing a massive shift of investment and employment from the advanced to the developing countries. Rather foreign direct investment (FDI) is highly concentrated among the advanced industrial economies and the Third World remains marginal in both investment and trade, a small minority of newly industrializing countries apart.
4 As some of the extreme advocates of globalization recognize, the world economy is far from being genuinely 'global'. Rather trade, investment and financial flows are concentrated in the Triad of Europe, Japan and North America and this dominance seems set to continue.
5 These major economic powers, the G3, thus have the capacity, especially if they coordinate policy, to exert powerful governance pressures over financial markets and other economic tendencies. Global markets are thus by no means beyond regulation and control, even though the current scope and objectives of economic governance are limited by the divergent interests of the great powers and the economic doctrines prevalent among their elites.

[. . .] We are well aware that there is a wide variety of views that use the term 'globalization'. Even among those analysts who confine themselves to strictly economic processes some make far more radical claims about changes in the international economy than others. It might therefore be argued that we are focusing too narrowly in concentrating on delineating and challenging the most extreme version of the thesis of economic globalization. Indeed, in criticizing such positions we might be held to be demolishing a straw man. On the contrary, we see these extreme views as strong, relatively coherent and capable of being developed into a clear ideal-typical conception of a globalized economic system. Such views are also important in that they have become politically highly consequential. The most eloquent proponents of the extreme view are very influential and have tended to set the tone for discussion in business and political circles. Views that shape the perception of key decision-makers are important, and thus are a primary target rather than a marginal one. The advocates of 'globalization' have proposed the further liberalization of the international economy and the deregulation of domestic economies. This advocacy has had serious effects in Asia and in emerging financial markets, leading to economic crisis, unemployment and impoverishment. The view we attack may have been dented by the Asian crisis but it is not dead. It remains strong in the developed countries, where it has sustained the rhetoric of 'competitiveness' and the belief that the extensive welfare states of Northern and Western Europe are a constraint on economic performance that they can no longer afford in an internationalized economy. These myths still need puncturing before they do impossible damage to both social stability and economic performance.

Some less extreme and more nuanced analyses that employ the term globalization are well established in the academic community and concentrate on the relative internationalization of major financial markets, of technology and of certain important sectors of manufacturing and services, particularly since the 1970s. Emphasis is given in many of these analyses to the increasing constraints on national-level governance that prevent ambitious macroeconomic policies that diverge significantly from the norms acceptable to international financial markets. Indeed, we ourselves have over some time drawn attention to such phenomena in our own work.

Obviously, it is no part of our aim here to deny that such trends to increased internationalization have occurred or to ignore the constraints on certain types of national economic strategy. Our point in assessing the significance of the internationalization that has occurred is to argue that it is well short of dissolving distinct national economies in the major advanced industrial countries, or of preventing the development of new forms of economic governance at the national and international levels. There are, however, very real dangers in not distinguishing clearly between certain trends towards internationalization and the strong version of the globalization thesis. It is particularly unfortunate if the two become confused by using the same word, 'globalization', to describe both. Often we feel that evidence from more cautious arguments is then used carelessly to bolster more extreme ones, to build a community of usage when there needs to be strict differentiation of meanings. It also confuses public discussion and policy-making, reinforcing the view that political actors can accomplish less than is actually possible in a global system.

The strong version of the globalization thesis requires a new view of the international economy, as we shall shortly see, one that subsumes and subordinates national-level processes. Whereas tendencies towards internationalization can be accommodated within a modified view of the world economic system, that still gives a major role to national-level policies and economic actors. Undoubtedly this implies some greater or lesser degree of change; firms, governments and international agencies are being forced to behave differently, but in the main they can use existing institutions and practices to do so. In this way we feel it makes more sense to consider the international economic system in a longer historical perspective, to recognize that current changes, while significant and distinctive, are not unprecedented and do not necessarily involve a move towards a new type of economic system. The strong economic versions of the globalization thesis have the advantage that they clearly and sharply pose the possibility of such a change. If they are wrong they are still of some value in enabling us to think out what *is* happening and why. In this sense, challenging the strong version of the thesis is not merely negative but helps us to develop our own ideas.

However, the question remains to be considered of how the myth of the globalization of economic activity became established as and when it did. In answering, one must begin with the ending of the post-1945 era in the turbulence of 1972–3. A period of prolonged economic growth and full employment in the advanced countries, sustained by strategies of active national state intervention and a managed multilateral regime for trade and monetary policy under US hegemony, was brought to an end by a number of significant changes. Thus we can point to:

1 The effects of the collapse of the Bretton Woods system and the 1973 and 1979 OPEC oil crises (which massively increased oil prices) in producing turbulence and volatility in all the major economies through the 1970s into the early 1980s. Significant in generating such turbulence and undermining previous policy regimes was the rapid rise in inflation in the advanced countries brought about by domestic policy failures, the international impact of US involvement in the Vietnam War, and the oil price hikes of 1973 and 1979.

2 The efforts of financial institutions and manufacturers, in this period of turbulence and inflationary pressure, to compensate for domestic uncertainty by seeking wider outlets for investments and additional markets; hence the widespread bank lending to the Third World during the inflationary 1970s, the growth of the Eurodollar market, and the increasing ratios of foreign trade to GDP in the advanced countries.

3 The public policy acceleration of the internationalization of financial markets by the widespread abandonment of exchange controls and other market deregulation in the late 1970s and early 1980s, even as the

more extreme forms of volatility in currency markets were being brought under control by, for example, the development of the European Monetary System (EMS) in 1979 and the Louvre and Plaza accords in the 1980s.

4   The tendency towards 'deindustrialization' in Britain and the United States and the growth of long-term unemployment in Europe, promoting fears of foreign competition, especially from Japan.

5   The relatively rapid development of a number of newly industrializing countries (NICs) in the Third World and their penetration of First World markets.

6   The shift from standardized mass production to more flexible production methods, and the change from the perception of the large, nationally rooted, oligopolistic corporation as the unchallengeably dominant economic agent towards a more complex world of multinational enterprises, less rigidly structured firms and the increased salience of smaller firms – summed up in the widespread and popular concept of 'post-Fordism'.

These changes are undoubted and they were highly disturbing to those conditioned by the unprecedented success and security of the post-1945 period in the advanced industrial states. The perceived loss of national control, the increased uncertainty and unpredictability of economic relations, and rapid institutional change were a shock to minds conditioned to believe that poverty, unemployment and economic cycles could all be controlled or eliminated in a market economy based on the profit motive. If the widespread consensus of the 1950s and 1960s was that the future belonged to a capitalism without losers, securely managed by national governments acting in concert, then the later 1980s and 1990s have been dominated by a consensus based on contrary assumptions, that global markets are uncontrollable and that the only way to avoid becoming a loser – whether as nation, firm or individual – is to be as competitive as possible. The notion of an ungovernable world economy is a response to the collapse of expectations schooled by Keynesianism and sobered by the failure of monetarism to provide an alternative route to broad-based prosperity and stable growth. 'Globalization' is a myth suitable for a world without illusions, but it is also one that robs us of hope. Global markets are dominant, and they face no threat from any viable contrary political project, for it is held that Western social democracy and socialism of the Soviet bloc are both finished.

One can only call the political impact of 'globalization' the pathology of overdiminished expectations. Many overenthusiastic analysts and politicians have gone beyond the evidence in overstating the extent of the dominance of world markets and their ungovernability. If this is so, then we should seek to break the spell of this uncomforting myth. The old rationalist explanation for primitive myths was that they were a way of masking and compensating for humanity's helplessness in the face of the power of nature. In this case we have a myth that exaggerates the degree of our helplessness in the face of contemporary economic forces. If economic relations are more governable (at both the national and international levels) than many contemporary analysts suppose, then we should explore the possible scale and scope of that governance. It is not currently the case that radical goals are attainable: full employment in the advanced countries, a fair deal for the poorer developing countries and widespread democratic control over economic affairs for the world's people. But this should not lead us to dismiss or ignore the forms of control and social improvement that could be achieved relatively rapidly with a modest change in attitudes on the part of key elites. It is thus essential to persuade reformers of the left and conservatives who care for the fabric of their societies that we are not helpless before uncontrollable global processes. If this happens, then changing attitudes and expectations might make these more radical goals acceptable.

Paul Hirst and Grahame Thompson (1990) *Globalization in Question*, Cambridge: Polity Press, pp. 1–7.

RECLAIMING THE COMMONS: NAOMI KLEIN (2004)

Naomi Klein (1970–) is a Canadian journalist and political activist most recognized for her writings on economic globalization and corporate consumer culture. She is author of *No Logo, Fences and Windows*, and, most recently, *The Shock Doctrine*. Since bursting onto the political scene in 1999, Klein has been particularly influential among what has been popularly termed the "anti-globalization movement." A common theme that runs throughout her work is the censuring of multinational corporations for their role in exacerbating global poverties. The selection is taken from a speech Klein gave at UCLA in 2001 on the state of globalization at the time. According to her, the only way to effectively fight back against the cold profit-seeking logics of corporate globalization is if social justice movements are formed across national boundaries. This is because the exploitation of human welfare for profits is also conducted at the level of the transnational. As such, social justice is something that must be fought for globally. It is not enough today to secure rights in one country if the same does not also apply elsewhere.

What is the Anti-Globalization Movement?

What is 'the anti-globalization movement'?[1] I put the phrase in quotemarks because I immediately have two doubts about it. Is it really a movement? If it is a movement, is it anti-globalization? Let me start with the first issue. We can easily convince ourselves it is a movement by talking it into existence at a forum like this – I spend far too much time at them – acting as if we can see it, hold it in our hands. Of course, we have seen it – and we know it's come back in Quebec, and on the US–Mexican border during the Summit of the Americas and the discussion for a hemispheric Free Trade Area. But then we leave rooms like this, go home, watch some TV, do a little shopping and any sense that it exists disappears, and we feel like maybe we're going nuts. Seattle – was that a movement or a collective hallucination? To most of us here, Seattle meant a kind of coming-out party for a global resistance movement, or the 'globalization of hope', as someone described it during the World Social Forum at Porto Alegre. But to everyone else Seattle still means limitless frothy coffee, Asian-fusion cuisine, e-commerce billionaires and sappy Meg Ryan movies. Or perhaps it is both, and one Seattle bred the other Seattle – and now they awkwardly coexist.

This movement we sometimes conjure into being goes by many names: anti-corporate, anti-capitalist, anti-free-trade, anti-imperialist. Many say that it started in Seattle. Others maintain it began five hundred years ago – when colonialists first told indigenous peoples that they were going to have to do things differently if they were to 'develop' or be eligible for 'trade'. Others again say it began on 1 January 1994 when the Zapatistas launched their uprising with the words Ya Basta! on the night NAFTA became law in Mexico. It all depends on whom you ask. But I think it is more accurate to picture a movement of many movements – coalitions of coalitions. Thousands of groups today are all working against forces whose common thread is what might broadly be described as the privatization of every aspect of life, and the transformation of every activity and value into a commodity. We often speak of the privatization of education, of healthcare, of natural resources. But the process is much vaster. It includes the way powerful ideas are turned into advertising slogans and public streets into shopping malls; new generations being target-marketed at birth; schools being invaded by ads; basic human necessities like water being sold as commodities; basic labour rights being rolled back; genes are patented and designer babies loom; seeds are genetically altered and bought; politicians are bought and altered.

At the same time there are oppositional threads, taking form in many different campaigns and movements. The spirit they share is a radical reclaiming of the commons. As our communal spaces – town squares, streets, schools, farms, plants – are displaced by the ballooning marketplace, a spirit of resistance is taking hold around the world. People are reclaiming bits of nature and of culture, and saying 'this is going to be public space'. American students are kicking ads out of the classrooms. European environmentalists and ravers are throwing parties at busy intersections. Landless Thai peasants are planting organic vegetables on over-irrigated golf courses. Bolivian workers are reversing the privatization of their water supply. [. . .]

In short, activists aren't waiting for the revolution, they are acting right now, where they live, where they study, where they work, where they farm.

But some formal proposals are also emerging whose aim is to turn such radical reclamations of the commons into law. When NAFTA and the like were cooked up, there was much talk of adding on 'side agreements' to the free-trade agenda, that were supposed to encompass the environment, labour and human rights. Now the fight-back is about taking them out. José Bové – along with the Via Campesina, a global association of small farmers – has launched a campaign to remove food safety and agricultural products from all trade agreements, under the slogan 'The World is Not for Sale'. [. . .]

What this means is that the discourse has shifted. During the battles against NAFTA, there emerged the first signs of a coalition between organized labour, environmentalists, farmers and consumer groups within the countries concerned. In Canada, most of us felt we were fighting to keep something distinctive about our nation from 'Americanization'. In the United States, the talk was very protectionist: workers were worried that Mexicans would 'steal' away 'our' jobs and drive down 'our' environmental standards. All the while, the voices of Mexicans opposed to the deal were virtually off the public radar – yet these were the strongest voices of all. But only a few years later, the debate over trade has been transformed. The fight against globalization has morphed into a struggle against corporatization and, for some, against capitalism itself. It has also become a fight for democracy. Maude Barlow spearheaded the campaign against NAFTA in Canada twelve years ago. Since NAFTA became law, she's been working with organizers and activists from other countries, and anarchists suspicious of the state in her own country. She was once seen as very much the face of a Canadian nationalism. Today, she has moved away from that discourse. 'I've changed', she says, 'I used to see this fight as saving a nation. Now I see it as saving democracy.' This is a cause that transcends nationality and state borders. The real news out of Seattle is that organizers around the world are beginning to see their local and national struggles – for better funded public schools, against union-busting and casualization, for family farms, and against the widening gap between rich and poor – through a global lens. That is the most significant shift we have seen in years.

How did this happen? Who or what convened this new international people's movement? Who sent out the memos? Who built these complex coalitions? It is tempting to pretend that someone did dream up a master plan for mobilization at Seattle. But I think it was much more a matter of large-scale coincidence. A lot of smaller groups organized to get themselves there and then found to their surprise just how broad and diverse a coalition they had become part of. Still, if there is one force we can thank for bringing this front into being, it is the multinational corporations. As one of the organizers of Reclaim the Streets has remarked, we should be grateful to the CEOs for helping us see the problems more quickly. Thanks to the sheer imperialist ambition of the corporate project at this moment in history – the boundless drive for profit, liberated by trade deregulation, and the wave of mergers and buy-outs, liberated by weakened anti-trust laws – multinationals have grown so blindingly rich, so vast in their holdings, so global in their reach, that they have created our coalitions for us. [. . .]

By focusing on corporations, organizers can demonstrate graphically how so many issues of social, ecological and economic justice are inter-connected. No activist I've met believes that the world economy can be changed one corporation at a time, but the campaigns have opened a door into the arcane world of international trade and finance. Where they are leading is to the central institutions that write the rules of global commerce: the WTO, the IMF, the FTAA, and for some the market itself. Here too the unifying threat is privatization – the loss of the commons. [. . .]

The biggest challenge facing us is to distil all of this into a message that is widely accessible. Many campaigners understand the connexions binding together the various issues almost intuitively – much as Subcomandante Marcos says, 'Zapatismo isn't an ideology, it's an intuition.' But to outsiders, the mere scope of modern protests can be a bit mystifying. If you eavesdrop on the movement from the outside, which is what most people do, you are liable to hear what seems to be a cacophony of disjointed slogans, a jumbled laundry list of disparate grievances without clear goals. [. . .]

This kind of impression is reinforced by the decentralized, non-hierarchical structure of the movement, which always disconcerts the traditional media. Well-organized press conferences are rare, there is no charismatic leadership, protests tend to pile on top of each other. Rather than forming a pyramid, as most movements do, with leaders up on top and followers down below, it looks more like an elaborate web. In part, this web-like structure is the result of internet-based organizing. But it is also a response to the very political realities that sparked the protests in the first place: the utter failure of traditional party politics. All over the world, citizens have worked to elect social-democratic and workers' parties, only to watch them plead impotence in the face of market forces and IMF dictates. In these conditions, modern activists are not so naïve as to believe change will come from electoral politics. That's why they are more interested in challenging the structures that make democracy toothless, like the IMF's structural adjustment policies, the WTO's ability to override national sovereignty, corrupt campaign financing, and so on. This is not just making a virtue of necessity. It responds at the ideological level to an understanding that globalization is in essence a crisis in representative democracy. What has caused this crisis? One of the basic reasons for it is the way power and decision-making have been handed along to points ever further away from citizens: from local to provincial, from provincial to national, from national to international institutions, that lack all transparency or accountability. What is the solution? To articulate an alternative, participatory democracy. [. . .]

So the question we are asking today, in the run-up to the FTAA, is not: are you for or against trade? The question is: do we have the right to negotiate the terms of our relationship to foreign capital and investment? Can we decide how we want to protect ourselves from the dangers inherent in deregulated markets – or do we have to contract out those decisions?

Note

1   This is a transcript of a talk given at the Center for Social Theory and Comparative History, UCLA, in April 2001. It has been abridged as marked by the editor. "Reclaiming the Commons" by Naomi Klein, copyright © 2001 by Naomi Klein.

Naomi Klein (2004) "Reclaiming the Commons," in Tom Mertes (ed.) *A Movement of Movements*, London: Verso, pp. 219–226.

THE CHALLENGE OF GLOBAL CAPITALISM: ROBERT GILPIN (2000)

Robert Gilpin (1930–) is Emeritus Dwight D. Eisenhower Professor of Public and International Affairs at Princeton University. His most recent work has focused on the political dimension of contemporary globalization and is informed by the "realist" position. Gilpin's thinking about globalization, which is found in his two works *The Challenge of Global Capitalism* and *Global Political Economy*, typically stresses the tenuous and intensely political nature of the current global financial system – a point revealed in the selection. For Gilpin, economic globalization is largely determined by (self-interested) political actors, contrary to the prevalent view which posits an inverse relationship.

The New Global Economic Order

Since the end of the Cold War, globalization has been the most outstanding characteristic of international economic affairs and, to a considerable extent, of political affairs as well. Yet, as I shall argue throughout this book, although globalization had become the defining feature of the international economy at the beginning of the twenty-first century, the extent and significance of economic globalization have been greatly exaggerated and misunderstood in both public and professional discussions; globalization in fact is not nearly as extensive nor as sweeping in its consequences (negative or positive) as many contemporary observers believe. This is still a world where national policies and domestic economies are the principal determinants of economic affairs. Globalization and increasing economic interdependence among national economies are indeed very important; yet, as Vincent Cable of the Royal Institute of International Affairs has pointed out, the major economic achievement of the post-World War II era has been to restore the level of international economic integration that existed prior to World War I.[1] [. . .]

Economic globalization has entailed a few key developments in trade, finance, and foreign direct investment by multinational corporations.[2] International trade has grown more rapidly than the global economic output. In addition to the great expansion of merchandise trade (goods), trade in services (banking, information, etc.) has also significantly increased. With the decreasing cost of transportation, more and more goods are becoming "tradeables." With the immense expansion of world trade, international competition has greatly increased. Although consumers and export sectors within individual nations benefit from increased openness, many businesses find themselves competing against foreign firms that have improved their efficiency. During the 1980s and 1990s, trade competition became even more intense as a growing number of industrializing economies in East Asia and elsewhere shifted from an import substitution to an export-led growth strategy. Nevertheless, the major competitors for almost all American firms remain other American firms. [. . .]

Since the mid-1970s, financial deregulation and the creation of new financial instruments, such as derivatives, and technological advances in communications have contributed to a much more highly integrated international financial system. The volume of foreign exchange trading (buying and selling national currencies) in the late 1990s reached approximately $1.5 trillion per day, an eightfold increase since 1986; by contrast, the global volume of exports (goods and services) for all of 1997 was $6.6 trillion, or $25 billion per day! In addition, the amount of investment capital seeking higher returns has grown enormously; by the mid-1990s, mutual funds, pension funds and the like totaled $20 trillion, ten times the 1980 figure. Moreover, the significance of these huge investments is greatly magnified by the fact that a large portion of foreign investments is leveraged; that is, they are investments made with borrowed funds. Finally, derivatives or repackaged securities and other financial assets play an important role in international finance. Valued at $360 trillion (larger than the value of the entire global economy), they have contributed to the complexity and the instability of international finance. It is obvious that international finance has a profound impact on the global economy.

This financial revolution has linked national economies much more closely to one another and increased the capital available for developing countries. As many of these financial flows are short-term, highly volatile, and speculative, international finance has become the most unstable aspect of the global capitalist economy. The immense scale, velocity, and speculative nature of financial movements across national borders have made governments more vulnerable to sudden shifts in these movements. Governments can therefore easily fall prey to currency speculators, as happened in the 1992 European financial crisis, which caused Great Britain to withdraw from the European Exchange Rate Mechanism, and in the 1994–95 punishing collapse of the Mexican peso, as well as in the devastating East Asian financial crisis in the late 1990s. Whereas, for some, financial globalization exemplifies the healthy and beneficial triumph of global capitalism, for others the international financial system is "out of control" and must be better regulated. Either way, international finance is the one area to which the term "globalization" is most appropriately applied.

The term "globalization" came into popular usage in the second half of the 1980s in connection with the huge surge of foreign direct investment (FDI) by multinational corporations. MNCs and FDI have been around for several centuries in the form of the East India Company and other "merchant adventurers." In the early postwar decades, most FDI was made by American firms, and the United States was host to only a small amount of FDI from non-American firms. Then, in the 1980s, FDI expanded significantly and much more rapidly than world trade and global economic output. In the early postwar decades, Japanese, West European, and other nationalities became major investors and the United States became both the world's largest home and host economy. As a consequence of these developments, FDI outflows from the major industrialized countries to the industrializing countries rose to approximately 15 percent annually. The largest fraction of FDI, however, goes to the industrialized countries, especially the United States and those in Western Europe. The cumulative value of FDI amounts to hundreds of billions of dollars. The greatest portion of this investment has been in services and especially in high-tech industries such as automobiles and information technology. Information, in fact, has itself become a "tradeable," and this raises such new issues in international commerce as the protection of intellectual property rights and market access for service industries. In combination with increased trade and financial flows, the increasing importance of MNCs has significantly transformed the international economy. [. . .]

Although most economists and many others welcome this development, critics emphasize the "high costs" of economic globalization, including growing income inequality both among and within nations, high chronic levels of unemployment in Western Europe and elsewhere, and, most of all, environmental degradation, widespread exploitation, and the devastating consequences for national economies wrought by unregulated international financial flows. These critics charge that national societies are being integrated into a global economic system and are buffeted by economic and technological forces over which they have little or no control. They view global economic problems as proof that the costs of globalization are much greater than its benefits. Foreseeing a world characterized by intense economic conflict at both the domestic and international levels, and believing that an open world economy will inevitably produce more losers than winners, critics argue that unleashing market and other economic forces has caused an intense struggle among individual nations, economic classes, and powerful groups. Many assert that what former German chancellor Helmut Schmidt called "the struggle for the world product" could result in competing regional blocs dominated by one or another of the major economic powers.

The idea that globalization is responsible for most of the world's economic, political, and other problems is either patently false or greatly exaggerated. In fact, other factors such as technological developments and imprudent national policies are much more important than globalization as causes of many, if not most, of the problems for which globalization is held responsible. Unfortunately, misunderstandings regarding globalization and its effects have contributed to growing disillusionment with borders open to trade and investment and have led to the belief that globalization has had a very negative impact on workers, the environment, and less developed countries. According to an American poll taken in April 1999, 52 percent of the respondents had negative views regarding globalization.[3] Yet, even though globalization is an important feature of the international economy that has changed many aspects of the subject of international political economy, the fact is that globalization is not as pervasive, extensive, or significant as many would have us believe. Most national economies are still mainly self-contained rather than globalized; globalization is also restricted to a limited, albeit rapidly increasing, number of economic sectors. Moreover, globalization is largely restricted to the triad of industrialized countries – the United States, Western Europe, and, to a much lesser extent, Japan – and to the emerging markets of East Asia. Most importantly, many of the attacks on globalization by its critics are misplaced; many, if not most, of its "evils" are really due to changes that have little or nothing to do with globalization.

Notes

1 Vincent Cable, "The Diminished Nation-State: A Study in the Loss of Economic Power," in *What Future for the State?*, *Daedalus* 124, no. 2 (spring 1995): 24.

2 For a strong attack on globalization and its alleged evils, see Richard Falk, *Predatory Globalization* (Oxford: Polity Press, 1999).

3 Andrew Kohut, "Globalization and the Wage Gap," *New York Times*, 3 December 1999, sec. 1, reporting on a Pew Research Center's national survey in April 1999, which found that 52 percent of all respondents were negative toward globalization. Low-income families were much more negative than wealthier ones.

Robert Gilpin (2000) *The Challenge of Global Capitalism: The World Economy in the Twenty-First Century*, Princeton NJ: Princeton University Press, pp. 3, 5–10.

GLOBALIZATION AND INTERNATIONAL INTERDEPENDENCE: R.J. BARRY JONES (1995)

R.J. Barry Jones is Emeritus Professor of International Relations at the University of Reading. His recent research is focused on the extent to which globalization transforms the existing international relations paradigm. His work, *Globalization and Interdependence in the International Political Economy*, investigates the definitional controversies of globalization. Against those who believe that globalization is an inevitable process that involves greater interconnectedness and interdependence among states, Jones claims that it is better to take a more voluntaristic perspective. This is because the view that globalization is an inexorable phenomenon is itself a constructed maneuver – one which is driven by those who benefit most from perpetuating such an idea into a self-fulfilling prophecy.

The Role of Politics in the Global Economy

Reflection upon the future of international interdependence and globalisation is a complex matter. The definitional nature, empirical character and ultimate significance of interdependence and globalisation are all matters of considerable controversy and potential confusion. These difficulties should not, however, detract from the central significance of the issues raised and the conditions suggested by notions of interdependence and globalisation.

The future of international interdependence, or globalisation, is partly a matter of the definitions applied to these terms. It is entirely possible that the interconnectedness of separate states could increase without any corresponding increase in real dependencies, interdependencies, or qualitative globalisation. Dependencies and interdependencies could, in their turn, intensify in the absence of any general increase in interconnectedness or globalisation. Central, here, is the distinction between sensitivity and vulnerability in relationships of dependence or interdependence and, within the realm of sensitivity, the distinction between 'objective' sensitivity (with its close connection to interconnectedness) and the more complex phenomenon of 'subjective' sensitivity. The definitional distinctions between interconnectedness and interdependence must, therefore, be maintained, as must the controversial, qualitative implications of many usages of the term globalisation.

Definitional issues aside, the empirical world is likely to exhibit complex patterns of association amongst developments in patterns of interconnectedness, interdependence and globalisation. These associations do not mean, however, that such developments are always closely correlated, or regular and irreversible. Considerable unevenness has been exhibited by all patterns of international economic association in the past and substantial reversals have occurred at times of major political and economic disturbances. Many interconnections have been broken by political decisions and developments. State policies have often been directed towards the modification, elimination or even reversal of existing external dependencies. Impersonal forces sometimes mould the longer-term development of patterns of interconnectedness and interdependence, but usually only within a framework of 'suitable' policies and institutions. [. . .]

The tension between globalisation and regionalisation highlights the wider issue of deterministic versus voluntaristic perspectives upon human affairs. Much of the discussion of interdependence, complex interdependence and globalisation carried, whether intentionally or not, a sense of the inevitable consequences of irresistible, and often impersonal, forces. Globalisation thus suggests the remorseless advance of interests and pressures that will progressively undermine 'national' frontiers, the autonomy of states and the distinctiveness of different cultures. The hint of determinism, whether contextual or inherent, in such a vision is both unacceptable to a number of students of the human condition and a highly selective interpretation of highly complex processes.

First-order accounts of central developments within the international political economy often serve to reinforce interpretations in terms of the automatic consequences of prevailing conditions. A second-order analysis, however, opens up questions about the origins of apparently decisive conditions and influences. It is at this stage that the central significance of 'political' factors can often be identified. Militarily and politically dominant states can be seen to set the 'rules of the game' for the international system, globally or regionally. While theories of hegemonical influence may suffer from both ambiguities and controversies,[1] few dispute the central influence over the international political economy exerted by Great Britain in the late nineteenth century and the United States of America since the Second World War.

Carefully constructed bargains amongst political authorities can, as in the case of the European Community, establish a significantly 'new' reality within which other actors subsequently have to operate. Such politically constructed frameworks for economic activity establish new, distinctive sets of opportunities and constraints for all actors. Indeed, even the political actors that have exercised a dominant influence on the establishment of the new framework may find their subsequent room for manoeuvre constrained by the fruits of their own efforts.

The relative strengths of globalising and regionalising forces in the international political economy will thus reflect, in large part, the decisions of those charged with policy-making responsibilities within the most influential states and the forces that bear upon those decisions. Indeed, one of the fundamental features of the international political economy is the central role of 'self-fulfilling prophecy'. If advocates of further integration within Europe do so because of their perceptions of regionalising tendencies within the wider international political economy, then the resulting intensification of defensive European integration could provide a major stimulus to the regionalisation that was initially feared. Equally, political leaders who become convinced of the inevitability of greater globalisation in economic matters, may well mould national policies in the direction of greater openness, thereby encouraging actions by economic actors, such as Transnational Corporations and financial institutions, that reinforce tendencies towards globalisation.

Economic frictions can, however, be generated both by movement towards greater interdependence and globalisation and thereby stimulate divisive political reactions. In the extreme, conflicts can then emerge which alter the established patterns of interdependence and international association: severing some whilst stimulating other, and often new, dependencies. Such adverse reactions to rising international interdependence can add their weight to persisting political and ideological sources of international hostilities.

'Politics' thus plays a central role in the shaping of the future of the international political economy. It is at this stage, however, that the third-order level of analysis must be addressed, for it is possible that the 'political' actions of leading states will, themselves, be moulded by impersonal forces and/or the influence of other dominant interests. Traditional Marxism highlighted the role of the economic infrastructure as an impersonal force; an interpretation that continues to find diluted echoes in the World System of Capitalism and Dependency perspectives upon the international political economy. Modern Gramscian 'Marxists' adopt a more hybrid approach, that accords leading economic interests a central, though not strictly deterministic, role in the shaping of the prevailing ideologies that mould the basic perspectives and preferences of political decision-makers. Economic liberals generally believe in the steady pressures of economic opportunities, and competitive forces, that progressively ease the path towards greater economic globalisation and political liberalisation.

Interpretations derived from third-order levels of analysis cannot be discounted as possibly dominant influences over the political realm. Neither, however, can such meta-theoretical propositions be verified by any simple empirical tests. Just as any, or all, such interpretations may encompass elements of truth, so it is possible that they will be falsified by future developments.

Note

1   See, in particular: Bruce Russett, 'The mysterious case of vanishing hegemony: or; Is Mark Twain really dead?', *International Organization*, Vol. 39, No. 2 (Spring 1985), pp. 207–31; Duncan Snidal, 'The limits of hegemonic stability theory', *International Organization*, Vol. 39, No. 4 (Autumn 1985), pp. 579–614; M.C. Webb and S.D. Krasner, 'Hegemonic stability theory: an empirical assessment', *Review of International Studies*, Vol. 15, No. 2, (April 1989), pp. 183–98; Andrew Walter, *World Power and World Money: The Role of Hegemony and International Monetary Order* (Hemel

Hempstead: Harvester/Wheatsheaf, 1991), esp. Ch. 1; and P.K. O'Brien and G.A. Pigman, 'Free trade, British hegemony and the international economic order in the nineteenth century', *Review of International Studies*, Vol. 18, No. 2 (April 1992), pp. 89–113.

R.J. Barry Jones (1995) *Globalization and Interdependence in the International Political Economy*, London: Pinter Publishers, pp. 219–221.

THE END OF GLOBAL STRATEGY: ALAN M. RUGMAN AND RICHARD HODGETTS (2001)

Alan M. Rugman (1945–) is L. Leslie Waters Chair of International Business at Indiana University. Along with former Canadian Prime Minister Brian Mulroney, he co-authored the North American Free Trade Agreement (NAFTA). Today, Rugman is considered a central authority on foreign trade policy. He is also regarded as a leading expert in the operations of multinational corporations. Richard Hodgetts (1942–2001) was Professor of Management at Florida International University. His work was mainly centered on corporate management and international business strategy. The selection is taken from Rugman and Hodgetts's co-authored article, 'The End of Global Strategy,' which aims to debunk a number of common myths about globalization. At the core of their argument is the claim that globalization is by no means a monolithic or all-consuming phenomenon. As evidence, they cite the fact that multinational enterprises (MNEs) are typically confined to a particular region. Also, they examine the ways in which MNEs do not develop homogenous products for the world market. Instead, products are usually adapted to local places. Thus, this is why Rugman and Hodgetts believe successful MNEs are those which still design business strategies on a regional basis. Unsuccessful ones are those who have the globe as their only frame of reference.

Global Failures and Regional Successes

Recent research suggests that globalization is a myth. Far from taking place in a single global market, most business activity by large firms takes place in regional blocks. There is no uniform spread of American market capitalism nor are global markets becoming homogenized. Government regulations and cultural differences divide the world into the triad blocks of North America, the European Union and Japan. Rival multinational enterprises from the triad compete for regional market share and so enhance economic efficiency. Only in a few sectors, such as consumer electronics, is a global strategy of economic integration viable. For most other manufacturing, such as automobiles, and for all services, strategies of national respon-siveness are required, often coupled with integration strategies, as explained in the matrix framework of this article. Successful multinationals now design strategies on a regional basis; unsuccessful ones pursue global strategies. © 2001 Elsevier Science Ltd. All rights reserved.

Common 'global' misunderstandings

Globalization has been defined in business schools as the production and distribution of products and services of a homogenous type and quality on a worldwide basis.[1] Simply put – providing the same output to countries everywhere. And in recent years it has become increasingly common to hear business executives, industry analysts, and even university professors talk about the emergence of globalization and the dominance of international business by giant, multinational enterprises (MNEs) that are selling uniform products from Cairo, Illinois to Cairo, Egypt and from Lima, Ohio to Lima, Peru.[2]

To back up their claims, these individuals often point to the fact that foreign sales account for more than 50 per cent of the annual revenues of companies such as Dow Chemical, Exxon, Hewlett Packard, IBM, Johnson and Johnson, Mobil, Motorola, Procter and Gamble, and Texaco.[3] These are accurate statements – but they fail to explain that most of the sales of 'global' companies are made on a 'triad-regional' basis. For example, most MNEs that are headquartered in North America earn the bulk of their revenue within their home country or by selling to members of the triad: NAFTA, the European Union (EU), or Japan and a small group of Asian and Oceania nations.[4] In fact, recent research shows that:

1. More than 85 per cent of all automobiles produced in North America are built in North American factories owned by General Motors, Ford, Daimler-Chrysler, or European or Japanese MNEs; over 90 per cent of the cars produced in the EU are sold there; and more than 93 per cent of all cars registered in Japan are manufactured domestically.
2. In the specialty chemicals sector over 90 per cent of all paint is made and used regionally by triad based MNEs and the same is true for steel, heavy electrical equipment, energy, and transportation.
3. In the services sector, which now employs approximately 70 per cent of the workforce in North America, Western Europe, and Japan, these activities are all essentially local or regional.[5] As a result, top managers now need to design triad-based regional strategies, not global ones.

The real drivers of 'globalization' are the network managers of large multinational enterprises. But their business strategies are triad/regional and responsive to local consumers, rather than global and uniform. For example, the automobile and specialty chemicals business are triad-based, not global. There is no global car. Instead, over 90 per cent of all cars produced in Europe are sold in Europe. Regional production and large local sales also occur in North America and Japan.

Another misunderstanding about globalization is the belief that MNEs are globally monolithic and excessively powerful in political terms. Research shows this is not so. MNEs are not monolithic; in fact, the largest 500 multinationals are spread across the triad economies of NAFTA, the EU, and Japan/Asia. Recent research shows that of these 500, there are 198 headquartered in NAFTA countries, 156 in the EU, and 125 in Japan/Asia.[6] Additionally, these triad-based MNEs compete for global market shares and profits across a wide variety of industrial sectors and trade services. And this process of regional competition erodes the possibility of sustainable long-term profits and the possibility of building strong, sustainable political advantage (Rugman, 1996; Rugman and D'Cruz, 2000).

A third misunderstanding about globalization is the belief that MNEs develop homogeneous products for the world market and through their efficient production techniques are able to dominate local markets everywhere. In truth, multinationals have to adapt their products for the local market. For example, there is no worldwide, global car. Rather, there are regionally-based American, European, and Japanese factories that are supported by local regional suppliers who provide steel, plastic, paint, and other necessary inputs for producing autos for that geographic triad region. Additionally, the car designs that are popular in one area of the world are often rejected by customers in other geographic areas. The Toyota Camry that dominates the American auto market is a poor seller in Japan. The Volkswagen Golf that was the largest selling car in Europe did not make an impact in North America. Even pharmaceuticals, which manufacture medicines that are often referred to as 'universal products,' have to modify their goods to satisfy national and state regulations thus making centralized production and worldwide distribution economically difficult. [. . .]

'Global' failures

Over the past decade a number of MNEs that should have known better have tried to succeed with a globalization strategy. Some of the best-known include Coca-Cola, the Walt Disney Company, and Saatchi and Saatchi. In all three cases, these MNEs have developed a global strategy based on Quadrant 1 of Figure 1, i.e. one where the benefits of global integration are sought and the need to adapt products to local markets is largely ignored.

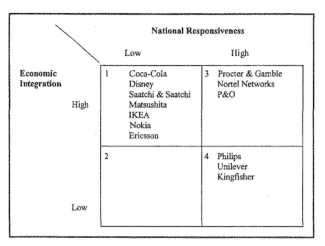

Figure 1 MNE Strategies and the International Management Strategy Matrix.

Coca-Cola: global is out, local is in

After decades of continued success, Coca-Cola found itself facing a series of problems as it entered the millennium. During the 1970s and 1980s the firm had expanded its global reach into almost 200 countries. At the same time the company began to centralize control and to encourage consolidation among all bottling partners. In the 1990s, however, the world began to change. Many national and local leaders began seeking sovereignty over their political, economic, and cultural futures. As a result, the very forces that were making the world more connected and homogeneous were also triggering a powerful desire for local autonomy and the preservation of unique cultural identity. Simply put, the world was demanding more nimbleness, responsiveness, and sensitivity from MNEs, while Coca-Cola was centralizing decision-making, standardizing operating practices, and insulating itself from this changing environment. Coke was going global, when it should have been going local (Daft, 2000).

Today Coca-Cola is beginning to turn things around. In particular, the firm has begun implementing three principles that are designed to make it more locally responsive. First, Coke is instituting a strategy of 'think local, act local' by putting increased decision-making in the hands of local managers. Second, the company is focusing itself as a pure marketing company that pushes its brands on a regional and local basis. Third, the firm is working to become a model citizen by reaching out to the local communities and getting involved in civic and charitable activities. In the past Coke succeeded because it understood and appealed to global commonalties. In the future it hopes to succeed by better understanding and appealing to local differences.

Disney: learning to say oui not yes

Between 1988 and 1990 three $150 million amusement parks opened in France. By 1991 two of them were bankrupt and one was doing poorly. This track record did not concern the Walt Disney Company, which planned to open Europe's first Disneyland in 1992 on a site 20 miles east of Paris. There were over 100 million people within six hours driving distance of the park and company officials were certain that Euro Disney would be a major success. They were quite wrong.

From opening day there were problems with the operation, as the company tried to implement a global strategy rather than a local one that accommodated the needs of Europeans. One of the problems was that workers were required to speak English at meetings, even if most people in attendance were French. Another was that liquor was not sold in the park, although many visitors were accustomed to having a drink with lunch or dinner. A third was that many of the exhibits and rides did not have a local theme, they were the same as those in Disneyland USA and thus did not appeal to Europeans. A fourth was that labor policies were at odds with worker expectations, resulting in 3000 employees leaving over pay and working conditions within a month of opening day.

By 1994, after heavy losses, Euro Disney was in such poor shape that some observers believed that it would be shut down. Forced to reevaluate its approach, however, the company began making a series of changes, abandoning its global approach, and substituting one that appealed to local tastes. The name of the park was officially changed to 'Disneyland Paris' and the company started to stress the regional origins of the fairy tale characters. In addition, the firm began creating European-specific attractions such as history movie shows and a science fiction tour based on Jules Verne's stories; the rules and regulations governing employee behavior were radically altered; and the services provided in the park, including the serving of alcoholic beverages, were changed to reflect local tastes. Today Disneyland Paris is profitable and local anti-Disney hostility is all but gone. The firm has come to realize that what works well in the US cannot be directly transported overseas, as seen by its new regionally-focused strategy. [. . .]

Regionalization and strategic successes

Successful MNEs do not always use the pure globalization, one-size-fits-all strategy of Quadrant 1. Rather they seek an optimal balance of economic integration and national responsiveness. In some cases MNEs employ high economic integration and low national responsiveness (Quadrant 1); in other instances they use high national responsiveness and low economic integration (Quadrant 4); and in still others they have a high focus on both areas (Quadrant 3). The most famous example of such a Quadrant 3 strategy is ABB, widely discussed in the literature.[7] This section reports on examples of 10 MNEs that are using one or other of these three strategies. (See Figure 1, which also shows the three MNEs discussed in the previous section.)

Philips and Matsushita: global gladiators

In terms of triad-based competition, the 1980s saw the emergence of Japanese winners in the consumer electronics industry. One of the most successful Japanese MNEs is Matsushita. Initially successful with color televisions (Panasonic TVs), its best known product was the video cassette recorder (VCR), a field which it denominates by using the VHS system instead of Sony's betamax format and others produced by European and American rivals. In order to dominate world business in VCRs, Matsushita made the VHS format the industry standard. It achieved this, not just by its own massive production and worldwide sales, but by licensing the VHS format to other MNEs such as Hitachi, Sharp, Mitsubishi and even its great European-based rival, Philips. Other companies like GE, RCA and Zenith (who sold VCRs under their own brand name) were tied into the VHS format because of the production and process technology retained by Matsushita in its strong Japanese home base. Massive global economies of scale enabled the firm to cut VCR prices by a half over its first five years. It operates a global strategy in Quadrant 1 of Figure 1.

In contrast to Matsushita, Philips was in desperate trouble by the 1980s. Built up in the inter-war period of protectionism and strong government regulations it had developed a very decentralized organizational structure. Individual national country managers held the power in Philips and they were slow to respond to the Japanese threat in the post-war period. As a result Philips lacked economies of scale and its radios, TVs and VCRs were all too expensive, compared with similar Japanese products. Philips had over 600 manufacturing plants across the world, all developing products for local markets. The challenge facing Philips was how to restructure its entire business away from Quadrant 4 of Figure 1 (a locally responsive national organization), towards becoming a more integrated and leaner manufacturer capable of reaping the necessary economies of scale through a standard production in the triad markets. This required a move to Quadrant 3 or even to Quadrant 1, to compete with its Japanese rival.

In essence, the Japanese had changed the rules of the game in the consumer electronics business. Matsushita, as a centralized, high quality, low price and innovative company was beating the decentralized and nationally responsive European firm. One response by European firms was to lobby their governments for protection in the form of anti-dumping actions and tougher customs inspection of Japanese products. But such triad-based 'shelter' only buys some breathing room before MNEs like Philips need to restructure and fit their organizational capability to the required industry strategy.

Finally, the response of Matsushita to more protection has been to switch overseas sales from the export mode to one of foreign direct investment. This means that the Japanese firm can evade European trade barriers such as anti-dumping actions, since it actually manufactures in European countries, such as the United Kingdom, where it has a major plant in Cardiff, Wales. But this also means that Matsushita needs to make its foreign subsidiaries as useful as possible by encouraging local initiatives, (moving from Quadrant 1 to Quadrant 3), even where these conflict with its international, centralized Japanese-based management culture. The same government regulations which made Philips too decentralized are now being reapplied half a century later to make Matsushita less global and more local.

IKEA: Low cost – and designed to stay that way

In less than 50 years IKEA has grown from a small, privately-held, Swedish furniture retailer into a $7 billion multinational corporation with 140 stores in 30 countries. Focusing heavily on an economic integration strategy, the company introduced knockdown kits that customers can buy at the store and assemble at home. IKEA also brought innovation to the logistics of furniture production by establishing groups of key suppliers to produce components at low cost, while maintaining tight control over product design and quality in order to maintain the IKEA brand name and the distinctive identity of its products.

After establishing itself in Sweden as a high quality, low cost producer of modern, functional, durable, and competitively priced furniture, the company began to 'internationalize' and become a strong regional player in Europe and, in more recent years, across the triad. During the 1970s it moved into Switzerland, Germany, Australia, and Canada. In the 1980s it expanded into Europe at large, as well as into the United States. In the past few years it has begun establishing operations in Shanghai. This is a Quadrant 1 strategy of building upon a strong home-based Swedish concept of clean, efficient, well designed, functional, durable and modern furniture. The product is not adapted as international expansion takes place.

Today IKEA continues to focus on the high economic integration, low national responsiveness strategy of Quadrant 1. It has been successful by introducing highly differentiated products into a traditional industry and has now established a universally recognized brand name for high quality, inexpensive, and attractive furniture. By combining the generic strategies of differentiation, low cost, and niching (Porter, 1980), the firm has been able to maintain its success as a Quadrant 1 player.

Nokia and Ericsson: Small phones but big markets

Nokia, headquartered in one of the smallest countries in Europe, Finland, is the world's largest producer of mobile phones. It is the leader in Europe and second only to Motorola in the United States. In the 1970s Nokia transformed itself from a forest products firm into a high technology producer of electronic products, especially cellular phones; and by the end of the millennium the company was operating in 130 countries with annual sales of almost $20 billion.[8]

Because there are only 3 million people in Finland, Nokia has actively pursued a Quadrant 1 internationalization strategy and today 95 per cent of all revenues are generated outside of its borders. A large degree of this success can be attributed to its research and development (R and D) efforts which have resulted in mobile phones that employ 'global roaming,' thus allowing the unit to be used across different telecom systems worldwide. Nokia has also been very successful in forming strategic alliances with US distributors such as Radio Shack and American telecom companies such as AT and T, thus providing it with access to large markets where it can successfully employ its economic integration strategy.

In addition, Nokia has worked closely with governments to develop an industry standard (a Quadrant 1 strategy) and has entered into a joint venture with its major rival, Ericsson, for this purpose. The two firms are working to establish GSM (Groupe Spéciale Mobile) as the standard for mobile phones across Europe, in addition to its becoming one of the key standards globally.

L.M. Ericsson is one of the world's largest producers of digital mobile phones. Like Nokia, its small phones have a worldwide market. Only 6 per cent of its $24 billion annual revenue is earned in its home country of Sweden.[9] Its biggest revenue markets are Europe (40 per cent), Asia (27 per cent), and North America (16 per cent). Like Nokia, the firm places major emphasis on R and D and innovation and, among other things, has developed telephone switches that compete effectively with Canada's Nortel Networks and France's Alcatel. Ericsson has also formed alliances with firms such as Compaq, Intel, Hewlett Packard, and Texas Instruments. These firms serve as key suppliers of components and products that Ericson uses for voice and data transmission. This out-sourcing approach also helps the company, like its competitor Nokia, maintain a successful Quadrant 1 strategy. Both Nokia and Ericsson are working for the development of standardized global telecom services which will make Quadrant 1 viable in the long term. At present, different national regulations affecting telecommunications raises the possibility of a Quadrant 3 strategy being necessary. [. . .]

Lessons learned

The case examples provided here show clearly that a pure globalization strategy of Quadrant 1 that is typified by high economic integration and low national responsiveness will not always work in the twenty-first century. In fact, firms that attempt this approach tend to be from strong triad-based home markets in consumer electronics or retailing, or hope to develop a global standard (as in mobile phones). Some MNEs in Quadrant 1 have significantly lower returns on their foreign assets than do MNEs that balance a concern for economic integration with that of national responsiveness (Gestrin *et al.*, 2000). For example, recently Japanese MNEs have used the globalization approach (Quadrant 1 of Figure 4.2) with disastrous results. The relatively more successful European MNEs tend to opt for strategies in Quadrants 1 and 4, although recent research shows that some of them are now beginning to move into Quadrant 3. Successful American MNEs also tend to adopt a Quadrant 3, transnational approach.

What are the lessons to be learned from analysis of these 10 MNEs?

- Philips has been in trouble as its country managers were too powerful and the firm was too decentralized, in Quadrant 4. The push for a single EU market to provide a 'home-base' to offset the advantages of US and Japanese rivals is a logical response.
- In contrast, Matsushita has successfully penetrated the US and European triad markets in Quadrant 1 but is now attempting to get more value out of its subsidiaries and be a little nationally responsive.
- IKEA has followed a Quadrant 1 home-based internationalization strategy whereas Kingfisher has not followed a standardized approach but rather left its French and German acquisitions alone to deal with triad retail customers, a Quadrant 4 approach.
- Nokia and Ericsson. The two mobile phone producers are successful as domestic champions and have been able to internationalize into larger triad markets, despite strong national telecom regulations, as they are attempting to develop a Quadrant 1 'global standard' for mobile phones.
- Nortel has already developed into a Quadrant 3 'transnational' MNE with strong decentralization within a network combined with integration skills in terms of communication and common strategy. P and O has

also developed a Quadrant 3 strategy of decentralized cruise ships combined with centralized global logistics.
- Unilever has been moving to consolidate its many national and regional brands into a manageable number and it is operating on a regional basis.
- In contrast, Procter and Gamble is attempting to set up seven worldwide product groups, the top management of which is spread around the triad. Both companies are nationally responsive; Unilever in Quadrant 4 and P and G in Quadrant 3.

What quadrant is best? This will depend on the specific situation, but it is possible to offer some practical strategies for managers who want to increase their company's international revenues and profits. Five of the most useful lessons learned are these:

1. Do not assume an integrated global market. There is more to strategy than Quadrant 1. Instead, be prepared to design strategies that take into account regional trade and investment agreements such as NAFTA or the single market of the EU. Also learn to deal with different cultures and become 'nationally responsive' when necessary.
2. Design organization structures for Quadrants 3 and 4 which recognize triad-based internal know-how capability and develop network organizational competencies, rather than always rely on international divisions or global product divisions, in Quadrant 1.
3. Develop new thinking and knowledge about regional business networks and triad-based clusters and assess the similar attributes of triad competitors, rather than always developing pure global strategies. The foreign market is not always the same as your home market. Make alliances and foster cross-cultural awareness in your senior managers.
4. Develop analytical methods for assessing regional drivers of success rather than globalization drivers because the former may be more useful in the future in gaining and holding market share.
5. Encourage all your managers to think regional, act local – and forget global!

Notes

1 Rugman and Hodgetts (2000). The definition of 'globalization' is a subject of intense academic debate. Most business school scholars would adopt the economics-based definition used here, where integration across national borders yields the potential for firm-level economies of scale and/or global brand name products. Contingent upon this definition of 'pure' economic globalization is the need for products to be uniform across markets. A much broader definition of globalization is used by other writers such as Anthony Giddens, a sociologist. He defines globalization as 'the worldwide interconnection at the cultural, political and economic level resulting from the elimination of communication and trade barriers' and he states that 'globalization is a process of convergence of cultural, political and economic aspects of life' (Giddens, 1999). Again, convergence (of cultures, tastes, regulations etc) is an extreme version of homogeneity of products and services. The thesis of this article is that such convergence and homogeneity has not occurred; instead of globalization we observe regional/trial production and distribution. Therefore, MNEs do not need global strategies; regional ones are more relevant.
2 Yip (1995). However, Schlie and Yip (2000) have suggested that automobile firms can be observed as following a 'regional' strategy (equivalent to our 'triad' regional strategy.) They argue that, first, any firms develop globally and only selectively regionalize as a second step. Examples of triad products are the Honda Accord (with the flexible-width platform), the VW group cars, and the old Ford and GM European versions of their cars. See Schlie and Yip (2000).
3 For more on these firms see the 'Top 100 TNCs Ranked by Foreign Assets' (Anon, 1997).
4 NAFTA consists of the United States, Canada, and Mexico. The European Union is made up of Belgium, France, Italy, Luxembourg, the Netherlands, Germany, Great Britain, Denmark, Greece, Ireland, Portugal, Spain, Austria, Finland, and Sweden. The major Asian countries included here include Australia, China, India, Indonesia, Malaysia, New Zealand, the Philippines, Singapore, South Korea, Taiwan, and Thailand as well as Japan.
5 Rugman (2000) (This book is to be published by AMACOM/McGraw-Hill, 2001 in North America).
6 These data have been adapted from Fortune (1999).
7 ABB is one of the core nine cases discussed by Bartlett and Ghoshal (1989). It is also discussed in Ghoshal and Bartlett

(1997), in which the former CEO of ABB, Percy Barnevik is used as a spokesperson for a Quadrant 3 transnational solution.

8   Nokia annual report, 1999.
9   Ericsson annual report, 1999.

Alan Rugman and Richard Hodgetts (2001) "The End of Global Strategy," *European Management Journal*, vol. 19, no. 4, pp. 333–343.

RUNAWAY WORLD: ANTHONY GIDDENS (1999)

Anthony Giddens (1937–), previously Professor of Sociology at Cambridge University and subsequently Director of the London School of Economics, is a member of the House of Lords. The most cited social scientist in the world today, Giddens achieved significant worldwide attention in political circles for his ideas of a "radical center" or "Third Way" in progressive politics during the 1990s. In this period, he acted as an advisor to British Prime Minister Tony Blair, and was a key figure in bringing New Labour into dialogue with the New Democrats under President Bill Clinton. This selection comes from his 1999 BBC Reith Lectures, where Giddens confronts the dilemmas of a globalizing world of both dizzying opportunity and terrifying risk. Globalization for Giddens becomes radically intensified in our own time of communications technology, in which the circularity of knowledge and information swirls as never before. Unlike both pro-globalists and anti-globalists, Giddens views globalization as at once enabling and constraining. The task for progressive politics in the global age, according to Giddens, is to foster transnational coalitions committed to the extension and deepening of global governance and social justice.

Globalisation Outruns Transformations

We live in a world of transformations, affecting almost every aspect of what we do. For better or worse, we are being propelled into a global order that no one fully understands, but which is making its effects felt upon all of us.

Globalisation may not be a particularly attractive or elegant word. But absolutely no one who wants to understand our prospects at century's end can ignore it. I travel a lot to speak abroad. I haven't been to a single country recently where globalisation isn't being intensively discussed. In France, the word is *mondialisation*. In Spain and Latin America, it is *globalización*. The Germans say *Globalisierung*.

The global spread of the term is evidence of the very developments to which it refers. Every business guru talks about it. No political speech is complete without reference to it. Yet even in the late 1980s the term was hardly used, either in the academic literature or in everyday language. It has come from nowhere to be almost everywhere.

Given its sudden popularity, we shouldn't be surprised that the meaning of the notion isn't always clear, or that an intellectual reaction has set in against it. Globalisation has something to do with the thesis that we now all live in one world – but in what ways exactly, and is the idea really valid? Different thinkers have taken almost completely opposite views about globalisation in debates that have sprung up over the past few years. Some dispute the whole thing. I'll call them the sceptics.

According to the sceptics, all the talk about globalisation is only that – just talk. Whatever its benefits, its trials and tribulations, the global economy isn't especially different from that which existed at previous periods. The world carries on much the same as it has done for many years.

Most countries, the sceptics argue, gain only a small amount of their income from external trade. Moreover, a good deal of economic exchange is between regions, rather than being truly world-wide. The countries of the European Union, for example, mostly trade among themselves. The same is true of the other main trading blocs, such as those of Asia-Pacific or North America.

Others take a very different position. I'll label them the radicals. The radicals argue that not only is globalisation very real, but that its consequences can be felt everywhere. The global market-place, they say, is much more developed than even in the 1960s and 1970s and is indifferent to national borders. Nations have lost most of the sovereignty they once had, and politicians have lost most of their capability to influence events. It isn't surprising that no one respects political leaders any more, or has much interest in what they have to say. The era of the nation-state is over. Nations, as the Japanese business writer Kenichi Ohmae puts it, have become mere 'fictions'. Authors such as Ohmae see the economic difficulties of the 1998 Asian crisis as demonstrating the reality of globalisation, albeit seen from its disruptive side.

The sceptics tend to be on the political left, especially the old left. For if all of this is essentially a myth, governments can still control economic life and the welfare state remain intact. The notion of globalisation, according to the sceptics, is an ideology put about by free-marketeers who wish to dismantle welfare systems and cut back on state expenditures. What has happened is at most a reversion to how the world was a century ago. In the late nineteenth century there was already an open global economy, with a great deal of trade, including trade in currencies.

Well, who is right in this debate? I think it is the radicals. The level of world trade today is much higher than it ever was before, and involves a much wider range of goods and services. But the biggest difference is in the level of finance and capital flows. Geared as it is to electronic money – money that exists only as digits in computers – the current world economy has no parallels in earlier times.

In the new global electronic economy, fund managers, banks, corporations, as well as millions of individual investors, can transfer vast amounts of capital from one side of the world to another at the click of a mouse. As they do so, they can destabilise what might have seemed rock-solid economies – as happened in the events in Asia.

The volume of world financial transactions is usually measured in US dollars. A million dollars is a lot of money for most people. Measured as a stack of hundred-dollar notes, it would be eight inches high. A billion dollars – in other words, a thousand million – would stand higher than St Paul's Cathedral. A trillion dollars – a million million – would be over 120 miles high, 20 times higher than Mount Everest.

Yet far more than a trillion dollars is now turned over *each day* on global currency markets. This is a massive increase from only the late 1980s, let alone the more distant past. The value of whatever money we may have in our pockets, or our bank accounts, shifts from moment to moment according to fluctuations in such markets.

I would have no hesitation, therefore, in saying that globalisation, as we are experiencing it, is in many respects not only new, but also revolutionary. Yet I don't believe that either the sceptics or the radicals have properly understood either what it is or its implications for us. Both groups see the phenomenon almost solely in economic terms. This is a mistake. Globalisation is political, technological and cultural, as well as economic. It has been influenced above all by developments in systems of communication, dating back only to the late 1960s. [. . .]

Globalisation is a complex set of processes, not a single one. And these operate in a contradictory or oppositional fashion. Most people think of globalisation as simply 'pulling away' power or influence from local communities and nations into the global arena. And indeed this is one of its consequences. Nations do lose some of the economic power they once had. Yet it also has an opposite effect. Globalisation not only pulls upwards, but also pushes downwards, creating new pressures for local autonomy. The American sociologist Daniel Bell describes this very well when he says that the nation becomes not only too small to solve the big problems, but also too large to solve the small ones.

Globalisation is the reason for the revival of local cultural identities in different parts of the world. If one asks, for example, why the Scots want more independence in the UK, or why there is a strong separatist movement in Quebec, the answer is not to be found only in their cultural history. Local nationalisms spring up as a response to globalising tendencies, as the hold of older nation-states weakens.

Globalisation also squeezes sideways. It creates new economic and cultural zones within and across nations. Examples are the Hong Kong region, northern Italy, and Silicon Valley in California. Or consider the Barcelona region. The area around Barcelona in northern Spain extends into France. Catalonia, where Barcelona is located, is closely integrated into the European Union. It is part of Spain, yet also looks outwards. [. . .]

Globalisation, of course, isn't developing in an even-handed way, and is by no means wholly benign in its consequences. To many living outside Europe and North America, it looks uncomfortably like Westernisation – or, perhaps, Americanisation, since the US is now the sole superpower, with a dominant economic, cultural and military position in the global order. Many of the most visible cultural expressions of globalisation are American – Coca-Cola, McDonald's, CNN.

Most of the giant multinational companies are based in the US too. Those that aren't all come from the rich countries, not the poorer areas of the world. A pessimistic view of globalisation would consider it largely an affair of the industrial North, in which the developing societies of the South play little or no active part. It would see it as destroying local cultures, widening world inequalities and worsening the lot of the impoverished. Globalisation, some argue, creates a world of winners and losers, a few on the fast track to prosperity, the majority condemned to a life of misery and despair.

Indeed, the statistics are daunting. The share of the poorest fifth of the world's population in global income has dropped, from 2.3 per cent to 1.4 per cent between 1989 and 1998. The proportion taken by the richest fifth, on the other hand, has risen. In sub-Saharan Africa, 20 countries have lower incomes per head in real terms than they had in the late 1970s. In many less developed countries, safety and environmental regulations are low or virtually non-existent. Some transnational companies sell goods there that are controlled or banned in the industrial countries – poor-quality medical drugs, destructive pesticides or high tar and nicotine content cigarettes. Rather than a global village, one might say, this is more like global pillage.

Along with ecological risk, to which it is related, expanding inequality is the most serious problem facing world society. It will not do, however, merely to blame it on the wealthy. It is fundamental to my argument that globalisation today is only partly Westernisation. Of course the Western nations, and more generally the industrial countries, still have far more influence over world affairs than do the poorer states. But globalisation is becoming increasingly decentred – not under the control of any group of nations, and still less of the large corporations. Its effects are felt as much in Western countries as elsewhere.

This is true of the global financial system, and of changes affecting the nature of government itself. What one could call 'reverse colonisation' is becoming more and more common. Reverse colonisation means that non-Western countries influence developments in the West. Examples abound – such as the latinising of Los Angeles, the emergence of a globally oriented high-tech sector in India, or the selling of Brazilian television programmes to Portugal.

Is globalisation a force promoting the general good? The question can't be answered in a simple way, given the complexity of the phenomenon. People who ask it, and who blame globalisation for deepening world inequalities, usually have in mind economic globalisation and, within that, free trade. Now, it is surely obvious that free trade is not an unalloyed benefit. This is especially so as concerns the less developed countries. Opening up a country, or regions within it, to free trade can undermine a local subsistence economy. An area that becomes dependent upon a few products sold on world markets is very vulnerable to shifts in prices as well as to technological change.

Trade always needs a framework of institutions, as do other forms of economic development. Markets cannot be created by purely economic means, and how far a given economy should be exposed to the world market-place must depend upon a range of criteria. Yet to oppose economic globalisation, and to opt for economic protectionism, would be a misplaced tactic for rich and poor nations alike. Protectionism may be a necessary strategy at some times and in some countries. In my view, for example, Malaysia was correct to introduce controls in 1998, to stem the flood of capital from the country. But more permanent forms of protectionism will not help the development of the poor countries, and among the rich would lead to warring trade blocs.

The debates about globalisation I mentioned at the beginning have concentrated mainly upon its implications for the nation-state. Are nation-states, and hence national political leaders, still powerful, or are they becoming largely irrelevant to the forces shaping the world? Nation-states are indeed still powerful and political leaders have a large role to play in the world. Yet at the same time the nation-state is being reshaped before our eyes. National economic policy can't be as effective as it once was. More importantly, nations have to rethink their identities now the older forms of geopolitics are becoming obsolete. Although this is a contentious point, I would say that, following the dissolving of the Cold War, most nations no longer have enemies. Who are the enemies of Britain, or France, or Brazil? The war in Kosovo didn't pit nation against nation. It was a conflict between old-style territorial nationalism and a new, ethically driven interventionism.

Nations today face risks and dangers rather than enemies, a massive shift in their very nature. It isn't only of the nation that such comments could be made. Everywhere we look, we see institutions that appear the same as they used to be from the outside, and carry the same names, but inside have become quite different. We continue to talk of the nation, the family, work, tradition, nature, as if they were all the same as in the past. They are not. The outer shell remains, but inside they have changed – and this is happening not only in the US, Britain, or France, but almost everywhere. They are what I call 'shell institutions'. They are institutions that have become inadequate to the tasks they are called upon to perform.

As the changes I have described in this chapter gather weight, they are creating something that has never existed before, a global cosmopolitan society. We are the first generation to live in this society, whose contours we can as yet only dimly see. It is shaking up our existing ways of life, no matter where we happen to be. This is not – at least at the moment – a global order driven by collective human will. Instead, it is emerging in an anarchic, haphazard, fashion, carried along by a mixture of influences.

It is not settled or secure, but fraught with anxieties, as well as scarred by deep divisions. Many of us feel in the grip of forces over which we have no power. Can we reimpose our will upon them? I believe we can. The powerlessness we experience is not a sign of personal failings, but reflects the incapacities of our institutions. We need to reconstruct those we have, or create new ones. For globalisation is not incidental to our lives today. It is a shift in our very life circumstances. It is the way we now live.

Anthony Giddens (1999) *Runaway World*, Cambridge: Polity Press, pp. 6–10, 12–13, 15–19.

GLOBAL TRANSFORMATIONS: DAVID HELD AND ANTHONY MCGREW (1999)

David Held (1951–) is Graham Wallis Professor of Political Science at the London School of Economics, and Anthony McGrew is Professor of International Relations at the University of Southampton, UK. Working together over many years and co-authoring a number of books, Held and McGrew have developed a novel critique of globalization that they term "transformationalist." Dismissive of global skeptics, but equally wary of some of the more overblown claims by radical globalists that we have entered a new period of world history, the transformationalist standpoint proceeds from the claim that globalism inaugurates a "shake-out" within the realms of the nation-state, politics, the economy, and culture. Such a "shake-out" involves a radical transformation of traditional social and political structures, so much so that orthodox distinctions between internal and external affairs, between the domestic and the international, dissolve. In one more notable section, from Held and McGrew's pathbreaking *Global Transformations* (1999), the transformationalist analysis of globalization is said to comprise four key elements: (1) the extensity of global networks; (2) the intensity of global interconnectedness; (3) the velocity of global flows; and (4) the impact propensity of global interconnectedness. The transformationalist position set out by Held and McGrew derives, in some considerable part, from the social-theoretical research of Anthony Giddens, Manuel Castells, and James

Rosenau. By integrating the insights of these scholars on globalization, Held and McGrew have forged a powerful position of their own — one that confronts the distinctive institutional features of contemporary globalizations cutting across and transforming all dimensions of the planet.

Transforming the Globalization Debate

At the heart of the transformationalist thesis is a conviction that, at the dawn of a new millennium, globalization is a central driving force behind the rapid social, political and economic changes that are reshaping modern societies and world order (Giddens, 1990; Scholte, 1993; Castells, 1996). According to the proponents of this view, contemporary processes of globalization are historically unprecedented such that governments and societies across the globe are having to adjust to a world in which there is no longer a clear distinction between international and domestic, external and internal affairs (Rosenau, 1990; Cammilleri and Falk, 1992; Ruggie, 1993; Linklater and MacMillan, 1995; Sassen, 1996). For Rosenau, the growth of 'intermestic' affairs define a 'new frontier', the expanding political, economic and social space in which the fate of societies and communities is decided (1997, pp. 4–5). In this respect, globalization is conceived as a powerful transformative force which is responsible for a 'massive shake-out' of societies, economies, institutions of governance and world order (Giddens, 1996).

In the transformationalist account, however, the direction of this 'shake-out' remains uncertain, since globalization is conceived as an essentially contingent historical process replete with contradictions (Mann, 1997). At issue is a dynamic and open-ended conception of where globalization might be leading and the kind of world order which it might prefigure. In comparison with the sceptical and hyperglobalist accounts, the transformationalists make no claims about the future trajectory of globalization; nor do they seek to evaluate the present in relation to some single, fixed ideal-type 'globalized world', whether a global market or a global civilization. Rather, transformationalist accounts emphasize globalization as a long-term historical process which is inscribed with contradictions and which is significantly shaped by conjunctural factors.

Such caution about the exact future of globalization is matched, nonetheless, by the conviction that contemporary patterns of global economic, military, technological, ecological, migratory, political and cultural flows are historically unprecedented. As Nierop puts it, 'virtually all countries in the world, if not all parts of their territory and all segments of their society, are now functionally part of that larger [global] system in one or more respects' (1994, p. 171). But the existence of a single global system is not taken as evidence of global convergence or of the arrival of single world society. On the contrary, for the transformationalists, globalization is associated with new patterns of global stratification in which some states, societies and communities are becoming increasingly enmeshed in the global order while others are becoming increasingly marginalized. A new configuration of global power relations is held to be crystallizing as the North–South division rapidly gives way to a new international division of labour such that the 'familiar pyramid of the core–periphery hierarchy is no longer a geographic but a social division of the world economy' (Hoogvelt, 1997, p. xii). To talk of North and South, of First World and Third World, is to overlook the ways in which globalization has recast traditional patterns of inclusion and exclusion between countries by forging new hierarchies which cut across and penetrate all societies and regions of the world. North and South, First World and Third World, are no longer 'out there' but nestled together within all the world's major cities. Rather than the traditional pyramid analogy of the world social structure, with a tiny top echelon and spreading mass base, the global social structure can be envisaged as a three-tier arrangement of concentric circles, each cutting across national boundaries, representing respectively the elites, the contented and the marginalized (Hoogvelt, 1997).

The recasting of patterns of global stratification is linked with the growing deterritorialization of economic activity as production and finance increasingly acquire a global and transnational dimension. From somewhat different starting points, Castells and Ruggie, among others, argue that national economies are being reorganized by processes of economic globalization such that national economic space no longer coincides with national territorial borders (Castells, 1996; Ruggie, 1996). In this globalizing economy, systems of transnational production, exchange and finance weave together ever more tightly the fortunes of communities and households on different continents.

At the core of the transformationalist case is a belief that contemporary globalization is reconstituting or 're-engineering' the power, functions and authority of national governments. While not disputing that states still retain the ultimate legal claim to 'effective supremacy over what occurs within their own territories', the transformationalists argue that this is juxtaposed, to varying degrees, with the expanding jurisdiction of institutions of international governance and the constraints of, as well as the obligations derived from, international law. This is especially evident in the EU, where sovereign power is divided between international, national and local authorities, but it is also evident in the operation of the World Trade Organization (WTO) (Goodman, 1997). However, even where sovereignty still appears intact, states no longer, if they ever did, retain sole command of what transpires within their own territorial boundaries. Complex global systems, from the financial to the ecological, connect the fate of communities in one locale to the fate of communities in distant regions of the world. Furthermore, global infrastructures of communication and transport support new forms of economic and social organization which transcend national boundaries without any consequent diminution of efficiency or control. Sites of power and the subjects of power may be literally, as well as metaphorically, oceans apart. In these circumstances, the notion of the nation-state as a self-governing, autonomous unit appears to be more a normative claim than a descriptive statement. The modern institution of territorially circumscribed sovereign rule appears somewhat anomalous juxtaposed with the transnational organization of many aspects of contemporary economic and social life (Sandel, 1996). Globalization, in this account, is therefore associated with a transformation or, to use Ruggie's term, an 'unbundling' of the relationship between sovereignty, territoriality and state power (Ruggie, 1993; Sassen, 1996).

Of course, few states have ever exercised complete or absolute sovereignty within their own territorial boundaries, as the practice of diplomatic immunity highlights (Sassen, 1996). Indeed the practice, as opposed to the doctrine, of sovereign statehood has always readily adapted to changing historical realities (Murphy, 1996). In arguing that globalization is transforming or reconstituting the power and authority of national governments, the transformationalists reject both the hyperglobalist rhetoric of the end of the sovereign nation-state and the sceptics' claim that 'nothing much has changed.' Instead, they assert that a new 'sovereignty regime' is displacing traditional conceptions of statehood as an absolute, indivisible, territorially exclusive and zero-sum form of public power (Held, 1991). Accordingly, sovereignty today is, they suggest, best understood 'less as a territorially defined barrier than a bargaining resource for a politics characterized by complex transnational networks' (Keohane, 1995).

This is not to argue that territorial boundaries retain no political, military or symbolic significance but rather to acknowledge that, conceived as the primary spatial markers of modern life, they have become increasingly problematic in an era of intensified globalization. Sovereignty, state power and territoriality thus stand today in a more complex relationship than in the epoch during which the modern nation-state was being forged. Indeed, the argument of the transformationalists is that globalization is associated not only with a new 'sovereignty regime' but also with the emergence of powerful new non-territorial forms of economic and political organization in the global domain, such as multinational corporations, transnational social movements, international regulatory agencies, etc. In this sense, world order can no longer be conceived as purely state-centric or even primarily state governed, as authority has become increasingly diffused among public and private agencies at the local, national, regional and global levels. Nation-states are no longer the sole centres or the principal forms of governance or authority in the world (Rosenau, 1997).

Given this changing global order, the form and functions of the state are having to adapt as governments seek coherent strategies of engaging with a globalizing world. Distinctive strategies are being followed from the model of the neoliberal minimal state to the models of the developmental state (government as the central promoter of economic expansion) and the catalytic state (government as facilitator of coordinated and collective action). In addition, governments have become increasingly outward looking as they seek to pursue cooperative strategies and to construct international regulatory regimes to manage more effectively the growing array of cross-border issues which regularly surface on national agendas. Rather than globalization bringing about the 'end of the state', it has encouraged a spectrum of adjustment strategies and, in certain respects, a more activist state. Accordingly, the power of national governments is not necessarily diminished by globalization but on the contrary is being reconstituted and restructured in response to the growing complexity of processes of governance in a more interconnected world (Rosenau, 1997).

David Held and Anthony McGrew (1999) *Global Transformations*, Cambridge: Polity Press, pp. 7–9.

■ ■ ■ ■ ■ ■

GLOBALIZATION AS AMERICANIZATION: PROJECT FOR THE NEW AMERICAN CENTURY (1997)

The Project for the New American Century (1997–2006) was a conservative American think tank founded by William Kristol and Robert Kagan to promote "American global leadership." The selection is their "Statement of Principles" which argue that the United States is the leading world power and should maintain that position through the rebuilding of the US military as a key instrument of international order. This position has been referred to positively as "Pax Americana" and negatively as "American Empire." The group, whose members included former US Vice President Dick Cheney and former US Secretary of Defense Robert Rumsfeld, exerted significant political and strategic influence on the administration of US President George W. Bush and his military policies.

Project for the New American Century: Statement of Principles, June 3, 1997

American foreign and defense policy is adrift. Conservatives have criticized the incoherent policies of the Clinton Administration. They have also resisted isolationist impulses from within their own ranks. But conservatives have not confidently advanced a strategic vision of America's role in the world. They have not set forth guiding principles for American foreign policy. They have allowed differences over tactics to obscure potential agreement on strategic objectives. And they have not fought for a defense budget that would maintain American security and advance American interests in the new century.

We aim to change this. We aim to make the case and rally support for American global leadership.

As the twentieth century draws to a close, the United States stands as the world's preeminent power. Having led the West to victory in the Cold War, America faces an opportunity and a challenge: Does the United States have the vision to build upon the achievements of past decades? Does the United States have the resolve to shape a new century favorable to American principles and interests?

We are in danger of squandering the opportunity and failing the challenge. We are living off the capital – both the military investments and the foreign policy achievements – built up by past administrations. Cuts in foreign affairs and defense spending, inattention to the tools of statecraft, and inconstant leadership are making it increasingly difficult to sustain American influence around the world. And the promise of short-term commercial benefits threatens to override strategic considerations. As a consequence, we are jeopardizing the nation's ability to meet present threats and to deal with potentially greater challenges that lie ahead.

We seem to have forgotten the essential elements of the Reagan Administration's success: a military that is strong and ready to meet both present and future challenges; a foreign policy that boldly and purposefully promotes American principles abroad; and national leadership that accepts the United States' global responsibilities.

Of course, the United States must be prudent in how it exercises its power. But we cannot safely avoid the responsibilities of global leadership or the costs that are associated with its exercise. America has a vital role in maintaining peace and security in Europe, Asia, and the Middle East. If we shirk our responsibilities, we invite challenges to our fundamental interests. The history of the twentieth century should have taught us that it is important to shape circumstances before crises emerge, and to meet threats before they become dire. The history of this century should have taught us to embrace the cause of American leadership.

Our aim is to remind Americans of these lessons and to draw their consequences for today. Here are four consequences:

- we need to increase defense spending significantly if we are to carry out our global responsibilities today and modernize our armed forces for the future;
- we need to strengthen our ties to democratic allies and to challenge regimes hostile to our interests and values;
- we need to promote the cause of political and economic freedom abroad;
- we need to accept responsibility for America's unique role in preserving and extending an international order friendly to our security, our prosperity, and our principles.

Such a Reaganite policy of military strength and moral clarity may not be fashionable today. But it is necessary if the United States is to build on the successes of this past century and to ensure our security and our greatness in the next.

"Statement of Principles, June 3, 1997." Source: http://www.newamericancentury.org/statementofprinciples.htm.

NEOLIBERALISM AS EXCEPTION: AIHWA ONG (2006)

Aihwa Ong grew up in Malaysia, was educated at Columbia University, and today is Professor of Anthropology and Southeast Asian Studies at the University of California, Berkeley. She is regarded the world over as a foremost interpreter of global history in respect to urgent issues of neoliberalism's evacuating of whatever may have remained of liberal, democratic, and market values. She is a particularly compelling critic of the exceptions taken to law and norm in the name of neoliberal market interests. Among her many books is *Neoliberalism as Exception: Mutations in Citizenship and Sovereignty* (2006), from which the selection is taken.

Neoliberalism, Citizenship, and Sovereignty

Since the 1970s, "American neoliberalism" has become a global phenomenon that has been variously received and critiqued overseas.

Neoliberalism and exceptions

As a new mode of political optimization, neoliberalism – with a small *n* – is reconfiguring relationships between governing and the governed, power and knowledge, and sovereignty and territoriality. Neoliberalism is often discussed as an economic doctrine with a negative relation to state power, a market ideology that seeks to limit the scope and activity of governing. But neoliberalism can also be conceptualized as a new relationship between government and knowledge through which governing activities are recast as nonpolitical and non-ideological problems that need technical solutions.[1] Indeed, neoliberalism considered as a technology of government is a profoundly active way of rationalizing governing and self-governing in order to "optimize." The spread of neoliberal calculation as a governing technology is thus a historical process that unevenly articulates situated political constellations. An ethnographic perspective reveals specific alignments of market rationality, sovereignty, and citizenship that mutually constitute distinctive milieus of labor and life at the edge of emergence.

I focus on the active, interventionist aspect of neoliberalism in non-Western contexts, where *neoliberalism as exception* articulates sovereign rule and regimes of citizenship. Of course, the difference between *neoliberalism as exception* and *exceptions to neoliberalism* hinges on what the "normative order" is in a particular milieu of investigation. This book focuses on the interplay of exceptions in emerging countries where neoliberalism itself is not the general characteristic of technologies of governing. We find neoliberal interventions in liberal democracies as well as in postcolonial, authoritarian, and post-socialist situations in East and Southeast Asia. Thus neoliberalism as exception is introduced in sites of transformation where market-driven calculations are bring introduced in the management of populations and the administration of special spaces. The articulation of neoliberal exceptions, citizenship, and sovereignty produces a range of possible anthropological problems and outcomes.[2]

At the same time, *exceptions to neoliberalism* are also invoked, in political decisions, to exclude populations and places from neoliberal calculations and choices. Exceptions to neoliberalism can be modes for protecting social safety nets or for stripping away all forms of political protection. In Russia, for instance, subsidized housing and social rights are preserved even when neoliberal techniques are introduced in urban budgetary practices.[3] At the same time, in Southeast Asia, exceptions to neoliberalism exclude migrant workers from the living standards created by market-driven policies. In other words, exceptions to neoliberalism can both preserve welfare benefits for citizens and exclude noncitizens from the benefits of capitalist development.

But there is an overlap in the workings of neoliberal exceptions and exceptions to market calculations. Populations governed by neoliberal technologies are dependent on others who are excluded from neoliberal considerations. The articulation of populations and spaces subjected to neoliberal norms and those outside the preview of these norms crystallizes ethical dilemmas, threatening to displace basic values of social equality and shared fate. The chapters that follow present diverse ethnographic milieus where the interplay of exceptions, politics, and ethics constitutes a field of vibrating relationships. New forms of governing and being governed and new notions of what it means to be human are at the edge of emergence. [. . .]

In contrast, I conceptualize the exception more broadly, as an extraordinary departure in policy that can be deployed to include as well as to exclude. As conventionally understood, the sovereign exception marks out excludable subjects who are denied protections. But the exception can also be a positive decision to include selected populations and spaces as targets of "calculative choices and value-orientation"[4] associated with neoliberal reform. In my formulation, we need to explore the hinge between neoliberalism as exception and exception to neoliberalism, the interplay among technologies of governing and of disciplining, of inclusion and exclusion, of giving value or denying value to human conduct. The politics of exception in an era of globalization has disquieting ethicopolitical implications for those who are included as well as those who are excluded in shifting technologies of governing and of demarcation. This book will explore how the market-driven logic of exception is deployed in a variety of ethnographic contexts and the ethical risks and interrogations set in motion, unsettling established practices of citizenship and sovereignty.

Interrelationships among exceptions, politics, and citizenship crystallize problems of contemporary living, and they also frame ethical debates over what it means to be human today. For instance, neoliberal exceptions have been variously invoked in Asian settings to recalculate social criteria of citizenship, to remoralize economic action, and to redefine spaces in relation to market-driven choices. These articulations have engendered a range of contingent and ambiguous outcomes that cannot be predicted beforehand. Neoliberal decisions have created new forms of inclusion, setting apart some citizen-subjects, and creating new spaces that enjoy extraordinary political benefits and economic gain. There is the Schmittian exception that abandons certain populations and places them outside political normativity. But articulations between neoliberal exceptions and exceptions to neoliberalism have multiplied possibilities for moral claims and values assigned to various human categories, so that different degrees of protection can be negotiated for the politically excluded. [. . .]

As an intervention of optimization, neoliberalism interacts with regimes of ruling and regimes of citizenship to produce conditions that change administrative strategies and citizenship practices. It follows that the infiltration of market logic into politics conceptually unsettles the notion of citizenship as a legal status rooted in a nation-state, and in stark opposition to a condition of statelessness.[5] Furthermore, the neoliberal exception articulates citizenship elements in political spaces that may be less than the national territory in some cases, or exceed national borders in others.

The elements that we think of as coming together to create citizenship – rights, entitlements, territoriality, a nation – are becoming disarticulated and rearticulated with forces set into motion by market forces. On the one hand, citizenship elements such as entitlements and benefits are increasingly associated with neoliberal criteria, so that mobile individuals who possess human capital or expertise are highly valued and can exercise citizenship-like claims in diverse locations. Meanwhile, citizens who are judged not to have such tradable competence or potential become devalued and thus vulnerable to exclusionary practices. On the other hand, the territoriality of citizenship, that is, the national space of the homeland, has become partially embedded in the territoriality of global capitalism, as well as in spaces mapped by the interventions of nongovernmental organizations (NGOS). Such overlapping spaces of exception create conditions for diverse claims of human value that do not fit neatly into a conventional notion of citizenship, or of a universal regime of human rights. In short, components of citizenship have developed separate links to new spaces, becoming rearticulated, redefined, and reimagined in relation to diverse locations and ethical situations. Such de- and relinking of citizenship elements, actors, and spaces have been occasioned by the dispersion and realignment of market strategies, resources, and actors.

Second, neoliberalism as exception refines the study of state sovereignty, long conceptualized as a political singularity. One view is of the state as a machine that steamrolls across the terrain of the nation, or that will eventually impose a uniform state bureaucracy.[6] In actual practice, sovereignty is manifested in multiple, often contradictory strategies that encounter diverse claims and contestations, and produce diverse and contingent outcomes. In the course of interactions with global markets and regulatory institutions, I maintain, sovereign rule invokes the exception to create new economic possibilities, spaces, and techniques for governing the population. The neoliberal exception allows for a measure of sovereign flexibility in ways that both fragment and extend the space of the nation-state. For instance, in Southeast and East Asia, zoning technologies have carved special spaces in order to achieve strategic goals of regulating groups in relation to market forces. The spatial concentration of strategic political, economic, and social conditions attracts foreign investment, technology transfer, and international expertise to particular zones of high growth. Market-driven strategies of spatial fragmentation respond to the demands of global capital for diverse categories of human capital, thus engendering a pattern of noncontiguous, differently administered spaces of "graduated" or "variegated sovereignty." Furthermore, as corporations and NGOS exert indirect power over various populations at different political scales, we have an emergent situation of overlapping sovereignties.

Notes

1   Rose and Miller, 'Political Power beyond the State.'
2   Collier and Ong, 'Ethics of the Concern for Self,' 300.
3   Collier, 'Spatial Forms and Social Norms.'
4   Collier, 'Spatial Forms and Social Norms.'
5   Arendt, *Human Condition*.
6   See, e.g. Scott, *Seeing Like a State*; and Ferguson, *Anti-politics Machine*.

Aihwa Ong (2006) *Neoliberalism as Exception: Mutations in Citizenship and Sovereignty*, Durham NC and London: Duke University Press, pp. 3–7.

STATES OF EMERGENCY: AL GORE (2007)

Al Gore (1948–) served as the 45th Vice President of the United States of America under President Bill Clinton from 1993 to 2001. After losing a highly controversial presidential election in 2000 to George W. Bush, Gore went on to become an environmental activist, focusing in particular on climate change and the need for alternative fuel energies. Since then, he has received many awards that recognize his work as an advocate for environmental causes. Some of these include the Nobel Peace Prize (which Gore shared with the Intergovernmental Panel on Climate Change) and an Academy Award for Best Documentary for *An Inconvenient Truth*, for which Gore served as the chief writer. The selection is taken from Gore's Nobel Prize acceptance speech which calls upon all nations and peoples to act in unison on global climate change. Unless there is cooperative action, Gore believes that current and future generations will stand a worse chance of surviving this oncoming ecological disaster.

The Nobel Peace Prize Lecture, 2007

We, the human species, are confronting a planetary emergency – a threat to the survival of our civilization that is gathering ominous and destructive potential even as we gather here. But there is hopeful news as well: we have the ability to solve this crisis and avoid the worst – though not all – of its consequences, if we act boldly, decisively and quickly. [. . .]

It has been harder and harder to misinterpret the signs that our world is spinning out of kilter. Major cities in North and South America, Asia and Australia are nearly out of water due to massive droughts and melting glaciers. Desperate farmers are losing their livelihoods. Peoples in the frozen Arctic and on low-lying Pacific islands are planning evacuations of places they have long called home. Unprecedented wildfires have forced a half million people from their homes in one country and caused a national emergency that almost brought down the government in another. Climate refugees have migrated into areas already inhabited by people with different cultures, religions, and traditions, increasing the potential for conflict. Stronger storms in the Pacific and Atlantic have threatened whole cities. Millions have been displaced by massive flooding in South Asia, Mexico, and 18 countries in Africa. As temperature extremes have increased, tens of thousands have lost their lives. We are recklessly burning and clearing our forests and driving more and more species into extinction. The very web of life on which we depend is being ripped and frayed. [. . .]

Now science is warning us that if we do not quickly reduce the global warming pollution that is trapping so much of the heat our planet normally radiates back out of the atmosphere, we are in danger of creating a permanent "carbon summer."

As the American poet Robert Frost wrote, "Some say the world will end in fire; some say in ice." Either, he notes, "would suffice."

But neither need be our fate. It is time to make peace with the planet.

We must quickly mobilize our civilization with the urgency and resolve that has previously been seen only when nations mobilized for war. These prior struggles for survival were won when leaders found words at the 11th hour that released a mighty surge of courage, hope and readiness to sacrifice for a protracted and mortal challenge. [. . .]

The way ahead is difficult. The outer boundary of what we currently believe is feasible is still far short of what we actually must do. Moreover, between here and there, across the unknown, falls the shadow.

That is just another way of saying that we have to expand the boundaries of what is possible. In the words of the Spanish poet, Antonio Machado, "Pathwalker, there is no path. You must make the path as you walk."

We are standing at the most fateful fork in that path. So I want to end as I began, with a vision of two futures – each a palpable possibility – and with a prayer that we will see with vivid clarity the necessity of choosing between those two futures, and the urgency of making the right choice now.

The great Norwegian playwright, Henrik Ibsen, wrote, "One of these days, the younger generation will come knocking at my door."

The future is knocking at our door right now. Make no mistake, the next generation will ask us one of two questions. Either they will ask: "What were you thinking; why didn't you act?"

Or they will ask instead: "How did you find the moral courage to rise and successfully resolve a crisis that so many said was impossible to solve?"

We have everything we need to get started, save perhaps political will, but political will is a renewable resource.

So let us renew it, and say together: "We have a purpose. We are many. For this purpose we will rise, and we will act."

Al Gore (2007) "The Nobel Peace Prize Lecture, 2007," Nobel Lecture, Oslo, 10 December. © The Nobel Foundation. Source: http://nobelprize.org/nobel_prizes/peace/laureates/2007/gore-lecture_en.html.

GLOBALITY AND GLOBALIZATION: ULRICH BECK (1999)

Ulrich Beck (1944–), Professor of Sociology at the University of Munich and Visiting Professor at the London School of Economics, is widely hailed for his research on "risk society" – involving processes of transformation from industrial to reflexive modernization. In this selection, "What is Globalization?", Beck situates globalism beyond the confines of the nation-state and squarely within the realm of what he terms "sub-politics" – a form of political activity at once transnational and multiregional. Beck, in suitably transformationalist style, says that sub-politics are fundamental to the advancement of global democracy and social justice. On the other hand, he notes that new institutions for the provision of global public goals re-involve states and national publics in new ways.

What is Globalization?

Globality means that *we have been living for a long time in a world society*, in the sense that the notion of closed spaces has become illusory. No country or group can shut itself off from others. Various economic, cultural and political forms therefore collide with one another, and things that used to be taken for granted (including in the Western model) will have to be justified anew. 'World society', then, denotes the totality of social relationships which are *not* integrated into or determined (or determinable) by national-state politics. Self-perceptions, as staged by the national mass media, here play a crucial role, so that world society in the narrower sense – to propose a still politically relevant operational criterion – means *perceived* or *reflexive* world society. The question of how far it exists may therefore (in accordance with the Thomas theorem that what people believe to be real becomes real in its consequences) be empirically turned into the question of how, and to what extent, people and cultures around the world relate to one another in their differences, and to what extent this self-perception of world society is relevant to how they behave.[1]

'World' in the combination 'world society' thus means *difference* or *multiplicity*, and 'society' means *non-*integration, so that we may (together with M. Albrow) conceive world society as *multiplicity without unity*. As we shall see, this presupposes a number of very different things: transnational forms of production and labour market competition, global reporting in the media, transnational consumer boycotts, transnational ways of life, as well as 'globally' perceived crises and wars, military and peaceful use of atomic energy, destruction of nature, and so on.

Globalization, on the other hand, denotes the *processes* through which sovereign national states are crisscrossed and undermined by transnational actors with varying prospects of power, orientations, identities and networks.

One essential feature distinguishing the second from the first modernity is the fact that *the new globality cannot be reversed*. This means that the various autonomous logics of globalization – the logics of ecology, culture, economics, politics and civil society – exist side by side and cannot be reduced or collapsed into one another. Rather, each must be independently decoded and grasped in its interdependences. The guiding supposition is that only in this way can the perspective and the space for political action be opened up. Why? Because only then can the depoliticizing spell of globalism be broken; only with a multidimensional view of globality can the globalist ideology of 'material compulsion' be broken down. But what is it that makes globality irreversible? Eight reasons may be given under the following headings:

1 The geographical expansion and ever greater density of international trade, as well as the global network-ing of finance markets and the growing power of transnational corporations.
2 The ongoing revolution of information and communications technology.
3 The universal *demands* for human rights – the (lip service paid to the) principle of democracy.
4 The stream of images from the global culture industries.
5 The emergence of a postnational, polycentric world politics, in which transnational actors (corporations, non-governmental organizations, United Nations) are growing in power and number alongside governments.
6 The question of world poverty.
7 The issue of global environmental destruction.
8 Transcultural conflicts in one and the same place.

In these circumstances, sociology acquires new significance as an exploration of what human life means in the trap that the world has become. Globality means that from now on nothing which happens on our planet is only a limited local event; all inventions, victories and catastrophes affect the whole world, and we must reorient and reorganize our lives and actions, our organizations and institutions, along a 'local-global' axis. Globality, understood in this way, denotes the new situation of the second modernity. This concept also concentrates elementary reasons why the stock answers of the first modernity are inapplicable and contra-dictory for the second modernity, where politics will have to be refounded or reinvented.

This concept of globality may be distinguished from the concept of a *globalization process* (a dialectical process, one would say in old-fashioned language), which creates transnational social links and spaces, revalues local cultures and promotes third cultures ('a little of this, a little of that, is the way new things come into the world' – Salman Rushdie). Within this complex framework, the question of the *extent* of successful globalization as well as of its *limits* may be posed anew in relation to three parameters: (a) extension in *space*; (b) stability over *time*; and (c) social *density* of the transnational networks, relationships and image-flows.

This conceptual horizon makes it possible to answer a further question: namely, what is historically specific about contemporary globalization and its paradoxes at a particular place (for example, in comparison with the 'capitalist world-system' that was already under construction in the age of colonialism)?[2]

The peculiarity of the present, and future, globalization process lies in the empirically ascertainable *scale, density and stability of regional-global relationship networks and their self-definition through the mass media, as well as of social spaces and of image-flows at a cultural, political, economic and military level*.[3] World society is thus not a mega-national society containing and dissolving all national societies within itself, but a world horizon charac-terized by multiplicity and non-integration which opens out when it is produced and preserved in communica-tion and action.

Sceptics will ask what is new about this, and answer: nothing really important. But they are wrong: historic-ally, empirically and theoretically. What is new is not only the everyday life and interaction across national frontiers, in dense networks with a high degree of mutual dependence and obligation. New, too, is the self-perception of this transnationality (in the mass media, consumption or tourism); new is the 'placelessness' of community, labour and capital; new are the awareness of global ecological dangers and the corresponding arenas of action; new is the inescapable perception of transcultural Others in one's own life, with all the contradictory certainties resulting from it; new is the level at which 'global culture industries' circulate (Scott Lash and John Urry); new are the rise of a European structure of states, and the number and power of transnational actors, institutions and agreements; and new, finally, is the degree of economic concentration, which is nevertheless slowed down by cross-frontier competition in the world market.

Globalization, then, also means *no* world state – or, to be more precise, world society *without a world state* and *without world government*. A globally *disorganized* capitalism is continually spreading out. For there is no hegemonic power and no international regime, either economic or political.

Notes

1 See below, pp. 38f., 47f., 68–70, 88–93. See also U. Beck, 'The Cosmopolitan Perspective. On the Sociology of the Second Age of Modernity', *British Journal of Sociology*, 1, 2000.
2 Wallerstein's 'world-system' analysis is discussed below, pp. 31–4.
3 This is stressed by the group around David Held. See D. Held, *Democracy and Global Order*, Cambridge, 1995, pp. 99–136.

Ulrich Beck (1999) *What is Globalization?* transl. by Patrick Camiller, Cambridge: Polity Press, pp. 10–13.

Post-Globalists

HUMAN CONSEQUENCES OF GLOBALIZATION: ZYGMUNT BAUMAN (1998)

Zygmunt Bauman (1925–) is Emeritus Professor of Sociology at the University of Leeds and the University of Warsaw. Widely celebrated for both his sociology of postmodernity and his more recent claim that the contemporary era is driven by processes of "social liquidization" (that is, the liquidizing of politics, culture, society, and human relationships more generally), Bauman has established himself as one of the most original social thinkers of our time. His approach to the question of globalization is highly sophisticated and nuanced: the new global arena of communications technology and multinational consumer capitalism penetrates not only social institutions and cultural processes, but also the core of our private lives. There is no "outside" to globalization, no secluded locale in which to retreat and hide away. Hence, Bauman speaks of the "human consequences" of globalism. His sociology of globalization underscores the point that today people live their lives within a liquid frame of experience – experience of the self and others, of space and time, of life's possibilities and risks – that erodes "long-term" thinking and fractures human bonds. He also argues that the separation of power and sovereignty from the politics of the territorial nation-state escalates in conditions of intensive globalization, which is linked to the collapse of "society" as a bounded complex, or set of structures, as well as the outsourcing of public political functions to non-political, deregulated market forces.

Global Speed and Polarization

The term 'time/space compression' encapsulates the ongoing multi-faceted transformation of the parameters of the human condition. Once the social causes and outcomes of that compression are looked into, it will become evident that the globalizing processes lack the commonly assumed unity of effects. The uses of time and space are sharply differentiated as well as differentiating. Globalization divides as much as it unites; it divides as it unites – the causes of division being identical with those which promote the uniformity of the globe. Alongside the emerging planetary dimensions of business, finance, trade and information flow, a 'localizing', space-fixing process is set in motion. Between them, the two closely interconnected processes sharply differentiate the existential conditions of whole populations and of various segments of each one of the populations. What appears as globalization for some means localization for others; signalling a new freedom for some, upon many others it descends as an uninvited and cruel fate. Mobility climbs to the rank of the uppermost among the coveted values – and the freedom to move, perpetually a scarce and unequally distributed commodity, fast becomes the main stratifying factor of our late-modern or postmodern times.

All of us are, willy-nilly, by design or by default, on the move. We are on the move even if, physically, we stay put: immobility is not a realistic option in a world of permanent change. And yet the effects of that new condition are radically unequal. Some of us become fully and truly 'global'; some are fixed in their 'locality' – a predicament neither pleasurable nor endurable in the world in which the 'globals' set the tone and compose the rules of the life-game.

Being local in a globalized world is a sign of social deprivation and degradation. The discomforts of localized existence are compounded by the fact that with public spaces removed beyond the reaches of localized life, localities are losing their meaning-generating and meaning-negotiating capacity and are increasingly dependent on sense-giving and interpreting actions which they do not control – so much for the communitarianist dreams/consolations of the globalized intellectuals.

An integral part of the globalizing processes is progressive spatial segregation, separation and exclusion. Neo-tribal and fundamentalist tendencies, which reflect and articulate the experience of people on the receiving and of globalization, are as much legitimate offspring of globalization as the widely acclaimed 'hybridization' of top culture – the culture at the globalized top. A particular cause for worry is the progressive breakdown in communication between the increasingly global and extraterritorial elites and the ever more 'localized' rest. The centres of meaning-and-value production are today exterritorial and emancipated from local constraints – this does not apply, though, to the human condition which such values and meanings are to inform and make sense of.

With the freedom of mobility at its centre, the present-day polarization has many dimensions; the new centre puts a new gloss on the time-honoured distinctions between rich and poor, the nomads and the settled, the 'normal' and the abnormal or those in breach of law. Just how these various dimensions of polarity intertwine and influence each other is another complex problem this book attempts to unpack. . . .

The mobility acquired by 'people who invest' – those with capital, with money which the investment requires – means the new, indeed unprecedented in its radical unconditionality, disconnection of power from obligations: duties towards employees, but also towards the younger and weaker, towards yet unborn generations and towards the self-reproduction of the living conditions of all; in short, freedom from the duty to contribute to daily life and the perpetuation of the community. There is a new asymmetry emerging between exterritorial nature of power and the continuing territoriality of the 'whole life' – which the now unanchored power, able to move at short notice or without warning, is free to exploit and abandon to the consequences of that exploitation. Shedding the responsibility for the consequences is the most coveted and cherished gain which the new mobility brings to free-floating, locally unbound capital. The costs of coping with the consequences need not be now counted in the calculation of the 'effectiveness' of investment.

New speed, new polarization

To put it in a nutshell: *rather than homogenizing the human condition, the technological annulment of temporal/ spatial distances tends to polarize it.* It emancipates certain humans from territorial constraints and renders certain community-generating meanings exterritorial – while denuding the territory, to which other people go on being confined, of its meaning and its identity-endowing capacity. For some people it augurs an unprecedented freedom from physical obstacles and unheard-of ability to move and act from a distance. For others, it portends the impossibility of appropriating and domesticating the locality from which they have little chance of cutting themselves free in order to move elsewhere. With 'distances no longer meaning anything', localities, separated by distances, also lose their meanings. This, however, augurs freedom of meaning-creation for some, but portends ascription to meaning-lessness for others. Some can now move out of the locality – any locality – at will. Others watch helplessly the sole locality they inhabit moving away from under their feet.

Information now floats independently from its carriers; shifting of bodies and rearrangement of bodies in physical space is less than ever necessary to reorder meanings and relationships. For some people – for the mobile elite, the elite of mobility – this means, literally, the 'dephysicalization', the new weightlessness of power. Elites travel in space, and travel faster than ever before – but the spread and density of the power web they weave is not dependent on that travel. Thanks to new 'bodylessness' of power in its mainly financial form, the power-holders become truly exterritorial even if, bodily, they happen to stay 'in place'. Their power is, fully and truly, not 'out of this world' – not of the physical world in which they build their heavily guarded homes and offices, themselves exterritorial, free from intrusion of unwelcome neighbours, cut out from whatever may be called a *local* community, inaccessible to whoever is, unlike them, confined to it.

Zygmunt Bauman (1998) *Globalization: The Human Consequences*, New York: Columbia University Press, pp. 2–3, 9–10, 18–19.

THE GLOBAL CULTURAL ECONOMY: ARJUN APPADURAI (1990)

Arjun Appadurai (1949–) is Goddard Professor of Media, Culture, and Communication at New York University. Born and educated in India before moving to the United States, Appadurai's work foregrounds the centrality of the "social imaginary" as an organized field of social practices operating within processes of globalization. As a radical, Appadurai believes that social change and political transformation intensifies in conditions of advanced globalization, and his own work represents an extraordinary interdisciplinary engagement with both the cultural and the personal consequences of globalism. In this selection, he identifies five imaginary dimensions underpinning the new global order: ethnoscapes, mediascapes, technoscapes, finanscapes and ideoscapes.

Disjuncture and Difference in the Global Cultural Economy

The new global cultural economy has to be understood as a complex, overlapping, disjunctive order, which cannot any longer be understood in terms of existing center-periphery models (even those that might account for multiple centers and peripheries). Nor is it susceptible to simple models of push and pull (in terms of migration theory) or of surpluses and deficits (as in traditional models of balance of trade), or of consumers and producers (as in most neo-Marxist theories of development). Even the most complex and flexible theories of global development which have come out of the Marxist tradition (Amin, 1980; Mandel, 1978; Wallerstein, 1974; Wolf, 1982) are inadequately quirky, and they have not come to terms with what Lash and Urry (1987) have recently called 'disorganized capitalism'. The complexity of the current global economy has to do with certain fundamental disjunctures between economy, culture and politics which we have barely begun to theorize.

I propose that an elementary framework for exploring such disjunctures is to look at the relationship between five dimensions of global cultural flow which can be termed: (a) ethnoscapes; (b) mediascapes; (c) technoscapes; (d) finanscapes; and (e) ideoscapes. [. . .]

By 'ethnoscape', I mean the landscape of persons who constitute the shifting world in which we live: tourists, immigrants, refugees, exiles, guestworkers and other moving groups and persons constitute an essential feature of the world, and appear to affect the politics of and between nations to a hitherto unprecedented degree. This is not to say that there are not anywhere relatively stable communities and networks, of kinship, of friendship, of work and of leisure, as well as of birth, residence and other filiative forms. But it is to say that the warp of these stabilities is everywhere shot through with the woof of human motion, as more persons and groups deal with the realities of having to move, or the fantasies of wanting to move. What is more, both these realities as well as these fantasies now function on larger scales, as men and women from villages in India think not just of moving to Poona or Madras, but of moving to Dubai and Houston, and refugees from Sri Lanka find themselves in South India as well as in Canada, just as the Hmong are driven to London as well as to Philadelphia. And as international capital shifts its needs, as production and technology generate different needs, as nation-states shift their policies on refugee populations, these moving groups can never afford to let their imaginations rest too long, even if they wished to.

By 'technoscape', I mean the global configuration, also ever fluid, of technology, and of the fact that technology, both high and low, both mechanical and informational, now moves at high speeds across various kinds of previously impervious boundaries. Many countries now are the roots of multinational enterprise: a huge steel complex in Libya may involve interests from India, China, Russia and Japan, providing different components of new technological configurations. The odd distribution of technologies, and thus the peculiarities of these technoscapes, are increasingly driven not by any obvious economies of scale, of political control, or of market rationality, but of increasingly complex relationships between money flows, political possibilities and the availability of both low and highly-skilled labor. So, while India exports waiters and chauffeurs to Dubai and Sharjah, it also exports software engineers to the United States (indentured briefly to Tata-Burroughs or the World Bank), then laundered through the State Department to become wealthy 'resident aliens', who are in turn objects of seductive messages to invest their money and know-how in federal and state projects in India. The global economy can still be described in terms of traditional 'indicators' (as the World Bank continues to do) and studied in terms of traditional comparisions (as in Project Link at the University of Pennsylvania), but the complicated technoscapes (and the shifting ethnoscapes), which underlie these 'indicators' and 'comparisions' are further out of the reach of the 'queen of the social sciences' than ever before. How is one to make a meaningful comparision of wages in Japan and the United States, or of real estate costs in New York and Tokyo, without taking sophisticated account of the very complex fiscal and investment flows that link the two economies, through a global grid of currency speculation and capital transfer?

Thus it is useful to speak as well of 'finanscapes', since the disposition of global capital is now a more mysterious, rapid and difficult landscape to follow than ever before, as currency markets, national stock exchanges, and commodity speculations move megamonies through national turnstiles at blinding speed, with vast absolute implications for small differences in percentage points and time units. But the critical point is that the global relationship between ethnoscapes, technoscapes and finanscapes is deeply disjunctive and profoundly unpredictable, since each of these landscapes is subject to its own constraints and incentives (some political, some informational and some techno-environmental), at the same time as each acts as a constraint and a parameter for movements in the other. Thus, even an elementary model of global political economy must take into account the shifting relationship between perspectives on human movement, technological flow, and financial transfers, which can accommodate their deeply disjunctive relationships with one another.

Built upon these disjunctures (which hardly form a simple mechanical global 'infrastructure' in any case) are what I have called 'mediascapes' and 'ideoscapes', though the latter two are closely related landscapes of images. 'Mediascapes' refer both to the distribution of the electronic capabilities to produce and disseminate information (newspapers, magazines, television stations, film production studios, etc.), which are now available to a growing number of private and public interests throughout the world; and to the images of the world created by these media. These images of the world involve many complicated inflections, depending on their mode (documentary or entertainment), their hardware (electronic or pre-electronic), their audiences (local, national or transnational) and the interests of those who own and control them. What is most important about these mediascapes is that they provide (especially in their television, film and cassette forms) large and complex repertoires of images, narratives and 'ethnoscapes' to viewers throughout the world, in which the world of commodities and the world of 'news' and politics are profoundly mixed. What this means is that many audiences throughout the world experience the media themselves as a complicated and interconnected repertoire of print, celluloid, electronic screens and billboards. The lines between the 'realistic' and the fictional landscapes they see are blurred, so that the further away these audiences are from the direct experiences of metropolitan life, the more likely they are to construct 'imagined worlds' which are chimerical, aesthetic, even fantastic objects, particularly if assessed by the criteria of some other perspective, some other 'imagined world'.

'Mediascapes', whether produced by private or state interests, tend to be image-centered, narrative-based accounts of strips of reality, and what they offer to those who experience and transform them is a series of elements (such as characters, plots and textual forms) out of which scripts can be formed of imagined lives, their own as well as those of others living in other places. These scripts can and do get disaggregated into complex sets of metaphors by which people live (Lakoff and Johnson, 1980) as they help to constitute narratives of the 'other' and proto-narratives of possible lives, fantasies which could become prologemena to the desire for acquisition and movement.

'Ideoscsapes' are also concatenations of images, but they are often directly political and frequently have to do with the ideologies of states and the counter-ideologies of movements explicitly oriented to capturing state power or a piece of it. These ideoscapes are composed of elements of the Enlightenment world-view, which consists of a concatenation of ideas, terms and images, including 'freedom', 'welfare', 'rights', 'sovereignty', 'representation' and the master-term 'democracy'. The master-narrative of the Enlightenment (and its many variants in England, France and the United States) was constructed with a certain internal logic and presupposed a certain relationship between reading, representation and the public sphere (for the dynamics of this process in the early history of the United States, see Warner, 1990). But their diaspora across the world, especially since the nineteenth century, has loosened the internal coherence which held these terms and images together in a Euro-American master-narrative, and provided instead a loosely structured synopticon of politics, in which different nation-states, as part of their evolution, have organized their political cultures around different 'keywords' (Williams, 1976). [. . .]

This extended terminological discussion of the five terms I have coined sets the basis for a tentative formulation about the conditions under which current global flows occur: *they occur in and through the growing disjunctures between ethnoscapes, technoscapes, finanscapes, mediascapes and ideoscapes.* This formulation, the core of my model of global cultural flow, needs some explanation. First, people, machinery, money, images, and ideas now follow increasingly non-isomorphic paths: of course, at all periods in human history, there have been some disjunctures between the flows of these things, but the sheer speed, scale and volume of each of these flows is now so great that the disjunctures have become central to the politics of global culture. The Japanese are notoriously hospitable to ideas and are stereotyped as inclined to export (all) and import (some) goods, but they are also notoriously closed to immigration, like the Swiss, the Swedes and the Saudis. Yet the Swiss and Saudis accept populations of guestworkers, thus creating labor diasporas of Turks, Italians and other circum-mediterranean groups. Some such guestworker groups maintain continuous contact with their home-nations, like the Turks, but others, like high-level South Asian migrants tend to desire lives in their new homes, raising anew the problem of reproduction in a deterritorialized context.

Deterritorialization, in general, is one of the central forces of the modern world, since it brings laboring populations into the lower class sectors and spaces of relatively wealthy societies, while sometimes creating exaggerated and intensified senses of criticism or attachment to politics in the home-state. Deterritorialization, whether of Hindus, Sikhs, Palestinians or Ukranians, is now at the core of a variety of global fundamentalisms, including Islamic and Hindu fundamentalism. In the Hindu case for example (Appadurai and Breckenridge, forthcoming) it is clear that the overseas movement of Indians has been exploited by a variety of interests both within and outside India to create a complicated network of finances and religious identifications, in which the problems of cultural reproduction for Hindus abroad has become tied to the politics of Hindu fundamentalism at home.

At the same time, deterritorialization creates new markets for film companies, art impressarios and travel agencies, who thrive on the need of the deterritorialized population for contact with its homeland. Naturally, these invented homelands, which constitute the mediascapes of deterritorialized groups, can often become sufficiently fantastic and one-sided that they provide the material for new ideoscapes in which ethnic conflicts can begin to erupt. The creation of 'Khalistan', an invented homeland of the deterritorialized Sikh population of England, Canada and the United States, is one example of the bloody potential in such mediascapes, as they interact with the 'internal colonialisms' (Hechter, 1974) of the nation-state. The West Bank, Namibia and Eritrea are other theaters for the enactment of the bloody negotiation between existing nation-states and various deterritorialized groupings.

The idea of deterritorialization may also be applied to money and finance, as money managers seek the best markets for their investments, independent of national boundaries. In turn, these movements of monies are the basis of new kinds of conflict, as Los Angelenos worry about the Japanese buying up their city, and people in Bombay worry about the rich Arabs from the Gulf States who have not only transformed the prices of mangoes in Bombay, but have also substantially altered the profile of hotels, restaurants and other services in the eyes of the local population, just as they continue to do in London. Yet, most residents of Bombay are ambivalent about the Arab presence there, for the flip side of their presence is the absence of friends and kinsmen earning big money in the Middle East and bringing back both money and luxury commodities to Bombay and other cities in India. Such commodities transform consumer taste in these cities, and also often end up smuggled through air and sea ports and peddled in the gray markets of Bombay's streets. In these gray markets, some members of Bombay's middle-classes and of its lumpenproletariat can buy some of these goods, ranging from cartons of Marlboro cigarettes, to Old Spice shaving cream and tapes of Madonna. Similarly gray routes, often subsidized by the moonlighting activities of sailors, diplomats, and airline stewardesses who get to move in and out of the country regularly, keep the gray markets of Bombay, Madras and Calcutta filled with goods not only from the West, but also from the Middle East, Hong Kong and Singapore.

It is this fertile ground of deterritorialization, in which money, commodities and persons are involved in ceaselessly chasing each other around the world, that the mediascapes and ideoscapes of the modern world find their fractured and fragmented counterpart. For the ideas and images produced by mass media often are only partial guides to the goods and experiences that deterritorialized populations transfer to one another. In Mira Nair's brilliant film, *India Cabaret*, we see the multiple loops of this fractured deterritorialization as young women, barely competent in Bombay's metropolitan glitz, come to seek their fortunes as cabaret dancers and prostitutes in Bombay, entertaining men in clubs with dance formats derived wholly from the prurient dance sequences of Hindi films. These scenes cater in turn to ideas about Western and foreign women and their 'looseness', while they provide tawdry career alibis for these women. Some of these women come from Kerala, where cabaret clubs and the pornograpic film industry have blossomed, partly in response to the purses and tastes of Keralites returned from the Middle East, where their diasporic lives away from women distort their very sense of what the relations between men and women might be. These tragedies of displacement could certainly be replayed in a more detailed analysis of the relations between the Japanese and German sex tours to Thailand and the tragedies of the sex trade in Bangkok, and in other similar loops which tie together fantasies about the other, the conveniences and seductions of travel, the economics of global trade and the brutal mobility fantasies that dominate gender politics in many parts of Asia and the world at large.

Arjun Appadurai (1990) "Disjuncture and Difference in the Global Cultural Economy," *Theory, Culture and Society*, vol. 7, pp. 296–300, 301–303.

GLOBALIZATION AND LATE CAPITALISM: FREDRIC JAMESON (1998)

Fredric Jameson (1934–), one of the most widely discussed post-Marxist theoreticians in the United States, is William A. Lane Professor in Literature at Duke University. Best known for his account of postmodernism as the cultural manifestation of advanced capitalism, Jameson has also focused on the problematic of globalization as a complex interplay of communication, culture, and capitalism. Examining both celebrations and critiques of globalism, Jameson contends that globalism is the very "lingua franca" of corporate power and mass culture in our own time of advanced capitalist cultural production.

Notes on Globalization as a Philosophical Issue

I believe that globalization is a communicational concept, which alternately masks and transmits cultural or economic meanings. We have a sense that there are both denser and more extensive communicational networks all over the world today, networks that are on the one hand the result of remarkable innovations in communicational technologies of all kinds, and on the other have as their foundation the tendentially greater degree of modernization in all the countries of the world, or at least in their big cities, which includes the implantation of such technologies.

But the communicational focus of the concept of globalization is essentially incomplete: I defy anyone to try to think it in exclusively media or communicational terms; and we can find a point of contrast and distinction in the images of the media in the earlier twentieth century, that is to say, in the modernist period. There did then seem to be a certain semiautonomy about the development of the media: radio did seem to penetrate for the first time into remote areas (both at home and abroad); the progress of film around the world was both swift and startling, and seemed to bring some new kind of mass consciousness with it; journalism and reporting, meanwhile, were somehow at their outer reaches heroic acts, which shed new light and brought back new information. No one can feel that the cybernetic revolution is like that, if only because it builds on those first, already established networks. The communicational development today is no longer one of "enlightenment" in all its connotations, but rather of new technologies.

This is why, along with the communicational concept of globalization, one always finds other dimensions smuggled in. Thus, if the newer phenomenon essentially distinguishes itself from the older, modern one by technology rather than by information (even though this term is then itself reappropriated and ideologically developed today on a grand scale), what happens is that the technology and what the computer people call information begin to slip insensibly in the direction of advertisements and publicity, of postmodern marketing, and finally of the export of TV programs, rather than the return of startling reports from remote places. But this is to say that the surface concept, the communicational one, has suddenly acquired a whole cultural dimension: the communicational signifier has been endowed with a more properly cultural signified or signification. Now the positing of an enlargement of communicational nets has secretly been transformed into some kind of message about a new world culture.

But the slippage can also take another direction: the economic. Thus, in our attempt to think this new, still purely communicational concept, we begin to fill in the empty signifier with visions of financial transfers and investments all over the world, and the new networks begin to swell with the commerce of some new and allegedly more flexible capitalism (I have to confess that I have always found this a ludicrous expression). We begin remembering that the newly flexible production was made possible precisely by computerization (a loop back to the technological again), and we also remember that computers and their programs and the like are themselves among the most hotly exchanged forms of goods among the nations today. In this variant, then, the ostensibly communicational concept has secretly been transformed into a vision of the world market and its newfound interdependence, a global division of labor on an extraordinary scale, new electronic trade routes tirelessly plied by commerce and finance alike.

Now I think we are better equipped to understand the flows of debate and ideology around this slippery concept, whose twin and not altogether commensurable faces now seem to produce two distinct types of position, which are however themselves reversible. Thus, if you insist on the cultural contents of this new communicational form, I think you will slowly emerge into a postmodern celebration of difference and differentiation: suddenly all the cultures around the world are placed in tolerant contact with each other in a kind of immense cultural pluralism which it would be very difficult not to welcome. Beyond that, beyond the dawning celebration of cultural difference, and often very closely linked to it, is a celebration of the emergence of a whole immense range of groups, races, genders, ethnicities, into the speech of the public sphere; a falling away of those structures that condemned whole segments of the population to silence and to subalternity; a worldwide growth of popular democratization – why not? – which seems to have some relationship to the evolution of the media, but which is immediately expressed by a new richness and variety of cultures in the new world space.

If, on the other hand, your thoughts turn economic, and the concept of globalization becomes colored by those codes and meanings, I think you will find the concept darkening and growing more opaque. Now what comes to the fore is increasing identity (rather than difference): the rapid assimilation of hitherto autonomous national markets and productive zones into a single sphere, the disappearance of national subsistence (in food, for example), the forced integration of countries all over the globe into precisely that new global division of labor I mentioned before. Here what begins to infuse our thinking of globalization is a picture of standardization on an unparalleled new scale; of forced integration as well, into a world-system from which "delinking" (to use Samir Amin's term) is henceforth impossible and even unthinkable and inconceivable. This is obviously a far more baleful prospect than the preceding joyous vision of heterogeneity and difference, but I'm not sure that these visions are logically incompatible; indeed, they seem somehow to be dialectically related, at least on the mode of the unresolvable antinomy.

But now, having achieved these first twin positions, having in some first moment rotated the concept in such a way that it takes on these distinct kinds of content, its surface now glittering in light, and then obscured again by darkness and shadow – now it is important to add that the transfers can begin. Now, after having secured these initial structural possibilities, you can project their axes upon each other. Now, in a second moment, the baleful vision of Identity can be transferred onto the cultural realm: and what will be affirmed, in some gloomy Frankfurt School fashion, is the worldwide Americanization or standardization of culture, the destruction of local differences, the massification of all the peoples on the planet.

But you are equally free to do the inverse, and to transfer the joyous and celebratory Difference and multiple heterogeneities of the first, cultural dimension onto the economic sphere: where, as you may well imagine, the rhetoricians of the market pop up and feverishly reassure us as to the richness and excitement of the new free market all over the world: the increase in sheer productivity that open markets will lead to, the transcendental satisfaction that human beings have finally begun to grasp exchange, the market, and capitalism as their most fundamental human possibilities and the surest sources of freedom.

Such are the multiple structural possibilities and combinations made available by this most ambiguous ideological concept and its alternating contents, through which we may now provisionally explore a few paths.

One obvious path is the sense in which globalization means the export and import of culture. This is, no doubt, a matter of business; yet it also presumably foretells the contact and interpenetration of national cultures at an intensity scarcely conceivable in older, slower epochs.

It is enough to think of all the people around the world who watch exported Northamerican television programs to realize that this cultural intervention is deeper than anything known in earlier forms of colonization or imperialism, or simple tourism. A great Indian filmmaker once described the ways in which the gestures and the allure of walking of his teenage son were modified by watching American television: one supposes that his ideas and values were also modified. Does this mean that the rest of the world is becoming Americanized? and if so, what do we think about that; or perhaps one should ask, what does the rest of the world think about that, and what might Americans think about it?

For I must now add here a basic point about cultural pluralism and diversity, even about linguistic pluralism and diversity. We have to understand, in this country, something that is difficult for us to realize: namely, that the United States is not just one country, or one culture, among others, any more than English is just one language among others. There is a fundamental dissymmetry in the relationship between the United States and every other country in the world, not only third-world countries, but even Japan and those of Western Europe, as I will suggest in a moment. [. . .]

This is indeed the sense in which the new explosion of world culture has seemed to so many to be an occasion for celebration; nor is it desirable to choose between the two very different views of the matter, but rather to intensify their incompatibility and opposition such that we can live this particular contradiction as our own historic form of Hegel's "unhappy consciousness." On the one hand, there is the view according to which globalization essentially means unification and standardization. By the intermediaries of the great, mostly American-based transnational or multinational corporations, a standard form of American material life, along with Northamerican values and cultural forms, is being systematically transmitted to other cultures. Nor is this simply a matter of machinery and buildings, which increasingly make all the places of the world look alike. It is not only a matter of values either – although Americans always find it shocking when foreigners suggest that human rights, feminist values, and even parliamentary democracy are not necessarily to be seen as universals, but rather merely local American cultural characteristics that have been exported as practices valid for all peoples in the world.

That kind of shock is good for us, I want to say; but I have not yet mentioned the supreme form in which American economic interest and American cultural influence coincide to produce the export of a way of life itself. People often evoke "corrosive individualism" and also consumerist "materialism" as a way of accounting for the destructiveness of the new globalization process. But I think these moralizing concepts are inadequate to the task, and do not sufficiently identify the destructive forces that are North American in origin and result from the unchallenged primacy of the United States today and thus the "American way of life" and American mass media culture. This is *consumerism* as such, the very linchpin of our economic system, and also the mode of daily life in which all our mass culture and entertainment industries train us ceaselessly day after day, in an image and media barrage quite unparalleled in history. Since the discrediting of socialism by the collapse of Russian communism, only religious fundamentalism has seemed to offer an alternative way of life – let us not, heaven help us, call it a lifestyle – to American consumerism. But is it certain that all of human history has been, as Fukuyama and others believe, a tortuous progression toward the American consumer as a climax? And is it meanwhile so sure that the benefits of the market can be extended so far as to make this new way of life available for everyone on the globe? If not, we will have destroyed their cultures without offering any alternatives; but it has also been argued that all the other recrudescences of what people think of as local and nationalist violence are themselves reactions and defense mechanisms in the face of heightened globalization. [. . .]

It is hard to give voice now to more positive views after such catastrophic visions without trivializing the other side of the coin: the celebration of globalization and postmodernity. But this is also a very persuasive view that I think many of us, particularly in the United States, tend to share unconsciously and practically to the degree to which we are ourselves the recipients of the new world culture. [. . .]

My sense is that the old and fundamental opposition, in the colonized world, between Westernizers and traditionalists, has almost completely disappeared in this new postmodern moment of capitalism. That opposition was, so to speak, a modernist one, and it no longer holds for the very simple reason that tradition in that form has everywhere been wiped out. Neo-Confucianism and Islamic and Hindu fundamentalism themselves are new, are postmodern inventions, not survivals of ancient ways of life. In that sense also the opposition between the metropolis and the provinces has also disappeared, both nationally and on a global scale; and this not necessarily for a very good reason either, as it is essentially standardization that effaces the difference between the center and the margins. And although it may be an exaggeration to claim that we are all marginals now, all decentered in the current good senses of those words, certainly many new freedoms have been won in the process whereby globalization has meant a decentering and a proliferation of differences. You see how this view grasps the arrival of globalization in exactly the opposite way from the pessimistic one, for which it meant unification and standardization; yet these are indeed the two antithetical features of that elephant we are here blindly attempting to characterize.

In the realm of culture, no one has given a more powerful expression to the celebratory picture of globalization than the Mexican theorist Néstor García Canclini in his conception of culture as hybridization:[1] in his view, the eclectic contacts and borrowings enabled by globalization are progressive and healthy, they positively encourage the proliferation of new cultures (and indeed, I think it is implied by this view that in any case culture always functioned this way, by impure and disorderly combinations, and not by situations of isolation and regulated tradition). García Canclini's work thus gives ammunition to the most vital utopian visions of our own time, of an immense global urban intercultural festival without a center or even any longer a dominant cultural mode. I myself think this view needs a little economic specificity and is rather inconsistent with the quality and impoverishment of what has to be called corporate culture on a global scale.

But its clash with the previous pessimistic view of the globalization process is the shock from which I hope the sparks will fly, and in any case, this is surely one of the most important debates of the current period.

(The other very important and surely related opposition is that which obtains between the older values of autonomy and self-sufficiency – both in culture and economics – and current visions of systemic interdependence in which we are all points in a net or global web. There, too, powerful cases can be made on both sides, but I mention this particular debate only in passing and in order to read it onto some enlarged agenda.)

But now I need to move back to the trilateral possibility, and say why, if García Canclini proves to be wrong about the continuing cultural vitality and production of the so-called third world, we might not continue to expect a counterbalance to Americanization in the two other great world centers of Europe and Japan.

In the present context, I would rather present that as a problem than a mere opinion: namely, whether, in our time, the relationship between culture and economics has not fundamentally altered. At any rate, it does seem to me that fresh cultural production and innovation – and this means in the area of mass-consumed culture – are the crucial index of the centrality of a given area and not its wealth or productive power. This is why it was extraordinarily significant when the ultimate Japanese moves to incorporate the U.S. entertainment industry – Sony's acquisition of Columbia Pictures and Matsushita's buyout of MCA – both failed: it meant that despite immense wealth and technological and industrial production, even despite ownership itself and private property, the Japanese were unable to master the essentially cultural productivity required to secure the globalization process for any given competitor. Whoever says the production of culture says the production of everyday life – and without that, your economic system can scarcely continue to expand and implant itself.

As for Europe – more wealthy and culturally elegant than ever, a glittering museum to a remarkable past, most immediately the past of modernism itself – I want also to suggest that its failure to generate its own forms of mass cultural production is an ominous sign. Is it possible that the death of modernism also meant a certain end for a certain type of hegemonic European art and culture? I happen to find the effort, stimulated by the EEC, to conjure up a new European cultural synthesis, with Milan Kundera substituting for T. S. Eliot, an equally ominous, if more pathetic, symptom. The emergence of a host of local popular and ethnic or oppositional cultures all over Europe is a welcome bonus of postmodernity, as it is everywhere in the world, but by definition renounces the old European hegemonic project.

By the same token, the former socialist countries have seemed largely unable to generate an original culture and a distinctive way of life capable of standing as an alternative, while, as I have already suggested, in the third world the older traditionalisms are equally enfeebled and mummified, and only a religious fundamentalism seems to have the strength and the will to resist Americanization. But here the operative word is surely *seems;* for we have yet to see whether these experiments offer positive social alternatives, or merely reactive and repressive violence.

Note

1   Néstor García Canclini, *Culturas Hibridas* (Mexico City, 1989).

Fredric Jameson (1998) "Notes on Globalization as a Philosophical Issue," in Fredric Jameson and Masao Miyoshi (eds) *The Cultures of Globalization*, Durham and London: Duke University Press, pp. 55–58, 64–68.

■ ■ ■ ■ ■ ■

A POSTMORTEM FOR GLOBALIZATION: JUSTIN ROSENBERG (2005)

Justin Rosenberg is Reader in International Relations and Politics at the University of Sussex. He is most well known for his polemical arguments against globalization as a useful concept. The selection is taken from one of these critiques and it outlines the basis for Rosenberg's dissatisfaction. One reason why Rosenberg is skeptical of globalization's explanatory power is that many of the novel areas that it supposedly touches upon are actually quite redundant. Another reason is that talk about globalization always involves a whole host of qualifiers (e.g., citizenship, capitalism). Ultimately, this leads Rosenberg to believe that globalization is a rather empty notion and unworthy of any further attention.

Theoretical Postmortem

Looking back from the present day onto the literature of Globalization Theory, is it now possible to pin-point the intellectual problems that made it liable to the fate described in the Introduction above? Arguably there were at least two such problems–problems that were, in fact, perfectly visible throughout the 1990s, even before we knew the historical end of the story. The first of these concerns its ambitions regarding social theory in general, while the second is bound up with its implied historical sociology of modernity in particular. Let us consider each of these in turn.

Globalization and social theory

The problem of 'globalization' and social theory may be summarized briefly in three steps.[1] First, the word 'globalization' is a geographical term, denoting a process over time of spatial change – the process of becoming worldwide. Twist and turn this word as you will, space, time and a reference to the shape of the planet are its only intrinsic contents. *Prima facie*, it contains nothing else which can be drawn upon in order to explain any real-world phenomena it is used to describe.

In this respect, it differs markedly from, for example, the word 'capitalism', which specifies a particular nexus of social relationships – centred upon private property and wage labour – from which spatial and temporal implications, among others, might be argued to follow. . . .

By contrast, the term 'globalization' in itself specifies no particular kind of society at all, but simply denotes a process of worldwide spatial expansion and integration *per se*.

Second, and for this reason, any attempt to involve this term in the explanation of large-scale social change faces an inevitable choice: either it must – consciously or otherwise – incorporate a social theory drawn from elsewhere, of what is being 'globalized', why, and with what effect – for none of these is visibly intrinsic to the term; or, alternatively, it must – again, consciously or otherwise – claim that the necessary social theory can after all be derived within the term, because space and time themselves are the foundational parameters of social explanation.

In the former case, the explanatory standing of 'globalization', however great, is ultimately derivative. Indeed in the overall scheme of explanation, it remains a primarily descriptive term, identifying an *explanandum*. In the latter case, however, it becomes itself the *explanans* of the argument, and can legitimately function as such only insofar as a spatio-temporal reformulation of social theory succeeds. In this contrast lies the distinction between a 'theory of globalization' and Globalization Theory. And when that distinction is applied to the literature, it reveals a substantial body of writers for whom 'theories of globalization' were not enough: convinced of the world-historic significance of contemporary developments, they believed that a fundamental revision of social theory was indeed necessitated; and, reversing the polarity of *explanans* and *explanandum* identified above, they took up the challenge of Globalization Theory. From this point onwards, the direction of the resulting argumentation was set ineluctably by the intellectual requirements of that challenge. One way or another, the starting point was always, and necessarily, the purification of 'globalization' into a spatio-temporal concept; and claims for the real world significance of 'globalization' as an empirical phenomenon then became dependent upon the successful application of this concept to explain contemporary social change.

Yet here, thirdly, lay the nub of the problem. There is no question that the relational form of any given society is inseparable from particular orderings (practical and imaginative) of space and time. Both classical social theory and the contemporary disciplines of Anthropology, History, Geography and Sociology furnish rich explorations of how and why different kinds of society have 'produced' space and time in different ways. However, the call for a spatio-temporal problematic for social science as a whole demanded more than this. For, as we have already noted, it implied a claim that the spatio-temporal dimension of human social reproduction is in some way ontologically prior to other dimensions – and therefore legitimately constitutes the starting point for social explanation. And once again, we should remind ourselves that (for example) Giddens' theory of 'time–space distanciation' rested ultimately on just such a claim: social analysis, he argued, should proceed by identifying the ways in which different societies achieve the 'binding' of space and time through which the ontological security of their members is maintained (1990, 14).

Now, it is not easy to say in principle why such claims are invalid – not, at any rate, without presupposing alternative starting points (such as 'relations of production'), which themselves can have no *a priori* justification. Indeed, this whole line of criticism might initially seem rather obscure and even pedantic to the point of triviality. Yet the error being identified here has a familiar name: misplaced concreteness. And its consequences, here as elsewhere, were anything but trivial. For again and again in this literature, the attempt to ground sociological explanation in a spatio-temporal definition of social structures produced instead a systematic reification of space and time themselves: the causal properties of particular social relations that were undergoing spatio-temporal expansion or compression were instead attributed to the expansion or compression itself. This in turn placed an explanatory weight on the phenomenon of time-space compression *per se* which it could not possibly bear: just how much causality, for example, could one really squeeze out of the fact of real-time communication between stockmarkets in itself, without including (knowingly or not) the causal properties of the specifically capitalist social relations which are the substance of the communication (and arguably also the source of its acceleration)?

Consequently, explanations of social phenomena, which claimed to be based on spatio-temporal analyses, were always beset by one of two problems. Either they were indifferent to the qualitative form of specific social relations, which rendered them incapable of explaining the sources of power and causation to which these forms gave rise (Giddens' discussion of the 'disembedding' properties of 'abstract systems' had this characteristic); or, alternatively (as in the case of Bauman), the explanation turned out to have included these other sources of causality all along, in which case its self-designation as a specifically spatio-temporal explanation was heavily vitiated – together with the grounds it supposedly provided for the pursuit of a new problematic.

In the writings of Globalization Theory, this negative antimony led to intellectual difficulties that were so severe that the outright collapse of the argument was only ever avoided in one of two ways: either the spatio-temporal claims were tacitly withdrawn before the end of the argument (as indeed occurred in the writings of both Giddens and Bauman); or they were so heavily qualified from the start that no clear argument could emerge at all (a spectacle which could be observed variously in the works of Held *et al.*, Castells, and Jan Aart Scholte). Either way, the resulting argumentation came to resemble the intellectual equivalent of an architectural folly – the structure could not be completed without destroying the effect; it was necessarily built as a ruin. To be sure, no concept is without explanatory limits and weaknesses, and these always need to be acknowledged through qualification when it is applied. But that process ought to clarify and strengthen the argument being made. What distinguishes a concept as an intellectual 'folly' is that the qualifications involved in its application are necessarily of such a kind that they add up to a *retraction* of the argument itself, without however being recognised as such by their author.[2]

This phenomenon of the folly recurred so regularly in these writings that, in the absence of other explanations, it seems reasonable to conclude that it reflected a systematic flaw in the entire enterprise of Globalization Theory. And, given what has been said above, it seems likely that this flaw lay in the common starting point of these writings, a bold inversion of the normal designation of *explanans* and *explanandum*: sociological explanation of spatio-temporal phenomena was not just supplemented with but actually displaced by attempted spatio-temporal explanation of social change. Nothing less, to be sure, could have vindicated the elevation of 'globalization' from an empirical, descriptive category to an alternative problematic for social theory *tout court*. But the penalty was all too clear: there was, and is, a limit to how deeply the categories of space and time may safely be inserted into the logical structure of social explanation. The foundational claims of Globalization Theory themselves carried it over that limit. This was its general problem – a problem that was never overcome. Towards the end of the 1990s, the authors of *Global Transformations* reported 'somewhat surprisingly' that there still existed 'no cogent theory of globalization, nor even a systematic analysis of its primary features' (Held *et al.*, 1999, 1). But this was not for want of trying.

To conclude this opening section of the argument: the concept of 'globalization' remained intellectually unstable from its arrival at the start of the 1990s right up till it faded from the screen at their end. But this was not simply, as was sometimes implied, because writers disagreed over the measurement or even the significance of various quantitative indicators. The cause was at once deeper and more straightforward than that. Quite simply, the enormous subjective plausibility of the idea was never matched by an equivalent theoretical potential for orienting coherent social analysis. Worldwide social changes were indeed occurring during the 1990s; and these changes do indeed, as will be argued later on, explain the rise of the idea of 'globalization'. But the reverse never applied. The idea of 'globalization' could not in turn explain the changes. It was a *Zeitgeist*, not a proto-scientific concept. And the attempt to turn it into the latter, however understandable, could only generate confusion and equivocation, in short, 'follies'.

Perhaps, however, we should turn the force of those last two sentences around: with intellectual liabilities like these, such an idea could spread across the social sciences only if, as *Zeitgeister* do, it corresponded powerfully, in all its inner confusion, to the subjective experience of the times. And spread it certainly did.

Notes

1   This theme is elaborated and pursued in detail in Rosenberg (2000). Rosenberg, J. 2000 *The Follies of Globalization Theory*, Polemical Essays, London: Verso.
2   I am grateful to Babak Bahador (2001) for alerting me to the need for this clarification. Bahador, B. (2001) 'Review of The Follies of GlobalizationTheory', *Millennium* 30(3): 887–889.

Justin Rosenberg (2005) "Globalization Theory: A Postmortem," *International Politics*, vol. 42, pp. 11–15.

PART FIVE

Contemporary globalization, 1996–2010

INTRODUCTION TO
PART FIVE

Conflicts over globalization, we have argued throughout this book, are not only academic or scholarly ones. For the nature of globalization, its conditions and consequences, has become the central political debate of our times and of our lives in these times. Throughout the late 1990s, as globalists battled anti-globalists throughout the academy, globalization remained a matter of intense controversy and conflict in politics, the economy, and culture. Indeed, globalization was taken to the streets – in protests from Seattle to Genoa, leveled against a transnational elite class as represented in forums from G8 summits to WTO meetings. Such anti-globalist mass street protests sought to confront the economic interests of global capital and the political domination of Western (especially US) hegemony. Reflecting on the protests that erupted in Seattle in 1999, Devinder Sharma, a New Dehli-based food and trade policy analyst, wrote: "While the strong-arm tactics of the American government in the streets is muffling the voice of the peaceful protesters, the high-handedness of the American bureaucracy in the convention centre is silencing the voice of developing countries."[1] Like many other voices emergent across a transnational public sphere, Sharma's comments were part of a new politics of "globalization from below" – the deploy-ment of global activism and global civil society to question and critique the dominant financial structures of globalization.

All of this changed on September 11, 2001. The day that the planes crashed into the World Trade Center and Pentagon has been said to be the day when "globalization from below" was undone. Certainly in the aftermath of 9/11, as well as the wars in Afghanistan and Iraq, there was considerable talk about the "democratic deficit" of globalism, and indeed of a new era of militarized or imperial globalization. Since 9/11, the political dimensions of globalization have been portrayed by some critics as increasingly thin and brittle, with trends toward militarization, unilateralism, and imperialism. Sharma captures the fall-out from 9/11 well: "The tragic events of 9/11 changed the world in such a dramatic way that globalization – that links trade with corporate interests – became much easier." "Easier," Sharma argues, because the terrain of geopolitics, capital flows, and foreign investment were subjected to American hegemony, imposed largely through military unilateralism and discriminatory one-way regional trade agreements. Globally speaking, what has unfolded in the wake of 9/11 – at least according to this standpoint – was a thorough rewriting of economic globalization as defined, regulated, and controlled by the United States. For globalization post-9/11, at least in its more instrumental economic, political, and policy aspects, involved transformations from multilateralism to unilateralism, democratic order to militarized insecurity, and geopolitical cooperation to neo-liberal competition.

There is, however, a profound paradox in this shift from multilateral to unilateral globalization. On the one hand, the New York terror attacks unleashed through Al-Qaeda's brand of Islamic fundamentalism undoubtedly led to the remaking of globalization in a more restrictive sense – both geopolitically and culturally. The much celebrated "borderless world" of globalism was at once hijacked and brought low by global terrorism – or, at least, this was certainly the outcome once President Bush took the unilateral decision to fire rockets into Afghanistan and Iraq. On the other hand, however, there was a much deeper affinity between terrorism and globalization than initially recognized. From Romantic-anarchist violence to the Algerian FLN and the Irish Republican Army, terrorism has been inextricably interwoven with the wider global ambitions of a kind of anti-politics that attempts to overthrow social order as such. Even so, it is the advent of new information technologies and the network society that dramatically reconstitutes terrorism in our own time as global. As an intensively transnational terror network, Al-Qaeda has deftly pursued its goals of sickening mass violence through global decentralized networks. This hi-tech, mobile, satellite-phone version of terrorism has been one in which the global and the technological have been pivotal to the orchestration of attacks around the world. Bin Laden and his associates may claim to be revolted by capitalist globalization and its consumerist logics, but Al-Qaeda's fanatical, fundamentalist assault on globalism as such has been deeply constituted by the network dynamics of globalization itself.

There are other ways, however, in which globalization in the era post-9/11 has been theorized. The relations between the national state, territorial power, and geopolitics have witnessed such a profound and massive restructuring during the early years of the twenty-first century that the outcome, in effect, is the "end of globalization" as we know it. Or, at least, this is what some global skeptics have argued. The obituaries for globalization have been many and varied. Political theorist John Gray contends "the era of globalization is over." Historian Niall Ferguson has spoken of "sinking globalization." Rosenberg argues that "the age of globalization is unexpectedly over." And economist Joseph Stiglitz claims that "globalization today has been oversold." Whether oversold, sunk, jeopardized, or dead, the claims of global skeptics revolve around two interrelated claims concerning the demise of globalization: (1) that today's post-globalist world has returned to traditional, territorially defined geopolitics – structured by militarism, violence, and imperialism; and (2) that this reassertion of national boundaries and borders has produced a dramatic fall in levels of global trade and a reassertion of economic regionalization. There is no need to imagine that we inhabit the financial, political, or cultural orders of globalism, simply because "globalization" as a descriptor of social reality is well and truly bankrupt. The catastrophic events of 9/11, the War on Terror, as well as new wars in Afghanistan and Iraq, have demonstrated loudly and clearly that globalization as a concept is at odds with current political realities.

Alternatively, some critics have viewed these post-9/11 political and economic developments in a more optimistic, though nevertheless highly critical, fashion. The strife between terrorism, militarization, state power, and territoriality need not be grasped as a matter of the global or universal versus the local or particular, since nations, peoples, and organizations are always enmeshed in complex systems of regional, transnational, and global governance. Identities, institutions, and cultures may be global, but they are also usually nation-based: the structures of our social life take place in local settings, but they may also be as global in scope as Catholicism or postmodernism. From this angle, global skeptics are in error to suppose that a resurgence of territorial militarism or American unilateralism spells the demise of globalization writ large. Among others, the IT revolution and digital communications, the spread of global markets in goods and services, the rapid growth in migration and the movement of peoples, the flexibilization of work required by multinational corporations, and the spread of democratic and environmental values throughout many parts of the world are just some of the core transformations driven by today's dense patterns of global interconnectedness. In all of this, it is hard to see exactly what has disappeared or come unstuck as a result of world changes since 9/11. From the standpoint of this more globalist analysis, the world is not only global, it is set to remain so for the foreseeable future.

Even so, it is acknowledged that the political conflict between globalization and fundamentalism is increasingly socio-economic as well as a geopolitical. But the most important upshot of this conflict is not between globalization and post-globalism, but between cosmopolitan global governance and the narrow security agenda promoted by the Washington Consensus and the War on Terror. As various critics associated with this standpoint have contended, including the writings reproduced here in Part Five by David Held, Joseph S. Nye, and James N. Rosenau, the interconnected events of 9/11, the war in Iraq, and the Washington security doctrine were defining moments in a weakening of international law and of multilateral institutions promoted by globalization. The terrorist attacks on the World Trade Center and the Pentagon could have resulted in a strengthening of international law, multilateral governance, and the globalizing of democracy. The unleashing of global terror by Al-Qaeda could have resulted in a deepening and strengthening of multilateral political institutions, and of global civil society more generally. In the face of the terrorist attacks of 9/11, however, the opposite in fact happened: as a consequence of the misguided policy response of the Washington security doctrine promoted by the Bush administration, the world became more polarized, the global economy more regionalized, international law weaker, and multilateral institutions deglobalized.

Cosmopolitanism emerged in various critical circles as an understandable response to economic neo-liberalism and global market integration (or, in short, the Washington Consensus) in order to address anew the challenges posed by 9/11. In the perspective detailed by Held, cosmopolitan social democracy is inseparable from the global governing capacity of multilateral institutions for peacemaking and peace-keeping, with a universal human rights regime acknowledged as the fundamental common value. This requires an ethic of common responsibility, social justice, and legal impartiality, as well as full democratic participation at all levels of social and political life, including representative and responsible global govern-ance. For Held, a cosmopolitan social democracy is one continuously remade and reconstituted by a commitment to the rule of law of its multilateral institutional members, not one in which dominant institutional actors seek the prosecution of wars as a counter-response. No state power can or should assume the global role of policeman and jury; the movement toward global justice requires multilateral political activity based on common rules and principles and seeking the advancement of global security, governance, and peace building. But the process of building international democratic institutions demands, crucially, recognition of the massive global disparity between rich and poor as well as of geopolitical asymmetries of life chances. Held makes the point that the plight of the poorest and most vulnerable across the globe cannot be left to market forces to resolve. In this sense, the project of cosmopolitan global democracy is at one with social justice.

Cosmopolitanism, at least in its more theoretical and utopian dimensions, has provided some valuable insights regarding the gross limitations and excesses of the new post-9/11 phase of militarized globaliza-tion. But it arguably does less well as a conceptual diagnosis of the current global order when applied to political topics such as culture, race, ethnicity, post-colonialism, and the Third World. The political concern of some critics is that the most cosmopolitan mentality, with its incessant celebration of representation, rights, responsibilities, and rules, actually reflects the imprint of a profoundly Eurocentric metaphysics. For such critics, the Eurocentrism of cosmopolitanism is that, beyond the expensive cities of the West, global political realities are more to do with enforced migrations, homelessness, and bare life than it has to do with dialogic democracy, formal political procedures, or multilateral governance. More pointedly, some critics – such as Stuart Hall, Mike Featherstone, and Tyler Cowen – are concerned that cosmopolitanism as a political doctrine has been deployed as a kind of cover for drawing post-colonial states and Third World nations into the current economic instabilities and human devastations of capitalist globalization. For by universalising the very idea of cosmopolitanism, this doctrine has also tended to ditch notions of particularist identities, forms of life, ethnicities, life-styles, and local experiences. In short, if cosmo-politanism represents the elitist culture of global capitalism, then anything outside or beyond that terrain (revolutionary nationalism, post-colonial states, Third World nations) can only appear as a form of resistance to it.

If post-colonial theory has been in general suspect of all talk of cosmopolitanism, or at least the formalized version of cosmoplitanism rendered up by contemporary political theory, it has been less wary of the discourse of globalization itself. Indeed, some of the most astute assessments of the relations between post-colonial theory and globalization, as represented in Part Five in the writings of Albert Paolini, seek to shift attention from state to subjectivity, internationalism to intersubjectivity. For the intertwining of intersubjectivity, modernity, and globalization has been to the forefront of recent post-colonial analyses of the Third World in the multinational world-system of capitalist globalization. Certainly for Paolini, what is at stake in recent debates about modernity, postmodernism, and globalization is not simply power politics, but rather a profound reflexive encounter with the ontological and epistemological co-ordinates of social-theoretical discourses that have underpinned the disciplinary terrain and political practice of international relations itself. Advancing beyond formulaic pronouncements about the "Westernization of the world" or the "end of history," such a standpoint seeks to address head-on the momentous subjective and institutional transformations of individual life and collective experience in an age of intensive globalization. Seeking to move beyond linear narratives of Enlightenment, post-colonial theory – in its dialogue with globalization studies – underscores the point that colonized peoples and subaltern groups cannot be "imported" back into Western theoretical models without considerable symbolic violence; the complex, unbalanced relations between the North and South of the globe cannot be grasped through "culturalism" alone. For the relations between North and South are also, and fundamentally, about labor, goods, commodities, exploitation, and excess.

As far as post-colonial culture goes, there are those who see processes of globalization as heralding an amazing swirl of identities, ethnicities, colors, creeds, and socio-economic interests. If for such critics this is thought to be beneficial to humankind, it is partly because contemporary life is best lived as free-floating or contingent. The contemporary period, or so some imagined after the postmodern 1990s, is one of radical political experimentation in a world without firm foundations – moral, ethical, religious, or cultural. This is one of the reasons why a cultural temper of irony fits well with the fluid connections promoted by deregulated, privatizing, neo-liberal globalisms of various kinds. But if this reforging of culture as permanently plural and pluralizing has been celebrated by some, it remains alarmingly frightening to others. Indeed, global terrorism might be said to serve as a kind of brake or limit to the excesses of Western arrogance in the face of a globe fast dissolving all its traditional social structures – or, at least, this is how some critics have sought to interpret the ongoing spread of fanatic, fundamentalist ideologies in the early decades of the twenty-first century. Certainly the unleashing of suicide bombings and terrorist operations post-9/11 in Madrid, London, Istanbul, Amman, Casablanca, Riyadh, and Cairo has been understood by some commentators as a purist, essentialist, and extremist reassertion of fixed principles and self-evident truths in a world of anything goes.

The globalization of terrorism – from Islamic fundamentalism to the War on Terror – might thus be cast as a battle of the grand narratives of Western high culture on the one hand and Islamic theology on the other. For Samuel Huntington, the essential political antagonism of our era – between universal freedom and fanatical fundamentalism – is a battle between the West and its Others. On this view, the most violent, death-dealing fault lines are between Western peoples on the one side and Islam and its Hindu, Orthodox, and African neighbors on the other. Huntington approaches the force-field of geopolitics thus in terms of civilization absolutism. The fanatical, extremist activities promoted by Islamic fundamentalism represent an obscene excess of cruelty, violence, and arbitrary destruction. It is a raging, lethal assault on the very idea of Western freedom, which in its nihilistic overload manages to deflate and diminish forms of international cooperation and global stability. The aim of Western coalitions, by contrast, is for Huntington and other conservative critics not merely the defense of capitalist institutions and global processes but to reassert universal Western culture. Fundamentalism is to be brought low by the much-vaunted civilizing powers of Western culture, with its universal order of values to strike right at the heart of Islamic fundamentalist anxieties over pluralism, cultural difference, social diversity, and individualism. The question of how authoritarian cultures fearful of difference might be brought into a full-blooded dialogue with the discourse of human rights law or international agreements on social justice, among other urgent matters, is nowhere adequately detailed from this standpoint – although Huntington does acknowledge that the reassertion of universal Western culture faces the somewhat troubling obstacle of weakened confidence in public authority and trust in government – nationally, regionally, and globally – as a result of global terrorism.

A lot of the critiques of globalization which emerged in the early 2000s were, fortunately, more upbeat than the approaches just mentioned. Certainly new connections were forged between globalization theories and cosmopolitanism. Some others sought to root the cause of cosmopolitan social democracy specifically in the European Union, as a globalizing experiment in new cross-regional coalitions. The sociologists Anthony Giddens and Ulrich Beck were two of the more prominent transformationalist globalizers arguing that Europe had a special role to play in advancing both cosmopolitan democracy and global civil society. From this standpoint, the heady abstractions of cosmopolitan theories of justice and democracy gave way to the more pressing political realities of the enlargement of the EU as a means of spreading peace, human rights, and open markets. For Giddens and Beck, the EU was less an "incomplete federal state" than a cosmopolitan operation comprising a loose confederation of states that hold out the hope for promoting global governance beyond the traditional structures of the nation-state. Through interregional dialogues, the EU is best placed to promote the national interests of its members – from finance and law and order to the environment; indeed, through crossing national frontiers, the EU is better placed to do this than member nations might ever do through traditional state functions. The inescapable conclusion that follows from this, of course, is that enlargement of the EU is intrinsically beneficial not only for global markets but also for global governance. Giddens and Beck dislike the idea of EU "integration": their arguments for cosmopolitan social democracy disapprove of notions of eliminating cultural differences in order to foster a federal state of fixed rules and uniform regulations. Rather, they wish to speak up, in suitably cosmopolitan style, for social diversity and cultural difference. Politically speaking, the EU is thus well placed to play a leading global role in governance through its regional building of constituencies for the protection of human rights, the expansion of international law and the rule of law, the fostering of democratic values, and the establishment and entrenchment of complex governance systems. This kind of reflexive, cosmopolitan form of cross-regional coalitions for Giddens and Beck just *is* globalization in action at the level of politics today.

Note

1 http://www.inmotionmagazine.com/opin/devsh_911.html.

GLOBAL JIHAD: OSAMA BIN LADEN (1996)

Osama bin Laden (1957–) was born in Saudi Arabia to a wealthy family. He was raised as a devout Wahhabi Muslim and received both a religious and a secular education. After leaving college in 1979, bin Laden went to Afghanistan to join the fight against invading Soviet Forces. Afterward, he would rise to prominence as a strong advocate in the Muslim diaspora for the restoration of Sharia Law and many tenets of Qutbism. However, he was quite controversial as to his means of doing so and this is reflected in his having to move from country to country throughout the 1980s and 1990s. Today, bin Laden is most well known for being the founder and ceremonial figurehead of the Al-Qaeda organization. Al-Qaeda is a transnational network that aids and facilitates acts of terrorism, most notably the September 11 attacks that led to the deaths of almost 3,000 people. Although Al-Qaeda is not a wholly homogenous organization, one of its core beliefs is that all other forms of ideology (e.g., Western, capitalism, communism) must be defeated so that a more righteous society based on certain interpretations of Islam can be actualized. Such a mindset has been informed by many of bin Laden's speeches and writings.

The selection is taken from one of bin Laden's public letters. Specifically, it addresses the ways in which the holy war (jihad) is global in nature. Thus, an attack against a Saudi Arabian soldier or a newly trained policeman in Afghanistan will still nevertheless hurt Western forces. The same can be said about attacks on Western soil. When something happens there, this can also weaken regimes that reside in the Middle East region.

Bin Laden's Fatwa

Praise be to Allah, reporting the saying of the prophet Shu'aib: {I desire nothing but reform so far as I am able, and with none but Allah is the direction of my affair to the right and successful path; on him do I rely and to him do I turn} (Hud; 11:88).

Praise be to Allah, saying: {You are the best of the nations raised up for – the benefit of – men; you enjoin what is right and forbid the wrong and believe in Allah} (Aal-Imraan; 3: 110). Allah's blessing and salutations on His slave and messenger who said: (The people are close to an all encompassing punishment from Allah if they see the oppressor and fail to restrain him.)

It should not be hidden from you that the people of Islam had suffered from aggression, iniquity and injustice imposed on them by the Zionist-Crusaders alliance and their collaborators; to the extent that the Muslims blood became the cheapest and their wealth as loot in the hands of the enemies. Their blood was spilled in Palestine and Iraq. The horrifying pictures of the massacre of Qana, in Lebanon are still fresh in our memory. Massacres in Tajakestan, Burma, Cashmere, Assam, Philippine, Fatani, Ogadin, Somalia, Erithria, Chechnia and in Bosnia-Herzegovina took place, massacres that send shivers in the body and shake the conscience. All of this and the world watch and hear, and not only didn't respond to these atrocities, but also with a clear conspiracy between the USA and its allies and under the cover of the iniquitous United Nations, the dispossessed people were even prevented from obtaining arms to defend themselves.

The people of Islam awakened and realised that they are the main target for the aggression of the Zionist-Crusaders alliance. All false claims and propaganda about "Human Rights" were hammered down and exposed by the massacres that took place against the Muslims in every part of the world. [. . .]

Today your brothers and sons, the sons of the two Holy Places, have started their Jihad in the cause of Allah, to expel the occupying enemy from of the country of the two Holy places. And there is no doubt you would like to carry out this mission too, in order to re-establish the greatness of this Ummah and to liberate its occupied sanctities. Nevertheless, it must be obvious to you that, due to the imbalance of power between our armed forces and the enemy forces, a suitable means of fighting must be adopted i.e. using fast moving light forces that work under complete secrecy. In other word to initiate a guerrilla warfare, were the sons of the nation, and not the military forces, take part in it. And as you know, it is wise, in the present circumstances, for the armed military forces not to be engaged in a conventional fighting with the forces of the crusader enemy (the exceptions are the bold and the forceful operations carried out by the members of the armed forces individually, that is without the movement of the formal forces in its conventional shape and hence the responses will not be directed, strongly, against the army) unless a big advantages is likely to be achieved; and great losses induced on the enemy side (that would shaken and destroy its foundations and infrastructures) that will help to expel the defeated enemy from the country. [. . .]

Muslims Brothers of land of the two Holy Places:

It is incredible that our country is the world largest buyer of arms from the USA and the area biggest commercial partners of the Americans who are assisting their Zionist brothers in occupying Palestine and in evicting and killing the Muslims there, by providing arms, men and financial supports.

To deny these occupiers from the enormous revenues of their trading with our country is a very important help for our Jihad against them. To express our anger and hate to them is a very important moral gesture. By doing so we would have taken part in (the process of) cleansing our sanctities from the crusaders and the Zionists and forcing them, by the Permission of Allah, to leave disappointed and defeated.

We expect the woman of the land of the two Holy Places and other countries to carry out their role in boycotting the American goods.

If economical boycotting is intertwined with the military operations of the Mujahideen, then defeating the enemy will be even nearer, by the Permission of Allah. However if Muslims don't co-operate and support their Mujahideen brothers then, in effect, they are supplying the army of the enemy with financial help and extending the war and increasing the suffering of the Muslims.

The security and the intelligence services of the entire world can not force a single citizen to buy the goods of his/her enemy. Economical boycotting of the American goods is a very effective weapon of hitting and weakening the enemy, and it is not under the control of the security forces of the regime. [. . .]

My Muslim Brothers of The World:

Your brothers in Palestine and in the land of the two Holy Places are calling upon your help and asking you to take part in fighting against the enemy – your enemy and their enemy – the Americans and the Israelis. they are asking you to do whatever you can, with one own means and ability, to expel the enemy, humiliated and defeated, out of the sanctities of Islam. Exalted be to Allah said in His book: {and if they ask your support, because they are oppressed in their faith, then support them!} (Anfaal; 8:72)

Osama bin Laden (1996) "Declaration of War Against The Americas Occupying The Land of the Two Holy Places." Source: http://www.pbs.org/newshour/terrorism/international/fatwa_1996.html.

TRAUMAS OF THE GLOBAL: SLAVOJ ŽIŽEK (2001)

Slavoj Žižek (1949–) is a Slovenian critic whose interweaving of Lacanian psychoanalysis, post-structuralist discourse, and post-Marxism has powerfully addressed the manifold social antagonisms and cultural traumas arising in an age of advanced globalization. Witty, playful, ironic, and politically engaged, Žižek places "ideology" at the center of the self's experience of the global capitalist economy. He contends that ideology is not an escape from the painful realities of society, but rather a medium through which social reality is constructed as a displacement of the emotional traumas of human life itself. In a powerful cross of the French psychoanalyst Jacques Lacan and the Marxist theoretician Louis Althusser, Žižek sees identity as marked by lack, gap, and antagonism. In this selection, which Žižek delivered as a lecture in New York City in the aftermath of the collapse of the twin towers on 9/11, the "First World" reactions and fantasies of people throughout the expensive cities of the West to terrorism are subjected to psychoanalytic criticism. Deconstructing global terrorism and its terrifying, traumatic, and obscene nature, Žižek draws from American cinema, television, and journalistic media to probe the dynamic evil of terror.

Welcome to the Desert of the Real

The ultimate American paranoiac fantasy is that of an individual living in a small idyllic Californian city, a consumerist paradise, who suddenly starts to suspect that the world he lives in is a fake, a spectacle staged to convince him that he lives in a real world, while all people around him are effectively actors and extras in a gigantic show. The most recent example of this is Peter Weir's The Truman Show (1998), with Jim Carrey playing the small town clerk who gradually discovers the truth that he is the hero of a 24-hours permanent TV show: his hometown is constructed on a gigantic studio set, with cameras following him permanently. Among its predecessors, it is worth mentioning Philip Dick's Time Out of Joint (1959), in which a hero living a modest daily life in a small idyllic Californian city of the late 50s, gradually discovers that the whole town is a fake staged to keep him satisfied . . . The underlying experience of Time Out of Joint and of The Truman Show is that the late capitalist consumerist Californian paradise is, in its very hyper-reality, in a way IRREAL, substance-less, deprived of the material inertia.

So it is not only that Hollywood stages a semblance of real life deprived of the weight and inertia of materiality – in the late capitalist consumerist society, "real social life" itself somehow acquires the features of a staged fake, with our neighbors behaving in "real" life as stage actors and extras . . . Again, the ultimate truth of the capitalist utilitarian de-spiritualized universe is the de-materialization of the "real life" itself, its reversal into a spectral show. Among others, Christopher Isherwood gave expression to this unreality of the American daily life, exemplified in the motel room: "American motels are unreal. /. . ./ they are deliberately designed to be unreal. /. . ./ The Europeans hate us because we've retired to live inside our advertisements, like hermits going into caves to contemplate." Peter Sloterdijk's notion of the "sphere" is here literally realized, as the gigantic metal sphere that envelopes and isolates the entire city. Years ago, a series of science-fiction films like Zardoz or Logan's Run forecasted today's postmodern predicament by extending this fantasy to the community itself: the isolated group living an aseptic life in a secluded area longs for the experience of the real world of material decay.

The Wachowski brothers' hit Matrix (1999) brought this logic to its climax: the material reality we all experience and see around us is a virtual one, generated and coordinated by a gigantic mega-computer to which we are all attached; when the hero (played by Keanu Reeves) awakens into the "real reality," he sees a desolate landscape littered with burned ruins – what remained of Chicago after a global war. The resistance leader Morpheus utters the ironic greeting: "Welcome to the desert of the real."

Was it not something of the similar order that took place in New York on September 11? Its citizens were introduced to the "desert of the real" – to us, corrupted by Hollywood, the landscape and the shots we saw of the collapsing towers could not but remind us of the most breathtaking scenes in the catastrophe big productions. When we hear how the bombings were a totally unexpected shock, how the unimaginable Impossible happened, one should recall the other defining catastrophe from the beginning of the XXth century, that of Titanic: it was also a shock, but the space for it was already prepared in ideological fantasizing, since Titanic was the symbol of the might of the XIXth century industrial civilization. Does the same not hold also for these bombings? Not only were the media bombarding us all the time with the talk about the terrorist threat; this threat was also obviously libidinally invested – just recall the series of movies from Escape From New York to Independence Day. Therein resides the rationale of the often-mentioned association of the attacks with the Hollywood disaster movies: the unthinkable which happened was the object of fantasy, so that, in a way, America got what it fantasized about, and this was the greatest surprise.

It is precisely now, when we are dealing with the raw Real of a catastrophe, that we should bear in mind the ideological and fantasmatic coordinates which determine its perception. If there is any symbolism in the collapse of the WTC towers, it is not so much the old-fashioned notion of the "center of financial capitalism," but, rather, the notion that the two WTC towers stood for the center of the VIRTUAL capitalism, of financial speculations disconnected from the sphere of material production. The shattering impact of the bombings can only be accounted for only against the background of the borderline which today separates the digitalized First World from the Third World "desert of the Real." It is the awareness that we live in an insulated artificial universe which generates the notion that some ominous agent is threatening us all the time with total destruction.

Is, consequently, Osama Bin Laden, the suspected mastermind behind the bombings, not the real-life counterpart of Ernst Stavro Blofeld, the master-criminal in most of the James Bond films, involved in the acts of global destruction. What one should recall here is that the only place in Hollywood films where we see the production process in all its intensity is when James Bond penetrates the master-criminal's secret domain and locates there the site of intense labor (distilling and packaging the drugs, constructing a rocket that will destroy New York . . .). When the master-criminal, after capturing Bond, usually takes him on a tour of his illegal factory, is this not the closest Hollywood comes to the socialist-realist proud presentation of the production in a factory? And the function of Bond's intervention, of course, is to explode in firecraks this site of production, allowing us to return to the daily semblance of our existence in a world with the "disappearing working class." Is it not that, in the exploding WTC towers, this violence directed at the threatening Outside turned back at us?

The safe Sphere in which Americans live is experienced as under threat from the Outside of terrorist attackers who are ruthlessly self-sacrificing AND cowards, cunningly intelligent AND primitive barbarians. Whenever we encounter such a purely evil Outside, we should gather the courage to endorse the Hegelian lesson: in this pure Outside, we should recognize the distilled version of-our own essence. For the last five centuries, the (relative) prosperity and peace of the "civilized" West was bought by the export of ruthless violence and destruction into the "barbarian" Outside: the long story from the conquest of America to the slaughter in Congo. Cruel and indifferent as it may sound, we should also, now more than ever, bear in mind that the actual effect of these bombings is much more symbolic than real: in Africa, EVERY SINGLE DAY more people die of AIDS than all the victims of the WTC collapse, and their death could have been easily cut back with relatively small financial means. The US just got the taste of what goes on around the world on a daily basis, from Sarajevo to Grozny, from Ruanda and Congo to Sierra Leone. If one adds to the situation in New York rapist gangs and a dozen or so snipers blindly targeting people who walk along the streets, one gets an idea about what Sarajevo was a decade ago.

It is when we watched on TV screen the two WTC towers collapsing, that it became possible to experience the falsity of the "reality TV shows": even if these shows are "for real," people still act in them – they simply play themselves. The standard disclaimer in a novel ("characters in this text are a fiction, every resemblance with the real life characters is purely contingent") holds also for the participants of the reality soaps: what we see there are fictional characters, even if they play themselves for the real. Of course, the "return to the Real" can be given different twists: one already hears some conservatives claim that what made us so vulnerable is our very openness – with the inevitable conclusion lurking in the background that, if we are to protect our "way of life," we will have to sacrifice some of our freedoms which were "misused" by the enemies of freedom. This logic should be rejected tout court: is it not a fact that our First World "open" countries are the most controlled countries in the entire history of humanity? In the United Kingdom, all public spaces, from buses to shopping malls, are constantly videotaped, not to mention the almost total control of all forms of digital communication.

Along the same lines, Rightist commentators like George Will also immediately proclaimed the end of the American "holiday from history" – the impact of reality shattering the isolated tower of the liberal tolerant attitude and the Cultural Studies focus on textuality. Now, we are forced to strike back, to deal with real enemies in the real world . . . However, WHOM to strike? Whatever the response, it will never hit the RIGHT target, bringing us full satisfaction. The ridicule of America attacking Afghanistan cannot but strike the eye: if the greatest power in the world will destroy one of the poorest countries in which peasant barely survive on barren hills, will this not be the ultimate case of the impotent acting out? Afghanistan is otherwise an ideal target: a country ALREADY reduced to rubble, with no infrastructure, repeatedly destroyed by war for the last two decades . . . one cannot avoid the surmise that the choice of Afghanistan will be also determined by economic considerations: is it not the best procedure to act out one's anger at a country for which no one cares and where there is nothing to destroy? Unfortunately, the possible choice of Afghanistan recalls the anecdote about the madman who searches for the lost key beneath a street light; when asked why there when he lost the key in a dark corner backwards, he answers: "But it is easier to search under strong light!"

To succumb to the urge to act now and retaliate means precisely to avoid confronting the true dimensions of what occurred on September 11 – it means an act whose true aim is to lull us into the secure conviction that nothing has REALLY changed. The true long-term threat are further acts of mass terror in comparison to which the memory of the WTC collapse will pale – acts less spectacular, but much more horrifying. What about bacteriological warfare, what about the use of lethal gas, what about the prospect of the DNA terrorism (developing poisons which will affect only people who share a determinate genome)? Instead of a quick acting out, one should confront these difficult questions: what will "war" mean in the XXIst century? Who will be "them," if they are, clearly, neither states nor criminal gangs?

There is a partial truth in the notion of the "clash of civilizations" attested here – witness the surprise of the average American: "How is it possible that these people display and practice such a disregard for their own lives?" Is the obverse of this surprise not the rather sad fact that we, in the First World countries, find it more and more difficult even to imagine a public or universal Cause for which one would be ready to sacrifice one's life? When, after the bombings, even the Taliban foreign minister said that he can "feel the pain" of the American children, did he not thereby confirm the hegemonic ideological role of this Bill Clinton's trademark phrase? It effectively appears as if the split between First World and Third World runs more and more along the lines of the opposition between leading a long satisfying life full of material and cultural wealth, and dedicating one's life to some transcendent Cause. However, this notion of the "clash of civilizations" has to be thoroughly rejected: what we are witnessing today are rather clashes WITHIN each civilization. Furthermore, a brief look at the comparative history of Islam and Christianity tells us that the "human rights record" of Islam (to use this anachronistic term) is much better than that of Christianity: in the past centuries, Islam was significantly more tolerant towards other religions than Christianity. NOW it is also the time to remember that it was through the Arabs that, in the Middle Ages, we in the Western Europe regained access to our Ancient Greek legacy. While in no way excusing today's horror acts, these facts nonetheless clearly demonstrate that we are not dealing with a feature inscribed into Islam "as such," but with the outcome of modern socio-political conditions.

Every feature attributed to the Other is already present in the very heart of the US: murderous fanaticism? There are today in the US itself more than two millions of the Rightist populist "fundamentalists" who also practice the terror of their own, legitimized by (their understanding of) Christianity. Since America is in a way "harboring" them, should the US Army have punished the US themselves after the Oklahoma bombing? And what about the way Jerry Falwell and Pat Robertson reacted to the bombings, perceiving them as a sign that God lifted up its protection of the US because of the sinful lives of the Americans, putting the blame on hedonist materialism, liberalism, and rampant sexuality, and claiming that America got what it deserved?

America as a safe haven? When a New Yorker commented on how, after the bombings, one can no longer walk safely on the city's streets, the irony of it was that, well before the bombings, the streets of New York were well-known for the dangers of being attacked or, at least, mugged – if anything, the bombings gave rise to a new sense of solidarity, with the scenes of young African-Americans helping an old Jewish gentlemen to cross the street, scenes unimaginable a couple of days ago.

Now, in the days immediately following the bombings, it is as if we dwell in the unique time between a traumatic event and its symbolic impact, like in those brief moment after we are deeply cut, and before the full extent of the pain strikes us – it is open how the events will be symbolized, what their symbolic efficiency will be, what acts they will be evoked to justify. Even here, in these moments of utmost tension, this link is not automatic but contingent. There are already the first bad omens, like the sudden resurrection, in the public discourse, of the old Cold war term "free world": the struggle is now the one between the "free world" and the forces of darkness and terror. The question to be asked here is, of course: who then belongs to the UNFREE world? Are, say, China or Egypt part of this free world? The actual message is, of course, that the old division between the Western liberal-democratic countries and all the others is again enforced. [. . .]

So what about the phrase which reverberates everywhere, "Nothing will be the same after September 11"? Significantly, this phrase is never further elaborated – it just an empty gesture of saying something "deep" without really knowing what we want to say. So our first reaction to it should be: Really? Is it, rather, not that the only thing that effectively changed was that America was forced to realize the kind of world it was part of? On the other hand, such changes in perception are never without consequences, since the way we perceive our situation determines the way we act in it. Recall the processes of collapse of a political regime, say, the collapse of the Communist regimes in the Eastern Europe in 1990: at a certain moment, people all of a sudden became aware that the game is over, that the Communists are lost. The break was purely symbolic, nothing changed "in reality" – and, nonetheless, from this moment on, the final collapse of the regime was just a question of days . . . What if something of the same order DID occur on September 11?

Slavoj Žižek (2001) "Welcome to the Desert of the Real." Source: http://www.theglobalsite.ac.uk/times/109zizek.htm.

GLOBALIZATION'S DEMOCRATIC DEFICIT: JOSEPH S. NYE, JR (2001)

Joseph Nye (1937–) is Distinguished Service Professor and Sultan of Oman Professor of International Relations at Harvard University. Previously, Nye has occupied a number of positions in the US federal government such as Deputy to the Undersecretary of State for Security Assistance, Science, and Technology from 1977 to 1979 and Assistant Secretary of Defense for International Security Affairs from 1994 to 1995. In recent times, his ideas have been quite influential to US political, military, and economic policy – especially those concerning "soft" and "smart" power, which the current Obama administration has made reference to. Nye's work has also engaged the issue of democracy in the age of contemporary globalization. This is a theme he explores in the selection. Here, he tries to wrestle with the problem of how global institutions currently hold a "democratic deficit." And in doing so, he proposes that globalization should be thought about differently from the way some supporters and detractors have typically thought about the matter.

Globalization and the Problem of Democracy

Seattle; Washington, D.C.; Prague; Québec City. It is becoming difficult for international economic organizations to meet without attracting crowds of protesters decrying globalization. These protesters are a diverse lot, coming mainly from rich countries, and their coalition has not always been internally consistent. They have included trade unionists worried about losing jobs and students who want to help the underdeveloped world gain them, environmentalists concerned about ecological degradation and anarchists who object to all forms of international regulation. Some protesters claim to represent poor countries but simultaneously defend agricultural protectionism in wealthy countries. Some reject corporate capitalism, whereas others accept the benefits of international markets but worry that globalization is destroying democracy. [. . .]

Antiglobalization protesters complain that international institutions are illegitimate because they are undemocratic. But the existing global institutions are quite weak and hardly threatening. Even the much-maligned World Trade Organization (WTO) has only a small budget and staff. Moreover, unlike self-appointed nongovernmental organizations (NGO), international institutions tend to be highly responsive to national governments and can thus claim some real, if indirect, democratic legitimacy. International economic institutions, moreover, merely facilitate cooperation among member states and derive some authority from their efficacy.

Even so, in a world of transnational politics where democracy has become the touchstone of legitimacy, these arguments probably will not be enough to protect any but the most technical organizations from attack. International institutions may be weak, but their rules and resources can have powerful effects. The protesters, moreover, make some valid points. Not all member states of international organizations are themselves democratic. Long lines of delegation from multiple governments, combined with a lack of transparency, often weaken accountability. And although the organizations may be agents of states, they often represent only certain parts of those states. Thus trade ministers attend WTO meetings, finance ministers attend the meetings of the International Monetary Fund (IMF), and central bankers meet at the Bank for International Settlements in Basel. To outsiders, even within the same government, these institutions can look like closed and secretive clubs. Increasing the perceived legitimacy of international governance is therefore an important objective and requires three things: greater clarity about democracy, a richer understanding of accountability, and a willingness to experiment.

We, the people

Democracy requires government by officials who are accountable and removable by the majority of people in a jurisdiction, together with protections for individual and minority rights. But who are "we the people" in a world where political identity at the global level is so weak? "One state, one vote" is not democratic. By that formula, a citizen of the Maldive Islands would have a thousand times more voting power than would a citizen of China. On the other hand, treating the world as a single global constituency in which the majority ruled would mean that the more than 2 billion Chinese and Indians could usually get their way. (Ironically, such a world would be a nightmare for those antiglobalization NGOs that seek international environmental and labor standards, since such measures draw little support from Indian or Chinese officials.)

In a democratic system, minorities acquiesce to the will of the majority when they feel they are generally full-fledged participants in the larger community. There is little evidence, however, that such a strong sense of community exists at the global level today, or that it could soon be created. In its absence, the extension of domestic voting procedures to the global level makes little practical or normative sense. A stronger European Parliament may reduce the "democratic deficit" within a union of relatively homogenous European states, but it is doubtful that such an institution makes sense for the world at large. Alfred, Lord Tennyson's "Parliament of man" made for great Victorian poetry, but it does not stand up to contemporary political analysis. Democracy, moreover, exists today only in certain well-ordered nation-states, and that condition is likely to change only slowly.

Still, governments can do several things to respond to the concerns about a global democratic deficit. First, they can try to design international institutions that preserve as much space as possible for domestic political processes to operate. In the WTO, for example, the procedures for settling disputes can intrude on domestic sovereignty, but a country can reject a judgment if it pays carefully limited compensation to the trade partners injured by its actions. And if a country does defect from its WTO trade agreements, the settlement procedure limits the kind of tit-for-tat downward spiral of retaliation that so devastated the world economy in the 1930s.

In a sense, the procedure is like having a fuse in the electrical system of a house: better the fuse blow than the house burn down. The danger with the WTO, therefore, is not that it prevents member states from accommodating domestic political choices but rather that members will be tempted to litigate too many disputes instead of resolving them through the more flexible route of political negotiations.

Clearer connections

Better accountability can and should start at home. If people believe that WTO meetings do not adequately account for environmental standards, they can press their governments to include environment ministers or officials in their WTO delegations. Legislatures can hold hearings before or after meetings, and legislators can themselves become national delegates to various organizations.

Governments should also make clear that democratic accountability can be quite indirect. Accountability is often assured through means other than voting, even in well-functioning democracies. In the United States, for example, the Supreme Court and the Federal Reserve Board respond to elections indirectly through a long chain of delegation, and judges and government bankers are kept accountable by professional norms and standards, as well. There is no reason that indirect accountability cannot be consistent with democracy, or that international institutions such as the IMF and the World Bank should be held to a higher standard than are domestic institutions.

Increased transparency is also essential. In addition to voting, people in democracies debate issues using a variety of means, from letters to polls to protests. Interest groups and a free press play important roles in creating transparency in domestic democratic politics and can do so at the international level as well. NGOs are self-selected, not democratically elected, but they too can play a positive role in increasing transparency. They deserve a voice, but not a vote. For them to fill this role, they need information from and dialogue with international institutions. [. . .]

In the end, there is no single answer to the question of how to reconcile the necessary global institutions with democratic accountability. Highly technical organizations may be able to derive their legitimacy from their efficacy alone. But the more an institution deals with broad values, the more its democratic legitimacy becomes relevant. People concerned about democracy will need to think harder about norms and procedures for the governance of globalization. Neither denying the problem nor yielding to demagogues in the streets will do.

Joseph S. Nye (2001) "Globalization's Democratic Deficit: How to Make International Institutions More Accountable," *Foreign Affairs*, July/August, pp. 2–6.

FAILED STATES: NOAM CHOMSKY (2006)

Noam Chomsky (1928–) is an American public intellectual and political commentator who is currently one of the most cited authors in the world. In his long and storied professional life, Chomsky has explored many different fields and topics. These include his early groundbreaking contributions to the disciplines of linguistics and cognitive psychology to his later shift to the realm of political commentary. While Chomsky is said to wear many political hats, one of his main pre-occupations has been to criticize the inherently unjust and deceptive nature of the capitalist system. This has also led him to excoriate the rise of neo-liberalism and corporate globalization beginning in the twentieth century. Chomsky has also gained notoriety for his criticisms of US foreign policy – a theme which Chomsky picks up in his work *Failed States*, from which the selection is taken. Here, Chomsky aims to disprove the idea that the US has always acted in an altruistic fashion – seeking instead to paint the US as a self-interested roguish empire.

Failed Systems and the States

The selection of issues that should rank high on the agenda of concern for human welfare and rights is, naturally, a subjective matter. But there are a few choices that seem unavoidable, because they bear so directly on the prospects for decent survival. Among them are at least these three: nuclear war, environmental disaster, and the fact that the government of the world's leading power is acting in ways that increase the likelihood of these catastrophes. It is important to stress the *government*, because the population, not surprisingly, does not agree. That brings up a fourth issue that should deeply concern Americans, and the world: the sharp divide between public opinion and public policy, one of the reasons for the fear, which cannot casually be put aside, that "the American 'system' as a whole is in real trouble – that it is heading in a direction that spells the end of its historic values [of] equality, liberty, and meaningful democracy."[1]

The "system" is coming to have some of the features of failed states, to adopt a currently fashionable notion that is conventionally applied to states regarded as potential threats to our security (like Iraq) or as needing our intervention to rescue the population from severe internal threats (like Haiti). Though the concept is recognized to be "frustratingly imprecise," some of the primary characteristics of failed states can be identified. One is their inability or unwillingness to protect their citizens from violence and perhaps even destruction. Another is their tendency to regard themselves as beyond the reach of domestic or international law, and hence free to carry out aggression and violence. And if they have democratic forms, they suffer from a serious "democratic deficit" that deprives their formal democratic institutions of real substance.[2]

Among the hardest tasks that anyone can undertake, and one of the most important, is to look honestly in the mirror. If we allow ourselves to do so, we should have little difficulty in finding the characteristics of "failed states" right at home. That recognition of reality should be deeply troubling to those who care about their countries and future generations. "Countries," plural, because of the enormous reach of US power, but also because the threats are not localized in space or time. [. . .]

No one familiar with history should be surprised that the growing democratic deficit in the United States is accompanied by declaration of messianic missions to bring democracy to a suffering world. Declarations of noble intent by systems of power are rarely complete fabrication, and the same is true in this case. Under some conditions, forms of democracy are indeed acceptable. Abroad, as the leading scholar-advocate of "democracy promotion" concludes, we find a "strong line of continuity": democracy is acceptable *if and only if* it is consistent with strategic and economic interests (Thomas Carothers). In modified form, the doctrine holds at home as well.

The basic dilemma facing policy makers is sometimes candidly recognized at the dovish liberal extreme of the spectrum, for example, by Robert Pastor, President Carter's national security advisor for Latin America. He explained why the administration had to support the murderous and corrupt Somoza regime in Nicaragua, and, when that proved impossible, to try at least to maintain the US-trained National Guard even as it was massacring the population "with a brutality a nation usually reserves for its enemy," killing some forty thousand people. The reason was the familiar one: "The United States did not want to control Nicaragua or the other nations of the region, but it also did not want developments to get out of control. It wanted Nicaraguans to act independently, *except* when doing so would affect U.S. interests adversely."[3] [. . .]

The persistence of the strong line of continuity to the present again reveals that the United States is very much like other powerful states. It pursues the strategic and economic interests of dominant sectors of the domestic population, to the accompaniment of rhetorical flourishes about its dedication to the highest values. That is practically a historical universal, and the reason why sensible people pay scant attention to declarations of noble intent by leaders, or accolades by their followers.

One commonly hears that carping critics complain about what is wrong, but do not present solutions. There is an accurate translation for that charge: "They present solutions, but I don't like them." In addition to the proposals that should be familiar about dealing with the crises that reach to the level of survival, a few simple suggestions for the United States have already been mentioned: (1) accept the jurisdiction of the International Criminal Court and the World Court; (2) sign and carry forward the Kyoto protocols; (3) let the UN take the lead in international crises; (4) rely on diplomatic and economic measures rather than military ones in confronting terror; (5) keep to the traditional interpretation of the UN Charter; (6) give up the Security Council veto and have "a decent respect for the opinion of mankind," as the Declaration of Independence advises, even if power centers disagree; (7) cut back sharply on military spending and sharply increase social spending. For people who believe in democracy, these are very conservative suggestions: they appear to be the opinions of the majority of the US population, in most cases the overwhelming majority. They are in radical opposition to public policy. To be sure, we cannot be very confident about the state of public opinion on such matters because of another feature of the democratic deficit: the topics scarcely enter into public discussion and the basic facts are little known. In a highly atomized society, the public is therefore largely deprived of the opportunity to form considered opinions.

Another conservative suggestion is that facts, logic, and elementary moral principles should matter. Those who take the trouble to adhere to that suggestion will soon be led to abandon a good part of familiar doctrine, though it is surely much easier to repeat self-serving mantras. Such simple truths carry us some distance toward developing more specific and detailed answers. More important, they open the way to implement them, opportunities that are readily within our grasp if we can free ourselves from the shackles of doctrine and imposed illusion.

Though it is natural for doctrinal systems to seek to induce pessimism, hopelessness, and despair, reality is different. There has been substantial progress in the unending quest for justice and freedom in recent years, leaving a legacy that can be carried forward from a higher plane than before. Opportunities for education and organizing abound. As in the past, rights are not likely to be granted by benevolent authorities, or won by intermittent actions – attending a few demonstrations or pushing a lever in the personalized quadrennial extravaganzas that are depicted as "democratic politics." As always in the past, the tasks require dedicated day-by-day engagement to create – in part re-create – the basis for a functioning democratic culture in which the public plays some role in determining policies, not only in the political arena, from which it is largely excluded, but also in the crucial economic arena, from which it is excluded in principle. There are many ways to promote democracy at home, carrying it to new dimensions. Opportunities are ample, and failure to grasp them is likely to have ominous repercussions: for the country, for the world, and for future generations.

Notes

1   Gar Alperovitz, *America Beyond Capitalism* (Wiley, 2005). The "historic values" are those professed. On the operative values for the powerful, there is, as always, a good deal more to say.
2   Stuart Eizenstat, John Edward Porter, and Jeremy Weinstein, *Foreign Affairs*, January–February 2005.
3   Robert Pastor, *Condemned to Repetition* (Princeton, 1987), his emphasis.

Noam Chomsky (2006) *Failed States: The Abuse of Power and the Assault on Democracy*, London: Allen and Unwin, pp. 1–2, 252, 263–4.

Global Governance

OUR GLOBAL NEIGHBORHOOD: THE COMMISSION ON GLOBAL GOVERNANCE (2002)

The Commission on Global Governance was originally founded in 1991 by three co-chairmen: Ingvar Carlsson, a former Swedish prime minister, Jan Pronk, a former government minister for Holland, and Shirdath Ramphal, a former Guyanian secretary-general of the Commonwealth. Together, at the urging of many world leaders, Carlsson, Pronk, and Ramphal established a commission to survey the state of global governance at the turn of the twenty-first century. They finally did so in 1992 with the establishment of a 28-member panel that received backing from the UN secretary general as well as other international organizations. In 1995, the Commission produced "Our Global Neighborhood," a report which made recommendations on how to realize a more globalized vision of international relations. The report's release garnered praise from some and provoked criticism from others. For example, some social thinkers have criticized the ideals put forth by the Commission as being too lofty and abstract to ever be realized. However, paradoxically, the report has been lauded by others for those very same reasons.

Governance, change, and values

Global governance, once viewed primarily as concerned with intergovernmental relationships, now involves not only governments and intergovernmental institutions but also non-governmental organizations (NGOs), citizens' movements, transnational corporations, academia, and the mass media. The emergence of a global civil society, with many movements reinforcing a sense of human solidarity, reflects a large increase in the capacity and will of people to take control of their own lives.

States remain primary actors but have to work with others. The United Nations must play a vital role, but it cannot do all the work. Global governance does not imply world government or world federalism. Effective global governance calls for a new vision, challenging people as well as governments to realize that there is no alternative to working together to create the kind of world they want for themselves and their children. It requires a strong commitment to democracy grounded in civil society.

The changes of the last half-century have brought the global neighbourhood nearer to reality – a world in which citizens are increasingly dependent on one another and need to cooperate. Matters calling for global neighbourhood action keep multiplying. What happens far away matters much more now.

We believe that a global civic ethic to guide action within the global neighbourhood and leadership infused with that ethic are vital to the quality of global governance. We call for a common commitment to core values that all humanity could uphold: respect for life, liberty, justice and equity, mutual respect, caring, and integrity.

We further believe humanity as a whole will be best served by recognition of a set of common rights and responsibilities.

It should encompass the right of all people to:

- a secure life,
- equitable treatment,
- an opportunity to earn a fair living and provide for their own welfare,
- the definition and preservation of their differences through peaceful means,
- participation in governance at all levels,
- free and fair petition for redress of gross injustices,
- equal access to information, and
- equal access to the global commons.

At the same time, all people share a responsibility to:

- contribute to the common good;
- consider the impact of their actions on the security and welfare of others;
- promote equity, including gender equity;
- protect the interests of future generations by pursuing sustainable development and safeguarding the global commons;
- free and fair petition for redress of gross injustices,
- equal access to information, and
- equal access to the global commons.

At the same time, all people share a responsibility to:

- contribute to the common good;
- consider the impact of their actions on the security and welfare of others;
- promote equity, including gender equity;
- protect the interests of future generations by pursuing sustainable development and safeguarding the global commons;
- preserve humanity's cultural and intellectual heritage;
- be active participants in governance; and
- work to eliminate corruption.

Democracy provides the environment within which the fundamental rights of citizens are best safeguarded and offers the most favourable foundation for peace and stability. The world needs, however, to ensure the rights of minorities, and to guard against the ascendence of the military and corruption. Democracy is more than just the right to vote in regular elections. And as within nations, so globally, the democratic principle must be ascendant.

Sovereignty has been the cornerstone of the interstate system. In an increasingly interdependent world, however, the notions of territoriality, independence, and non-intervention have lost some of their meaning. In certain areas, sovereignty must be exercised collectively, particularly in relation to the global commons. Moreover, the most serious threats to national sovereignty and territorial integrity now often have internal roots.

The principles of sovereignty and non-intervention must be adapted in ways that recognize the need to balance the rights of states with the rights of people, and the interests of nations with the interests of the global neighbourhood. It is time also to think about self-determination in the emerging context of a global neighbourhood rather than the traditional context of a world of separate states.

Against this backdrop of an emerging global neighbourhood and the values that should guide its governance, we explored four specific areas of governance central to the challenges of the new era the world has entered: security, economic interdependence, the United Nations, and the rule of law. In each case we have sought to focus on governance aspects, but these are often

- The development of military capabilities beyond that required for national defence and support of UN action is a potential threat to the security of people.
- Weapons of mass destruction are not legitimate instruments of national defence.
- The production and trade in arms should be controlled by the international community. [. . .]

Managing economic interdependence

The globalization process is in danger of widening the gap between rich and poor. A sophisticated, globalized, increasingly affluent world currently coexists with a marginalized global underclass.

The pace of globalization of financial and other markets is outstripping the capacity of governments to provide the necessary framework of rules and co-operative arrangements. There are severe limits to national solutions to such failures within a globalized economy, yet the structures of global governance for pursuing international public policy objectives are underdeveloped. [. . .]

A start must be made in establishing schemes of global financing of global purposes, including charges for the use of global resources such as flight lanes, sea-lanes, and ocean fishing areas and the collection of global revenues agreed globally and implemented by treaty. An international tax on foreign currency transactions should be explored as one option, as should the creation of an international corporate tax base among multinational companies. It is time for the evolution of a consensus on the concept of global taxation for servicing the needs of the global neighbourhood.

Reforming the United Nations

We do not subscribe to the notion that the UN should be dismantled to make way for a new architecture of global governance. Much of the necessary reform of the United Nations system can be effected without amending the Charter, provided governments are willing. But some Charter amendments are necessary for better global governance, and those we propose will help to create an environment propitious to a return to the spirit of the Charter.

UN reform must reflect the realities of change, including the new capacity of global civil society to contribute to global governance. [. . .]

The world community can take pride in UN achievements in the economic and social sectors through the specialized agencies and the programmes and funds. But there is scope for improvement in responding to new needs and in efficiency. There is also need to improve co-ordination and for the specialized agencies to enhance their position as centres of authority. The various programmes and funds require more efficient governance structures and improved funding systems, with fairer burden – sharing among a wider range of donor countries. [. . .]

The UN must gear itself for a time when regionalism becomes more ascendant world-wide and assist the process in advance of that time. Regional co-operation and integration should be seen as an important and integral part of a balanced system of global governance. However, the continuing utility of the UN Regional Economic Commissions now needs to be closely examined and their future determined in consultation with the respective regions. [. . .]

Strengthening the rule of law world-wide

The global neighbourhood of the future must be characterized by law and the reality that all, including the weakest, are equal under the law and none, including the strongest, is above it. Our recommendations are directed to strengthening international law and the International Court of Justice in particular. [. . .]

The next steps

If reform is left to normal processes, only piecemeal and inadequate action will result.

We have made many recommendations, some of them far-reaching. We would like in this chapter to go one step further by suggesting a process through which the world community could consider these and similar recommendations. [. . .]

We call on international civil society, NGOs, the business sector, academia, the professions, and especially young people to join in a drive for change in the international system.

Governments can be made to initiate change if people demand it. That has been the story of major change in our time; the liberation of women and the environmental movement provide examples. If people are to live in a global neighbourhood and live by neighbourhood values, they have to prepare the ground. We believe that they are ready to do so.

We urge governments to set in motion a process of change that can give hope to people everywhere, and particularly to the young. Despite today's many complexities and hazards, the world has a unique opportunity to take human civilization to higher levels and to make the global neighbourhood a more peaceful, just, and habitable place for all, now and in the future.

The Commission on Global Governance (2002) "Our Global Neighborhood." Source: http://web.archive.org/web/20020225083552/www.cgg.ch/ch7.htm.

GOVERNANCE WITHOUT GOVERNMENT: JAMES N. ROSENAU (1992)

James Rosenau (1924–) is University Professor of International Affairs at the George Washington University. As the author of *Turbulence in World Politics*, *Along the Domestic-Foreign Frontier*, and *The Study of World Politics*, Rosenau is widely considered to be a leading expert on the impact of globalization on the international political landscape. A common theme in Rosenau's work is the belief that globalization has blurred the lines between what is domestic and what is international. This is evident in his piece "Governance, Order and Change in World Politics" from which the selection is taken. Here, Rosenau lays out the claim that governance is not synonymous with government – a fact he believes is thrown into sharp relief because of recent developments.

Governance, Order and Change in World Politics

To presume the presence of governance without government is to conceive of functions that have to be performed in any viable human system irrespective of whether the system has evolved organizations and institutions explicitly charged with performing them. Among the many necessary functions, for example, are the needs wherein any system has to cope with external challenges, to prevent conflicts among its members or factions from tearing it irretrievably apart, to procure resources necessary to its preservation and well-being, and to frame goals and policies designed to achieve them. Whether the systems are local or global in scope, these functional needs are ever present if a system is to persist intact through time.

Activities designed to service a system's functional necessities are readily self-evident in the operations of governments which, normally, either evolve constitutions to regulate their conduct domestically or sign treaties to guide their performance internationally. During the present period of rapid and extensive global change, however, the constitutions of national governments and their treaties have been undermined by the demands and greater coherence of ethnic and other subgroups, the globalization of economies, the advent of broad social movements, the shrinking of political distances by microelectronic technologies, and the mushrooming of global interdependencies fostered by currency crises, environmental pollution, terrorism, the drug trade, AIDS, and a host of other transnational issues that are crowding the global agenda. These centralizing and decentralizing dynamics have undermined constitutions and treaties in the sense that they have contributed to the shifts in the loci of authority. Governments still operate and they are still sovereign in a number of ways; but, as noted above, some of their authority has been relocated toward subnational collectivities. Some of the functions of governance, in other words, are now being performed by activities that do not originate with governments.

What, then, is an appropriate way of formulating the concept of governance as it operates in world politics? Is it merely a synonym for international institutions and regimes? Can governance be effective in the absence of central authority? To what extent is the stability of a global order dependent on the presence of governance?

Such questions invite a lengthy disquisition on the nature of government and how sovereign national systems are so much more conducive to governmental operations than international systems that are not endowed with sovereign powers. And, indeed, the collapse of the Cold War and the many other changes that mark our time readily justify such a disquisition. Given the profound transformations in the nature and location of authority, legitimacy, and compliance, and given the emergent roles and structures of the modern state, transnational organizations, social movements, common markets, and political parties, the basis for extensive re-examinations of government and governance in an increasingly interdependent world is surely compelling. Obviously, however, this is not the occasion to undertake this task. Here we can only take note of possible meanings of governance in the emergent international context and how it is linked into the prevailing order and the prospects for change.[1]

As indicated by the title of this book, governance is not synonymous with government. Both refer to purposive behavior, to goal-oriented activities, to systems of rule; but government suggests activities that are backed by formal authority, by police powers to insure the implementation of duly constituted policies, whereas governance refers to activities backed by shared goals that may or may not derive from legal and formally prescribed responsibilities and that do not necessarily rely on police powers to overcome defiance and attain compliance. Governance, in other words, is a more encompassing phenomenon than government. It embraces governmental institutions, but it also subsumes informal, non-governmental mechanisms whereby those persons and organizations within its purview move ahead, satisfy their needs, and fulfill their wants.

Governance is thus a system of rule that is as dependent on inter-subjective meanings as on formally sanctioned constitutions and charters. Put more emphatically, governance is a system of rule that works only if it is accepted by the majority (or, at least, by the most powerful of those it affects), whereas governments can function even in the face of widespread opposition to their policies. In this sense governance is always effective in performing the functions necessary to systemic persistence, else it is not conceived to exist (since instead of referring to ineffective governance, one speaks of anarchy or chaos). Governments, on the other hand, can be quite ineffective without being regarded as non-existent (they are viewed simply as "weak"). Thus it is possible to conceive of governance without government – of regulatory mechanisms in a sphere of activity which function effectively even though they are not endowed with formal authority.

Nor is it far-fetched to derive from this line of reasoning a plausible scenario marked by government without governance. Indeed, if one ponders all the deeply divided countries whose politics are paralyzed and stale-mated, it can readily be concluded that the world is populated with more than a few formal authorities who lack the regulatory mechanisms to function effectively, that is, with governments without governance. One might even argue, given all the noxious policies governments pursue, that governance without government is in some ways preferable to governments that are capable of governance. As one exasperated analyst has succinctly and tellingly observed, "Governance has been usurped by governments."[2]

To suggest that governance is always effective is to posit a close link between governance and order. It might even be said that governance is order plus intentionality. Global order consists of those routinized arrangements through which world politics gets from one moment in time to the next. Some of the arrangements are fundamental (such as the dispersion of power among key actors, the hierarchical differences among them, the rules which bound their interactions, and the premises they share about the role of force, diplomacy, cooperation, and conflict) and some are quite routinized (such as trade, postal, and passport procedures). But irrespective of whether they are fundamental or routinized, not all of the arrangements are the result of self-conscious efforts on the part of those who sustain them. Some of the arrangements derive, rather, from the aggregation of individual decisions that are designed to serve immediate subsystem concerns but that cumulate to system-wide orderly arrangements. The setting of prices in a market place exemplifies a self-regulating aggregation that facilitates order: sellers are concerned with receiving the highest possible amount for their goods and buyers seek to pay the lowest possible amount, but the result of their individual bargains is normally a stable and orderly system-wide market for the commodity. Similarly, individual members of Amnesty International work on specific cases of illegal imprisonment and torture, but the collective sum of their efforts makes a substantial contribution to that dimension of global order through which a modicum of human rights is preserved. Or consider the example of the flight of East Germans to the West in the fall of 1989: as participants in the Cold War order they previously acquiesced in the prohibition against movement across the East–West border, but that consensus unraveled with the decision of each family to flee to West Germany and, within only weeks, the cumulative impact of these decisions hastened an end to that system of governance and initiated a new one that is still very much in the process of formation.

On the other hand, some of the arrangements underlying a global order spring from activities that are self-consciously designed to maintain the order. Most markets have created rules and officials charged with monitoring and preventing unfair practices; Amnesty International has an executive committee that assigns cases to individuals and issues periodic reports on overall patterns in the human rights field; during the Cold War East Germany had officials and laws that relied on police powers to insure the continuance of the consensus that kept East Germans from emigrating, just as the subsequent breakdown of that consensus was facilitated by West German, Hungarian, and other authorities who sought to encourage the emergence of a new order. And it is here, in those dimensions of order suffused with intentionality, that its close links to governance are most readily discernible.

While examples help to clarify the concept of governance and how it is more encompassing than that of government, they obviously do not guarantee the resolution of conceptual ambiguity. The distinction between governance and government and the links between governance and order are not self-evident. In some languages (German for one), in fact, there is no readily identifiable word that signifies governance. The notion of intersubjective systems of rule not backed by legal and constitutional authority is too improbable an aspect of political processes in the cultures that employ these languages to have allowed for convergence around a simplified, single-word designation of the concept. But even those whose language includes such a designation can easily encounter difficulty in using the concept. A host of diverse (but not incompatible) nuances attach to the use of "governance" in English. As indicated above, some formulations conceive of governance in functional terms, that is, in terms of the tasks that have to be performed to sustain the routinized arrangements of the prevailing order and that may or may not be performed by governments. For other observers governance is linked to the capacity to regulate the arrangements so that they remain routinized. For still others governance is associated with occasions when power is exercised independently of the authority of government. Some distinguish governance as a mode of allocating values while viewing government as operating the mechanisms through which the allocation is accomplished. In some instances governance is equated with the emergence of rule-like systems and problem-solving devices.[3]

Notwithstanding the various shades of meaning attached to the concept, there is one dimension of governance about which all of the ensuing chapters fully agree. It is that while a focus on "governance without government" does not require the exclusion of national or sub-national governments from the analysis, it does necessitate inquiry that presumes the absence of some overarching governmental authority at the international level. Put differently, the concept of governance without government is especially conducive to the study of world politics inasmuch as centralized authority is conspicuously absent from this domain of human affairs even though it is equally obvious that a modicum of order, of routinized arrangements, is normally present in the conduct of global life. Given an order that lacks a centralized authority with the capacity to enforce decisions on a global scale, it follows that a prime task of inquiry is that of probing the extent to which the functions normally associated with governance are performed in world politics without the institutions of government.

Many students of world politics are inclined to use the term "anarchy" to designate the absence of a centralized authority in world politics. For them anarchy has neither good nor bad connotations. Nor does it necessarily imply that the prevailing global order is marked by pervasive disarray and commotion. Rather, "anarchy" is employed simply as a descriptive term for the lack of a centralized authority that stands over national governments and has the capacity, including the use of force if necessary, to direct their conduct. For some analysts, however, anarchy implies a lack of patterned rule, a tendency for actors to go their own separate ways without regard for common principles, norms, rules, and procedures. Such an implication seems highly questionable. As one observer puts it, noting the authority that attached to many treaties, international legal precedents, and international organizations, "the international system (in spite of its lack of an overarching regime or world government) is several steps beyond anarchy."[4]

In sum, governance and order are clearly interactive phenomena. As intentional activities designed to regularize the arrangements which sustain world affairs, governance obviously shapes the nature of the prevailing global order. It could not do so, however, if the patterns constituting the order did not facilitate governance. Thus order is both a precondition and a consequence of government. Neither comes first and each helps explain the other. There can be no governance without order and there can be no order without governance (unless periods of disorder are regarded as forms of order).

Notes

1 For another, more extensive and cogent inquiry into the meaning of the governance concept, see Lawrence S. Finkelstein, "What Is International Governance?," a paper presented at the Annual Meeting of the International Studies Association (Vancouver: March 21, 1991).
2 Rajhi Kothari, "On Human Governance," *Alternatives*, 12 (1987), p. 277.
3 For an inquiry that identifies sixteen different types of situations in which governance operates as a system of rule, see James N. Rosenau, "Governance without Government: Systems of Rule in World Politics" (Los Angeles: Institute for Transnational Studies, University of Southern California, November 1987). An extended critique of this essay is developed in Richard K. Ashley, "Imposing International Purpose: Notes on a Problematic of Governance," in Ernst-Otto Czempiel and James N. Rosenau, eds., *Global Changes and Theoretical Challenges: Approaches to World Politics for the 1990s* (Lexington, MA: Lexington Books, 1989), ch. 13.
4 Robert C. North, *War, Peace, Survival: Global Politics and Conceptual Synthesis* (Boulder, CO. Westview Press, 1990), p. 136.

James N. Rosenau (1992) "Governance, Order and Change in World Politics," in J. Rosenau and E. Czempiel (eds) *Governance Without Government: Order and Change in World Politics*, Cambridge: Cambridge University Press, pp. 3–8.

GLOBAL COVENANT: DAVID HELD (2004)

David Held (1951–), whose highly influential work on global transformations appeared in Part IV, is also a key proponent of global governance as a means of achieving political and social justice. He has been particularly influential in debates surrounding cosmopolitanism, and indeed his own writings in this area are both analytically subtle and politically scintillating. He is impatient with the limits and dead-ends of neo-liberalism and its tireless promotion of consumerist freedoms, and instead posits a new internationalism transformed by emergent cosmopolitan values and standards. For Held, cosmopolitan principles – focused, for example, on the claims of each person as an individual or member of humanity as a whole – are the guiding ethical ground of global social democracy. In this selection, Held puts the claims of global social democracy and cosmopolitanism into dialogue with that brand of neo-liberalism (what he terms "the Washington Consensus") which dominated global politics in the aftermath of 9/11 and the wars on Afghanistan and Iraq. In an age which has fetishized the doctrine of pre-emptive war, according to Held, a brave new global covenant aimed at political, social, and economic reform is demanded for our global age.

Towards a Global Covenant

The contemporary phase of globalization is transforming the foundations of world order, leading away from a world based exclusively on state politics to a new and more complex form of global politics and multilayered governance. At the beginning of the twenty-first century there are good reasons for believing that the traditional international order of states cannot be restored and that the deep drivers of globalization are unlikely to be halted. Accordingly, a fundamental change in political orientation is unavoidable. Changes of outlook are clearly demarcated in the contest between the principal variants in the politics of globalization. Two leading positions – neoliberalism and that of the anti-globalization movement – are both deeply problematic. Whereas neoliberalism simply perpetuates existing economic and political systems and offers no substantial policies to deal with the problems of market failure, the radical anti-globalist position appears deeply naive about the potential for locally based action to resolve, or engage with, the governance agenda generated by the forces of globalization. How can such a politics cope with the challenges posed by overlapping communities of fate?

The same can be said, of course, about the current position of the US administration. If the US acts alone in the world, it cannot deliver core global public goods, such as free trade, financial stability and environmental sustainability, which it depends on for its overall development and prosperity. Moreover, if it acts alone it cannot achieve key domestic objectives, including leading national security goals. The fight against global terrorism requires the global pooling of intelligence, information and resources; the policing of what is left of a secure Afghanistan (Kabul) needs internationally generated resources (financial and personnel); and Iraq itself cannot be legitimately pacified and rebuilt without international cooperation, globally sourced investment and collaboration among many countries helping to supply skilled people of all kinds, from soldiers to engineers.

The alternative position is global social democracy. It seeks to build on the project of social democracy while embracing the achievements of the post-Holocaust multilateral order. Its aim is to adopt some of the values and insights of social democracy while applying them to the new global constellation of economics and politics. National social bargains, as noted in the Introduction, are insufficient to ensure an effective trade-off between the values of social solidarity, the politics of democracy and the efficiencies of the market. The challenge today, as Kofi Annan has written (1999), is to devise a similar bargain or project to underpin the new global economy. The project of global social democracy addresses this call. It is a basis for promoting the rule of international law; greater transparency, accountability and democracy in global governance; a deeper commitment to social justice; the protection and reinvention of community at diverse levels; and the transformation of the global economy into a free and fair rule-based economic order. The politics of global social democracy contains clear possibilities of dialogue between different segments of the 'pro-globalization/anti-globalization' political spectrum, although it will, of course, be contested by opinion at the extreme ends of the spectrum.

Box 5 summarizes the project of global social democracy – the basis of a new global covenant. It does not present an all-or-nothing choice, but rather lays down a direction of change with clear points of orientation. In so doing, it draws together some of the main threads of this book, highlighting the core recommendations made in the areas of economics, politics and law. Since security considerations were confronted in both parts II and III, these have been drawn out under a separate heading in the box. Although steps taken to implement the reform programme in each of these areas would constitute a major step forward for progressive politics, it is only by addressing the policy packages in all of them that the programme of global social democracy can ultimately be fulfilled. One of the principal political questions of our time is how such a programme can best be carried out, and how global public goods can best be provided.

Box 5 Towards a new global covenant: global social democracy

Guiding ethical principles

Equal moral worth, equal liberty, equal political status, collective decision-making about public affairs, amelioration of urgent need, development for all, environmental sustainability

Institutional goals

Rule of law, political equality, democratic politics, global social justice, social soldiarity and community, economic efficiency, global ecological balance

Priority measures

Economy

- Regulating global markets: salvaging the Doha trade negotiating round; removal of EU and US subsidies of agriculture and textiles; reforming TRIPS; expansion of the terms of reference of the Global Compact
- Promoting development: phasing in trade and financial global market integration (particularly of portfolio capital markets); expanding the negotiating capacity of developing countries at the WTO; enhancing developing country participation in international financial institutions; abolition of debt for highly indebted poor countries (HIPCs); linking debt cancellation to the funding of children's education and basic health; meeting UN aid targets of 0.7 per cent GNP; establishing new international finance facility to aid investment in poorest countries

Governance

- Reform of global governance: establishing a representative Security Council; establishment of Economic and Social Security Council to coordinate poverty reduction and global development policies; creation of environmental IGO; establishment of global issue networks on pressing social and economic problems; strengthening the negotiating capacity of developing countries; developing criteria for fair negotiations among states and non-state actors; improving cooperation among IGOs; enhanced parliamentary scrutiny of regional and international bodies

Law

- Convene an international convention to begin the process of reconnecting the security and human rights agendas through the consolidation of international humanitarian law

Security

- Developing UN Security Council principles and procedures in relation to threats to the peace and the use of armed force to intervene in the affairs of another state; enhancing monitoring capacity of the risks of, and developments concerning, humanitarian crises; implementation of existing global poverty reduction and human development commitments and policies; strengthening of arms control and arms trade regulation

Long-term measures

Economy
- Taming global markets: global antitrust authority; world financial authority; mandatory codes of conduct for MNCs
- Market correcting: mandatory global labour and environmental standards; foreign investment codes and standards
- Market promoting: privileged market access for developing countries where fledgling industries require protection; convention on global labour mobility and economic migration

Governance
- Democratization of national and suprastate governance (multi-level citizenship); global constitutional convention to explore the rules and mandates of new democratic global bodies; establishment of new international tax mechanism; creation of negotiating arenas for new priority issues (e.g. world water court); enhanced global public goods provision

Law
- Establishment of international human rights court with strong supporting regional courts; the expansion of the jurisdictions of the ICC and ICJ; the entrenchment of labour, welfare and environmental standards in the *modus operandi* of corporate practice

Security
- Establishment of permanent peace-making and peacekeeping forces; developing security and human rights threshold tests for membership in key IGOs; security, social exclusion and equity impact reviews of all global development measures

A coalition of political groupings could develop to push the agenda of global social democracy further. It could comprise European countries with strong liberal and social democratic traditions; liberal groups in the US which support multilateralism and the rule of law in international affairs; developing countries struggling for freer and fairer trade rules in the world economic system; non-governmental organizations, from Amnesty International to Oxfam, campaigning for a more just, democratic and equitable world order; transnational social movements contesting the nature and form of contemporary globalization; and those economic forces that desire a more stable and managed global economy.

A complex set of parties and commitments would be needed to make a compelling coalition for global social democracy. But while it would be complex, it is not impossible to envisage. In fact, some of its core ingredients could be stipulated as follows:

- leading European powers need to commit to the creation of a multilateral order, and not a multipolar one in which they simply pursue their own state interests above all else;
- the EU must address its weak geopolitical and strategic capacity via the development of a rapid reaction force and the creation of a common European defence force;
- the US needs to acknowledge that its long-term strategic, economic and environmental interests can only be achieved collaboratively, and it must, as a matter of principle, accept the opportunities and constraints afforded by multilateral institutions and international regimes;
- developing countries, seeking major aid and overseas investments (public and private), need to accept the establishment of transparent and good governance as part of the requirements to attract investment in the infrastructure of their economies and societies;

- INGOs need to understand that, while their voices in global affairs are important, they represent particular interests which need to be articulated with, and harnessed within, wider frameworks of accountability and justice;
- IGOs utilizing and advocating greater public funding have to recognize that they are part of an international civil service delivering core public goods – and not outposts of particular nation-states or sectional interests. The confusing and conflicting mandates and jurisdictions of IGOs need to be streamlined and clarified;
- regional governance structures, while enhancing and expanding the developmental opportunities of their member states, must commit to keeping regions open for economic and diplomatic engagement with others – in short, they need to nurture open forms of regionalism;
- national governments must recognize that they are stakeholders in global problems and that ownership of these is a crucial first stage in their resolution – national and regional parliaments need to enhance their communication with, understanding of and engagement with supranational governance.

Europe could have a distinctive role in pursuing the cause of global social democracy (McGrew, 2002a). As the home of both social democracy and a historic experiment in governance beyond the state, Europe has accumulated a wealth of experience in considering institutional designs for suprastate governance. It offers novel ways of thinking about governance beyond the state which encourage a more accountable and rule-bound – as opposed to more neoliberal or unilateralist – approach to global governance. This is not to suggest that the EU should lead an anti-US coalition of transnational and international forces. On the contrary, it is crucial to recognize the complexity of US domestic politics and the existence of progressive social, political and economic forces seeking to advance a rather different kind of world order from that championed by the current neoconservatives (Nye, 2002).

While some of those who might coalesce around a movement for global social democracy would inevitably have divergent interests on a wide range of issues, there is potentially an important over-lapping sphere of concern among them for the strengthening of multilateralism, building new institutions for providing global public goods, regulating global markets, deepening accountability, protecting the environment and urgently remedying social injustices that kill thousands of men, women and children daily. And there is evidence that the thrust of such a coalition would resonate with people's attitudes to globalization in many parts of the world. A recent poll highlights that while many people have positive views about the broad benefits of globalization, they want a different kind of globalization from the one currently on offer: the integration of economies and societies has to be balanced with the protection of local traditions, with a sustainable pace of life, and with a global safety net to help ensure equitable life chances (see Stokes, 2003; www.people-press.org).

High stakes

Over the last one hundred years political power has been reshaped and reconfigured. It has been diffused below, above and alongside the nation-state. Globalization has brought large swathes of the world's population 'closer together' in overlapping communities of fate. Yet there are, obviously enough, many reasons for pessimism. There are storm clouds ahead. Globalization has not just integrated peoples and nations, but created new forms of antagonism. The globalization of communications does not just make it easier to establish mutual understanding, but often highlights what it is that people do not have in common and how and why differences matter. The dominant political game in the 'transnational town' remains geopolitics. Ethnic self-centredness, right-wing nationalism and unilateralist politics are once again on the rise, and not just in the West. However, the circumstances and nature of politics have changed. Like national culture and state traditions, a vibrant internationalism and global social democracy are a cultural and political project, but with one difference: they are better adapted and suited to our regional and global age. Unfortunately, the arguments in support of them have yet to be fully articulated in many parts of the world; and we fail here at our peril.

It is important to return to the themes of the Preface – 9/11 and the war in Iraq – and to say what they mean in this context. One cannot accept the burden of putting accountability and justice right in one realm of life – physical security and political cooperation among defence establishments – without at the same time seeking to put it right elsewhere. If the political and the security, the social and the economic dimensions of accountability and justice are separated in the long term – as is the tendency in the global order today – the prospects of a peaceful and civil society will be bleak indeed. Popular support against terrorism, as well as against political violence and exclusionary politics of all kinds, depends on convincing people that there is a legal, responsive and specific way of addressing their grievances. For this reason, globalization without global social democracy could fail.

Against the background of 9/11, the current unilateralist stance of the US and the desperate cycle of violence in the Middle East and elsewhere, the advocacy of global social democracy may appear like an attempt to defy gravity or to walk on water! And, indeed, if it were a case of having to adopt global social democracy all at once or not at all, this would be true. But it is no more the case than was the pursuit of the modern state at the time of its founders. Over the last several decades the growth of multilateralism and the development of international law have created social democratic anchors for the world. These are the basis for the furhter consolidation of social democratic principles and institutions. Moreover, a coalition of political groupings could emerge to push these achievements further. Of course, how far such forces can unite around these objectives – and can overcome fierce opposition from well-entrenched geopolitical and geoeconomic interests – remains to be seen. The stakes are high, but so too are the potential gains for human security and development if the aspirations for global social democracy can be realized. One thing is clear; existing security and development policies are not working well enough and the case for a new politics and policy mix is overwhelming.

David Held (2004) *Global Covenant: The Social Democratic Alternative to the Washington Consensus*, Cambridge: Polity Press, pp. 162–169.

CHINA AND THE GLOBAL ORDER: G. JOHN IKENBERRY (2008)

G. John Ikenberry (1954–) is the Albert G. Milbank Professor of Politics and International Affairs at Princeton University in the Woodrow Wilson School and Department of Politics. He has worked with the U.S. State Department, the Council of Foreign Relations, and Carnegie Commission on the Reorganization of Government for the Conduct of Foreign Policy. He is known as a critic of U.S. imperialism, arguing that the imperial project is pragmatically unsustainable. This selection argues that the U.S. system is part of a Western order of market societies that have been drawn closer together. The rise of China, often seen through the lens of traditional international relations as a threat to US-led global order, might rather be an asset if China is welcomed into the global economic market.

The Rise of China and the Future of the West

The rise of China will undoubtedly be one of the great dramas of the twenty-first century. China's extraordinary economic growth and active diplomacy are already transforming East Asia, and future decades will see even greater increases in Chinese power and influence. But exactly how this drama will play out is an open question. Will China overthrow the existing order or become a part of it? And what, if anything, can the United States do to maintain its position as China rises?

Some observers believe that the American era is coming to an end, as the Western-oriented world order is replaced by one increasingly dominated by the East. The historian Niall Ferguson has written that the bloody twentieth century witnessed "the descent of the West" and "a reorientation of the world" toward the East. Realists go on to note that as China gets more powerful and the United States' position erodes, two things are likely to happen: China will try to use its growing influence to reshape the rules and institutions of the international system to better serve its interests, and other states in the system – especially the declining hegemon – will start to see China as a growing security threat. The result of these developments, they predict, will be tension, distrust, and conflict, the typical features of a power transition. In this view, the drama of China's rise will feature an increasingly powerful China and a declining United States locked in an epic battle over the rules and leadership of the international system. And as the world's largest country emerges not from within but outside the established post-World War II international order, it is a drama that will end with the grand ascendance of China and the onset of an Asian-centered world order.

That course, however, is not inevitable. The rise of China does not have to trigger a wrenching hegemonic transition. The U.S.–Chinese power transition can be very different from those of the past because China faces an international order that is fundamentally different from those that past rising states confronted. China does not just face the United States; it faces a Western-centered system that is open, integrated, and rule-based, with wide and deep political foundations. The nuclear revolution, meanwhile, has made war among great powers unlikely – eliminating the major tool that rising powers have used to overturn international systems defended by declining hegemonic states. Today's Western order, in short, is hard to overturn and easy to join.

This unusually durable and expansive order is itself the product of farsighted U.S. leadership. After World War II, the United States did not simply establish itself as the leading world power. It led in the creation of universal institutions that not only invited global membership but also brought democracies and market societies closer together. It built an order that facilitated the participation and integration of both established great powers and newly independent states. (It is often forgotten that this postwar order was designed in large part to reintegrate the defeated Axis states and the beleaguered Allied states into a unified international system.) Today, China can gain full access to and thrive within this system. And if it does, China will rise, but the Western order – if managed properly – will live on.

As it faces an ascendant China, the United States should remember that its leadership of the Western order allows it to shape the environment in which China will make critical strategic choices. If it wants to preserve this leadership, Washington must work to strengthen the rules and institutions that underpin that order – making it even easier to join and harder to overturn. U.S. grand strategy should be built around the motto "The road to the East runs through the West." It must sink the roots of this order as deeply as possible, giving China greater incentives for integration than for opposition and increasing the chances that the system will survive even after U.S. relative power has declined.

The United States' "unipolar moment" will inevitably end. If the defining struggle of the twenty-first century is between China and the United States, China will have the advantage. If the defining struggle is between China and a revived Western system, the West will triumph. [. . .]

The postwar Western order is historically unique. Any international order dominated by a powerful state is based on a mix of coercion and consent, but the U.S.-led order is distinctive in that it has been more liberal than imperial – and so unusually accessible, legitimate, and durable. Its rules and institutions are rooted in, and thus reinforced by, the evolving global forces of democracy and capitalism. It is expansive, with a wide and widening array of participants and stakeholders. It is capable of generating tremendous economic growth and power while also signaling restraint – all of which make it hard to overturn and easy to join.

It was the explicit intention of the Western order's architects in the 1940s to make that order integrative and expansive. Before the Cold War split the world into competing camps, Franklin Roosevelt sought to create a one-world system managed by cooperative great powers that would rebuild war-ravaged Europe, integrate the defeated states, and establish mechanisms for security cooperation and expansive economic growth. In fact, it was Roosevelt who urged – over the opposition of Winston Churchill – that China be included as a permanent member of the UN Security Council. [. . .]

After the Cold War, the Western order once again managed the integration of a new wave of countries, this time from the formerly communist world. Three particular features of the Western order have been critical to this success and longevity.

First, unlike the imperial systems of the past, the Western order is built around rules and norms of nondiscrimination and market openness, creating conditions for rising states to advance their expanding economic and political goals within it. Across history, international orders have varied widely in terms of whether the material benefits that are generated accrue disproportionately to the leading state or are widely shared. In the Western system, the barriers to economic participation are low, and the potential benefits are high. China has already discovered the massive economic returns that are possible by operating within this open-market system.

Second is the coalition-based character of its leadership. Past orders have tended to be dominated by one state. The stakeholders of the current Western order include a coalition of powers arrayed around the United States – an important distinction. These leading states, most of them advanced liberal democracies, do not always agree, but they are engaged in a continuous process of give-and-take over economics, politics, and security. Power transitions are typically seen as being played out between two countries, a rising state and a declining hegemon, and the order falls as soon as the power balance shifts. But in the current order, the larger aggregation of democratic capitalist states – and the resulting accumulation of geopolitical power – shifts the balance in the order's favor.

Third, the postwar Western order has an unusually dense, encompassing, and broadly endorsed system of rules and institutions. Whatever its shortcomings, it is more open and rule-based than any previous order. State sovereignty and the rule of law are not just norms enshrined in the United Nations Charter. They are part of the deep operating logic of the order. To be sure, these norms are evolving, and the United States itself has historically been ambivalent about binding itself to international law and institutions – and at no time more so than today. But the overall system is dense with multilateral rules and institutions – global and regional, economic, political, and security-related. These represent one of the great breakthroughs of the postwar era. They have laid the basis for unprecedented levels of cooperation and shared authority over the global system.

The incentives these features create for China to integrate into the liberal international order are reinforced by the changed nature of the international economic environment – especially the new interdependence driven by technology. The most farsighted Chinese leaders understand that globalization has changed the game and that China accordingly needs strong, prosperous partners around the world. From the United States' perspective, a healthy Chinese economy is vital to the United States and the rest of the world. Technology and the global economic revolution have created a logic of economic relations that is different from the past – making the political and institutional logic of the current order all the more powerful. [. . .]

The United States must reinvest in the Western order, reinforcing the features of that order that encourage engagement, integration, and restraint. The more this order binds together capitalist democratic states in deeply rooted institutions; the more open, consensual, and rule-based it is; and the more widely spread its benefits, the more likely it will be that rising powers can and will secure their interests through integration and accommodation rather than through war. And if the Western system offers rules and institutions that benefit the full range of states – rising and falling, weak and strong, emerging and mature – its dominance as an international order is all but certain.

The first thing the United States must do is reestablish itself as the foremost supporter of the global system of governance that underpins the Western order. Doing so will first of all facilitate the kind of collective problem solving that makes all countries better off. At the same time, when other countries see the United States using its power to strengthen existing rules and institutions, that power is rendered more legitimate – and U.S. authority is strengthened. Countries within the West become more inclined to work with, rather than resist, U.S. power, which reinforces the centrality and dominance of the West itself. [. . .]

In addition to maintaining the openness and durability of the order, the United States must redouble its efforts to integrate rising developing countries into key global institutions. Bringing emerging countries into the governance of the international order will give it new life. The United States and Europe must find room at the table not only for China but also for countries such as Brazil, India, and South Africa. A Goldman Sachs report on the so-called BRICs (Brazil, Russia, India, and China) noted that by 2050 these countries' economies could together be larger than those of the original G-6 countries (Germany, France, Italy, Japan, the United Kingdom, and the United States) combined. Each international institution presents its own challenges. The UN Security Council is perhaps the hardest to deal with, but its reform would also bring the greatest returns. Less formal bodies – the so-called G-20 and various other intergovernmental networks – can provide alternative avenues for voice and representation. [. . .]

The key thing for U.S. leaders to remember is that it may be possible for China to overtake the United States alone, but it is much less likely that China will ever manage to overtake the Western order.

G. John Ikenberry (2008) "The Rise of China and the Future of the West: Can the Liberal System Survive?" *Foreign Affairs*, Jan/Feb.

REALIST CRITIQUE OF GLOBAL CITIZENSHIP: DANILO ZOLO (2007)

Danilo Zolo (1936–) is Professor of Jurisprudence and Political Theory at the University of Florence, Italy. On top of his work on complexity and democracy, Zolo is best known for his criticism of political and legal cosmopolitanism. As the selection reveals, he appeals to the political "realist" view of globalization. The realist standpoint proceeds from the notion that power is always the primary end of political action. And as such, realists believe that cosmopolitanism is neither as universalistic nor as altruistic as it might initially seem. This is because, as Zolo argues, cosmopolitanism is itself just another way that power is being exerted. Specifically, it is the West trying to "universalize" its own standpoint without regard for other perspectives.

Global Citizenship: A Realist Critique

Realist interpretations of the globalisation process

As is well known, both political realism and legal realism are opposed to the ethical rationalism and the legal idealism of the Kantian tradition. A realist interpretation of the globalisation processes questions that they lead to the establishment of the so-called 'global village'. Instead, realists suggest that the processes of global integration largely coincide with the phenomenon of the Americanisation of the West and with the Western-isation of the world (Bauman 1998; Latouche 1989). This phenomenon produces an approval of existential models, styles of thought, and production practices that cannot be properly interpreted as a trend towards cultural integration of world society. Neither can it be read as foreshadowing the formation of a global civil society and enabling the advent of 'world constitutionalism'. Global citizenship, in this view, is not teleologically secure but is at most a contingent possibility. According to some sociologists (Robertson 1992; Featherstone 1991; Turner 1990), the contemporary compression of the world produces frames of cultural reference that cannot be termed 'global culture'. Rather, what is occurring on a world scale is a process of 'creolization'. This involves the adoption by a large number of indigenous populations of a foreign culture (technical, scientific and industrial) which does not produce order and community integration, but pollution, reaction and disorder. Or, it may lead to the emergence of 'third cultures' without territory linked by fast exchanges, international tourism and consumerism, all developed and promoted by those in the West who are cosmopolitan for professional reasons. Sociologically, this is quite a narrow phenomenon that lacks any intrinsic or profound universality.

In short, globalisation does not produce a cultural homogenisation of the world, as modernisation and convergence theorists have alleged. Instead, it stimulates particularist reactions that lay claim to the identity of cultural codes which are deep-rooted in nations and ethnic groups. A classic example of this type of reaction – important and ambiguous at the same time – is the argument by such Asian leaders as the Singaporean Lee Kuan Yew and the Malaysian Mohamad Mahatir, which gave rise to the theoretical debate about Asian values.

Optimistic prophecies of global harmony are also contradicted by the ways that the expansion of the market economy and its unstoppable propelling force throughout the world has significant effects on the increasingly disproportionate international distribution of power and wealth between states, world regions, and within individual countries. New and deeper differences in wealth, information, scientific and technological power, and work opportunities make the select groups of wealthy individuals increasingly wealthier and the majority of the poor increasingly poorer. This is what Eric Hobsbawn aptly terms the 'new wall of poverty'. The process of global economic and financial disproportion also uproots millions of individuals from their lands and social connections, and dumps them in the desert of metropolitan urbanisation, either as internal or external migrants. Growing masses of disinherited men and women, deprived of any social context and cultural identity, devoid of citizenship, migrate seeking asylum and besieging wealthy countries. This migratory drift destroys and disperses their roots, but does not integrate them, except marginally, in the processes of industrialisation, technological change, and bureaucratisation which accompany it: nor does it include them in a 'global citizenship'. In terms of the expanding international division of labour and the growth of technical and scientific specialisation, there is an increase in functional differentiation, but as social particularisms dissolve, there is no authentic cultural universalism, no core of shared values, no collective imaginary emerging to replace them. Indeed, Serge Latouche (1989) maintains that one can legitimately speak of a real failure of the 'modernization' project and of a setback for its Promethean universalisation with respect to these effects of 'deculturation', 'deterritorialization' and 'planetary uprooting'. Similarly, Zygmunt Bauman (1998) posits a new stratification of the world's population into the globalised rich and localised poor, and denounces the impotence of neo-liberal politics to remedy the global disintegration of cultures, social groups, and their 'citizenships', while Ulrich Beck (1997) reminds us that this phenomenon occurs even in highly civilised and wealthy Europe, which today accounts for 50 million poor, 20 million unemployed, and 5 million homeless individuals. Globalisation does not lead only to happy consequences.

Legal and political globalism?

Intentionally, globalisation is also not necessarily good news. On the contrary, the international divergence of economic power is accompanied by a drift towards further hierarchisation of international relations, the breaking down of standards of legitimation of international political power, the increasingly more frequent recourse to the use of military force by the great powers, and the spread of hardened and effective 'global terrorism'. Against the background of such processes, the hegemonic strategy of industrial powers led by the US stands out clearly. Indeed, documents written by US strategists from the early 1990s reveal that these strategists believe that globalisation is not a spontaneous process of world unification generated by the laws of the market, but rather requires constant military vigilance to secure its realisation.

In this context, the whole international law system, including international criminal justice, has been subordinated to the needs of 'global security' and the new modalities of the war against terrorism. Such developments lead to the marginalisation of the United Nations, and the undermining of international law in the name of the irrevocable *jus ad bellum*,[1] which the Great Powers arrogated to themselves. The result is that even international criminal justice has suffered discredit. The Hague Tribunal has provided irrefutable proof of its dependence on the political decisions, besides the financing and military assistance, of NATO and the United States. It is highly unrealistic, of course, to think that a legal process that aims to apply sanctions against single individuals held responsible for international crimes could impact on the macro-structural dimensions of war.

It is significant for realists that Western political and legal cultures are so singularly indifferent to other cultural, political and legal traditions, even while they attempt to elaborate a project for world unification. Thus, India and China are almost wholly distant from legal positivism, individualism, and the technical and scientific determinism of Western civilisation to the point where it may be suggested that the theory of human rights can only be considered 'universal' in the context of Western legal and political language (*koiné*).

From a realist perspective, the idea of a global citizenship is both difficult to achieve and perhaps not altogether desirable. This is because social homogeneity and political unification of the world cannot be guaranteed through the use of coercive instruments (legal, economic, or military) at least while the current trend that heightens disparities in power, wealth, and scientific and technological resources persists in the international arena. On the other hand, the Kantian model of humanity's spiritual and moral unity does not provide a useful basis for reappraising ethnic-national identities, the function of states and their limited sovereignty. It is, therefore, of genuine interest that values such as political pluralism, cultural differentiation, and the self-determination of peoples are promoted.

Towards an imperial citizenship?

In *Empire*, Michael Hardt and Antonio Negri (2000) argue that globalisation is taking us towards 'imperial citizenship'. That is, political cosmopolitanism and legal globalism ends in an 'imperial constitution' of the world. Their thesis deserves careful consideration.

After 9/11, the United States declared a 'new war' against global terrorism. This raised the prospect of permanent war, without territorial boundaries or time limits, largely secretive, and operating outside the rules of the traditional international law of war. It is now clear that the war in Afghanistan was only the beginning of a total war against the 'axis of evil'. In March 2003, the USA with a 'coalition of the willing' attacked Iraq, without UN approval, based on the assumption that it possessed weapons of mass destruction. As revealed in the *Quadrennial Defence Review Report* of the US Department of State, the strategic objective of the United States and their closest Western allies was to consolidate their global hegemony, and ensure a stable military presence in the heart of Central Asia. This project involves gaining control of the massive energy resources in the territories of the former Soviet Republics in the Caucasian, Caspic and trans-Caspic regions, and above all, completing the double military encirclement from Russia to the West, and from China to the East. After the Cold War period and the ephemeral liberation of colonial countries in Africa and Asia, it seems that the age-old Western aspiration to the control, occupation, and 'civilisation' of the non-Western world is regaining full vigour.

In these emerging circumstances (*rebus sic stantibus*), it is not unwarranted to talk of a failure of the neo-Kantian philosophy of 'global citizenship'. From Kant to Kelsen to Habermas, this philosophy sets up international law and international institutions as the principal, if not exclusive, instruments for the attainment of world peace and the protection of fundamental rights. The Kelsenian formula of 'peace through law', with its normative optimism and ingenuous cosmopolitical universalism, has never been so clearly exposed as an illusion of European Enlightenment. It follows that it is illusory to think that the project on cosmopolitical citizenship can be effectively opposed to the clash between hegemonic power and global terrorism. Rather, a realistic assessment of the globalisation processes suggests that a more prudent attitude would be taken towards the potential and possible outcomes of the cosmopolitical project. As Kenichi Ohmae (1995) has shown, there are enormous economic forces that oppose such a project in the interest of the (alleged) sovereignty of self-regulating mechanisms of global markets. Moreover, there are many justifiable doubts about the benefits of a project for political unification of the world in conditions of growing differentiation and agitation of the international arena. We are left, then, with the shimmer of cosmopolitan hopes and few firm reserves to be confident that an idealistic universalism will, in fact, lead to positive enactments of either liberty or citizenship.

Note

1 *Jus ad bellum*, law on the prevention of war; *jus in bello*, law in war.

Danilo Zolo (2007) "Global Citizenship: a Realist Critique," in Stephen Slaughter and Wayne Hudsons (eds) *Globalisation and Citizenship: The Transnational Challenge*, London and New York: Routledge, pp. 80–83.

Cultural Globalization, Global Culture

CULTURE AND GLOBALIZATION: JOHN TOMLINSON (1999)

John Tomlinson (1949–) is Professor of Cultural Sociology and Director of the Institute of Cultural Analysis at Nottingham Trent University and has taught at a few European, East Asian, and U.S. universities. As author of *Cultural Imperialism* and *Globalization and Culture*, Tomlinson is widely considered to be a leading authority on theories about cultural globalization. One of his more recent works, *The Culture of Speed*, has tried to bring the cultural issue of speed more into the purview of contemporary social thought. In doing so, Tomlinson highlights the relative dearth of research that has been explicitly devoted to the topic. Another highly novel contribution that Tomlinson has recently made to contemporary social theory can be found in his other work, *Globalization and Culture*. Here, he is noted for the idea that culture plays a vital role in understanding globalization as a complex, multi-form phenomenon. This view stems from Tomlinson's observation that culture and globalization dually inform one another; just as culture offers us new insights into understanding the nature of globalization, globalization also offers new ways of looking at culture – of which the notion of deterritorialization looms large. While Tomlinson has explored many different issues in his academic career, a constant interest of his has been to emphasize this complex, multifaceted quality of cultural matters – whether applied to globalization, speed or Western imperialism.

Globalization Disturbs Culture

Globalization disturbs the way we conceptualize 'culture'. For culture has long had connotations tying it to the idea of a fixed locality. The idea of 'a culture' implicitly connects meaning construction with particularity and location. As Eade (1997: 25) notes, 'an emphasis on boundedness and coherence traditionally dominated the sociological treatment of the idea of culture', particularly in the functionalist tradition where collective meaning construction was dealt with largely as serving the purposes of social integration.

So 'a culture' parallels the problematic notion of 'a society' as a bounded entity (Mann 1986) occupying a physical territory mapped as a political territory (predominantly the nation-state) and binding individual meaning constructions into this circumscribed social, political space. The connectivity of globalization is clearly threatening to such conceptualizations, not only because the multiform penetration of localities breaks into this binding of meanings to place, but because it undermines the thinking through which culture and fixity of location are originally paired.

In anthropology, James Clifford's work on 'travelling cultures' (Clifford 1992, 1997) has focused on prising culture apart from location. Writing of the 'practices of crossing and interaction that troubled the localism of many common assumptions about culture' he argues: 'In these assumptions authentic social existence is, or should be, centred in circumscribed places – like the gardens where the word "culture" derived its European meanings. Dwelling was understood to be the local ground of collective life, travel a supplement; roots always precede routes' (1997:3). (Clifford demonstrates how the practices of anthropological fieldwork have contributed to the localizing of the concept of culture: 'centering the *culture* around a particular locus, the *village*, and around a certain spatial practice of dwelling/research which itself depended on a complementary localization – that of the *field*' (1997: 20). So the traditional research methods of anthropology – the village taken as a 'manageable unit' for cultural analysis, the practice of ethnography as 'dwelling' with the community – have contributed to a synecdoche in which location (village) is taken for culture. And, Clifford argues, this has endured into contemporary ethnographic fieldwork practices where the locations may be, 'hospitals, labs, urban neighbourhoods, tourist hotels' rather than remote villages, but the informing assumption for the researcher and subject is one of 'localized dwelling'.

Clifford goes against the grain of this inheritance to think of culture as essentially *mobile* rather than static, to treat 'practices of displacement . . . as constitutive of cultural meanings'. And in this he raises something very close to the conceptual challenge globalization makes to culture. Culture cannot be thought of as having these inevitable *conceptual* ties to location, for meanings are equally generated by people 'on the move' and in the flows and connections between 'cultures'.

Yet the notion of 'travelling culture' can also be tendentious. It's not that we have to *reverse* the priority between 'roots and routes', insisting on the essence of culture as restless nomadic movement. Rather we need to see 'roots and routes' as always coexistent in culture, and both as subject to transformation in global modernity. To return to the earlier discussion of travel, we have to remember that a huge proportion of cultural experience is still for the majority the day-to-day experience of physical location, rather than of constant movement. In fact Clifford admits this point in describing an objection to the trope of 'travel', made by another anthropologist, Christina Turner. Turner pointed to the obvious limitations on movement that vast numbers are subject to – being 'kept in their place' by their class and gender position. Her ethnographic work with female Japanese factory workers, 'women who have not "travelled" by any standard definition', led her to question Clifford's stress on 'literal travel'. But these women's 'local' cultural experience and practice also disturbed the culture-locality connection: 'They do watch TV; they do have a global/local sense; they do contradict the anthropologist's typifications; and they don't simply enact a culture' (Clifford 1997: 28). In accepting this, Clifford concedes that the notion of travelling culture 'can involve forces that pass powerfully through – television, radio, tourists, commodities, armies' (ibid.).

This is precisely the point I want to stress: globalization promotes much more physical mobility than ever before, but the key to its cultural impact is in the transformation of localities themselves. It is important to keep to the fore the material conditions of physical embodiment and of political-economic necessity that 'keep people in their place', and so for me the transformation of culture is not grasped in the trope of travel but in the idea of *deterritorialization*. What I . . . understand by this . . . is that complex connectivity weakens the ties of culture to place. This is in many ways a troubling phenomenon, involving the simultaneous penetration of local worlds by distant forces, and the dislodging of everyday meanings from their 'anchors' in the local environment. Embodiment and the forces of material circumstance keep most of us, most of the time, situated, but in places that are changing around us and gradually, subtly, losing their power to define the terms of our existence. This is undoubtedly an uneven and often contradictory business, felt more forcibly in some places than others, and sometimes met by countervailing tendencies to re-establish the power of locality. Nevertheless deterritorialization is, I believe, the major cultural impact of global connectivity. And it's not all bad news.

For the final point to make is that connectivity also furnishes people with a *cultural resource* that they lacked before its expansion: a cultural awareness which is, in various senses, 'global'. Roland Robertson has always stressed that globalization intrinsically involves 'the intensification of consciousness of the world as a whole' (1992: 8) and Giddens (1991: 187) also argues that people's 'phenomenal worlds', though situated locally, 'for the most part are truly global'. This doesn't mean that we all experience the world as cultural cosmopolitans, much less that a 'global culture' is emerging. But it does imply that 'the global' increasingly exists as a cultural horizon within which we (to varying degrees) frame our existence. The penetration of localities which connectivity brings is thus double-edged: as it dissolves the securities of locality, it offers new understandings of experience in wider – ultimately global – terms.

Grasping the nature and significance of this global consciousness constitutes an important agenda in the cultural analysis of globalization. The Japanese women Christina Turner describes are surely not unusual in having a 'global/local sense' as part of their everyday life, and one obvious source of this is the images and information that flows to them – as to millions of us – through the routine use of globalizing media technologies like television. One task for cultural analysis is therefore to understand the 'phenomenology' of this global consciousness, particularly in the mediated form in which it mostly appears to us. And it is not difficult to see that the horizon of significance made available by the connectivity of media technologies suggests possibilities not only for the reconstitution of the cultural meanings and identities depleted by deterritorialization, but also for associated forms of global cultural politics. A sense of our mutual interdependency combined with the means for communicating across distance is producing new forms of cultural/political alliance and solidarity. These are undoubtedly weakly developed at present in comparison with the concentrations of power within, for instance, transnational capitalism. But as some argue (Castells 1997), the global perspective of the 'new social movements' may prove to be embryonic forms of a wider, more powerful order of social resistance to the repressive aspects of globalization. However this turns out, it is clear that the reconfiguration of cultural experience that connectivity produces will be crucial to the possibilities of a cosmopolitan politics. Globalization therefore matters for culture in the sense that it brings the negotiation of cultural experience into the centre of strategies for intervention in the other realms of connectivity: the political, the environmental, the economic. [. . .]

John Tomlinson (1999) *Globalization and Culture*, Cambridge: Polity Press, pp. 27–31.

CREATIVE DESTRUCTION: TYLER COWEN (2002)

Tyler Cowen (1962–) is Holbert C. Harris Professor of Economics at George Mason University. He is author of *Creative Destruction, Markets and Cultural Voices*, and *Discover Your Inner Economics* as well as co-founder of the influential blog *Marginal Revolution*. Cowen has spent most of his academic career analyzing culture through the prism of economic theory. This approach is evident in his work on globalization, which is principally found in his book *Creative Destruction*. Here, Cowen argues against the belief that economic globalization closes down on cultural diversity. Instead, he believes that cross-cultural exchange is a much more dynamic process, whereby forms of cultural expressions are not only destroyed but also created when different cultures come into contact with one another.

The Tragedy of Cultural Loss

Cross-cultural contact often mobilizes the creative fruits of an ethos before disrupting or destroying it. In this regard trade plays a critical and neglected role in converting an ethos into creative artistic achievement.

We see a common pattern. The initial meeting of cultures produces a creative boom, as individuals trade materials, technologies, and ideas. Often the materially wealthier culture provides financial support for the creations of the poorer culture, while the native aesthetic and ethos remains largely intact. For a while we have the best of both worlds from a cultural point of view. The core of the poorer or smaller culture remains intact, while it benefits from trade. Over time, however, the larger or wealthier culture upsets the balance of forces that ruled in the smaller or poorer culture. The poorer culture begins to direct its outputs towards the tastes of the richer culture. Communication with the outside world makes the prevailing ethos less distinct. The smaller culture "forgets" how to make the high-quality goods it once specialized in, and we observe cultural decline.

I refer to this as the *Minerva model*. In this scenario a burst of creative flowering also brings the decline of a culture and an ethos. Even when two (or more) cultures do not prove compatible in the long run, they may produce remarkable short-run gains from trade. "Minerva" refers to Hegel's famous statement that "the owl of Minerva flies only at dusk," by which he meant that philosophic understanding of a civilization comes only when that civilization has already realized its potential and is in decline. I reinterpret the metaphor to refer to cultural brilliance instead, which in this context occurs just when a particular culture is starting its decline. Alternatively, it may be said that cultural blossomings contain the seeds of their own destruction.

The culture of the Hawaiian Islands, rather than withering immediately with foreign contact, blossomed in the late nineteenth and early twentieth centuries. The combination of Pacific, American, Japanese, and Chinese influences created a fertile creative environment. In music Hawaiian performers have been seminal influences behind the development of country and western, pedal steel guitar, blues, jazz, and fingerpicking guitar styles, as well as modern "lounge" music. In each case the Hawaiians innovated within established Western forms, or relied partly on Western inspiration. The Hawaiian steel guitar, for instance, was invented by a Czech immigrant living in California. Hawaii also produced many superb hand-woven quilts in the latter part of the nineteenth century and in the early part of the twentieth. Like Hawaiian music, these works were synthetic products of American, Asian, and Polynesian styles.[1]

This fertile period for Hawaiian culture, however, did not last forever. American dominance of the island – in cultural, economic, and political terms – was only a matter of time. The vital indigenous Hawaiian culture has since dwindled precipitously, having been swamped by the greater numbers and wealth of mainland Americans and Asians. Contemporary Hawaii is hardly a cultural desert (witness the architecture at Diamond Head), but it is more like mainland America than in times past. The region is not producing a stream of distinctive creative achievement comparable to its peak years earlier in this century.

To damn modernity for this development, however, ignores the original role of cross-cultural contact in stimulating the creative environment. Virtually all of the Hawaiian innovations were synthetic in nature and based in cultural trade. In part, modernity destroys so many cultural communities only by creating so many in the first place. And the original sources behind Hawaiian culture – such as the Chinese, Japanese, and Polynesian components – were themselves synthetic products of earlier eras. They arose from earlier processes of creative destruction, which had left many cultural victims in their wake as well.

The Minerva model applies most frequently when gains from trade are based on a severe cultural imbalance. For instance, American Indian arts and crafts flourished until shortly before their (temporary) collapse early in the twentieth century. The most accomplished arts of the Plains Indians used European crayons, pencils, clothes, metals, bright paint-pigments, papers, dyed-wool yarns, mirrors, bells, brass tacks, and glass beads. The wood-splint basketry technique of many Indian tribes appears to have been European in origin, probably Swedish. The kachina dolls of the Hopi flowered in the nineteenth century, when the Hopi tribe came into contact with Spanish and Mexican folk art, and sought to meet touristic demands for dolls.[2]

Indian totem poles became common in the middle of the nineteenth century when the Northwest fur trade brought new wealth to Indian communities. Indian chiefs and nobles competed for status by commissioning large poles; a major village would have as many as seventy. Large numbers of impressive poles became feasible only after settlers introduced the metal knife, a prerequisite for effective large-scale Indian carving. Across North America, trade relations gave an unprecedented boost to Indian artistic production in the eighteenth and nineteenth centuries. This was exactly when the North American Indian cultures, viewed more broadly as a way of life, were declining precipitously.[3]

The tradition of Andean textiles was badly damaged by Spanish conquest, but Andean weaving boomed during the early years of contact with Europeans. On the demand side, some of the Spaniards recognized that Andean textiles were of very high quality and bought them eagerly, thus stimulating production. On the supply side, the Andean weavers drew upon new materials, styles, and ideas. The Spaniards introduced silk, linen, sheep's wool, and metal-wrapped threads, in addition to bringing stylistic inspiration in the forms of textiles and designs from Europe, the Arab world, Turkey, and China. In particular, the Andean weavers innovated with their use of color, which they started using in complex patterns to create effects of depth and dimensionality.

Chinese silk tapestries and embroideries, brought in through the Philippines, were especially influential. Until the Spanish toll on the Andean societies became decisively high and destroyed their social infrastructure, the cross-cultural contact proved fruitful for the textile arts.[4]

The Minerva model implies that it may be worthwhile to "cash in" the potential creativity embedded in a culture. By accepting the eventual decline of the culture, we also are mobilizing its creative forces to unprecedented levels, at least for a while.

The modern world may be cashing in cultures too quickly, or too many at once, but we should not measure failure by the number of declining cultures. Casual observers too quickly conclude that an observed decline suggests a problem. But the absence of observed cultural decline could be a sign of failure rather than success. The absence of decline might reflect a world that attained less diversity in the first place and reached lower and fewer peaks. Conversely, a large number of declining artistic genres might be a symptom of cultural wealth and vitality, rather than a harbinger of complete and absolute decay for all time.

Most generally, almost all of today's disappearing cultures evolved out of earlier processes of remixing and "cashing in" of cultures. The spread of the Chinese across Southeast Asia, the extension of the Roman Empire, or the European folk migrations in the Dark Ages, whatever their cultural benefits, all wrought great havoc on the cultures of their time. In reality today's so-called indigenous cultures are regroupings, yesterday's remixed version of previous cultural expansions. Cross-cultural contact cashes in some cultures while others germinate. Subsequent exchanges will bring out the virtues of these cultures-in-waiting, while simultaneously heralding their later declines.

Notes

1 On Hawaiian quilts, see Wild (1987). On the guitar, see Clifford (1997, p. 26).
2 On Hopi kachina, see Furst and Furst (1982, p. 31). Some scholars note the possibility that the kachina may have preceded Spanish contact, but even they admit a strong influence; see, for instance, Dockstader (1954, p. 98). On the Plains Indians arts, see Feder (1986, p. 93, passim), and Brody (1971, p. 25); on basketry techniques, see J.G.H. King (1986, p. 82), and Sturtevant (1986, p. 33). For other examples of Indian synthesis, see Feest (1992, pp. 42–44, 107). Egan (1993, chap. 6) and Damian (1995, pp. 44–45) discusses the role of Indian painters and craftsmen in colonial art in South America.
3 See Woodcock (1977, p. 25), and H. Stewart (1990, pp. 20–21). On the roles of knives, see Feder (1971, p. 18). The totem pole tradition was discontinued in the later-nineteenth century when the fur trade slowed down, smallpox eradicated many villages, the rifle led to bloody intertribal warfare, and the Canadian government outlawed many elements of Indian culture.
4 See Stone-Miller (1992, pp. 51–60, 185–86, 193–96, 201).

Tyler Cowen (2002) *Creative Destruction: How Globalization is Changing the World Cultures*, Princeton, NJ: Princeton University Press, pp. 55–59.

■ ■ ■ ■ ■ ■

THE LOCAL AND THE GLOBAL: STUART HALL (1991)

Stuart Hall (1932–) is Professor Emeritus of Sociology at the Open University. He has played an influential role in developing the field of cultural studies within and beyond the British academy. In particular, his work has helped expand the purview of cultural studies to include questions of race and ethnicity. The selection below, which is drawn from Hall's later work on globalization, discusses the possibility that globalization is 'nothing but the triumph and closure of history by the West.' Hall, however, is immensely skeptical of such sentiments – something he discusses in great detail.

The Postmodern and the Local Global

Not everywhere, by any means, but in some of the most advanced parts of the globalization process what one finds are new regimes of accumulation, much more flexible regimes founded not simply on the logics of mass production and of mass consumption but on new flexible accumulation strategies, on segmented markets, on post-Fordist styles of organization, on lifestyle and identify-specific forms of marketing, driven by the market, driven by just-in-time production, driven by the ability to address not the mass audience, or the mass consumer, but penetrating to the very specific smaller groups, to individuals, in its appeal.

From one point of view, you might say that this is just the old enemy in a new disguise and that actually is the question I am going to pose. Is this just the old enemy in a new disguise? Is this the ever-rolling march of the old form of commodification, the old form of globalization, fully in the keeping of capital, fully in the keeping of the West, which is simply able to absorb everybody else within its drive? Or is there something important about the fact that, at a certain point, globalization cannot proceed without learning to live with and working through difference?

If you look at one of the places to see this speaking itself, or beginning to represent itself, it is in the forms of modern advertising. If you look at these what you will see is that certain forms of modern advertising are still grounded on the exclusive, powerful, dominant, highly masculinist, old Fordist imagery, of a very exclusive set of identities. But side by side with them are the new exotics, and the most sophisticated thing is to be in the new exotica. To be at the leading edge of modern capitalism is to eat fifteen different cuisines in any one week, not to eat one. It is no longer important to have boiled beef and carrots and Yorkshire pudding every Sunday. Who needs that? Because if you are just jetting in from Tokyo, via Harare, you come in loaded, not with "how everything is the same" but how wonderful it is, that everything is different. In one trip around the world, in one weekend, you can see every wonder of the ancient world. You take it in as you go by, all in one, living with difference, wondering at pluralism, this concentrated, corporate, over-corporate, over-integrated, over-concentrated, and condensed form of economic power which lives culturally through difference and which is constantly teasing itself with the pleasures of the transgressive Other. [. . .]

Now, the regime I am talking about does not have this pleasure/pain economy built into it. It is pleasure endlessly. Pleasure to begin with, pleasure in the middle, pleasure at the end, nothing but pleasure: the proliferation of difference, questions of gender and sexuality. It lives with the new man. It produced the new man before anyone was ever convinced he even existed. Advertising produced the image of the post-feminist man. Some of us cannot find him, but he is certainly there in the advertising. I do not know whether anybody is living with him currently but he's there, out there in the advertising.

In England it is these new forms of globalized power that are most sensitive to questions of feminism. It says, "Of course, there'll be women working with us. We must think about the question of creches. We must think about equal opportunities for Black people. Of course, everybody knows somebody of different skin. How boring it would be just to know people like us. We don't know people like us. We can go anywhere in the world and we have friends who are Japanese, you know. We were in East Africa last week and then we were on safari and we always go to the Caribbean, etc.?"

This is what I call the world of the global post-modern. Some parts of the modern globalization process are producing the global post-modern. The global post-modern is not a unitary regime because it is still in tension within itself with an older, embattled, more corporate, more unitary, more homogenous conception of its own identity. That struggle is being fought out within itself and you may not see it actually. If you don't see it, you ought to. Because you ought to be able to hear the way in which, in American society, in American culture, those two voices speak at one and the same time. The voice of infinite pleasurable consumption and what I call "the exotic cuisine" and, on the other hand, the voice of the moral majority, the more fundamental and traditional conservative ideas. They are not coming out of different places, they are coming out of the same place. It is the same balancing act which Thatcherism is trying to conduct by releasing Rupert Murdoch and Sir William Rees Mogg at one and the same time, in the hope that they will kind of hold on to one another. An old petite bourgeois morality will constrain the already deregulated Rupert Murdoch. Somehow, these two people are going to live in the same universe – together.

So, the notion of globalization as a non-contradictory, uncontested space in which everything is fully within the keeping of the institutions, so that they perfectly know where it is going, I simply do not believe. I think the story points to something else: that in order to maintain its global position, capital has had to negotiate and by negotiate I mean it had to incorporate and partly reflect the differences it was trying to overcome. It had to try to get hold of, and neutralize, to some degree, the differences. It is trying to constitute a world in which things are different. And that is the pleasure of it but the differences do not matter.

Now the question is: is this simply the final triumph, the closure of history by the West? Is globalization nothing but the triumph and closure of history by the West? Is this the final moment of a global post-modern where it now gets hold of everybody, of everything, where there is no difference which it cannot contain, no otherness it cannot speak, no marginality which it cannot take pleasure out of?

It's clear, of course, that when I speak about the exotic cuisine, they are not eating the exotic cuisine in Calcutta. They're eating it in Manhattan. So do not imagine this is evenly and equally spread throughout the world. I am talking about a process of profound unevenness. But I am nevertheless saying that we shouldn't resolve that question too quickly. It is just another face of the final triumph of the West. I know that position. I know it is very tempting. It is what I call ideological post-modernism: I can't see round the edge of it and so history must have just ended. That form of post-modernism I don't buy. It is what happens to ex-Marxist French intellectuals when they head for the desert.

But there is another reason why one should not see this form of globalization as simply unproblematic and uncontradictory, because I have been talking about what is happening within its own regimes, within its own discourses. I have not yet talked about what is happening outside it, what is happening at the margins. So, in the conclusion of this talk, I want to look at the process from the point of view, not of globalization, but of the local. I want to talk about two forms of globalization, still struggling with one another: an older, corporate, enclosed, increasingly defensive one which has to go back to nationalism and national cultural identity in a highly defensive way, and to try to build barriers around it before it is eroded. And then this other form of the global post-modern which is trying to live with, and at the same moment, overcome, sublate, get hold of, and incorporate difference.

What has been happening out there in the local? What about the people who did not go above the globalization but went underneath, to the local?

The return to the local is often a response to globalization. It is what people do when, in the face of a particular form of modernity which confronts them in the form of the globalization I have described, they opt out of that and say "I don't know anything about that any more. I can't control it. I know no politics which can get hold of it. It's too big. It's too inclusive. Everything is on its side. There are some terrains in between, little interstices, the smaller spaces within which I have to work." Though, of course, one has to see this always in terms of the relationship between unevenly-balanced discourses and regimes. But that is not all that we have to say about the local.

For it would be an extremely odd and peculiar history of this part of the twentieth century if we were not to say that the most profound cultural revolution has come about as a consequence of the margins coming into representation – in art, in painting, in film, in music, in literature, in the modern arts everywhere, in politics, and in social life generally. Our lives have been transformed by the struggle of the margins to come into representation. Not just to be placed by the regime of some other, or imperializing eye but to reclaim some form of representation for themselves.

Paradoxically in our world, marginality has become a powerful space. It is a space of weak power but it is a space of power, nonetheless. In the contemporary arts, I would go so far as to say that, increasingly, anybody who cares for what is creatively emergent in the modern arts will find that it has something to do with the languages of the margin.

The emergence of new subjects, new genders, new ethnicities, new regions, new communities, hitherto excluded from the major forms of cultural representation, unable to locate themselves except as de-centered or subaltern, have acquired through struggle, sometimes in very marginalized ways, the means to speak for themselves for the first time. And the discourses of power in our society, the discourses of the dominant regimes, have been certainly threatened by this de-centered cultural empowerment of the marginal and the local.

Just as I tried to talk about homogenization and absorption, and then plurality and diversity as characteristic of the new forms of the dominant cultural post-modern, so in the same way one can see forms of local opposition and resistance going through exactly the same moment.

Face to face with a culture, an economy and a set of histories which seem to be written or inscribed elsewhere, and which are so immense, transmitted from one continent to another with such extraordinary speed, the subjects of the local, of the margin, can only come into representation by, as it were, recovering their own hidden histories. They have to try to retell the story from the bottom up, instead of from the top down. And this moment has been of such profound significance in the post-war world that you could not describe the post-war world without it. You could not describe the movements of colonial nationalism without that moment when the unspoken discovered that they had a history which they could speak; they had languages other than the languages of the master, of the tribe. It is an enormous moment. The world begins to be decolonized at that moment. You could not understand the movements of modern feminism precisely without the recovery of the hidden histories.

These are the hidden histories of the majority that never got told. History without the majority inside it, history as a minority event. You could not discover, or try to discuss, the Black movements, civil rights movements, the movements of Black cultural politics in the modern world, without that notion of the rediscovery of where people came from, the return to some kind of roots, the speaking of a past which previously had no language. The attempt to snatch from the hidden histories another place to stand in, another place to speak from, and that moment is an extremely important moment. It is a moment which always tends to be overrun and to be marginalized by the dominant forces of globalization.

But do not misunderstand me. I am not talking about some ideal free space in which everybody says, "Come on in. Tell us what you think. I'm glad to hear from you." They did not say that. But those languages, those discourses, it has not been possible to silence in the last twenty years.

Those movements also have an extraordinarily complex history. Because at some time, in the histories of many of them over the last twenty years, they have become locked into counter-identities of their own. It is a respect for local roots which is brought to bear against the anonymous, impersonal world of the globalized forces which we do not understand. "I can't speak of the world but I can speak of my village. I can speak of my neighborhood, I can speak of my community." The face-to-face communities that are knowable, that are locatable, one can give them a place. One knows what the voices are. One knows what the faces are. The recreation, the reconstruction of imaginary, knowable places in the face of the global post-modern which has, as it were, destroyed the identities of specific places, absorbed them into this post-modern flux of diversity. So one understands the moment when people reach for those groundings, as it were, and the reach for those groundings is what I call ethnicity.

Ethnicity is the necessary place or space from which people speak. It is a very important moment in the birth and development of all the local and marginal movements which have transformed the last twenty years, that moment of the rediscovery of their own ethnicities.

But just as, when one looks at the global post-modern, one sees that it can go in both an expansive and a defensive way, in the same sense one sees that the local, the marginal, can also go in two different ways. When the movements of the margins are so profoundly threatened by the global forces of postmodernity, they can themselves retreat into their own exclusivist and defensive enclaves. And at that point, local ethnicities become as dangerous as national ones. We have seen that happen: the refusal of modernity which takes the form of a return, a rediscovery of identity which constitutes a form of fundamentalism.

But that is not the only way in which the rediscovery of ethnicity has to go. Modern theories of enunciation always oblige us to recognize that enunciation comes from somewhere. It cannot be unplaced, it cannot be unpositioned, it is always positioned in a discourse. It is when a discourse forgets that it is placed that it tries to speak everybody else. It is exactly when Englishness is the world identity, to which everything else is only a small ethnicity. That is the moment when it mistakes itself as a universal language. But in fact, it comes from a place, out of a specific history, out of a specific set of power relationships. It speaks within a tradition. Discourse, in that sense, is always placed. So the moment of the rediscovery of a place, a past, of one's roots, of one's context, seems to me a necessary moment of enunciation. I do not think the margins could speak up without first grounding themselves somewhere.

Stuart Hall (1991) "The Local and the Global: Globalization and Ethnicity," in Anthony King (ed.) *Culture and Globalization and the World System: Contemporary Representation of Identity*, London: Macmillan, pp. 30–36.

INCORPORATING THE THIRD WORLD: ALBERT PAOLINI (1999)

Albert Paolini (1963–1996) was born in Australia. He taught politics at the University of Melbourne and La Trobe University, and his research on the complex connections between globalization and postcolonial identities was not to be widely reviewed until after his untimely death at the young age of 33 as a result of leukemia. In this selection, Paolini develops a critically reflexive approach to globalization – one that maps forces of globality, hybridity, and ambivalence in the structuration of the Third World and its relations to world politics. He emphasizes the problem of ambivalence and resistance – that is, the ways in which individuals and groups develop strategies of appropriation and distance in response to globalization and its structures of domination. Deploying conceptual insights from both post-structuralism and postmodernism, Paolini elucidates the emancipatory promises and repressive lures of globality in the context of postcolonialist discourses and Third World experiences.

Navigating Modernity

The tendency to view globalization from the vantage point of the West has led critics such as Massey and Stuart Hall to note how "un-global" is the perspective from which the nature of globalization has been analyzed.[1] How global processes are played out on the ground in a specific locale, be it Lagos, Dar es Salaam, or the myriad of villages in sub-Saharan Africa, or in the so-called Fourth World conditions evident in Central and South American cities such as Mexico City and São Paulo, is left out of account despite the implicit assumption in most analyses that the impact is pervasive and homogeneous. No one doubts that globalized modernity is a real phenomenon in these places, albeit at times modernity may constitute anything from Green Revolution technology to the humble transistor radio or bicycle rather than CNN, the Internet, or the TGV fast train. Although relations of space and time are effected by all of these modern innovations, obviously there is a vast difference in the degree of, not to mention a significant economic differential in terms of access to, these technologies. [. . .]

> From above the clouds we can observe, with all the detail of a laboratory test, the Amazon on fire, Abyssinia starving, Afghanistan suffering, Armenia struck by an earthquake at the very moment the Mir satellite station was proudly overflying it and sending its triumphal messages to the open-mouthed gapers below. From high in the sky, the wretched of the earth seem far away.[2]

[. . .] Even if the existence of a global condition is conceded, the key question remains, where exactly do Africa and the Third World in general fit into this globalization scenario? Featherstone's Western representation of the local has already been explored. There seems to be three basic representations of the Third World's place in late modernity. Africa is mostly ignored in this literature. Certain references are made to a cross-cultural traffic in music and fashion, but aside from these attempts to suggest an African presence in global space (in Hannerz and Friedman, for example), Africa simply does not figure in accounts of globalization, except as an adjunct to the Third World in general. Even in this way, the understanding of the Third World tends to be amorphous and poorly informed. It is thus necessary to explore conceptions of the place of the Third World in globalization discourses that by extension include, however tenuously, the African continent. I will then return to a consideration of how globalization is to be understood as it impinges on Africa.

First, the Third World is mostly either incorporated by default or simply ignored. In this respect it becomes a significant blind spot in global projections, a repository for what Jameson views as the "political unconscious" of the global narrative: silences and omissions that act as "repressions" or "strategies of containment." Robertson's "inclusion" of the Third World in the latest phase of globalization is one such instance. Similarly, Cox points to the liberal/laissez-faire paradigm, which preaches the virtues of a global free market and the necessity for various structural adjustment programs, as an instance of incorporating the non-Western world into the global camp. Even when the Third World is incorporated into the new globality on its own terms, there is an insufficient attempt to distinguish its radical heterogeneity. The result is that the Third World is understood quite selectively and with reference to what are essentially atypical examples, such as Brazil, Mexico, or the newly industrialized countries. The Third World is thus flattened into a single dimension and read off mostly unrepresentative case studies. What is distinctive about Hong Kong or parts of Brazil does not equate to much of sub-Saharan Africa.

Part of the problem relates to the inadequacy of the rubric "Third World,"[3] particularly when Africa is considered. Cities across developing countries may appear, as King argues, locked into an interconnecting global space, yet this is not true of all cities or all parts of these cities, nor of the many villages and towns outside their orbit. There are different modernities operating in these sites that do not yet make for one world. One needs to keep in mind that it is only of late that more people across the globe live in the city rather than the countryside. In fact, if the First World were removed from the picture, the countryside would still predominate as the most common form of modern living. In Africa, the move to the cities has been unfolding since colonial times, but the village or rural town is still significant. This situation is suggestive of Julius Nyerere's argument in *Freedom and Socialism* of the necessity to view Tanzania's immediate and long-term future in a rural context and thus base the economy around the village (hence Ujaama). Rural life should be the focus of government policy and planning because society was likely to remain agricultural for a long time to come.[4] The limits of Western concepts of modernity in Africa are evident, as is the need to temper assumptions about globalization and the importance of cities in societies that have a substantial rural population.

The second representation of the Third World in globalization discourses is typically postmodern. In this representation, the significance of the Third World is located in its otherness and its capacity to work as a discursive rupture in the narrative of Western dominance. The Third World is seen mostly in terms of a metaphorical, representational space on the outside of or opposite to the West. It becomes what Bhabha (borrowing from Michel de Certeau) has referred to in a different context as a "non-place" in the discourse of modernity. It is not merely "terra nulla," but a "time-lag" in the understanding of modernity, "a lag which all histories must encounter in order to make a beginning."[5] In this respect, the wish is not to ostensibly deny its place in the modern, but to reinscribe its otherness and emphasize its difference. It exists on the outside of globalization/modernity as an other that forces the global and the modern to encounter themselves and interrogate and interrupt their assumptions about the non-European world. The desire behind such a reading, evident in Jameson and Nandy, for example (and prevalent across postcolonialism), is actually to empower the Third World and cast it as a subversive place of resistance to Western hegemony. Thus, as already noted, Santiago Colas argues that part of the Third World's "paradoxical double function" in Jameson's theory of postmodernism is to exist outside the cultural logic of late capitalism.[6] The same view is apparent in Featherstone's notion that one possible response to globalization is an immersion in the local: remaining undiscovered and ignoring the outside as strategies open to local cultures in the Third World.

In a similar vein, Nandy, not a theorist of globalization but one subscriber to the existence of a global civilization, has argued that the Third World has become the other of the West and that this otherness opens up, theoretically at least, many possibilities, one of which is that the Third World "holds in trust the rejected selves of the First and Second Worlds."[7] Nandy opens his critique with the observation: "We are living in a global civilization, even if it does not look to us sufficiently global. This civilization has certain features and 'ground rules' and those who want to consolidate, transcend or dismantle it, must first identify them." The first criterion of this global civilization is that "all surviving civilizations define themselves with reference to it." For Nandy, "the recovery of the other selves and cultures and communities, *selves not defined by the dominant consciousness*, may turnout to be the first task of social criticism and political activism and the first responsibility of intellectual stock-taking in the first decades of the coming century."[8]

Both Nandy and Jameson, in attempting to confront the Third World directly as part of their taking globalization to task, present the flip side of the dominant tendency outlined in the first representation, which is to repress or incorporate the Third World. Yet this flip side is also problematic: By placing the Third World outside modernity in some mystical or pure state of non-modernity, they are not only effectively denying its engagement with the modern but setting up an untenable binarism that effectively marginalizes the Third World. The danger is that the Third World merely becomes a narrative or representational technique of deconstruction that systematically ignores the key factor of how the many cultures of the Third World already navigate the processes of the modern and the global, albeit in differing degrees. It is one thing for the marginalization of the Third World to serve as a discomfort to globalization; it is quite another for this nonplace to imply an existence outside the influence of global processes. At the very least, it seems a peculiar denial of the economic reach of global capitalism.

A third approach to the place of the Third World in globalization is propelled by a more traditional concern to expose the inequality and injustice of the contemporary North-South relationship. Not surprisingly, the emphasis is on the material basis of this relationship and the economic structure of globalization that under-pins it. In this account globalization is accepted as the logic of late modernity, and Western hegemony is seen to drive global processes. However, the Third World is not left out of the account as either a nonplace or an inclusion. Rather, the marginal and peripheral position of the Third World is directly confronted and held up as indicating the unevenness of globalization's reach. The critique here is not of the existence of globalization per se but its failure to properly address the exploited position of the Third World. Thus Aijaz Ahmad, regarding the Third World in general, and Colin Leys, focusing on Africa specifically, both attempt to temper the celebratory, triumphal tone of global capitalism. Ahmad argues that globalization leads not to homogenization between and within the First and Third Worlds but to increased differentiation between the haves and the have-nots in the global system, with the gaps likely to increase as globalization intensifies.[9] Similarly, Leys's summary of the "African collapse" paints a bleak portrait of economic weakness and exploitation with the "logic of global capitalism" merely reinforcing Africa's decline.[10] [. . .]

These three representations of the Third World's place in globalization are only partly useful in explaining how the various cultures and identities in Africa and beyond confront and make sense of the global forces of modernity in the here and now. Certainly the latter two representations contribute to our knowledge of the Third World's position. The radical commitment of the materialist approach is perhaps a necessary and initial step in exposing the myth of globalization's homogeneity. Likewise, the postmodern approach is a reminder of the complexity and ambiguity of the Third World's place within the modern. However, one could argue that the material account over-emphasizes the very real systemic considerations that need to be addressed in any analysis of the North-South divide. The postmodern reading is perhaps too detached from what is happening on the ground and experiences what one critic has termed a "distancing effect" from material realities.[11] Both, in their own ways, provide little sense of a way forward out of the respective impasse they each describe. Further, they each strike me as inadequately addressing the reception of the modern and the global in the everyday experience of peoples and cultures in Africa.

I instead posit an intermediate path that takes into account the material realities of modernity, which have long been present on the African continent, while according a prominent place to the subjective and the cultural. In this respect, I want to avoid the implicit reductionism of Dirlik: "Concrete problems of the everyday world" involve questions of subjectivity and identity as much as they refer to material considerations.[12] Further, pointing to the necessity for resistance and the insidiousness of globalization does not obviate the need to acknowledge the local strategies already in place that empower Third World agents, not so much to resist modernity outright but to modify, distort, or bend it to their particular desires via processes of appropriation, indigenization, and creolization. Terence Ranger has long argued for the creative and resilient pluralism of

African societies during and after colonial capitalism that have witnessed "cheerful adaptations to urban life, the innovation of new structures of fraternity and association, the evolution of an urban popular culture," as well as the capacity of religions to transform themselves.[13] Even if Chesneaux is correct in arguing that politics has been reduced to "navigation by sight" under globalized modernity, so that people can only manage or steer global forces rather than reject or resist them,[14] this navigation politics allows for a significant range of possibilities and maneuvering under globalization, indicating the existence of a space for agency. Finally, othering the Third World merely distances it further from the mediation of modernity that takes place, so that concepts of difference, authenticity, and essentialism that often lurk beneath constructions of otherness are as misleading as the notion that globalization inevitably leads to a homogenized global culture.

Notes

1 Doreen Massey, 'A Place Called Home?' *New Formations*, 17 Summer, 1992, p. 10, and Stuart Hall, 'The Local and the Global: Globalization and Ethnicity,' in Anthony D. King, ed., *Culture, Globalization and the World-System: Contemporary Conditions for the Representation of Identity* (London: Macmillan, 1991), pp. 24–5. It is interesting to compare this to an earlier piece by Hall in which he advances the provocative notion that marginality and migranthood become both centered and *the* representative (post)modern experience. See 'Minimal Selves,' in *Postmodernism and the Question of Identity* (London: Institute of Contemporary Arts), pp. 44–46. See also Chapter 4, pp. 100–101, for the extended quote and analysis of Hall's position.

2 Chesneaux, *Brave Modern World*, p. 88.

3 This problem of accurately defining the Third World is alluded to in Paul Rabinow's 'A Modern Tour of Brazil,' in Scott Lash and Jonathan Friedman, eds., *Modernity and Identity* (Oxford and Cambridge, MA: Blackwood, 1992).

4 See Julius K. Nyerere, *Freedom and Socialism/Uhuru na Ujamaa: A Selection of Wrigins and Speeches, 1965–1967* (Dar es Salaam, Nairobi, London, and New York: Oxford University Press, 1968). See especially the essay 'Socialism and Rural Development,' pp. 337–366. In his analysis of contemporary African cities, Alessandro Triulzi, citing UNDP figures, commends: 'By 2015 half of the "Third World" population will be living in cities and already today the population of many African cities, such as Nairobi, Dar es Salaam, Lago, Lusaka and Kinshasa, has multiplied sevenfold. . . . Forty per cent of today's African population lives in cities.' Thus, as we approach the new millennium, the majority still live in villages and towns outside the major cities and urban centers. See Alessandro Triulzi, 'African Cities, Historical Memory and Street Buzz,' in Iain Chambers and Lidia Curti, eds., *The Post-Colonial Question: Common Skies, Divided Horizons* (London and New York: Routledge, 1996), p. 80.

5 Bhabha, *The Location of Culture* (London and New York: Routledge, 1996), p. 246.

6 See Santiago Colas, 'The "Third World" in Jameson's *Postmodernism, or the Cultural Logic of Late Capitalism*,' *Social Text*, 31/32, 1992, p. 14.

7 Ashis Nandy, 'Shamans, Savages and the Wilderness: On the Audibility of Dissent and the Future of Civilizations,' *Alternatives*, 15(3), 1989, p. 273.

8 Ibid., pp. 263–265.

9 Ahmad, *In Theory*, pp. 313–6.

10 Leys, 'Confronting the African Tragedy,' *New Left Review*, 204, March/April 1994, pp. 44–47.

11 Leys, 'Confronting the African Tragedy,' p. 43. Leys juxtaposes his material realism with the hope and commitment of Basil Davidson and the poststructual approach of Jean-Francois Bayart, whom he sees as producing the 'distancing effect' referred to. See pp. 41–44.

12 See A. Dirlik, 'Culturalism as Hegemonic Ideology and Liberating Practice,' *Cultural Critique*, 6, Spring 1987, pp. 13–50; and A. Dirlik, 'The Postcolonial Aura: Third World Criticism in the Age of Global Capitalism,' *Critical Inquiry*, 20, Winter, 1994, pp. 328–356.

13 See Terence Ranger, 'Concluding Summary: Religion, Development and Identity,' in Kirsten Holst Petersen, ed., *Religion, Development and African Identity* (Uppsala: Scandinavian Institute of African Studies, Seminar Proceedings No. 12, 1987) pp. 150–151.

14 Chesneaux, *Brave Modern World*, p. 117.

Albert Paolini (1999) *Navigating Modernity: Postcolonialism, Identity, and International Relations*, Anthony Elliott and Anthony Moran (eds), Boulder, CA, and London: Lynne Rienner Publishers, pp. 157–164.

GLOCALIZATION: ROLAND ROBERTSON (1995)

Roland Robertson (1938–) is Professor of Sociology and Global Society at the University of Aberdeen. Within contemporary social thought, he is considered one of the pioneering voices on globalization. Throughout his career, he has developed many novel theories on globalization that have been highly influential such as his conceptualization of globalization as "the compression of the world into a single place" and his use of the Japanese business term "glocalization." It is the latter which forms the basis of the selection. Robertson's research into this term has caused many to rethink the typical understanding of globalization as an overarching phenomenon that supercedes local differences. Instead, what the term "glocalization" captures is the fact that global transformations always involve a local dimension. This is also true vice versa.

Time-Space Homogeneity-Heterogeneity

According to *The Oxford Dictionary of New Words* (1991: 134) the term 'glocal' and the process noun 'glocalization' are 'formed by telescoping *global* and *local* to make a blend'. Also according to the *Dictionary* that idea has been 'modelled on Japanese *dochakuka* (deriving from *dochaku* "living on one's own land"), originally the agricultural principle of adapting one's farming techniques to local conditions, but also adopted in Japanese business for *global localization*, a global outlook adapted to local conditions' (emphasis in original). More specifically, the terms 'glocal' and 'glocalization' became aspects of business jargon during the 1980s, but their major locus of origin was in fact Japan, a country which has for a very long time strongly cultivated the spatio-cultural significance of Japan itself and where the general issue of the relationship between the particular and the universal has historically received almost obsessive attention (Miyoshi and Harootunian, 1989). By now it has become, again in the words of *The Oxford Dictionary of New Words* (1991: 134), 'one of the main marketing buzzwords of the beginning of the nineties'.

   The idea of glocalization in its business sense is closely related to what in some contexts is called, in more straightforwardly economic terms, micromarketing: the tailoring and advertising of goods and services on a global or near-global basis to increasingly differentiated local and particular markets. Almost needless to say, in the world of capitalistic production for increasingly global markets the adaptation to local and other particular conditions is not simply a case of business responses to existing global variety – to civilizational, regional, societal, ethnic, gender and still other types of differentiated consumers – as if such variety or heterogeneity existed simply 'in itself'. To a considerable extent micromarketing – or, in the more comprehensive phrase, glocalization – involves *the construction* of increasingly differentiated consumers, the 'invention' of 'consumer traditions' (of which tourism, arguably the biggest 'industry' of the contemporary world, is undoubtedly the most clear-cut example). To put it very simply, diversity sells. From the consumer's point of view it can be a significant basis of cultural capital formation (Bourdieu, 1984). This, it should be emphasized, is not its only function. The proliferation of, for example, 'ethnic' supermarkets in California and elsewhere does to a large extent cater not so much to difference for the sake of difference, but to the desire for the familiar and/or to nostalgic wishes. On the other hand, these too can also be bases of cultural capital formation.

   It is not my purpose here to delve into the comparative history of capitalistic business practices. Thus the accuracy of the etymology concerning 'glocalization' provided by *The Oxford Dictionary of New Words* is not a crucial issue.[1] Rather I want to use the general idea of glocalization to make a number of points about the global-local problematic. There is a widespread tendency to regard this problematic as straightforwardly involving a polarity, which assumes its most acute form in the claim that we live in a world of local assertions *against* globalizing trends, a world in which the very idea of locality is sometimes cast as a form of opposition or resistance to the hegemonically global (or one in which the assertion of 'locality' or *Gemeinschaft* is seen as the pitting of subaltern 'universals' against the 'hegemonic universal' of dominant cultures and/or classes). An interesting variant of this general view is to be found in the replication of the German culture-civilization distinction at the global level: the old notion of ('good') culture is pitted against the ('bad') notion of civilization. In this traditional German perspective local culture becomes, in effect, national culture, while civilization is given a distinctively global, world-wide colouring.

We have, in my judgement, to be much more subtle about the dynamics of the production and reproduction of difference and, in the broadest sense, locality. Speaking in reference to the local-cosmopolitan distinction, Hannerz (1990: 250) has remarked that for locals diversity 'happens to be the principle which allows all locals to stick to their respective cultures'. At the same time, cosmopolitans largely depend on 'other people' carving out 'special niches' for their cultures. Thus 'there can be no cosmopolitans without locals'. This point has some bearing on the particular nature of the intellectual interest in and the approach to the local-global issue. In relation to Hannerz's general argument, however, we should note that in the contemporary world, or at least in the West, the current counter-urbanization trend (Champion, 1989), much of which in the USA is producing 'fortress communities', proceeds in terms of the standardization of locality, rather than straightforwardly in terms of 'the principle of difference'.[2]

In any case, we should become much more historically conscious of the various ways in which the deceptively modern, or postmodern, problem of the relationship between the global and the local, the universal and the particular, and so on, is not by any means as unique to the second half of the twentieth century as many would have us believe. This is clearly shown in Greenfeld's (1992) recent study of the origins of nationalism in England, France, Germany, Russia and America. With the notable exception of English nationalism, she shows that the emergence of all national identities – such constituting 'the most common and salient form of particularism in the modern world' (Greenfeld, 1992: 8) – developed as a part of an 'essentially international process' (Greenfeld, 1992: 14).

The more extreme or adamant claims concerning the contemporary uniqueness of these alleged opposites is a refraction of what some have called the nostalgic paradigm in Western social science (Phillips, 1993; Robertson, 1990; Turner, 1987). It is a manifestation of the not always implicit world view that suggests that we – the global we – once lived in and were distributed not so long ago across a multitude of ontologically secure, collective 'homes'. Now, according to this narrative – or, perhaps, a metanarrative – our sense of home is rapidly being destroyed by waves of (Western?) 'globalization'. In contrast I maintain – although I can present here only part of my overall argument – that globalization has involved the reconstruction, in a sense the production, of 'home', 'community' and 'locality' (cf. J. Abu-Lughod, 1994). To that extent the local is not best seen, at least as an analytic or interpretative departure point, as a counterpoint to the global. Indeed it can be regarded, subject to some qualifications, as *an aspect* of globalization. [. . .]

Thus the notion of glocalization actually conveys much of what I myself have previously written about globalization. From my own analytic and interpretative standpoint the concept of globalization has involved the simultaneity and the interpenetration of what are conventionally called the global and the local, or – in more abstract vein – the universal and the particular. (Talking strictly of my own position in the current debate about and the discourse of globalization, it may even become necessary to substitute the term 'glocalization' for the contested term 'globalization' in order to make my argument more precise.) I certainly do not wish to fall victim, cognitive or otherwise, to a particular brand of current marketing terminology. Insofar as we regard the idea of glocalization as simply a capitalistic business term (of apparent Japanese origin) then I would of course reject it as, *inter alia*, not having sufficient analytic-interpretative leverage. On the other hand, we are surely coming to recognize that seemingly autonomous economic terms frequently have deep cultural roots (for example, Sahlins, 1976). In the Japanese and other societal cases the cognitive and moral 'struggle' even to recognize the economic domain as relatively autonomous has never really been 'won'. In any case, we live in a world which increasingly acknowledges the quotidian conflation of the economic and the cultural. But we inherited from classical social theory, particularly in its German version in the decades from about 1880 to about 1920, a view that talk of 'culture' and 'cultivation' was distinctly at odds with 'materialism' and the rhetoric of economics and instrumental rationality.

My deliberations . . . on the local-global problematic hinge upon the view that contemporary conceptions of locality are largely produced in something like global terms, but this certainly does not mean that all forms of locality are thus substantively homogenized (notwithstanding the standardization, for example, of relatively new suburban, fortress communities). An important thing to recognize in this connection is that there is an increasingly globe-wide discourse of locality, community, home and the like. One of the ways of considering the idea of *global culture* is in terms of its being constituted by the increasing interconnectedness of many local cultures both large and small (Hannerz, 1990), although I certainly do not myself think that global culture is entirely constituted by such interconnectedness. In any case we should be careful *not to equate the communicative and interactional connecting of such cultures* – including very asymmetrical forms of such communication and interaction, as well as 'third cultures' of mediation – *with the notion of homogenization of all cultures.*

I have in mind the rapid, recent development of a relatively autonomous discourse of 'intercultural communication'. This discourse is being promoted by a growing number of professionals, along the lines of an older genre of 'how to' literature. So it is not simply a question of social and cultural theorists talking about cultural difference and countervailing forces of homogenization. One of the 'proper objects' of study here is the phenomenon of 'experts' who specialize in the 'instrumentally rational' promotion of intercultural communication. These 'experts' have in fact a vested interest in the promotion and protection of variety and diversity. Their jobs and their profession depend upon the expansion and reproduction of heterogeneity. The same seems to apply to strong themes in modern American business practice (Rhinesmith, 1993; Simons et al., 1993).

We should also be more interested in the conditions for the production of cultural pluralism (Moore, 1989) – as well as geographical pluralism. Let me also say that the idea of locality, indeed of globality, is very relative. In spatial terms a village community is of course local relative to a region of a society, while a society is local relative to a civilizational area, and so on. Relativity also arises in temporal terms. Contrasting the well-known pair consisting of locals and cosmopolitans, Hannerz (1990: 236) has written that 'what was cosmopolitan in the early 1940s may be counted as a moderate form of localism by now'. I do not in the present context get explicitly involved in the problem of relativity (or relativism). But sensitivity to the problem does inform much of what I say.

There are certain conditions that are currently promoting the production of concern with the local-global problematic within the academy. King (1991: 420) has addressed an important aspect of this. In talking specifically of the spatial compression dimension of globalization he remarks on the increasing numbers of 'protoprofessionals from so-called "Third World" societies' who are travelling to 'the core' for professional education. The educational sector of 'core' countries 'depends increasingly on this input of students from the global periphery'. It is the experience of 'flying round the world and needing schemata to make sense of what they see' on the one hand, and encountering students from all over the world in the classroom on the other, which forms an important experiential basis for academics of what King (1991: 401–2) calls totalizing and global theories. I would maintain, however, that it is *interest in 'the local'* as much as the 'totally global' which is promoted in this way.

Notes

1 My colleague, Akiko Hashimoto, informs me that in 'non-business' Japanese *dochakuka* conveys the idea of 'making something indigenous'. For some provocative comments on the connections between multiculturalism (especially in debates about the university curriculum), consumer culture and current trends in commodification and product diversification in contemporary capitalism, see Rieff (1993). [Rieff, D. (1993) 'Multiculturalism's silent partner: it's the newly globalized economy stupid', *Harper's*, 287.]

2 This trend is, or course, partly facilitated by the 'electronic cottage' phenomenon, which increasingly enables those who can afford it to be vicinally distant from urban centres, but communicationally close to increasingly large numbers of people. Various aspects of geographic dispersal in relation to financial globalization and centralization are explored at

length in Sassen (1991). [Sassen, S. (1991) *The Global City: New York, London, Tokyo*. Princeton: Princeton University Press.]

Roland Robertson (1995) "Glocalization: Time-Space Homogeneity-Heterogeneity," in Mike Featherstone *et al.* (eds) *Global Modernities*. London: Sage Publications, pp. 28–32.

Globalizing Regions

THE END OF HISTORY: FRANCIS FUKUYAMA (1989)

Francis Fukuyama (1952–) is a Japanese-American scholar who is the Bernard L. Schwartz Professor of International Political Economy at Johns Hopkins University. Fukuyama is most recognized for his "end of history" thesis, which suggests that no ideological revolutions remain in the world we now live in. All that is left is the prospect of liberal democracy. And this is not only true for those in the West, but also for the whole of humanity. Fukuyama's claim is thus that there will eventually be a global convergence of values – one where the master/slave dialectic no longer finds relevance. However, as the selection below indicates, Fukuyama does not discount that global wars and conflicts will still take place in his vision of the coming future. This is because we have not yet reached the end of history altogether. There are those who will try to hold onto their nostalgia and, in turn, this will fuel conflict and competition among those in the international political arena. But Fukuyama remains convinced that liberal democracy is still the only viable political form of government in the long run. Obstacles to this destiny are just hiccups.

Western Liberalism and the End of Contradictions

IN WATCHING the flow of events over the past decade or so, it is hard to avoid the feeling that something very fundamental has happened in world history. The past year has seen a flood of articles commemorating the end of the Cold War, and the fact that "peace" seems to be breaking out in many regions of the world. Most of these analyses lack any larger conceptual framework for distinguishing between what is essential and what is contingent or accidental in world history, and are predictably superficial. If Mr. Gorbachev were ousted from the Kremlin or a new Ayatollah proclaimed the millennium from a desolate Middle Eastern capital, these same commentators would scramble to announce the rebirth of a new era of conflict.

And yet, all of these people sense dimly that there is some larger process at work, a process that gives coherence and order to the daily headlines. The twentieth century saw the developed world descend into a paroxysm of ideological violence, as liberalism contended first with the remnants of absolutism, then bolshevism and fascism, and finally an updated Marxism that threatened to lead to the ultimate apocalypse of nuclear war. But the century that began full of self-confidence in the ultimate triumph of Western liberal democracy seems at its close to be returning full circle to where it started: not to an "end of ideology" or a convergence between capitalism and socialism, as earlier predicted, but to an unabashed victory of economic and political liberalism.

The triumph of the West, of the Western *idea*, is evident first of all in the total exhaustion of viable systematic alternatives to Western liberalism. In the past decade, there have been unmistakable changes in the intellectual climate of the world's two largest communist countries, and the beginnings of significant reform movements in both. But this phenomenon extends beyond high politics and it can be seen also in the ineluctable spread of consumerist Western culture in such diverse contexts as the peasants' markets and color television sets now omnipresent throughout China, the cooperative restaurants and clothing stores opened in the past year in Moscow, the Beethoven piped into Japanese department stores, and the rock music enjoyed alike in Prague, Rangoon, and Tehran.

What we may be witnessing is not just the end of the Cold War, or the passing of a particular period of postwar history, but the end of history as such: that is, the end point of mankind's ideological evolution and the universalization of Western liberal democracy as the final form of human government. This is not to say that there will no longer be events to fill the pages of *Foreign Affairs*'s yearly summaries of international relations, for the victory of liberalism has occurred primarily in the realm of ideas or consciousness and is as yet incomplete in the real or material world. But there are powerful reasons for believing that it is the ideal that will govern the material world *in the long run*. [. . .]

HAVE WE in fact reached the end of history? Are there, in other words, any fundamental "contradictions" in human life that cannot be resolved in the context of modern liberalism, that would be resolvable by an alternative political-economic structure? If we accept the idealist premises laid out above, we must seek an answer to this question in the realm of ideology and consciousness. Our task is not to answer exhaustively the challenges to liberalism promoted by every crackpot messiah around the world, but only those that are embodied in important social or political forces and movements, and which are therefore part of world history. For our purposes, it matters very little what strange thoughts occur to people in Albania or Burkina Faso, for we are interested in what one could in some sense call the common ideological heritage of mankind.

In the past century, there have been two major challenges to liberalism, those of fascism and of communism. The former[1] saw the political weakness, materialism, anomie, and lack of community of the West as fundamental contradictions in liberal societies that could only be resolved by a strong state that forged a new "people" on the basis of national exclusiveness. Fascism was destroyed as a living ideology by World War II. This was a defeat, of course, on a very material level, but it amounted to a defeat of the idea as well. What destroyed fascism as an idea was not universal moral revulsion against it, since plenty of people were willing to endorse the idea as long as it seemed the wave of the future, but its lack of success. After the war, it seemed to most people that German fascism as well as its other European and Asian variants were bound to self-destruct. There was no material reason why new fascist movements could not have sprung up again after the war in other locales, but for the fact that expansionist ultranationalism, with its promise of unending conflict leading to disastrous military defeat, had completely lost its appeal. The ruins of the Reich chancellory as well as the atomic bombs dropped on Hiroshima and Nagasaki killed this ideology on the level of consciousness as well as materially, and all of the proto-fascist movements spawned by the German and Japanese examples like the Peronist movement in Argentina or Subhas Chandra Bose's Indian National Army withered after the war.

The ideological challenge mounted by the other great alternative to liberalism, communism, was far more serious. Marx, speaking Hegel's language, asserted that liberal society contained a fundamental contradiction that could not be resolved within its context, that between capital and labor, and this contradiction has constituted the chief accusation against liberalism ever since. But surely, the class issue has actually been successfully resolved in the West. As Kojève (among others) noted, the egalitarianism of modern America represents the essential achievement of the classless society envisioned by Marx. This is not to say that there are not rich people and poor people in the United States, or that the gap between them has not grown in recent years. But the root causes of economic inequality do not have to do with the underlying legal and social structure of our society, which remains fundamentally egalitarian and moderately redistributionist, so much as with the cultural and social characteristics of the groups that make it up, which are in turn the historical legacy of premodern conditions. Thus black poverty in the United States is not the inherent product of liberalism, but is rather the "legacy of slavery and racism" which persisted long after the formal abolition of slavery.

As a result of the receding of the class issue, the appeal of communism in the developed Western world, it is safe to say, is lower today than any time since the end of the First World War. This can be measured in any number of ways: in the declining membership and electoral pull of the major European communist parties, and their overtly revisionist programs; in the corresponding electoral success of conservative parties from Britain and Germany to the United States and Japan, which are unabashedly pro-market and antistatist; and in an intellectual climate whose most "advanced" members no longer believe that bourgeois society is something that ultimately needs to be overcome. This is not to say that the opinions of progressive intellectuals in Western countries are not deeply pathological in any number of ways. But those who believe that the future must inevitably be socialist tend to be very old, or very marginal to the real political discourse of their societies. [. . .]

THE PASSING of Marxism-Leninism first from China and then from the Soviet Union will mean its death as a living ideology of world historical significance. For while there may be some isolated true believers left in places like Managua, Pyongyang, or Cambridge, Massachusetts, the fact that there is not a single large state in which it is a going concern undermines completely its pretensions to being in the vanguard of human history. And the death of this ideology means the growing "Common Marketization" of international relations, and the diminution of the likelihood of large-scale conflict between states.

This does not by any means imply the end of international conflict *per se*. For the world at that point would be divided between a part that was historical and a part that was post-historical. Conflict between states still in history, and between those states and those at the end of history, would still be possible. There would still be a high and perhaps rising level of ethnic and nationalist violence, since those are impulses incompletely played out, even in parts of the post-historical world. Palestinians and Kurds, Sikhs and Tamils, Irish Catholics and Walloons, Armenians and Azeris, will continue to have their unresolved grievances. This implies that terrorism and wars of national liberation will continue to be an important item on the international agenda. But large-scale conflict must involve large states still caught in the grip of history, and they are what appear to be passing from the scene.

The end of history will be a very sad time. The struggle for recognition, the willingness to risk one's life for a purely abstract goal, the worldwide ideological struggle that called forth daring, courage, imagination, and idealism, will be replaced by economic calculation, the endless solving of technical problems, environmental concerns, and the satisfaction of sophisticated consumer demands. In the post-historical period there will be neither art nor philosophy, just the perpetual caretaking of the museum of human history. I can feel in myself, and see in others around me, a powerful nostalgia for the time when history existed. Such nostalgia, in fact, will continue to fuel competition and conflict even in the post-historical world for some time to come. Even though I recognize its inevitability, I have the most ambivalent feelings for the civilization that has been created in Europe since 1945, with its north Atlantic and Asian offshoots. Perhaps this very prospect of centuries of boredom at the end of history will serve to get history started once again.

Note

1   I am not using the term "fascism" here in its most precise sense, fully aware of the frequent misuse of this term to denounce anyone to the right of the user. "Fascism" here denotes any organized ultra-nationalist movement with universalistic pretensions – not universalistic with regard to its nationalism, of course, since the latter is exclusive by definition, but with regard to the movement's belief in its right to rule other people. Hence Imperial Japan would qualify as fascist while former strongman Stoessner's Paraguay or Pinochet's Chile would not. Obviously fascist ideologies cannot be universalistic in the sense of Marxism or liberalism, but the structure of the doctrine can be transferred from country to country.

Francis Fukayama (1989) "The End of History?" *The National Interest*, Summer.

CLASH OF CIVILIZATIONS: SAMUEL HUNTINGTON (1993)

Samuel Huntington (1927–2008) was born in New York City and eventually educated at Harvard University where, in due course, he became a distinguished professor of political science until his death. Huntington's "Clash of Civilizations" first appeared as an essay in a prominent international affairs publication, then as a 1993 book of the same title. Coming as it did on the heels of the 1991 end of the Cold War, Huntington's Clash-thesis was in effect a Hegelian reinterpretation of the triumph of the West's liberal synthesis. At its worst, the argument presented as a naïve defense of the West against "the Rest." At its best, it was a brilliant illustration of the best defense of Western liberal politics that might be made.

The Next Pattern of Conflict

WORLD POLITICS IS entering a new phase, and intellectuals have not hesitated to proliferate visions of what it will be – the end of history, the return of traditional rivalries between nation states, and the decline of the nation state from the conflicting pulls of tribalism and globalism, among others. Each of these visions catches aspects of the emerging reality. Yet they all miss a crucial, indeed a central, aspect of what global politics is likely to be in the coming years.

It is my hypothesis that the fundamental source of conflict in this new world will not be primarily ideological or primarily economic. The great divisions among humankind and the dominating source of conflict will be cultural. Nation states will remain the most powerful actors in world affairs, but the principal conflicts of global politics will occur between nations and groups of different civilizations. The clash of civilizations will dominate global politics. The fault lines between civilizations will be the battle lines of the future.

Conflict between civilizations will be the latest phase in the evolution of conflict in the modern world. For a century and a half after the emergence of the modern international system with the Peace of Westphalia, the conflicts of the Western world were largely among princes – emperors, absolute monarchs and constitutional monarchs attempting to expand their bureaucracies, their armies, their mercantilist economic strength and, most important, the territory they ruled. In the process they created nation states, and beginning with the French Revolution the principal lines of conflict were between nations rather than princes. In 1793, as R. R. Palmer put it, "The wars of kings were over; the wars of peoples had begun." This nineteenth-century pattern lasted until the end of World War I. Then, as a result of the Russian Revolution and the reaction against it, the conflict of nations yielded to the conflict of ideologies, first among communism, fascism-Nazism and liberal democracy, and then between communism and liberal democracy. During the Cold War, this latter conflict became embodied in the struggle between the two superpowers, neither of which was a nation state in the classical European sense and each of which defined its identity in terms of its ideology.

These conflicts between princes, nation states and ideologies were primarily conflicts within Western civilization, "Western civil wars," as William Lind has labeled them. This was as true of the Cold War as it was of the world wars and the earlier wars of the seventeenth, eighteenth and nineteenth centuries. With the end of the Cold War, international politics moves out of its Western phase, and its centerpiece becomes the interaction between the West and non-Western civilizations and among non-Western civilizations. In the politics of civilizations, the peoples and governments of non-Western civilizations no longer remain the objects of history as targets of Western colonialism but join the West as movers and shapers of history.

The Nature of Civilizations

DURING THE COLD WAR the world was divided into the First, Second and Third Worlds. Those divisions are no longer relevant. It is far more meaningful now to group countries not in terms of their political or economic systems or in terms of their level of economic development but rather in terms of their culture and civilization.

What do we mean when we talk of a civilization? A civilization is a cultural entity. Villages, regions, ethnic groups, nationalities, religious groups, all have distinct cultures at different levels of cultural heterogeneity. The culture of a village in southern Italy may be different from that of a village in northern Italy, but both will share in a common Italian culture that distinguishes them from German villages. European communities, in turn, will share cultural features that distinguish them from Arab or Chinese communities. Arabs, Chinese and Westerners, however, are not part of any broader cultural entity. They constitute civilizations. A civilization is thus the highest cultural grouping of people and the broadest level of cultural identity people have short of that which distinguishes humans from other species. It is defined both by common objective elements, such as language, history, religion, customs, institutions, and by the subjective self-identification of people. People have levels of identity: a resident of Rome may define himself with varying degrees of intensity as a Roman, an Italian, a Catholic, a Christian, a European, a Westerner. The civilization to which he belongs is the broadest level of identification with which he intensely identifies. People can and do redefine their identities and, as a result, the composition and boundaries of civilizations change.

Civilizations may involve a large number of people, as with China ("a civilization pretending to be a state," as Lucian Pye put it), or a very small number of people, such as the Anglophone Caribbean. A civilization may include several nation states, as is the case with Western, Latin American and Arab civilizations, or only one, as is the case with Japanese civilization. Civilizations obviously blend and overlap, and may include subcivilizations. Western civilization has two major variants, European and North American, and Islam has its Arab, Turkic and Malay subdivisions. Civilizations are nonetheless meaningful entities, and while the lines between them are seldom sharp, they are real. Civilizations are dynamic; they rise and fall; they divide and merge. And, as any student of history knows, civilizations disappear and are buried in the sands of time.

Westerners tend to think of nation states as the principal actors in global affairs. They have been that, however, for only a few centuries. The broader reaches of human history have been the history of civilizations. In *A Study of History*, Arnold Toynbee identified 21 major civilizations; only six of them exist in the contemporary world.

Why Civilizations Will Clash

CIVILIZATION IDENTITY will be increasingly important in the future, and the world will be shaped in large measure by the interactions among seven or eight major civilizations. These include Western, Confucian, Japanese, Islamic, Hindu, Slavic-Orthodox, Latin American and possibly African civilization. The most important conflicts of the future will occur along the cultural fault lines separating these civilizations from one another.

Why will this be the case?

First, differences among civilizations are not only real; they are basic. Civilizations are differentiated from each other by history, language, culture, tradition and, most important, religion. The people of different civilizations have different views on the relations between God and man, the individual and the group, the citizen and the state, parents and children, husband and wife, as well as differing views of the relative importance of rights and responsibilities, liberty and authority, equality and hierarchy. These differences are the product of centuries. They will not soon disappear. They are far more fundamental than differences among political ideologies and political regimes. Differences do not necessarily mean conflict, and conflict does not necessarily mean violence. Over the centuries, however, differences among civilizations have generated the most prolonged and the most violent conflicts.

Second, the world is becoming a smaller place. The interactions between peoples of different civilizations are increasing; these increasing interactions intensify civilization consciousness and awareness of differences between civilizations and commonalities within civilizations. North African immigration to France generates hostility among Frenchmen and at the same time increased receptivity to immigration by "good" European

Catholic Poles. Americans react far more negatively to Japanese investment than to larger investments from Canada and European countries. Similarly, as Donald Horowitz has pointed out, "An Ibo may be . . . an Owerri Ibo or an Onitsha Ibo in what was the Eastern region of Nigeria. In Lagos, he is simply an Ibo. In London, he is a Nigerian. In New York, he is an African." The interactions among peoples of different civilizations enhance the civilization-consciousness of people that, in turn, invigorates differences and animosities stretching or thought to stretch back deep into history.

Third, the processes of economic modernization and social change throughout the world are separating people from longstanding local identities. They also weaken the nation state as a source of identity. In much of the world religion has moved in to fill this gap, often in the form of movements that are labeled "fundamental- ist." Such movements are found in Western Christianity, Judaism, Buddhism and Hinduism, as well as in Islam. In most countries and most religions the people active in fundamentalist movements are young, college- educated, middle-class technicians, professionals and business persons. The "unsecularization of the world," George Weigel has remarked, "is one of the dominant social facts of life in the late twentieth century." The revival of religion, "la revanche de Dieu," as Gilles Kepel labeled it, provides a basis for identity and commit- ment that transcends national boundaries and unites civilizations.

Fourth, the growth of civilization-consciousness is enhanced by the dual role of the West. On the one hand, the West is at a peak of power. At the same time, however, and perhaps as a result, a return to the roots phenomenon is occurring among non-Western civilizations. Increasingly one hears references to trends toward a turning inward and "Asianization" in Japan, the end of the Nehru legacy and the "Hinduization" of India, the failure of Western ideas of socialism and nationalism and hence "re-Islamization" of the Middle East, and now a debate over Westernization versus Russianization in Boris Yeltsin's country. A West at the peak of its power confronts non-Wests that increasingly have the desire, the will and the resources to shape the world in non-Western ways.

The West versus the Rest

THE WEST IS NOW at an extraordinary peak of power in relation to other civilizations. Its superpower opponent has disappeared from the map. Military conflict among Western states is unthinkable, and Western military power is unrivaled. Apart from Japan, the West faces no economic challenge. It dominates international political and security institutions and with Japan international economic institutions. Global political and security issues are effectively settled by a directorate of the United States, Britain and France, world economic issues by a directorate of the United States, Germany and Japan, all of which maintain extraordinarily close relations with each other to the exclusion of lesser and largely non-Western countries. Decisions made at the U.N. Security Council or in the International Monetary Fund that reflect the interests of the West are presented to the world as reflecting the desires of the world community. The very phrase "the world community" has become the euphemistic collective noun (replacing "the Free World") to give global legitimacy to actions reflecting the interests of the United States and other Western powers.[1] Through the IMF and other inter- national economic institutions, the West promotes its economic interests and imposes on other nations the economic policies it thinks appropriate. In any poll of non-Western peoples, the IMF undoubtedly would win the support of finance ministers and a few others, but get an overwhelmingly unfavorable rating from just about everyone else, who would agree with Georgy Arbatov's characterization of IMF officials as "neo-Bolsheviks who love expropriating other people's money, imposing undemocratic and alien rules of economic and political conduct and stifling economic freedom."

Western domination of the U.N. Security Council and its decisions, tempered only by occasional abstention by China, produced U.N. legitimation of the West's use of force to drive Iraq out of Kuwait and its elimination of Iraq's sophisticated weapons and capacity to produce such weapons. It also produced the quite unprecedented action by the United States, Britain and France in getting the Security Council to demand that Libya hand over the Pan Am 103 bombing suspects and then to impose sanctions when Libya refused. After defeating the largest Arab army, the West did not hesitate to throw its weight around in the Arab world. The

West in effect is using international institutions, military power and economic resources to run the world in ways that will maintain Western pre-dominance, protect Western interests and promote Western political and economic values.

That at least is the way in which non-Westerners see the new world, and there is a significant element of truth in their view. Differences in power and struggles for military, economic and institutional power are thus one source of conflict between the West and other civilizations. Differences in culture, that is basic values and beliefs, are a second source of conflict. V. S. Naipaul has argued that Western civilization is the "universal civilization" that "fits all men." At a superficial level much of Western culture has indeed permeated the rest of the world. At a more basic level, however, Western concepts differ fundamentally from those prevalent in other civilizations. Western ideas of individualism, liberalism, constitutionalism, human rights, equality, liberty, the rule of law, democracy, free markets, the separation of church and state, often have little resonance in Islamic, Confucian, Japanese, Hindu, Buddhist or Orthodox cultures. Western efforts to propagate such ideas produce instead a reaction against "human rights imperialism" and a reaffirmation of indigenous values, as can be seen in the support for religious fundamentalism by the younger generation in non-Western cultures. The very notion that there could be a "universal civilization" is a Western idea, directly at odds with the particularism of most Asian societies and their emphasis on what distinguishes one people from another. Indeed, the author of a review of 100 comparative studies of values in different societies concluded that "the values that are most important in the West are least important worldwide."[2] In the political realm, of course, these differences are most manifest in the efforts of the United States and other Western powers to induce other peoples to adopt Western ideas concerning democracy and human rights. Modern democratic government originated in the West. When it has developed in non-Western societies it has usually been the product of Western colonialism or imposition.

The central axis of world politics in the future is likely to be, in Kishore Mahbubani's phrase, the conflict between "the West and the Rest" and the responses of non-Western civilizations to Western power and values.[3] Those responses generally take one or a combination of three forms. At one extreme, non-Western states can, like Burma and North Korea, attempt to pursue a course of isolation, to insulate their societies from penetration or "corruption" by the West, and, in effect, to opt out of participation in the Western-dominated global community. The costs of this course, however, are high, and few states have pursued it exclusively. A second alternative, the equivalent of "band-wagoning" in international relations theory, is to attempt to join the West and accept its values and institutions. The third alternative is to attempt to "balance" the West by developing economic and military power and cooperating with other non-Western societies against the West, while preserving indigenous values and institutions; in short, to modernize but not to Westernize.

Notes

1   Almost invariably Western leaders claim they are acting on behalf of "the world community." One minor lapse occurred during the run-up to the Gulf War. In an interview on "Good Morning America," Dec. 21, 1990, British Prime Minister John Major referred to the actions "the West" was taking against Saddam Hussein. He quickly corrected himself and subsequently referred to "the world community." He was, however, right when he erred.
2   Harry C. Triandis, *The New York Times*, Dec. 25, 1990, p. 41, and "Cross-Cultural Studies of Individualism and Collectivism," Nebraska Symposium on Motivation, vol. 37, 1989, pp. 41–133.
3   Kishore Mahbubani, "The West and the Rest," *The National Interest*, Summer 1992, pp. 3–13.

Samuel Huntington (1993) "The Clash of Civilizations?" *Foreign Affairs*, vol. 22, Summer, pp. 22–26, 39–41.

CLASH OF GLOBALIZATIONS: STANLEY HOFFMAN (2002)

Stanley Hoffman (1928–) is currently the Paul and Catherine Buttenwieser University Professor at Harvard University, where he has taught for over fifty years. Before that, Hoffman studied and taught at the Institut d'Etudes Politiques of Paris. As author of many books including *The State of War: Essays on the Theory and Practice of International Politics* and *World Disorders: Troubled Peace in the Post-Cold War Era*, Hoffman is commonly recognized for his work on French political and social history as well as his research into American foreign policy and international relations. In more recent times, Hoffman has directed his attention to the topic of international terrorism. Specifically, he is interested in the role terrorism plays in shaping the new global order, which forms the basis of the selection.

Imagined Communities

AMONG the many effects of globalization on international politics, three hold particular importance. The first concerns institutions. Contrary to realist predictions, most states are not perpetually at war with each other. Many regions and countries live in peace; in other cases, violence is internal rather than state-to-state. And since no government can do everything by itself, interstate organisms have emerged. The result, which can be termed "global society," seeks to reduce the potentially destructive effects of national regulations on the forces of integration. But it also seeks to ensure fairness in the world market and create international regulatory regimes in such areas as trade, communications, human rights, migration, and refugees. The main obstacle to this effort is the reluctance of states to accept global directives that might constrain the market or further reduce their sovereignty. Thus the UN's powers remain limited and sometimes only purely theoretical. International criminal justice is still only a spotty and contested last resort. In the world economy – where the market, not global governance, has been the main beneficiary of the state's retreat – the network of global institutions is fragmented and incomplete. Foreign investment remains ruled by bilateral agreements. Environmental protection is badly ensured, and issues such as migration and population growth are largely ignored. Institutional networks are not powerful enough to address unfettered short-term capital movements, the lack of international regulation on bankruptcy and competition, and primitive coordination among rich countries. In turn, the global "governance" that does exist is partial and weak at a time when economic globalization deprives many states of independent monetary and fiscal policies, or it obliges them to make cruel choices between economic competitiveness and the preservation of social safety nets. All the while, the United States displays an increasing impatience toward institutions that weigh on American freedom of action. Movement toward a world state looks increasingly unlikely. The more state sovereignty crumbles under the blows of globalization or such recent developments as humanitarian intervention and the fight against terrorism, the more states cling to what is left to them.

Second, globalization has not profoundly challenged the enduring national nature of citizenship. Economic life takes place on a global scale, but human identity remains national – hence the strong resistance to cultural homogenization. Over the centuries, increasingly centralized states have expanded their functions and tried to forge a sense of common identity for their subjects. But no central power in the world can do the same thing today, even in the European Union. There, a single currency and advanced economic coordination have not yet produced a unified economy or strong central institutions endowed with legal autonomy, nor have they resulted in a sense of postnational citizenship. The march from national identity to one that would be both national and European has only just begun. A world very partially unified by technology still has no collective consciousness or collective solidarity. What states are unwilling to do the world market cannot do all by itself, especially in engendering a sense of world citizenship.

Third, there is the relationship between globalization and violence. The traditional state of war, even if it is limited in scope, still persists. There are high risks of regional explosions in the Middle East and in East Asia, and these could seriously affect relations between the major powers. Because of this threat, and because modern arms are increasingly costly, the "anarchical society" of states lacks the resources to correct some of globalization's most flagrant flaws. These very costs, combined with the classic distrust among international actors who prefer to try to preserve their security alone or through traditional alliances, prevent a more satisfactory institutionalization of world politics – for example, an increase of the UN's powers. This step could happen if global society were provided with sufficient forces to prevent a conflict or restore peace – but it is not.

Globalization, far from spreading peace, thus seems to foster conflicts and resentments. The lowering of various barriers celebrated by Friedman, especially the spread of global media, makes it possible for the most deprived or oppressed to compare their fate with that of the free and well-off. These dispossessed then ask for help from others with common resentments, ethnic origin, or religious faith. Insofar as globalization enriches some and uproots many, those who are both poor and uprooted may seek revenge and self-esteem in terrorism.

Globalization and Terror

TERRORISM is the poisoned fruit of several forces. It can be the weapon of the weak in a classic conflict among states or within a state, as in Kashmir or the Palestinian territories. But it can also be seen as a product of globalization. Transnational terrorism is made possible by the vast array of communication tools. Islamic terrorism, for example, is not only based on support for the Palestinian struggle and opposition to an invasive American presence. It is also fueled by a resistance to "unjust" economic globalization and to a Western culture deemed threatening to local religions and cultures.

If globalization often facilitates terrorist violence, the fight against this war without borders is potentially disastrous for both economic development and globalization. Antiterrorist measures restrict mobility and financial flows, while new terrorist attacks could lead the way for an antiglobalist reaction comparable to the chauvinistic paroxysms of the 1930s. Global terrorism is not the simple extension of war among states to nonstates. It is the subversion of traditional ways of war because it does not care about the sovereignty of either its enemies or the allies who shelter them. It provokes its victims to take measures that, in the name of legitimate defense, violate knowingly the sovereignty of those states accused of encouraging terror. [. . .]

But all those trespasses against the sacred principles of sovereignty do not constitute progress toward global society, which has yet to agree on a common definition of terrorism or on a common policy against it. Indeed, the beneficiaries of the antiterrorist "war" have been the illiberal, poorer states that have lost so much of their sovereignty of late. Now the crackdown on terror allows them to tighten their controls on their own people, products, and money. They can give themselves new reasons to violate individual rights in the name of common defense against insecurity – and thus stop the slow, hesitant march toward international criminal justice.

Another main beneficiary will be the United States, the only actor capable of carrying the war against terrorism into all corners of the world. Despite its power, however, America cannot fully protect itself against future terrorist acts, nor can it fully overcome its ambivalence toward forms of interstate cooperation that might restrict U.S. freedom of action. Thus terrorism is a global phenomenon that ultimately reinforces the enemy – the state – at the same time as it tries to destroy it. The states that are its targets have no interest in applying the laws of war to their fight against terrorists; they have every interest in treating terrorists as outlaws and pariahs. The champions of globalization have sometimes glimpsed the "jungle" aspects of economic globalization, but few observers foresaw similar aspects in global terrorist and antiterrorist violence.

Finally, the unique position of the United States raises a serious question over the future of world affairs. In the realm of interstate problems, American behavior will determine whether the non-superpowers and weak states will continue to look at the United States as a friendly power (or at least a tolerable hegemon), or whether they are provoked by Washington's hubris into coalescing against American preponderance. America may be a hegemon, but combining rhetorical overkill and ill-defined designs is full of risks. Washington has yet to understand that nothing is more dangerous for a "hyperpower" than the temptation of unilateralism. It may well believe that the constraints of international agreements and organizations are not necessary, since U.S. values and power are all that is needed for world order. But in reality, those same international constraints provide far better opportunities for leadership than arrogant demonstrations of contempt for others' views, and they offer useful ways of restraining unilateralist behavior in other states. A hegemon concerned with prolonging its rule should be especially interested in using internationalist methods and institutions, for the gain in influence far exceeds the loss in freedom of action.

In the realm of global society, much will depend on whether the United States will overcome its frequent indifference to the costs that globalization imposes on poorer countries. For now, Washington is too reluctant to make resources available for economic development, and it remains hostile to agencies that monitor and regulate the global market. All too often, the right-leaning tendencies of the American political system push U.S. diplomacy toward an excessive reliance on America's greatest asset – military strength – as well as an excessive reliance on market capitalism and a "sovereigntism" that offends and alienates. That the mighty United States is so afraid of the world's imposing its "inferior" values on Americans is often a source of ridicule and indignation abroad.

Odd Man Out

FOR ALL THESE TENSIONS, it is still possible that the American war on terrorism will be contained by prudence, and that other governments will give priority to the many internal problems created by interstate rivalries and the flaws of globalization. But the world risks being squeezed between a new Scylla and Charybdis. The Charybdis is universal intervention, unilaterally decided by American leaders who are convinced that they have found a global mission provided by a colossal threat. Presentable as an epic contest between good and evil, this struggle offers the best way of rallying the population and overcoming domestic divisions. The Scylla is resignation to universal chaos in the form of new attacks by future bin Ladens, fresh humanitarian disasters, or regional wars that risk escalation. Only through wise judgment can the path between them be charted.

We can analyze the present, but we cannot predict the future. We live in a world where a society of uneven and often virtual states overlaps with a global society burdened by weak public institutions and under-developed civil society. A single power dominates, but its economy could become unmanageable or disrupted by future terrorist attacks. Thus to predict the future confidently would be highly incautious or naive. To be sure, the world has survived many crises, but it has done so at a very high price, even in times when WMD were not available.

Precisely because the future is neither decipherable nor determined, students of international relations face two missions. They must try to understand what goes on by taking an inventory of current goods and disentangling the threads of present networks. But the fear of confusing the empirical with the normative should not prevent them from writing as political philosophers at a time when many philosophers are extending their conceptions of just society to international relations. How can one make the global house more livable? The answer presupposes a political philosophy that would be both just and acceptable even to those whose values have other foundations. As the late philosopher Judith Shklar did, we can take as a point of departure and as a guiding thread the fate of the victims of violence, oppression, and misery; as a goal, we should seek material and moral emancipation. While taking into account the formidable constraints of the world as it is, it is possible to loosen them.

Stanley Hoffman (2002) "Clash of Globalizations," *Foreign Affairs*, vol. 81, no. 4, July/August, pp. 110–115.

GLOBALIZING HONG KONG: PETER KWONG AND DUSANKA MISCEVIC (2002)

Peter Kwong is Professor of Asian American Studies, Urban Affairs and Planning, and Sociology at the City University of New York. Dusanka Miscevic is a freelance writer with a Ph.D. in Chinese History from Columbia University. Together, they are recognized for their writings on Chinese Americans and contemporary Chinese politics. In the selection below, which is taken from their co-authored article "Globalization and Hong Kong's Future," Kwong and Miscevic are interested in Hong Kong's changing status as an economic center. Here, they ironically note that what has traditionally produced Hong Kong's wealth is also what has put the city in its current predicament. In large part, this is because Hong Kong's erstwhile status as the "financial center of the world" has now become somewhat a mark of detriment. With the increasing uncertainty and speculative nature of global capital today, fewer and fewer people want to put all of their eggs into one basket. As result, this has put Hong Kong in the position of having to compete with other Chinese cities such as Shanghai and Shenzhen – a reality that Hong Kong has not been able to cope particularly well with. And in turn, this has caused the city to experience a number of new social problems. Taken as a lesson, for Kwong and Miscevic, this exposes the true nature of contemporary globalization: as it is revealed in a Chinese context, global economic predators at any moment can also become victims.

Globalization and Hong Kong's Future

In 1998 the new Hong Kong international airport was opened to public at Chek Lap Kok – a piece of land reclaimed from the sea when two small islands were first destroyed and then rebuilt into an enormous flat field, creating enough space for 38 aircraft bays and 20 remote aircraft gates.[1] The new airport terminal is built of glass to bring in its dramatic surroundings and is one of the largest in the world. An underground train shuttles passengers within the terminal; an expressway and a high-speed railroad cross a series of bridges and islands to connect it to the metropolitan area and provide a most efficient municipal link. Chek Lap Kok may well be the most technologically advanced air hub in the world. Envisaged before the so-called handover to China in 1997 as a guarantee that Hong Kong would continue its forward thrust into the brave new world of global markets even under the mainland rule.

In the spring of 2001, a few months short of four years since the handover, Hong Kong projects an aura of opulence, efficiency, and high-tech competence. It flies high the flag flaunting its trading expertise and global managerial know-how – the skills needed to compete in the twenty-first century. With only 6.7 million people and an area one third larger than New York City, it has US$26,325 per capita GDP, making it one of the richest places in the world, only slightly behind the US and higher than most European states. Its per capita income had already caught up with that of its colonial master, Great Britain by the mid-1980s.[2] By 1996, Hong Kong had the world's seventh largest stock market, and was the fifth largest banking center and the world's busiest container port.

Named by the Heritage Foundation "the world's freest economy,"[3] Hong Kong is almost universally lauded for hard work, flexibility and the rule of law, and its success has been largely attributed to its willingness to transform itself and its ability to harness rather than resist the forces of globalization. As the last 50 years of its uninterrupted growth attest – from a humble trading entry port for China at the end of World War 2, to a low-cost manufacturing center for cheap clothing, electronics, plastic goods and toys in the late 1960s, through the restructuring in the 1980s which turned it into a premier business and financial center – Hong Kong has been quick to adapt and has gained a reputation for its remarkable strength and resilience in the face of economic and political shocks. If Deng Xiaoping, who visited Hong Kong as one of his last acts before he passed away, had it his way, he would have made the whole of China into Hong Kong.

The handover blues

As soon as the British folded their flags and sailed away, however, the vibrant stock market, which up to that point had been soaring toward the stratosphere, went into relentless decline and lost half of its value, wiping out a generation of investors who had come to believe that the Hang Seng index went only one way – up. During the Asian financial crisis in 1997 and 1998, the drop in stock prices was so alarming that the newly established SAR government (under Mainland China, Hong Kong is administered as a Special Administrative Region [SAR]) decided to intervene in the stock market by pumping over US$15 billion to prop it up and frustrate the attempts at shorting by the traders who were selling Hong Kong dollars – an intervention rather shocking in a place promoting its free enterprise image.[4]

Tourism – a vital industry in the restructured economy of post-manufacturing Hong Kong, experienced a drop in hotel bookings of 25%. Many Japanese department stores in Causeway Bay, including the highly visible Daimaru and Yaohan, closed down. All of a sudden, the maverick billionaire Li Kaishing's real estate conglomerate flagship, Cheung Kong, was worth less than the apartment buildings and land that it owns.[5] Up to that time everyone had assumed that real estate prices in space-starved Hong Kong could only go up; professionals with a bit of disposable income thought they were savvy when they invested it in property. But one-room flats in Happy Valley that had been valued at more than US$600,000 just before the bubble burst were now worth less then US$300,000. Those who took out mortgages were stuck with negative assets. In the words of Andy Xie, a regional economist at Morgan Stanley Dean Witter, "The middle class has been crushed by capital loss." In less than a year, according to Standard Chartered Bank, wealth of more than US$551 billion was wiped from the territory's real estate and shares – some US$256,500 lost for each household.[6]

But it was the ordinary working people that really got hurt by the economic downturn of late 1990s. The unemployment went up to 6.3% in 1999, in a place where anything beyond 3% had previously been considered a disaster. It has since come down, but remains above 5% in late 2001. Older workers were let go off, younger ones were forced into retrenchment, and at the same time wages were cut in many sectors by 5–30%.[7]

No wonder that Hong Kongers often strike outside observers as cheerless people. In a survey taken by the polling firm Roper Starch, a mere 6% of Hong Kong residents described themselves as happy; only the frigidly cold and mafia-ridden Russia and Ukraine scored lower.[8]

What is wrong?

Hong Kong's problems started a long time before the former British colony's handover to China and the Asian economic crisis of 1997. They can be traced back to the 1980s and the opening of China to foreign invest-ment, when the Hong Kong capital started taking advantage of China's cheap labor by moving almost all labor-intensive manufacturing operations, such as the clothing, electronics, toys, and plastics industries, to the mainland. The result of this early "globalization" next-door was a high unemployment effecting Hong Kong's manufacturing workers, particularly women in garment industry. The younger unskilled workers were shifted to service jobs, gaining on the average 10% less in salary. Women largely returned to homework. Many older workers, particularly those between the ages of 40 and 55, were forced into chronic unemployment.

The economic restructuring benefited the rich and the professionals, however, who were able to capitalize on China's opening to invest, trade and wheel and deal with Chinese officials who were slowly turning state properties into private enterprises. The endless deals and mergers were making millionaires and billionaires overnight. Reminiscent of tycoons who made huge profits in the economic restructuring in New York in 1980s, Hong Kong's investors plowed their growing assets into real estate, turning the entire colony into a huge construction site, prompting observers to declare construction crane the "official bird" of Hong Kong. The unprecedented construction boom was aided by large real estate purchases by Mainland China, in an attempt to counter the effects of the pre-reversion panic by projecting "confidence in Hong Kong." The results of the go-go years were spectacular: by 1997, Hong Kong's top ten richest people were worth about US$100 billion, while six of the world's 141 billionaires called Hong Kong home. The city acquired a Mercedes Benz fleet second only to Germany's. It was about to open the world's most expensive airport, and introduced the first cellular phone system that could be used on underground trains.[9] The well-paid professionals enjoyed high living standards. With added benefits after taxes, even a humble professor had an income three times higher than he would in America.

But such affluence came at a cost. This one-time center of diverse economic activities – not unlike New York City – was now left to survive on finance and services industries. When the Asian financial crisis hit, Hong Kong realized that it is not easy to be a financial center in the midst of a modern-day speculative storm. Like Malaysia's, Hong Kong's money-men discovered that their entire currency reserves and capital investments can be swept away in a couple of days. Worst of all, the speculative real estate "bubble" burst at the same time, and Hong Kong was stuck with an over-supply of houses: many who had been burnt by speculative purchases were no longer buying; those without money could not afford to buy even at deflated prices. Today, despite many unsold flats in glitzy "estates," as the apartment complexes in Hong Kong are called, plenty of old-time hard-pressed residents are still trapped in chicken coops of a bygone era.

Hong Kong's claim to be a world-class financial center lies in ruins: the huge real estate mortgage debts have crippled Hong Kong's ability to invest in more productive ventures. It is looking a slow and painful recovery, if at all. [. . .]

Many members of the business community believe that the most critical problem Hong Kong faces if it is to find its future in the global economy by fostering innovative technology is the shortage of qualified human resources, due to its incompetent educational system in need of reform. In response, Chief Executive Tung Chee-hwa has proposed improving the quality of education by injecting US$15.5 million into the institutions of higher education over the next five years to develop information technology, biotechnology, economic and business strategies.[10] For, despite its glossy, high-tech image, Hong Kong does not have quality professionals to back it up. Some of its best managers and scientist left for Europe, Australia and North America before the former British colony reverted to Mainland China. In order to reverse the brain-drain, the new SAR government started out by spending heavily on college education in the first few years after the handover, with special emphasis on training information technology specialists. Its avowed aim for the beginning of the millennium is to have 25% of the curriculum taught through computers within five years. It has also announced a plan to increase college enrollment from the current 25% (including those enrolled in non-degree courses) to 60% of 17–20 year olds in Hong Kong within ten years. [. . .]

In the meantime, Hong Kong is spending millions of dollars in promoting itself as a tourist destination under the label "City of Life" to win back lost business. A public campaign is under way reminding the locals, particularly the service personnel, of the need to smile and be polite if Hong Kong is to attract more visitors. (A bit of local wisdom: if you see a smiling face on a Hong Kong street, it is bound to belong to a Filipina maid.) Surrounded by dour citizenry, a visitor cannot but feel that smiles and courtesy will definitely help, but they will not be enough. In the past, tourists used to flock to Hong Kong because of its main attraction – shopping at bargain prices. These days all the bargains are to be found across the border in Shenzhen. And the service personnel there is much more eager to please.

And so it goes in this "globalized" world: the one-time predator is now the victim. Is there a way out? Contrary to Hong Kong government's propaganda, says the Executive director of Hong Kong Women Workers' Association, Wu Mei Lin, "the impacts of the government's economic strategies under globalization have all been negative," creating hundred of thousands of unemployable and marginalized workers in Hong Kong. Like other labour leaders, she argues that the gap between the rich and the poor appears to keep widening.[11] She and hundreds of other grass-root community organizations scattered across working class neighborhoods are fighting for employment and safety-net protections for these workers. Some groups are even experimenting with forming workers' co-ops. It is they, perhaps, who hold the answers to the growing search by progressive forces around the world for viable alternatives to globalization.

Notes

1. Lane Boyd, "International Airport Design (the new Hong Kong airport)," *Computer Graphics World*, September 1998.
2. See "Introduction and Overview" *International Monetary Fund – Occasional Paper 152 – Hong Kong, China*, also in *Business Week*, 9 June 1997.
3. Heritage Foundation, "Global Economic Freedom Continues to Gain Survey Shows," Heritage News, 1 November 2000 (http://www.heritage.org/news/2000/nr110100indexoverview.html).
4. John Ridding, "Trouble Stirs in the Capitalist Paradise," *Financial Times*, 29 June 1998.
5. Li Kaishing's name is spelt in different ways. It can also be found as Li Kashing or Li Ka-Shing.
6. David Lague, "Flagging Fortune," *The Age*, 30 June 1998, p. 1; also Edward Chan, "Prices of Flats Fall by More Than Half," *Hong Kong iMail*, 15 March 2001.
7. "Union Battles Economic Downturn," *Turning Point*, published by Hong Kong Confederation of Trade Unions, 22 March 2001.
8. Mark Mitchell, "Cappuccino Capitalism: You work hard for a living, don't you?" *Far Eastern Economic Review*, 10 August 2000.
9. Some Facts about Hong Kong,' *Welcome-to-Hong Kong 96–97*, Hong Kong: Blue Bridge Enterprises, Inc., 1997.
10. "Hong Kong must be competitive or decline, Tung says," *Asian Economic News*, Kyodo News International, Inc. 11 October 1999, p. 2.
11. Even some business leaders agree and are worried. See *South China Morning Post*, 22 October 2001, p. 7.

Peter Kwong and Duskana Miscevic (2002) "Globalization and Hong Kong's Future," *Journal of Contemporary Asia*, vol. 32, no. 3. pp. 323–325, 328, 335–336.

■ ■ ■ ■ ■ ■

GLOBALIZING CHINA: DOUG GUTHRIE (2006)

Doug Guthrie (1969–) is a Professor of Sociology and Department of Management and Organization (Stern School of Business) at New York University. His research is on social and economic change in China. In his work on *China and Globalization*, he investigates the structural changes that have driven China's global rise. While many argue that the global economic marketplace has driven reform and change in China, Guthrie argues that state involvement in reforms has been critical. The economic and cultural changes happening in China have been because of global involvement, and that this process will continue, involving a gradual process of democratization.

China and Globalization

Not only is China the most populous nation on earth, but it has also, in recent years, stormed onto the world economic stage. The country has accomplished in twenty-five years what many developing nations have taken half a century or more to achieve. For the better part of the last two-and-a-half decades, China has had the fastest growing economy in the world, sustaining double-digit growth figures for much of the 1980s and '90s. [. . .]

Where China was a third-world developing economy two short decades ago, today it has the sixth largest economy in the world overall in terms of gross domestic product (GDP), and it is second only to the United States when GDP is adjusted for purchasing power within the country. To the extent that economic and political power are intimately intertwined, China's sizable role as a political force on the world stage is all but guaranteed. It is no longer a question of whether China is going to play a major role in world economic and political arenas; it is only a question of what role China will play. [. . .]

The concerns over abuses of human rights and labor that are inextricably tied to China's reputation in the global economy are significant, and it is not my purpose here to dismiss the importance of the harm that the

Chinese government has inflicted on its people. However, it is also the case that gradually implemented reforms have transformed labor relations in China in fundamental ways, and it is important to depict an accurate and empirically grounded picture of those changes. By looking beyond the workplace, we can begin to understand the forces pushing these reforms forward. The programs of reform-minded elites, who are creating the "quiet revolution" occurring within China, are reshaping the institutional terrain within which labor relations occur. Pressure from foreign investors to show commitments to the rational principles of the international economy are reshaping the normative environments in which managers make decisions about labor. Changing labor market dynamics afford the most talented workers to test the boundaries of the rational-legal reforms that are transforming labor. As China continues to evolve under the normative pressures of the international economy, these changes are likely to become even more widespread. [. . .]

It is no longer controversial to state that China will play a pivotal role in the political and economic structure of the world in the twenty-first century; the question that remains is what that role will be. China's reform process has been an inherently global one, and all indications are that China's growth will continue to integrate the country into the global economy. The reforms of the last two-and-a-half decades have radically transformed China's economy and society. From the agricultural policies that transformed rural China and the transformation of the state sector to the institutional changes that have transformed social life in China, the changes have been radical and deep.

This is not a story about the ways that markets lead to liberal policies. Rather, it is about the ways in which reform minded elites have engineered a gradual reform process, slowly liberalizing economic, political, and social realms. In this book, I have emphasized four key points about the economic reforms in China. First, changes in China are much more radical than is often understood by outside observers.

Second, the enacting of China's reforms has fundamentally been a state-led process. For decades, we have been skeptical about the possibility of a successful transition to capitalism in which the state plays a key role. China's reforms not only show that states can be effective in this process, they suggest that state-led development may be far superior to letting the market work its magic. The reasons for this, I argue, are stability and experimentation. New economic and political systems take time to learn, and it is important for states to provide stability as societies make the transition between the two. These processes of change are driven by state-led initiatives that have gradually transformed the rules of society across the board. Experimentation has emphasized getting the institutions right rather than blindly assuming that one path of institutional change – rapid privatization – will necessarily lead to the successful development of a market economy. The state begins this process of gradual experimentation that is then codified in broad-based institutional changes (in the form of laws and policies). As the state gradually implements these new policies, Chinese citizens adapt to these new rules, and the social worlds that they live in are transformed as well.

Third, economic reform in China will lead to democratization, but not because of what some neoliberals argue is the fundamental connection between liberal economic and political systems. Rather, China will become a democracy because that is the agenda some of the key powerful leaders in China have had over the course of the economic reforms. They have used the economic reforms to bring this change about. They have not talked about it openly, because, since 1989, they have lived in the shadow of Zhao Ziyang's fate. But both Zhao Ziyang and Zhu Rongji were clearly pushing radical reform agendas. Markets do not, in and of themselves, breed liberalism; liberal-minded leaders do. Finally, this process of change in China has been a fundamentally global one. Chinese leaders have leveraged the process of global integration to transform China from within.

As the twenty-first century unfolds, China's role in the global economy will continue to grow and transform, and that role will also continue to transform China from within.

Doug Guthrie (2006) *China and Globalization: The Social, Economic and Political Transformation of Chinese Society*, New York and London: Routledge, pp. 3–4, 255, 329–31.

EUROPE AS NOT-AMERICA: TIMOTHY GARTON ASH (2004)

Timothy Garton Ash (1955–) is Professor of European Studies at the University of Oxford. He is a noted expert and commentator on recent historical developments in European politics. His work *Free World*, which the selection draws from, contends that the most significant argument today for Europe is between the Euro-Gaullists and the Euro-Atlanticists. While both groups generally agree that the time is ripe for Europe to play a more influential role in the world, they disagree about what the future of Europe should look like. Whether one view will gain ultimate prominence throughout Europe remains to be seen, but in Garton Ash's view, it is likely that any resolution of this debate will have grave consequences for not only the future direction of Europe but also the broader global landscape.

The Battle for New Europe

"On Saturday, February 15, a new nation was born on the street. This new nation is the European nation."[1] Such was the conclusion drawn by Dominique Strauss-Kahn, a former French finance minister, from the simultaneous demonstrations across Europe on February 15, 2003, protesting against the Bush administration's advance to war with Iraq. Europeans already knew, wrote Strauss-Kahn, when they strolled down the main street of a European town or watched a European film, that they were in Europe. Anyone who was ill, old, or unemployed appreciated the value of that social security which characterized the European model, and distinguished it from the prevailing models in the United States, Japan, India, and China. But this was something more: "the birth of a European nation. On one and the same continent, on one and the same day, and for one and the same cause, the peoples rose up. And suddenly we realize that these peoples are one." We – but who exactly were we? – realized too that "the Europeans have a common view of the organization of the world: far removed from solitary decisions in an Oval Office, instead preferring collective decisions in the framework of international institutions." At the invitation of the President of the European Commission, Dominique Strauss-Kahn was at this time chairing a roundtable of eminent Europeans searching for a new project or, as he put it, "myth" for tomorrow's Europe.[2]

That summer there appeared in many European newspapers an appeal for the rebirth of Europe, cosigned by Jacques Derrida and Jürgen Habermas, two of the Continent's most famous living philosophers. In an introductory note, Derrida said they felt it to be both "necessary and urgent" for "German and French philosophers to raise their voices together."[3] The text, written by Habermas, began by contrasting two recent moments. First, there was the publication in various newspapers of the Letter of Eight pro-Atlanticist European leaders, described by Habermas as a "declaration of loyalty to Bush," which, he claimed, the Spanish prime minister had invited "those European governments bent on war" to sign "behind the backs of their E.U. colleagues." Then there was February 15, 2003, "when the demonstrating masses in London and Rome, Madrid and Barcelona, Berlin and Paris, reacted to this surprise attack." While acknowledging the divisions within Europe, and the existence of a larger West as a "spiritual contour," Habermas, like Strauss-Kahn, argued that what happened on February 15 can help to catalyze the formation of a European identity – if Europeans want it to. We can forge this identity by consciously "making our own" some parts of our historical heritage, while rejecting others.

He went on to list what he called six candidates for building a European identity. First, there is the European separation of religion from politics: "in our latitudes it's hard to imagine a president who begins his daily business with public prayer and relates his momentous political decisions to a divine mission." Then there's the European belief in the formative power of the state to correct the failures of the market. Third, since the French Revolution Europe has developed a political party system – composed of conservatives, liberals, and socialists – which continually confronts the "sociopathological consequences of capitalist modernization." The legacy of Europe's labor movements and its Christian-social tradition, meanwhile, is an ethos of solidarity, an insistent demand for more social justice against "an individualist performance ethos which accepts crass social inequalities." A moral sensibility, informed by the memory of the totalitarian regimes of the twentieth century and the Holocaust, is reflected "among other things in the fact that the Council of Europe and the E.U. have made the renunciation of the death penalty a condition of entry." Finally, the way Europe has overcome its warlike past in forms of supranational cooperation has strengthened Europeans' conviction that internationally, too, the domestication of the state's use of force requires a mutual limitation of sovereignty. Having lived through the rise and fall of empires, Europeans can now carry "the Kantian hope of a world domestic policy."

What Habermas argues with philosophical density, and Strauss-Kahn with eloquent political hyperbole, is that Europe is *different* from the United States, that in these differences Europe is, on the whole, *better* than the United States, and that a European *identity* can and should be built upon these differences – or superiorities. Europe, in short, is the Not-America. This triple claim is quite popular in Europe today. You see and hear it made repeatedly, often in cruder forms, but always with some of the same themes: solidarity and social justice, the welfare state, secularism, no death penalty, the environment and international law, peaceful solutions and multilateralism, transcending sovereignty, counterbalancing the U.S. Moving the motion "This House would rather be European than American" at the Oxford Union, a university debating society, one student charmingly summed up the advantages of being European thus: "You're less likely to get shot. This is a good thing. And if you are going to get shot, you're going to have social provision in the hospital."[4]

The arguments for Europe as Not-America can be heard at every turn in Paris, but they are also the stuff of pleas by British authors such as Will Hutton for Janus Britain to choose Europe. Even before George W. Bush came to power, a senior and respected German journalist, Claus Koch, was admonishing Europe to face up to the fact that "the American empire must be declared the enemy."[5] More sophisticated protagonists of the Not-America school, like Habermas, do not deny the existence of an overarching West. But, says the most agile dialectician of German foreign policy, Egon Bahr, there are two Wests: a European West and an American West.[6] Responding to the U.S. Defense Secretary Donald Rumsfeld's famous dismissal of France and Germany as "old Europe,"[7] the German philosopher Peter Sloterdijk wrote: "old Europe, honourably represented by France and Germany, is the advanced faction of the West, which, learning the lessons of the twentieth century, has turned to a post-heroic cultural style, and a corresponding policy; the United States, by contrast, is stuck in the conventions of heroism."[8] America itself. According to the American writer Robert Kagan, Americans still operate in "an anarchic Hobbesian world," where individual nations have to use military might, while Europeans are moving on to a world "of laws and rules and transnational negotiation . . . a post-historical paradise of peace and relative prosperity, the realization of Immanuel Kant's 'perpetual peace.' "[9] What came to be known as "the Kagan thesis" appeared, with perfect timing, just as America was gearing up to go to war on Iraq, and made a large impact in Europe. "Yes," excited Europeans exclaimed, "that's who we are: systematic peace-loving Kantians!" (Derrida and Habermas also invoked Kant.) The fact that this confirmation came from a right-wing American – indeed, one of the fabled, demonized cabal of neoconservatives – doubled the impact. It was as if the devil had just certified the status of the angels.

Europeans had already derived their two biggest political ideas of the post-Cold War era from the United States: Francis Fukuyama's End of History and Samuel Huntington's Clash of Civilizations. Like Kagan's *boutade*, both had started as journal articles with a striking, deliberately overstated thesis. The authors' subsequent caveats and qualifications in the longer book versions passed largely unnoticed. But this was something more. For here, Europeans were getting their own idea of themselves played back to them by an American, in an exaggerated form. We come from different planets! Americans are from Mars! And it must be true, because an *American* tells us so . . .

But which Europeans are we talking about? To leap from a scrapbook of quotations to a sweeping generalization about Europeans or, worse still, *the* Europeans, is to make precisely the mistake I've already criticized. In fact, it would take a whole essay to do justice to the views of a single European intellectual such as Jürgen Habermas.[*] It would call for a whole book to describe the variety of German approaches to this problem, another for France, yet another for Poland – and in geographical Europe there are at least forty countries, so we would need as many books. If you were serious, you would have to consider the governments, which change;

the intellectuals, who write and talk so much; and the peoples, whose views may be tracked (we fondly imagine) in opinion polls and referendums. Combine those three levels, over time, in more than forty countries, and you have a moving matrix impossible to draw. [. . .]

My conclusion, nonetheless, is simple: the whole of the new, enlarged Europe is engaged in a great argument between the forces of Euro-Gaullism and Euroatlanticism. This is the argument of the decade. On its outcome will depend the future of the West. [. . .]

Euroatlanticists and Euro-Gaullists generally agree on one thing: Europe should play a bigger role in the world. So, apparently, do most Europeans. More than two-thirds of those asked in a poll in the summer of 2003 said the European Union should become a superpower.[10] After all, this enlarged E.U. of twenty-five states has far more inhabitants than the United States, and a combined economy of comparable size. The draft European constitution envisages a European foreign minister, and a common foreign and security policy, "including the progressive framing of a common defence policy."[11] But a power for what?

At one extreme are those who want the European Union to become a secbert Védrine.[12] Few of these European nationalists (that is, protagonists of a European nation) say outright that they want it to be a rival to the United States. The senior German journalist who wrote "the American empire must be declared the enemy" is an exception.[13] This is not considered politic – or polite. After all, did not the French intellectual Jacques Attali observe, in a defense of "old Europe," that politeness is a European invention?[14] (The Chinese of Confucius's time might have been surprised.) So the Gaullist president of the Convention on the Future of Europe, Valéry Giscard d'Estaing, pleaded for Europe to acquire "the power to take on the giants of this world."[15] Euro-Gaullists talk of *l'Europe puissance* and, at their most explicit, of the E.U. as a counterweight to the U.S.; Americans are not wrong to suspect in this more than meets the eye.

However, the European nationalist or Euro-Gaullist aspiration is not simply directed against the United States. There are those, especially among the elites of the former European great powers, for whom world power status is an end in itself. De Gaulle expressed this almost as a syllogism when he said that France "because she can, because everything invites her to do so, *because she is France*, must carry out in the world policies that are on a world scale" (my italics).[16] Churchill would have said much the same for Britain. And I will never forget hearing the passion with which a distinguished white-haired former president of Germany spoke of how Europe might one day become a *Weltmacht* (a pre-1945 German term for world power). In this view, France, Britain, and Germany can no longer be world powers on their own – but together, as Europe, perhaps they might. An aspiration that is both unrealistic and discredited for individual European nation-states is somehow considered realistic and respectable for Europe as a whole.

Then there are Europeans who want Europe to play a larger role in the world for almost the opposite reason. Europe, they feel, has learned from its terrible history of competing nation-states, each aspiring to mastery. After giving the world the curse of the nation-state, Europe should now offer the global antidote. The European Union is a model of how nation-states can overcome their differences, in a law-based transnational community of peaceful cooperation. That model is now ripe for export. It's already embracing many post-communist democracies of Europe. It exercises a benign magne-diplomat confesses that his ultimate ideal would be "the Europeanization of the world." If America has a universalist aspiration, born of the Enlightenment, so do France and Germany.

In the same spirit, such patriots of transnational Europeanism emphasize Europe's contribution to promoting "global public good." Europe gives nearly three times as much as the United States in foreign development aid.[17] Europeans are involved in peacekeeping operations and reconstruction after conflicts around the world. They support the International Criminal Court. They wish to implement the Kyoto Protocol on climate change and are altogether more solicitous of the environment. Here the claim of difference from, and even superiority to, the United States does not amount to hostility; it is, so to speak, friendly rivalry in a good cause.

Finally, at the other extreme from the European nationalists, there are those who believe, like Tony Blair, that in shaping its own foreign and security policy Europe must always stay close to the United States. Its goal should be to try and broaden Washington's agenda by neo-Churchillian engagement. Those global public goods can be achieved only if Europe and America work together.

Typically you hear more French and German voices at one end of this spectrum, and more British and Polish ones at the other. When the French commentator Bernard Guetta challenged the Polish writer Adam Michnik to agree that Europe should become a world power as a counterweight to the United States, Michnik crisply replied: "Power, Yes. Counterweight, No."[18] But the division is not simply along national lines. If Americans are confused about Europe's intentions, they have every reason to be, because Europe is itself confused. Millions of Europeans are swinging between the two poles of Euro-Gaullism and Euroatlanticism, in the argument of the decade.

Notes

1. *Le Monde*, February 26, 2003.
2. Letter to the author from Dominique Strauss-Kahn, July 23, 2003, and background papers of the Round Table.
3. *Frankfurter Allgemeine Zeitung*, May 31, 2003. All following quotations also came from this source.
4. Oxford Union debate, June 12, 2003. My notes.
5. Claus Koch in *Merkur*, Sonderheft 9/10, September/October 2000, pp. 980–90, at p. 990.
6. In a television discussion on *Das philosophische Quartett,* ZDF, March 30, 2003.
7. At a press conference on January 22, 2003.
8. One of many indignant responses by European intellectuals to Rumsfeld's 'old Europe' remark in the *Feuilleton* of the *Frankfurter Allgemeine Zeitung*, January 24, 2003.
9. Robert Kagan, *Of Paradise and Power: American and Europe in the New World Order* (New York: Knopf, 2003), p. 3. The book's U.S. publication date was February 5, 2003. The original article appeared in *Policy Review* No. 113, June/July 2002.
10. German Marshall Fund et al., *Transatlantic Trends*, p. 9.
11. Article II–11.4 of the *Draft Treaty Establishing a Constitution for Europe* (Brussels: European Convention, 2003), p. 17.
12. Hubert Vedrine, 'The Europe of the Future,' *Newsweek*, Special Davos edition, December 2002–February 2003, p. 34.
13. See note 5, above.
14. In the *Feuilleton* of the *Frankfurter Allgemeine Zeitung*, January 24, 2003.
15. In his introductory speech to the Convention on February 26, 2002, available on http://european-convention.eu.int.
16. Quoted in Lacourture, *De Gaulle: The Ruler*, p. 393.
17. Calculations for 2001 by Marton Benedek from figures provided by OECD Development Assistance Committee.
18. *Gazeta Wyborcza*, February 8–9, 2003.

Timothy Garton Ash (2004) *Free World: America, Europe, and the Surprising Future of the West*, New York: Random House, pp. 46–50, 80–2.

THE FUTURE OF EUROPE: ANTHONY GIDDENS AND ULRICH BECK (2007)

Anthony Giddens (1937–) and Ulrich Beck (1944–), whose influential writings on globalization have been included in earlier selections, came together in 2005 to write this text on the future of the European social model. The impacts of European enlargement, transnational economic innovation, and political invention are considered by Giddens and Beck in the sociological context of accelerated globalization. Nationalism in a globalizing world, argue Giddens and Beck, is the enemy of European nations. Too often people tend to think of the EU as some kind of super-state, cast in the image of American hegemony. Yet another way of thinking about the EU, arising as a consequence of globalism, is the emergence of a new kind of cosmopolitan political project. From this angle for Giddens and Beck, the EU is not about uniformity, but rather cultural difference and political diversity.

Open Letter on the Future of Europe

The proposed European Constitution is dead. The people of France and the Netherlands have spoken. But what sentiments underlay their 'non' and their 'nee'? A confusion of ideas and feelings, probably: 'Help, we don't understand Europe any more'; 'Where are Europe's boundaries?'; 'Europe is not doing enough for us'; 'Our way of life is being swamped.'

The Constitution is dead. Long live . . .! What? It's up to pro-Europeans to say. We shouldn't allow the Euro-sceptics to seize the agenda. We have to react to and cope with the 'no' in a positive and constructive way.

The EU is the most original and successful experiment in political institution-building since the Second World War. It has reunited Europe after the fall of the Berlin Wall. It has influenced political change as far away as Ukraine and Turkey – not, as in the past, by military, but by peaceful means. Through its economic innovations, it has played a part in bringing prosperity to millions, even if its recent level of growth has been disappointing. It has helped one of the very poorest countries in Europe, Ireland, to become among the richest. It has been instrumental in bringing democracy to Spain, Portugal and Greece, countries that had previously been dictatorships.

It is often said by its supporters that the EU has sustained peace in Europe for more than 50 years. This claim is dubious. NATO and the presence of the Americans have been most important. But what the Union has achieved is in fact more profound. It has turned malign influences in European history – nationalism, colonialism, military adventurism – inside out. It has set up or supported institutions – such as the European Court of Human Rights – that not only reject, but legislate against, the very barbarisms that have marked Europe's own past.

It is not the EU's failure, but its very successes that trouble people. Reuniting Western and Eastern Europe would have seemed an impossible dream less than 20 years ago. But even in the new member states, people ask: 'Where does all this stop?' These feelings tend to stimulate an emotional return to the apparent safe haven of the nation. Yet if the EU were abolished overnight, people would feel less rather than more secure in their national and cultural identities. Let's say, for example, that the Euro-sceptics in Britain got their way and the UK quit the EU altogether. Would the British then have a clearer sense of identity? Would they have more sovereignty to run their own affairs?

No they would not, is the answer to both questions. The Scots and Welsh would almost certainly continue to look to the EU anyway, perhaps leading to the break-up of the United Kingdom. And Britain – or England – would lose rather than gain sovereignty, if sovereignty means real power to influence the wider world. For so many issues and problems today originate above the level of the nation-state and cannot be solved within the boundaries of the nation-state.

The paradox is that, in the contemporary world, nationalist or isolationist thinking can be the worst enemy of the nation and its interests. The EU is an arena where formal sovereignty can be exchanged for real power, national cultures nurtured and economic success improved. The EU is better placed to advance national interests than nations could possibly do acting alone: in commerce, immigration, law and order, the environment, defence and many other areas.

Let us start to think of the EU not as an 'unfinished nation' or an 'incomplete federal state', but instead as a new type of cosmopolitan project. People feel afraid of a possible federal superstate and they are right to do so. A resurgent Europe can't rise up from the ruins of nations. The persistence of the nation is the condition of a cosmopolitan Europe; and today, for reasons just given, the reverse is true too. For a long time the process of European integration took place mainly by means of eliminating difference. But unity is not the same as uniformity. From a cosmopolitan point of view, diversity is not the problem, it is the solution.

Following the blocking of the Constitution, the future of the EU suddenly seems amorphous and uncertain. But it shouldn't do! Pro-Europeans should ask themselves three questions: Do we want a Europe that stands up for its values in the world? Do we want a Europe that is economically strong? Do we want a Europe that is fair and socially just? The questions are close to rhetorical, because everyone who wishes the EU to succeed must answer positively to all three.

Various quite concrete consequences follow. If Europe is to be heard and valued on the world scene, we cannot suddenly declare an end to expansion, nor can we leave the EU's system of governance as it is. The Union is a means of promoting the spread of peace, democracy and open markets. There is virtually no hope of stabilizing the Balkans, for example, if the prospect of EU accession is cut off. The eruption of further conflict there would be a disaster. The EU will lose massive potential influence geopolitically if it decides to keep Turkey out.

Similar considerations apply to governance. The EU cannot play an effective global role without more political innovation. The proposals to reform the leadership of the Council, and to have a single EU foreign minister, should be kept in play. More effective means of taking mutual decisions are needed than the cumbersome method left over from the Nice agreements. And the proposals in the Constitution to have more consultation with national parliaments before EU policies are instituted are surely both democratic and sensible.

Political and diplomatic influence, however, always reflect economic weight. It is here above all that pro-Europeans must urge the Commission and the leaders of member states to action. We know that the 'no' votes in France and the Netherlands were motivated substantially by social and economic anxieties – anxieties that fed into the larger fears noted above. Despite its other successes, the European Union is simply not performing well enough economically. It has much lower growth levels than the US, not to mention less developed countries like India and China.

Europe simply must gear up for change. But along with reform we must preserve, and indeed deepen, our concern with social justice. The British Prime Minister, Tony Blair, has called for a Europe-wide debate on this issue. We believe he is right to do so. Some countries have been remarkably successful in combining economic growth with high levels of social protection and equality – especially the Nordic countries. Let's see what the rest of Europe can learn from them, as well as from other successful countries around the world.

The rejection of the Constitution does allow – let's hope it forces – Europeans to face up to some basic realities and respond to them. The European Union can be a major influence on the global scene in the current century. It is what pro-Europeans should want to happen. Let's make it happen.

Anthony Giddens and Ulrich Beck (2007) "Open Letter on the Future of Europe," in Anthony Giddens (ed.) *The Future of Europe*, Cambridge: Polity Press, pp. 231–234.

PART SIX

Global futures: time and tense, 1980–2010, and beyond

INTRODUCTION TO PART SIX

"Why do men obey?" Why, that is, if I am meant to be a free individual, must I obey others, any others? No one stated this question better than Max Weber in his justifiably famous essays on political authority. If there is a single defining question put to the human species by the modern age, it would be hard to think of one more basic than this one. Weber was a genius at capturing the ironies of the modern era.

Why do people obey? The irony is that this is a question of moral and practical urgency *only* in modern times. Before, when slaveholders, lords, princes, despots, and prophets ruled, obedience was not perfect but its reasons were not hard to discern. Then, one obeyed according to fear of punishment, unthinking regard for traditions, or infatuation with charismatic powers. By contrast, after the modern took hold, especially after the long eighteenth century (or the short seventeenth, as you wish), political cultures were inclined to stipulate what they held to be more sane and dignified theories of the power of authority to incite obedience. With rare exception, modern political theories encourage individuals to think of themselves as masters of their own destinies and inventors of themselves as uniquely important individuals. In principle, modern political order (in the classically liberal sense) is founded on a preternatural grammar that is very hard to put into practical play – that the people are the source of power and authority in a democracy. Several different modern political systems have been devised to effect this ideal. Some work better than others. But none works perfectly well because the principle, by relying on the power of the people, relies on an illusion. In other words, modern liberal ideas of authority are confused as to how to join freedoms with real political powers. As it happens, the sore point is *the people*.

The people are nobodies in particular. They are, if they are anything, an unruly collection of individuals who come together only in theories or ideologies. This is why, as Giorgio Agamben most recently has pointed out, *the people* is a duplicitous abstraction used, at once, to signify *the people* in whose name a democracy is ruled and *the people* in the sense of the masses, the populous, ultimately the poor and ill-bred. The two variant forms merge under extreme historical circumstances when the people are the impoverished masses and their equivalents that are put to rhetorical service for politically vile ends – notably nationalisms that turn the state into a machine for governing that, incredibly, entails the right to kill *the people* themselves – either individually or collectively or according to some partial equation. It could be said – as Agamben has, commenting on Hannah Arendt and Michel Foucault in *Homo Sacer* (1995) – that the death camps are the paradigm of modern life. The Nazis, thus, implemented the potential of the most imprecise, thus plastic, concept in the wordbook of modern culture.

Even under the best possible historical circumstances, the ideal of a people puts the modern individual in an impossible situation. Moderns are meant to be individuals; and the *individual* (herself an abstraction of a different kind) strives in practical reality to be different from all others – at least to the extent that she means to take the concept *individual* seriously. Naturally (even obviously), it is not possible for any given individual to be unique in every important detail, any more than it is possible for the people as an abstract whole to act in coherent concert, each with the others. A people comprising hypothetically free individuals will govern itself at best unevenly, at worst cruelly.

Hence, in practical terms, the dilemma of the modern is that its two core principles − free individuals and government by the people − are all but impossible to hold together except in the rarest and most ephemeral of situations. They are concepts, ideals, rules, principles; in practice they are, when forced together, so unstable as to yield poor, often exceedingly bad, results; only occasionally do they do good − hence the sad history of the twentieth century and its aftermath.

One would suppose that in a real world, however well or poorly organized, *the people* would want to do something about the trouble provoked by the rules they are expected to obey. Why do men obey? In reality, for the most part, they don't. The whole system sorely needs an overhaul. Still, should it be possible, the overhaul (dare we call it a restructuring?) would be at the nub of the problems associated with attempts to understand globalization. Globalization might well turn out to be the human animal's necessary, if unwitting, attempt to remake the social order of things in global terms.

If, somehow or another, globalization is that which comes *after* the modern − or, in some less radical way, that which is brewed *out of* the modern and its failures − then you would expect global things to be, if not post-modern, at least more than − or different from − modern things. If this, then among other things the core concepts of modern culture − that the *individual* is meant to be free, that *the people* are meant to govern themselves − would require, at the least, revision. (How, and by whom, is still another matter.)

If this is so (or, if only one grants that it *could* be so), then there are, as in most things social, relatively few ways to repair the principles such that they might work better than they have in the last century or two. Tentatively, in the abstract, we would suggest the following are more or less the central issues that modern political culture needs somehow to fix. First, *the individual* (and, generally speaking, individualism, the ethical norm) has proven itself a weak timber out of which to build complex structures − and this, we have seen, is a matter that many realized had to be addressed after the terrible failures of nineteenth-century values, beginning with the Great War, to prevent war, economic misery, and political chaos. In other words, the moral agency of self-interested subjects is not an answer to the dilemma of modern political cultures. Second, assuming something realistic can be done about the first of these then, some-how, it would be necessary to invent a concept of democracy that relies on a social category more modest than anything so vaporously splendid as *the people* − and this would entail any and all cognates of peopleness, including the masses, civil society, society plain-and-simple, the community, and so forth. In other words, unregulated market freedoms, state ownerships of the means of production, and grassroots populisms are not answers. Thirdly, assuming the first two can be addressed, then something has to be done about the way people think about the relations among themselves as individuals and society as somehow resources for how (and why) individuals in all their various quests for freedom obey social norms, when they do, at a cost to their individual freedoms. In other words, rational choice utilitarianisms are not an answer.

The list could go on, but these three are enough for the time being. No short list of ideas and norms has been more thoroughly tested and failed over, say, the two centuries of industrial capitalism. The names and nuances may differ but the overall failure of modern political cultures is beyond serious argument except in the minds of unrecombinant nostalgics and fantasy-prone utopians. As it happens, even this short list of concepts or principles that might require some attention is enough for the simple reason that no one should assume that the issues that must be dealt with are a matter of theory, or ethics, or political values, or such like. Weber, often thought of as a theorist, was not asking a theoretical question when he wondered why modern people obey. He was acutely concerned, near the end of the long nineteenth century, with the moral and political consequences of obedience and, in particular, he was concerned that the systems of modern society could not sustain the dual responsibility of satisfying the needs of individuals to find meaning as individuals and the demands of political society to govern rationally in diverging spheres of modern life − social, cultural, economic, among others. Had Weber lived to see it, the Nazi regime would not have surprised him; it was the coming into being of the very iron cage he abhorred.

In our time – a good century and more after Weber wrote of the iron cage of the modern world, of the bureaucratic machine, and of the troubles the modern democratic state has maintaining its legitimacy – social things are vastly more complicated. This could well be enough to account for the globalization debates that began in the 1990s and the crises of global differences that came to world-wide consciousness early in the 2000s. Any attempt to interpret the history of the present is, as we have said, fraught with difficulties, not least of which is that it is impossible to know, in any scientific or political sense, what exactly is taking place in the present and just how whatever it is might be different from what came before.

Still, any question of true urgency for human life must be asked and answers, however incomplete, must be sought. Otherwise, human being would no longer be human after all these perturbations. It may be, as some in our day have begun to suggest, that human life is something very different from the grand narrative of the Human that, since at least the Enlightenment, the modern had told and trusted. Modern culture supposed that the unique virtue of the human was precisely its capacity for consciousness of self – of selves individually; but also of the human as such. Thus, for even the best and most daring of moderns it is human nature to ask questions of the nature of the human. Though long neglected, one such question – a decidedly counterintuitive one in modern cultures – has begun to edge into the public sphere. Is the human, after all, a discrete category defining a true and discernible distinction interior to the class of creatures party to life itself?

Why, exactly, it took as long as it did – well into the twenty-first century – for questions like these to be taken with increasing seriousness is hard, but not impossible, to say. First of all, the ordinal problem of assessing changing times is that the mental categories available for the assessment are predisposed to encourage resistance to change. For the modern to worm its way out from under the premodern, many thousands of martyrs were hung, burned, guillotined, or otherwise excommunicated from the then prevailing race of living humans. Martyrs are hated not because they are unorthodox but because the orthodox are unable to imagine what they are driving at. *If the earth is not the flat firmament of God's world, then God cannot be as we were taught He is, thus these people must be, if not exactly sociopaths, evil in some freshly dangerous way.* Martyrs, whatever their mental state, are those who represent changes so severe that people with official responsibility for policing the norms can only envisage them as heretics whose punishment must be expulsion, which is to say social death by whatever means. Were not the camps and gulags of the twentieth century themselves punishments for unorthodox ideas that threatened the prevailing orthodoxies? And what, many ask, was Guantanamo and other prisons for the politically obnoxious if they are not disposal centers for those of whom the normal cannot be sure? Dumps for wasted humanity, like all garbage dumps, are landfills located outside of town, often in a dark forest, usually beyond view from the roadways. They are crude but ubiquitous in the backwoods and marshes of human communities.

In the long history of the West – and especially of the modern West – the cultural resource used to define, identify, and process heretics has been ethics. Ethics are, thus, the meeting ground of the people (*ethos*, hence *ethics*) and the righteous individual; as such ethics are simultaneously social (even sociological) and personal (even psychological). Shared social norms define *the good life* which, like *the people*, is a vague abstraction meant to organize individuals into conformity. In this respect, one could go so far, as we do, to suggest that the dilemma of the modern is an ethical one – the incommensurability of pure, practical individualism and rational democratic authority. Men (Weber's word) do not in fact obey. They do not, but not because individual humans in community are by nature rebels but because, in point of practical effect, obedience in democracies is all but impossible. The only exceptions to this shocking fact of social life are any and all conditions where collective death is threatened due to the disintegration of the social – war, pandemics, natural catastrophe, the wrath of the gods, solar eclipses, rampant heresy, apocalyptic visions, and such like. Or, otherwise put, to look for a solution to the threefold dilemma of the modern is to look for a way around modern ethics. But ways around are hard and rocky.

If ethical coherence is the moral method by which theoretically free individuals are to obey their ideologies of themselves as the source of collective authority, then, in effect, a large amount of political and social theory must be thrown overboard. For one, the notion that something called "agency" is the means by which individuals act thoughtfully in relation to the people must be called what it is – just another nice idea that makes very little practical sense. An agent is one who acts – this from the Medieval Latin, *agens*, "to do." Yet, when politically hip characters use "agency" to polish the sheen of *the individual* as the one who must do something about the collective messes, the usage entails a degradation of the original meaning of the word, "agency." One need not consult an etymological dictionary to know that in the real practical world agencies are hard institutional forms, muscle-bound by self-aggrandizing authority. To use "agency" as a slogan does not get to the heart of the political trouble. In the long run (and most short runs), to mouth platitudes about the agency of individuals to do something about the way modern agencies (in the institutional sense) actually make agency (in the liberal sense) does little or no good. Agencies are tough. Agencies certify their own agents. Uncertified "free" individuals are, with rare exception, not permitted past the front desk. Hence, the dilemma of obedience in the modern age – that free agency is a pitiful wail against the pull of obedience.

Individuals are meant to obey a ghost of themselves which turns out to be, as Weber put it, a bureau-cratic machine that cannot be stopped. If there were *a people*, then it is they who made this machine and set it in motion according to some magical formula known only to officials of formal agencies. Like the sorcerer's apprentice, the only way to stop the thing from drowning them all is to call in the Master Sorcerer who alone knows the secret words. This is the worst case that even Hobbes did not foresee. People obey because they do not and are not permitted to know the secret for containing the people they claim to be but surely realize that this is no more than an abracadabra.

To come to terms with the global – hence, to make sense of what globalization might mean – is, thus, to accept that the modern, however fine in the ideal, was always a pluperfect, a perfect past deployed as a hedge against the future. *We knew we were meant to be free to govern ourselves.* The pure perfect freedoms the liberal-modern set forth as the standard by which they were to do good things were, and are, hard to come by in any actual present. The pluperfect is, thus, an unadulterated narrative tense – a poetic device for describing a perfect past as a future event in the story being told. *The Kennedy boys knew they were expected to be president.* Or, more generally, *the English people were destined for greatness.*

The future of the global is, one might say, a question of time and tense. To question a future is entirely different from a serious study of the past. Neither is a sure bet, but in respect to the past there is at least good and sufficient reason to trust that things happened, however uncertain the record of them may be. The problem is that to speak of those things always involves language, needless to say; and the problem with language in speaking (or writing) about events is that it requires exactness in the use of terms and grammar. To say that "The Twin Towers will crash on 9/11" makes sense only in certain atypical forms of literary or cinematic expression. To speak of events that took place on September 11, 2001 in New York City is to speak in one of the several available past tenses: "The towers fell on 9/11" or "The towers fell just as we were going to class that morning." Formally, this is to say that in speaking of events occurring in time is, among other things, to speak in a correct tense. Thus it is that to speak of past events, whatever the facts at hand, is to speak in a past tense or, if you are telling a story of what conclusively happened in a past time, you may speak in the pluperfect – of the events that occurred utterly in the past, the occurrence of which is not at issue or in question: "My friend Niki was in second period at Stuyvesant High School when the Towers fell and no one really believed what had happened." This latter is a story – a true story – but it is story told me by Niki in which the fact of the past event in time is taken as a given.

This may seem a needlessly obscure way to introduce the question of the future of the global, yet to speak of *the* future is to contend with complexities of an unyielding sort. The best you can hope for when speaking of the future is to make a good guess. Such a guess may be called an extrapolation from data points or a projection of trends but the underlying fact of future time is that there are no future factuals. As a result, to speak or write of future time is to speak, of course, in a future tense: "I will be there tomorrow morning at 9 am" or "The world will come to an end on December 21, 2012–12/21/12." If the former is more reasonable in your book (the latter being a common religious prophecy), something always can happen to disavow the tense of future time: "Sorry, my kid is sick, I can't make it." When the future time of which one speaks is by its nature complicated and (even in the present) a relatively new kind of thing, then one can only speak of it in a conditional or subjunctive tense – "The world might come to an end on 12/21/12" or "I wish this world would die." It is possible to tell of a story that banks on the gullibility of those to whom it is told: "In 2112 the Vulcans helped form the United Federation of Planets and a new era of peace was established." Yet, even in science fiction, to speak of the future is to speak of what might-have-beens – of beliefs, wishes, or desires. To speak of the future of the global is not science fiction, but it does require an appreciation that future time is tense and that the tense of the future is always beholden to human imagination and animal desire which, in turn, is always at least subjunctive, and definitely conditional.

The global future is a state of desire, of longing, of hope. The modern might have done better had it been more subjunctive. Still it would have had to have been more perfectly modest in respect to itself. The political form of the global is the conditional subjunctive: *If only we could, we would like to*. As in: *If only we could eliminate poverty, we would like to*. The recognition that the global might require not just a new political vocabulary but a new grammar of tentativeness will shock many on both sides of the political fence. Yet, who would say that practical, public political thought would not do better were it more humble, less certain, more open, less hampered by prior prejudices?

Complicated or not, the link between time and tense clarifies the crucial difference between the modern and the global. We, thus, bring this collection to a subjunctive conclusion by sampling some of the prominent ideas bearing on globalization that may anticipate the revisions of modern thinking that may be necessary. Of these, roughly put, there are four basic issues among others: (1) What is to become of the modern ideal of a perfect world in the face of the global future's mechanization of democratic authority and the impossible complications arising therefrom? (2) What accordingly is to become of the claims of the modern to secure civil identities in sheltering nations free of destructive violence? (3) How will the already troubled notions of personal life and individualism as a way of life survive the global future's pressures toward nomadic life migrating and mobility? (4) What, indeed, is to become of the ideal of the Human as the end for which social life and its achievements have for so long been directed? The selections gathered here under these four questions are notable precisely because they are, at once, sober and imaginative attempts to take stock of the moth already breaking out of the chrysalis. Whether they will be butterflies or pests remains to be seen.

Our classification of the issues at stake in the global future may not correspond, point-for-point, to the three elements of the failure of the modern: How are individuals to think and act democratically in relation to *the people*? However, the tense of this kind of future is necessarily not neat. At the least, we will see that the old modern formulas – particularly those concerning individualism, democracy, and political agency – are being tested as never before. The writings here illustrate the better – if not entirely satisfying – attempts to rethink the modern in terms at once responsible and humble – which is to say subjunctive.

The past was pluperfect in the sense that so much of modern political culture was founded on an unproven assumption that the world began in a pure past in which, as John Rawls rephrased the classical figure, Man in the Original Position was the guide to all things political. By contrast, as the global future unfolds, the early evidence contradicts this elementary figure of thought.

Today, you might say that the global realities as they are coming into sight are not pluperfect – that is to say, they are not expressions of a perfect ideal. It is far more evident that the new world is coming apart; or, better, that the world is worlds – and that the global future is one without a singular unity. One of the signs that this condition is considered a likely feature of the global future is the recurrence of the concept *assemblages* – normally in the plural, commonly in reference to cities or nations, almost always with reference to globalization or its equivalent. The origin of the concept as it is used now was in a work that, at the time of its appearance (1980), was widely deemed outlandishly unreadable. Yet, 30 years later, Gilles Deleuze's and Felix Guattari's *A Thousand Plateaus: Capitalism and Schizophrenia* is, readable or not, a most influential book. As have many other writers represented here, Deleuze and Guattari are proposing, without demanding, a new political logic – one that abandons claims of territorial order, legitimate govern-ance, and dominant states.

Assemblages are, in effect, the accidental coming together of masses of people – not as *a people*, nor even as discernible individuals. Assemblages move irregularly and settle, when they do, without regard for spatial logics. They seek what life can be had. They are outside the sanctions of a state. Their numbers may be great but are not organized into cities, much less nations. Assemblages in which there are no citizens, no rights, no rules, no social benefits. Assemblages are outside social order and populated by nomads.

"With the nomad," as Deleuze and Guattari say in the selection, "it is deterritorialization that constitutes the relation to the earth." For any who might at first find this an odd way to speak, just consider the fact of a growing number of global assemblages in and around Lagos in Nigeria, Mexico City, Jakarta in Indonesia, Sao Paulo in Brazil, Shenzhen in South China, Bishkek in Kyrgyzstan where nomads fleeing deadly illnesses, civil wars, or poverty come to a temporary stopping place in a nomadic life. They are not, thus, migrants because their fate (if fate is still a word that applies) is created for them. Migrants, whether in groups or as individuals, decide to move from point to point, as does the nomad seeking an oasis; but the nomad does not resettle around a watering hole because there is nothing there – there is, that is, no social or political order whereby goods, such as they are, may be distributed and heretics driven away. At Bishek's most prestigious research and learning institution the vast majority of scholars and students know that there is an assemblage outside the city near the American Air Force base. But I could find no one who knew very much more about these nomads beyond the general scientific explanations for such a place. Kyrgyzstan is a bleak nation. It leads the world in the percentage of its GDP derived from remittances (close to 30 percent). Should the global economy hiccup, the people of Kyrgyzstan choke. The poorest among them move where they can to find what they can to survive for so long as they might.

Saskia Sassen is surely more plain-spoken, if not quite so subtle, in her application of assemblage theory to the global future. She is universally well-regarded for her probing analysis of the causes and effects of globalization. But in all her many writings, none is more challenging than her persuasive inter-pretation of the effects of deterritorialization on the single most salient political institution of the modern era, the nation-state. Many, as we have seen, hold the view that globalization is eroding the power and authority of the nation-state as the principal guarantor of political rights. But, as Sassen says clearly in the selection, the future may well be headed toward a new series of partial political and extra-political assemblages that operate without respect for territories (in both the political and the conceptual senses) – without, that is, being either national or global, either simply local or powerfully global. As do many, she seeks to transcend the modern method of thinking in binaries – of either-ors like state or interstate, national or global. Again, like Deleuze and Guattari (to whom she acknowledges a debt of a distant sort), Sassen emphasizes the strange way globalization forces a redefinition of political spaces. The state was and for the most part remains a source of authority and rights because it controls the borders of a national territory. Yet, as everyone to some degree knows, it is increasingly difficult to patrol territorial borders. Information, capital, culture, and more flow without regard to territorial borders. As a con-sequence, the state and its agencies in any given nation are less able to determine who possesses which rights and goods normally assumed (or advertised) to come and go with citizenship. Hence, again, deter-ritorialization refigures global space in ways that simultaneously localize and globalize many of the effects that determine the fates of individuals. Under these conditions, to speak of individuals as agents of their own governance is not quite nonsense (the people of various nations still insist on their independence and their rights), but neither does it make the sense it once did.

Though their approach to the issues of the global future are very different from Sassen's, Michael Hardt and Antonio Negri's *Empire* (1990) is still another instance of roughly the same set of ideas – deter-ritorialization leads to, as they say, "hybrid identities, flexible hierarchies, and plural exchanges through modulating networks of command." These, they argue, are the warnings of a resurgence of empire in a new – utterly new – form from empires of old. Central to the Hardt and Negri argument is the idea that the new global empires, far from being territorially centered in nation-states, are in fact information-based.

They speak of a mode of information production as the dynamo that drives multiplicities that, so to speak, dis-order the world. Disorder, in this line of thought, may be chaotic but, if so (as surely it is), then the chaos is typical of the global future where neither the one nor the many control the field of political and social values.

What Deleuze and Guattari started in 1980 in *Thousand Plateaus* was decidedly distinctive but it was also much more than an intellectual fad. One can never say for certain when and how it happens that books and the ideas they express are related to the particular social milieu of their origin. In retrospect, when the thought dawns that ideas are conditioned by their times, it dawns because in the intervening time what at the earlier time may have seemed weirdly out of order comes to assume an importance that then would never have occurred even to the most arduous of readers. This is true of the lineage of influences from Foucault, then Deleuze and Guattari to Hardt and Negri, Sassen, and many others. But, it can be, as it is in this case, also true of thinking that takes shape quite apart from this line of influence.

If there is a single idea that is unique to the twentieth century and more important to scientific thinking, it is one with roots in the early writings of Albert Einstein. Today, more than a century later, most educated people know at least something of his special and general theories of relativity. We even know something of the general concept of *time-space*. For, if we did not, millions of us would not flock to iterations of the *Star Trek* saga and other variations such as the *Star Wars* films or even the underlying mysteries of the *Harry Potter* series or, at the bottom of barrel, *Back to the Future*. In these and other instances (not all of them technically science fiction), stories play with the indefiniteness of time's relations to spaces. I once assigned a popular essay on the subject by Stephen Hawking, the world's greatest living theoretical physicist. The point of the essay was to explain for the lay reader how the evidence of modern physics makes time-travel theoretically possible. The essay from *A Brief History of Time* is stunningly clear and scientifically authoritative. Yet, one of my better students wrote me a note to say how much he liked the assignment because he was "into" science fiction. I did not have the heart to rebuke him or to say that among scientists Hawking is as much a household name as Einstein's.

Still, what is the line between science and science fiction? In part, this is the methodological question of theories of all kinds for which there is not yet or unlikely ever to be sufficient empirical evidence. Yet, this condition of theory – that it is always, necessarily fictive to some degree – is not sufficient cause for it to be ignored. As it happens, Einstein's theories of time-space enjoyed, after 1922, excellent empirical verification. This is important to our subject because, surprisingly, it took the social sciences a very long time to embrace the idea that time and space are not independent variables in real world time but aspects of the same, if not singular, set of natural processes. When objects move in space so fast that their velocity comes close to being immeasurable, time exceeds the natural limits of space, warping one against the other. It is true that when it comes to social things, speeds never, so far as we know, achieve the levels of, say, interstellar light. This may alone be a good enough reason to explain why social thought took so long to consider time-space. Social and historical things are too slow to consider the possibility that they could change rapidly enough to curve back on themselves. Yet, slow or not, it is also true that social thought has been so deeply beholden to modern analytic categories as to have failed even to contemplate the reversibility of history. This is a bit surprising in light of the twentieth century itself which was, if not a reversal in historical time, at least a regression to states of violence and deadliness the modern had thought were in the past.

Yet, all this reluctance on the part of social science to rethink time's relation to space began to change in the 1980s. The immediate influence then was Ilya Prigogine, a physical chemist whose prize-winning work included contributions to complexity theory. In one sense, complexity theory is straightforward – nothing in nature is determined. This, of course, is consistent with relativity theories of time-space. In the 1980s, Immanuel Wallerstein, most notably, introduced complexity theory into his world-systems analysis to the effect of proposing that even world-systems can come to a point where the complexity of the system is too great to bear, causing it to lapse into long periods of chaos and uncertainty. This idea was one of the reasons Wallerstein was the first important social scientist to prophesy (or, at least, to explain) the collapse of the modern system after 1990. This is saying something because the work allowed Wallerstein to use his own theory of modern world-system to interpret the early signs of its collapse. This is not a scientific attribute normally found among sociologists.

In time, others picked up the idea, from Prigogine, if not from Wallerstein. Among them is John Urry whose book *Global Complexity* (2003) is one of the first systematic interpretations of globalization according to a general theory of complexity (or, at least, the first since Wallerstein). In particular, Urry's theory of the global future allows centrally for the bifurcation (another of Prigogine's ideas) of global systems. Some will conclude that Urry stops a bit short of fully developing the implications of complexity theory. He seems, at times, to speak of complexity as a metaphor more than as a natural attribute of the global order. Yet, again, it is quite exceptional for a sociologist to be as bold in breaking conceptual molds and Urry deserves in this respect to be mentioned in the same breath with Wallerstein. Even more than Wallerstein, perhaps because he came at the topic early in 2000s after a good bit of thinking in other fields had matured, Urry took very seriously work done outside his primary field – including the ideas of Prigogine and Deleuze. To read Urry in the context of other attempts to think about the global future is to open up connections to assemblage theory and related developments that embolden the seriousness with which it is necessary to think of the world as a series of disjointed, heterogeneous assemblages that may in some subterranean way be connected while at the same time moving according to historical vectors not likely to be commensurable.

If, over the time of modern political theory, there was a single embracing term to describe the territory considered essential to the securing of individual freedoms and viable democracies, that term was "civil society." But to consider the concept civil society in light of the beginnings of theories of the global future one begins to see the tremendous value, even necessity, of what might be called a *positive* theory of deterritorialization. Political and social theories of collective life may concretely refer to political territories such as the bordered spaces of nation-states, but when it comes to describing what goes on in those spaces – or, better put, what is *meant* to go on in them – theory must abandon hard geographies of territory to explore the more imaginative, yet-to-be (if-at-all) spaces that are beyond the time-spaces of past and present. The details of what deterritorialization might come to be have yet to be worked out. Still, there could be no better example than the rethinking of civil society in the ways our understanding of the global future can be assembled out of the scrap left behind in the ruins of the modern.

Civil societies, such as they have been and might come to be, are irremediably deterritorialized in the sense that they are, when concrete, utterly local. Yet, when a civil society does what it is ideally supposed to do, its effects cut a wide but vaporous swath through the thickets of a given territorial society. The term "society" is, of course, a source of this miasmatic fog. It sounds so real, but says so little. How, truth be told, did social science ever suppose that the attributes of high society (low society is an oxymoron) could be enlarged to encompass the whole of a nation or, more modestly, a region of relatively coherent social attitudes and behaviors? The answer no doubt is that in earlier modern times, when social thought had its start, a society was in fact governed and organized by members of high bourgeois society. Still, this gets us nowhere. But to add the modifier "civil" to stipulate a civil society has a salutary, if not class-neutral, benefit.

Civil society refers to the normal terms of civic participation that, in democracies, must be, at once, *civic* – in the sense of for the common good – and *civil* – in the sense of well-mannered or civilized. What, thereby, saves civil society from being mere fog is the particulate gravity of these dual meanings – for a society to be civilly civic is for its adherents to be at once under a political and ethical obligation. Even if civility is a somewhat puffy moral principle, it is one that can be brought to bear on the civically uncouth. At the very least this aspect allows local participants to call the wayward to account without, by the way, their assuming free license to excommunicate those they do not like well enough. In modern and after-modern political cultures this is quite a lot, if not quite enough to settle the realities of any civil society as grand as a national one. And this small, but real, leverage may be why civil society enjoys, for the time being, a healthy after life in the adolescence of the global future.

Mary Kaldor and John Keane, in the selections here, are two of the foremost proponents of *global* civil society. Kaldor, for one, offers common sense and clarity in her glossary of the five possible applications of the ideal of civil society to the global situation. Two of them, she states, are tied directly to the usages of the modern era. The other three are, if not exactly radical, compelling alternatives for the global future: activist, neo-liberal, and postmodern. She, for herself, identifies with activist civil society – participation in global social movements aimed at establishing a global public sphere. Kaldor's two remaining categories have, at least, the merit of describing global structures known to exist and having discernible effects. Neo-liberalism duplicitously offers to create global markets out of private energies and capital wealth to the end of bringing a rebirth of humanitarianism. The fifth type is what she calls, rather chunkily, post-modern civil society and is not so much a movement as a consequence of the obvious condition of global life – that the fractious and fractured nature of geopolitics encourage networks that serve to aggravate social and human differences to the end of generating a beneficial dynamism. Immanuel Wallerstein, from a very different point of view, might refer to these last two (neo-liberal markets and contentious social differences) as the alternatives posed respectively by the neo-liberal World Economic Forum and the more social democratic World Social Forum. In either case, Kaldor, whatever her preferences, gives good account of the range of alternatives for a global civil society, in respect to which she cites John Keane's interesting comment to the effect that the widespread discussion of global civil society is itself evidence that such a thing is gaining momentum in the real world.

The very title of John Keane's earlier book is a question, *Global Civil Society?*. To begin the exploration by inquiring into its possibility is, thus, an exemplary attitude for thinking subjunctively of the global future. It is possible, however, that, unlike Mary Kaldor, when push comes to shove, Keane is a bit too definitive in his idea of global civil society as "a dynamic non-governmental system of interconnected socio-economic institutions that straddle the whole earth, and that have complex effects that are felt in all corners." Whether global realities are so settled as to be straddled (much less confined to four corners) is itself a question; still Keane puts coherent emphasis on the importance of building a global civil society out of specific global institutions such as the plethora of nongovernment agencies that spread across the field of global life while forming a series of networks that can connect otherwise disparate parts. "The heterogeneity of global civil society," he says, "works against enforced unity ... spontaneous sympathy and automatic consensus." Again, one must respect the circumspect humility of both the analysis and the political proposal. With Keane, as with Kaldor, global civil society is understood as different in nature and tone from the traditional civil society of modern nations which, all too often, are put forth as if it were evident that *the people* in a given nation were self-evidently capable of deploying their freedoms to good civil effect.

Amartya Sen and Kwame Anthony Appiah – both subjects of post-colonial worlds – put a considerable damper on all attempts to argue for anything like an unbridled global civil sphere. Yet, neither is a pessimist, pure and simple. Sen, a Nobel laureate in economics, is justifiably respected for his empirically hard-nosed assessment of the relations between economic development and freedom. In the selection here, "Violence, Identity, and Poverty," Sen offers respectful criticism of the bipolar terms in the debate over the nature of the global future's two most-pressing uncertainties – poverty and violence. It would be hard to say which, if either, is the more troubling, but it is not hard to own the evidence that both are fully, tragically global.

Sen challenges the two most prominent liberal explanations for poverty and violence – that poverty is implicated in questions of collective identity and that violence is, in turn, an issue of economic deprivation. In this distinction, Sen powerfully insists that violence and poverty must not be "decoupled" – that each feeds the other and, thus, that global economic policy must see them, so to speak, as complicated aspects of the same set of issues. Sen, in other of his writings on violence and collective identity, comes eventually (as most must) to the neo-classic cases of ethnic violence, of which none is more terrible than those between Muslim and Hindu in South Asia, Hutu and Tutsi in Rwanda, and Serb and Muslim in Bosnia and Kosovo. In cases such as these, violence arises because Rwanda, for example, is not a sufficiently collective identity to override Hutu sensibilities. Collective identities play a part, but not an overriding part.

Anthony Appiah, a Princeton philosophy professor who grew up in Ghana, comes, quite naturally, to a similar point on the link between cultural identity and civil violence. Sen's attentions are on the ameliorative potential of economic development to relieve poverty and thus to encourage the freedom that the new theories of global civil society are attempting to refresh. Somewhat differently, Appiah focuses on a philosophic ethic of cosmopolitan patriotism. Appiah, like others, means to recover patriotism from the evils latent to hard nationalisms – this by outlining what he calls a rooted cosmopolitanism in which the evident global values of national identities are hedged by what is, in effect, a global patriotism.

We offer this variety of approaches to the role of civic virtues to the global future in order to illustrate the energies currently devoted to a sensible rethinking of modern values. As with all questions of the global future, we shall see what we shall see. Still what will be seen will surely have to account for the most deadly consequences of the full package of modern civic ideals – violence and civil strife; as well as the scourge of nationalisms; and of the failure of the civil society ideal to come anywhere near a solution to global poverty.

Pheng Cheah's now famous, if a bit overwrought, essay, *Spectral Nationality*, has for a good while now served to chasten optimism as to civil society or, in the term he uses, nation-people by which he means to identify the historical drift of any political system that so trusts *the people* as to lapse into nationalism. He opens with an honest appraisal of the evidence culled from the sad history of the twentieth century that "nationalism is probably one of the few phenomena we associate most closely with death." In this, as we illustrate in the last group of selections, the eerily potent question of the uncertainties of life itself against the deadlier forces of political process – whether national or global enters as a consideration that cannot be ignored. Pheng Cheah argues, with acute appreciation of the realities of the post-colonial world, that the colonizing nations will not anytime soon be able to outlive the ghosts of their origins as colonial powers. He concludes that the post-colonial nation, with all the degradations visited upon it and which it has become is a "specter that haunts global capital, for it is the undecidable neuralgic point within the global capitalist system that refuses to be exorcised." The ghost of modern nationalities and their corruption into nationalisms are, as Cheah says, deadly.

For the most part, globalization has been treated as an "out there" phenomenon. From one angle, this is entirely understandable. To work on the topic of multinational corporate finance or transnational governance frameworks is to take seriously the conventional wisdom that globalization is all about large-scale institutions. That is to say, globalization is primarily an institutional order comprising complex systems, abstract organizational processes, communication networks, and immense technological transformations. From such a standpoint there appears a seamless linkage between globalization, organizations, and institutions. It is rather like believing that globalism is a solely institutional affair, only having to do with the most pressing, "hard" facts of finance, militarization, capitalist expansion, empire, the nation-state, and technology. As such, the idea that globalization likewise affects everyday emotional life, and profoundly so, does not get much consideration. Even on the wilder shores of academic and public debate, it is as if the most that might be acknowledged is that globalization is somehow transformative of culture, ideology, or religion.

Today, such conventional wisdom is in doubt. For one of the significant achievements of recent cultural debate has been to consider afresh the intricate interconnections between globalization and identity as a topic of study. Above all, new cultural ideas have sprung up which suggest that globalization extends into the core of the self. Indeed, globalism has been redefined as an "in here" phenomenon. That is to say, globalization is about identities and not just institutions, feelings and not just finance, sexualities and not just systems. On this view, globalization initiates significant psychic reorganization, cultivates new emotional dispositions and significantly alters the self. Changes in psychic aspects of personal identity, in other words, are directly connected to social changes that are increasingly global in scope. This is perhaps but another way of saying that continuous shifts of capital across the globe, the transnational spread of multipurpose production, the privatization of all things social, the rise of new technologies and the thrills and spills of 24/7 stock markets all bring starkly into focus the degree to which people are remaking their identities (whether by design or default), and daily. That is to say that the big institutional changes associated with globalism seep deeply into psychic life, and are affecting greater and greater numbers of people.

Don DeLillo, in *Underworld: A Novel*, has put this unsettling prospect to fiction – that today's globalism generates transformations in our personal lives at "the speed of light." As the readings of Dennis Altman, Nikos Papastergiadis, and other authors in the section "Globalization and Personal Life" demonstrate, our present global order is based upon profound (and often traumatic) transformations to identities and the personal sphere. From the global trade in sex trafficking to the enforced brutal migration of peoples arising as a result of the techno-industrialization of war, there is little doubt that the destructive edges of globalization leave a substantial part of the world's population feeling increasingly worthless, depleted, and degraded. Caught in a savagely despairing circle, it is as if the very logics of globalization exhibit a fascination with dispossession, destruction, and death. Certainly, one extremely powerful contemporary manifestation of how globalism rewrites the texture of our emotional worlds is to be found in the figure of the suicide bomber. Another is to be found in the dark, dystopic images of global climate change and of the ravages to humanity wrought by high-carbon economies and societies.

There are, however, plenty of other ways of conceiving of the impacts of globalization on personal life – some of them (like those above) momentous, others less threatening, some even enticing or exhilarating. For if the "speed of light" global transformations to personal life underscored above scoop up everything from economic production to militarization, another part of what we mean by "intimate globalism" concerns the global atmospherics and esthetics through what we live by – the very emotional air by which we breathe. Again, DeLillo is highly illuminating here, arguing that globalization infuses "everything from architecture to leisure time to the way people eat and sleep and dream."[1] Globalization, as we have argued and sought to demonstrate throughout this book, is a very slippery term. A United Nations resolution is the upshot of globalizing social forces, but so too is last night's dream of a friend living in distant lands. Globalization is thus recast as all about desire and the emotions.

The European psychoanalytic feminist Julia Kristeva underscores powerfully and provocatively how globalization is marked by such dreams, desires, affects, emotional states, sexual politics, and the unleashing of the unconscious. In the reading selected in Part Six, as well as in many seminal works over recent years, Kristeva has sought to show – both by embracing and by pushing psychoanalysis to its conceptual limits – that the unconscious is the deepest link between the global and the personal. The unconscious for Kristeva is a kind of proto-language (comprising libidinal desires, somatic dispositions, affects) which faces outward while always turned back on the self, toward the global and the personal simultaneously. There is a kind of rhythm to the unconscious – what Kristeva has previously termed "the semiotic" – which organizes the astonishing blend of personal and global transformations occurring all around us. Prose and poetry are symbolic forms that Kristeva has psychoanalytically deconstructed to try to capture something of the repressed unconscious, or semiotic realm, that remains truly inexpressible. She finds in acts of artistic expression that press language to its limits – that is, in the ruins of the symbolic – a zone, by definition incommunicable, in which desire bursts forth. Something of the same can be said for various new political forces that shape globalization, from discourses of cosmopolitanization to resurgent nationalism.

A related issue in contemporary cultural debate concerns the impact of globalizing social forces upon the complex array of mournful, melancholic, and mimetic aspects of subjectivity. In theoretical terms, this was an issue first noted by Freud in his studies of narcissism. In his essay of 1915, "Mourning and Melancholia," Freud reconstructed the connections between love and loss on the one hand, and the limits of identification and identity on the other. The loss of a loved person, he argued, brings with it ambivalence and aggression. Distinguishing between "normal mourning" and the "complex of melancholia," Freud considered mourning a normal response to the loss of a loved person. In "normal mourning," the self incorporates aspects of the other person and then gradually detaches itself from the lost love. By acknowledging the pain of absence, the mourner emotionally draws from the lost love; he or she borrows, as it were, personality traits and feelings associated with the loved person, and in so doing is able to work through these feelings of loss. In the "complex of melancholia," the individual fails to break from the lost love, keeping hold of the object through identification. Unable to mourn, the melancholic cannot express love and hate directly toward the lost love, and instead denigrates its own ego. Whereas the mourner gradually accepts that the lost love no longer exists, the melancholic engages in denial in order to protect the self from loss.

A good deal of the psychoanalytic debate on mourning and melancholia has been excessively pre-occupied with the "internal states" of subjectivity, as if desire or passion is, magically, self-contained and cut-off from communication with the surrounding world. But there have been some wider cultural studies of the traffic between psychic mourning and social meanings, and the recent contributions of American feminist Judith Butler, whose text from her widely read book *Precarious Life: The Powers of Mourning and Violence* is selected here, are of singular importance in this connection. In the wake of such global violence as 9/11 and the wars in Afghanistan and Iraq, Butler deploys psychoanalytic notions of mourning and melancholia to rethink the relations between identities, communities, and otherness. Theory of this kind becomes directly political when, as with Butler, psychoanalytic notions of mourning and grief are deployed to critically interrogate the global spread of militarization, practices of extreme incarceration (such as Guantanamo Bay) as well as the erosion of human rights under new extra-legal modalities of "states of exception." Globalism, in Butler's hands, is intricately interwoven with violence and vulnerability, and the urgent political task is for social theory to explore what an ethic of non-violence would look like in terms of global relations of power. Such an ethics would radically alter our current politics of globalization almost beyond recognition.

Jean-Luc Nancy, in the selection from his *Creation of the World*, or *Globalization*, reminds us that the "out there" of globalization and the "in here" of personal life are, among the dimensions of human living, uniquely unsettled. Instead of assemblage, he writes of the global future as an agglomeration – thus to suggest the ever more bitter aspect of the world's condition. Agglomerations, he says, stack events upon events, people on people, to the point of squeezing out the civil orders once offered by cities and states, proliferating with "what bears the quite simple and unmerciful name of misery."

"Thanks to computers and the advances of bio-technology, the life sciences are able to threaten the species . . . by the control of the sources of life, the origin of the individual." This image of the global future, from Paul Virilio's *The Information Bomb*, selected here, is disturbing, but as theories of the global future go it is anything but crazy or even out of line.

Virilio is far from alone in thinking that the global future will be composed by technosciences which, in the modern gaze, seemed to promise so much for humankind. But, the argument continues, the promises will be paid out at a cost to the survival of human life *as we have known it.* Subjunctively speak, we tend to believe that sciences and technologies will serve, not supplant, human life. Yet, pluperfectly speaking, the Human was an idea bound tightly to the modern past, an idea beholden to the power of the individual to think, act, govern, invent, and make the world better. The condition under which the modern theory of the Human suffered was the restriction of its ability to account for its role in life itself. The idea of the Human in liberal cultures – as in mankind, humanism, the rights of Man, and so forth – was never seriously about life as such. It was, in a word, not just extra-biological it was *anti*-biological. Man was the One, the master of history, who by his (so to speak) capacity for self-conscious individualism, was (still is, for the most part, culturally speaking) not really an animal (though some of the alleged species have been know to exhibit the properties of certain sluggish vegetables). Animals for the most part defecate and fornicate in public. They harvest or slaughter their food sources with keen, if passive, regard for their scarcities. They live for longer or shorter whiles, then die quietly with a sad knowing stare of acceptance in their eyes. Modern humans trained in the arts of self-consciousness may admit that, in the end, they are animals with all the responsibilities and limitations appertaining thereto. Yet, if well trained as they have been in the modern era, they will defecate and fornicate in private, kill and harvest with scant regard for the food sources of their progeny, and they are known to suffer mightily when confronted with pending death.

Technosciences, including the bio-technologies Virilio refers to, are thus dimly understood by humans who, lacking very much native consciousness of their relations to life itself, assume that if a technoscience can make the infertile fertile, the genetically doomed aware of their life chances, the starving sated by engineered crops and desalinated water, and so forth, then all this must be good. Virilio, among others, is seriously skeptical as to the prospect that the superficial benefits of information technologies and the miracles they make possible are to the good. This kind of liberal innocence forms, as we have seen, one very powerful element in the globalization debates – the idea that information technologies are nothing but good, even to the extent of promising a global unity of all men. By contrast, Virilio sees them as information, even biological, bombs that are in fact weapons threatening life as we knew it. Is this right-wing cookery? Not so much if you consider how slow we humanoids have been to appreciate global warming, how short the supply of available food sources, how little we know about cancers and other perturbations of our biological systems, how little troubled we are (even after the appalling twentieth century) by the epidemic of deadly violence done in the name of human identity.

No one has done more than Giorgio Agamben to probe the historical origins of the threat the living pose to life itself. Since the mid-1990s, Agamben has been advancing our understanding of politics of life and death (an idea first introduced by Michel Foucault in the 1970s). Agamben's contribution to what Foucault called biopolitics is conveyed in his most famous concept, *naked life* (in some places also translated as "bare life"). At the core of his thinking is the idea that the modern state, the protector of the rights of citizens, has in fact proven to be a death machine. Drawing upon earlier discussions of the sovereign, Agamben develops a philosophical view that is well-grounded in the history of the modern state – that it alone reserves unto itself the right to declare exceptions to its own high-minded laws and particularly those governing the right to kill or let die even those over whom it exercises political responsibility.

Naked life, thus, is the condition of all those subjected to the modern Sovereign and, here again, Weber's question arises. Prior to the modern era, it would not be shocking that a sovereign – whether lord, prince, despot, or slave-holder – would kill those subject to his authority. Subjects obeyed, then, because not to obey was to put their lives at risk. The claim of modern democratic politics was that this sort of ruthlessness was at an end because the modern state was the authority defined by the legitimate right to govern, a right that dwelled in the will of the people. In fact, Agamben explains, even those subject to the modern state (including those with legitimate citizenship claims) suffer the risk and reality of naked life. Naked life, thus, is a political consequence of the historical fact that the rights of modern political authority were illusory – illusions derived from the magical thinking that believed, all too subjunctively, that free individuals were the agents of the people and thus their own authority. The reality – and Agamben is quite specific on this – is that the major modern states of all nations have always declared exceptions to whatever laws governing individual rights there may have been – none more horribly that Hitler who assumed power by democratic measures and suspended the rights to life of Jews by legal decree; hence Agamben's view that the death camps are the paradigm of the modern.

Agamben, thus, is among those who see the precarious balance between life and death as the original, actual condition of the so-called rights of Man which, by implication were rights that artificially distinguished man from his animal circumstances. If so, then what is to be done politically may be the central question of the global future. And that future is one, he states, in which the form of life is a "life in which it is never possible to isolate something such as naked life." It is, thus, a life that flies in the face of the allegedly humane state that abandons "naked life to 'Man' and to the 'Citizen,' who clothe it temporarily and represent it with their 'rights.'" This is Agamben's idea of "the coming politics" – clearly a politics deeply skeptical of liberal ideologies and one that attends (as Foucault had earlier insisted we should) to the politics of life and death in which the sheer nakedness of human life locates it closer to the bare life of death camps than to the glorious utopias of a civil society.

Manuel DeLanda, an architect among many other talents, is one of the first to attempt to outline a systematic assemblage theory. Like others, Urry and Wallerstein included, he draws heavily on complexity theory (though with a decidedly more direct dependence on Deleuze). DeLanda's writings, selected here from *A New Philosophy of Society* (his not entirely successful outline of a global sociology and social theory), are particularly apt to the concluding sections of this book because he so eloquently interprets global structural flaws as at the interior of the modern world system from, at least, the long sixteenth century. DeLanda does not engage the globalization debate in so many words. What he does is to begin to work through the thinking necessary to the global future – a future in which, again, deterritorialized human assemblages replace not just the centering nation-state but all prior spatial and social forms for building coherent global empires, commonly centered in a focal city such as Rome, Constantinople, or London. DeLanda diagnoses very well the fate of late modern empires: "Territorial states born from the collapse of a previous empire or from the break-up of former colonial possessions can find themselves with unstable frontiers cutting across areas heterogeneous in language, ethnicity, or religion." What Westphalia sought to overcome comes back to haunt in terms very close to Pheng Cheah's idea that the remains of the capital system continue to be haunted by the failed post-colonial states they created.

There is a risk taken when one reads works that refer to heterogeneity or fragmentation as structural features of the near and present future. For one, the words can be (and have been) sneered at as foolish fads by those with a stake in the old order. More seriously, the problem is the one we have referred to earlier: since most who engage in the science of social histories are by training and disposition wedded to the modern cultural categories – the ever-present challenge is how to think that which is, in effect, unthinkable, that which, in other words, is outside the normal terms of conceptual discipline. This is the foremost methodological problem of global futures. The final two selections in the book are exemplars of just how it might be possible to meet this challenge.

Achille Mbembe, for one, puts forward the stunningly counterintuitive theme of *necropolitics* – meaning in effect that the politics of the present future are the politics of death. "My concern is with the figures of sovereignty whose central project is not the struggle for autonomy but *the generalized instrumentalization of human existence and the material destruction of human bodies and populations*." It is easy enough to detect in the selection echoes of all of the texts we have collected here to represent new theories of global futures. What distinguishes Mbembe's now famous essay is, however, that, as it develops beyond the selection, necropolitics are interpreted quite specifically as neither an accidental distortion of the modern state nor as a local historical entailment of Euro-American nation-states. Rather necropolitics are the politics of the whole – the agglomerated in assemblages and the movers and shakes of the whole of the modern global enterprise: "The historical self-creation of humankind is itself a life-and-death conflict, that is, a conflict over what paths should lead to the truth of history: the overcoming of capitalism and the commodity form and the contradictions associated with both." One might suppose, even in scanning a line like this, that here again we have a dusting off of familiar radical thought. Yet, looking closer, it is possible to see not only a stark turn in the argument – one that is related to others we have presented here, but also one that raises the ante in a significant way. The moral failure of the modern State and its entailments (including civil society) is historical in its effect, but it represents just as much a historical *mis*understanding of life itself. Life, he says, referring to George Bataille, "*is* the domain of sovereignty ... death is therefore the very principle of excess." Death is, thus, a luxury which is to say that the politics of the global future (our term, not his) are vastly beyond biopolitics. Life and death are on unspeakably, even erotically, intimate terms.

Mbembe agrees with Agamben on naked life, with Pheng Cheah on the ghosts of the colonial system, with Deleuze and DeLanda on disjointed assemblages; but he goes beyond them by identifying the primacy of death. This is, from the modern point of view, a tragic pessimism, but from Mbembe's it is neither optimism nor pessimism. It is the way life is – above all his native Cameroon, which (not entirely by coincidence) is the subject of the final selection in the book. Africa, more perhaps than any other continent on the face of the globe, points to the global future – its most miserable degradations, but also its most unexpected possibilities.

AbdouMaliq Simone, in the concluding selection, writes with gripping honesty of his first-hand experiences in, among other African cities, Douala, Cameroon. It is, we think, entirely proper to end with a story – one that asks the reader to think differently about urban assemblages as sites of naked life, but also as places where a remarkable creativity is at work both in resistance to the prevailing powers and as a sign of political work and, even, community building that, to the naked modern eye, is invisible. Reading Simone, one cannot be sure what exactly is going on in Douala or, for that matter, other of the global assemblages he has studied and of which he has written elsewhere. Nor can we know with certainty what this future will bring. But one thing is certain: whatever the global future is becoming, we shall not know much at all if we are not willing to look, even without the glasses we may need, to the invisible stirrings the ear cannot hear nor the eye see.

Note

1   Don DeLillo (1998) *Underworld: A Novel*, New York: Scribner, p. 786.

NOMADOLOGY: GILLES DELEUZE AND FELIX GUATTARI (1986)

Gilles Deleuze (1925–1995) and Felix Guattari (1930–1995) were joint authors of two books that today are prominently considered among the most important, if inscrutable, texts to come down from the intellectual ferment of the 1970s in Paris. One was *Anti-Oedipus* (1972). The second, from which the selection is taken, was *Thousand Plateaus* (1980). Together the two books might be said to be radical rethinkings of Marxist and Freudian ideas. In fact, as they endure into our day, they are also profound challenges to modern intellectual assumptions and experiments (if the word applies) that yield deeply challenging prospects for reconsidering how one rethinks thought itself through a definitively fresh global perspective.

The War Machine

The nomad has a territory, he follows customary paths, he goes from one point to another, he is not ignorant of points (water points, dwelling points, assembly points, etc.). But the question is what in nomad life is a principle and what is only a consequence. To begin with, although the points determine paths, they are strictly subordinated to the paths they determine, the reverse of what happens with the sedentary. The water point is reached only in order to be left behind, every point is a relay and exists only as a relay. A path is always between two points, but the in-between has taken on all the consistency, and enjoys both an autonomy and a direction of its own. The life of the nomad is the intermezzo. Even the elements of his dwelling are conceived in terms of the trajectory that is forever mobilizing them. The nomad is not at all the same as the migrant; for the migrant goes principally from one point to another, even if the second point is uncertain, unforseen or not well localized. But the nomad only goes from point to point as a consequence and as a factual necessity: in principle, points for him are relays along a trajectory. Nomads and migrants can mix in many ways, or form a common aggregate; their causes and conditions are no less distinct for that (for example, those who joined Mohammed at Medina had a choice between a nomadic or bedouin pledge, and pledge of hegira or emigration).

Secondly, even though the nomadic trajectory may follow trails or customary routes, it does not fulfill the function of the sedentary road, which is to *parcel out a closed space to people*, assigning each person a share and regulating the communication between shares. The nomadic trajectory does the opposite, it *distributes people (or animals) in an open space*, one that is indefinite and noncommunicating. The *nomos* came to designate the law, but that was originally because it was distribution, a mode of distribution. It is a very special kind of distribution, one without division into shares, in a space without borders or enclosure. The *nomos* is the consistency of a fuzzy aggregate: it is in this sense that it stands in opposition to the law or the *polis*, as the backcountry, a mountainside or the vague expanse around a city ("either nomos or polis"). There is therefore, and this is the third point, a significant difference between the spaces: sedentary space is striated, by walls, enclosures and roads between enclosures, while nomad space is smooth, marked only by "traits" that are effaced and displaced with the trajectory. Even the lamella of the desert slide over each other, producing an inimitable sound. The nomad distributes himself in a smooth space, he occupies, inhabits, holds that space; that is his territorial principle. It is therefore false to define the nomad by movement. Toynbee is profoundly right to suggest that the nomad is on the contrary *he who does not move*. Whereas the migrant leaves behind a milieu that has become amorphous or hostile, the nomad is one who does not depart, does not want to depart, who clings to the smooth space left by the receding forest, where the steppe or the desert advance, and who invents nomadism as a response to this challenge. Of course, the nomad moves, but while seated, and he is only seated while moving (the Bedouin galloping, knees on the saddle, sitting on the soles of his upturned feet, "a feat of balance"). The nomad knows how to wait, he has infinite patience. Immobility and speed, catatonia and rush, a "stationary process," station as process – these traits of Kleist's are eminently those of the nomad. It is thus necessary to make a distinction between *speed* and *movement*: a movement may be very fast, but that does not give it speed; a speed may be very slow, or even immobile, yet it is still speed. Movement is extensive, speed is intensive. Movement designates the relative character of a body considered as "one," and which goes from point to point; *speed, on the contrary, constitutes the absolute character of a body whose irreducible parts (atoms) occupy or fill a smooth space in the manner of a vortex*, with the possibility of springing up at any point. (It is therefore not surprising that reference has been made to spiritual voyages effected without relative movement, but in intensity, in one place: these are part of nomadism.) In short, we will say by convention that only the nomad has absolute movement, in other words speed; vortical or swirling movement is an essential feature of his war machine.

It is in this sense that the nomad has no points, paths or land, even though he does by all appearances. If the nomad can be called the Deterritorialized *par excellence*, it is precisely because there is no reterritorialization *afterwards* as with the migrant, or upon *something else* as with the sedentary (the sedentary's relation with the earth is mediatized by something else, a property regime, a State apparatus . . .). With the nomad, on the contrary, it is deterritorialization that constitutes the relation to the earth, to such a degree that the nomad reterritorializes on deterritorialization itself. It is the earth that deterritorializes itself, in a way that provides the nomad with a territory. The land ceases to be land, tending to become simply ground *(sol)* or support. The earth does not become deterritorialized in its global and relative movement, but at specific locations, at the spot where the forest recedes, or where the steppe and the desert advance. Hubac is right to say that nomadism is explainable less by universal changes in climate (which relate instead to migrations) as by the "divagation of local climates." The nomad is there, on the land, wherever there forms a smooth space that gnaws, and tends to grow, in all directions. The nomad inhabits these places, he remains in them, and he himself makes them grow, for it has been established that the nomad makes the desert no less than he is made by it. He is a vector of deterritorialization. He adds desert to desert, steppe to steppe, by a series of local operations the orientation and direction of which endlessly vary. The sand desert does not only have oases, which are like fixed points, but also rhizomatic vegetation that is temporary and shifts location according to local rains, bringing changes in the direction of the crossings. The same terms are used to describe ice deserts as sand deserts: there is no line separating earth and sky; there is no intermediate distance, no perspective or contour, visibility is limited; and yet there is an extraordinarily fine topology that does not rely on points or objects, but on haecceities, on sets of relations (winds, undulations of snow or sand, the song of the sand or the creaking of ice, the tactile qualities of both); it is a tactile space, or rather "haptic," a sonorous much more than a visual space . . . The variability, the polyvocity of directions, is an essential feature of smooth spaces of the rhizome type, and it alters their cartography.

The nomad, nomad space, is localized and not de-limited. What is both limited and limiting is striated space, the *relative global*: it is limited in its parts, which are assigned constant directions, are oriented in relation to one another, divisible by boundaries, and can be fit together; what is limiting (*limes* or wall, and no longer boundary), is this composite in relation to the smooth spaces it "contains," the growth of which it slows or prevents, and which it restricts or places outside. Even when the nomad sustains its effects, he does not belong to this relative global, where one passes from one point to another, from one region to another. Rather, he is in a *local absolute*, an absolute that is manifested locally, and engendered in a series of local operations of varying orientations: desert, steppe, ice, sea.

Gilles Deleuze and Felix Guattari (1986) *Nomadology: The War Machine*, New York: Semiotext(e), pp. 50–54.

EMPIRE: MICHAEL HARDT AND ANTONIO NEGRI (2000)

Michael Hardt (1960–) and Antonio Negri (1933–) are the authors, most famously, of *Empire* (2000) a wildly popular book among readers seeking fresh understanding of the qualities of empire that seem at once to be consistent with Marxist ideas as with global informatics and culture. *Empire* is praised by many for its daring reinvention of the terms of political debate in a global era and scorned by others who find it a somewhat fanciful adventure that plays loose with evidence and the sources cited. Either way, Antonio Negri is one of Italy's and Europe's best-known Marxists and political philosophers whose many writings, over decades, are made all the more acute for their having been written, in many instances, from prison. Hardt, an American literary and social theorist, is the younger of the two but brilliant in his own way. The selection represents the core claims made in *Empire*.

The Return of Empire

Empire is materializing before our very eyes. Over the past several decades, as colonial regimes were overthrown and then precipitously after the Soviet barriers to the capitalist world market finally collapsed, we have witnessed an irresistible and irreversible globalization of economic and cultural exchanges. Along with the global market and global circuits of production has emerged a global order, a new logic and structure of rule – in short, a new form of sovereignty. Empire is the political subject that effectively regulates these global exchanges, the sovereign power that governs the world.

Many argue that the globalization of capitalist production and exchange means that economic relations have become more autonomous from political controls, and consequently that political sovereignty has declined. Some celebrate this new era as the liberation of the capitalist economy from the restrictions and distortions that political forces have imposed on it; others lament it as the closing of the institutional channels through which workers and citizens can influence or contest the cold logic of capitalist profit. It is certainly true that, in step with the processes of globalization, the sovereignty of nation-states, while still effective, has progressively declined. The primary factors of production and exchange – money, technology, people, and goods – move with increasing ease across national boundaries; hence the nation-state has less and less power to regulate these flows and impose its authority over the economy. Even the most dominant nation-states should no longer be thought of as supreme and sovereign authorities, either outside or even within their own borders. *The decline in sovereignty of nation-states, however, does not mean that sovereignty as such has declined.*[1] Throughout the contemporary transformations, political controls, state functions, and regulatory mechanisms have continued to rule the realm of economic and social production and exchange. Our basic hypothesis is that sovereignty has taken a new form, composed of a series of national and supranational organisms united under a single logic of rule. This new global form of sovereignty is what we call Empire.

The declining sovereignty of nation-states and their increasing inability to regulate economic and cultural exchanges is in fact one of the primary symptoms of the coming of Empire. The sovereignty of the nation-state was the cornerstone of the imperialisms that European powers constructed throughout the modern era. By "Empire," however, we understand something altogether different from "imperialism." The boundaries defined by the modern system of nation-states were fundamental to European colonialism and economic expansion: the territorial boundaries of the nation delimited the center of power from which rule was exerted over external foreign territories through a system of channels and barriers that alternately facilitated and obstructed the flows of production and circulation. Imperialism was really an extension of the sovereignty of the European nation-states beyond their own boundaries. Eventually nearly all the world's territories could be parceled out and the entire world map could be coded in European colors: red for British territory, blue for French, green for Portuguese, and so forth. Wherever modern sovereignty took root, it constructed a Leviathan that overarched its social domain and imposed hierarchical territorial boundaries, both to police the purity of its own identity and to exclude all that was other.

The passage to Empire emerges from the twilight of modern sovereignty. In contrast to imperialism, Empire establishes no territorial center of power and does not rely on fixed boundaries or barriers. It is a *decentered* and *deterritorializing* apparatus of rule that progressively incorporates the entire global realm within its open, expanding frontiers. Empire manages hybrid identities, flexible hierarchies, and plural exchanges through modulating networks of command. The distinct national colors of the imperialist map of the world have merged and blended in the imperial global rainbow.

The transformation of the modern imperialist geography of the globe and the realization of the world market signal a passage within the capitalist mode of production. Most significant, the spatial divisions of the three Worlds (First, Second, and Third) have been scrambled so that we continually find the First World in the Third, the Third in the First, and the Second almost nowhere at all. Capital seems to be faced with a smooth world – or really, a world defined by new and complex regimes of differentiation and homogenization, deterritorialization and reterritorialization. The construction of the paths and limits of these new global flows has been accompanied by a transformation of the dominant productive processes themselves, with the result that the role of industrial factory labor has been reduced and priority given instead to communicative, cooperative, and affective labor. In the postmodernization of the global economy, the creation of wealth tends ever more toward what we will call biopolitical production, the production of social life itself, in which the economic, the political, and the cultural increasingly overlap and invest one another. [. . .]

We should emphasize that we use "Empire" here not as a *metaphor*, which would require demonstration of the resemblances between today's world order and the Empires of Rome, China, the Americas, and so forth, but rather as a *concept*, which calls primarily for a theoretical approach.[2] The concept of Empire is characterized fundamentally by a lack of boundaries: Empire's rule has no limits. First and foremost, then, the concept of Empire posits a regime that effectively encompasses the spatial totality, or really that rules over the entire "civilized" world. No territorial boundaries limit its reign. Second, the concept of Empire presents itself not as a historical regime originating in conquest, but rather as an order that effectively suspends history and thereby fixes the existing state of affairs for eternity. From the perspective of Empire, this is the way things will always be and the way they were always meant to be. In other words, Empire presents its rule not as a transitory moment in the movement of history, but as a regime with no temporal boundaries and in this sense outside of history or at the end of history. Third, the rule of Empire operates on all registers of the social order extending down to the depths of the social world. Empire not only manages a territory and a population but also creates the very world it inhabits. It not only regulates human interactions but also seeks directly to rule over human nature. The object of its rule is social life in its entirety, and thus Empire presents the paradigmatic form of biopower. Finally, although the practice of Empire is continually bathed in blood, the concept of Empire is always dedicated to peace – a perpetual and universal peace outside of history.

The Empire we are faced with wields enormous powers of oppression and destruction, but that fact should not make us nostalgic in any way for the old forms of domination. The passage to Empire and its processes of globalization offer new possibilities to the forces of liberation. Globalization, of course, is not one thing, and the multiple processes that we recognize as globalization are not unified or univocal. Our political task, we will argue, is not simply to resist these processes but to reorganize them and redirect them toward new ends. The creative forces of the multitude that sustain Empire are also capable of autonomously constructing a counter-Empire, an alternative political organization of global flows and exchanges. The struggles to contest and subvert Empire, as well as those to construct a real alternative, will thus take place on the imperial terrain itself – indeed, such new struggles have already begun to emerge. Through these struggles and many more like them, the multitude will have to invent new democratic forms and a new constituent power that will one day take us through and beyond Empire. [. . .]

More important, the forces that contest Empire and effectively prefigure an alternative global society are themselves not limited to any geographical region. The geography of these alternative powers, the new cartography, is still waiting to be written – or really, it is being written today through the resistances, struggles, and desires of the multitude. [. . .]

Empire is formed not on the basis of force itself but on the basis of the capacity to present force as being in the service of right and peace. All interventions of the imperial armies are solicited by one or more of the parties involved in an already existing conflict. Empire is not born of its own will but rather it is *called* into being and constituted on the basis of its capacity to resolve conflicts. Empire is formed and its intervention becomes juridically legitimate only when it is already inserted into the chain of international consensuses aimed at resolving existing conflicts. [. . .]

Imperial power can no longer resolve the conflict of social forces through mediatory schemata that displace the terms of conflict. The social conflicts that constitute the political confront one another directly, without mediations of any sort. This is the essential novelty of the imperial situation. Empire creates a greater potential for revolution than did the modern regimes of power because it presents us, alongside the machine of command, with an alternative: the set of all the exploited and the subjugated, a multitude that is directly opposed to Empire, with no mediation between them.

Notes

1 On the declining sovereignty of nation-states and the transformation of sovereignty in the contemporary global system, see Saskia Sassen, *Losing Control? Sovereignty in an Age of Globalization* (New York: Columbia University Press, 1996).

2 On the concept of Empire, see Maurice Duverger, "Le concept d'empire," in Maurice Duverger, ed., *Le concept d'empire* (Paris: PUF, 1980), pp. 5–23. Duverger divides the historical examples into two primary models, with the Roman Empire on one side and the Chinese, Arab, Mesoamerican, and other Empires on the other. Our analyses pertain primarily to the Roman side because this is the model that has animated the Euro-American tradition that has led to the contemporary world order.

Michael Hardt and Antonio Negri (2000) *Empire*, Cambridge, MA: Harvard University Press, pp. xi–xiii, xiv–xv, 15, 392.

GLOBAL ASSEMBLAGES: SASKIA SASSEN (2008)

Saskia Sassen (1949–) is Professor of Sociology at the London School of Economics and Columbia University. She is most well known for her work in urban sociology, in particular the way that global flows of capital and labor impact cities. Her book, *The Global City*, argues that certain cities have become important nodes, strategic places where global connections take place. This selection, about territory, rights, and assemblages, investigates further her notion of understanding how globalization happens in specific places and the institutional and economic means by which people are centralized or marginalized. In particular, her focus is on transnationalism, and how previously disadvantaged people fare in the global economic marketplace. Assemblages offers a new political possibility for those disadvantaged as even the disadvantaged are aggregated into global networks.

Neither Global Nor National[1]

A key yet much overlooked feature of the current period is the multiplication of a broad range of partial, often highly specialized, global assemblages of bits of territory, authority, and rights (TAR) that begin to escape the grip of national institutional frames.[2] These assemblages cut across the binary of national versus global. They continue to inhabit national institutional and territorial settings but are no longer part of the national as historically constructed. They exit the national through a process of denationalization that may or may not lead to the formation of global arrangements.

These assemblages are enormously diverse. At one end we find private, often very narrow, frameworks such as the *lex constructionis*, a private 'law' developed by the major engineering companies in the world to establish a common mode of dealing with the strengthening of environmental standards in a growing number of countries, in most of which these firms are building.[3] At the other end of the range they include far more complex (and experimental) entities, such as the first ever global public court, the International Criminal Court; this court is not part of the established supranational system and has universal jurisdiction among signatory countries.[4] Beyond the fact of the diversity of these assemblages, there is the increasingly weighty fact of their numbers – over 125 according to the best recent count.[5] Their proliferation does not represent the end of national states, but it does begin to disassemble the national. [. . .]

One of the consequences of the sharpening differentiation among domains once suffused with the national, or the supranational, is that this can enable a proliferation of temporal and spatial framings and a proliferation of normative orders where once the dominant logic was toward producing unitary spatial, temporal, and normative framings. A synthesizing image we might use to capture these dynamics is that we see a movement from centripetal nation-state articulation to a centrifugal multiplication of specialized assemblages. This multiplication in turn can lead to a sort of simplification of normative structures: these assemblages are partial and often highly specialized formations centered in particular utilities and purposes. The valence of these particular utilities and purposes can range from the search for justice (the ICC) to narrow self-interest (Lex constructionis).

What distinguishes these novel assemblages is that they can de-border, and even exit, what are today still ruling normative orders. Further, and equally important if not more so, they can constitute particularized 'normative' orders internal to each assemblage which easily amount to mere utility logics. These assemblages are not only highly specialized or particular, they are also without much internal differentiation, thereby further reducing normative orders to somewhat elementary utilities. This is still a minor process in the larger scale of our geopolity. But it may well be the beginning of a multi-sited disruption of its existing formal architecture. It is a process that lifts a variety of segments (involving dimensions of TAR) out of their nation-state normative framing, thereby reshuffling their constitutional alignments. Not even well-functioning states with their powerful raison d'etat can quite counteract the particularized normativities of each of these assemblages, and their easy slide into narrower utilitarian logics.

This slide into utilitarian logics is not always bad. In the case of a single-minded pursuit of human rights, we can see many positive outcomes. But a similarly single-minded pursuit of profits and disregard of state welfare functions is troubling. There is, then, multivalence in this process of multiplying lower-order normative framings. But whether good or bad, the de-bordering of national normative frames is a change, and it carries implications for how we are to handle the often complex interactions of larger normative issues.

My argument is then that these developments signal the emergence of new types of orderings that can coexist with older orderings, such as the nation-state and the interstate system, but nonetheless bring consequences that may well be strategic for larger normative questions. These developments are both strategic and particular, and hence often illegible, requiring diverse modes of decoding.

Emphasizing this multiplication of partial assemblages contrasts with much of the globalization literature. That literature has tended to assume the binary of the global versus the national, and hence to focus on the powerful global institutions that have played a critical role in implementing the global corporate economy and have reduced the power of 'the state'. I rather emphasize that the global can also be constituted inside the national, i.e. the global city, and that particular components of the state have actually gained power because they have to do the work of implementing policies necessary for a global corporate economy. [. . .]

Specialized assemblages as new types of territoriality

[. . .] A first type of territoriality is being constituted through the development of new jurisdictional geographies. Legal frameworks for rights and guarantees, and more generally the rule of law, were largely developed in the context of the formation of national states. But now some of these instruments are strengthening a non-national organizing logic. As they become part of new types of transnational systems they alter the valence of older national state capabilities. Further, in so doing, they are often pushing these national states to go against the interests of national capital. A second type of instance is the formation of triangular cross-border jurisdictions for political action, which once would have been confined to the national. Electronic activists often use global campaigns and international organizations to secure rights and guarantees from their national states. Furthermore, a variety of national legal actions involving multiple geographic sites across the globe can today be launched from national courts, producing a transnational geography for national lawsuits.

The critical articulation is between the national (as in national court, national law) and a global geography outside the terms of traditional international law or treaty law. A good example is the lawsuit launched by the Washington-based Center for Constitutional Rights in a national court against nine multinational corporations, both American and foreign, for abuses of workers' rights in their offshore industrial operations, using as the national legal instrument the Alien Torts Claims Act. In other words, this is a global three-sited jurisdiction, with several locations in at least two of those sites – the locations of the headquarters (both the US and other countries), the locations of the offshore factories (several countries), and the court in Washington. Even if these lawsuits do not quite achieve their full goal, they signal it is possible to use the national judiciary for suing US and foreign firms for questionable practices in their operations outside their home countries. Thus, besides the much noted new courts and instruments (e.g. the new International Criminal Court, the European Court of Human Rights), what this example shows is that components of the national rule of law that once served to build the strength of the national state, are today contributing to the formation of transnational jurisdictions. Another instance is the US practice of 'exporting' prisoners to third countries (rendition), *de facto* to facilitate their torture. This is yet another instance of a territoriality that is both national and transnational. Finally, diverse jurisdictional geographies can also be used to manipulate temporal dimensions. Reinserting a conflict in the national legal system may ensure a slower progression than in the private jurisdiction of international commercial arbitration.[6] Diverse jurisdictional geographies can also be used to manipulate temporal dimensions. Reinserting a conflict in the national legal system may ensure a slower progression than in the private jurisdiction of international commercial arbitration.

A second type of specialized assemblage that is contributing to a novel type of territoriality is the work of national states across the globe to construct a standardized global space for the operations of firms and markets. What this means is that components of legal frameworks for rights and guarantees, and more generally the rule of law, largely developed in the process of national state formation, can now strengthen non-national organizing logics. As these components become part of new types of transnational systems they alter the valence of (rather than destroy, as is often argued) older national state capabilities. Where the rule of law once built the strength of the national state and national corporations, key components of that rule of law are now contributing to the partial, often highly specialized, denationalizing of particular national state orders. For instance, corporate actors operating globally have pushed hard for the development of new types of formal instruments, notably intellectual property rights and standardized accounting principles. But they need not only the support, but also the actual work of each individual state where they operate to develop and implement such instruments in the specific context of each country. In their aggregate this and other emergent orderings contribute to produce an operational space partly embedded in particular components of national legal systems which have been subjected to specialized denationalizations;[7] thereby these orderings become capabilities of an organizing logic that is not quite part of the national state even as that logic installs itself in that state. Further, in so doing, they often go against the interests of national capital. This is a very different way of representing economic globalization than the common notion of the withdrawal of the state at the hands of the global system. Indeed, to a large extent it is the executive branch of government that is getting aligned with global corporate capital and ensuring this work gets done.

A third type of specialized assemblage can be detected in the formation of a global network of financial centers. We can conceive of financial centers that are part of global financial markets as constituting a distinct kind of territoriality, simultaneously pulled in by the larger electronic networks and functioning as localized micro-infrastructures for those networks. These financial centers inhabit national territories, but they cannot be seen as simply national in the historical sense of the term, nor can they be reduced to the administrative unit encompassing the actual terrain (e.g. a city), one that is part of a nation-state. In their aggregate they house significant components of the global, partly electronic market for capital. As localities they are denationalized in specific and partial ways. In this sense they can be seen as constituting the elements of a novel type of multi-sited territoriality, one that diverges sharply from the territoriality of the historic nation-state.

A fourth type of assemblage can be found in the global networks of local activists and, more generally, in the concrete and often place-specific social infrastructure of 'global civil society'.[8] Global civil society is enabled by global digital networks and the associated imaginaries. But this does not preclude that localized actors, organizations, and causes are key building blocks of global civil society as it is shaping up today. The localized involvements of activists are critical no matter how universal and planetary the aims of the various struggles – in their aggregate these localized involvements are constitutive. Global electronic networks actually push the possibility of this local–global dynamic further. Elsewhere I have examined[9] the possibility for even resource-poor and *immobile* individuals or organizations to become part of a type of horizontal globality centered on diverse localities. When supplied with the key capabilities of the new technologies – decentralized access, interconnectivity, and simultaneity of transactions – localized, immobilized individuals and organizations can be part of a global public space, one that is partly a subjective condition, but only partly because it is rooted in the concrete struggles of localities.

In principle, we can posit that those who are immobile might be more likely to experience their globality through this (abstract) space than individuals and organizations that have the resources and the options to travel across the globe. These globalities can assume complex forms, as is the case with first-nation people demanding direct representation in international fora, bypassing national state authority, a longstanding cause that has been significantly enabled by global electronic networking. They can also be more indirect, as is the case with the Forest Watch network which uses indigenous residents in rain forests around the world who can detect forest abuse long before it becomes visible to the average observer. They then pass on this information to what are often long chains of activists eventually ending in the central office; the early links in the chain, where the deep knowledge resides, are typically not via digital media nor are they in English.

We can see here at work a particular type of interaction between placeless digital networks and deeply localized actors/users. One common pattern is the formation of triangular cross-border jurisdictions for political action which once would have been confined to the national. Local activists often use global campaigns and international organizations to secure rights and guarantees from their national states; they now have the option to incorporate a non-national or global site in their national struggles. These instances point to the emergence of a particular type of territoriality in the context of the imbrications of digital and non-digital conditions. This territoriality partly inhabits specific subnational spaces and partly gets constituted as a variety of somewhat specialized or partial global publics.

While the third and fourth types of territoriality might seem similar, they are actually not. The subnational spaces of these localized actors have not been denationalized as have the financial centers discussed earlier. The global publics that get constituted are barely institutionalized and mostly informal, unlike the global capital market, which is a highly institutionalized space both through national and international law, and through private governance systems. In their informality, however, these global publics can be seen as spaces for empowerment of the resource-poor or of not very powerful actors. In this sense the subjectivities that are emerging through these global publics constitute capabilities for new organizing logics.

These emergent assemblages begin to unbundle the traditional territoriality of the national, albeit in partial, often highly specialized ways. In cases where the global is rich in content or subject to multiple conditionalities, its insertion in an institutional world that has been historically constructed overwhelmingly as a national unitary spatio-temporal domain is eventful. It is the combination of this embeddedness of the global along with its specificity.

Although these four types of emergent territorialities are diverse, each containing multiple, often highly specialized and partial instances, all three evince specific features. First, they are not exclusively national or global but are assemblages of elements of each. Second, in this assembling they bring together what are often different spatio-temporal orders, that is, different velocities and different scopes. Third, this can produce an eventful engagement, including contestations and the frontier zone effect, a space that makes possible kinds of engagements for which there are no clear rules. The resolution of these encounters can become the occasion for playing out conflicts that cannot easily be engaged in other spaces. Fourth, novel types of actors can emerge in this assembling, often with the option to access domains once exclusive to older established actors, notably national states. Finally, in the juxtaposition of the different temporal orders that come together in these novel territorialities, existing capabilities can get redeployed to domains with novel organizing logics.

These emergent assemblages begin to unbundle the traditional territoriality of the national historically constructed overwhelmingly as a national unitary spatio-temporal domain.

Avoiding old binaries

A major methodological, theoretical and political implication of the type of analysis I am proposing is that it is insufficient to focus on the nation-state and the global system as two mutually exclusive and distinct entities. There are global formations that are indeed distinct and mutually exclusive with the nation-state, and I have studied these as well. But the transformations that concern me here criss-cross this binary, and enter the national and even the state apparatus itself. They may be a global conditions that gets endogenized into the nation-state or they may be endogenous to the nation-state but become denationalized in this process of change.

To historicize both the national and the global as constructed conditions, I have taken three transhistorical components present in almost all societies and examined how they became assembled into different historical formations. [. . .]

These three components are territory, authority, and rights (TAR). Each can assume specific contents, shapes, and interdependencies across diverse historical formations. The choice of these three rests partly on their foundational character and partly on the contingency of my fields of knowledge. One could choose additional components or replace one or another of these.

TAR are complex institutionalizations arising from specific processes, struggles, and competing interests. They are not simply attributes. They are interdependent, even as they maintain their specificity. Each can, thus, be identified. Specificity is partly conditioned by levels of formalization and institutionalization. Across time and space, TAR have been assembled into distinct formations within which they have had variable levels of performance. Further, the types of instruments and capabilities through which each gets constituted vary, as do the sites where each is in turn embedded – private or public, law or custom, metropolitan or colonial, national or supranational, and so on.

Using these three foundational components as analytic pathways into the two distinct formations that concern me in the larger project – the national and the global – helps avoid the endogeneity trap that so affects the globalization literature. Scholars have generally looked at these two complex formations *in toto*, and compared them to establish their differences. This is not where I start. Rather than comparing what are posited as two wholes – the national and the global – I disaggregate each into these three foundational components (TAR). They are my starting point. I dislodge them from their particular historically constructed encasements (in this case, the national and the global) and examine their constitution and institutional location in these different historical formations, and their possible shifting valence as the global grows. An example is the shift of what were once components of public authority into a growing array of forms of private authority. One thesis that arises out of this type of analysis is that particular national capabilities can be dislodged from their national institutional encasement and become constitutive of, rather than being destroyed or sidelined by, globalization.[10]

This type of approach produces an analytics that can be used by others to examine be it countries in the context of today's globalization, be it diverse or different types of assemblages across time and space.[11] In the modern state, TAR evolve into what we now can recognize as a centripetal scaling where one scale, the national, aggregates most of what there is to be had in terms of TAR. Although never absolutely, each of the three components is constituted overwhelmingly as a national domain and, further, exclusively so. Whereas in the past most territories were subject to multiple systems of rule, the modern state gains exclusive authority over a given territory and at the same time this territory is constructed as coterminous with that authority, in principle ensuring a similar dynamic in other nation-states. This in turn gives the sovereign the possibility of functioning as the exclusive grantor of rights. Territory is perhaps the most critical capability for the formation of the nation-state. But it is not for today's new type of global regulators, for whom authority is more critical than territory. Nor is it for the human rights regime, for which rights are more critical than territory.

Globalization can be seen as destabilizing the particular scalar assemblage represented by the nation-state. What scholars have noticed is the fact that the nation-state has lost some of its exclusive territorial authority to new global institutions.[12] What they have mostly failed to examine in depth are the specific, often specialized rearrangements inside the highly formalized and institutionalized national state apparatus aimed at instituting the authority of global institutions. This shift is not simply a question of policymaking – it is about making a novel type of institutional space inside the state. In overlooking such rearrangements, or interpreting them as simply national changes, it is also easy to overlook the extent to which critical components of the global are structured inside the national, producing what I refer to as a partial, and often highly specialized, denationalizing of what historically was constructed as national.

Thus today particular elements of TAR are becoming reassembled into novel global configurations. Therewith, their mutual interactions and interdependencies are altered as are their institutional encasements. These shifts take place both within the nation-state, for example, shifts from public to private, and through shifts to the inter- and supra-national and global levels. What was bundled up and experienced as a unitary condition (the national assemblage of TAR) now increasingly reveals itself to be a set of distinct elements, with variable capacities for becoming denationalized. For instance, we might say that particular components of authority and of rights are evincing a greater capacity to partial denationalization than territory; geographic boundaries have changed far less (except in cases such as the disintegration of the Soviet Union) than authority (i.e. the greater power of global regulators over national economies) and rights (the further institutionalizing of the international human rights regime). It points to possibly sharp divergence between the organizing logics of the earlier international and current global phases; these two phases are often seen as analogous to the current global phase, but I argue this understanding may be based on a confusion of analytical levels. In earlier periods that international logic was geared toward building national states, typically through imperial geographies. In today's phase, it is geared toward setting up global systems *inside* national states and national economies, and in that sense, at least partly denationalizing what had historically been constructed as national. This denationalizing can take multiple concrete forms. Two critical ones are global cities and specific policies and institutions within the state itself, including such different regimes as instituting human rights and instituting the rights of foreign firms. The Bretton Woods agreement, often seen as the beginning of the current global era, in my interpretation is not part of the current phase because it sought to protect national states from excessive fluctuations in the international economy.

The scholarship on the state and globalization contains three basic positions: one finds the state is victimized by globalization and loses significance; a second one finds that nothing much has changed and states basically keep on doing what they have always done; and a third, a variant on the second, finds that the state adapts and may even be transformed, thereby ensuring that it does not decline and remains the critical actor. There is research to support critical aspects of each one of these three positions, partly because much of their difference hinges on interpretation. For some, states remain as the key actors no matter how the context has changed, and hence not much has changed about states and the interstate system.[13] For others, even if states remain important there are today other key actors, and globalization has changed some important features of states and the interstate system.[14] But notwithstanding their diversity these scholarships tend to share the assumption that the national and the global are mutually exclusive.

A second line of argumentation concerns what has changed. Thus for Mann, the present era is merely a continuation of a long history of changes that have not altered the fundamental fact of state primacy.[15] Both the 'strong' and the 'weak' version of neo-Weberian state theory[16] share certain dimensions of this conceptualization of the state. While acknowledging that the primacy of the state may vary given different structural conditions between state and society, these authors tend to understand state power as basically denoting the same conditions throughout history: the ability successfully to implement explicitly formulated policies. A second type of literature[17] interprets deregulation and privatization as the incorporation by the state of its own shrinking role. In its most formalized version this position emphasizes the state's constitution-alization of its own diminished role. In this literature economic globalization is not confined to capital crossing geographic borders as is captured in measures of international investment and trade, but is in fact conceptualized as a politico-economic system. A third, growing literature emphasizes the relocation of national public governance functions to private actors both within national and global domains.[18] Key institutions of the supranational system, such as the World Trade Organization, are emblematic of this shift. Cutting across these types of literatures are the issues raised earlier as to whether states are declining, are remaining as strong as they have ever been, or, have changed but as part of an adaptation to the new conditions rather than a loss of power.

Given my effort to expand the analytic terrain within which to map the question of the global and the national, the larger research and theorization agenda needs to address aspects of globalization and the state which are lost in these dualized accounts about their relationship. In these accounts, the spheres of influence of, respectively, the national and the global are seen as mutually exclusive. While there are indeed many components of each the national and the global that are mutually exclusive, there is a growing, often specific set of components that does not fit in this dual structure.

Factoring in these types of conditions amounts to a fourth position alongside the three referred to above. While this fourth type of approach does not necessarily preclude all propositions in the other three, it is nonetheless markedly different in its foundational assumptions. For instance, in my own research I find that far from being mutually exclusive, the state is one of the strategic institutional domains where critical work for developing globalization takes place. This does not necessarily produce the decline of the state but neither does it keep the state going as usual, or produce merely adaptations to the new conditions. The state becomes the site for foundational transformations in the relation between the private and the public domains, in the state's internal balance of power, and in the larger field of both national and global forces within which the state now has to function.[19]

Notes

1 This is based on a larger project published as *Territory, Authority, Rights: From Medieval to Global Assemblages* (Princeton University Press 2006; new updated edition 2008), henceforth referred to as *Territory*. There readers can find full bibliographic elaboration of the issues raised here.

2 This is clearly an analysis that emerges from European history, with all the limitations that entails. Critical here is Gayatri Spivak's thinking about the diverse positions that can structure an 'author's stance. Donna Landry and Geral MacLean (Eds) (1996) *The Spivak Reader*. New York and London, Routledge.

3 See generally Teubner, Gunther (Ed.) (1997) *Global Law Without a State*. Aldershot, UK: Dartmouth Publishing.

4 See Sadat, Leila Nadya, and Richard Carden, S. (2000) The new international criminal court, *Georgetown Law Journal*, 88(3), 381–474.

5 See http://www.pict.org

6 *Territory*, Chapter 5.

7 *Territory*, Chapters 4 and 5.

8 This term remains underspecified in the view of many. But there is now a vast scholarship that has documented various features, measures and interpretations. See for instance, the Annual Global Civil Society volumes published by Oxford University Press.

9 *Territory*, Chapter 7.

10 In the larger project (*Territory*, Chapters 1, 8, and 9) there are lengthy discussion of method and interpretation. I propose a distinction between capabilities (for example, the rule of law) and the organizing logics (the national, the global) within which they are located. Thus capabilities are multivalent: as they switch organizing logics their valence changes. But they may look the same, and detecting their change may well require decoding.

11 I use the concept assemblage in its most descriptive sense. However, several scholars have developed theoretical constructs around this term. Most significant for the purposes of this book is the work of Deleuze and Guattari, for whom 'assemblage' is a contingent ensemble of practices and things that can be differentiated (that is, they are not collections of similar practices and things) and that can be aligned along the axes of territoriality and deterritorialization. More specifically, they posit that particular mixes of technical and administrative practices 'extract and give intelligibility to new spaces by decoding and encoding milieux'. Deleuze and Guattari (1987) *A Thousand Plateaux: Capitalism and Schizophrenia*. Minneapolis: University of Minnesota Press, 504–505. There are many more elaborations around the concept of assemblage, including not surprisingly, among architects and urbanists (vide the journal *Assemblages*). While I find many of these elaborations extremely important and illuminating, and while some of the assemblages I identify may evince some of these features, my usage is profoundly untheoretical compared to that of the above-cited authors. I simply want the dictionary term. I locate my theorization elsewhere, not on this term.

12 For a number of critical scholars, even if states remain important there are today other key actors, and globalization has changed some important features of states and the interstate system. Phillip G. Cerny (2000) 'Structuring the political arena: public goods, states and governance in a globalizing world', in Ronen Palan (Ed.) *Global Political Economy: Contemporary Theories*, 21–35. London: Routledge. Phillip G. Cerny (1990) *The Changing Architecture of Politics*. London and Newbury, CA: Sage. Ferguson, Y.H. and Barry Jones, R.J. (Eds) (2002) *Political Space. Frontiers of Change and Governace in a Globalizing World*. Albany, NH: SUNY Press; Susan Strange (1996) *The Retreat of the State*. Cambridge, Cambridge University Press; Cutler, A. Claire, Virginia Haufler and Tony Porter (Eds) *Private Authority and International Affairs*. Albany, NH: SUNY Press. For others more centered in canonical propositions, states remain as the key actors no matter how the context has changed, and hence not much has changed about states and the interstate system. Stephen Krasner (2003) 'Globalization and the state', in Edwards and Sisson (Eds) *Contemporary Debates in International Relations*. Ohio University Press; Eric Helleiner (1999) 'Sovereignty, territoriality and the globalization of finance', in Smith, D., Solinger, D. and Topic, S. (Eds) *States and Sovereignty in the Global Economy*. London: Routledge; Pauly (2002) 'Who governs the bankers', in Rodney Bruce Hall and Thomas J. Biersteker (Eds) *The Emergence of Private Authority in Global Governance*. Cambridge: Cambridge University Press, op. cit.

13 Krasner, 'Globalization and the State'; Pauly, 'Who Governs the Bankers'; Helleiner, 'Sovereignty, territoriality and the globalization of finance'.

14 For example, Cerny, 'Structure the Political Arena'; Cerny, *The Changing Architecture*; Strange 1996; Cutler *et al.* 1999; Ferguson and Jones, *Political Space*.

15 Michael Mann (1997) 'Has globalization ended the rise and rise of the nation state?', *Review of International Political Economy*, 4(3), 472–496.

16 Skocpol, Theda (1985) 'Bringing the state back in: strategies of analysis in current research', in: Peter Evans, Dietrich Rueschemeyer and Theda Skocpol (Eds) *Bringing the State Back In*. Cambridge and New York, Cambridge University Press. Evans, Peter (1997) 'The eclipse of the state? Reflections on stateness in an era of globalization,' *World Politics*, 50 (1), 62–87.

17 Panitch, Leo (1996) 'Rethinking the role of the state', in James Mittelman (Ed.) *Globalization: Critical Reflections*, 83–113. Boulder, CO: Lynne Rienner Publishers. Gill, S. (1996) 'Globalization, democratization, and the politics of indifference', in J. Mittelman *Globalization: Critical Reflections*, 205–228; Mittelman, James H. (2000) *The Globalization Syndrome: Transformation and Resistance*. Princeton: Princeton University Press.

18 For example, Hall and Biersteker (2002) and Cutler *et al.* (1999).

19 *Territory*, Chapters 4 and 5.

Saskia Sassen (2008) "Neither Global Nor National: Novel Assemblages of Territory, Authority and Rights," *Ethics and Global Politics*, vol. 1, no. 2, pp. 61–71.

GLOBAL COMPLEXITY: JOHN URRY (2003)

The British social theorist John Urry (1946–) is Distinguished Professor of Sociology at Lancaster University, UK. Widely celebrated for his elaboration of a "mobilities paradigm" in social science, Urry portrays today's global landscape as a complex of subjects, signs, power, money, risks, images, and information. How globalization reconstitutes individuals to live life "on the move" is the core question animating his books *Sociology Beyond Societies* (2000), *Global Complexity* (2003), and *Mobilities* (2007). In this text, Urry draws from "complexity theory" to argue against accounts of globalization as homogeneous or monolithic. Globally complex systems, he says, comprise numerous, diverse, and multiple processes, units, networks, velocities, and performances.

No Single Set of Effects

There is no global society or single centre of global power and hence no clear-cut global 'region'. There is also no unambiguous set of outcomes providing evidence of the power of 'global' processes. I thus argue against those who maintain that globalization produces a set of linear effects, such as the heightened homogenization of culture, or increased socio-economic inequalities, or the worldwide growth of democracies.

What is treated here as the 'global' produces no single set of effects, although it is bound up with all those processes just mentioned. The development of the attractor of glocalization entails a wholesale shifting in the very structure of economic, social and political relations across the globe. However, the evidence for this does not consist of a set of effects that can provide a direct 'test' or 'measurement' of the 'global'. Of course, there must be substantial programmes of research examining these sets of putatively 'global' relations.

According to Abbott (2001: ch.1), much social science assumes a 'linear reality' in which the social world consists of fixed entities with variable attributes, that these attributes have only one meaning, that the past sequencing of events is irrelevant and that context does not affect these attributes. He makes a general argument against such a position, but global processes and especially the global-local processes that construct and reconstruct the *relations* between the global and local further undermine the notion that there are or indeed could be clear and unambiguous fixed entities with variable properties whose history is irrelevant. Indeed the 'evidence' that relationships across the globe are being globalized is necessarily ambivalent, contradictory and contestable. If it is right to argue for a complexity formulation of the emerging system, then the research needs to reflect and capture uneven, far-from-equilibrium sets of interdependent processes involved in the very making of the global and especially of the glocalizing attractor (as Duffield (2001) argues for global governance).

Held et al. (1999: 17) do provide massive evidence of an extensivity of global networks and flows, an intensity of interconnectedness, a velocity of mobilities around the globe and the high impact of such interconnectedness. And these have powerful effects, especially of powerful local perturbations in the system that result in unpredictable branching emerging across the global system. Examples of these local perturbations include the demolition of the Berlin Wall, the invention of the first Web browser in the USA, the release from a South African prison of Nelson Mandela, and the presence of twenty bombers on four American planes on 11 September 2001.

But such emergent effects are often produced by 'small causes' and these get relayed through the diverse and overlapping global networks and fluids that interact physically, and especially informationally, under, over and across the earth's surface, stretching over hugely different temporal scales. These interactions are rich, non-linear and move towards the attractor of 'glocalization'. There is no simple empirical research here of unambiguous global or local entities. Rather, the processes are much more like 'gravity'. There is an increasingly powerful gravity effect upon numerous, diverse localized patterns. Such globally complex systems, especially developing from around 1990 and the desubstantiation of information, involve positive feedback loops that render the global far from equilibrium as many entities are drawn into the attractor relationships.

Further, this set of global systems is like no other social system. Its emergent features make it different from anything that has gone before. Paradoxically it does have some similarities with feudal Europe. Some have described the globalizing world as 'neo-feudal'. In the global world there are *multiple* political units beyond individual societies (see Walby 2001); there are *empires*, such as Coca-Cola, Microsoft or Disney, more powerful than societies (see Klein 2000); there are competing *city states*, such as London, Sydney or Los Angeles (see Roche 2000); and there are many *wandering intellectuals, sports stars, musicians and so on*, as well as international *vagrants*, with declining national attachments (see Urry 2002a). But there are also many differences between emergent global ordering and European feudalism, especially in terms of the technologies of the household and of warfare, production, circulation, distribution, and exchange, such that few useful lessons can be drawn from such a comparison.

Likewise the system of nation states seems to bear few resemblances to global systems. The former is organized through a nation state that 'governs' its citizens, there are clear boundaries and memberships, they possess a self-organizing character, and each derives a unity from opposition to each 'other'. There is a *system* of competing, self-organizing nation states that characterized the twentieth century (albeit with plenty of exceptions). Global systems, by contrast, are not governed by a central state, although there are very significant attempts by the corporate world to draw up various rules for global governance in their interests. Monbiot rather brilliantly describes the 'corporate bid for world domination' (2000: ch. 10).

Thus we are confronted with a global social laboratory but one within which we have almost no guides to appropriate investigation. Three things are sure. Developments towards the global are irreversible but unpredictable. The global possesses systemic characteristics that urgently demand investigation and are distinct from those of other social systems. And, since the global is like nothing else, the social sciences have to start more or less from scratch. Existing theories such as that of class domination will not work when converted onto the global level. Hence there are significant limitations of Sklair's hugely ambitious efforts (2001) to write class theories as global.

Complexity has thus been drawn on here, since it deals with odd and unpredictable systems often far from equilibrium and without a central 'governor'. Complexity we have seen emphasizes that no distinctions should be drawn between structure and process, stability and change, and a system and its environment (see Duffield's analogous formulation from security studies: 2001).

I have resisted defining 'globalization' as a single, clear and unambiguous 'causal' entity. Jessop similarly argues that globalization is 'best interpreted as the complex resultant of many different processes rather than as a distinctive causal process in its own right' (2000: 339). If we resist distinguishing between structure and process, stability and change, a system and its environment, then there is indeed no 'globalization' as a causal entity involved in 'contests' with various other regions. There are in more formal language no such entities with variable attributes (Abbott 2001). There are 'many different processes', but the key question is how they are organized within certain emergent irreversible global outcomes that move backwards and forwards between the more localized and more global levels. On such an account then globalization is a characterization of the system as 'effect' rather than as in any sense a 'cause', although I have noted the likely inappropriateness of such causal language (Rosenberg 2000). This leads me to thinking the global through the lens of performativity. I will now consider such a way of thinking the global.

First, the 'globe' is an object of concern for many citizens across many different countries. I noted above the remarkably widespread availability of *global* images, in TV programmes, branding by global corporations, adverts and especially political campaigns. Also countless oppositional organizations concerned with aspects of global governance have developed since the 1960s. There are also many more formal organizations, especially since the founding of the UN in 1948, that take the whole earth as an object of reflexive concern. The globe has become an object of widespread reflexivity stretching across the world in the face of what has been termed the 'world risk society' (Beck 1998). With such a development we can experience at least putatively the 'end of the other'. [. . .]

Furthermore, scientists (and other groups of professionals) are increasingly organized in a post-national manner. They are almost 'quasi-nations', with their own system of globally organized events, timetables and rewards (such as Nobel and other prizes). And, as modern electronic communications develop, so these quasi-nations become more important, widespread and drawn into the attractor of glocalization. Professionals indeed see the global village as replacing the nation state, as electronic communication supplants written communication and the 'whole earth' replaces the 'territory with borders'. There is a widespread sense of the increasing role that communities that cut across national boundaries play in the lives of ordinary people (Rotblat 1997b). Various authorities have talked of the growth of a 'transnational civil society as an arena for struggle' (Keck and Sikkink 1998: 33), as well as massively extensive and self-organizing 'ungrounded empires' like the overseas Chinese (Ong and Nonini 1997).

Some analysts also argue that women are more likely to be drawn to notions of global citizenship. Women appear to be more opposed to wars (on the Gulf War, see Shaw 1994: 127). They often find the maleness of symbols of national power particularly alienating (Yuval-Davis 1997). Survey evidence shows that they are particularly committed to conservation and environmental issues (Anderson 1997: 174). Thus women are more likely to convince others of the superiority of a relatively countryless notion of citizenship and indeed to advance a notion of universal rights under which specific women's rights, such as freedom from sexual violence, can be lodged (Shiva 1989; Kaplan 1996; Walby 2001).

So various social practices, of science, the media, international groupings, women and so on, which stem from the putative universalism of the globe as an object of reflexive concern, may begin to make or perform the global. *Global Nature, Global Culture* formulates a conception of the global as 'performance' (Franklin et al. 2000). Indeed, it uses various complexity notions: of ideas of catastrophe, chaos and fractals, of how global culture is partially self-organizing, of the open character of the global system, of the importance of iteration and of the generally disruptive effects of specific informational flows. There is a strong recognition of the complex, non-linear and temporally irreversible character of global processes.

The authors draw especially on Butler's claim that performativity 'must be understood not as a singular or deliberative "act", but rather, as the reiterative and citational practice by which discourse produces the effects that it names' (1993: 2). Butler brings out the crucial importance of iteration for performance. Structures are never fixed or given for good. They always have to be worked at over time. And naming something (such as the global) is itself partly to call that which is named into being. Franklin, Lury and Stacey argue that the global is 'performed' by itself and is not caused by something outside itself, not does it cause effects external to it. The global is seen as auto-enabled or auto-reproduced, although they do not use the term 'autopoeisis' from complexity . . . . Thus they examine how the global is being brought into being as an emergent effect, as it comes to constitute its own domain especially through various materialsemiotic practices (Franklin et al. 2000: 5). The global is shown to be 'performed, imagined and practised' across numerous domains that are operating at enormously different scales or levels.

The authors also describe how the global 'enters' the self through what they portray as the 'intimate global'. Because of the shift from 'kind' to 'brand', they describe how nature is being drawn into the attractor of globalization. Nature gets commodified, technologized, reanimated and rebranded. And many material-semiotic practices – from the economic, to politics, to medical science, to theme parks, to computer technology – are involved in the global remaking of culture and nature and especially the increasing fusion of the two.

Does this therefore mean that we should conceive of the global system as autopoietic? Is the global system self-making? Maturana writes how autopoietic systems 'are defined as networks of productions of components that recursively, through their interactions, generate and realize the network that produces them and constitute, in the space in which they exist, the boundaries of the network as components that participate in the realization of the network' (1981: 21). Such a system is thus not a set of relations between static components with fixed attributes. Rather there are processes of self-making through iteration over time of the production of components that are in fact necessary to make up that very system. There is continuous regeneration of the processes of production through an array of feedback mechanisms (Capra 1996: 168).

In a sociological context Luhmann has most deployed this notion of autopoiesis. He defines it thus: 'everything that is used as a unit by the system is produced as a unit by the system itself. This applies to elements, processes, boundaries, and other structures and, last but not least, to the unity of the system itself'

(Luhmann 1990: 3; see also Mingers 1995). Such systems deploy 'communications' as the 'particular mode of autopoietic reproduction', since only communications are necessarily social. A theory of autopoietic systems involves the development of communications as the elementary component of each system. Such communications are not living or conscious units but involve three elements, information, utterance and understanding. Luhmann understands these as co-created within the processes of communication. Social systems are not 'closed systems' but open systems that are recursively closed with respect to such communications. Such communications result, he says, in the self-making of 'our well-known society' (Luhmann 1990: 13; see also P. Stewart 2001). These systems increase their complexity and their selectivity in order to reduce the complexity of the environment in which they have to operate (Luhmann 1990: 84).

How relevant is autopoiesis to examining the nature of *global systems*? Certainly, the notion of autopoiesis bears some similarities with analyses in *Global Nature, Global Culture* as to the spreading of global communications and consequential remarking of the natural and cultural domains around the world. Autopoiesis also bears a resemblance to the argument that it is through naming the global, and through billions of iterations, that the global is then brought into being. Luhmann talks of the differentiations involved in the development of 'world society'.

However, Luhmann's argument is couched at too high a level of abstraction to grasp the very specific character of the global networks and fluids that I outlined and defended above (for a more circumscribed application, see Medd 2000). Luhmann's account is functionalist, not capturing the contingent, far-from-equlibrium processes implicated in the current world 'on the edge of chaos'. Feedbacks are predominantly negative rather than positive. Luhmann refers to 'our well-known society'. But this suggests that the general concept of self-making cannot be connected to the very detailed workings of networked phenomena that are complex, fractured entities often operating far from equilibrium. These limitations are even more problematic where such notions of self-making weakly capture the extensivity of global networks and flows, the intensity of global interconnectedness, the heightened velocity of mobilities around the globe and the massive impact of such interconnectedness.

Indeed, applying Luhmann's autopoeitic formulation to the global or 'world society' would result in a 'global functionalism' where everything that affects the system across the globe is seen as contributing to its self-making. Thus the massive inequalities that accompany globalization, or the rising of global temperatures through 'global warming', or the growth of global terrorism might all be viewed as necessary functional components of the processes of global self-making. This position is unconvincing. But so too is an alternative view that treats the global as the clear and determinant outcome of a partially self-conscious transnational capitalist class (Sklair 2001).

John Urry (2003) *Global Complexity*, Cambridge: Polity Press, pp. 93–101.

Global Civil Society in the Cosmopolitan Age

GLOBAL CIVIL SOCIETY: JOHN KEANE (2003)

John Keane (1949–) is Professor of Politics at the University of Westminster, UK and at the Wissenschaftszentrum Berlin, Germany. Born in Australia and educated at Cambridge University, he has become one of the UK's leading political writers and has researched extensively the intricate connections between globalization and processes of democratization. In this reading on the emergence of what he terms "global civil society," Keane argues that the notion implies a less violent political world, based upon emergent forms of cultural cosmopolitanism, transnational networks, and post-national developments. The dialectic at the heart of Keane's political theory is one between universalism and difference, which he places center-stage with the advent of globalization.

Global Civil Society?

The term global civil society properly refers to *a dynamic non-governmental system of interconnected socio-economic institutions that straddle the whole earth, and that have complex effects that are felt in its four corners. Global civil society is neither a static object nor a* fait accompli. *It is an unfinished project that consists of sometimes thick, sometimes thinly stretched networks, pyramids and hub-and-spoke clusters of socio-economic institutions and actors who organise themselves across borders, with the deliberate aim of drawing the world together in new ways. These non-governmental institutions and actors tend to pluralise power and to problematise violence; consequently, their peaceful or 'civil' effects are felt everywhere, here and there, far and wide, to and from local areas, through wider regions, to the planetary level itself.*

We need to look carefully at the elements of this rather abstract definition. Considered together, *five* tightly coupled features of this global civil society mark it off as historically distinctive. To begin with, the term global civil society refers to *non-governmental* structures and activities. It comprises individuals, households, profit-seeking businesses, not-for-profit non-governmental organisations, coalitions, social movements and linguistic communities and cultural identities. It feeds upon the work of media celebrities and past or present public personalities – from Gandhi, Bill Gates, Primo Levi and Martin Luther King to Bono and Aung San Suu Kyi, Bishop Ximenes Belo, Naomi Klein and al-Waleed bin Talal. It includes charities, think-tanks, prominent intellectuals (like Tu Wei-ming and Abdolkarim Soroush), campaigning and lobby groups; citizens' protests responsible for 'clusters of performances',[1] small and large corporate firms, independent media, Internet groups and websites, employers' federations, trades unions, international commissions, parallel summits and sporting organisations. It comprises bodies like Amnesty International, Sony, Falun Gong, Christian Aid, al Jazeera, the Catholic Relief Services, the Indigenous Peoples Bio-Diversity Network, FIFA, Transparency International, Sufi networks like Qadiriyya and Naqsha-bandiyya, the International Red Cross, the Global Coral

Reef Monitoring Network, the Ford Foundation, Shack/Slum Dwellers International, Women Living Under Muslim Laws, News Corporation International, Open Democracy.net, and unnamed circles of Buddhist monks, dressed in crimson robes, keeping the mind mindful. Considered together, these institutions and actors constitute a vast, interconnected and multi-layered non-governmental space that comprises many hundreds of thousands of more-or-less self-directing ways of life. All of these forms of life have at least one thing in common: across vast geographic distances and despite barriers of time, they deliberately organise themselves and conduct their cross-border social activities, business and politics outside the boundaries of governmental structures.

Sometimes those who use and defend the term global civil society – the World Passport initiative, for instance[2] – think of it in no other way than as a synonym for an unbounded space of non-governmental institutions and actors. This rather monistic understanding has the advantage of highlighting one of its principal qualities – that it is neither an appendage nor a puppet of governmental power. Yet the price that is paid for this limited definition is high: it enables the critics of the vision of global civil society to accuse their opponents of careless blindness. These critics insist, with some justification, that the term global civil society is too often used as a residual or dustbin category that describes everything and nothing. The term is used to refer to all those parts of life that are *not* the state; it seems that it is a synonym for everything that exists outside of and beyond the reach of the territorial state and other institutions of governance – that it includes not only business and not-for-profit organisations and initiatives, but 'mafias, extremist networks of various kinds, and terrorists'.[3] The picture presented by the critics is overdrawn, even inaccurate, for global civil society, when carefully defined, is not a simple-minded *alter ego* of 'the state'. The truth is that in a descriptive sense global civil society is only *one* special set of 'non-state' institutions. Hunting and gathering societies and tribal orders, insofar as they have survived under modern conditions, comprise 'non-state' institutions, but it would be wrong to describe them as 'civil society' orders. The same point applies to mafias and mafia-dominated structures, which have *destructive* effects upon civil society institutions precisely because *mafiosi* rely upon kinship bonds, blood imagery, violence and intrigue to *dissolve* the boundaries between the governmental and civilian domains.[4] The same point can be put in another way: global civil society is indeed an extra-governmental space, but it is much more than that. It is defined by other qualities that beg us to see it with different eyes . . .

To say that global civil society is not merely a non-governmental phenomenon, for instance, is to confirm – this is its second feature – that it is also a form of *society*. Global civil society is a dynamic ensemble of more or less tightly interlinked *social* processes.[5] The quest to unlock its secrets cannot be pursued through the biological or mechanical sciences, for this emergent social order is neither an organism nor a mechanism. It is not a thing that grows according to the blind logic of dividing cells, untouched by human judgement and human will, by recursive reflection and self-generated learning; global civil society is also not a piece of machinery which can be assembled and re-assembled according to human design. The processes and methods through which it is produced and reproduced are unique.

So what does it mean then to speak of global civil *society*? The word 'society' is one of those household concepts that help us economise on lengthy and pedantic explanations – by hiding away or setting aside their complicated (sometimes self-contradictory) genealogy. The concept of society certainly has a complicated history, with two distinct and tensely related connotations. During the nineteenth and twentieth centuries, especially in the Atlantic region, the term came to be used as a signifier of a whole totality of interrelated processes and events, stretching from (and including) households to governmental institutions. This understanding of 'society' as a whole way of life, as a 'social organism, a holistic system of social relations, the social formation' (Lenin), can be thought of as a depoliticised, less normative version of the much older, early modern idea of a Civil Society, which referred to a well-governed, legally ordered whole way of life. Both usages of 'society' differ from a second, originally medieval meaning of the term: society as a particular fellowship or partnership of equals. St Augustine's description of the Church as the true 'society of the Father and the Son', identical neither with the City of Man nor with the City of God, pointed in this direction. 'Society' means sociable interaction at a distance from government and law. Vocational fellowships and commercial partnerships, the Dutch *matshappeij*, the German *Gesellschaft*, the English 'Societie of Saynt George' (1548) and the Anti-Slavery Society, or today's Society of Authors or the Society of Black Lawyers, all fall in this category. So do eighteenth-century references to the style-setting circles of the upper class, *le Monde*, or what the Germans called 'Die Sozietät', the same group described in Byron's *Don Juan*: 'Society is now one polished horde, Formed of two mighty tribes, the Bores and the Bored.'

We can say that global civil *society* means something quite different from these older usages, to which it is nevertheless genealogically related. It refers to a vast, sprawling non-governmental constellation of many institutionalised structures, associations and networks within which individual and group actors are interrelated and functionally interdependent. As a society of societies, it is 'bigger' and 'weightier' than any individual actor or organisation or combined sum of its thousands of constituent parts – most of whom, paradoxically, neither 'know' each other nor have any chance of ever meeting each other face-to-face. Global civil society is a highly complex ensemble of differently sized, overlapping forms of structured social action; like a Tolstoy novel, it is a vast scenario in which hundreds of thousands and millions of individual and group adventures unfold, sometimes harmoniously through cooperation and compromise, and sometimes conflictually. The key point is that General Motors plus Amnesty International plus the Ruckus Society plus DAWN (Development Alternatives With Women for a New Era) does not equal global civil society. Its social dynamics are more intricate, more dynamic, and more interesting than that.

Like all societies in the strict sense, it has a marked life or momentum or power of its own. Its institutions and rules have a definite durability, in that at least some of them can and do persist through long cycles of time. Global civil society, as we shall see in the coming pages, has much older roots. Most non-European civilisations have made contributions to it, and the effects upon our own times of early modern European developments – the ground-breaking pacifist tradition[6] and the growth spurt of globalisation during the half-century before the First World War – are easily observed. The institutions of present-day global civil society, like those of any functioning society, both predate the living and outlive the life-span of this society's individual members, every one of whom is shaped and carried along in life by the social customs and *traditions* of this global society. In various ways, the social actors of global civil society are both constrained and empowered by this society. These actors are enmeshed within codes of unwritten and written rules that both enable and restrict their action-in-the-world; they understand that many things are possible, but that not everything goes, that some things are desirable, and that some things are not possible, or that they are forbidden. Within global civil society – which is only one particular form of society – social actors' involvement in institutions obliges them to refrain from certain actions, as well as to observe certain *norms*, for instance those that define what counts as civility. [. . .]

The heterogeneity of global civil society works against enforced unity. It throws into question presumptions about spontaneous sympathy and automatic consensus.[7] It heaps doubt upon claims (famously associated with Seneca) that all human beings are 'social animals',[8] or that they stand firm upon some bedrock of essential 'humanity'. This complex society is not a space wherein people naturally touch and feel good about the world. Certainly that happens. Dressed in the clothing of honest pilgrims, young people take time off, travel the world, odd-job, sleep rough, sleep around, wonder and marvel at the complexity and beauty of the world, just like a satisfied botanist observing and contemplating the extraordinary complexity of plant life. Others meanwhile dedicate their lives to charitable or volunteer work by putting their minds and hearts to work with others. They speak of compassion, and practise it. Yet despite all this, the world of global civil society can be tough, calculating and rough n tumble. It looks and feels expansive and polyarchic, full of horizontal push and pull, vertical conflict and compromise. Take a stroll through the heart of Riyadh, a city of astonishing contrasts between ancient social customs and ultra-modern norms: women shrouded in black *abayas* shop at Harvey Nichols inside a Norman Foster building, their eyes fully covered; the street corner McDonald's close five times a day for prayers; men crowd into mosques surrounded by giant neon signs advertising Sony. Global civil society – to use a term of psychoanalysis – is richly conflicted. That fact helps many participants within this society to know and to understand that it is neither self-reproducing nor spontaneously self-regulating. They are more or less reflexively aware of its *contingency*. They sense that its dynamic structures and rules and various identities – even supposedly 'ascriptive' primary groups like kinship ties – are not somehow naturally given, for all time; they see that they are subject to strenuous negotiation and modification, through complex processes – parallel summits, blockades, media events, for instance – whose consequences are often better understood after the fact, with hindsight. This shared sense of contingency defies presumptions about the 'natural sociability of humans'.[9] It also feeds social conflict, thus ensuring that global civil society stands precariously between the boundaries of orderly equilibrium and disorder at the edge of chaos.

The volume of this worldly self-awareness of the complexity of the world, should not be exaggerated. It is hard to estimate its extent, but probably only 5 per cent of the world's population has an acute awareness of the tightening interdependence of the world, its ecosystems, institutions and peoples. Perhaps another 25 per cent are moderately or dimly aware of this interdependence.[10] While most others have not (yet) thought over the matter, or don't much care, or are too cynical or self-preoccupied to open their eyes and ears, the aggregate numbers of those who are globally aware are weighty enough to spread awareness that global civil society exists; that it is a force to be reckoned with; that it both operates within, and resembles, a patchwork quilt of power relations. Global civil society is most definitely riddled with power relations.[11] Its social groups and organisations and movements lobby states, bargain with international organisations, pressure and bounce off other non-state bodies, invest in new forms of production, champion different ways of life and engage in charitable direct action in distant local communities, for instance through 'capacity-building' programmes that supply jobs, clean running water, sporting facilities, hospitals and schools. In these various ways, the members of global civil society help to conserve or to alter the power relations embedded in the chains of interaction linking the local, regional and planetary orders. Their cross-border links and networks help to define and redefine who gets what, when, and how in the world. Of great importance is the fact that these cross-border patterns have the power to stimulate awareness among the world's inhabitants that mutual understanding of different ways of life is a practical necessity, that we are being drawn into the first genuinely bottom-up transnational order, a global civil society, in which millions of people come to realise, in effect, that they are incarnations of world-wide webs of interdependence, whose complexity is riddled with opportunity, as well as danger.

To say this is to note – this fifth point is obvious, but most crucial – that global civil society is *global*. To speak of a *global* civil society is to refer to politically framed and circumscribed social relations that stretch across and underneath state boundaries and other governmental forms. This 'macro-society' or 'society of interlocking societies' consists of a myriad of social interactions stretched across vast geographic distances. Global civil society is the most complex society in the history of the human species. It comprises a multitude of different parts, which are connected in a multitude of different ways. These diverse components interact both serially and in parallel, and they produce effects that are often both simultaneous and sequential. These effects, while normally generated by local interactions and events, have emergent properties that tend to be global. We are not exactly speaking here of a 'vast empire of human society, as it is spread over the whole earth' (Wordsworth[12]) – global civil society is neither a new form of empire nor encompassing of the whole earth[13] – but it certainly is a special form of *unbounded* society marked by constant feedback among its many components.

Notes

1 Charles Tilly, 'From Interactions to Outcomes in Social Movements', in Marco Giugni *et al.* (eds.), *How Social Movements Matter* (Minneapolis and London, 1999), p. 263.

2 www.worldservice.org/docpass.html: 'The World Passport is . . . a meaningful symbol and sometimes powerful tool for the implementation of the fundamental human right of freedom of travel. By its very existence, it challenges the exclusive assumption of sovereignty of the nation-state system.'

3 Barry Buzan, 'An English School Perspective on Global Civil Society', unpublished paper (Centre for the Study of Democracy, 17 January 2002), p. 1; cf. p. 3: 'In descriptive mode, civil society = non-state, and therefore includes mafias, pornography merchants, terrorists and a host of other dark side entities as well as the nicer side of civil society represented by humanitarian, animal welfare and humanitarian organizations.'

4 Anton Blok, *Honour and Violence* (Oxford 2001), chapter 5.

5 On the sociological concept of 'society', see Claus Offe, 'Is There, or Can There Be, a "European Society"?', in John Keane (ed.), *Civil Society: Berlin Perspectives* (London, 2004), forthcoming.

6 A good discussion of the long-term impact of the world's first peace movement, which appeared during the 1790s, as a reaction against the French wars, is Martin Ceadl, *The Origins of War Prevention. The British Peace Movement and International Relations, 1730–1854* (Oxford, 1996).

7 Francis Fukuyama, *The Great Disruption. Human Nature and the Reconstitution of Social Order* (London, 1999), chapter 13.

8 Seneca, *De Beneficiis* (Cambridge, MA and London, 1935), book 7, section 1.

9 Buzan, 'An English School Perspective', p. 3.

10 Data generated by recent World Values Surveys suggests that 'almost one-fifth of the baby boomers born after World War II see themselves as cosmopolitan citizens of the globe, identifying with their continent or the world as a whole, but this is true of only one in ten of the group brought up in the interwar years, and of even fewer of the prewar generation'; see Pippa Norris, 'Global Governance and Cosmopolitan Citizens', in Joseph S. Nye and John D. Donahue (eds.), *Governance in a Globalizing World* (Cambridge, MA and Washington, DC, 2000), p. 175. From a global civil society perspective, the concept of 'cosmopolitan citizens' is unfortunate, if only because awareness of the *interdependence* of the world is both more subtle and different than positive 'identification' with one's own 'continent' or 'the world'.

11 On the concept of power and its wide variety of forms, see my *Václav Havel: A Political Tragedy in Six Acts* (London and New York, 1999).

12 From William Wordsworth's Preface to the *Lyrical Ballads, with Other Poems* (2nd edn., London, 1800).

13 Compare the claim that there is a spreading new form of empire – a 'global society of control' – ruled by global capital in Michael Hardt and Antonio Negri, *Empire* (Cambridge, MA and London, 2000), esp. pp. 325–50.

John Keane (2003) *Global Civil Society?* Cambridge: Cambridge University Press, pp. 8–12, 15–17.

--- --- --- ▪ --- ---

VERSIONS OF GLOBAL CIVIL SOCIETY: MARY KALDOR (2003)

Mary Kaldor (1946–) is a Professor at the London School of Economics, where she is Director of the Centre for the Study of Global Governance. Her research has focused on violence, war, nuclear disarmament, and citizenship – all in the wider context of current debates over the politics of globalization. In this selection, Kaldor argues that civil society must necessarily undergo profound transformation as a consequence of globalization. There is, she argues, a profound paradox to civil society in conditions of advanced globalism. On the one hand, it allows individuals and groups to address their demands beyond the sphere of national governments and reach global institutions, and thus opens new possibilities for human freedom – especially escape from the sickening trauma of territorial wars. On the other hand, global civil society entails news risks and dangers – especially as evil, death, and destruction become "global" and as never before.

Global Civil Society: An Answer to War

Definitions of global civil society

I propose to set out five different versions of the concept of civil society in common usage and to say something about what they imply in a global context. This is a non-exhaustive and abbreviated (but not altogether arbitrary) list. The civil society literature is much richer and more complex than this summary would suggest; the aim is to set up some parameters for the rest of the book.

  The first two versions are drawn from past versions of the concept; the last three are contemporary versions, with echoes of historical usage. It is not straightforward to transpose the concept of civil society into the concept of global civil society, since, as I have argued, the key to understanding what is new about contemporary meanings is precisely their global character. Yet the exercise may be illuminating since I do believe that there is a common core of meaning and we can investigate the nature of the contemporary phenomenon by trying to understand the relevance of past meanings.

Societas civilis

Here I am referring to what could be described as the original version of the term – civil society as a rule of law and a political community, a peaceful order based on implicit or explicit consent of individuals, a zone of 'civility'. Civility is defined not just as 'good manners' or 'polite society' but as a state of affairs where violence has been minimized as a way of organizing social relations. It is public security that creates the basis for more 'civil' procedures for settling conflicts – legal arrangements, for example, or public deliberation. Most later definitions of civil society are predicated on the assumption of a rule of law and the relative absence of coercion in human affairs at least within the boundaries of the state. Thus, it is assumed that such a *societas civilis* requires a state, with a public monopoly of legitimate violence. According to this definition, the meaning of civil society cannot be separated from the existence of a state. Civil society is distinguished not from the state but from non-civil societies – the state of nature or absolutist empires – and from war.

One of the main objections to the notion of global civil society is the absence of a world state.[1] However, it can be argued that the coming together of humanitarian and human rights law, the establishment of an international criminal court, the expansion of international peacekeeping, betoken an emerging framework of global governance, what Immanuel Kant described as a universal civil society, in the sense of a cosmopolitan rule of law, guaranteed by a combination of international treaties and institutions.

Bourgeois society (*Bürgerliche Gesellschaft*)

For Hegel and Marx, civil society was that arena of ethical life in between the state and the family. It was a historically produced phenomenon linked to the emergence of capitalism. They drew on the insights of the Scottish enlightenment, especially Adam Smith and Adam Ferguson, who argued that the advent of commercial society created the individuals who were the necessary condition for civil society. Markets, social classes, civil law and welfare organizations were all part of civil society. Civil society was, for the first time, contrasted with the state. For Hegel, civil society was the 'achievement of the modern age'. And for Marx, civil society was the 'theatre of history'.[2]

Transposed to a global level, civil society could be more or less equated with 'globalization from below' – all those aspects of global developments below and beyond the state and international political institutions, including transnational corporations, foreign investment, migration, global culture, etc.[3]

The activist version

The activist perspective is probably closest to the version of civil society that emerged from the opposition in Central Europe in the 1970s and 1980s. It is sometimes described as the post-Marxist or utopian version of the concept. It is a definition that presupposes a state or rule of law, but insists not only on restraints on state power but on a redistribution of power. It is a radicalization of democracy and an extension of participation and autonomy. On this definition, civil society refers to active citizenship, to growing self-organization outside formal political circles, and expanded space in which individual citizens can influence the conditions in which they live both directly through self-organization and through political pressure.

What is important, according to this definition, at a transnational level is the existence of a global public sphere – a global space where non-instrumental communication can take place, inhabited by transnational advocacy networks like Greenpeace or Amnesty International, global social movements like the protestors in

Seattle, Prague and Genoa, international media through which their campaigns can be brought to global attention, new global 'civic religions' like human rights or environmentalism.

The neoliberal version

In the aftermath of 1989, neoliberals claimed their victory and began to popularize the term 'civil society' as what the West has, or even what the United States has. This version might be described as *'laissez-faire* politics', a kind of market in politics. According to this definition, civil society consists of associational life – a non-profit, voluntary 'third sector' – that not only restrains state power but also actually provides a substitute for many of the functions performed by the state. Thus charities and voluntary associations carry out functions in the field of welfare which the state can no longer afford to perform. This definition is perhaps the easiest to transpose to the global arena; it is viewed as the political or social counterpart of the process of globalization understood as economic globalization, liberalization, privatization, deregulation and the growing mobility of capital and goods. In the absence of a global state, an army of NGOs (non-governmental organizations) perform the functions necessary to smooth the path of economic globalization. Humanitarian NGOs provide the safety net to deal with the casualties of liberalization and privatization strategies in the economic field. Funding for democracy-building and human rights NGOs is somehow supposed to help establish a rule of law and respect for human rights. Thus critics have charged that the term is reactionary, a way of evading the responsibilities of states for welfare or security.[4]

The postmodern version

The postmodern definition of civil society departs from the universalism of the activist and neoliberal versions, although even this version requires one universal principle – that of tolerance.[5] Civil society is an arena of pluralism and contestation, a source of incivility as well as civility. Some postmodernists criticize the concept of civil society as Eurocentric; a product of a specific Western culture that is imposed on the rest of the world. Others suggest a reformulation so as to encompass other more communalist understandings of political culture. In particular, it is argued that classic Islamic society represented a form of civil society in the balance between religion, the bazaar and the ruler.

For the activist version, the inhabitants of civil society can be roughly equated with civic-minded or public-spirited groups. Those active in civil society would be those concerned about public affairs and public debate. For the postmodernists, civic-minded groups are only one component of civil society. In particular, post-modernists emphasize the importance of national and religious identities as well as multiple identities as a precondition for civil society, whereas for the activists, a shared cosmopolitanism is more important. Whether or not groups advocating violence should be included is open to question.

From this perspective, it is possible to talk about global civil society in the sense of the global spread of fields of contestation. Indeed, one might talk about a plurality of global civil societies through different globally organized networks. These might include Islam, nationalist Diaspora networks, as well as human rights networks etc.

These five versions are summarized in table 6.1. My own understanding of global civil society, which I shall explore in this book, incorporates much of these different meanings. I do believe that both the first two versions, a rule of law and a market society, or at least the aspiration for a rule of law and for economic autonomy, are constituted and constituted by what we now tend to mean by civil society; for civil society to exist there has to be a relationship with markets, which secure economic autonomy, and the rule of law, which provides security. I also think that the various actors that inhabit contemporary versions of civil society are all part of global civil society – the social movements and the civic networks of the activist version; the charities, voluntary associations and what I shall call the 'tamed' NGOs of the neo-liberal version; and the nationalist and fundamentalist groups that are included in the postmodern version.

Table 6.1 The five versions of civil society

Type of society	Territorially bounded	Global
Societas civilis	Rule of law/Civility	Cosmopolitan order
Bürgerliche Gesellschaft	All organized social life between the state and the family	Economic, social and cultural globalization
Activist	Social movements, civic activists	A global public sphere
Neoliberal	Charities, voluntary associations, third sector	Privatization of democracy building, humanitarianism
Postmodern	Nationalists, fundamentalists as well as above	Plurality of global networks of contestation

In terms of normative considerations, however, I am closest to the activist version. All versions of civil society are both normative and descriptive. They describe a political project i.e. a goal, and at the same time an actually existing reality, which may not measure up to the goal. *Societas civilis* expressed the goal of public security, of a civilized, i.e. non-violent, society. *Bürgerliche Gesellschaft* was about the rise of market society as a condition for individual freedom, and the balance between the state and the market. For Hegel, this was the *telos* (end goal) of history; for Marx, civil society was merely a stage towards the *telos* of communism.

The contemporary versions of civil society all have normative goals, which can only be fully explained in the context of globalization. The neoliberal version is about the benefits of Western, especially American, society; thus the goal is the spread of this type of society to the rest of the world. Globalization, the spread of global capitalism, is viewed as a positive development, the vehicle, supplemented by global civil society, for achieving global Westernization or 'the end of history'.

The postmodern version has to be related to the break with modernity of which a key component was the nation-state. Even though the postmodernists are anti-teleological, they would see the contestation that is currently taking place on a global scale as a way of breaking with grand narratives, teleological political projects that were associated with states. The rise of the Internet allows for a riot of virtuality and for a denial of the existence of something called the real.

The activist version is about political emancipation. It is about the empowerment of individuals and the extension of democracy. I will argue that war and the threat of war always represented a limitation on democracy. Globalization offers the possibility of overcoming that limitation and, at the same time, the global extension of democracy has become, as a consequence of globalization, the necessary condition for political emancipation. For activists, globalization is not an unqualified benefit. It offers possibilities for emancipation on a global scale. But in practice, it involves growing inequality and insecurity and new forms of violence. Global civil society, for the activists, therefore, is about 'civilizing' or democratizing globalization, about the process through which groups, movements and individuals can demand a global rule of law, global justice and global empowerment. Global civil society does, of course, in my own version, include those who are opposed to globalization and those who do not see the need for regulation. Thus my version of global civil society is based on the belief that a genuinely free conversation, a rational critical dialogue, will favour the 'civilizing' option.

Notes

1   Brown, 'Cosmopolitanism'; David Rieff, 'The False Dawn of Civil Society', *Nation*, 22 Feb. 1999.

2   See ch. 2.

3   This version of global civil society is exemplified in John Keane's essay 'Global Civil Society?', in Helmut Anheier, Marlies Glasius and Mary Kaldor (eds), *Global Civil Society 2001* (Oxford University Press, Oxford, 2001). The term

'globalization from below' is sometimes used in a narrower sense to refer to global social movements, NGOs and networks. See Mario Piantia, *Globalizzazione dal Basso: Economia Mondiale e Movimenti Sociali* (Manifestolibri, Rome, 2001).

4   Rieff, 'The False Dawn'.
5   Keane, 'Global Civil Society?'.

Mary Kaldor (2003) *Global Civil Society: An Answer to War*, Cambridge: Polity Press, pp. 6–12.

COSMOPOLITAN PATRIOTS: KWAME ANTHONY APPIAH (1997)

Kwame Anthony Appiah (1954–) was born in London to Peggy Cripps, a well known English children's author, and Joe Appiah, a prominent Ghanaian politician. At the time, his birth caused something of a stir within the British media for its cross-racial and cultural implications. Soon after he was born, Appiah was taken by his parents to be raised in Ghana. However, years later Appiah would return to the U.K. to receive much of his formal schooling, culminating in a Ph.D. in philosophy from Cambridge. Appiah's own biography often figures prominently in his own work. This is particularly true of his research into the idea of cosmopolitanism, for which he is considered one of the world's leading thinkers on the topic. His book, *Cosmopolitanism: Ethics in a World of Strangers* (2006) is often celebrated as one of the most significant contemporary contributions to cosmopolitan philosophy. Currently, Appiah is Laurance S. Rockefeller University Professor of Philosophy at Princeton University.

Everyone is Cosmopolitan

My father was a Ghanaian patriot. He once published a column in the *Pioneer*, our local newspaper in Kumasi, under the headline "Is Ghana Worth Dying For?" and I know that his heart's answer was yes.[1] But he also loved Asante, the region of Ghana where he and I both grew up, a kingdom absorbed within a British colony and, then, a region of a new multiethnic republic: a once-kingdom that he and his father also both loved and served. And, like so many African nationalists of his class and generation, he always loved an enchanting abstraction they called Africa. [. . .]

When he died, my sisters and I found a note he had drafted and never quite finished, last words of love and wisdom for his children. After a summary reminder of our double ancestry – in Ghana and in England – he wrote: "Remember that you are citizens of the world." And he went on to tell us that this meant that – wherever we chose to live, and, as citizens of the world, we could surely choose to live anywhere – we should make sure we left that place "better than you found it." "Deep inside of me," he went on, "is a great love for mankind and an abiding desire to see mankind, under God, fulfil its highest destiny."

The favorite slander of the narrow nationalist against us cosmopolitans is that we are rootless. What my father believed in, however, was a rooted cosmopolitanism, or, if you like, a cosmopolitan patriotism. Like Gertrude Stein, he thought there was no point in roots if you couldn't take them with you. "America is my country and Paris is my hometown," Stein said.[2] My father would have understood her.

We cosmopolitans face a familiar litany of objections. Some, for example, have complained that our cosmopolitanism must be parasitic: where, they ask, could Stein have gotten her roots in a fully cosmopolitan world? Where, in other words, would all the diversity we cosmopolitans celebrate come from in a world where there were only cosmopolitans?

The answer is straightforward: the cosmopolitan patriot can entertain the possibility of a world in which *everyone* is a rooted cosmopolitan, attached to a home of one's own, with its own cultural particularities, but taking pleasure from the presence of other, different places that are home to other, different people. The cosmopolitan also imagines that in such a world not everyone will find it best to stay in their natal patria, so that the circulation of people among different localities will involve not only cultural tourism (which the cosmopolitan admits to enjoying) but migration, nomadism, diaspora. In the past, these processes have too often been the result of forces we should deplore; the old migrants were often refugees, and older diasporas often began in an involuntary exile. But what can be hateful, if coerced, can be celebrated when it flows from the free decisions of individuals or of groups.

In a world of cosmopolitan patriots, people would accept the citizen's responsibility to nurture the culture and the politics of their homes. Many would, no doubt, spend their lives in the places that shaped them; and that is one of the reasons local cultural practices would be sustained and transmitted. But many would move; and that would mean that cultural practices would travel also (as they have always travelled). The result would be a world in which each local form of human life was the result of long-term and persistent processes of cultural hybridization: a world, in that respect, much like the world we live in now.

Behind the objection that cosmopolitanism is parasitic there is, in any case, an anxiety we should dispel: an uneasiness caused by an exaggerated estimate of the rate of disappearance of cultural heterogeneity. In the global system of cultural exchanges there are, indeed, somewhat asymmetrical processes of homogenization going on, and there are forms of human life disappearing. Neither of these phenomena is particularly new, but their range and speed probably is. Nevertheless, as forms of culture disappear, new forms are created, and they are created locally, which means they have exactly the regional inflections that the cosmopolitan celebrates. The disappearance of old cultural forms is consistent with a rich variety of forms of human life, just because new cultural forms, which differ from each other, are being created all the time as well. [. . .]

I have been arguing, in essence, that you can be cosmopolitan – celebrating the variety of human cultures; rooted – loyal to one local society (or a few) that you count as home; liberal – convinced of the value of the individual; and patriotic – celebrating the institutions of the state (or states) within which you live. The cosmopolitanism flows from the same sources that nourish the liberalism, for it is the variety of human forms of life that provides the vocabulary of the language of individual choice. And the patriotism flows from the liberalism because the state carves out the space within which we explore the possibilities of freedom. For rooted cosmopolitans, all this is of a single piece.

But I have also been arguing that we do not need to insist that all of our fellow citizens be cosmopolitans, or patriots, or loyal to the nation; we need them only to share the political culture of the state. And sharing that political culture does not require you to be centered on it and certainly doesn't require you to be centered on a culture wider than the political.[3] What *is* essential is only – though this is, in fact, a great deal – that all of us share respect for the political culture of liberalism and the constitutional order it entails.

This formula courts misunderstanding: for the word *liberal* has been both divested of its original content and denied a solid new meaning. So let me remind you again that, for me, the essence of this liberal culture lies in respect for the dignity and autonomy of individual persons.[4] There is much to be said about the meaning of autonomy and of dignity; there is much to be said, too, about how, in practice, individuals are to live with other values, political and not, that we cherish. This is not the place for that exploration. But let me say one thing: since I believe that the state can be an instrument for autonomy I do not share the current distaste for the state that drives much of what in America is now called conservatism; and so I am often a liberal in the more colloquial sense as well.

The point, in sum, is this: it is important that citizens should share a political culture; it is not important (in America, without massive coercion, it is not even possible) that the political culture be important to all citizens, let alone that it matter to all of them in the same way. (Indeed, one of the great freedoms that a civilized society provides is the freedom *not* to preoccupy yourself with the political.) Only politicians and political theorists are likely to think the best state is one where every citizen is a politician (and when Western theorists think this, it may be because they are overinfluenced by the view of politics taken by some in the small self-governing town of Athens in the fifth century B.C.E.).

Not being political is not the same as being unsociable (though that is something we should be legally free to be also!). Many people express concern for their communities by acting through churches and charities, and, as observers of America since Tocqueville have pointed out, this is a distinctively American tradition. Part of what makes this tradition attractive is that it reflects elective affinities rather than state-imposed obligation.

Notes

1   This questions was first put to him by J.B. Danquah, leader of the major opposition party in Kwame Nkrumah's Ghana in 1962. See Joseph Appiah: *Joe Appiah: The Autobiography of an African Patriot* (New York, 1990), p. 266. My Father's column is reprinted in Appiah, *Antiochus Lives Again! (Political Essays of Joe Appiah)*, ed. Ivor Agyeman-Duah (Khumasi, Ghana, 1992).

2   Gertrude Stein, "An American and France" (1936). *What Are Masterpieces?* (Los Angeles, 1940), p. 61.

3   I think that in the United States that grasp of the political culture probably requires knowing (some) English. But since English, like the rest of the political culture, needn't center your life, speaking and even loving other languages is consistent with participating in the political culture.

4   Despite recent communitarian arguments to the contrary, I do not think that the liberal respect for autonomy is inconsistent with recognizing the role of society in creating the options in respect to which free individuals exercise their freedom. As Taylor has argued so powerfully, it is in dialogue with other people's understandings of who I am that I develop a conception of my own identity; and my identity is crucially constituted through concepts and practices made available to me by religion, society, school, and state and mediated to varying degrees by the family. But all of this can, in my view, be accepted by someone who sees autonomy as a central value. See my "Identity, Authenticity, Survival: Multicultural Societies and Social Reproduction," in *Multiculturalism: Examining "The Politics of Recognition,"* ed. Amy Gutmann (Princeton, N.J., 1996), pp. 149–63.

Kwame Anthony Appiah (1997) "Cosmopolitan Patriots," *Critical Inquiry*, vol. 23, spring, pp. 617–19, 633–4.

VIOLENCE, IDENTITY, AND POVERTY: AMARTYA SEN (2008)

Amartya Kumar Sen (1933–) is an Indian economist and global public intellectual. He studied at Presidency College in Calcutta, India, and at Trinity College, Cambridge, where he was until recently a Master. He is currently the Thomas W. Lamont University Professor and Professor of Economics and Philosophy at Harvard University and an Honorary Advisor to Oxfam. His work serves as a powerful critique of the mechanisms of poverty by illuminating the operations of welfare economics. In 1998, he was awarded the Nobel Prize in economics for his contributions to this field.

Violence is Everywhere

Violence is omnipresent in the world around us. On the root causes of contemporary global violence, theories abound – as theories are prone to. However, two particular lines of theorizing have come to receive much more attention than most others: one approach concentrates on the culture of societies, and the other on the political economy of poverty and inequality. Each approach has some plausibility, at least in some forms, and yet both are, I would argue, ultimately inadequate and in need of supplementation. Indeed, neither works on its own, and we need to see the two sets of influences together, in an integrated way. [. . .]

Underlying the approach of civilizational clash is an oddly artificial view of history, according to which these distinct civilizations have grown separately, like trees on different plots of land, with very little overlap and interaction. And today, as these disparate civilizations, with their divergent histories, face one another in the global world, they are firmly inclined, we are told, to clash with each other – a tale, indeed a gripping tale, of what can be, I suppose, called 'hate at first sight'. This make-believe account has little use for the actual history of extensive – and persistent – interactions through history, and constructive movements of ideas and influences across the borders of countries, in so many different fields – literature, arts, music, mathematics, science, engineering, trade, commerce and other human engagements. [. . .]

What about the other approach, the one of political economy? This line of reasoning sees poverty and inequality as the root cause of violence, and it certainly is – or at least seems like – a momentous approach that rivals cultural explanations of violence. It is not hard to see that the injustice of inequality can generate intolerance and that the suffering of poverty can provoke anger and fury. That connection has been pointed out extensively in the social approach to understanding the prevalence of violence and disorder. There have been some statistical attempts to bring out the factual basis of this 'economic reductionism', but the connection has appeared to be so obviously credible that the paucity of definitive empirical evidence has not discouraged the frequent invoking of this way of understanding the recurrence of violent crime in countries with much poverty and inequality. [. . .]

It would be, I think, a huge mistake to see economic inequality and poverty as being automatically responsible for violence – indeed, it would be just as serious a mistake as the assumption that inequality and poverty have nothing to do with the possibility of violence.

So what are my general conclusions? First, economic, social and cultural issues related to violence demand serious efforts at integration, an exercise that is spurned both by the fatalistic theorists of civilizational clash and by the hurried advocates of economic reductionism. Cultural and social factors, as well as features of political economy, are all quite important in understanding violence in the world today. But they do not work in isolation from each other, and we have to resist the tempting shortcuts that claim to deliver insight through their single-minded concentration on some one factor or another, ignoring other central features of an integrated picture.

Second, while identity politics can certainly be mobilized very powerfully in the cause of violence, that violence can also be effectively resisted through a broader understanding of the richness of human identities. Our disparate associations may divide us in particular ways, and yet there are other identities, other affiliations, that encourage us to defy the isolationist demands of any singular division, no matter how lionized that division might be in some particular versions of identity politics. A Hutu who is recruited in the cause of chastising a Tutsi is, in fact, also a Rwandan, and an African, possibly a Kigalian, and indubitably a human being – identities that the Tutsis also share. The process of such cultivated violence cannot be readily translated into the unfolding of something like human destiny.

Third, even as far as identity divisions are concerned, no matter how momentous the religious differences may appear to be in the context of warfare today, there are other divisions that also have the potential for creating strife and carnage. The violence of solitarist identity can have a tremendously varying reach. Indeed, the obsession with religions and so-called civilizations has been so strong in contemporary global politics that there is a tendency to forget how other lines of identity divisions have been exploited in the past – indeed, not so long ago – to generate very different types of violence and war, causing millions of deaths.

For example, appeals to country and nationality played an intoxicating role in the immensely bloody war in Europe between 1914 and 1918, and a shared Western or European background of Christianity did nothing to stop the Germans, the British and the French from tearing each other apart. The identities that were championed then were those of nationalities, with the patriotic fervour that they generated. Before the horrors of the First World War took the life of Wilfred Owen, he wrote his own protest about values that glorify violent combat in the cause of one's identity with one's nation and fatherland:

My friend, you will not tell with such high zest
To children ardent for some desperate glory,
The old lie: Dulce et Decorum est
Pro Patria Mori.

Horace's ringing endorsement of the honour of death for (or *allegedly* for) one's country could be seen as catering to the violence of nationalism, and it was this invocation against which Wilfred Owen was emphatically protesting.

Europeans today may not easily appreciate Owen's profound sense of frustration, pessimism and protest. The Germans, the French and the British work with each other today in peace and tranquillity and sit together to decide what to do in their continent without reaching for their guns. This would have seemed highly implausible when Owen was writing his poem of protest. A similar vulnerability is present in many other divisions of identities that may, at one level, be made to look like an unstoppable march of violence based on its unique claim of importance, but which, at another broader level, may be nothing other than an artificially fostered avowal that can be disputed and displaced by a great many other solidarities and loyalties associated with different identities, including, of course, the broad commonality of our shared humanity.

Amartya Sen (2008) "Violence, Identity and Poverty," *Journal of Peace Research*, vol. 45, no. 5, pp. 5–7, 13–15.

SPECTRAL NATIONALITY: PHENG CHEAH (1999)

Pheng Cheah is still a relatively young social and cultural theorist who teaches rhetoric and East Asian studies at the University of California at Berkeley. The selection is from an early portion of what became his 2003 book *Spectral Nationality* that – along with other books, essays, and public lectures – have shaken established thinking on questions of the postcolonial under the conditions of neo-liberal globalization. By fusing received ideas with daring new theoretical modifications – some borrowed, some seemingly invented out of his learning and intellectual creativity – Cheah's theories of the nation, the citizen, and the cosmopolitan have introduced fresh air into a line of thought once at risk of becoming a new orthodoxy. His other books include *Cosmopolitics: Thinking and Feeling Beyond the Nation* (1998) and *Inhuman Conditions: On Cosmopolitanism and Human Rights* (2006).

Life–Death in the Postcolonial

In the late twentieth century, nationalism is probably one of the few phenomena we associate most closely with death. The end of this millennium is marked (and marred) by endless acts of fanaticist intolerance, ethnic violence, and even genocidal destruction that are widely regarded as extreme expressions of nationalism: patriarchal fundamentalism in Afghanistan and other parts of the "Islamic world"; the atrocities designated by the proper names of Rwanda, Bosnia, and Kosovo; the recent revival of the nuclear race in South Asia as a result of religious official nationalism in India and Pakistan, to name only a few examples. Indeed, one might even say that in our age, nationalism has become the exemplary figure for death. The common association of nationalism with recidivism and the desire for the archaic implies that nationalism destroys human life and whatever futures we may have because its gaze is fixed on the frozen past.

Yet the nation's seemingly inevitable affinity with death is paradoxically inseparable from the desire for life. For the destructive, or, better yet, sacrificial, tendencies of nationalism are part of an attempt to protect or maximize the capacity for life. In nationalist discourse, the nation is not only conceived in analogy with a living organic being but is also regarded as the enduring medium or substrate through which individuals are guaranteed a certain life beyond finite or merely biological life, and, hence, also beyond mortality and death.[1] The nation, in other words, guarantees an eternal future. Its alleged organic power of birth and origination is intimated by its etymological link with the words *nativity* and *natality*. What is presupposed is a vitalist ontology that opposes life to death, spirit to matter/mechanism, and, ultimately, living concrete actuality to abstract ghostly form.

We would, however, be mistaken to assume that this vitalist ontology is peculiar to nationalist discourse. As I will suggest, this ontology of life underwrites the discourse of revolutionary decolonization and contemporary theories of postcolonial nationalism regardless of whether they are organicist or sociological, or whether they defend the nation-form or denounce it as an ideological construct. Indeed, the familiar thematic oppositions we use to describe all forms of political community – oppositions that pit either the state against the nation, the people, or civil society, or capital against labor – rely on ontological metaphors that subordinate the dead to the living.

In this essay, I want to explore the question of whether this vitalist ontology, which conceives of the future in terms of eternal present life, provides an adequate basis for understanding the persistence of the nation-form in the current neocolonial global conjuncture and the future of postcolonial nationalism as an emancipatory project. I will argue that the modality of becoming of the decolonizing and postcolonial nation cannot be understood in terms of any human, natural, or even organic form of life in the conventional meaning of these terms. [. . .]

Put another way, I am suggesting that the relationship between the people and the postcolonial nation-state (Chatterjee, Said) or the people-nation and the postcolonial state (Fanon, Anderson) cannot be adequately understood in terms of the contamination of a living spirit by *techne*, in terms of a perverse diversion, detour, or deferral of a true becoming as the result of the intrusion of an external or contingent artificial foreign body. For if the people and living national culture need the state to survive, and the state comes into being and continues to exist within a neocolonial capitalist world order, the transcendence of which is not in sight, then the contamination of national culture by the bourgeois state is not a matter of the intrusion of an artificial alien body that can be either sublated or permanently removed. The contamination of national culture involves a more original susceptibility to infection by the technical: an a priori receptivity of the people, the people's opening out onto that which is other to it, the people's welcoming of an other that dislocates it even as this other constitutes the self-identity of the people.

The questions I have posed about these influential accounts of post-colonial nationalism amount to a philosophical problem insofar as I have attempted to question the ontology of life that underpins these accounts. When the state is characterized as an abstraction, or when national culture is described as an ideology, we think of them as creatures of death or phantoms that invade the living body of the people and obstruct its life. However, if these prostheses turn out to be necessary supplements to the living national body, then the line between life and death can no longer be drawn with clarity because death would be inscribed within the heart of life. The living people would be constitutively susceptible to a certain kind of death that can no longer be thought within a vitalist ontology that asserts the unequivocal delimitation of death by life and the victory of the latter over the former. It is a death that must be interminably negotiated. [. . .]

But speaking more generally, if we consider the precarious life of the postcolonial nation-people in terms of the current economic conditions within which this body, conceived in analogy with a living body, has to maximize its capabilities and well-being, then, its relation by means of the bourgeois state to the outside in uneven globalization – flows of technology, flows of foreign direct investment, flows of cultural images, and so on – is a case of spectrality, or the interminable experience of the aporia of life-death. For uneven globalization produces a polarized world in which national development in the periphery is frustrated because of state adjustment to the dictates of transnational capital. But in a global capitalist system, the transcendence of which is not in imaginary sight, transnational forces are also a means for the development of the national body. The state, however, can resist capitulation to transnational forces only if it is transformed from a comprador regime into a popular nation-state. This is the hope we saw in Fanon, Anderson, and others – the belief that popular rearticulations of the nation can be ethically imperative and not automatically dismissed as ideologies, even though the exclusionary dimension of popular nationalism can always be manipulated by state elites.

The point here is not to reject these projects of postcolonial national *Bildung* as ideologies. For if I understand Derrida correctly, the specter is neither living nor dead, neither ideology nor the spontaneous will of the people, but the sliding movement or flickering between the two. And the spectrality of the nation is especially pronounced in contemporary globalization. As long as we continue to think of "the people" or "the people-nation" in analogy with a living body or a source of ever present life, then the postcolonial state qua political and economic agent is always the necessary supplement of the revolutionary nation-people, the condition for its living on after decolonization. The nation-people can come into freedom only by attaching itself to the postcolonial bourgeois state. It can live on only through this kind of death. The state is an uncontrollable specter that the nation-people must welcome within itself, and direct, at once *for itself and against itself*, because this specter can possess the nation-people and bend it toward global capitalist interests. [. . .]

I have argued that we might see the postcolonial nation as a creature of life-death because, by virtue of its aporetic inscription within neocolonial globalization, the neocolonial state stands between the living nation-people and dead global capital, pulling on both even as it is pulled by both. I want to end this speculative essay with a brief coda, a concrete example that is also a promise of work to come. As is well known, the financial crisis that is still sweeping across Asia today "began" in June 1997, triggered by a massive attack on the Thai baht by currency speculators on 14–15 May 1997. This crisis has become a free fall into deep economic recession across industrialized and industrializing Southeast Asia and East Asia, indicated by increased inflation, declining production, and rising unemployment. What is so surprising about the collapse of the "Asian economic miracle" is its suddenness. Almost overnight, the strong economic fundamentals of many of these countries – the economic well-being of the nation conceived as an organic body – which were widely regarded by international financial and economic authorities such as the World Bank not only as sound but also as models for less-developed countries to follow,[2] were driven down by global financialization.

Clearly, the ghost of money has contaminated the realm of real production. But more importantly, these rapidly developing postcolonial national bodies have been spectralized by the ghost of foreign money, which they cannot *not* welcome within themselves in order to develop, even though this autoimmunization is precisely also a certain kind of death. Indeed, prior to the collapse, in their official cultural self-representations in the international public sphere, those countries had ironically colluded with the Northern liberal picture of the fiscalization of the globe, world trade liberalization, and foreign direct investment – "growth for all, leading to transnational solidarity" – by fouting themselves as success stories of flexible or disorganized global capitalism.

Here are instances of both sides of the aporia, where the postcolonial national body must accept the other within itself but cannot clearly discriminate between what it welcomes into itself: On the one hand, as Dr. Mahathir Mohamad, the prime minister of Malaysia, notes even after the crash, Malaysia regards "genuine foreign direct investors" as *vital* contributors to the country's industrial development. "We have always treated them as *special guests* of the country."[3] On the other hand, the very conditions that can secure future foreign direct investment, such as acquiescence to directives from the international Monetary Fund (IMF), are themselves harmful. Using Indonesia as an example, one commentator notes that "some of the IMF policies are wrong and deadly. Asking the IMF for assistance may well cause a moderately sick patient to develop a serious and life-threatening disease that will take much suffering and many years to get out of, it at all."[4]

Far from being rendered obsolete by globalization, the living on of the postcolonial nation in the wake of the currency crash can be seen in the rise of both popular and official nationalisms in Southeast Asia in response to economic necolonialism and IMF manipulation: protest by the Malaysian state against unregulated currency speculation, peasant protest in Thailand, and student radicalism in Indonesia that led to the ousting of President Suharto. The postcolonial nation must be seen as a specter of global capital (double genitive – both objective and subjective genitive): It always runs the risk of being an epiphenomenon or reflection of global capital to the extent that it is originally infected by the prosthesis of the bourgeois state qua terminal of capital. But it is also a specter that haunts global capital, for it is the undecidable neuralgic point within the global capitalist system that refuses to be exorcised.

Notes

1   For philosophical arguments about how the nation-people and the ideal state embody the transcendence of human finitude, see, respectively, Johann Gottlieb Flohte. *Addresses to the German Nation*, trans. R. F. Jones and G. H. Turnbull, ed. George Armstrong Kelly (New York: Harper and Row, 1968), and G. W. F. Hegel, *Philosophy of Right*, trans. T. M. Knox (London and New York: Oxford University Press, 1967), §§325–28. Ernst H. Kantorowicz makes a similar historical argument about the ontotheological character of the European state by linking both patriotism and the absolutist idea of the mysteries of the state to the *corpus mysticum* in medieval theology. See his "*Pro Patria Mori* in Medieval Political Thought," in *Selected Studies* (Locust Valley, N.Y.: J. J. Augustin, 1965), 320–21: "Once the *corpus mysticum* has been identified with the *corpus morale et pollicum* of the people and has become synonymous with nation and 'fatherland,' death *pro patria* that is for a mystical body corporate, regains its former nobility. Death for the fatherland now is viewed in a truly religious perspective; it appears as a sacrifice for the *corpus mysticum* of the state which is no less a reality than the *corpus mysticum* of the church. . . . [T]he quasi-religious aspects of death for the fatherland clearly derived from the Christian faith, the forces of which now were activated in the service of the secular *corpus mysticum* of the state." In the same volume, see also "Mysteries of the State: An Absolutist Concept and Its Late Mediaeval Origins," 381–98.
2   See, for instance, Howard Stein, ed., *Asian Industrialization and Africa: Studies in Policy Alternatives to Structural Adjustment* (New York: St. Martin's, 1995).
3   "Dr. M: We Don't Need 'Hot Money,'" *Star* (Kuala Lumpur, Malaysia), Sunday, 14 June 1998; my emphasis.
4   Martin Khor, "IMF 'Cure' Pushes Indonesia to Crisis," *Star* (Kuala Lumpur, Malaysia), Monday, 11 May 1998.

Pheng Cheah (1999) "Spectral Nationality: The Living on [sur-vie] of the Postcolonial Nation in . . ." *Boundary 2*, vol. 26, no. 3. pp. 226–7, 239–40, 247, 251–2.

NEW MALADIES OF THE SOUL: JULIA KRISTEVA (1995)

Julia Kristeva (1941–) is Professor of Linguistics at the Université de Paris VII. She is a world renowned Bulgarian/French social thinker, psychoanalyst, and novelist whose work has spanned five decades. Since the 1969 publication of her first work, *Semeiotikè*, Kristeva has been lauded as a highly influential figure in an array of academic disciplines as well as more broadly in the general public. Principally, this has to do with her unique ability to blend philosophy, semiotics, psychoanalysis, theology, art history, and literary theory together to understand a host of social phenomena. Her work *New Maladies of the Soul*, from which the selection is taken, builds upon her earlier investigations into how individuals are currently constituted. Specifically, she is interested in new kinds of subjectivities and psycho-pathologies that come to the fore today.

Comeback of the Soul and Reduction of Private Life

Progress in the natural sciences, notably in biology and neurobiology, has enabled us to envision the death of the soul. Since we are continually decoding the secrets of neurons, their tendencies and their electrical dynamics, do we still have a need for this age-old chimera? Have we not come up with cognitive constructs that can account for cellular as well as human behavior?

However that may be, one cannot help noticing that the subject, whose soul was considered banished from the "pure" sciences, is making a triumphant comeback in the most sophisticated biological theories that make up cognitive science. "The image is present in the brain before the object," claim biologists. "Cognitive architecture is not limited by the nervous system; on the contrary, the nervous system is penetrated by the cognitive architecture that takes place there." "We cannot dispense with a teleonomy here." "I cannot see how we might conceive of mental functioning that did not include a representation of the goal, that is, that did not imply a subject that attempts to represent both itself and its expected goal."[1]

Image before object, subject, teleonomy, representation: where is the soul to be found? If cognitive science is not to lead biology toward a spiritualist rebirth, we must ask how a soul is made. What kinds of representations and which logical varieties constitute the soul? Psychoanalysis does not necessarily have the answers to these questions, but it is the one discipline that is searching for them.

Can we speak of new patients?

At the same time, everyday experience points to a spectacular reduction of private life. These days, who still has a soul? We are all too familiar with the sort of emotional blackmail that reminds us of television serials, but this coercion is merely a by-product of the hysterical failure of psychic life that romantic dissatisfaction and middle-class domestic comedy have already depicted for us. As for the renewed interest in religion, we have reason to wonder if it stems from a legitimate quest, or from a psychological poverty that requests that faith give it an artificial soul that might replace an amputated subjectivity. For an affirmation emerges: today's men and women – who are stress-ridden and eager to achieve, to spend money, have fun, and die – dispense with the representation of their experience that we call psychic life. Actions and their imminent abandonment have replaced the interpretation of meaning.

We have neither the time nor the space needed to create a soul for ourselves, and the mere hint of such activity seems frivolous and ill-advised. Held back by his aloofness, modern man is a narcissist – a narcissist who may suffer, but who feels no remorse. He manifests his suffering in his body and he is afflicted with somatic symptoms. His problems serve to justify his refuge in the very problems that his own desire paradoxically solicits. When he is not depressed, he becomes swept away by insignificant and valueless objects that offer a perverse pleasure, but no satisfaction. Living in a piecemeal and accelerated space and time, he often has trouble acknowledging his own physiognomy; left without a sexual, subjective, or moral identity, this amphibian is a being of boundaries, a borderline, or a "false self" – a body that acts, often without even the joys of such performative drunkenness. Modern man is losing his soul, but he does not know it, for the psychic apparatus is what registers representations and their meaningful values for the subject. Unfortunately, that darkroom needs repair.

Of course, the society that shapes modern individuals does not leave them stranded. They can find one possibly effective solution for their problems in neurochemistry, whose methods can often treat insomnia, anxieties, certain psychotic states, and some forms of depression. And who could find fault with that? The body conquers the invisible territory of the soul. Let it stand for the record. There is nothing you can do about it. You are overwhelmed with images. They carry you away, they replace you, you are dreaming. The rapture of the hallucination originates in the absence of boundaries between pleasure and reality, between truth and falsehood. The spectacle is life as a dream – we all want this. Do this "you" and this "we" exist? Your expression is standardized, your discourse becomes normalized. For that matter, do you really have a discourse of your own?

If drugs do not take over your life, your wounds are "healed" with images, and before you can speak about your states of the soul, you drown them in the world of mass media. The image has an extraordinary power to harness your anxieties and desires, to take on their intensity and to suspend their meaning. It works by itself. As a result, the psychic life of modern individuals wavers between somatic symptoms (getting sick and going to the hospital)' and the visual depiction of their desires (daydreaming in front of the TV). In such a situation, psychic life is blocked, inhibited, and destroyed.

We see all too easily, however, that this mutation may be beneficial. More than just a commodity or a new variant of the "opium of the people," the current transformation of psychic life may foreshadow a new humanity, one whose psychological conveniences will be able to overcome metaphysical anxiety and the need for meaning. Wouldn't it be great to be satisfied with just a pill and a television screen?

The problem is that the path of such a superman is strewn with traps. A wide variety of troubles can bring new patients to the analyst's couch: sexual and relationship difficulties, somatic symptoms, a difficulty in expressing oneself, and a general malaise caused by a language experienced as "artificial," "empty," or "mechanical." These patients often resemble "traditional" analysands, but "maladies of the soul" soon break through their hysterical and obsessional allure – "maladies of the soul" that are not necessarily psychoses, but that evoke the psychotic patient's inability to symbolize his unbearable traumas.

As a result, analysts must come up with new classification systems that take into account wounded "narcissisms," "false personalities," "borderline states," and "psychosomatic conditions."[2] Whatever their differences, all these symptomatologies share a common denominator – the inability to represent. Whether it takes the form of psychic mutism or adopts various signs experienced as "empty" or "artificial," such a deficiency of psychic representation hinders sensory, sexual, and intellectual life. Moreover, it may strike a blow to biological functioning itself. In a roundabout manner, the psychoanalyst is then asked to restore psychic life and to enable the speaking entity to live life to its fullest.

Are these new patients a product of contemporary life, which exacerbates our familial situations and infantile difficulties and makes them into symptoms of a particular era? If not, are dependence on medicines and refuge in the image merely modern renditions of the narcissistic inadequacies common to all times? Finally, have patients changed or has analytic practice changed, such that analysts have sharpened their interpretations of previously neglected symptomatologies? These questions as well as others will be asked by the readers of this book, just as they are asked by its author. The fact remains, however, that analysts who do not discover a *new malady of the soul* in each of their patients do not fully appreciate the uniqueness of each individual. Similarly, we can place ourselves at the heart of the analytic project by realizing that these new maladies of the soul go beyond traditional classification systems and their inevitable overhaul. What is more important, they embody difficulties or obstacles in psychic representation, difficulties that end up destroying psychic life. Revitalizing grammar and rhetoric, and enriching the style of those who wish to speak with us because they can no longer remain silent and brushed aside: do such projects not mirror the new life and new psyche that psychoanalysis wishes to unearth?

Notes

1 Jacques Hochmann and Marc Jennerot, *Espirit où es-tu? Psychanalyse et neuroscience* (Paris: Odile Jacob, 1991), p. 53.
2 I indicate here some of the best-known nosographical contributions:
   * Helene Deutsch 'Some forms of emotional disturbances and their relationship to schizophrenia' (1942, *Neurosis and Character Types*. New York: International Universities Press, 1965.
   * D.W. Winnicott, 'Distortion of the ego as a function of the true and false self,' *The Maturational Processes and the Facilitating Environment*. London: Hogarth Press, 1965.
   * P. Marty, *L'Ordre psychosomatique*. Paris: Payot, 1980.
   * Otto Kernberg, *Borderline Conditions and Pathological Narcissism*. New York: Jeffery Aronson, 1976.
   * André Green, *Narcissisme de vie, narcissisme de mort*. Paris: Éditions de Minuit, 1983.

Kristeva Julia (1995) *New Maladies of the Soul*, Trans. by Ross Guberman, New York: Columbia University Press, pp. 6–10.

GLOBAL SEX: DENNIS ALTMAN (2001)

Dennis Altman (1943–) is Professor of Politics at La Trobe University, Australia, and the author of many widely read books on homosexuality, gay politics, and sexualities. In this selection from his outstanding book *Global Sex*, Altman reviews some of the key personal and cultural transformations at work in the globalization of sexual identities. In fueling a shift from production to consumption throughout various contemporary societies, globalization for Altman heralds a new range of identities, as individuals seek to make sense of their lives (and the social conditions of their lives) in the context of the global electronic economy. Against this conceptual backcloth, Altman considers the discursive shift in terminology from "prostitute" to "sex worker" as part of the degraded logics of intimate globalism.

Sex and the Global Crisis of Identities

A growing globalization of both identities and human rights is reflected in the growth of sex-worker groups and the regulation of prostitution. In recent years there have been legislative attempts in a number of first-world countries to decriminalize prostitution and at the same time to control certain forms of sex work, especially that involving enforced prostitution or children.[1] There is a bitter division between those who argue that human rights should mean the end of prostitution (understood as "sex-slavery" to use Kathleen Barry's phrase)[2] and those who argue that adults should have the right to use their bodies to make money, and should be protected from exploitation and danger in making use of that right. Indeed the use of the term "sex worker" is a deliberate ploy to demystify the category of "prostitute," and the terms "sex work" and "sex worker" "have been coined by sex-workers themselves to redefine commercial sex, not as the social or psychological characteristic of a class of women, but as an income-generating activity or form of employment for women and men."[3] [. . .]

This shift toward seeing prostitution as work is reflected in the development of "sex-work" organizations in some developing countries, the first of which seems to have been in Ecuador, followed by groups in a number of other Latin American countries[4] and a couple in Southeast Asia such as Talikala in Davao City, the Philippines. The women who founded Talikala were concerned from the outset to empower sex workers, and were attacked by conservative Catholics for "promoting prostitution," ironic as the initial funding for the project came from the Maryknoll Fathers. In 1995 sex workers in the Sonagachi area of Calcutta organized the Durbar Mahila Samanwaya Committee, which claims to be the registered organization of more than 40,000 female, male, and transsexual sex workers of West Bengal[5] and with the Usha Co-operative runs its own STI clinics, a cooperative credit union, literacy classes, and a crèche. One report suggested 3,000 people attended the first national prostitution conference in India in 1997.[6] Even if this sort of organizing was in part inspired by western ideas, does that make it less significant? One might remember that the Indian independence movement was also influenced by western concepts of nation and democracy – and itself became a major inspiration for the American and South African civil rights movements. In the same way the Durbar Mahila Samanwaya Committee has taken the mobilization of sex workers to a scale beyond that reached in any western country.

During the 1990s an international network of sex-work projects (NSWP) has sought to link sex-worker groups in both rich and poor countries, often organizing around international HIV/AIDS conferences. By the end of the decade the network linked groups in forty countries, but was limited by huge difficulty in getting resources, and the dependence on a handful of dedicated volunteers.[7] Gaining acceptance for sex-worker groups has been a tough ongoing struggle, with only a few governments being willing to accord any recognition at all. In both Australia and New Zealand the national organizations have at times played a role in national AIDS advisory bodies, but this is rare, nor have better-established community AIDS organizations always been particularly supportive. Guenter Frankenberg's comment about Germany applies elsewhere: "The gay dominated AIDS-Hilfen have effectively colonized junkies, prostitutes and prisoners, speaking for them instead of enabling them to be their own advocates."[8] The recognition of representatives of both sex workers and lesbians in the 1998 Indonesian Women's Congress which followed the downfall of Suharto was therefore particularly significant,[9] as was the inclusion of lesbianism on the official agenda of the 1998 All National Women's Conference in India.

Most people who engage in sex for money have no sense of this comprising their central identity, and they may well be repelled by attempts to organize around an identity they would strongly reject. It is a fact that money will be involved in a great many sexual encounters in almost any cash economy, and that the great majority of such transactions will not involve people who identify themselves as professional sex workers, but see it rather as one among a number of strategies to survive.[10] This is true of young African girls who find "sugar daddies" (sometimes known as "spare tyres") to help with their school fees, as it is of American beach bums who accept hospitality and gifts in exchange for sexual favors. We should be skeptical of those studies which claim to tell us that 36% of sex workers are positive/negative/use condoms or whatever: this assumes a fixed population, which is a dangerous fiction. It seems useful to think of prostitution not as a fixed state or identity, but rather as a continuum ranging from organized prostitution, through brothels, escort agencies, and so forth, to unpremeditated transactions resulting from chance encounters.

This does not mean that organization around conditions of employment and protection from abuse may not be successful. Speaking of drug users, Chris Jones suggested the idea of a "pragmatic community . . . a community in action affected by various forces producing potentially pro-active responses to various situations."[11] We need to know more about organizations which may well include sex workers without making this a central definition, as in the example of the Ghana Widows' Association, which according to at least one account includes large numbers of women in Accra working in commercial sex.[12] In early 1998 a group known as the Henao Sisters was established in Port Moresby (Papua New Guinea) for women known as *raun-raun* girls, those who move in and out of prostitution. While the group grew out of a peer-education program established by a government-supported program for HIV-prevention education, the initiative for its development appears to have come from the women themselves who are faced with ongoing issues of survival, violence, and police harassment.

As both the examples of gay/lesbian and sex-worker identities show, socioeconomic change will produce new ways of understanding ourselves and our place in the world. The breakdown of the extended family household as both an economic and social unit was one of the most important consequences of industrialization in the western world. In turn the growth of affluence, and the shifting emphasis from production to consumption, has meant a steady shrinking in households as even the nuclear family is replaced by large numbers of unmarried couples, of single-parent families, of people living large parts of their lives alone or in shared households. With this has come a new range of identities, as people seek to make sense of their lives as divorced, single, unmarried, or sole parents. Both commercial pressures to target specific "demographics" and the personal need to define one's identity in psychological terms means the growth of new sorts of support and social groups for, say, divorcées, single fathers, people living in multiple relationships (for which the word "polyandry" has been revived).

Unlike identities based on sexuality such as "lesbian" or "transvestite," these are identities based on relationship status and can in fact cross over definitions of sexuality. In Harvey Fierstein's play *Torch Song Trilogy* there is an angry argument where Arnold tries to make his mother accept that the loss of his lover is equivalent to her loss of her husband. There are small signs that this emphasis on relationship identities is spreading beyond the rich world, such as a report of an attempt to found "the Divorced Women's Tea-house" in Beijing in 1995. The association foundered on Chinese government restrictions on the creation of nongovernmental organizations.[13]

Underlying all these developments is an increasing stress on ideas of individual identity and satisfaction, and the linking of these concepts to sexuality. One of the dominant themes in post-Freudian western thinking about sex has been to explain why sexuality is so central to our sense of self, and thus the basis of both psychological and political identity. These assumptions about sexuality are far from universal; as Heather Montgomery warned, speaking of children in the sex industry in Thailand: "Sexuality was never identified with personal fulfilment or individual pleasure . . . Prostitution was an incidental way of constructing their identities."[14] Similarly Lenore Manderson wrote, also of Thailand: "For women, commercial sex is the mechanism by which many women today fulfill their obligations as mothers and daughters. For them, the body and its sexual expression in work are a means of production rather than a mirror to the self."[15]

That last phrase is crucial, for it sums up the dominant script by which westerners have interpreted sexuality for the past century, whether they have sought genetic and biological explanations or, like the radical Freudian school derived from thinkers like Wilhelm Reich and Herbert Marcuse, have sought to develop concepts of repression and sublimation to explain political attitudes and behavior.[16] In some ways Frantz Fanon also belongs to this tradition, and the fact that he wrote from the position of a colonized Algerian has made him particularly attractive to postcolonial theorists, who tend to ignore his strong homophobia.[17] This attempt to link sexuality with the political is far less fashionable today, where sexuality is more commonly linked with contemporary capitalism, and we increasingly think of ourselves as consumers rather than citizens. Indeed it is the Right who seem to set the agenda for sexual politics, through attacks on abortion, contraception, and homosexuality, which they link clearly to dissatisfaction with the whole tenor of modern life, yet refusing, except for a small group of religious thinkers, to see the connection between contemporary capitalism and the changes in the sex/gender order they so abhor.

Notes

1 This legislation, it might be argued, is another form of western discourse being deployed to counter a largely western-generated phenomenon. See Eliza Noh, ' "Amazing Grace, Come Sit on My Face," or Christian Ecumenical Representation of the Asian Sex Tour Industry,' *Positions* 5:2 (1997): 439–65.

2 Kathleen Barry, *Female Sexual Slavery* (New York: New York University Press, 1984). This should be read alongside the very different views of G. Phetersen, ed., *A Vindication of the Rights of Whores* (Seattle: Seal Press, 1989). A more contemporary statement drawing on Barry's work is Sheila's Jeffreys, *The Idea of Prostitution* (Melbourne: Spinifex, 1997). For an overview of some of the relevant literature see Lynn Sharon Chancer, 'Prostitution, Feminist Theory and Ambivalence,' *Social Text*, no. 37 (1993): 143–71; Wendy Chapkis, *Live Sex Acts* (London: Cassell, 1997).

3 Jo Bindman with Jo Doezema, *Redefining Prostitution as Sex Work on the International Agenda* (London: Anti-Slavery International, 1997), 1. See also Cheryl Overs and Paulo Longo, *Making Sex Work Safe* (London: Network of Sex Work Projects, 1997).

4 See Kemala Kempadoo, 'Introduction: Globalizing Sex Workers' Rights,' and Angelita Abad et al., 'The Association of Autonomous Women Workers, Ecuador,' in K. Kempadoo and J. Doezema, eds., *Global Sex Workers* (New York: Routledge, 1998), 1–28, 172–77.

5 'The "Fallen" Learn to Rise,' and 'Sex Worker's Co-operative,' publications of Durbar Mahila Samanwaya Committee, Calcutta, 1998–99.

6 'Prostitutes Seek Workmen Status,' *Statesman Weekly*, November 22, 1997.

7 There is an interview with the central figure in the development of NSWP, Cheryl Overs, in Kempadoo and Doezema, *Global Sex Workers*, 204–9. Overs here pays tribute both to her 'mates in the global village' and to her Australian background.

8 Guenter Frankberg, 'Germany: The Uneasy Triumph of Pragmatism,' in D. Kirp and R. Bayer, eds., *AIDS in the Industrialized Democracies* (New Brunswick: Rutgers University Press, 1992), 121.

9 'Sex Appeal,' *Far Eastern Economic Review*, February 4, 1999, 29–31.

10 This sort of 'transactional sex' is discussed in Lori Heise and Chris Elias, 'Transforming AIDS Prevention to Meet Women's Needs,' *Social Science and Medicine* 40 (1995): 931–43.

11 Chris Jones, 'Making a Users Voice,' paper presented at the Fifth International Conference on Drug-Related Harm, Toronto, March 1994, 7.

12 See Alfred Neequaye, 'Prostitution in Accra,' in M. Plant, ed., *AIDS, Drugs, and Prostitution* (London: Routledge, 1993), 178–79.

13 Matt Forney, 'Voice of the People,' *Far Eastern Economic Review*, May 7, 1998, 10.

14 Heather Montgomery, 'Children, Prostitution, and Identity,' in Kempadoo and Doezema, *Global Sex Workers*, 147.

15 Lenore Manderson, 'Public Sex Performances in Patpong and Explorations of the Edges of Imagination,' *Journal of Sex Research* 29:4 (1992): 473. See also Barbara Zalduondo, 'Prostitution Viewed Cross-Culturally: Toward Recontextualizing Sex Work in AIDS Intervention Research,' *Journal of Sex Research* 28:2 (1991): 232–48.

16 On the sexual radicals see Paul Robinson, *The Freudian Left* (New York: Harper and Row, 1969).

17 See Frantz Fanon, *Black Skin White Masks* (London: Pluto, 1986), and the introduction to that volume by Homi Bhabha, vii–xxvi.

Dennis Altman (2001) *Global Sex*, Chicago: University of Chicago Press, pp. 100–105.

TURBULENCE OF MIGRATION: NIKOS PAPASTERGIADIS (2000)

Nikos Papastergiadis (1962–) is Professor of English at the University of Melbourne, Australia. In this selection, from his engaging book *The Turbulence of Migration* (2000), Papastergiadis demonstrates a radical disjuncture between globalization and geo-political borders, between modernity and migration. In mapping patterns of global migration, Papastergiadis tracks the differential patterns between mobility and economic production as regards wealthy, shielded transients on the one hand, and tragic, dispossessed illegals of contemporary global systems on the other. From the global trade in prostitution to people smuggling, Papastergiadis is keenly alert to the emotional costs of illegal migration, cultural exclusion, and political displacement as core aspects of the "intimate global."

Migration, Mobility, and Global Movements

The link between globalization of the economy and the international labour market is not a clear one. Deregulation in one area does not automatically imply a loosening of restrictions in the other. The one form of international migration which does resemble the new flows of capital is the circulation of 'skilled transients'.[1] There is now a significant flow of corporate managers, consultants and technicians who are highly mobile. They frequently move between countries with minimal restrictions, or find themselves being relocated according to the needs of a transnational corporation. Intra-company transfers and the attraction to global cities for 'skilled transients' is now exerting a significant economic and political role in the global migration systems.

At the other end of the socio-economic spectrum there is not such a direct link between patterns of mobility and economic production. The tragic stories of women being lured to the west with the promise of marriage, only to find their passports confiscated, their children abducted, and themselves coerced into working as prostitutes, are no longer uncommon. According to Anita Gradin, the European Union Justice Commissioner, between 200,000 and 500,000 women, mostly from Asia, Africa, Latin America and the former Eastern bloc, have become victims of traffickers in sex slaves.[2] On the promise of work or marriage, they have been drugged, beaten and condemned to work for pimps across Europe. They are sold from brothel to brothel, fetching from $500 to $5,000.[3] Their earnings and movements monitored by ruthless pimps, forced into living and working in appalling conditions, these women have few rights and are often too intimidated to call for help. Their pimps not only threaten them with reprisals but also convince them that they would be severely punished by the state if they were caught working illegally as prostitutes. A further strategy is the possession of humiliating videotapes which they threaten to show to their families back home. [. . .]

The relationship between movement and settlement has become increasingly jagged. The contrast between earlier policies of migration, which were motivated by selective resettlement, and the current phase, which is driven by economic advantage can also be illustrated by the shifts in attitudes in places like Australia. Until the early 1960s the Australian government offered British people assisted passage schemes to encourage 'white immigration'. Fares were heavily subsidized, and preferential opportunities for housing and work were made available. These racialized policies were eventually dismantled only to be replaced with new criteria which predominantly linked entry to economic benefit. The most notable example of this policy is the creation of special 'fast tracks' for citizenship to attract wealthy Asian entrepreneurs. Yet, owing to the circuitous loops of global speculation, the money that is brought in to secure citizenship rarely trickles down to the national economy. Shifting in no longer implies a commitment to stay.

The ability of certain Asian entrepreneurs to buy citizenship in a second and sometimes third country presents a different image from the conventional category of the migrant as victim. These new middle-class migrants have a far greater flexibility in their ability to move and in their selection of destination. Countries like Canada and Australia now actively compete with each other in offering inducements that bypass the current restrictions on immigration from Asia. However, as some commentators have noted, the integration of the entrepreneurs within the new host country has created hostility from members of the established Asian immigrant communities, as well as stimulating broader resentments from the hegemonic groups in the host societies.

The commitment of these immigrants has also been questioned as their relationship to place has been described in terms of 'bi-locality'. The flow of movement is not one-way. There is a high rate of return as well as many forms of ongoing exchange. For political or educational reasons children and older members of the family are often 'parachuted' into one country while the 'astronaut' breadwinners continue to commute across the Pacific. Decisions over the spatial location of the family are often made in terms of security and economic opportunity, and given their resources, the decision to move on to another country is not a difficult one. These transnational migrants, who use different locations to create the optimal conditions for their own prosperity and family security, have forced commentators to rethink the 'classical' factors of migration. In these instances, the model of push-pull fails to address the patterns of mobility and the decisions for integration into a host society. Given the complexity of high finance and flux in political security, sociologists have gained very little insight into the forms of agency that operate in these forms of migration. [. . .]

The degree to which migrants can move varies considerably. In most cases it depends on the status and resources of the migrant and, in some instances, it relates to the degree to which territorial boundaries are actively policed. In some regions communities are either settled across borders or move freely between them. The Lapps in northern Scandinavia and the loosely guarded borders of West Africa are examples where political regulations are not a restraint on movement. However, the majority of nation-states in the world are increasingly tightening entry and exit from their territories. There is a temptation to relate the movement of migrant labour with the broader flows of capital and information across the world. To make such a connection would certainly draw attention to the links between demographic, economic and cultural changes. Yet there can be no direct correspondence between the circulation of money with the movement of people. The tracks on which they move and the barriers imposed on them are often contradictory.

A more useful way of thinking of borders and flows in the contemporary migration patterns is from a dual perspective, one which focuses on both regional political regulations and specific cultural prohibitions, while also recognizing the global pressures and motivations for movement. No nation-state can completely close its borders. All borders are both permeable and selective. Certain categories of migrants will be encouraged at given times; and at all times, if the inducements for migration are strong, some people will find other ways to bypass the official border controls. This dual perspective will need to acknowledge the effectiveness of some states in regulating movement across their borders, as well as being cognizant of the ways in which migrants target their destinations and on arrival develop new expectations of settlement. Neither the historical routes established by colonial links, nor the proximity of neighbouring states, provide the main clues for the paths that future migrants will take. Sociologists have underestimated the extent to which migration is based on the transmission of ideas, stories told by other migrants, rumours of opportunity, the strutting of returnees, as well as the more conventional practices of recruiting agencies and the complex levels of influence exerted by the media, collectively stimulating the thought that life is better elsewhere. The directions and sources of migration have multiplied dramatically, and these can only be accounted for by taking a perspective which draws attention to both the global perception of mobility and the local strategies of selectivity across borders.

It is perhaps necessary to think of migratory movements beyond the binarism of either long-term resettlement, or short-term contracted labour. Both at the level of skilled and unskilled, legal and illegal workers, migration has generated new relationships between place and belonging. During the period of the 'classical migration' to the New World, the stereotypical vision of the migrant was either as the young man who left to make his fortune and return as a hero, or as the man who left to set up a home and enterprise in a new country. Migration was either a one-way trip, or a temporary sojourn. It represented the opportunity to start a new life elsewhere, or to provide the resources for getting a better foothold in the original homeland.

The self-image of settler societies in the New World was built on the unacknowledged genocide of the indigenous people and the ambivalent promise that a new nation could be built by migrants from other nations. Not all migrants were granted the same privileges, but there was the underlying assumption that a selective form of diversity was a positive force in national unity. In countries like the United States, Canada, Australia and New Zealand the formation of a new national culture was premised at first on the assimilation of the minorities to the hegemonic Anglo-Celtic culture, and then redefined in terms of pluralist models of cultural integration. Given that the foundational scars of genocide have far from healed in these countries, and the promise of equality under the policies are far from the daily realities of the diasporic communities in these countries, there is little confidence that the west can furnish a universal model for managing the future of global migration.

The driving motivation for contemporary migrants is rarely expressed in the masculinist narrative of the pioneer that dominated the hopes and sentiments of settlers in the New World. The experiences of Third World women, a key force in the international labour market, cannot be described in such pioneering terms. Their presence in the national imaginary of their host country is confined to cheap and temporary labour. There is no social space which beckons the migrant as a positive and permanent feature. According to the United Nations Population Division (1990), women make up half the world's migrants. In countries like the Philippines, women account for up to 80 per cent of the migrant population. The restructuring of the global economies with a demand for services in the First World, and the increasing feminization of manufacturing industries in the Third World, have led to a dramatic realignment of gender relations. These women are often seen as double victims. Shouldering inherited family debts and exploited by the agencies that contract them to overseas companies, they have no opportunities to create a new sense of community in their migrant homes. They have short-term contracts and live, for the most part, in isolation from other migrants with whom they could form social bonds. Yet their experience of alienation is often accompanied by a broader rethinking of their identity and social position. In places like Britain, immigrant women, particularly from the Indian sub-continent, have been at the forefront of initiating cultural change. But these cultural and political initiatives in Britain have to be seen in the context of extended migration and the complexities of multicultural policies.[4] The position of immigrant workers in Britain is significantly different from the contract workers in the Gulf States.

Across Europe and Asia we see new patterns of migrants entering countries both legally and illegally for limited periods. Despite the existence of strict border controls, vast numbers of migrants oscillate between their homeland and workplace(s). The scale of illegal migration has grown dramatically in the 1990s. In the USA illegal migrants tend to settle for more extensive stays. Skeldon estimates that the smuggling of people into the USA is a business worth $3 billion a year.[5] In 1993 the General Accounting Office reported that there were from 3.4 to 5.5 million illegal workers in the USA.[6] This growth in illegal migration reflects the broader inequalities and turbulent phase of global politics. However, as Mark Miller argues, the pattern of movement of illegal migrants cannot be explained by a neat binarism which presupposes that illegals are impelled to move because of economic stagnation and political crisis in the homeland, and then lured by the high wages and prosperity of the host country:

> Rarely, however, does it suffice to account for illegal immigration in such bald terms. A great deal of illegal immigration occurs between developing countries and fits poorly into a south to north schema. Indeed, two of the most striking points to be made about the late twentieth century illegal migration are its globalization, with transportation and communication advances facilitating migration that was scarcely possible several decades earlier, and its decoupling from historically set patterns.[7]

The historical links forged under colonialism still provide some of the axial routes of migration. Algerians continue to head for France, while Pakistanis try their luck in Britain. However, the recent trends reveal that migrants, in particular those from the former Eastern bloc countries, are heading for new destinations on the basis of covert agencies, or messages sent along complex information chains that link friends and families across diverse locations. The diversity in the sources of migration implies that there are more limited possi-bilities for migrants to form ethnic bonds. The established immigrant communities can be as foreign to them as the hegemonic community. Despite the growing militarization of national boundaries to ward off illegal migration, the more draconian visa restrictions and the possible penalization of employers who fail to check the status of their workers, the international battle against migration is far from won. How can a state defend itself against a process which is so deeply implicated within its own development? With a rapid feedback system that informs potential migrants about the various means of entry, how do immigration officials develop clear rules that will legitimately distinguish the legal from the illegal migrant?

> Thus while restricting the entry of aliens for permanent settlement, states may simultaneously encourage or even promote the entry of tourists, business men, artists, social workers, scientists, skilled workers, students, diplomats, or even a certain number of unskilled workers. In addition, the entry of refugees,

though generally not encouraged, may be tolerated for humanitarian reasons. Consequently, unless external controls are reinforced by strong and effective internal controls, illegal migration is likely to emerge as a relatively viable option for a person denied access to *bona fide* migration opportunities.[8]

Government policy in terms of the relationship between globalization and migration can be characterized as contradictory. Deregulation and casualization in the workforce may make the labour markets more competitive on a global scale, but they also stimulate the informal economy, towards which migrants gravitate with greater intensity than the indigenous labour force. The evisceration of inner cities and the dismantling of welfare services have also created more hostile and more divided urban spaces. Urban planning is now more concerned with surveillance and segregation than with inspiring any form of civic integration. The decline of local economies and social services has fuelled a new dimension of scapegoating within the racist ideologies that proliferate in these inner cities. This tense environment of conflict and competition could produce far more explosive and exploitative forms of social relations than political leaders anticipate. Global cities like New York, London and Sydney often proudly parade the vitality of 'their' multiculturalism, by displaying variety at the level of ethnic cuisine. Yet this gastronomic boast would have greater social credibility if it were matched by a commitment to promote the conditions by which different cultures are sustained and new cultural forms articulated. What would a multicultural workplace look like? How do urban planners accomodate cultural differences in domestic situations? Who will judge, when there is a legal conflict between competing cultural codes? Global migration has heightened the urgency of such questions, as it has cleaved open the gulf in the political rhetoric, which seemingly endorses multiculturalism, but also denies the need to rethink the terms of social inclusion and spatial belonging:

> Cities and communities are increasingly conflicted about immigration. Residents often do not mind including those who fit into the self-image of a prosperous, technologically innovative and democratic society, but wish to exclude the workers who are, in fact, necessary for the reproduction of society. Immigrants are more likely to belong to the excluded. But the groups are more closely bound together than they think: the corporate elite profit from illegal immigrants, and the prosperous suburbanites use the labor of poorer immigrants they find so threatening. It is out of this contradiction and multi-layered character of the postmodern city that its enormous energy, its cultural dynamism, and its innovative capability emerge.[9]

Before these changes, government agencies respond in conflicting ways. They seek to strike the impossible balance between satisfying the global interests of capital as well as protecting the local needs of labour. The patterns of migration that emerge from these contradictory aspirations are so multiple and of such a complex nature that it is now impossible either to generalize about the logic which determines its causes, or to map its flows according to the binary co-ordinates of departure and destination. Migrants have become more mobile and the story of migration is even more jagged. Flexibility in the marketplace has not meant more diversity in the workplace, but has only stretched the capacity of labour to endure insecurity and to see opportunity in displacement. A current map of global migration would have to be as complex as all the migrant biographies.

Notes

1 Allan Findlay, 'Skilled Transients: The Invisible Phenomenon?' in Cohen, *Cambridge Survey of World Migration*, p. 515.
2 European Commission Conference on Trafficking in Women, 10 June 1996.
3 Massimo Calabresi, 'Of Human Bondage', *Time* (Februrary 1998), p. 26.
4 Avtar Brah, *Cartographies of Diaspora* (Routledge, London, 1996), pp. 67–83.
5 Skeldon, 'Trans-Pacific Migration', p. 535.
6 Mark Miller, 'Illegal Migration', in Cohen, *Cambridge Survey of World Migration*, p. 537.
7 Ibid., p. 538.

8   M. Kritz and H. Zlotnik, 'Global Interactions: Migration Systems, Processes and Policies', in M. Kritz, L. Lim and H. Zlotnik (eds), *International Migration System: A Global Approach* (Clarendon Press, Oxford, 1992).

9   M. Douglass, *Global Migration – Beyond Multiculturalism* (unpublished paper, 1997), p.8.

Nikos Papastergiadis (2000) *Turbulence of Migration: Globalization, Deterritorialization and Hybridity*, Cambridge: Polity Press, pp. 40–41, 43–44, 46–50.

■ ■ ■ ■ ■ ■ ■

EVERYWHERE AND ANYWHERE: JEAN-LUC NANCY (2002)

Jean-Luc Nancy (1940–) is a philosopher who was educated in Paris where, ultimately, he completed a doctorate on Immanuel Kant. He has taught or lectured in Strasbourg, Berlin, other parts of Europe, the UK, and the United States, as well as the European Graduate School in Switzerland. He is noted especially for his literary sensibilities and his knowledge of psychoanalysis. Like many French and European philosophers, Nancy is deeply informed by classical languages and literature, a quality that is on display in the title of the book from which the selection is taken: *The Creation of the World* or *Globalization*. By juxtaposing an essentially religious theme with the over-used term "globalization," Nancy opens new vistas on concepts at once ancient and postmodern – here, the city as a global force articulated from a formative city that is, as he says, "everywhere and anywhere" and perhaps now nowhere exactly at all. Nancy's best-known works are *The Title of the Letter: A Reading of Lacan, The Literary Absolute*, and *Being Singular Plural* – but three of nearly 40 books published since the mid-1970s.

The Creation of the World or Globalization

Urbi et orbi: this formulation drawn from papal benediction has come to mean "everywhere and anywhere" in ordinary language. Rather than a mere shift in meaning, this is a genuine disintegration. This disintegration is not simply due to the dissolution of the religious Christian bond that (more or less) held the Western world together until around the middle of a twentieth century to which the nineteenth century effectively relinquished its certainties (history, science, conquering humanity – whether this took place with or against vestiges of Christianity). It is due to the fact that it is no longer possible to identify either a city that would be "The City" – as Rome was for so long – or an orb that would provide the contour of a world extended around this city. Even worse, it is no longer possible to identify either the city or the orb of the world in general. The city spreads and extends all the way to the point where, while it tends to cover the entire orb of the planet, it loses its properties as a city, and, of course with them, those properties that would allow it to be distinguished from a "country." That which extends in this way is no longer properly "urban" – either from the perspective of urbanism or from that of urbanity – but megapolitical, metropolitan, or co-urbational, or else caught in the loose net of what is called the "urban network." In such a network, the city crowds, the hyperbolic accumulation of construction projects (with their concomitant demolition) and of exchanges (of movements, products, and information) spread, and the inequality and apartheid concerning the access to the urban milieu (assuming that it is a dwelling, comfort, and culture), or these exclusions from the city that for a long time has produced its own rejections and outcasts, accumulate proportionally. The result can only be understood in terms of what is called an *agglomeration*, with its senses of conglomeration, of piling up, with the sense of accumulation that, on the one hand, simply concentrates (in a few neighborhoods, in a few houses, sometimes in a few protected mini-cities) the well-being that used to be urban or civil, while on the other hand, proliferates what bears the quite simple and unmerciful name of misery.

This network cast upon the planet – and already around it, in the orbital band of satellites along with their debris – deforms the *orbis* as much as the *urbs*. The agglomeration invades and erodes what used to be thought of as *globe* and which is nothing more now than its double, *glomus*. In such a *glomus*, we see the conjunction of an indefinite growth of techno-science, of a correlative exponential growth of populations, of a worsening of inequalities of all sorts within these populations – economic, biological, and cultural – and of a dissipation of the certainties, images, and identities of what the world was with its parts and humanity with its characteristics.

The civilization that has represented the universal and reason – also known as the West – cannot even encounter and recognize any longer the relativity of its norms and the doubt on its own certainty: this was already its situation two centuries ago. (Hegel wrote in 1802: "[T]he increasing range of acquaintance with alien peoples under the pressure of natural necessity; as, for example, becoming acquainted with a new continent, had this skeptical effect upon the dogmatic common sense of the Europeans down to that time, and upon their indubitable certainly about a mass of concepts concerning right and truth.") This skepticism, in which Hegel saw the fecundity of the destabilization of dogmatisms today, no longer harbors the resource of a future whose dialectic would advance reason farther, ahead or forward, toward a truth and a meaning of the world. On the contrary, it is in the same stroke that the confidence in historical progress weakened, the convergence of knowledge, ethics, and social well-being dissipated, and the domination of an empire made up of technological power and pure economic reason asserted itself.

The West has come to encompass the world, and in this movement it disappears as what was supposed to orient the course of this world. For all that, up until now, one cannot say that any other configuration of the world or any other philosophy of the universal and of reason have challenged that course. Even when, and perhaps especially when one demands a recourse to the "spiritual," unless it is to the "revolution" (is it so different?), the demand betrays itself as an empty wish, having lost all pretense of effective capacity, or else as a shameful escape – and even when it does not appear as a supplementary means of exploiting the conditions created by the economic and technological exploitation. (To take what is "positive" of the West and to infuse it with something new – "values" – on the basis of an African, Buddhist, Islamic, Taoist, perhaps supra-Christian or supra-communist soul, such has been for a long time the sterile theme of many a dissertation . . .).

The world has lost its capacity to "form a world" [*faire monde*]: it seems only to have gained that capacity of proliferating, to the extent of its means, the "unworld" [*immonde*], which, until now, and whatever one may think of retrospective illusions, has never in history impacted the totality of the orb to such an extent. In the end, everything takes place as if the world affected and permeated itself with a death drive that soon would have nothing else to destroy than the world itself.

It is not a question of "weighing in" for or leaning toward either the destruction or the salvation. For we do not even know what either can signify: neither what another civilization or another savagery arising out of the ruins of the West might be, nor what could be "safe/saved" when there is no space outside of the epidemic (in this respect, AIDS is an exemplary case, as are certain epizootic diseases on another level: the scale of the world, of its technologies and of its *habitus*, brings the terror of the plagues of the past to incommensurable heights).

The fact that the world is destroying itself is not a hypothesis: it is in a sense the fact from which any thinking of the world follows, to the point, however, that we do not exactly know what "to destroy" means, nor which world is destroying itself. Perhaps only one thing remains, that is to say, one thought with some certainty: what is taking place is really happening, which means that it happens and happens to us in this way more than a history, even more than an event. It is as if being itself – in whatever sense one understands it, as existence or as substance – surprised us from an unnamable beyond. It is, in fact, the ambivalence of the unnamable that makes us anxious: a beyond for which no alterity can give us the slightest analogy.

It is thus not only a question of being ready for the event – although this is also a necessary condition of thought, today as always. It is a question of owning up to the present, including its very withholding of the event, including its strange absence of presence: we must ask anew what the world wants of us, and what we want of it, everywhere, in all senses, *urbi et orbi*, all over the world and for the whole world, without (the) capital of the world but with the richness of the world.

Let us begin with a lengthy citation to which we must give our sustained attention:

In history up to the present it is certainly an empirical fact that separate individuals have, with the broadening of their activity into world-historical activity, become more and more enslaved under a power alien to them (a pressure which they have conceived of as a dirty trick on the part of the so-called world spirit [*Weltgeist*], etc.), a power which has become more and more enormous and, in the last instance, turns out to be the world market. But it is just as empirically established that, by the overthrow of the existing state of society by the communist revolution (of which more below) and the abolition of private property which is identical with it, this power, which so baffles the German theoreticians, will be dissolved; and that then the liberation of each single individual will be accomplished in the measure in which history becomes transformed into world history. From the above it is clear that the real intellectual wealth of the individual depends entirely on the wealth of his real connections. Only then will the separate individuals be liberated from the various national and local barriers, be brought into practical connection with the material and intellectual production of the whole world and be put in a position to acquire the capacity to enjoy this all-sided production of the whole earth (the creation of man).[1]

This text from *The German Ideology* dates from the time that is considered, not without reason, as that of the "early" Marx: he nevertheless formulates what was his conviction to the end according to which "communism" is nothing other than the actual movement of world history insofar as it becomes global and thus renders possible, and perhaps necessary, the passage to consciousness and enjoyment of human creation in its entirety by all human beings. Human beings would henceforth be freed from what limited the relation in which they mutually produce themselves as spirit and as body. In other words, it was his conviction that humanity is defined by the fact that it produces itself as a whole – not in general, but according to the concrete existence of each, and not in the end only humans, but with them the rest of nature. This, for Marx, is the world: that of the market metamorphosing itself or revolutionizing itself in reciprocal and mutual creation. What Marx will define later as "individual property," that is to say, neither private nor collective, will have to be precisely the property or the proper of each as both created and creator within this sharing of "real relations."

Thus, for Marx, globalization and the domination of capital converge in a revolution that inverts the direction [*sens*] of domination – but which can do so precisely because the global development of the market – the instrument and the field of play of capital – creates in and of itself the possibility of revealing the real connection between existences as their real sense. The commodity form, which is the fetishized form of value, must dissolve itself, sublimate or destroy itself – in any case revolutionize itself, whatever its exact concept – in its true form, which is not only the creation of value but value as creation. Transcribed in terms closer to our current linguistic usage (if we retain the distinction of senses between "globalization" [*globalisation*] and "world-forming" [*mondialisation*] – a distinction that sometimes in France in particular encompasses two usages of the same word *mondialisation* – these semantic complexities are the indicators of what is at stake): globalization makes world-forming possible, by way of a reversal of global domination consisting in the extortion of work, that is, of its value, therefore of value, absolutely. But if globalization has thus a necessity – the necessity that Marx designated as the "historical performance" of capital and that consists in nothing other than the creation by the market of the global dimension as such – it is because, through the interdependence of the exchange of value in its merchandise-form (which is the form of general equivalency, money), the interconnection of everyone in the production of humanity as such comes into view.

If I may focus even more on this point: commerce engenders communication, which requires community, communism. Or: human beings create the world, which produces the human, which creates itself as absolute value and enjoyment [*jouissance*] of that value.

Note

1   Karl Marx, *The German Ideology*, in *The Marx-Engels Reader*, ed. Robert C. Tucker (New York: W.W. Norton, 1978), 163–64. Translation slightly modified. (The German term translated by 'creation' is indeed its corresponding *Schöpfung*: one

could study in Marx the usages of this term and its relation with value in itself, that is to say, with work in itself, as well as its difference and its relations with the *Production* that pertain to the interdependency of work.)

Jean-Luc Nancy (2007) *The Creation of the World* or *Globalization*, trans. by Francois Raffoul and David Pettigrew, Albany, NY: State University of New York Press, pp. 33–37.

■ ■ ■ ■ ■ ■ ■

PRECARIOUS LIFE: JUDITH BUTLER (2004)

Judith Butler (1956–) is the Maxine Elliot Professor in the Departments of Rhetoric and Comparative Literature at the University of California, Berkeley. She is well known for her contributions to feminist theory, queer theory, gender, psychoanalysis, and sexual politics. Her work *Gender Trouble* (1990) is a modern classic in feminist and queer theory in which Butler challenges assumptions as to the stability of analytic categories such as gender and identity. This work is for many the key text of third-wave feminism as it is also a reference for the important and more general philosophies of the relation between power and knowledge. The selection is from *Precarious Life: The Powers of Mourning and Violence* (2004), one of many books in which Butler has engaged current controversies in social and political theory. Here she picks up on Giorgio Agamben's contribution to a critical theory of human life by examining life in respect to representation, war, and ethics.

The Powers of Mourning and Violence

It was my sense in the fall of 2001 that the United States was missing an opportunity to redefine itself as part of a global community when, instead, it heightened nationalist discourse, extended surveillance mechanisms, suspended constitutional rights, and developed forms of explicit and implicit censorship. These events led public intellectuals to waver in their public commitment to principles of justice and prompted journalists to take leave of the time-honored tradition of investigative journalism. That US boundaries were breached, that an unbearable vulnerability was exposed, that a terrible toll on human life was taken, were, and are, cause for fear and for mourning; they are also instigations for patient political reflection. These events posed the question, implicitly at least, as to what form political reflection and deliberation ought to take if we take injurability and aggression as two points of departure for political life.

That we can be injured, that others can be injured, that we are subject to death at the whim of another, are all reasons for both fear and grief. What is less certain, however, is whether the experiences of vulnerability and loss have to lead straightaway to military violence and retribution. There are other passages. If we are interested in arresting cycles of violence to produce less violent outcomes, it is no doubt important to ask what, politically, might be made of grief besides a cry for war.

One insight that injury affords is that there are others out there on whom my life depends, people I do not know and may never know. This fundamental dependency on anonymous others is not a condition that I can will away. No security measure will foreclose this dependency; no violent act of sovereignty will rid the world of this fact. What this means, concretely, will vary across the globe. There are ways of distributing vulnerability, differential forms of allocation that make some populations more subject to arbitrary violence than others. But in that order of things, it would not be possible to maintain that the US has greater security problems than some of the more contested and vulnerable nations and peoples of the world. To be injured means that one has the chance to reflect upon injury, to find out the mechanisms of its distribution, to find out who else suffers from permeable borders, unexpected violence, dispossession, and fear, and in what ways. If national sovereignty is challenged, that does not mean it must be shored up at all costs, if that results in suspending civil liberties and suppressing political dissent. Rather, the dislocation from First World privilege, however temporary, offers a chance to start to imagine a world in which that violence might be minimized, in which an inevitable interdependency becomes acknowledged as the basis for global political community. I confess to not knowing how to theorize that interdependency. I would suggest, however, that both our political and ethical responsibilities are rooted in the recognition that radical forms of self-sufficiency and unbridled sovereignty are, by definition, disrupted by the larger global processes of which they are a part, that no final control can be secured, and that final control is not, cannot be, an ultimate value. [. . .]

"Precarious Life" approaches the question of a non-violent ethics, one that is based upon an understanding of how easily human life is annulled. Emmanuel Levinas offers a conception of ethics that rests upon an apprehension of the precariousness of life, one that begins with the precarious life of the Other. He makes use of the "face" as a figure that communicates both the precariousness of life and the interdiction on violence. He gives us a way of understanding how aggression is *not* eradicated in an ethics of non-violence; aggression forms the incessant matter for ethical struggles. Levinas considers the fear and anxiety that aggression seeks to quell, but argues that ethics is precisely a struggle to keep fear and anxiety from turning into murderous action. Although his theological view conjures a scene between two humans each of which bears a face that delivers an ethical demand from a seemingly divine source, his view is nevertheless useful for those cultural analyses that seek to understand how best to depict the human, human grief and suffering, and how best to admit the "faces" of those against whom war is waged into public representation.

The Levinasian face is not precisely or exclusively a human face, although it communicates what is human, what is precarious, what is injurable. The media representations of the faces of the "enemy" efface what is most human about the "face" for Levinas. Through a cultural transposition of his philosophy, it is possible to see how dominant forms of representation can and must be disrupted for something about the precariousness of life to be apprehended. This has implications, once again, for the boundaries that constitute what will and will not appear within public life, the limits of a publicly acknowledged field of appearance. Those who remain faceless or whose faces are presented to us as so many symbols of evil, authorize us to become senseless before those lives we have eradicated, and whose grievability is indefinitely postponed. Certain faces must be admitted into public view, must be seen and heard for some keener sense of the value of life, all life, to take hold. So, it is not that mourning is the goal of politics, but that without the capacity to mourn, we lose that keener sense of life we need in order to oppose violence. And though for some, mourning can only be resolved through violence, it seems clear that violence only brings on more loss, and the failure to heed the claim of precarious life only leads, again and again, to the dry grief of an endless political rage. And whereas some forms of public mourning are protracted and ritualized, stoking nationalist fervor, reiterating the conditions of loss and victimization that come to justify a more or less permanent war, not all forms of mourning lead to that conclusion.

Dissent and debate depend upon the inclusion of those who maintain critical views of state policy and civic culture remaining part of a larger public discussion of the value of policies and politics. To charge those who voice critical views with treason, terrorist-sympathizing, anti-Semitism, moral relativism, postmodernism, juvenile behavior, collaboration, anachronistic Leftism, is to seek to destroy the credibility not of the views that are held, but of the persons who hold them. It produces the climate of fear in which to voice a certain view is to risk being branded and shamed with a heinous appellation. To continue to voice one's views under those conditions is not easy, since one must not only discount the truth of the appellation, but brave the stigma that seizes up from the public domain. Dissent is quelled, in part, through threatening the speaking subject with an uninhabitable identification. Because it would be heinous to identify as treasonous, as a collaborator, one fails to speak, or one speaks in throttled ways, in order to sidestep the terrorizing identification that threatens to take hold. This strategy for quelling dissent and limiting the reach of critical debate happens not only through a series of shaming tactics which have a certain psychological terrorization as their effect, but they work as well by producing what will and will not count as a viable speaking subject and a reasonable opinion within the public domain. It is precisely because one does not want to lose one's status as a viable speaking being that one does not say what one thinks. Under social conditions that regulate identifications and the sense of viability to this degree, censorship operates implicitly and forcefully. The line that circumscribes what is speakable and what is livable also functions as an instrument of censorship.

To decide what views will count as reasonable within the public domain, however, is to decide what will and will not count as the public sphere of debate. And if someone holds views that are not in line with the nationalist norm, that person comes to lack credibility as a speaking person, and the media is not open to him or her (though the internet, interestingly, is). The foreclosure of critique empties the public domain of debate and democratic contestation itself, so that debate becomes the exchange of views among the like-minded, and criticism, which ought to be central to any democracy, becomes a fugitive and suspect activity.

Public policy, including foreign policy, often seeks to restrain the public sphere from being open to certain forms of debate and the circulation of media coverage. One way a hegemonic understanding of politics is achieved is through circumscribing what will and will not be admissible as part of the public sphere itself. Without disposing populations in such a way that war seems good and right and true, no war can claim popular consent, and no administration can maintain its popularity. To produce what will constitute the public sphere, however, it is necessary to control the way in which people see, how they hear, what they see. The constraints are not only on content – certain images of dead bodies in Iraq, for instance, are considered unacceptable for public visual consumption – but on what "can" be heard, read, seen, felt, and known. The public sphere is constituted in part by what can appear, and the regulation of the sphere of appearance is one way to establish what will count as reality, and what will not. It is also a way of establishing whose lives can be marked as lives, and whose deaths will count as deaths. Our capacity to feel and to apprehend hangs in the balance. But so, too, does the fate of the reality of certain lives and deaths as well as the ability to think critically and publicly about the effects of war.

Judith Butler (2004) *Precarious Life: The Powers of Mourning and Violence*, London and New York: Verso, pp. xi–xiii, xvii–xxi.

Information Technology
and Assemblages

THE INTEGRAL ACCIDENT: PAUL VIRILIO (2006)

Paul Virilio (1932–) was born in Paris and studied phenomenology at the Sorbonne. He was originally an artist before becoming a prominent architect in France. Like so many of the European thinkers whose writings began to draw worldwide attention early in the 2000s, Virilio is also a philosopher, a social and cultural critic, and social theorist. He was influenced, as were others whose writings are represented in this section, by Gilles Deleuze to reconsider prevailing assumptions about war, science, technology, and techno-science. *The Information Bomb* is one of Virilio's shorter and relatively more accessible essays toward a theory of what many call the postmodern age. His appreciation of art and architecture – thus, also of space and time – is evident in books such as *Open Sky* (1995).

The Information Bomb

With the end of the twentieth century, it is not merely the second millennium which is reaching its close. The Earth too, the planet of the living, is being closed off.

Globalization is not so much, then, the *accomplishment* of the acceleration of history as the *completion*, the closure, of the field of possibilities of the terrestrial horizon.

The Earth is now double-locked by the endless round of satellites and we are running up against the invisible outer wall of habitable space, in the same way as we bump up against the envelope, the firm flesh, of a liveable body. As mere men and women, mere terrestrials, the world for us today is a dead-end and claustrophobia an agonizing threat. Our metaphysical hopes have wasted away and our desires for physical emancipation are similarly withered.

The Earth of the great multiplication of the species is becoming, then, the colony, the camp of the great ordeal. Babel is returning – as cosmic ghetto, city and world all in one – and perhaps this time it is indestructible.

Less than a thousand days before the end of a pitiless century, a series of facts, of events of all kinds, alerts us to an untimely emergence of limits, the end of a geophysical horizon which had till then set the tone of history.

Between the astrophysical suicide of the Heaven's Gate sect and the Assumption of Princess Diana, we had the announcement, the official annunciation of the genetic bomb, the unprecedented possibility of cloning human beings on the basis of a computer read-out of the map of the human genome.

Since then, thanks to the coupling of the life and information sciences, the outlines of a **cybernetic eugenicism** have emerged, a eugenicism which owes nothing to the politics of nations – as was still the case in the laboratories of the death camps – but everything, absolutely everything, to science – an economic techno-science in which the single market demands the commercialization of the whole of living matter, the privatization of the genetic heritage of humanity. Besides this, the proliferation of atomic weapons, freshly boosted by India, Pakistan and probably other destabilized countries on the Asian continent, is prompting the United States – the last great world power – to accelerate its famous 'revolution in military affairs' by developing that emergent strategy known as 'information war', which consists in using electronics as a hegemonic technology: a role it now takes over from nuclear physics.

The atom bomb can then be merely a last guarantee, provided of course that the information bomb effectively proves its credentials as the new absolute weapons system.

It is in this context of financial instability and military uncertainty, in which it is impossible to differentiate between information and disinformation, that the question of the **integral accident** arises once again and that we learn, at the Birmingham summit of May 1998, that the Central Intelligence Agency not only takes seriously the possibility of a 'widespread computer catastrophe' in the year 2000, but that it has scheduled this hypothetical event into its calendar, indicating on a state-by-state basis how far individual nations still have to go to forearm themselves against it.[1]

Similarly, the United States Senate announced the creation of a committee to assess this potential electronic disaster and the Bank of International Settlements in New York followed suit shortly afterwards, setting up a high-level committee to attempt to forestall a **computer crash** in which the damage caused by the serial downturns in the Asian economies might produce global meltdown.

As the first great global manoeuvre in 'Information Warfare',[2] what we see here is the launch of a new logistics, that of the cybernetic control of knowledge: politico-economic knowledge, in which the single market affords a glimpse of its military and strategic dimension in terms of 'information transfer'. To the point where the *systemic risk* of a chain reaction of the bankruptcy of the financial markets (for so long masked during the promotional launch of the Internet) is now officially acknowledged, showing that this *major risk* can also be used to exert pressure on those nations which are reluctant to give in to free-trade blackmail.[3]

As I pointed out some considerable time ago, if *interactivity* is to information what *radioactivity* is to energy, then we are confronted with the fearsome emergence of the 'Accident to end all accidents', an accident which is no longer *local* and precisely situated, but *global* and generalized. We are faced, in other words, with a phenomenon which may possibly occur everywhere simultaneously.

But what we might add today is that this *global systemic risk* is precisely what makes for the strategic supremacy of the future 'weapons systems' of the infowar, that electro-economic war declared on the world by the United States and that, far more than the viruses and other 'logical bombs' hidden away by hackers in the software of our computers, this **integral accident** is the true detonator of the **information bomb**, and hence of its future power of deterrence over the political autonomy of nations. [. . .]

The atom bomb, the information bomb and the demographic bomb – these three historical deflagrations evoked by Albert Einstein in the early 1960s are now on the agenda for the next millennium. The first is there, with the dangers of nuclear weapons becoming generally commonplace, as heralded in the Indian and Pakistani nuclear tests. And the second is also present, with the threat of cybernetic control of the politics of states, under the indirect threat of a *generalized accident*, as we have seen above.

As for the third, the *demographic bomb*, it is clear that if the use of computers is indispensable in the development of atomic weapons, it is equally indispensable in the decipherment of the genetic code and hence in the research aimed at drawing up *a physical map of the human genome*, thus opening up a new eugenicism promoting not the *natural* but the *artificial* selection of the human species.[4]

And given the considerable growth in the demography of our planet in the twenty-first century, are we not right to suspect that experiments on the *industrialization of living matter* will not be content merely to treat patients and assist infertile couples to have children, but will soon lead back to that old folly of the 'new man'? That is to say, the man who will deserve to survive (the superman), whereas the man without qualities, the primate of the new times, will have to disappear – just as the 'savage' had to disappear in the past to avoid cluttering up a small planet – and give way to the latest model of humanity, the **transhuman**, built on the lines of transgenic crops, which are so much better adapted to their environment than the natural products. That this is indeed the case is confirmed by the recent declarations of Professor Richard Seed on his attempt to achieve human cloning, or the statements of those who openly advocate the production of *living mutants*, which are likely to hasten the coming, after the extra-terrestrial, of the extra-human, another name for the superhuman race which still looms large in our memories. [. . .]

Transgenic, transhuman – these are all terms which mark the headlong charge forward, in spite of all the evidence, of a *transpolitical* community of scientists solely preoccupied with acrobatic performances. In this they are following the example of those fairground shows mounted in the nineteenth century by the self-styled 'mathemagicians' . . .

Ultimately, this so-called post-modern period is not so much the age in which industrial modernity has been surpassed, as the era of the sudden *industrialization of the end*, the all-out globalization of the havoc wreaked by progress.

To attempt to industrialize living matter by *bio-technological* procedures, as is done in the semi-official project of reproducing the individual in standard form, is to *turn the end into an enterprise*, into a Promethean factory.

In the age of the 'balance of nuclear terror' between East and West, the military-industrial complex had already succeeded in militarizing scientific research to ensure the capability of mutual destruction – the 'MAD' concept. *Genetic* engineering is now taking over from the *atomic* industry to invent *its own* bomb.

Thanks to computers and the advances of bio-technology, the life sciences are able to threaten the species no longer (as in the past) by the radioactive destruction of the human environment, but by clinical insemination, by the control of the sources of life, the origin of the individual.

Notes

1 Michel Alberganti, 'Un problème majeur pour la communauté internationale', *Le Monde*, 21 May 1998.
2 In English in the original. (Trans.)
3 As with the Multilateral Agreement on Investment and the New Transatlantic Market.
4 While Darwin, in *The Origin of Species*, had advanced the principle of the natural selection of the individuals fittest to survive, in 1860 his cousin, Francis Galton, proposed the principle of artificial selection or, in other words, a voluntary policy of the elimination of the least fit, thus institutionalizing the struggle against the alleged degeneracy of the human species.

Paul Virilio (2006) *The Information Bomb*, London: Verso, pp. 131–137, 139–140.

NAKED LIFE: GIORGIO AGAMBEN (1996)

Giorgio Agamben (1942–) was born in Rome and today teaches philosophy at the University of Verona, among other institutes and universities in Italy, the United States, France, and Switzerland. In the 2000s, Agamben is the one social philosopher who must be read as much as Michel Foucault was in the 1980s. One of the reasons for Agamben's worldwide importance is the remarkable classical learning whereby he is able to redefine the political and social significance of seemingly straightforward concepts such as "life" by examining their Greek and Latin origins. His most famous, if difficult, book is *Homo Sacer: Sovereign Power and Bare Life* (1995) in which he systematically develops a critical theory of life as bare (or naked) that simultaneously extends the key concepts in the German and French traditions of social thought. Naked life has become a central consideration in attempts to understand the role of modern nation-state in the light of its terrible history of having made exceptions to its own principles of human rights and the global assemblages of human misery and death. Agamben thereby brings together the deadly histories of death camps and prisons with the global exclusions of world's poorest populations.

Means without End: Notes on Politics

THE ANCIENT Greeks did not have only one term to express what we mean by the word *life*. They used two semantically and morphologically distinct terms: *zoē*, which expressed the simple fact of living common to all living beings (animals, humans, or gods), and *bios*, which signified the form or manner of living peculiar to a single individual or group. In modern languages this opposition has gradually disappeared from the lexicon (and where it is retained, as in *biology* and *zoology*, it no longer indicates any substantial difference); one term only – the opacity of which increases in proportion to the sacralization of its referent – designates that naked presupposed common element that it is always possible to isolate in each of the numerous forms of life.

By the term *form-of-life*, on the other hand, I mean a life that can never be separated from its form, a life in which it is never possible to isolate something such as naked life.

A life that cannot be separated from its form is a life for which what is at stake in its way of living is living itself. What does this formulation mean? It defines a life – human life – in which the single ways, acts, and processes of living are never simply *facts* but always and above all *possibilities* of life, always and above all power.[1] Each behavior and each form of human living is never prescribed by a specific biological vocation, nor is it assigned by whatever necessity; instead, no matter how customary, repeated, and socially compulsory, it always retains the character of a possibility; that is, it always puts at stake living itself. That is why human beings – as beings of power who can do or not do, succeed or fail, lose themselves or find themselves – are the only beings for whom happiness is always at stake in their living, the only beings whose life is irremediably and painfully assigned to happiness. But this immediately constitutes the form-of-life as political life. "Civitatem . . . communitatem esse institutam propter vivere et bene vivere hominum in ea" [The state is a community instituted for the sake of the living and the well living of men in it].

Political power as we know it, on the other hand, always founds itself – in the last instance – on the separation of a sphere of naked life from the context of the forms of life. In Roman law, *vita* [life] is not a juridical concept, but rather indicates the simple fact of living or a particular way of life. There is only one case in which the term *life* acquires a juridical meaning that transforms it into a veritable *terminus technicus*, and that is in the expression *vitae necisque potestas*, which designates the *pater*'s power of life and death over the male son. Yan Thomas has shown that, in this formula, *que* does not have disjunctive function and *vita* is nothing but a corollary of *nex*, the power to kill.

Thus, life originally appears in law only as the counterpart of a power that threatens death. But what is valid for the *pater*'s right of life and death is even more valid for sovereign power (imperium), of which the former constitutes the originary cell. Thus, in the Hobbesian foundation of sovereignty, life in the state of nature is defined only by its being unconditionally exposed to a death threat (the limitless right of everybody over everything) and political life – that is, the life that unfolds under the protection of the Leviathan – is nothing but this very same life always exposed to a threat that now rests exclusively in the hands of the sovereign. The *puissance absolue et perpétuelle*, which defines state power, is not founded – in the last instance – on a political will but rather on naked life, which is kept safe and protected only to the degree to which it submits itself to the sovereign's (or the law's) right of life and death. (This is precisely the originary meaning of the adjective *sacer* [sacred] when used to refer to human life.) The state of exception, which is what the sovereign each and every time decides, takes place precisely when naked life – which normally appears rejoined to the multifarious forms of social life – is explicitly put into question and revoked as the ultimate foundation of political power. The ultimate subject that needs to be at once turned into the exception and included in the city is always naked life.

"The tradition of the oppressed teaches us that the 'state of emergency' in which we live is not the exception but the rule. We must attain to a conception of history that is in keeping with this insight."[2] Walter Benjamin's diagnosis, which by now is more than fifty years old, has lost none of its relevance. And that is so not really or not only because power no longer has today any form of legitimization other than emergency, and because power everywhere and continuously refers and appeals to emergency as well as laboring secretly to produce it. (How could we not think that a system that can no longer function at all except on the basis of emergency would not also be interested in preserving such an emergency at any price?) This is the case also and above all because naked life, which was the hidden foundation of sovereignty, has meanwhile become the dominant form of life everywhere. Life – in its state of exception that has now become the norm – is the naked life that in every context separates the forms of life from their cohering into a form-of-life. The Marxian scission between man and citizen is thus superseded by the division between naked life (ultimate and opaque bearer of sovereignty) and the multifarious forms of life abstractly recodified as social-juridical identities (the voter, the worker, the journalist, the student, but also the HIV-positive, the transvestite, the porno star, the elderly, the parent, the woman) that all rest on naked life. (To have mistaken such a naked life separate from its form, in its abjection, for a superior principle – sovereignty or the sacred – is the limit of Bataille's thought, which makes it useless to us.)

Foucault's thesis – according to which "what is at stake today is life" and hence politics has become biopolitics – is, in this sense, substantially correct. What is decisive, however, is the way in which one understands the sense of this transformation. What is left unquestioned in the contemporary debates on bioethics and biopolitics, in fact, is precisely what would deserve to be questioned before anything else, that is, the very biological concept of life. Paul Rabinow conceives of two models of life as symmetrical opposites: on the one hand, the experimental life[3] of the scientist who is ill with leukemia and who turns his very life into a laboratory for unlimited research and experimentation, and, on the other hand, the one who, in the name of life's sacredness, exasperates the antinomy between individual ethics and technoscience. Both models, however, participate without being aware of it in the same concept of naked life. This concept – which today presents itself under the guise of a scientific notion – is actually a secularized political concept. (From a strictly scientific point of view, the concept of life makes no sense. Peter and Jean Medawar tell us that, in biology, discussions about the real meaning of the words *life* and *death* are an index of a low level of conversation. Such words have no intrinsic meaning and such a meaning, therefore, cannot be clarified by deeper and more careful studies.[4]

Such is the provenance of the (often unperceived and yet decisive) function of medical-scientific ideology within the system of power and the increasing use of pseudoscientific concepts for ends of political control. That same drawing of naked life that, in certain circumstances, the sovereign used to be able to exact from the forms of life is now massively and daily exacted by the pseudoscientific representations of the body, illness, and health, and by the "medicalization" of ever-widening spheres of life and of individual imagination.[5] Biological life, which is the secularized form of naked life and which shares its unutterability and impenetrability, thus constitutes the real forms of life literally as forms of *survival*: biological life remains inviolate in such forms as that obscure threat that can suddenly actualize itself in violence, in extraneousness, in illnesses, in accidents. It is the invisible sovereign that stares at us behind the dull-witted masks of the powerful who, whether or not they realize it, govern us in its name.

A political life, that is, a life directed toward the idea of happiness and cohesive with a form-of-life, is thinkable only starting from the emancipation from such a division, with the irrevocable exodus from any sovereignty. The question about the possibility of a nonstatist politics necessarily takes this form: Is today something like a form-of-life, a life for which living itself would be at stake in its own living, possible? Is today a *life of power* available?

I call *thought* the nexus that constitutes the forms of life in an inseparable context as form-of-life. I do not mean by this the individual exercise of an organ or of a psychic faculty, but rather an experience, an *experimentum* that has as its object the potential character of life and of human intelligence. To think does not mean merely to be affected by this or that thing, by this or that content of enacted thought, but rather at once to be affected by one's own receptiveness and experience in each and every thing that is thought a pure power of thinking. ("When thought has become each thing in the way in which a man who actually knows is said to do so . . . its condition is still one of potentiality . . . and thought is then able to think of itself.")[6]

Only if I am not always already and solely enacted, but rather delivered to a possibility and a power, only if living and intending and apprehending themselves are at stake each time in what I live and intend and apprehend – only if, in other words, there is thought – only then can a form of life become, in its own factness and thingness, *form-of-life*, in which it is never possible to isolate something like naked life.

The experience of thought that is here in question is always experience of a common power. Community and power identify one with the other without residues because the inherence of a communitarian principle to any power is a function of the necessarily potential character of any community. Among beings who would always already be enacted, who would always already be this or that thing, this or that identity, and who would have entirely exhausted their power in these things and identities – among such beings there could not be any community but only coincidences and factual partitions. We can communicate with others only through what in us – as much as in others – has remained potential, and any communication (as Benjamin perceives for language) is first of all communication not of something in common but of communicability itself. After all, if there existed one and only one being, it would be absolutely impotent. (That is why theologians affirm that God created the world ex nihilo, in other words, absolutely without power.) And there where I am capable, we are always already many (just as when, if there is a language, that is, a power of speech, there cannot then be one and only one being who speaks it.) [. . .]

The act of distinguishing between the mere, massive inscription of social knowledge into the productive processes (an inscription that characterizes the contemporary phase of capitalism, the society of the spectacle) and intellectuality as antagonistic power and form-of-life – such an act passes through the experience of this cohesion and this inseparability. Thought is form-of-life, life that cannot be segregated from its form; and anywhere the intimacy of this inseparable life appears, in the materiality of corporeal processes and of habitual ways of life no less than in theory, there and only there is there thought. And it is this thought, this form-of-life, that, abandoning naked life to "Man" and to the "Citizen," who clothe it temporarily and represent it with their "rights," must become the guiding concept and the unitary center of the coming politics.

Notes

1 The English term *power* corresponds to two distinct terms in Italian, *potenza* and *potere* (which roughly correspond to the French *puissance* and *pouvoir*, the German *Macht* and *Vermögen* and the Latin *potentia* and *potestas*, respectively). *Potenza* can often resonate with implications of potentiality as well as with decentralized or mass conceptions of force and strength. *Potere*, on the other hand, refers to the might or authority of an already structured and centralized capacity, often an institutional apparatus such as the state. [Translator's note by Vincenzo Binetti and Cesare Cesarino]
2 Walter Benjamin, 'Theses on the Philosophy of History,' in *Illuminations,* trans. Harry Zohn (New York: Shocken Book, 1989), p. 1989. In the Italian translation of Benjamin's passage, 'state of emergency' is translated as 'state of exception,' which is the phrase Agamben uses in the preceding section of this essay and which will be a crucial refrain in several of the other essays included in this volume.' [Translator's note.]
3 'Experimental life' is in English in the original. [Translator's note.]
4 See, for example, Peter Medawar and Jean Medawar, *Aristotle to Zoos* (Oxford: Oxford University Press, 1983), pp. 66–67.
5 The terminology in the original is the same as that used for bank transactions (and thus 'naked life' becomes here the cash reserve contained in accounts such as 'the forms of life'). [Translator's note.]
6 Aristotle, *On the Soul.*

Giorgio Agamben (2000) *Means without End: Notes on Politics*, trans. by Vincenzo Binetti and Cesare Casarino, Minneapolis and London: University of Minnesota Press, pp. 3–12.

SOCIAL COMPLEXITY AND ASSEMBLAGES: MANUEL DELANDA (2006)

Manuel DeLanda (1952–) was born in Mexico and today lives in New York City where he pursues a many-sided life in art, architecture, writing, philosophy, film-making, teaching, and lecturing. DeLanda is, perhaps, the foremost interpreter of Gilles Deleuze, from whom he has drawn, and developed, the theory of assemblages as the organizing principle of after-modern social life. His notable books include *Intensive*

Science and Virtual Philosophy (2002), an exposition of Deleuze's philosophy, and *A New Philosophy of Society: Assemblage Theory and Social Complexity* (2006), a daring (if not always persuasive) rethinking of social theory in relation to assemblage theory.

A New Philosophy of Society

Interpersonal networks and institutional organizations may be studied without reference to their location in space because communication technologies allow their defining linkages and formal positions to be created and maintained at a distance, but as we move to larger scales spatial relations become crucial. Social entities like cities, for example, composed of entire populations of persons, networks and organizations, can hardly be conceptualized without a physical infrastructure of buildings, streets and various conduits for the circulation of matter and energy, defined in part by their spatial relations to one another. [. . .]

In formal models of urban dynamics, assemblages of cities of different sizes emerge from a sequence of symmetry-breaking events, as each town confronts centripetal processes, like the capture of population, investment and other resources, as well as centrifugal ones, like congestion, pollution, traffic. At the tipping-point, when one set of forces begins to dominate the other, a town may grow explosively or shrink to a small size in the shadow of a larger one. In computer simulations the actual pattern that emerges *is not unique* – as if there existed a single optimal pattern to which the urban dynamics always tended – but is, on the contrary, highly sensitive to the actual historical sequence of events. For this reason, the emergent pattern of urban centres is like a memory of this symmetry-breaking sequence 'fossilized in the spatial structure of the system'.[1]

A recurrent emergent pattern in these formal models is one familiar to geographers: a hierarchy of *central places*. In its original formulation, central-place theory was an attempt to describe the hierarchical relations among regularly spaced urban centres, with larger ones displaying a greater degree of service differentiation than smaller ones. [. . .]

In addition to landlocked central-place hierarchies, trade among the European population of towns in the Middle Ages generated extensive *networks of maritime ports* in which cities were not geographically fixed centres but changing relays, junctions or outposts. [. . .]

The historical period that sealed the fate of autonomous cities can be framed by two critical dates, 1494 and 1648, a period that witnessed warfare increasing enormously in both intensity and geographical scope. The first date marks the year when the Italian city-states were first invaded and brought to their knees by armies from beyond the Alps: the French armies under Charles VIII whose goal was to enforce territorial claims on the kingdom of Naples. The second date celebrates the signing of the peace treaty of Westphalia, ending the Thirty Years War between the largest territorial entity at the time, the Catholic Habsburg empire, and an alliance between France, Sweden and a host of Protestant-aligned states. When the peace treaty was finally signed by the exhausted participants, a unified, geopolitically stabilizing Germany had been created at the centre of Europe, and the frontiers that defined the identity of territorial states, as well as the balance of power between them, were consolidated. Although the crucial legal concept of 'sovereignty' had been formal-ized prior to the war (by Jean Bodin in 1576) it was during the peace conference that it was first used in practice to define the identity of territorial states as legal entities.[2] Thus, international law may be said to have been the offspring of that war.

As I argued in the previous chapter, it is important not to confuse territorial states as *geopolitical entities* with the organizational hierarchies that govern them. Geopolitical factors are properties of the former but not of the latter. As Paul Kennedy argues, given the fact that after 1648 warfare typically involved many national actors, geography affected the fate of a nation not merely through

> such elements as a country's climate, raw materials, fertility of agriculture, and access to trade routes – important though they all were to its overall prosperity – but rather [via] the critical issue of strategic *location* during these multilateral wars. Was a particular nation able to concentrate its energies upon one front, or did it have to fight on several? Did it share common borders with weak states, or powerful ones?

Was it chiefly a land power, a sea power, or a hybrid – and what advantages and disadvantages did that bring? Could it easily pull out of a great war in Central Europe if it wished to? Could it secure additional resources from overseas?[3]

But if territorial states cannot be reduced to their civilian and military organizations, the latter do form the main actors whose routine activities give these largest of regionalized locales their temporal structure. A good example of the new organizational activities that were required after 1648 were the fiscal and monetary policies, as well as the overall system of public finance, needed to conduct large-scale warfare. On the economic side there were activities guided by a heterogeneous body of pragmatic beliefs referred to as 'mercantilism'. The central belief of this doctrine was that the wealth of a nation was based on the amount of precious metals (gold and silver) that accumulated within its borders. This monetary policy, it is clear today, is based on mistaken beliefs about the causal relations between economic factors. On the other hand, since one means of preventing the outward flow of precious metals was to discourage imports, and this, in turn, involved the promotion of local manufacture and of internal economic growth, mercantilism had collective unintended consequences that did benefit territorial states in the long run.[4] For this reason, however, it is hard to consider the people making mercantilist policy decisions the relevant social actors in this case. Another reason to consider the activities of organizations the main source of temporal structure for territorial states is that many of the capacities necessary to conduct a sound fiscal policy were the product of *slow organizational learning*, a feat first achieved in England between the years of 1688 and 1756. [. . .]

An assemblage analysis of organizational hierarchies has already been sketched in the previous chapter, so what remains to be analysed is the territorial states themselves. Among the components playing a material role we must list all the resources contained within a country's frontiers, not only its natural resources (agricultural land and mineral deposits of coal, oil, precious metals) but also its demographic ones, that is, its human populations viewed as reservoirs of army and navy recruits as well as of potential taxpayers. As with all locales, the material aspect also involves questions of connectivity between regions: questions that in this case involves the geographical regions previously organized by cities. Territorial states did not create these regions, nor the provinces that several such regions formed, but they did affect their interconnection through the building of new roads and canals. This is how, for example, Britain stitched together several provincial markets to create the first national market in the eighteenth century, a process in which its national capital played a key centralizing role. And, as Braudel argues, without the national market 'the modern state would be a pure fiction'.[5]

Other countries (France, Germany, the USA) accomplished this feat in the following century through the use of locomotives and telegraphs. The advent of steam endowed land transportation with the speed it had lacked for so long, changing the balance of power between landlocked and coastal regions and their cities, and giving national capitals a dominant position. [. . .]

The stability of the identity of territorial states depends in part on the degree of uniformity (ethnic, religious, linguistic, monetary, legal) that its organizations and cities manage to create within its borders. A good example of homogenization at this scale is the creation of standard languages. In the areas which had been latinized during the Roman Empire, for example, each central place hierarchy had its own dominant dialect, the product of the divergent evolution that spoken or vulgar Latin underwent after the imperial fall. Before the rise of national capitals the entire range of romance dialects that resulted from this divergent differentiation coexisted, even as some cities accumulated more prestige for their own versions. But as territorial states began to consolidate their grip, the balance of power changed. In some cases, special organizations (official language academies) were created to codify the dialects of the dominant capitals and to publish official dictionaries, grammars and books of correct pronunciation. This codification, however, did not manage to propagate the new artifical languages throughout the entire territory. That process had to wait until the nineteenth century for the creation of a nationwide system of compulsory elementary education in the standard. Even then, many regions and their cities resisted this imposition and managed to preserve their own linguistic identity, a resistance that was a source of centripetal forces. Although in some countries, such as

Switzerland, political stability coexists with multilingualism, in others (Canada, Belgium) even bilingualism has proved to be a destabilizing force.[6]

In addition to internal uniformity, territorialization at this scale has a more direct spatial meaning: the stability of the defining frontiers of a country. This stability has two aspects, the control of the different flows moving across the border, and the endurance of the frontiers themselves. The latter refers to the fact that the annexation (or secession) of a large piece of land changes the geographical identity of a territorial state. Although these events need not involve warfare aimed at territorial expansion (or civil war aimed at secession) they often do, and this shows the importance of deploying armies near the border or constructing special fortifications for the consolidation of frontiers. A few decades after the treaty of Westphalia was signed, for example, France redirected enormous resources to the creation of coherent, defensible boundaries, through the systematic construction of fortress towns, perimeter walls and citadels – separate star-shaped strongholds sited next to a town's perimeter. In the hands of Sebastien le Prestre de Vauban, the brilliant military engineer, France's defining borders became nearly impregnable, maintaining their defensive value until the French Revolution. Vauban built double rows of fortresses in the northern and southeastern frontiers, so systematically related to each other that one 'would be within earshot of French fortress guns all the way from the Swiss border to the Channel'.[7]

Migration and trade across national borders tend to complicate the effort to create a single national identity, and to this extent they may be considered deterritorializing. The ability to reduce the permeability of frontiers depends to a large degree on the conditions under which a territorial entity comes into being. Those kingdoms and empires that crystallized in the feudal areas of Europe had an easier task creating internal homogeneity than those in the densely urbanized areas that had to cope with the split sovereignty derived from the coexistence of many autonomous city-states.[8] Similarly, territorial states born from the collapse of a previous empire or from the break-up of former colonial possessions can find themselves with unstable frontiers cutting across areas heterogeneous in language, ethnicity or religion: a situation which militates against a stable identity and complicates border control. A more systematic challenge to border control and territorial stability has existed since at least the seventeenth century. As the identity of the modern international system was crystallizing during the Thirty Years War, the city of Amsterdam had become the dominant centre of a transnational trade and credit network that was almost as global as anything that exists today. If the rise of kingdoms, empires and nation-states exerted territorializing pressures on cities by reducing their autonomy, maritime networks not only resisted these pressures but were capable then, and still are today, of deterritorializing the constitutive boundaries of territorial states. The pressure on these boundaries has intensified in recent decades as the ease with which financial resources can flow across state boundaries, the degree of differentiation of the international division of labour, and the mobility of legal and illegal workers, have all increased.

That networks of cities, and the transnational organizations based on those cities, can operate over, and give coherence to, large geographical areas cutting across state boundaries, has been recognized since the pioneering work of Fernand Braudel, who refers to these areas as 'world-economies'.[9] It is too early, however, to tell whether these world-economies are as real as the other regionalized locales that have been analysed in this chapter. Some of the processes that are supposed to endow these economic locales with coherence, such as the synchronized movement of prices across large geographical areas following long temporal rhythms (the so-called 'Kondratieff waves'), remain controversial. But what is clear even at this stage of our understanding is that approaches based on reductionist social ontologies do not do justice to the historical data. This is particularly true of macro-reductionist approaches, such as the so-called 'world-systems analysis' pioneered by Immanuel Wallerstein, in which Braudel's original idea is combined with theories of uneven exchange developed by Latin American theorists.[10] In Wallerstein's view, for example, only one valid unit of social analysis has existed since the end of the Thirty Years War, the entire 'world-system'. Explanations at the level of nation-states are viewed as illegitimate since the position of countries in the world-system determines their very nature.[11] An assemblage approach, on the other hand, is more compatible with Braudel's original idea. Although he does not use the concept of 'assemblage', he views social wholes as 'sets of sets', giving each differently scaled entity its own relative autonomy without fusing it with the others into a seamless whole.[12]

It has been the purpose of this book to argue the merits of such a nonreductionist approach, an approach in which every social entity is shown to emerge from the interactions among entities operating at a smaller scale. The fact that the emergent wholes react back on their components to constrain them and enable them does not result in a seamless totality. Each level of scale retains a relative autonomy and can therefore be a legitimate unit of analysis. Preserving the ontological independence of each scale not only blocks attempts at micro-reductionism (as in neoclassical economics) and macro-reductionism (as in world-systems analysis) but also allows the integration of the valuable insights that different social scientists have developed while working at a specific spatiotemporal scale, from the extremely short duration of the small entities studied by Erving Goffman to the extremely long duration of the large entities studied by Fernand Braudel. Assemblage theory supplies the framework where the voices of these two authors, and of the many others whose work has influenced this book, can come together to form a chorus that does not harmonize its different components but interlocks them while respecting their heterogeneity.

Notes

1 Allen, *Cities and Regions as Self-Organizing System*, p. 53.
2 J. Craig Barker, *International Law and International Relations* (London: Continuum, 2000), pp. 5–8. For the five-year negotiation period see Geoffrey Parker, *The Thirty Years War* (London: Routledge and Kegan Paul, 1987), pp. 170–78.
3 Kennedy, *The Rise and Fall of the Great Powers*, p. 86 (emphasis in the original).
4 Fernand Braudel, *The Wheels of Commerce* (New York: Harper and Row, 1979), pp. 544–5.
5 Braudel, *The Structures of Everyday Life*, p. 527.
6 I attempted to synthesize all available materials on the political history of languages and dialects in Manuel DeLanda, *A Thousand Years of Nonlinear History* (New York: Zone Books, 1997), Ch. 3.
7 Christopher Duffy, *The Fortress in the Age of Vauban and Frederick the Great* (London: Routledge and Kegan Paul, 1985), p. 87.
8 Peter J. Taylor, *Political Geography* (New York: Longman, 1985), pp. 113–15.
9 Braudel introduced the term 'world-economy' to discuss the Mediterranean as a coherent economic area in Fernand Braudel, *The Mediterranean. And the Mediterranean World in the Age of Philip II*, Vol. 1. (Berkeley, CA: University of California Press, 1995), p. 419. Braudel attributes the original concept to two German scholars in Braudel, *The Perspective of the World*, p. 634, n. 4.
10 Immanuel Wallerstein, *World-Systems Analysis. An Introduction* (Durham, NC: Duke University Press, 2004), pp. 11–17.
11 Ibid., p. 16. Wallerstein's macro-reductionism derives directly from his use of Hegelian totalities to conceptualize large-scale social entities. See Immanuel Wallerstein, *The Capitalist World-Economy* (Cambridge: Cambridge University Press, 1993), p. 4.
12 Braudel, *The Wheels of Commerce*, p. 458.

Manuel DeLanda (2006) *A New Philosophy of Society: Assemblage Theory and Social Complexity*, London and New York: Continuum, pp. 94, 108–109 112–119.

NECROPOLITICS: ACHILLE MBEMBE (2003)

Achille Mbembe (1957–), a native of Cameroon, was educated in France where he received his Ph.D. in History from the Sorbonne. He currently teaches primarily at the University of Witwatersrand, Johannesburg and also at the University of California, Irvine. Mbembe is one of the world's leading post-colonial theorists. His long essay on necropolitics has made the term known the world over for the way his ideas advance the history and theory of biopower and death in the history of modern politics.

Politics of Sovereignty and Death

The aim of this essay is not to debate the singularity of the extermination of the Jews or to hold it up by way of example.[1] I start from the idea that modernity was at the origin of multiple concepts of sovereignty – and therefore of the biopolitical. Disregarding this multiplicity, late-modern political criticism has unfortunately privileged normative theories of democracy and has made the concept of reason one of the most important elements of both the project of modernity and of the topos of sovereignty.[2] From this perspective, the ultimate expression of sovereignty is the production of general norms by a body (the demos) made up of free and equal men and women. These men and women are posited as full subjects capable of self-understanding, self-consciousness, and self-representation. Politics, therefore, is defined as twofold: a project of autonomy and the achieving of agreement among a collectivity through communication and recognition. This, we are told, is what differentiates it from war.[3]

In other words, it is on the basis of a distinction between reason and unreason (passion, fantasy) that late-modern criticism has been able to articulate a certain idea of the political, the community, the subject – or, more fundamentally, of what the good life is all about, how to achieve it, and, in the process, to become a fully moral agent. Within this paradigm, reason is the truth of the subject and politics is the exercise of reason in the public sphere. The exercise of reason is tantamount to the exercise of freedom, a key element for individual autonomy. The romance of sovereignty, in this case, rests on the belief that the subject is the master and the controlling author of his or her own meaning. Sovereignty is therefore defined as a twofold process of *self-institution* and *self-limitation* (fixing one's own limits for oneself). The exercise of sovereignty, in turn, consists in society's capacity for self-creation through recourse to institutions inspired by specific social and imaginary significations.[4]

This strongly normative reading of the politics of sovereignty has been the object of numerous critiques, which I will not rehearse here.[5] My concern is those figures of sovereignty whose central project is not the struggle for autonomy but *the generalized instrumentalization of human existence and the material destruction of human bodies and populations*. Such figures of sovereignty are far from a piece of prodigious insanity or an expression of a rupture between the impulses and interests of the body and those of the mind. Indeed, they, like the death camps, are what constitute the *nomos* of the political space in which we still live. Furthermore, contemporary experiences of human destruction suggest that it is possible to develop a reading of politics, sovereignty, and the subject different from the one we inherited from the philosophical discourse of modernity. Instead of considering reason as the truth of the subject, we can look to other foundational categories that are less abstract and more tactile, such as life and death.

Significant for such a project is Hegel's discussion of the relation between death and the "becoming subject." Hegel's account of death centers on a bipartite concept of negativity. First, the human negates nature (a negation exteriorized in the human's effort to reduce nature to his or her own needs); and second, he or she transforms the negated element through work and struggle. In transforming nature, the human being creates a world; but in the process, he or she also is exposed to his or her own negativity. Within the Hegelian paradigm, human death is essentially voluntary. It is the result of risks consciously assumed by the subject. According to Hegel, in these risks the "animal" that constitutes the human subject's natural being is defeated.

In other words, the human being truly *becomes a subject* – that is, separated from the animal – in the struggle and the work through which he or she confronts death (understood as the violence of negativity). It is through this confrontation with death that he or she is cast into the incessant movement of history. Becoming subject therefore supposes upholding the work of death. To uphold the work of death is precisely how Hegel defines the life of the Spirit. The life of the Spirit, he says, is not that life which is frightened of death, and spares itself destruction, but that life which assumes death and lives with it. Spirit attains its truth only by finding itself in absolute dismemberment.[6] Politics is therefore death that lives a human life. Such, too, is the definition of absolute knowledge and sovereignty: risking the entirety of one's life. [. . .]

That *race* (or for that matter *racism*) figures so prominently in the calculus of biopower is entirely justifiable. After all, more so than class-thinking (the ideology that defines history as an economic struggle of classes), race has been the ever present shadow in Western political thought and practice, especially when it comes to imagining the inhumanity of, or rule over, foreign peoples. Referring to both this ever-presence and the phantomlike world of race in general, Arendt locates their roots in the shattering experience of otherness and suggests that the politics of race is ultimately linked to the politics of death.[7] Indeed, in Foucault's terms, racism is above all a technology aimed at permitting the exercise of biopower, "that old sovereign right of death."[8] In the economy of biopower, the function of racism is to regulate the distribution of death and to make possible the murderous functions of the state. It is, he says, "the condition for the acceptability of putting to death."[9]

Foucault states clearly that the sovereign right to kill (*droit de glaive*) and the mechanisms of biopower are inscribed in the way all modern states function;[10] indeed, they can be seen as constitutive elements of state power in modernity. According to Foucault, the Nazi state was the most complete example of a state exercising the right to kill. This state, he claims, made the management, protection, and cultivation of life coextensive with the sovereign right to kill. By biological extrapolation on the theme of the political enemy, in organizing the war against its adversaries and, at the same time, exposing its own citizens to war, the Nazi state is seen as having opened the way for a formidable consolidation of the right to kill, which culminated in the project of the "final solution." In doing so, it became the archetype of a power formation that combined the characteristics of the racist state, the murderous state, and the suicidal state.

It has been argued that the complete conflation of war and politics (and racism, homicide, and suicide), until they are indistinguishable from one another, is unique to the Nazi state. The perception of the existence of the Other as an attempt on my life, as a mortal threat or absolute danger whose biophysical elimination would strengthen my potential to life and security – this, I suggest, is one of the many imaginaries of sovereignty characteristic of both early and late modernity itself. Recognition of this perception to a large extent underpins most traditional critiques of modernity, whether they are dealing with nihilism and its proclamation of the will for power as the essence of the being; with reification understood as the *becoming-object* of the human being; or the subordination of everything to impersonal logic and to the reign of calculability and instrumental rationality.[11] Indeed, from an anthropological perspective, what these critiques implicitly contest is a definition of politics as the warlike relation par excellence. They also challenge the idea that, of necessity, the calculus of life passes through the death of the Other; or that sovereignty consists of the will and the capacity to kill in order to live.

Taking a historical perspective, a number of analysts have argued that the material premises of Nazi extermination are to be found in colonial imperialism on the one hand and, on the other, in the serialization of technical mechanisms for putting people to death – mechanisms developed between the Industrial Revolution and the First World War. According to Enzo Traverso, the gas chambers and the ovens were the culmination of a long process of dehumanizing and industrializing death, one of the original features of which was to integrate instrumental rationality with the productive and administrative rationality of the modern Western world (the factory, the bureaucracy, the prison, the army). Having become mechanized, serialized execution was transformed into a purely technical, impersonal, silent, and rapid procedure. This development was aided in part by racist stereotypes and the flourishing of a class-based racism that, in translating the social conflicts of the industrial world in racial terms, ended up comparing the working classes and "stateless people" of the industrial world to the "savages" of the colonial world.[12]

In reality, the links between modernity and terror spring from multiple sources. Some are to be found in the political practices of the ancien régime. From this perspective, the tension between the public's passion for blood and notions of justice and revenge is critical. Foucault shows in *Discipline and Punish* how the execution of the would-be regicide Damiens went on for hours, much to the satisfaction of the crowd.[13] Well known is the long procession of the condemned through the streets prior to execution, the parade of body parts – a ritual that became a standard feature of popular violence – and the final display of a severed head mounted on a pike. In France, the advent of the guillotine marks a new phase in the "democratization" of the means of disposing of the enemies of the state. Indeed, this form of execution that had once been the prerogative of the nobility is extended to all citizens. In a context in which decapitation is viewed as less demeaning than hanging, innovations in the technologies of murder aim not only at "civilizing" the ways of killing. They also aim at disposing of a large number of victims in a relatively short span of time. At the same time, a new cultural sensibility emerges in which killing the enemy of the state is an extension of play. More intimate, lurid, and leisurely forms of cruelty appear.

But nowhere is the conflation of reason and terror so manifest as during the French Revolution.[14] During the French Revolution, terror is construed as an almost necessary part of politics. An absolute transparency is claimed to exist between the state and the people. As a political category, "the people" is gradually displaced from concrete reality to rhetorical figure. As David Bates has shown, the theorists of terror believe it possible to distinguish between authentic expressions of sovereignty and the actions of the enemy. They also believe it possible to distinguish between the "error" of the citizen and the "crime" of the counterrevolutionary in the political sphere. Terror thus becomes a way of marking aberration in the body politic, and politics is read both as the mobile force of reason and as the errant attempt at creating a space where "error" would be reduced, truth enhanced, and the enemy disposed of.[15]

Finally, terror is not linked solely to the utopian belief in the unfettered power of human reason. It is also clearly related to various narratives of mastery and emancipation, most of which are underpinned by Enlightenment understandings of truth and error, the "real" and the symbolic. Marx, for example, conflates labor (the endless cycle of production and consumption required for the maintenance of human life) with work (the creation of lasting artifacts that add to the world of things). Labor is viewed as the vehicle for the historical self-creation of humankind. The historical self-creation of humankind is itself a life-and-death conflict, that is, a conflict over what paths should lead to the truth of history: the overcoming of capitalism and the commodity form and the contradictions associated with both. According to Marx, with the advent of communism and the abolition of exchange relations, things will appear as they really are; the "real" will present itself as it actually is, and the distinction between subject and object or being and consciousness will be transcended.[16] But by making human emancipation dependent upon the abolition of commodity production, Marx blurs the all-important divisions among the man-made realm of freedom, the nature-determined realm of necessity, and the contingent in history.

The commitment to the abolition of commodity production and the dream of direct and unmediated access to the "real" make these processes – the fulfillment of the so-called logic of history and the fabrication of humankind – almost necessarily violent processes. As shown by Stephen Louw, the central tenets of classical Marxism leave no choice but to "try to introduce communism by administrative fiat, which, in practice, means that social relations must be decommodified forcefully."[17] Historically, these attempts have taken such forms as labor militarization, the collapse of the distinction between state and society, and revolutionary terror.[18] It may be argued that they aimed at the eradication of the basic human condition of plurality. Indeed, the overcoming of class divisions, the withering away of the state, the flowering of a truly general will presuppose a view of human plurality as the chief obstacle to the eventual realization of a predetermined telos of history. In other words, the subject of Marxian modernity is, fundamentally, a subject who is intent on proving his or her sovereignty through the staging of a fight to the death. Just as with Hegel, the narrative of mastery and emancipation here is clearly linked to a narrative of truth and death. Terror and killing become the means of realizing the already known telos of history.

Notes

1 On these debates, see Saul Friedlander, ed., *Probing the Limits of Representation: Nazism and the "Final Solution"* (Cambridge: Harvard University Press, 1992); and, more recently, Bertrand Ogilvie, "Comparer l'incomparable," *Multitudes*, no. 7 (2001): 130–66.

2 See James Bohman and William Rehg, eds., *Deliberative Democracy: Essays on Reason and Politics* (Cambridge: MIT Press, 1997); Jürgen Habermas, *Between Facts and Norms* (Cambridge: MIT Press, 1996).

3 James Schmidt, ed., *What Is Enlightenment? Eighteenth-Century Answers and Twentieth-Century Questions* (Berkeley: University of California Press, 1996).

4 Cornelius Castoriadis, *L'institution imaginaire de la société* (Paris: Seuil, 1975) and *Figures du pensable* (Paris: Seuil, 1999).

5 See, in particular, Paul Gilroy, *The Black Atlantic: Modernity and Double Consciousness* (Cambridge: Harvard University Press, 1993), especially chap. 2.

6 G.W.F.Hegel, *Phénoménologie de l'esprit*, trans. J.P. Lefebvre (Paris: Aubier, 1991). See also the critique by Alexandrè Kojève, *Introduction à la lecture de Hegel* (Paris: Gallimard, 1947), especially Appendix II, "L'idée de la mort dans la philosophie de Hegel"; and Georges Bataille, *Oeuvres complètes XII* (Paris: Gallimard, 1988), especially "Hegel, la mort et le sacrifice," 326–48, and "Hegel, l'homme et l'histoire," 349–69.

7 "Race is, politically speaking, not the beginning of humanity but its end . . ., not the natural birth of man but his unnatural death." Arendt, *Origins of Totalitarianism*, 157.

8 Foucault, *Il faut défendre la société*, 214.

9 Foucault, *Il faut défendre la société*, 228.

10 Foucault, *Il faut défendre la société*, 227–32.

11 See Jürgen Habermas, *The Philosophical Discourse of Modernity: Twelve Lectures*, trans. Frederick G. Lawrence (Cambridge: MIT Press, 1987), especially chaps. 3, 5, 6.

12 Enzo Traverso, *La violence nazie: Une généalogie européenne* (Paris: La Fabrique Editions, 2002).

13 Michel Foucault, *Discipline and Punish: The Birth of the Prison* (New York: Pantheon, 1977).

14 See Robert Wokler, "Contextualizing Hegel's Phenomenology of the French Revolution and the Terror." *Political Theory* 26 (1998): 33–55.

15 David W. Bates, *Enlightenment Aberrations: Error and Revolution in France* (Ithaca, N.Y.: Cornell University Press, 2002), chap. 6.

16 Karl Marx, *Capital: A Critique of Political Economy*, vol. 3 (London: Lawrence and Wishart, 1984), 817. See also *Capital*, vol. 1, trans. Ben Fowkes (Harmondsworth, England: Penguin, 1986), 172.

17 Stephen Louw, "In the Shadow of the Pharaohs: The Militarization of Labour Debate and Classical Marxist Theory," *Economy and Society* (29) 2000: 240.

18 On labor militarization and the transition to communism, see Nikolai Bukharin, *The Politics and Economics of the Transition Period*, trans. Oliver Field (London: Routledge and Kegan Paul, 1979); and Leon Trotsky, *Terrorism and Communism: A Reply to Karl Kautsky* (Ann Arbor: University of Michigan Press, 1961). On the collapse of the distinction between state and society, see Karl Marx, *The Civil War in France* (Moscow: Progress, 1972); and Vladimir Il'ich Lenin, *Selected Works in Three Volumes*, vol. 2 (Moscow: Progress, 1977). For a critique of "revolutionary terror," see Maurice Merleau-Ponty, *Humanism and Terror: An Essay on the Communist Problem*, trans. John O'Neill (Boston: Beacon, 1969). For a more recent example of "revolutionary terror," see Steve J. Stern, ed., *Shining and Other Paths: War and Society in Peru, 1980–1995* (Durham, N.C.: Duke University Press, 1998).

Achille Mbembe (2003) "Necropolitics," trans. by Libby Meintjes, *Public Culture*, vol. 15, no. 1, pp. 13–15, 17–20.

THE DISAPPEARED: ABDOUMALIQ SIMONE (2003)

AbdouMaliq Simone teaches sociology at Goldsmith's College, University of London, and The New School University in New York City. An urbanist, Simone is noted for his close ethnographic study of cities of the South – notably Africa and South Asia. Simone brings to his first-hand knowledge of new forms of city life, an acute understanding of the most current theoretical work from psychoanalysis to social philosophy, as well as social theory. His recent books include *For the City Yet to Come* (2004) and *City Life from Jakarta to Dakar* (2009).

The Visible and the Invisible

Part two: Douala, Cameroon

The Disappeared President Paul Biya established Operation Command on February 20, 2000 as a means of rectifying the alarming increase in violent crime in Douala. At first residents across the city applauded this military operation, as they had become increasingly frightened of venturing anywhere in public, even during daylight hours. It was common for people from all walks of life and in all quarters to tell stories of being held up at work, on the street, or in their homes. Equipped with vast powers of search and seizure, as well as arbitrary detention, Operation Command quickly zeroed in on a huge network of warehouses harboring stolen goods, as well as illicit acquisitions of cars, houses, and consumer goods.

As the net widened, almost everyone came under suspicion. During raids on homes, if the residents were unable to immediately provide receipts for items like televisions or refrigerators, they would be confiscated. Increasingly, Operation Command appeared to Doualaise as organized military theft. There were also reports about large-scale extrajudicial killings, of detainees disappearing from prisons. Bodies of suspected criminals were often found in the streets with signs of torture and bullet wounds.

On January 23, 2001, nine youths from the Bapenda quarter were picked up after a neighbor had reported them as having stolen a gas canister. They were taken to a gendarme station in Bonanjo, on the other side of the city, where they were allowed to visit their families and correspond with them, although they reported being physically tortured. On January 28, they were transferred to an Operation Command post whereupon all communication from them stopped. The parents were unable to find out any information as to the location of their children. Following the disappearance of the "Bapenda 9," Douala witnessed the first in a series of marches and demonstrations which were brutally suppressed by the police.

During this time, there were many reputed sightings of the disappeared, usually at night and usually in quarters considered highly dangerous. The sightings would describe the boys as beaten and emaciated, but desperate to hide from the expected onslaught of Operation Command from which they inexplicably slipped. There was widespread concern that if there were any validity to these sightings, that all should be done to keep the boys alive as testimonials to what was assumed to be a practice killing thousands. As Marc Etaha, Frederic Ngouffo, Chatry Kuete, Eric Chia, Jean Roger Tchiwan, Charles Kouatou, Chia Effician, Elysee Kouatou, and Fabrice Kuate – the Bapenda 9[1] – served as a kind of "last straw" for public patience with Operation Command, there was an uneasy mixture of guilt, anger, impotence, and mysticism wrapped up in the larger public response to their disappearance.

Whether or not people actually believed the reputed sightings of the disappeared, in some quarters of the city a ritual developed where efforts were made to feed the disappeared. Because the sightings were most frequently in very dangerous parts of the city, households would send their girl domestics, often great distances, to deliver food. It is common in Douala to take in young girls from the rural areas as unpaid servants. Many rural households can no longer provide for their children and so either throw them out of the home or sell them to intermediaries. These girls remain the "property" of the households they work for and are usually badly mistreated and have little freedom of mobility. From one sighting of the disappeared to the next, from one part of the city to the other, these girls took the risk of their own disappearance on the feeding expeditions. In the process, they crossed Douala at night in ways that at the time were without precedent. Sometimes they would meet up with other girls they had met on previous journeys and share what they had seen, as well as embellish stories and invent new ones. The danger entailed was secondary to the flush of this sudden and usually daily freedom, for soon they would meet up in particular spots and go where they wanted, never mind whether it corresponded with the destination they were instructed to seek out.

They would leave ciphers and other marks on cars and household walls, on store windows and security grates, or pile up empty pots and pans at key intersections. They would then tell their respective employers that the disappeared were attempting to leave messages, to communicate with the residents of the city about what was really taking place. Word spread that these girls had become interlocutors between the disappeared and the city and not merely deliverers of food. Their capacities were greatly inflated in a city where the reputations of those able to navigate the world of the night were already inflated. And so several of the girls began to be sought out by various officials, businesspersons, and even top personnel of Operation Command itself. They came not so much for direct information about the disappeared themselves nor to interpret their supposed conveyances. Rather, they wanted interpretations of their dreams, advice on new ventures, insights on the wheeling and dealing of colleagues and competitors.

Girls of thirteen who not long before had gone hungry in rural areas experiencing thorough economic and social decline, bought and sold to fetch water, now suddenly found 10,000 CFA notes pressed in their hands, and started demanding more. Stories spread how one of the girls, Sally, would hold court by the pool at the Meridien Hotel, cellphone in hand and surrounded by her entourage of body guards.

Illuminating Nkongmondo Nkongmondo is set back from the intersection of two major roads, one leading into Douala, the other to Yaounde. During the rains, the area floods easily and is traversed with great difficulty. It is a quarter with a reputation for thieves, killers, and malaria. What success these neighborhood "emissaries" have had in the past has not been necessarily attributed to deft skill or astute planning. Instead, twenty guys will show up somewhere completely improbable – a formal luncheon for ambassadors' wives, payday at the bank – during times where places are either crowded or full of security and simply bully their way to some relatively modest cash, usually taking significant casualties on the way. Sometimes the ruthlessness will result in a big score. But the brutal intrusiveness and take-no-prisoners attitude is what has earned the quarter its characterization as a sullen dump of thuggery and its young male criminals the name "headbangers." Few attempts at quarter "improvement" are initiated, though both the police and security command have repeatedly tried to clean out the growing criminal element.

Given the number of schemes, syndicates, and confidence games that often have occasion to make use of such "blind determination," one might think there would be safer and more lucrative opportunities for the young men here. But there is a seeming insistence to stand apart, as very few are willing to work as brute force for more sophisticated networks or ringleaders. Detention and death are also not persuasive deterrents to the endless supply of youth from the area purportedly identified as assailants and perpetrators.

Not two minutes from the western entrance to the quarter stand the remains of what was once Douala's largest cinema, now closed for the past several years. Next door stands a four-story building that once housed one of the city's better Catholic high schools, now moved to another, more suburban location. The demise of both has a lot to do with the relationship between them. The school kids would skip out of classes and crowd matinee showings of an endless fare of cheap kung fu movies. The kids would barely pay attention to the films; it was more a place to smoke marijuana and have sex. Some efforts were made to get the authority to at least close the place during school hours. But this was to no avail, especially as the very popular soft-porn showings on the weekends drew crowds of functionaries already disappointed that they hadn't attained the positions which would entitle them to the special twice-monthly strip shows and beyond featuring Parisian women held in Bonanjo.

While over the years the cinema had been stripped clean of seats, carpet, even major sections of the roof, the locked projection booth strangely remained intact. Given its proximity to Nkongmondo, the cinema was a convenient hangout for neighborhood youth, a beguiling place of refuge given how, despite its present locked-down fortress appearance, its status as a gathering spot of criminals was well known to the police. But as far as I could make out, there were no raids, no arrests. Unlike the high school kids, these youth actually came to watch cinema, perhaps as a respite from just how much their lives had become clumsy imitations of grade C movies. The thing was that there were no movies per se to watch. Rather, they had managed to attach the projector to a small generator to simply get it running and would then sit, often for hours, watching the rays of light as they reached the surface of the screen. Afterwards, they would get beers and have long discussions about what they had seen, arguing over plot lines and characters. But what was clear was that an important way of life was being depicted. The landscape and composition of this life, imposed on the screen from their imaginations, was discussed in great detail following these "showings."

Like most Doualaise, they were fascinated with this specter of distant lands, and also like most, they were determined to save money any way they could in order to buy tickets and secure visas. But unlike these others, they never could identify the name of the destination or figure out how far away it really was, or conversely, the name and distance would change all the time, as would the relevant authorities and the ways of getting there. So it would never be clear just how much money they needed, what the cost would be. As it was always difficult to hide money or to keep from spending it either to be left alone or buy one's way out of trouble, the problems seemed endless.

In the summer of 2001, a new organization, Forum for Inhabitants, made a preliminary effort to organize some form of community association in Nkongmondo. It consulted the village chief and with his assistance put together an initial assembly of over fifty residents to talk about what they could do about the insalubrious conditions that prevailed. Unlike most such meetings across the city, and across most cities in the region today, the complaints about present conditions were muted. Sure there was flooding and the lack of basic services, but the community had long been able to get by with being what they were; their aspirations were neither great, nor did they think that, whatever they might do, anything significant would likely ensue. When asked if the large numbers of criminals who reputedly operated from the community and subjected the community to harassment and a bad name put a damper on their motivation, a gray bearded man of about seventy forcefully responded, "no, not at all, they are invisible to us."

How does one locate this invisibility and to what ends? Within cities, the process of making individuals strangers to each other has been critical to incorporating their bodies and energies as labor for production of increasingly ephemeral commodities without referenced value, and the consumption of which grows more frenetic and dissociated from the stabilization of place or livelihood. Even across the impoverished quarters of Douala, there is an obsession with eating well, and neighborhoods become identified through the particularities of the foods cooked and the ways in which they are presented. From fried plantains served on images of the President's bare ass in specific humorous newspapers to the specific colors of plastic forks which must be used to eat certain stews on specific days, this incorporation of bits and pieces of quotidian objects into a complex economy of consuming basic meals makes the act of eating something potentially fractal – spacing out in all directions without clear aleatory channels or implications.

On the other hand, the unleashing of signifiers also is deployed as an excessive marker of belonging; excessive evidence of narrow genealogies cited to explain just where residents should be fixed. Fixed in the sense of specifying clearly eligible domains where the "broken" nature that characterizes most residents lives can be "repaired." But also fixed in the sense of being able to be pinned down and summed up, even as kin and communitarian relationships have become increasingly murky and fragmented in how they actually operate. Autochthony increasingly becomes a vehicle through which claims on resources can be made and legitimated.

But between the estrangement of labor and the reparation of belonging is the space of remembrance. Between embellishing anticipation of the next meal with traces of the "news" of yesterday and the undoing of the news of yesterday with the conviction that one has not yet "eaten well," there remains the collective process of sitting down to eat. Increasing numbers of youth are forced to float across the city in search of livelihood or run in a constant cat-and-mouse game, chasing those who owe them money, running from those whose money they have stolen. To locate someone, then, is often to speculate about when and where they will eat. In the midst of this speculation, and the uncertainty as to who is allied with whom, who knows what in an economy of appropriation and theft, sudden accumulation and loss, those who stop to eat must be careful about what they say. They may inevitably share their food, but they will make sure to say nothing to give themselves away. Sitting down to eat is then engineered with a complex toolbox of declensions, fragmented words, smirks, tongue clicks, and grunts.

Pinned down by the oozing appearance of identity markers, yet footloose in the pursuit of those from whom one is escaping, there is little to be presented, and achievement is not based on the figuration of a more comprehensive narrative. The circulation of communication's materiality "clears the bush for the bush to return," as the Sawa residents would say. In other words, as Agamben points out in his notion of *decreation*, what could have been and was becomes indistinguishable from what could have been but was not.[2]

The Doualaise know that they cannot go it alone, but who exactly to go with is another matter. For we have seen the pulling apart of conventional social ties. This is the place, then, of remembrance. There are no maps, no grand visions for a viable future, as in turn, there is nothing intact from the "archive" to be returned to life or to be reinvented. Rather, the boundary between the actual and the possible is effaced, as that which never happened but could be remembered as if it were about to happen now. The flickering projection in the cinema, the punctuation of meals by unnecessary language, the feeding of the disappeared and subsequent valorization of domestic girls – all point to a repositioning to call upon possibilities that have been there all along. It is a repositioning that releases a multiplicity of active forces to be in play, rather than assigned to reiterate existing values and differentials.[3]

Concluding note

New trajectories of urban mobility and mobilization are taking place in the interstices of complex urban politics. Distinct groups and capacities are provisionally assembled into surprising, yet often dynamic, inter-sections outside of any formal opportunity the city presents for the interaction of diverse identities and situations.

Across urban Africa, there is a persistent tension as to what is possible to do within the city and the appropriate forms of social connections through which such possibilities can be pursued. Increasingly, more ephemeral forms of social collaboration are coming to the fore, and more effective formal governance partnerships often succeed to the degree to which they can draw on them. This emergence is a means of circumventing the intensifying contestation as to what kinds of social modalities and identities can legitimately mobilize resources and people's energies. Throughout these efforts lingers the question as to how urban residents reach a "larger world" of operations. What happens within the domain of the city itself that allows urban actors, often deeply rooted in specific places and ascriptions, to operate outside these confines? How are apparent realities of social coherence and cohesion maintained while opportunities, that would seemingly require behaviors and attitudes antithetical to the sustainability of such cohesion, are pursued?

Urban Africans are on the move, and the ability to move, through their quarters or cities or among cities, must draw on a capacity to see themselves as more than just marginal to prevalent global urban processes. Residents must see that deteriorating urban conditions do not simply mean that they become further removed from where the real power or opportunities lie, and that access to expanded domains of operation is not fixed to specific "development trajectories," institutional memberships, or transportation circuits. There are multiple geographies pieced together and navigated through the particular ways in which urban residents constitute the connections among themselves and the ways in which these connections are folded along a series of other daily interactions.

Notes

1   From reports of Christian Action Against Torture, Douala, March 3, 2001.
2   Glorgio Agamben, *Potentialities: Collected Essays in Philosophy*, ed. and trans. Daniel Heller-Roazen (Stanford: Stanford University Press, 1999).
3   Michel Serres, *Angels: A Modern Myth*, trans. Francis Cowper (Paris: Flammarion, 1995).

AbdouMaliq Simone (2003) "The Visible and the Invisible: Remaking Cites in Africa," in *Under Siege: Four African Cities – Freetown, Johannesburg, Kinshasa, Lagos: Documenta11_Platform4*, Hatje Cantz Publishers, pp. 37–41.

An Inconclusive Word,
After the Crash

If globalization turns out to be enduring – if, that is, over a long time it proves to be a structure of global salience – then the question to be asked of it early in the 2000s would be: What are we to make of disturbances in global structures that even in geological time shake and shape mountains as they are forming? "Mountains come first," Braudel once said. Still, when it comes to the *longue durée*, earthquakes move structural things about first. No less with global structures. The quakes prompt the fear that the world is coming to an end.

To think through the history of globalizing forces, as we have in this book, is to identify certain dates when the worlds shook and changed – among them: 410, 1439, 1522, 1640, 1789, 1848, 1914, 1968, 1991, 2001, and of course many before and between, not to mention those to come after. Whatever the list, dates are taken as if they were events, when in fact they are no more than data points along the trajectories of longer-term structural swings. None is as exact as event-history would like it to be. One supposes that the more they are in the past, the more precise are the dates. But this is not true. We can be cautious about assigning too much meaning to 9/11/2001 or 12/25/1991 for it is still too soon to tell whether Osama bin Laden's attack on New York on 9/11 or Mikhail Gorbachev's abdication of the Soviet Imperium on Christmas 1991 were anything like the turning points they are, even now already, supposed to have been. Thus, too, when the reach back over time is much longer, one might well ask, for example, when exactly did Rome collapse? With the fall of the Republic or the end of the Augustan era or centuries later when Rome retreated to Byzantium? The bigger the empire, the longer it takes the fall.

Jared Diamond's *Collapse* (2005) bears a sub-title easily misunderstood: *How Societies Choose to Fail or Succeed.* The subtitle catches the eye because of the key word "choose." How can it be that societies of any material and human scale choose to collapse? And, especially, how does it happen that well-documented factors in the more prominent collapses – overpopulation, overextension of territories in search of food, overharvesting of natural food and fuel sources, unintended scorching of native lands, disease, out-migration, ruin – can be characterized as choices. We usually think of choices as decisions at a time in a locale to drink too much vodka or not, to marry this one or that one, to enter this occupation or some other, to buy a burial plot or to leave the remains up to survivors, and so on.

Jared Diamond is a very serious scholar, a professor of Geography and Physiology at UCLA. Though his books have won numerous prizes and are best-sellers, Diamond's work is far from being pop-science or high journalism. Like Einstein and Hawking, among many others, his is a science that counts and thinks in respect to facts. If, then, Diamond is to be taken seriously on this account, what is to be made of his evidenced argument that societies choose to collapse? Where is the choice when all about are making babies or conquering vassals (thus to push the limits of the land to feed)? Where is the choice when babies are starving and the only apparent option is to start eating the sacred cows or mastodons? And who would not join the armies seeking more and better lands? Who in the end would not flee the homeland when its forests and animal life are gone?

The problem, here, is that against the collapse of the early modern idea of the individual as *the* agent – as the one who chooses – the wider question of choice itself is left up for grabs. Can groups or, more complicated still, societies choose? If so, do they choose rationally? Is the defense of a homeland, or flight from it, really a rational choice when the reasonable alternatives are so few and frightful? And what, then, becomes of the dilemma when the society in question might be, as so many today believe it is, a global society wherein membership rights are, at best, vague and metaphoric? This, effectively, is the barrier reef on which liberal hope in such possibilities as a global civil society stubs its toes.

Is the global civil society deciding, at this moment, not to stop the wreckage of the global environment? Some individuals, prominent or not, and the groups, big and small, they join clearly are thinking about this problem. But it is a matter of survival that requires more that right-thinking good people, but the whole – all, more or less, at once. What if, let us say, China and the United States – the leading environmental criminals on the planet – were somehow to decide by some act of political will to address the problems for which they are responsible? What would they do? Reduce emission levels? Is that enough? Refuse to build cars or prohibit their use? Make meat production and consumption illegal? Make bicycles mandatory or offer free access to trains or ships while grounding all forms of air travel? Colonize Mars or the Moon? How would this work without a Bruce Willis or a Will Smith to be our agents?

In the same way that dates are no more that data points representing a series of unknowable conclusions, so too are choices ephemera of the passing and past moments when, it is supposed, we might have followed a different course by making better choices. Would the Americas be somehow better off today if they had chosen not to invade Iraq in 2003, focusing instead on, let us say, more productive wars? Would the Soviets have survived had they decided not to invade Afghanistan in 1979 and instead turned their might and wealth to domestic goods? The regress of rational choice options is infinite: What if the Archduke had decided not to go to Sarajevo on a hot summer day in 1914 or, just a century before, on another June day Napoleon had said: "Shit it's raining, let Wellington have Waterloo." The questions become a fantastic exercise in virtual history. Yet, they do make one think about choices when they must be made in the name of, or even *by*, a society of any scale, much less a global one.

Returning, then, to the present moment, whenever that turns out to be, let us assume that something enduring changed in the interim between 1991 and 2001. And let us further assume that that change, as seems likely, had or has to do with what, for the time being, we are calling globalization. If this, then what is to be made of it much less any subsequent quake that comes to pass even closer to the time from which we are looking backward in order to look ahead? And what, if anything, can we decide to do about it?

Take, for example, the Crash of 2009, which began in earnest more or less early autumn 2008 and continued in a downward spiral through, at least, early summer 2009. Whether subsequent signs of economic upturn in the third quarter of 2009 will be enough to reverse the Crash itself, like all dramatic events in global history, will be told as time passes by. What is evident, if not new, is that the Crash of 2009 was: first, global; second, hard on all; third, hardest on the global poor; fourth, a threat to free markets; thus, also, fifth, a threat to neo-liberal globalism; sixth, stuff like that; seventh, and worse.

However long or short the list, few of right mind would argue that events such as these did happen and may still be happening. The striking thing is that those who make it their business to understand and comment on big structural changes of the kind, have not, since, been able to make up their collective minds as to the cause and extent of the, dare we say, collapse?

A random sample of the public wisdom from the first half of 2009 includes – "The Brave New World of Deglobalization" (*China Vortex*, 4 January 2009); "When Globalization Goes into Reverse" (*Financial Times*, February 3, Gideon Rachman); "The De-Globalization Question" (*Z-Net*, January 31, William H. Thornton); "A Global Retreat As Economies Dry Up" (*Washington Post*, March 5, Anthony Faiola); "Running Out of Planet to Exploit" (*New York Times*, April 21, Paul Krugman); "De-Globalization" (*New Yorker Online*, May 26, referring to Bill Gross); "The Dangers of 'Deglobalization'" (*Council on Foreign Relations*, March 16, Jayshree Bajoria); "The World is Bumpy" (*New Republic*, July 15, Joshua Kurlantzick); "Globalization in Retreat" (*Foreign Affairs*: July/August, Roger C. Altman). There are of course other opinions. The ones here listed, however, are all written by experts and wisemen whose opinions are meant to be respected. The drift of these commentaries, read in full, as in their titles, is that the Crash of 2009 was indeed a collapse of its own kind.

The keyword, of course, is "deglobalization," which, if anything, has the virtue of being philosophically pungent. "Globalization," we have seen, is a term of many ambiguities in as much as it may or may not be new as the modern was new. We simply do not, and cannot, know the extent to which the globalization that took off sometime early in the 1990s was an extension of the modern global economy or its destruction. But, by contrast, "deglobalization" makes a definite statement – that globalization whatever it was or is meant to be is reversible. Thus is illustrated the conundrum that has appeared time and again through this book.

To think about globalization is, on the one had, always to think about the past – about the modern, of which globalization might be the sign of collapse; about, the ancient past, in respect to which many want to know if this is a return to empire by whatever name; about the future, in respect to which anyone who thinks about globalization, whether skeptically or hopefully, wants to know if it might be bad or good for human life.

Jared Diamond's view is that all societies, however small or large, collapse – some in short order, others over time. When they collapse they do because somehow or another they *choose* to outrun their supplies of land, water, food, social order, and all the other goods needed for people to live as if they were one. Thus, when a relatively short-term perturbation like the Crash of 2009 rears its ugly head, the inclination is to wonder if this is *the* Collapse; and, if so, of what? Darfur is dead dessert. Haiti is completely deforested. Bishkek is a ghost town. South Australia is out of fresh water. Chernobyl is a dead zone. The Arctic ice shelves are breaking off. Douala is an assemblage the state cannot police. Rwanda is not enough to contain the tribes. Mumbai is a contradiction. Slum dogs are a global class. Iceland is broke. And so on. Are they local or global? Are they signs of a global collapse? Might deglobalization be a sign of global recovery? Where in the world are we meant to go? What are we to do?

Globalization, like so many concepts, may end up just being words; or it may stand for something. If so, what that something might be is less urgent than how, whatever terms are in play, we are made to think freshly about events as if, as they must be, they are all linked at some vanishing point in the time and tense of the human. Globalization, we have seen, forces a reconsideration of a great many taken-for-granted truths – that individuals can be free, that they are agents of their fates, that a people can rule itself, that the world is one, that what fates may lie before us in this world the choice is ours. What we do not know exactly is where this all leads or, if there are choices to be, how we are to make them.

Finally, globalization is an inconclusive thing. It serves for the time being to open up the worlds – to their parts, their differences, their limitations, their naïveties, their foolishnesses, and their possibilities. In the end, there is no final world, only the raw politics of life's agglomerating forces.

Bibliography

Agamben, Giorgio (2000) *Means without End: Notes on Politics*. Translated by Vincenzo Binetti and Cesare Casarino. Minneapolis: University of Minnesota Press, pp. 3–12.

Altman, Dennis (2001) *Global Sex*. Chicago: University of Chicago Press, pp. 100–105.

Andrews, Carol (1981) "The Rosetta Stone," London: The Trustees of the British Museum. pp. 25, 26, 27, 28. Available online at http://pw1.netcom.com/~qkstart/rosetta.html.

Appadurai, Arjun (1990) "Disjuncture and difference in the global cultural economy." *Theory, Culture and Society* 7(2), 296–300, 301–303.

Appiah, Kwame Anthony (1997) "Cosmopolitan Patriots," *Critical Inquiry* 23, spring. 617–9, 633–4.

Augustine of Hippo "The Folly of the Romans," City of God (I, 3) from Christian Classics Ethereal Library. Available online at www.ccel.org.

Augustus (1924) *Deeds of Augustus (Res Gestae Divi Augusti)* translated by F.W. Shipley. Loeb Classical Library Volume 152, Cambridge, MA: Harvard University Press.

Bauman, Zygmunt (1998) *Globalization: The Human Consequences*. New York: Columbia University Press. pp. 2–3, 9–10, 18–19.

Beck, Ulrich (1999) *What is Globalization*. translated by Patrick Camiller, Cambridge: Polity Press. pp. 10–13.

Benedict, Ruth (1946) *The Chrysanthemum and the Sword: Patterns of Japanese Culture*. Boston: Houghton Mifflin Company. pp. 29–33.

Bessemer, Henry (1856) "On The Manufacture of Malleable Iron and Steel without Fuel," *The Engineer*. August 15.

Bradford, William (1856) "Of Plimouth Plantation" in Charles Deane (ed.) *Collections of the Massachusetts Historical Society*, ser. 4, vol. 3, pp. 100–106.

Breasted, James Henry (2001 [1906]) "Ancient Records of Egypt: Vol. 3: The Nineteenth Dynasty," Champaign: University of Illinois Press.

Bruchac, Joseph (1985) "The coming of Gluskabi" in *The Wind Eagle and Other Abenaki Stories*. Greenfield Center, NY: Bowman Books.

Butler, Judith (2004) *Precarious Life: The Powers of Mourning and Violence*. London and New York: Verso. pp. xi–xiii, xvii–xxi.

Castells, Manuel (2006) "The Network Society: From Knowledge to Policy" in Castells, Manuel and Gustavo Cardoso (eds) *The Network Society: From Knowledge to Policy*. Washington DC: Johns Hopkins Center for Transatlantic Relations. pp. 3–5, 7, 15–16.

Castro, Fidel (1960) "To the U.N. General Assembly, the problem of Cuba and its revolutionary policy." *Castro Speech Database* [Embassy of Cuba], from, *Castro Internet Archive*. Available online at http:/www.marxists.org/history/cuba/archive/castro/1960/09/26.htm.

Chamberlain, Basil Hall (trans.) (1919) *Kojiki*. Vol. II. 1, (Sect. XLIV). Tuttle Publishing. p. 159–161.

Chomsky, Noam (2006) *Failed States: The Abuse of Power and the Assault on Democracy*. Allen and Unwin. pp. 1–2, 252, 263–4.

Cicero (1993) *de Re Publica* (trans. Richard Hooker). Available online at http://www.wsu.edu/~dee/rome/scipio.htm.

Cowen, Tyler (2002) *Creative Destruction: How Globalization is Changing the World Cultures*. Princeton, NJ: Princeton University Press, pp. 55–59.

Curl, John (2005) "Hymn Seven, Prayer for the Inca" in *Ancient American Poets* by John Curl, translator, Tempe, AZ: Bilingual Press/Editorial Bilingüe.

Darwin, Charles (1859) *On the Origin of Species by Means of Natural Selection* (2nd edition). Available online at http://www.gutenberg.org/files/22764/22764-h/22764-h.htm.

Dean, Patrick (1956) "The Protocol of Sèvres, 1956" (written in 1978). National Archive, Crown Copyright, catalogue reference: FCO/73/205.

DeLanda, Manuel (2006) *A New Philosophy of Society: Assemblage Theory and Social Complexity.* London: Continuum. pp. 95–6, 112–119.

Deleuze, Gilles, and Guattari, Felix (1986) *Nomadology: The War Machine.* New York: Semiotext(e). pp. 50–54.

Dhammika, Ven. S. "Edicts of King Ashoka, Pillar 13." The Buddhist Publication Society Inc. Available online at http://www.cs.colostate.edu/~malaiya/ashoka.html.

DeLillo, Don (1998) *Underworld: A Novel,* New York: Scribner, p. 786.

Dicken, Peter (1992) *Global Shift: The Internationalization of Economic Activity.* London: Paul Chapman, pp. 5–6, 10–13.

Dobson, W.A.C.H. (1963) *Mencius: a new translation arranged and annotated for the general reader.* University of Toronto Press.

Eliade, Mircea (1971) *Myth of the Eternal Return: Cosmos and History,* Princeton University Press.

Fanon, Frantz (1968) *Wretched of the Earth,* translated by Constance Farrington. New York: Grove Press. pp. 35–39.

Fernández-Armesto, Felipe (2003) *The Americas: A Hemispheric History.* New York: The Modern Library. pp. 90–95.

Foucault, Michel (1988) *Technologies of the Self: A Seminar With Michel Foucault,* Amherst, MA: University of Massachusetts Press, p. 17.

Frank, Andre Gunder (1998) *ReOrient: Global Economy in the Asia Age,* University of California Press, p. 5.

Freidman, Thomas (2000) *The Lexus and the Olive Tree.* London: Harpers Collins Publishers, pp. 104–106.

Fukuyama, Francis (1989) "The End of History?" *The National Interest.* Summer.

Fussell, Paul Interview on PBS. Available online at http://www.pbs.org/greatwar/historian/hist_fussell_03_trenches.html and http://www.pbs.org/greatwar/historian/hist_fussell_04_xmas.html.

Garton Ash, Timothy (2004) *Free World: America, Europe, and the Surprising Future of the West.* New York: Random House. pp. 46–50, 80–82.

George, Andrew (1999) *The Epic of Gilgamesh: The Babylonian Epic Poem and Other Texts in Akkadian and Sumerian.* Harmandsworth: Penguin.

Gerard, Chaliand (1994) "Napoleon, social and political thoughts," in Gerard Chaliand (ed.) *The Art of War in World History from Antiquity to the Nuclear Age,* Berkeley: University of California Press, pp. 646–651.

Giddens, Anthony (1999) *Runaway World.* Cambridge: Polity Press, pp. 6–10, 12–13, 15–19.

Giddens, Anthony and Ulrich Beck (2007) "Open Letter on the Future of Europe," in Anthony Giddens *The Future of Europe.* Cambridge: Polity Press, pp. 231–234.

Gilpin, Robert (2000) *The Challenge of Global Capitalism: The World Economy in the Twenty-First Century.* Princeton, NJ: Princeton University Press. pp. 3, 5–10.

Gilroy, Harry (1960) "Lumumba assails colonialism as Congo is freed" *New York Times,* July 1. Available online at http://partners.nytimes.com/library/world/africa/600701lumumba.html.

Gore, Al (2007) "The Nobel Peace Prize Lecture, 2007," Nobel Lecture, Oslo, 10 December 2007. Available online at http://nobelprize.org/nobel_prizes/peace/laureates/2007/gore-lecture_en.html.

Griffith, Ralph T.H. (1971) "Rig Veda 3.62 – Gayatri Mantra" in "The Hymns of the Rig-Veda," The *Chowkhamba Sanskrit Studies* vol. XXXV, Varanasi – 1 (India): The Chowkhamba Sanskrit Series Office, vol. 1, pp. 389–390.

Guthrie, Doug (2006) *China and Globalization: The Social, Economic and Political Transformation of Chinese Society,* New York: Routledge. pp. 3–4, 255, 329–331.

Hall, Stuart (1991) "The local and the global: globalization and ethnicity," in Anthony King (ed.) *Culture and Globalization and the World System: Contemporary Representation of Identity.* London: Macmillan. pp. 30–36.

Hannerz, Ulf (1996) *Transnational Connections: Culture, People, Places.* London and New York: Routledge. pp. 102, 107–111.

Hardt, Michael and Antonio Negri (2000) *Empire,* Cambridge, MA: Harvard University Press. pp. xi–xii, xv–xvi, 15, 392.

Havel, Václav (1992) "The End of the Modern Era," *The New York Times,* March 1. Available online at www.nytimes.com.

Held, David (2004) *Global Covenant: The Social Democratic Alternative to the Washington Consensus.* Cambridge: Polity Press. pp. 162–169.

Held, David and Anthony McGrew (1999) *Global Transformations.* Cambridge: Polity Press. pp. 7–9.

Hirst, Paul and Grahame Thompson (1990) *Globalization in Question,* Cambridge: Polity Press. pp. 1–7.

Hobsbawn, E.J. (2001) *The Age of Extremes: A History of the World, 1914–1991,* Gloucester, MA: Peter Smith Pub Inc.

Ho Chi Min, Part Two (1945–1954): To the Vietnamese people, the French people and the peoples of the allied nations

(December 21, 1946). The Gioi Publishers. Available online at http://www.cpv.org.vn/english/archives/details.asp?topic=14&subtopic=99&leader_topic=41&id=BT1970355632.

Hochschild, Adam (1999) *King Leopold's Ghost*. New York: Houghton Mifflin. pp. 6–18.

Hoffman, Stanley (2002) "Clash of Globalizations," *Foreign Affairs*, 81(4) July/August, 110–115.

Hopkins, J.F.P. (1981) "The Picture of the Earth," in *Corpus of Early Arabic Sources for West African History* translated by J.F.P. Hopkins, edited and annotated by N. Levtzion and J.F.P. Hopkins. Cambridge: Cambridge University Press. pp. 44–46.

Hughes, Robert (1966) *The Fatal Shore*. New York: Vintage Books. pp. 1–3.

Huntington, Samuel (1993) "The clash of civilizations?" *Foreign Affairs* 22, Summer, 22–26, 39–41.

Ikenberry, G. John (2008) "The rise of China and the future of the West: can the liberal system survive?" *Foreign Affairs* Jan/Feb 2008.

Jameson, Fredric (1998) "Notes on globalization as a philosophical issue" in *The Cultures of Globalization*, Fredric Jameson and Masao Miyoshi (eds), Durham, NC: Duke University Press. pp. 54–77.

Jones, R.J. Barry (1995) *Globalization and Interdependence in the International Political Economy*. London: Pinter Publishers. pp. 219–221.

Kaldor, Mary (2003) *Global Civil Society: An Answer to War*. Cambridge: Polity Press. pp. 6–12.

Keane, John (2003) *Global Civil Society?* Cambridge: Cambridge University Press. pp. 8–12, 16–17.

Kennan, George F. (1967) "The Long Telegram," in *Memoirs: 1925–1950*, Little Brown and Company.

King, Martin Luther (1986) "My trip to the land of Gandhi" in James Melvin Washington, *Testament of Hope: The Essential Writings of Martin Luther King, Jr.* San Francisco: Harper. pp. 25–26.

Klein, Naomi (2004) "Reclaiming the Commons" in Tom Mertes (ed.), *A Movement of Movements*. London: Verso. pp. 219–229.

Kristeva, Julia (1995) *New Maladies of the Soul*. Translated by Ross Guberman. New York: Columbia University Press, pp. 6–10.

Ku, Mei-Kao (1988) *Chinese Mirror for Magistrates: The Hsin-Yu of Lu Chia*. Canberra: Australian National University, Faculty of Asian Studies.

Kwong, Peter and Duskana Miscevic (2002) "Globalization and Hong Kong's Future," *Journal of Contemporary Asia*, 32(3), 323, 324, 325, 328, 335, 336.

Lee, Peter (ed.) (1993) "From 'Samguk Sagi: 41:394–43:406'" in *Sourcebook of Korean Civilization*. New York: Columbia University Press. p. 111–112.

Luce, Henry (1999) "The American Century," in Hogan, Michael J. (ed.) *The Ambiguous Legacy: U.S. Foreign Relations in the "American Century,"* New York: Time, pp. 11–30, 22–24.

Malcolm X (1992) "The Black Muslim Movement: An Assessment," in Betty Shabazz, *The Final Speeches*. New York: Pathfinder. pp. 16–19.

Mao Tse-tung (1949) "The chinese people have stood up!" September 21. Available online at http://www.marxists.org/reference/archive/mao/selected-works/volume–5/mswv5_01.htm.

Mbembe, Achille (2003) "Necropolitics" translated by Libby Meintjes. *Public Culture*, 15(1) 11–40.

Naipaul, V.S. (1975) "A new king for the Congo," *New York Review of Books*, 22(11) June 26, 1975.

Nancy, Jean-Luc (2007) *The Creation of the World or Globalization*. Translated by Francois Raffoul and David Pettigrew. Albany, NY: State University of New York Press. pp. 33–37.

New American Century (1997) "Statement of Principles, June 3, 1997". Available online at http://www.newamericancentury.org/statementofprinciples.htm.

Nye, Joseph S. (2001) "Globalization's Democratic Deficit: How to Make International Institutions More Accountable," *Foreign Affairs* July/August. 2–6.

Ohmae, Kenichi (1995) *The End of the Nation State: The Rise of the Regional Economies*. New York: Free Press Paperbacks. pp. 7, 28–30, 141–142.

Ong, Aihwa (2006) "Introduction," in *Neoliberalism as Exception: Mutations in Citizenship and Sovereignty*, Durham, NC: Duke University Press. pp. 1–27.

Paolini, Albert (1999) *Navigating Modernity: Postcolonialism, Identity, and International Relations*, edited by Anthony Elliott and Anthony Moran. Boulder, CO: Lynne Rienner.

Papastergiadis, Nikos (2000) *Turbulence of Migration: Globalization, Deterritorialization and Hybridity*. Cambridge: Polity Press, pp. 40–41, 44, 46–50.

Peterson, Joseph H. (1997) Zarathustra, *Avesta*, translation by Bartholomae, in I.J.S. Taraporewala, *The Divine Songs of Zarathustra*. Translation of excerpt from Zoroastrian text Yasna, by Joseph H. Peterson. Available online at http://www.avesta.org/.

Pheng Cheah (1999) "Spectral Nationality: The Living on [sur-vie] of the Postcolonial Nation in Neocolonial Globalization," *Boundary 2*, 26(3) 225–252.

Plutarch, Moralia. "On the Fortune or the Virtue of Alexander, bk. 1," *De Fortuna Alexandri by Plutarch* as published in Vol. IV of the Loeb Classical Library edition, 1936.

Pritchard, James B. (ed.) (1958) *Ancient Near East: An Anthology of Texts and Pictures*. Princeton, NJ: Princeton University Press.

Reginald, Robert and Elliott, Jeffrey M. (1983) "Argentinean Surrender, 14 June 1982," in R. Reginald and Dr Jeffrey M. Elliot *Tempest in a Teapot*, San Bernardino, CA: The Borgo Press. Available online at http://www.falklands.info/history/82doc013.html.

Robertson, Roland (1995) "Glocalization: time-space homogeneity heterogeneity," in Mike Featherstone *et al.* (eds) *Global Modernities*. London: Sage Publications. pp. 28–32.

Rosenau, James N. (1992) "Governance, order and change in world politics," in J. Rosenau and E. Czempiel (eds) *Governance Without Government: Order and Change in World Politics*. Cambridge: Cambridge University Press. pp. 3–8.

Rosenberg, Justin (2005) "Globalization theory: a postmortem," *International Politics*, 42, 11–15.

Rugman, Alan and Richard Hodgetts (2001) "The end of global strategy," *European Management Journal*, 19(4) 333–343.

Sahagún, Bernardino de (1989 translated by Howard F. Cline, edited with an introduction and notes by S.L. Cline) "Concerning other events that happened when the Mexicans, Tlatelolcans, and the lord of Mexico surrendered to the Spaniards," in *Conquest of New Spain:1585 Revisio*. Salt Lake City: University of Utah Press. pp. 137–139.

Sassen, Saskia (2008) "Neither Global Nor National: Novel Assemblages of Territory, Authority and Rights," *Ethics and Global Politics*, 1(2) 61–71. Available online at http://journals.sfu.ca/coaction/index.php/egp/article/view/1814/1809.

Scott, James C. (1998) *Seeing Like a State: How Certain Schemes to Improve the Human Condition Have Failed*, New Haven: Yale University Press. pp. 11–15, 25–29.

Sen, Amartya (2008) "Violence, Identity and Poverty," *Journal of Peace Research* 45(5), 5–7, 13–15.

Simone, AbdouMaliq (2003) "The visible and the invisible: remaking cites in Africa," in *Under Siege: Four African Cities–Freetown, Johannesburg, Kinshasa, Lagos: Documenta11_Platform4*. Ostfildern: Hatje Cantz Verlag. pp. 37–41.

Sobel, Dava (1995) *Longitude: The True Story of a Lone Genius Who Solved the Greatest Scientific Problem of His Times*. New York: Walker and Company. pp. 165–175.

Stalin, Joseph (1946) "Stalin Interview with Pravda on Churchill" in *New York Times*, March 14, 1946, p. 4.

The Commission on Global Governance (2002) *Our Global Neighborhood*. Oxford: Oxford University Press.

The World Social Forum "Note from the Organizing Committee on the Principles that Guide the WSF." Available online at http://www.forumsocialmundial.org.br/main.php?id_menu=4_2&cd_language=2.

Thucydides, "Funeral Oration of Pericles" in *History of the Peloponnesian War*, book 2. Translated by Richard Crawley in 1876. Available online at http://classics.mit.edu.

Tomlinson, John (1999) *Globalization and Culture*. Cambridge: Polity Press. pp. 27–31.

Treaty of Westphalia. Available online at http://avalon.law.yale.edu/17th_century/westphal.asp.

Urry, John (2003) *Global Complexity*. Cambridge: Polity Press. pp. 93–101.

Virilio, Paul (2005) *The Information Bomb*. London: Verso, pp. 130–137, 139–140.

Wallerstein, Immanuel (1974) *The Modern World System: Capitalist Agriculture and the Origins of the European World-Economy in the Sixteenth Century*. New York: Academic Press. pp. 15–17.

Watt, James, Patent. 1855. Printed by George Edward Eyre and William Spottiswoode.

Žižek, Slavoj (2001) *Welcome to the Desert of the Real*. New York: Verso.

Zolo, Davilo (2007) "Global citizenship: a realist critique," in Stephen Slaughter and Wayne Hudsons (eds), *Globalisation and Citizenship: The Transnational Challenge*. London and New York: Routledge. p. 80–83.

Index

Afghanistan 134, 138, 139, 269, 270, 274, 278, 291, 300, 310, 352, 384, 423
Agamben, Giorgio 69, 341, 353, 354, 401, **406–409**, 420, 421 (note 2)
AIDS 191, 277, 288, 391, 393 (notes) 399
    see also HIV
Ali, Muhammad 140
Al-Qaeda 269, 270, 271, 274
Althusser, Louis 276
Altman, Dennis 351, **390–393**
American Century 133–134
    selection on **157–158**
Americanization 82, 206, 226, 261, 263
Amnesty International 207, 289, 293, 372, 374, 377
anti-globalization movement 203, 205, 206, 225, 280, 291
Appadurai, Arjun 117, 119 (notes), **256–259**
Appiah, Kwame Anthony 219 (notes), 349–350, **380–382**
Archduke Ferdinand 134, 142
    assassination of **142–143**
Arendt, Hannah 249 (note 5), 341, 415, 417 (notes)
Asia Pacific Economic Cooperation 207
Assemblage(s) 14, 15, 30, 345–346, 348, 352–355
    Sassen, **360–367**
    DeLanda **410–413**

Balkanization 156
Balkans 134, 143, 338
Batista, Fulgencio 140, 186
Bauman, Zygmunt 73, 208, **254–256**, 265, 298, 299
Beck, Ulrich 206, **251–253**, 272–273, 299, **336–338**, 369
Benedict, Ruth 135, **153–155**
Bessemer, Sir Henry 74, **121–126**
bin Laden, Osama 6, 270, **274–275**, 277, 422
Blair, Tony 206, 240, 335, 338
Braudel, Fernand 77–78, 132, 411–413
Brazil 97, 98, 100, 185, 198–199, 242, 243, 298, 311, 346
Brazilian Workers' Party (PT) 198
Bush, President George H.W. 209
Bush, President George W. 246, 250, 269, 271, 333–334
Butler, Judith 352, 370, **401–403**

Castells, Manuel 204, 208, **211–213**, 214, 215 (notes), 243, 244, 265, 304
Castro, Fidel 138, 140, **185–187**
Cheah, Pheng 350, 354, **384–387**
Chiang Kai-Shek 137, 145, 182
    Generalissimo of China 181
Chomsky, Noam **281–283**
Churchill, Winston 137–138, **159–160**, 160–164, 296, 335
Clifford, James 302–306
Clinton, President Bill 206, 240, 246, 250, 278
Civil Rights Movement; American 140, 180, 188–190
    South African 391
Civilization 77, 80–81, 139, 183, 272, 277, 287, 305
    American 47, 54, 56–57
    ancient 5–8
    Chinese 44
    clash of 278, **321–324**, 334, 382–383
    classical 28–31
    global 191, 244, 250, 311, 314–316
    western 189, 320, 399
Cold War 3, 19, 132, 136–139, 141, 160, 164, 180, 186, 191, 219, 227, 243, 246, 279, 288, 296, 297, 300, 318, 319, 321, 325, 334
Colonial 33, 55–56, 80–82, 88, 94, 133, 139–140, 157, 179–180, 225, 252, 258, 300, 309, 321, 324, 328, 337, 358, 369, 395–396, 412, 415
    America **82–85**
    Australia **93–95**
    China 4
    Congo **184–186**
    Cuba **185–186**
    system of 62, 67–68, 71, 141, 179, 354
    Vietnam **176–177**
    see also post-colonial
The Commission on Global Governance **284–287**
Communism 138, 160, 163–164, 182, 262, 274, 319, 321, 379, 400, 416, 417 (notes)
    collapse of 190–192, 196–198
community 13, 20, 82, 182, 183, 189, 196, 214, 216, 223, 252, 255, 256, 291, 298, 302, 309–316, 319, 335, 345, 354, 392, 400–402

international community 286, 287, 323, 324
    political community 377, 385, 406–409
Congo 95–102, 130, 140–141, 183–185, 193–194, 277
    see also Zaire
consumer 208 (notes), 210, 228, 256, 259, 307, 314, 320,
    392, 418
    capitalism 254
    consumerism 208, 262, 298
    culture 225–226, 262, 270, 276, 291, 319
    electronics 232–237
Cosmopolitan(-ism) 215–219, 243, 271–273, 291, 298, 303,
    304, 316, 337, 350, 351, 372, 377, 379, 384
    critique of 298–300
    identity 380–382
Cowen, Tyler 271, **304–306**
creolization 215, 218, 219 (notes) 298, 312
cultural diversity 218, 261, 304, 309, 315, 337, 380

Dean, Sir Patrick **166–175**
Decolonization *see* colonial and post-colonial
DeLanda, Manuel 353–354, **409–413**
Deleuze, Gilles 345–348, 353–354, **356–358**, 367 (notes),
    404, 409, 410
Deng, Xiaoping 139, 328
deregulation 205, 208, 222–223, 226, 228, 366, 378, 394,
    397
deterritorialization 258–259, 299, 303–304, 359, 398
    Deleuze and Guattari's conceptualization 346,
    356–358
    economic 214, 244
    effect on the nation-state 346, 348, 412
Diamond, Jared 422, 424
Dicken, Peter 204, **213–215**

Eden, Sir Anthony 166, 169–175
Einstein, Albert 347, 405, 422
Eisenhower, Dwight D. 166, 227
Empire 3–9, 63, 71, 76–78, 88–90, 96, 102, 131, 142–143,
    156, 166, 181, 205, 246, 281, 306, 334–335, 354,
    369–370, 375–377, 399, 410–412, 422, 424
    Hardt and Negri's *Empire*, 134, 300, 346, **358–360**
Enlightenment 132, 136, 191, 258, 260, 272, 300, 343, 377,
    416
European Monetary System (EMS) 224
European Union (EU) 205, 212, 232–233, 237, 241–242,
    272–273, 292–294, 325, 335–338, 394

Fanon, Frantz 139–140, 141, **178–179**, 385, 392, 393
Featherstone, Mike 218 (note), 271, 298, 310, 317 (note)
Ferdinand, Archduke, assassination of **142–143**
Ferguson, Niall 249 (notes) 270, 295
Foreign Direct Investment (FDI) 222, 228, 236, 385–386
Foucault, Michel 68, 69, 75 (note 3), 118 (note 7), 341, 347,
    353, 406, 408, 415, 417 (notes)

Frank, Andre Gunder 5, 9 (note), 75 (note), 131
    critique of Wallerstein 62–63
free trade 242, 291
    see also North American Free Trade Agreement (NAFTA)
Free Trade of the Americas (FTAA) 225–226
Friedman, Thomas **219–220**, 310, 326
Fukuyama, Francis 262, **318–320**, 334, 376
Fussell, Paul 133, **143–145**

G8 (also G-8) 203, 206, 207, 212, 269
Gandhi, Mohandas K. 3, 139–140, 141, **180–181**, 188–189,
    190 (note), 372
Garton Ash, Timothy **333–336**
gender 259, 260, 285, 303, 307, 308, 314, 392, 396, 401
genetic engineering 225, 406
Geneva Convention 134
Giddens, Lord Anthony 206, 238 (notes) **240–243**, 244,
    265, 272–273, 303, **336–338**
Gilpin, Robert 205, **227–229**
Glasnost 141, 196–198
    in relation to modern 61–62
global cities 362, 365, 394, 397
global market 222, 224, 232–234, 238, 244, 249, 273, 300,
    314, 327, 349, 358
    market integration 270–271, 292–294
    marketplace 62, 204–205, 214, 241
Global Transnational Corporations, *see* transnational
    corporation (TNC), multinational enterprise, and
    multinational corporation
global village 214, 242, 298, 370, 393 (notes)
glocalization 368, 370
    selection by Robertson on **314–317**
Gorbachev, Mikhail 141, **196–198**, 318, 422
Gore, Al **250–251**
Gray, John 270
Guattari, Felix 345–347, **356–358**, 367 (notes)
Gulag 6, 68, 132, 160, 343
    selection by Hughes on Australia **93–95**
Gurion, Ben 172, 174
Guthrie, Doug **331–332**

Hall, Stuart 271, **306–310**, 313 (notes)
Hannerz, Ulf 204, **215–219**, 310, 315, 316
Hardt, Michael 134, 300, 346–347, **358–360**, 376 (notes)
Havel, Václav 141, **190–192**, 376 (notes)
Hawking, Stephen 347, 422
Hegel, G.F.W. 261, 277, 305, 319, 321, 387 (note), 399, 413
    (note), 417 (note)
    on civil society 377, 379
    on death 414
Held, David 204, 206–207, **243–246**, 253 (notes), 270, 271,
    291–295, 368
Hiroshima 3, 134, 135, 314
Hirst, Paul 205, **221–224**

Hitler, Adolf 6, 133, 135, 137, 149, 154, 155, **155–157**, 161–162, 353
  see also Nazi
HIV 391, 392, 408
  see also AIDS
Hobsbawn, E.J. 141 (notes), 299
Ho Chi-Minh 138, 139, 140, **176–177**
Hodgetts, Richard **232–239**
Hoffman, Stanley **325–327**
Holocaust 132, 135, 291, 334
Hong Kong 242, 259, 311
  selection on **328–331**
Hughes, Robert 68, **93–95**
Huntington, Samuel 272, **321–324**, 334

Ikenberry, G. John **295–298**
imperium 8, 40, 407
  Europe's lost **143–145**
  Soviet 134
India 3, 31, 93, 96, 126, 139, 141, 206, 242, 256, 261, 298, 300, 323, 333, 338, 382, 384, 391, 396, 405
  Ghandi's speech **180–181**
  Indian National Army 319
  Martin Luther King Jr's speech on visiting **188–189**
  Mauryan Empire **36–37**
  selection from Rig Veda **12–13**
intergovernmental organizations (IGOs) 207, 292–294
International Monetary Fund (IMF) 203, 206, 207, 212, 226, 227, 280, 281, 323, 331 (notes), 386, 387 (notes)
international non-governmental organizations (INGO) 207
  see also non-governmental organizations (NGO)
internationalization 205, 213, 222–223, 237
Internet 187, 227, 310, 372, 379, 403, 405
  web site 368, 372
Iraq 6, 139, 269, 270, 274, 282, 291, 295, 300, 323, 333–334, 352, 403
Islam 6, 8, 11, 48–49, 136, 140, 188, 190, 272, 278, 322–324, 326, 378, 384, 399
  bin Laden's Fatwa **274–275**
  fundamentalist 62, 252, 262, 269, 272, 322–323
  Muhammad, *Qur'an* **19–22**
  Nation of 188–190

Jameson, Fredric **259–263**, 311–312, 313 (notes)
jihad 274
  bin Laden's Fatwa **274–275**
Jones R.J.B., 205, **230–232**, 367 (notes), 387 (notes)
July Ultimatum 134, **142–143**

Kaldor, Mary 349, **376–380**
Keane, John 349, **372–376**, 379–380 (notes)
Kennan, George 137–138, 139, 159, **164–166**
Keynes, John Maynard 135–136, **149–151**, 151, 224

King, Martin Luther Jr. 140, 180, **188–189**, 372
Klein, Naomi **225–227**, 369, 372
Kristeva, Julia 351, **388–390**
Kwong, Peter **328–331**

Lenin, Vladimir 137, 150–151, **151–153**, 165, 373, 417 (notes)
  Leningrad 134
  Leninism 320
  Leninist State 181
Leopold II, King 68, 185
  Leopoldville 184, 185
  selection by Hochschild on **95–102**
liberal 154, 191, 247, 278, 333, 341, 344, 349, 381, 386
  cultural 63, 135, 278, 352
  economic 63, 72, 139, 231, 311
  ideological 63, 136–138, 353
  liberalization 205, 222, 231, 378, 386
  political 66, 73, 90, 278, 282, 293, 318–320, 321, 324, 332, 341
  selection on the survival of the liberal system **295–298**
  see also neoliberal
Lincoln, Abraham 145, 146
Locke, John 66–67, 69, 70, 71, **90–92**
Luce, Henry 133–134, **157–158**
Lumumba, Patrice 140
  selection by Harry Gilroy on **183–185**
Luther, Martin 69–70, **110**

Macmillan, Sir Harold 166, 174
Magellan, Ferdinand 65–66
Malcolm X 140, **188–190**
Mao Zedong 6, 137, 145, **181–183**, 219
Mau Mau 139
Mbembe, Achille 354, **413–417**
McGrew, Anthony 207, **243–246**, 294;
  as author of *Global Transformations* 265, 266, 368
Miscevic, Dusanka **328–331**
Mobutu Sese Seko 137, 140–141
  selection by V.S. Naipaul on **193–194**
modernity 70, 252–253, 264, 271, 303–305, 308–309, 379, 379, 393, 406, 414–417
  selection on "Navigating Modernity" **310–13**
Muhammad, Elijah 188, 190
multinational corporation (MNC) 198, 206, 225–226, 228–229, 232, 236, 245, 262, 270, 293, 350, 362
  see also multinational enterprise, transnational corporation
multinational enterprise (MNE) 224, 232, 233–237, 257
  see also multinational corporation, transnational corporation
Mumbai 198
  Bombay 180–181, 259

Naipaul, V.S. **193–194**, 324
Nancy, Jean-Luc 352, **398–401**
nationalism 136–137, 139, 142, 226, 242–243, 271, 294,
    308–309, 319–320, 323, 336–337, 341, 350–351
    in America **157–158**
    in China **145–148**, 181
    in Germany **155–157**
    in Russia 166
    spectral nationality **384–387**
nation-state 76, 205, 212–213, 221, 245, 249, 251, 254,
    257–258, 280, 294, 302, 335, 346, 348, 354, 363–365,
    379
    emergence of 3, 67, 73, 88
    reshaped by globalization 132, 205, 207, 241–243, 273,
        337, 350, 358–361, 385, 395, 406, 412
Nation of Islam 140, 188–190
Nazi (-ism) 133, 135, 137, 154, 160, 341, 342, 415
Negri, Antonio 134, 300, 346–347, **358–360**, 376 (notes)
neoliberal 198, 245, 269, 271–272, 294, 299, 332, 349,
    378–379, 384
    market 247, 269, 349
    neoliberalism 198, 281, 291, 349
    Neoliberalism as Exception, **247–249**
New York 9, 76, 140, 216, 256–257, 321, 323, 328, 328–329,
    397, 405, 409, 417
New York Times 138, 203, 219
    terror attacks 138, 203, 219
Niebuhr, Reinhold 133, 140, 188
non-governmental organization (NGO) 213, 249, 252, 280,
    281, 284, 287, 293, 294, 378, 380 (notes), 392
    see also international non-governmental organization
        (INGO)
North American Free Trade Agreement (NAFTA) 225–226,
    232–233, 238
Nye, Joseph S. Jr. 270, **279–281**, 294, 376 (notes)

Ohmae, Kenichi 205, **209–211**, 241, 300
Ong, Aihwa **247–249**, 370
Organization for Economic Co-operational and
    Development (OECD) 205, 336 (notes)

Paolini, Albert 271–272, **310–313**
Papastergiadis, Nicos 351, **393–398**
post-colonial 140, 184, 248, 349–350, 271–272, 354, 392,
    413
    post-colonialism and nationality, **384–387**
    Third World and **310–313**
    Zaire **193–194**
    see also colonialism
post-modern (-ism, -ity) 191, 192, 262, 263, 271, 272, 276,
    309, 310–313, 315, 349, 359
poverty, 30, 157, 188, 224, 252, 292–293, 299, 319, 345–346,
    349–350, 389
    selection on identity and poverty **382–384**

Project for the New American Century **246–247**
    see also American Century

rail(-road) 73, 121, 124, 131, 209, 328
    -way 81, 125, 147–188
Reagan, Ronald 134
    administration 246, 247
realpolitik 211
revolution 32, 69–71, 94, 132, 137, 156, 164, 194, 226, 228,
    241, 271, 304, 308, 318, 360, 385–386, 399–400;
    1960s 3, 140
    American 66–67, 71, 90, 157
    Chinese 6, 136, 139, 146–148, **182–183**, 332
    Cuban 138–9, **186–187**
    economic 228, 297
    European Revolution of 1848 3
    French 1789 3, 71, 111–112, 132, 321, 333, 412, 416
    industrial 119, 121, 415
    nuclear 296
    Russian 136, 143, **151–153**, 196–198, 321
    technological 204, 214, 252, 260, 270, 310, 405
    Velvet **190–192**
    Vietnamese 176
Robertson, Roland 298, 303, 311, **314–317**
Roosevelt, Franklin Delano 136, 159, 296
Rosenau, James N. 244, 245–246, 270, **287–290**
Rosenberg, Justin **264–266**, 270, 369
Rosenberg, Tina 203–204, 208 (note)
Rugman, Alan M. 205, **232–239**

Sartre, John Paul 178
Sassen, Saskia 244, 245, 317 (notes), 346–347, **360–367**
Seattle 203, 225–256, 269, 279, 387, 393 (notes)
Sen, Amartya 349–350, **382–384**
September 11, 2001 (9/11) 269–272, 291, 295, 300, 344,
    352, 368
    selection by Žižek on **276–279**
sex 419
    politics 351, 401
    selection on global sex **390–393**
    sexual identity 389
    sexuality 278, 307, 390, 392
    trafficking and violence 259, 251, 370, 394
Shenzen 328, 330, 346
Silk Road 5, 8, 9 (notes), 18, 63, 131, 210
Simone, AbdouMaliq 354–355, **417–421**
Smith, Adam 209, 377
socialism 136–138, 145–148, 152–153, 164–165, 191, 224,
    262, 311, 318, 323
    national socialism 6
Soviet Union 134, 136, 139–141, **151–153**, 159–166, 176,
    182–184, 186, 190, **196–198**, 212, 224, 274, 300, 320,
    358, 365, 422–423
    see also Cold War

Spivak, Gayatri Chakrovorty 140, 366 (notes)
Stalin, Joseph 6, 137–138, 159, **160–164**, 164, 166
Stiglitz, Joseph 270
Suez Canal 126, 139
    in relation to the Suez Crisis **166–175**
Sun Yat-Sen 136–137, **145–148**, 183

Third World 116, 205, 222–224, 263, 271, 278, 316, 321,
    396
    selection on **310–313**
Thompson, Grahame 205, **221–224**
Tiananmen Square 18, 14, 194–195
Tomlinson, John **302–304**
totalitarian 160, 163, 189, 334
transnational 205, 225, 237, 244–245, 251–253, 257,
    269, 288, 299, 304, 360, 362, 377, 385–386, 395,
    412
    organization 207, 240, 280
    politics 203, 212, 269–270, 274, 280, 326, 334–336, 350,
    370–372, 375
    selection by Hannerz on culture, **215–219**
    see also transnational corporation
transnational corporation (TNC) 204–205, 213, 221, 231,
    238, 252, 262, 284, 377, 394
    transnational company 222, 242
    see also multinational corporation, multinational
    enterprise

United Nations (UN) 25, 27, 140, 141, 160, 166, 181, 184,
    207, 212, 252, 275, 292, 297, 299, 300, 309, 351, 396
    Commission on Global Governance **282–287**
    Fidel Castro's speech to **185–187**
    Mikhail Gorbachev's speech to **196–198**
    Security Council 296, 298
United States of America (USA) 8, 22, 53, 81–82, 93, 101,
116, 127, 133–134, 136–140, 144, 146, 151, 160–162,
176, 185–187, 207, 212, 224, 226, 228–229, 231, 236,
246–247, 250, 256–259, 261–262, 269, 281, 282, 299,
300, 319, 320, 323–324, 325–327, 378, 395, 398, 401
    in relation to China 296–298
    in relation to Europe 333–336
    see also Americanization, American Century
Urry, John 253, 256, 348, 353, **368–371**

Virilio, Paul 352–353, **404–406**

Wallerstein, Immanual 4–5, 9 (notes), 62–64, 75 (notes)
    76–79, 88, 132, 178, 256, 347–349, 353, 412–413
    world-system theory as globalization 63–64
Washington Consensus 270, 271, 291
waste 4, 38, 73–75, 83, 90–92, 343, 404
Weber, Max 52, 61, 64, 68, 70, 341–344, 353, 366
Westernization 206, 272, 323, 379
Wilson, Woodrow 135, 145, 212, 257, 281
World Bank 203, 206, 212, 257, 281
World Social Forum (WSF) 141, **198–199**, 225,
    349
World Trade Center (WTC) 270, 277–278
World War I 54, 108, 132–138, 142, 145, 149, 151, 155, 160,
    164, 228, 319, 321, 374, 383, 415
    The Great War 3, 132, 133–135, **143–145**, 342, 411
World War II 50, 132–138, 145, 149, 153, 159, 160, 164,
    177, 228, 231, 296, 319, 321, 328, 337

Zaire 137, 140–141, 183, 193–194
    see also Congo
Zapatistas 225–226
Zhao Ziyang **194–196**, 332
Žižek, Slavoj **276–279**
Zolo, Danilo **298–301**